Table of Contents

*   The examiners classify Criminal Law and Criminal Procedure as one subject.

INTRODUCTION

GENERAL

This book contains outlines for the subjects tested on the Multistate Bar Examination ("MBE"). MBE questions should be answered according to general majority legal principles and the Federal Rules of Evidence, unless otherwise indicated.

The outlines in this book are focused on the legal issues that are testable on the MBE and generally follow the scope of testability provided by the National Conference of bar Examiners. The outlines have been specially developed to address the topics that are testable and to highlight the topics that are traditionally heavily tested. Additionally, the scope of the outlines has been limited to avoid wasted preparation time.

Developing an efficient and effective study plan is essential to passing the MBE. Although these outlines may be long, they cover the law that you should know in preparing for the MBE. Therefore, you should study these outlines slowly and carefully. You should also complete and review released and practice MBE questions.

QUESTION KEYS

Many of the topics in this book contain accompanying question keys. The questions for each subject are keyed to the questions for the subject contained in the Multistate Bar Examination Released Questions Book (not the mixed-subject MBE Practice Questions in the first part of the book). The question keys will allow you to immediately examine how the subject-matter you are reviewing has been tested in prior examinations.

On occasion, you may notice that some topics are keyed to questions testing other subjects. For example, some questions testing Contracts may be keyed to Property questions in the question book. The subject-matter classification of each question has been made by the National Conference of Bar Examiners. In such cases, we have elected not to change to examiner's classification.

STARRING SYSTEM

The starring system in this outline has been developed to assist students in allocating study resources during "crunch time." Students should *never* presume that a topic will not be tested if it does not contain at least one star. Everything covered in this book is potentially testable. Therefore, do not use the star system to limit coverage of subject-matter.

MULTISTATE BAR EXAMINATION

The Multistate Bar Examination (MBE) is developed by the National Conference of Bar Examiners (NCBE). The purpose of the MBE is to assess the extent to which an examinee can apply fundamental legal principles and legal reasoning to analyze a given fact pattern. The MBE contains 200 multiple-choice questions and is administered by participating jurisdictions on the last Wednesday in February and the last Wednesday in July of each year. The exam is divided into morning and afternoon periods of three hours each, with 100 questions in each period. The exam consists of questions in the following areas: Constitutional Law, Contracts, Criminal Law and Procedure, Evidence, Real Property, and Torts. Subject matter outlines for each area are provided in this booklet and online at www.ncbex.org/multistate-tests/mbe/.

INSTRUCTIONS TO EXAMINEES

Taking the Test

Each of the questions on the MBE is followed by four possible answers. Examinees should choose the best answer from the four stated alternatives. Each question on the MBE is designed to be answered according to the generally accepted view, unless noted otherwise in the question. Examinees should mark only one answer for each question; multiple answers will be scored as incorrect. Since scores are based on the number of questions answered correctly, examinees are advised to answer every question. If a question seems too difficult, the examinee is advised to go on to the next one and come back to the skipped question later. Each jurisdiction will provide specific instructions regarding the appropriate marking of answer sheets.

MBE CONTENT

In General

The MBE consists of 200 multiple-choice questions, 190 of which are scored. The 10 unscored questions are being evaluated for future use; because these questions are indistinguishable from scored questions, examinees should answer all 200 questions. The 190 scored questions on the MBE are distributed as follows: Constitutional Law (31), Contracts (33), Criminal Law and Procedure (31), Evidence (31), Real Property (31), and Torts (33).

MBE SCORES

Explanation of the Scoring Process

MBE answer sheets are centrally scored. Both raw scores and scaled scores are computed for each examinee. A raw score is the number of questions answered correctly. Raw scores from different administrations of the MBE are not comparable, primarily due to differences in the difficulty of the questions from one administration to the next. The statistical process of equating adjusts for variations in the difficulty of the questions, producing scaled scores that represent the same level of performance across all MBE administrations. For instance, if the questions appearing on the July MBE were more difficult than those appearing on the February MBE, then the scaled scores for the July MBE would be adjusted upward to account for this difference. These adjustments ensure that no examinee is unfairly penalized or rewarded for taking a more or less difficult exam.

DESCRIPTION OF THE MBE

The Multistate Bar Examination is an objective six-hour examination containing 200 questions. The examination is divided into two periods of three hours each, one in the morning and one in the afternoon, with 100 questions in each period. The examination includes 190 live test questions in the following areas: Constitutional Law, Contracts, Criminal Law and Procedure, Evidence, Real Property, and Torts. There are 33 questions each in Contracts and Torts and 31 questions each in Constitutional Law, Criminal Law and Procedure, Evidence, and Real Property. In addition the exam contains 10 pretest questions which are indistinguishable from the live test items, but will not be used for scoring purposes.

The questions on the examination are designed to be answered by applying fundamental legal principles rather than local case or statutory law. A given question may indicate the applicable statute, theory of liability, or comparable principle of law.

Many of the questions require applicants to analyze the legal relationships arising from a fact situation or to take a position as an advocate. Some questions call for suggestions about interpreting, drafting, or counseling that might lead to more effective structuring of a transaction.

All questions are multiple choice. Applicants are asked to choose the best answer from the four stated alternatives. The test is designed to give credit only when the applicant has selected the best answer. Therefore, applicants should mark only one answer for each question; multiple answers will not be counted.

Scores are based on the number of questions answered correctly. Applicants are, therefore, advised to answer every question. Time should be used effectively. Applicants should not hurry, but should work steadily and as quickly as possible without sacrificing accuracy. If a question seems too difficult, the applicant is advised to go on to the next one and come back to the skipped question later.

Answer sheets are centrally scored. Both raw scores and scaled scores are computed for each applicant. A raw score is the number of questions answered correctly. Raw scores on different forms of the test are not comparable primarily due to differences in the difficulty of the test forms. A statistical process called equating adjusts for variations in the difficulty of different forms of the examination so that any particular scaled score will represent the same level of performance from test to test.

For instance, if a test were more difficult than previous tests, then the scaled scores on that test would be adjusted upward to account for this difference. The purpose of these adjustments is to help ensure that no applicant is unfairly penalized (or rewarded) for taking a more (or less) difficult form of the test.

AMERIBAR BAR REVIEW

Multistate Bar Examination Preparation Course

CONSTITUTIONAL LAW

TABLE OF CONTENTS

We provide case names for reference purposes.
However, an examinee is not generally expected to know case names.

I.   THE NATURE OF JUDICIAL REVIEW

A.   Relationship of State and Federal Courts in a Federal System

1)   CONSTITUTIONAL BASIS

Article III of the *Constitution of the United States* (the *"U.S. Constitution"* or
"Constitution") empowers Congress to create all federal courts other than the Supreme
Court of the United States (the "Supreme Court" or "Court"). The *Constitution* itself
creates the Supreme Court. Specifically, Section 1 of Article III creates "one Supreme
Court." U.S. Const. art. III, § 1.

State courts may be authorized and created pursuant to state constitutions and laws based
on the powers that are reserved to the states under the Tenth Amendment to the
Constitution (the "Tenth Amendment").

a)   Respective Federal and State Judicial Jurisdiction

Both federal and state courts are subject to, and must apply to individual cases, any
applicable provisions of the *Constitution*.

Federal courts are authorized to determine the constitutionality of federal and state laws
pursuant to controlling precedents of the federal courts. The general function of the
federal judiciary is to uniformly construe federal law and maintain its supremacy over
contrary state laws.

State courts are authorized to decide the constitutionality of federal and state laws
pursuant to controlling precedents of state and federal courts. In this outline, unless
otherwise specified, all references to states, state courts, and state laws also include local
governmental entities, courts, and laws, which are all derived from the state's power.

b)   Comparative Roles of High Federal and State Courts

Generally, the decisions of both state and federal courts may be subject to review in the
Supreme Court.

State supreme courts construe and apply state constitutions and laws. The decisions of
state supreme courts may result in the provision of greater freedoms under state law than
those that are available under federal law.

A state's highest court is subject to an appellate relationship with the Supreme Court of
the United States. State supreme courts are not, however, bound to follow the decisions
of the lower courts of the federal judiciary regarding federal law issues.

Usually, the proper method to challenge a state trial court decision is to appeal to the state appellate court. Generally, a party may appeal to a federal court only after an initial appeal to the state's appellate or highest court. Congress possesses authority to determine and establish the ways that lower state court decisions upholding state law may be challenged to the Supreme Court. U.S. Const. art. III, § 2, cl. 2.

★   **B.   Jurisdiction**

> Question Key
> 144

1)   <u>CONSTITUTIONAL BASIS</u>

Article III describes the scope of authority of federal courts to adjudicate cases or controversies.

a)   Original Jurisdiction of the Supreme Court

Original jurisdiction of the Supreme Court refers to cases that may be initially filed in the Supreme Court.

(1)   Exclusive Jurisdiction

The original and exclusive jurisdiction of the Court (cases that may be brought only in the Supreme Court) includes cases or controversies between two or more states.

(2)   Discretionary Jurisdiction

The original and discretionary jurisdiction (cases that the Court may elect to hear originally) of the Supreme Court applies to cases or controversies that:

- involve ambassadors, public ministers, or consuls; or
- are between the United States and a state; or
- involve a state against aliens or citizens of another state.

These cases may be filed originally in a lower federal court or in the Supreme Court.

b)   Constitutional Scope of Subject Matter Jurisdiction

Article III provides that the federal judicial power (at both the trial and appellate levels) applies to all cases in equity or at law arising under the following subject matter:

- a federal statute, treaty, or the *Constitution*;
- ambassadors, public ministers, or consuls;
- maritime and admiralty law;
- controversies involving the United States as a party;
- disputes between two or more states;
- disputes between a state and citizens of different states;

- disputes between citizens of a state claiming land that different states granted; and
- disputes between a state or its citizens and a foreign country and its citizens.

U.S. Const. art. III, § 2, cl. 1.

★★   C.   **Congressional Power to Define and Limit Judicial Power**

★★   1)   <u>ARTICLE III COURTS</u>

Question Key
18,45,63,77,106

Under Article III, Congress may determine the Supreme Court's appellate jurisdiction, as well as the types of cases the lower federal courts may adjudicate. Section 1 of Article III, the Judicial Vesting Clause, provides that: "The judicial power of the United States, shall be vested in one Supreme Court, and in such inferior courts as the Congress may from time to time ordain and establish." U.S. Const. art. III, § 1.

a)   Congressional Power over Jurisdiction

(1)   Original Jurisdiction

The *Constitution* sets forth the original jurisdiction of the Supreme Court. Therefore, Congress may not statutorily expand or reduce the original jurisdiction of the Supreme Court.

(2)   Appellate Jurisdiction

Congress may reduce or expand the appellate jurisdiction of the Supreme Court. Specifically, the Exceptions Clause states in part: "In all other cases . . . , the Supreme Court shall have appellate Jurisdiction, both as to Law and Fact, with such Exceptions, and under such Regulations as the Congress shall make." U.S. Const. art. III, § 2, cl. 2.

However, Congress limiting the Supreme Court's appellate jurisdiction as to eliminate an entire area of law, rather than only an avenue of review (e.g., *habeas corpus*), may be unconstitutional. This is because such a congressional act violates the structure of the *Constitution* in that it seriously interferes with the establishment of a supreme and uniform body of federal constitutional law, and Article III was not meant to be interpreted this broadly.

b)   Congressional Power over the Lower Federal Courts

Congress may create any inferior court it deems necessary under Article III. Congress may establish the scope of those courts' jurisdiction (trial and appellate) and eliminate or proscribe it with respect to certain subject matter. Congress may not, however, alter the inferior courts' jurisdiction and obligation to interpret the *Constitution*. The inferior courts, such as the federal district courts and the federal circuit courts of appeal, are subordinate to the Supreme Court.

Congress may create inferior courts with a specialized and limited subject-matter jurisdiction, such as for regulating a certain type of interstate commerce. Congress appoints the judges of Article III federal courts for life, subject to impeachment for "high crimes and misdemeanors." Congress may not reduce the salary of such a judge.

           c)   Congressional Expansion of Jurisdiction

Congress may increase, and has expanded, the constitutionally provided subject-matter jurisdiction of the federal courts. For example, diversity jurisdiction based on the different state citizenship of parties to a federal lawsuit includes a non-constitutionally proscribed requirement of an amount in controversy. The following partial list illustrates the types of subject matter that are cognizable by the federal courts as national statutory law or treaties:

- federal intellectual property law (e.g., patent, copyright, and trademark);
- federal bankruptcy law;
- federal military law;
- federal international law;
- federal *Tort Claims Act* cases;
- *habeas corpus* cases; and
- nuclear energy regulation.

        2)   ARTICLE I TRIBUNALS

Article I of the *Constitution* ("Article I") authorizes Congress to establish legislative courts similar to those used by administrative agencies. U.S. Const. art. I, § 8, cl. 9. The purpose of Article I courts is to provide oversight of issues as an auxiliary extension of the congressional power to legislate. Examples of these tribunals include military courts, tax courts, and territorial courts such as those in the District of Columbia. The judges of Article I courts lack the guarantees of lifetime tenure and no decrease in salary possessed by the judges of Article III courts.

★★★   D.   **Judicial Review in Operation**

        1)   GROUNDS FOR JUDICIAL REVIEW

           a)   Review of Federal Law

In the landmark case *Marbury v. Madison*, the Supreme Court established its ultimate authority of judicial review. The Supreme Court exercises that power to evaluate, and potentially invalidate, a federal law, on the basis that it violates the *Constitution*.

           b)   Review of State Law

The Supreme Court also possesses the power and jurisdiction to review state law and local government action because state law and government action are subject to the *Constitution*, federal law, and international treaties. The Supreme Court's appellate jurisdiction extends to final decisions from state courts, federal courts, and federal tribunals.

     c)   Denying Judicial Review

Despite the Supreme Court's broad authority to conduct judicial review, its policy is to not hear or decide certain cases:

- if they are non-justiciable for certain reasons addressed later; or
- on the merits of a constitutional issue if a case could be decided on non-constitutional grounds.

These policies of denying judicial review are followed by the lower federal courts.

    2)   DISCRETIONARY JURISDICTION

     a)   Writ of *Certiorari*

The writ of *certiorari* is a special form of appellate pleading that petitions the Supreme Court for judicial review of a case. The Supreme Court exercises discretion regarding which appeals it will hear when those cases are presented by a writ of *certiorari*. A writ of *certiorari* is granted only if four of the Supreme Court's nine justices vote to accept for decision a case on indirect appeal. That standard is referred to as the "rule of four."

    3)   MANDATORY JURISDICTION

     a)   Direct Appeals – Special District Courts

The Supreme Court must hear direct appeals from decisions made a by three-judge panel of a federal district court.

     b)   Statutory Jurisdiction – Congressionally Conferred

Certain federal laws may provide for mandatory jurisdiction over specific issues that arise under those laws.

     c)   Certified Case – Circuit Court Approval

The federal circuit courts of appeal may certify a case for the Supreme Court's mandatory review.

★★★   4)   "CASE OR CONTROVERSY" REQUIREMENT

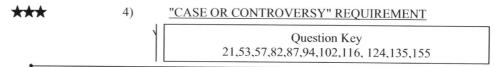

Question Key
21,53,57,82,87,94,102,116, 124,135,155

A federal court may only adjudicate a case or controversy. U.S. Const. art. III, § 2. There must be an actual dispute between the litigants. The case or controversy requirement is a jurisdictional requirement that either a court, or the parties in a case, may raise at any time during the proceedings. The Supreme Court may even raise the issue on appeal.

The *Constitution* prohibits advisory opinions. Advisory opinions are opinions that concern hypothetical facts and abstract issues that do not satisfy the requirements of standing. Particularly, they involve claims that are not based upon a constitutionally required "case or controversy," and accordingly are non-justiciable cases. A federal court is prohibited from issuing an advisory opinion arising from any hypothetical or abstract issue. Thus, a federal court cannot take jurisdiction of such a case. For example, a federal court cannot adjudicate the constitutionality of proposed legislation prior to its enactment. Therefore, Congress may not statutorily authorize the Supreme Court to render advisory opinions. *Muskrat v. United States*, 219 U.S. 346 (1911).

Several justiciability doctrines govern the scope of federal court adjudication of cases or controversies including standing, ripeness, and mootness.

      a) Standing

A party must possess standing to bring a federal case. Standing is a threshold question that a federal court may consider before adjudicating a civil legal proceeding.

★★★   (1) General Rule of Standing

In order for a plaintiff to possess standing to bring a civil action, the party must possess a significant stake in the proceeding and its outcome. The elements of standing include injury in fact, causation, and redressability.

- Injury in Fact

The plaintiff must demonstrate evidence of a threat of imminent injury or evidence of an actual injury in fact. The injury must constitute a violation of constitutional or statutory rights, an economic injury, or any other legally recognized harm.

- Causation

The plaintiff must demonstrate evidence that the defendant caused (or will cause) the injury.

- Redressability

The plaintiff must demonstrate that the court is capable of affording relief to a party (through judicial relief).

      (2) Standing of an Association

An association may bring an action in its own name, on behalf of its members, if:

- the members would individually possess standing; and
- the association desires to protect interests that relate to its objectives.

The members do not need to participate in bringing the claim or demanding the remedy.

(3)   Standing of States

If a state files an action in a federal court, it must generally meet the standing requirements of injury in fact, causation, and redressability. However, states occupy a special position of interest as compared to that of individuals in order to protect their quasi-sovereign interests subject to injury. For example, Massachusetts had standing to bring a suit seeking to protect its land from the rising level of the Atlantic Ocean attributed to global warming allegedly caused by the release of greenhouse gases into the atmosphere.

(4)   Collusion

The parties to a civil legal proceeding may neither collude to obtain standing nor waive the requirement of standing.

b)   Taxpayer Standing

Generally, a taxpayer lacks constitutional standing to challenge a federal government expenditure of tax revenue merely because of his status as a taxpayer. *Frothingham v. Mellon*, 262 U.S. 447 (1923). However, a taxpayer may obtain standing to challenge a specific federal expenditure on the basis that it exceeds a certain limitation of the *Constitution.* The general test to determine if a taxpayer possesses standing to challenge a federal expenditure is called the "double nexus" test. Under the test:

> First, the taxpayer must establish a logical link between that status and the type of legislative enactment attacked. Thus, a taxpayer will be a proper party to allege the unconstitutionality only of exercises of congressional power under the taxing and spending clause of Art. I, 8, of the *Constitution.* It will not be sufficient to allege an incidental expenditure of tax funds in the administration of an essentially regulatory statute. . . .

> Secondly, the taxpayer must establish a nexus between that status and the precise nature of the constitutional infringement alleged. Under this requirement, the taxpayer must show that the challenged enactment exceeds specific constitutional limitations imposed upon the exercise of the congressional taxing and spending power and not simply that the enactment is generally beyond the powers delegated to Congress by Art. I, 8. When both nexuses are established, the litigant will have

shown a taxpayer's stake in the outcome of the controversy and will be a proper and appropriate party to invoke a federal court's jurisdiction.

Flast v. Cohen, 392 U.S. 83, 103-4 (1968).

In *Flast v. Cohen,* the Supreme Court held that taxpayer standing existed to challenge congressional appropriations of funds under the Taxing and Spending Clause of Article I of the *U.S. Constitution* as violating the Establishment Clause of the First Amendment to the *U.S. Constitution.*

(1)   Executive Expenditures of Appropriations

Taxpayer standing does not exist to challenge an expenditure of congressionally appropriated funds by the executive branch. The Court has declined to review the expenditure of such funds by an executive agency because the expenditure constitutes "an administrative decision traditionally regarded as committed to agency discretion." *Hein v. Freedom from Religion Foundation,* 551 U.S. 587 (2007).

c)   Statutory Standing

If Congress has conferred standing upon an individual or entity through an express statutory provision, then usually the Supreme Court and federal courts will grant standing. Such a statutory right may be asserted without fulfilling all three of the usual elements of the standing test.

★   d)   Third-Party Standing

Generally, an injured person must file a lawsuit on his own behalf. A person generally lacks standing to assert the legal rights of a third party in a civil legal proceeding. However, a first party that has sustained a direct injury that did not result from a violation of the first party's constitutionally protected right may complain that the constitutional rights of the third party were violated. In order to obtain third party standing, the first party must satisfy the following test:

1a)   the third party is not likely to assert his own rights; or
1b)   the third party will experience difficulty in asserting his rights.

and

2a)   the first party suffered a direct injury; or
2b)   a special relationship exists between the third party and the first party.

The third party's rights must be "difficult if not impossible" to assert in order for a first party to fulfill the rule of third-party standing. Third-party standing may exist in several situations.

(1)   Associations

An association or similar organization may possess standing to raise both its own rights and the rights of another person who is not directly involved in a civil legal proceeding, such as its members.

(2)   Government Officials

A government official may have standing to challenge the constitutionality of a law if the official is faced with a difficult choice between the following two adverse outcomes:

- a refusal to enforce the law would result in removal from office; or
- enforcing the law would violate the oath to uphold the *Constitution.*

(3)   Seller of Contraceptives

A pharmacy may have third-party standing to assert the right of some of its customers to obtain contraceptives. For example, the pharmacy may challenge a law prohibiting a certain class of people, such as minors, from purchasing contraceptives.

(4)   Minor Children

A minor child's parent usually possesses standing to prosecute a lawsuit on behalf of the child. Generally, a parent must possess legal custody to bring an action on behalf of a minor child. Consequently, a non-custodial parent lacks standing to bring an action on behalf of a minor child. *Elk Grove Unified School District v. Newdow*, 542 U.S. 1 (2004). The Court reversed, on this procedural ground, a decision of the Ninth Circuit Court of Appeals finding that this defendant California school district's policy requiring all classes to daily recite the Pledge of Allegiance violated the Establishment Clause of the First Amendment to the *U.S. Constitution.*

e)   Ripeness

Ripeness is a requirement that a party litigant must have experienced an actual harm, or have been subject to an imminent threat of harm, in order for a civil legal proceeding to be adjudicated. A claim is not ripe for adjudication if it rests upon contingent future events that may not occur as anticipated, or may not occur at all. For example, if a threatened law has been enacted but never applied, a case challenging that law lacks ripeness and may be dismissed.

f)   Mootness

(1)   Legal Standard

A court may not hear a case that is moot. A case is moot when "there is no subject matter on which the judgment of the court's order can operate." *St. Pierre v. United States*, 319 U. S. 41 (1943). In other words, a case becomes moot if a controversy ceases to exist at any point during litigation, such that it is too late for adjudication of an action because it is unlikely that the controversy will be revived.

(a)   Voluntary Cessation

A voluntary cessation of a challenged practice may arise if a defendant, in a civil legal proceeding in which the plaintiff is seeking equitable relief, halts the conduct being challenged at some point during the proceedings. In that event, the proceeding will be considered as having become moot if the conduct probably will not re-occur.

(b)   Mootness on Appeal

Federal appellate court decisions that become moot on appeal may be vacated.

(2)   Exceptions to Mootness Doctrine

(a)   Capable of Repetition but Evading Review

A controversy that is capable of repetition but evading review will not be dismissed as moot. It is an exception to the general mootness doctrine.

For example, *Roe v. Wade*, a case initiated by a pregnant woman challenging a statute as unconstitutionally restricting her from obtaining an abortion, was not dismissed as moot despite her pregnancy having ended during that litigation. The plaintiff continued to have a stake in the outcome of the litigation. Because typical litigation lasts longer than nine months, if it were to be dismissed when the pregnancy ended, any such litigation would be a case that is capable of repetition but evading review.

(b)   Sham Mootness

Sham mootness is another exception to the mootness doctrine. Under the sham mootness exception, a defendant's unilateral cessation of wrongful activity will not render a plaintiff's case moot if a reasonable expectation exists that a wrong will be repeated.

5)   POLITICAL QUESTIONS AND JUSTICIABILITY

a)   General Constitutional Basis

| Question Key |
| 117 |

A federal court will not exercise jurisdiction over a case that seeks to resolve a political issue when the issue is considered either best addressed by another branch of the government or is considered inappropriate for judicial review. The political question doctrine promotes the federal constitutional principle of the separation of powers.

b)   Political Question Doctrine Analysis

A federal court may examine the following factors to determine whether a case involves a non-justiciable (i.e., a case that should not be adjudicated by a court) political question:

- "a textually demonstrable constitutional commitment of the issue to a coordinate political department;
- or a lack of judicially discoverable and manageable standards for resolving it;
- or the impossibility of deciding without an initial policy determination of a kind clearly for non-judicial discretion;
- or the impossibility of a court's undertaking independent resolution without expressing lack of the respect due coordinate branches of government or an unusual need for unquestioning adherence to a political decision already made;
- or the potentiality of embarrassment from multifarious pronouncements by various departments on one question."

Baker v. Carr, 369 U.S. 186 (1962).

          c)   Examples of Political Questions

Among other things, the following issues may be considered non-justiciable political questions:

- the decision to go to war.
- the congressional process of impeaching or removing the President.
- adoption of amendments to the *Constitution*.
- the President's general conduct of foreign policy.
- treaties entered into by the President.
- the composition, training, and discipline of the military forces.

★   6)   "ADEQUATE AND INDEPENDENT STATE GROUNDS"

★   a)   General Rule

Question Key
2,35,150

The adequate and independent state grounds rule is a doctrine of judicial review. The highest court of a state makes the ultimate determination of the meaning of the state's constitution and laws. Therefore, the Supreme Court of the United States will not entertain an appeal from a state court decision if an independent and adequate state ground supports the state court decision. When the Supreme Court reviews a state court decision, it usually considers the federal law issues, rather than the state law issues. If a review of the federal issues cannot change the result, then the Supreme Court of the United States will not hear the case.

For example, suppose the Florida Supreme Court decides an appeal involving a criminal defendant's challenge to police conduct. The defendant alleges that a police investigation violated his rights under the Florida and United States Constitutions. If the Florida Supreme Court rules that the government violated the defendant's rights under both federal and Florida law, then the government cannot appeal to the Supreme Court of the United States. This is because the Supreme Court of the United States cannot change the outcome of the case because it cannot overrule the Florida court's decision on Florida law (the Florida Supreme Court is the ultimate decision-maker regarding Florida law). As a result, any decision that the Supreme Court of the United State makes on the federal issues will be inconsequential. Therefore, the Supreme Court of the United States would decline to hear the appeal on the grounds that there is an adequate and independent state ground for the decision.

      b)   Exceptions

There are two exceptions to the rule of "adequate and independent state grounds," which apply if: 1) a state law incorporates a federal law by reference; or 2) important federal interests are included with substantive state law.

For example, in the prior example involving the Florida Supreme Court, suppose the Florida Supreme Court has held that the applicable Florida constitutional standard is identical to the federal constitutional standard. In that case, the Supreme Court of the United States may hear the appeal because its determination of the federal issue would, according to the Florida Supreme Court, be equally applicable to the violation of rights under state law.

      7)   <u>ELEVENTH AMENDMENT</u>

      a)   Sovereign Immunity

Under the Eleventh Amendment to the *Constitution* ("Eleventh Amendment"), a plaintiff does not possess standing in a federal court to file an action seeking damages "against any one of the states." U.S. Const. amend. XI. This provision is considered a basis of state sovereign immunity pursuant to which a state government will not be subject to a lawsuit unless the state government grants consent to it.

      (1)   Congressional Exceptions

Congress may establish exceptions to Eleventh Amendment immunity by enacting a statute that enforces the Fourteenth Amendment to the *Constitution* ("Fourteenth Amendment") and authorizes lawsuits in federal courts by a state's citizens against that state. *Fitzpatrick v. Bitzer*, 427 U.S. 445 (1976).

      (2)   Other Exceptions

The following exceptions apply to the Eleventh Amendment's general rule of immunity:

- Waiver

A state may waive Eleventh Amendment immunity.

- Injunction Against State Official

The Eleventh Amendment does not prevent a federal court from issuing an injunction against a state official who is violating federal law. A federal court can order the official to stop the action. The plaintiff may also obtain money damages as long as the damages are attributable to the actions of the officer and are not paid from the state treasury. *Scheuer v. Rhodes*, 416 U.S. 232 (1974).

- Local Government

The Eleventh Amendment does not automatically protect political subdivisions of the state (e.g., cities, counties, or school boards) from liability. However, if the state would have to pay for damages from the state treasury, then the Eleventh Amendment will serve as a shield from liability.

- Remedial Powers

The states surrendered a portion of the sovereign immunity when states passed the Fourteenth and Fifteenth Amendments. Therefore, Congress may authorize a private action against a state to enforce the constitutional guarantees of these amendments.

8)   ABSTENTION

An abstention doctrine is any one of several alternative doctrines a federal court may invoke to refuse to hear a case otherwise properly before it when hearing the case potentially would intrude upon the powers of state courts. In general, parties may proceed to judgment in a federal district court action without regard to the pendency of state proceedings that seek similar relief. *Kline v. Burke Construction Co.*, 260 U.S. 226 (1922). Indeed, a federal district court has a "duty . . . to adjudicate a controversy properly before it," and it may abstain "only in the exceptional circumstances where the order to the parties to repair to the State court would clearly serve an important countervailing interest." *Colorado River Water Conservation District v. United States*, 424 U.S. 800, 813 (1976).

There are four abstention doctrines.

a)   *Pullman* Abstention

Pullman abstention is an equitable doctrine that operates only when the state court's resolution of unsettled state law issues may eliminate the need of resolving a difficult federal law issue. Like all abstention doctrines, *Pullman* abstention is an extraordinary and narrow exception to the duty of a federal district court to adjudicate a controversy properly before it.

Two elements must be met to apply *Pullman* abstention:

1) The case must present an unsettled question of state law; and

2)   The question of state law must be dispositive (the deciding factor) of the case or would materially alter a question presented.

If a court invokes *Pullman* abstention, it should stay the federal constitutional question until the matter has been sent to a state court for a determination of the uncertain state law issue.

b)   *Burford* Abstention

Abstention under the *Burford* doctrine is appropriate only if federal adjudication would interfere with a state's administration of a complex regulatory scheme. The most commonly cited example of a complex regulatory scheme is state insurance regulation. The reason for abstaining under *Burford* is that the state courts possess a greater expertise in a particularly complex area of law, such as a complex state regulatory scheme. The *Burford* case, for example, dealt with the regulation of Texas oil drilling operations.

c)   *Younger* Abstention

Younger abstention may apply when the state's interest in the smooth functioning of its criminal justice system or its civil enforcement machinery is threatened by a federal court action that would interfere with those types of pending state proceedings.

There are three requirements for *Younger* abstention to apply:

1)   pending or ongoing state proceedings that are judicial in nature;
2)   the state proceedings must implicate an important state interest; and
3)   the state proceedings must afford an adequate opportunity to raise any constitutional issues.

d)   *Colorado River* Abstention

Colorado River abstention may be appropriate when both federal and state court proceedings are simultaneously being carried on to determine the rights of parties with respect to the same issues of law. Under these circumstances, it would waste judicial resources for both courts to carry on. Application of the doctrine is not governed by a rigid rule, but by the application of an elaborate balancing test. *Moses H. Cone Mem. Hosp. v. Mercury Const. Corp.*, 460 U.S. 1, 16 (1983).

There must be evidence of factors that disfavor proceeding with the federal litigation, such as the risk of inconsistent rulings with respect to a particular piece of property or clear evidence of a federal policy favoring unitary adjudication of the claims at issue. In conducting the balancing inquiry, the balance is weighted heavily in favor of the exercise of jurisdiction.

II.   THE SEPARATION OF POWERS

The *Constitution* expressly creates and establishes the rights and responsibilities of three separate political branches of the federal government: the legislative; the executive; and the judiciary. The doctrine of separation of powers precludes any of the branches from interfering with the respective function of each other. For example, the President may not utilize the legislative power, even in an emergency when Congress cannot function. In essence, the *Constitution* empowers Congress to make laws, authorizes the President to execute the laws, and enables the federal courts to interpret the laws. Therefore, if a power belongs to one of the three branches, any act by another branch to encroach or conduct a similar action will be barred by the doctrine of separation of powers.

A.   The Powers of Congress

Congress may not act unless authorized to do so in the *Constitution*. There are several different sources of Congressional power in the *Constitution*. On the exam, questions testing congressional powers focus on the authority of Congress to pass a law. It is important to consider the content of the law to determine whether it is permitted by the relevant grant of authority in the *Constitution*.

1)   COMPOSITION OF CONGRESS

Article I sets forth the organization and powers of Congress. Congress is made up of two separate bodies of elected officials. The House of Representatives consists of 435 members who represent voting districts of each state and are determined by each state legislature. Each state is allocated a certain number of the total members according to population. The Senate includes two members from each state, for a total of 100 Senators. The Senate has a president *pro tem*, who is the Vice President of the United States. Usually, a vote of the majority of the members of each body is required to enact legislation. The Senate may bar an elected member from participating in its activities if the member lacks the constitutionally required age, citizenship, and residency.

★★★   2)   COMMERCE, TAXING, AND SPENDING POWERS

★★★   a)   Commerce Clause

Question Key
6,10,11,28,35,40,51,92,105,113,142,158

The most heavily tested congressional power on the exam is the commerce power. The Commerce Clause of Article I of the *Constitution* ("Article I") provides that Congress has the power: "To regulate Commerce with foreign Nations, and among the several States." U.S. Const. art. I, § 8, cl. 3. In particular, Congress possesses exclusive power over foreign commerce such as overseas shipments and trade with foreign nations. It also possesses regulatory authority over interstate commerce.

(1)   Scope of Regulatory Power

The Commerce Clause grants Congress plenary (full and complete) power to regulate international and interstate commerce and activity, such as transportation and travel. That authority extends to include:

- instrumentalities of interstate commerce such as certain private or commercial trains, airplanes, and trucks;

- channels or facilities of interstate commerce such as certain private or commercial railroads, roads, and airports;
- noncommercial activity having a direct connection to interstate commerce, regardless of whether it has any cumulative or aggregate effect; and
- activities producing a substantial effect on interstate commerce in a cumulative manner or by inseverable aggregates.

(2)   Limits upon Congressional Power

(a)   Substantial Effect Rule

Commercial activity, even if it occurs on an intrastate or local level, is subject to congressional regulation if the aggregate impact of the activity has a substantial effect on interstate commerce. With minor exception, the Supreme Court has liberally construed the authority of Congress under the Commerce Clause. Therefore, it is rare that the Court invalidates commercial regulatory legislation on the ground that it is not authorized by the Commerce Clause.

(i)   Examples

The Commerce Clause empowers Congress to enact laws that prohibit small restaurants from engaging in racial discrimination because the cumulative economic activity of many small restaurants has a substantial effect on interstate commerce. In one case, members of a racial minority were denied service at a restaurant. Even though the operation of one restaurant did not, by itself, substantially impact interstate commerce, the type of discrimination that occurred there could be prohibited by Congress because the aggregate impact of restaurants obtaining a substantial amount of their food through interstate commerce has a substantial effect on interstate commerce.

In the landmark case *U.S. v. Lopez*, the Supreme Court struck down a federal statute that criminalized the possession of a firearm within a certain distance of a school. The Supreme Court concluded that the possession of a firearm neither constituted economic activity nor affected interstate commerce. Therefore, Congress lacked the authority to impose that law pursuant to the Commerce Clause. Conversely, however, federal regulations regarding the disposal of nuclear waste involve national economic activity that impacts all geographic areas of the United States.

(b)   Economic Regulation Review

A federal statute that regulates interstate commerce is subject to a form of rational basis review. The statute will be upheld if:

- it may be reasonably interpreted as a regulation;
- of the channels or facilities of interstate commerce; or
- of activities that in the aggregate produce a national economic effect; and
- the regulation does not violate other constitutional rights.

b)   Taxing Power

The congressional power of taxation arises under Article I, which states in part that "The Congress shall have Power to lay and collect Taxes." U.S. Const. art. I, § 8.

Congress possesses plenary power to impose and collect taxes for the primary purposes of obtaining funds to provide for national defense and public welfare. Congress may exercise the taxing power to enact taxes that are solely regulatory and have no genuine money-raising purposes.

(1)   Federal Tax Regulation Review

An act of Congress that imposes a tax will be sustained as a valid use of its taxation power if:

- objective test: the act in fact raises revenue; or
- subjective test: the act is intended to raise revenue.

A court will uphold a tax that adversely impacts the taxed activity if the tax satisfies either prong of the above alternative test and if:

- it lacks any provisions unrelated to the tax needs and purposes; and
- no language of the *Constitution* prohibits it.

A court will uphold a regulation that masquerades as a tax, provided the regulation is raising tax revenue.

(a)   No Taxing Exports

Congress is constitutionally prevented from taxing exports under Article I, the Export Clause, which provides in part that: "No Tax or Duty shall be laid on Articles exported from any State." U.S. Const. art. I, § 9, cl. 5.

★★   c)   Spending Power

> Question Key
> 9,50,66,83,84,88,138

The General Welfare or Spending Clause of Article I provides that "Congress shall have Power . . . to pay the Debts and provide for the common Defense and general Welfare of the United States." U.S. Const. art. I, § 8, cl. 1. Congress is constitutionally authorized to decide the amount and scope of federal fiscal appropriations and expenditures.

The obligation to provide for the general welfare includes, at a minimum, funding federal entitlement programs. The obligation to provide for the common defense includes, at least, expenditures on federal military programs. Congress may not make any expenditure that violates other constitutional provisions.

The examiners often provide incorrect answer choices citing a congressional authority or "obligation" to provide for the general welfare. Unlike legislative authority granted in many state constitutions, Congress does not possess an obligation or even the authority to pass general legislation to promote the general welfare. The general welfare language in the *Constitution* only imposes a limitation on the authority of Congress under the spending power. If Congress exercises the spending power, then any expenditure must provide for the common defense or general welfare of the public.

(1)   Federal Spending Regulation Review

A court would apply a rational basis standard of review to a congressional expenditure. Thus, a court would determine if it is reasonable to conclude that the expenditure will benefit or protect the public.

(a)   Standard of Review

A court applying this standard to a federal spending statute would inquire whether:

- a contested expenditure statute is reasonably related to the general welfare;
- it states concrete objectives; and
- it provides adequate administrative criteria.

A person challenging the law possesses the burden of demonstrating its invalidity.

★★   (2)   Conditional Federal Expenditures

A state or local government that takes federal money is required to spend it according to the federal government's requirements. Thus, pursuant to the spending power, Congress may condition a state or local government's receipt of federal funds on voluntary compliance with federal law when that law rationally relates to the objectives of a spending program. In other words, the spending power permits Congress to attach, as a condition of receiving federal funding, a requirement that a state voluntarily comply with a federal law.

(a)   Improper Conditions

Congress cannot impose the requirement of compliance using other coercive means. Of course, Congress cannot impose an unconstitutional condition upon receiving federal funding.

(b)   Examples

Congress may condition federal funding of an institution of higher education, such as a college, upon compliance with relevant federal regulations applicable to such institutions. Of course, any institution that declines this funding will not be subject to the federal regulation. Congress also may require, as a condition to receipt of federal funds, that a university afford to military recruiters equal access on campus and to its students as any other type of employer, rather than discriminate in favor of other employers and against military recruiters.

 ★★   3)   <u>POWER OVER FEDERAL PROPERTY</u>

| Question Key |
| 41,73,81, |
| 115,121,129 |

a)   Constitutional Basis

Congress possesses control over all federal property, including the District of Columbia, pursuant to the Property Clause (or Territorial Clause) of the *Constitution*. Congress may act pursuant to that provision to "dispose of and make all needful rules and regulations respecting the territory or other property of the United States." U.S. Const. art. IV, § 3, cl. 2.

b)   General Property Power

Under the Property Clause, Congress may acquire, maintain, and eliminate the federal government's real and personal property. The Property Clause authorizes Congress to make any laws and regulations necessary to protect federal real and personal property, including wild animals. By virtue of the Necessary and Proper Clause, the federal government also may legislate to protect wild animals on state property adjacent to federal property – if the law is necessary to protect the federal property including wild animals.

c)   Regulatory Authority

Congress has the authority to regulate the territory of the United States, including the District of Columbia. Congress holds sovereign authority in the District of Columbia under the Enclave Clause. U.S. Const. art. I, § 8, cl. 17. In that respect, Congress possesses the same police powers as a state legislature to regulate the District.

d)   Delegation of Property Power

Congress may delegate some of its power of control over property to other branches of government or administrative agencies. For example, Congress may create a commission to exercise that power by contracting with private individuals or entities to perform work on federal lands, and to control the activities of third parties on the property.

4)   WAR AND DEFENSE POWERS

Congresses possesses certain war and defense powers.

a)   Declare War

Congress is empowered "To declare War..." under the War Clause. U.S. Const. art. I, § 8, cl. 11.

b)   Establish and Maintain Armies

Congress is authorized to "To raise and support Armies. . . ." U.S. Const. art. I, § 8, cl. 12.

c)   Create and Supply Navy

Congress is required to "To provide and maintain a Navy. . . ." U.S. Const. art. I, § 8, cl. 13.

d)   Promulgate Military Regulations

Congress is enabled "To make Rules for the Government and Regulation of the land and naval Forces." U.S. Const. art. I, § 8, cl. 13.

★   5)   POWER TO ENFORCE THIRTEENTH, FOURTEENTH, AND FIFTEENTH AMENDMENTS

Question Key 33,46,110

Congress possesses, and has exercised, its power to enact laws that prohibit and remedy public and private denials and deprivations of rights guaranteed by the *Constitution* pursuant to three Amendments sometimes referred to as the Reconstruction Amendments.

a)   The Thirteenth Amendment

The Thirteenth Amendment to the *Constitution* ("Thirteenth Amendment") provides, in part, that: "Neither slavery nor involuntary servitude, except as a punishment for crime whereof the party shall have been duly convicted, shall exist within the United States, or any place subject to their jurisdiction." U.S. Const. amend. XIII, § 1.

The Thirteenth Amendment further provides that: "Congress shall have power to enforce this article by appropriate legislation." U.S. Const. amend. XIII, § 2. This provision authorizes Congress to enact statutes that further the purposes of the Thirteenth Amendment.

(1)   Examples

Pursuant to the Thirteenth Amendment, the Supreme Court upheld the *Civil Rights Act of 1866*, 42 U.S.C. § 1982, on the basis that it was rationally related to the purpose of the amendment (to end slavery). Congress is authorized to outlaw racial discrimination in the sale of real property by a private person. The Supreme Court construed the Thirteenth Amendment as authorizing Congress to identify "badges of slavery," and to enact laws that were "necessary and proper" to eliminate them. The *Civil Rights Act of 1866* applies to actions between parties who represent both different and the same racial groups.

Also pursuant to the Thirteenth Amendment, the Supreme Court upheld a law prohibiting conspiracies by private actors to interfere with the constitutional right of interstate travel. The Supreme Court eliminated the requirement of proving that an individual or entity acted improperly under the color of law. In other words, the law may regulate purely private action. The Supreme Court also expanded the scope of the law to include private conduct that involved racial discrimination beyond the limited category of property rights.

b)   The Fourteenth Amendment

(1)   Constitutional Basis

The Fourteenth Amendment provides, in part, that: "No State shall make or enforce any law which shall abridge the privileges or immunities of citizens of the United States; nor shall any State deprive any person of life, liberty, or property, without due process of law; nor deny to any person within its jurisdiction the equal protection of the laws." U.S. Const. amend. XIV, § 1.

The Fourteenth Amendment further states that: "The Congress shall have power to enforce, by appropriate legislation, the provisions of this article." U.S. Const. amend. XIV, § 5. This provision empowers Congress to create causes of action against the states to enforce the Fourteenth Amendment. Congress may enact laws under the Fourteenth Amendment that provide relief for or to prevent constitutional violations by state actors. That provision cannot be invoked with respect to the unlawful conduct of private actors.

The Fourteenth Amendment's enabling clause empowers Congress to enact laws that supersede state government conduct that limits the constitutional right of due process to the guarantee of equal protection. U.S. Const. amend. XIV, § 5. Such congressional legislation is appropriate if (1) the legislation seeks to prevent or remedy state or local government action that violates provisions of the Fourteenth Amendment; and (2) the requirements of the legislation are congruent with and proportional to the Fourteenth Amendment violations it addresses.

(2)   Mode of Redress against State Action

The federal courts are authorized to review state action to ascertain if any rights that the Fourteenth Amendment provides were violated and, if so, to award an appropriate remedy.

In the *Civil Rights Cases*, the Supreme Court described the congressional power to enforce the Fourteenth Amendment with respect to state action. The Supreme Court held that section 5, the Fourteenth Amendment's enabling clause, "does not invest Congress with power to legislate upon subjects which are within the domain of state legislation; but to provide modes of relief against state legislation, or state action. It does not authorize Congress to create a code of municipal law for the regulation of private rights; but to provide modes of redress against the operation of state laws, and the action of state officers."

(a)   Private Conduct not Actionable

Congress lacks the authority to prohibit private conduct that infringes upon a private person's equal protection and due process rights under the Fourteenth Amendment. Congress does, however, possess the authority to regulate private action that occurs in conjunction with state officials and results in state action.

c)   The Fifteenth Amendment

(1)   Constitutional Basis

The Fifteenth Amendment to the *Constitution* ("Fifteenth Amendment") states in part that: "The right of citizens of the United States to vote shall not be denied or abridged by the United States or by any State on account of race, color, or previous condition of servitude." U.S. Const. amend. XV, § 1.

The Fifteenth Amendment further provides that: "The Congress shall have power to enforce this article by appropriate legislation." U.S. Const. amend. XV, § 2.

(2)   State Cannot Deprive Right to Vote

The Fifteenth Amendment's enabling clause empowers Congress to enact laws to prohibit a state government from depriving anyone the right to vote based on color, race, or prior condition of servitude. The Supreme Court has relied on the Fifteenth Amendment to sustain a federal law that prohibits requiring a voter to pass a literacy test in order to exercise the right to vote in an election.

Pursuant to the Fifteenth Amendment, the Supreme Court upheld the *Voting Rights Act of 1965*. Congress may use any rational means to effectuate the constitutional prohibitions of racial discrimination in voting.

6)   NECESSARY AND PROPER CLAUSE

The Necessary and Proper Clause of the *Constitution* provides additional congressional authority beyond the other specifically enumerated powers in the *Constitution*. Congress is authorized:

> "To make all Laws which shall be necessary and proper for carrying into Execution the foregoing Powers, and all other Powers, vested by this *Constitution* in the government of the United States, or in any Department or Officer thereof."

U.S. Const. art. I, § 8, cl. 18.

The examiners often refer to the Necessary and Proper Clause as an incorrect answer choice on the exam. The Necessary and Proper Clause can only be used in conjunction with some other power. As the Constitution provides, Congress can make all laws necessary and proper "*for carrying into [e]xecution the foregoing [p]owers.*" (emphasis added). The Necessary and Proper Clause cannot, by itself, serve as a basis for congressional action.

7)   MISCELLANEOUS POWERS

Article I, Section 8 of the *Constitution* details several additional enumerated congressional powers. These powers are not tested as often as the other powers. These powers include the power:

- "to borrow money on the credit of the United States;
- to establish a uniform rule of naturalization, and uniform laws on the subject of bankruptcies throughout the United States;
- to coin money, regulate the value thereof, and of foreign coin, and fix the standard of weights and measures;

- to provide for the punishment of counterfeiting the securities and current coin of the United States;
- to establish post offices and post roads;
- to promote the progress of science and useful arts, by securing for limited times to authors and inventors the exclusive right to their respective writings and discoveries;
- to define and punish piracies and felonies committed on the high seas, and offenses against the law of nations;
- to provide for calling forth the militia to execute the laws of the union, suppress insurrections and repel invasions;
- to provide for organizing, arming, and disciplining, the militia, and for governing such part of them as may be employed in the service of the United States, reserving to the states respectively, the appointment of the officers, and the authority of training the militia according to the discipline prescribed by Congress; and
- to exercise exclusive legislation in all cases whatsoever" over the District of Columbia.

U.S. Const. art. I, § 8.

★★   **B.   The Powers of the President**

| Question Key |
| 27,49,75,108,143,147 |

Article II of the *Constitution* defines the powers and responsibilities of the President of the United States.

1)   AS CHIEF EXECUTIVE

a)   General Executive Power

(1)   Vesting Clause

Article II provides, in part, that "The executive power shall be vested in a President of the United States of America." U.S. Const. art. II, § 1. This Vesting Clause authorizes the President to engage in certain types of activity traditionally conducted by heads of state, generally within the scope of federal legal and historical bounds upon the executive branch. Of course, the President may not exercise the powers vested either in Congress (the legislative branch), or the federal courts (the judicial branch).

(2)   Take Care Clause

The Take Care Clause provides that the President must "take care that the laws be faithfully executed." U.S. Const. art. II, § 3. The President possesses power to execute the laws of the United States and to supervise the federal government's operation. The President is authorized to take any action that is expressly or implicitly permitted under the *Constitution* and not otherwise prohibited by law.

b)   Scope of Presidential Discretion

The President's obligation to execute the law includes the duty to fulfill the law's standards of execution. Those express standards may limit the manner in which the President administers and enforces the law. Congress may, alternatively, explicitly grant the President substantial discretion in determining how to execute the law. In the absence of express standards or explicit discretion, the President may exercise implied discretion in executing the law.

c)   Pardon Power

Article II provides the President with: "Power to grant Reprieves and Pardons for Offenses against the United States, except in Cases of Impeachment." U.S. Const. art. II, § 2. The power to pardon extends "to every offense known to the law, and [it] may be exercised at any time after its commission, either before legal proceedings are taken, or during their pendency, or after conviction and judgment." The President may pardon persons from convictions of federal offenses, subject to certain limitations imposed by the Supreme Court. Congress may not attempt to statutorily limit the President's right to pardon.

2)   AS COMMANDER IN CHIEF

Article II makes the President the Commander in Chief of all military forces of the United States. U.S. Const. art. II, § 2, cl. 1. As such, the President possesses the power to deploy military service members and equipment in operations around the world without a congressional declaration of war if that deployment:

- is necessary to protect Americans abroad; or
- is in furtherance of other national security interests.

3)   TREATY, FOREIGN AFFAIRS, AND OTHER POWERS

a)   Treaties

Under the Treaty Clause, the President is empowered to negotiate and execute treaties between the United States and foreign nations that are not contrary to federal law. U.S. Const. art. II, § 2, cl. 2. Those documents are not binding or effective unless ratified by a two-thirds vote of the Senate. Ratification makes a treaty the "supreme law of the land" if the treaty does not contravene any constitutional provisions. A treaty remains in effect until Congress enacts law that contravenes or controls the treaty.

b)   Foreign Affairs

The President is the sole officer of government in the field of international relations. The President, however, cannot take certain action regarding foreign commerce without congressional authorization. Congressional approval is required because Congress possesses the power to regulate foreign commerce under the Commerce Clause. The President may issue an executive order pursuant to, or in furtherance of, congressional regulation of foreign commerce.

c)   Executive Agreement

The President has broad authority to negotiate and sign executive agreements that are binding upon the United States when executed by a foreign nation's authorized leader and the President. An executive agreement is effective without ratification by Congress. An executive agreement cannot contravene or supersede federal law.

d)   Executive Order

Although the President lacks the power to make statutory law, the President has general authority to issue executive orders that are the law of the land. Those orders are effective without congressional approval. An executive order cannot contravene or supersede federal law. The President possesses the power to issue executive orders that impact employees of the administration. That power may not, however, be employed to violate the employees' rights under the *Constitution*, such as the freedom of speech.

(1)   Lawmaking Authority

An executive order may be invalidated if it constitutes an exercise of congressional lawmaking authority. For example, the Supreme Court invalidated the executive order of President Truman authorizing the federal government to seize and operate private steel mills to preclude strikes by workers during wartime. The majority opinion found that the President usurped the lawmaking power of Congress and lacked authority to issue this executive order pursuant to either the power to execute the laws or the power to serve as the commander-in-chief. *Youngstown Sheet & Tube Co. v. Sawyer*, 343 U.S. 579 (1952).

(a)   Levels of Executive Power

A prominent concurring opinion of the majority opinion in the case described the following three levels of presidential power to act.

- The President exercises the highest level of power when acting pursuant to express or implied congressional authority.
- The President exercises a lower level of power when acting in the absence of any congressional denial or grant of authority.
- The President exercises the lowest level of power when acting contrary to an express or implied will of congressional authority.

Courts differ with respect to when the President acts under the middle, intermediate level of power due to congressional silence about an issue. If Congress has rejected a proposed executive power without enacting legislation against the President's exercise of the power, this exercise probably would be subject to judicial disapproval and invalidation. However, if Congress has impliedly acquiesced in the President's exercise of power, then this may be considered when determining the constitutionality of that exercise of power.

e)   Priority of Conflicting Obligations

- The *U.S. Constitution* is the supreme law of the land. Any conflicting law is invalid.
- Treaties and federal statutes are the next highest authority. If a federal statute conflicts with a treaty, then the most recently adopted of the two

governs. If a treaty or federal statute conflicts with the *Constitution*, the *Constitution* governs.

- Executive orders and executive agreements are the next highest authority. If a statute or treaty conflicts with an executive order or agreement, the treaty or statute governs.
- State law is the lowest of these authorities. If a state law conflicts with any federal law, the federal law governs.

4) APPOINTMENT AND REMOVAL OF OFFICIALS

a) Appointment

Under the Appointment Clause, the President possesses authority to appoint ambassadors, certain federal officials, and members of the federal judiciary. U.S. Const. art. II, § 2, cl. 2. For example, the President may appoint federal officials who are empowered to enforce, or prosecute violations of, federal law. The President is empowered to appoint executive officials.

b) Impeachment / Removal

Article II provides the President with implied power to remove executive officers that he appointed. However, the President may not remove, at will, a quasi-judicial officer or a quasi-legislative officer, even if the President appointed the officer.

★★

C. Federal Interbranch Relationships

Question Key
3,67,68,76,111,120,161,164

1) CONGRESSIONAL LIMITS ON THE EXECUTIVE

★★   a)   Appointment

Under the Advice and Consent Clause in Article II, the President's power to appoint ambassadors, certain federal officials, and members of the federal judiciary is subject to the Senate's "advice and consent." U.S. Const. art. II, § 2, cl. 2. Congress may authorize the federal judiciary, the President, and Cabinet members to appoint other "inferior officers," for lower-level federal positions. Congress may not, however, provide that power to itself. Congress lacks any power of appointment. Any congressional appointment is void. Any congressional regulations or rules that purport to authorize or govern appointments by Congress are invalid.

b) Impeachment / Removal

Congress is authorized to impeach the President, the Vice President, certain federal officials, and members of the federal judiciary on the grounds of bribery, treason, high crimes, and misdemeanors. U.S. Const. art. II, § 4. A majority vote of the House is required to impeach the President or the other officials. A two-thirds majority vote of the Senate is required to convict and remove the President or other officials.

c) Investigation

(1)   Constitutional Basis of Authority

No constitutional provision expressly empowers Congress to conduct investigations. This authority, however, is derived from the Necessary and Proper Clause of the *Constitution*. The Supreme Court considers the power of investigation as essential to Congress' fulfillment of its legislative and oversight functions. The Supreme Court has approved Congress' exercise of the contempt power to enforce a congressional subpoena of a witness. Congress often conducts investigations in support of a legislative agenda or to oversee the activities of other branches of government or administrative agencies.

(2)   Permissible Scope of Investigations

The Necessary and Proper Clause empowers Congress to conduct investigations if the purpose and scope of the fact finding is relevant to the legislative function of Congress. On that basis, Congress may conduct hearings, issue subpoenas, and question witnesses. If the investigatory questions concern issues irrelevant to the legislative function, then a witness possesses a valid constitutional defense to answering the questions. Congress may appoint officials to conduct investigations on its behalf. Those officials are subject to the same limitations that apply to Congress. Generally, neither Congress nor its appointed officials are authorized to take law enforcement action as a result of these investigations.

d)   Appropriation

The congressional spending power may be exercised in a manner that limits the executive branch's power. Although the executive branch traditionally submits a proposed budget to Congress, Congress still must enact legislation to authorize funding by means of appropriations. Congress may establish various funding levels of the appropriations that are different from those of the President. Although the President may decide to veto an appropriations bill, Congress may override that veto to effectuate different appropriations than those that the President had proposed.

2)   <u>PRESENTMENT AND VETO</u>

Although the President may propose legislation for congressional enactment, the President lacks the exclusive power of Congress to legislate.

a)   Presentment

The Presentment Clause of Article I requires that if both the House and the Senate pass and reconcile related legislation, their final bill must be provided to the President for approval or veto. U.S. Const. art. I, § 7, cl. 2. The President's signature on the bill within 10 days completes its enactment into law as of its effective date.

b)   Veto

The President possesses the power to veto a bill simply by not signing it into law. The veto both disapproves of the legislation and prevents its enactment. Congress may override the veto only if both the House of Representatives and the Senate each obtain the vote of two-thirds of their members in favor of the legislation. In that event, the presentment requirement does not apply again, and the bill automatically becomes law on its effective date.

c)   Legislative Veto

The term legislative veto refers to the repeal by Congress of federal agency or presidential actions. In *INS v. Chadha,* the Supreme Court invalidated a federal law that provided for a legislative veto. The law unconstitutionally permitted a joint committee of Congress to overrule decisions of an executive branch agency.   A legislative veto violates the principle of separation of powers. Thus, Congress cannot legislatively obtain the power to veto the President's execution of federal law.

d)   Line-Item Veto

The term line-item veto refers to the power of the President to nullify specific provisions of a bill, most often budget appropriations, without vetoing the entire bill. The laws of several states possess line-item veto provisions.

The President briefly obtained the power by the *Line-Item Veto Act of 1996.* However, that law was struck down as an unconstitutional presidential exercise of legislative action.

★★   3)   THE DELEGATION DOCTRINE

a)   General Rule

Congress is the entity that conducts legislative actions. However, Congress may delegate limited legislative authority (i.e., legislative actions, but not the power to declare war) to members of the other branches, usually the executive branch or even to the President.

b)   Intelligible Standards

When Congress is permitted to delegate its authority, it must provide the delegate with intelligible standards and guidelines. The Supreme Court traditionally takes a deferential approach to applying the intelligible standards requirement.   Thus, usually most delegations of authority have been permitted.

★   4)   EXECUTIVE,   LEGISLATIVE,   AND   JUDICIAL
                    IMMUNITIES

a)   Executive Immunity

(1)   Immunity from Civil Actions

The President is protected by absolute immunity for civil actions seeking money damages arising from the President's conduct while in office. The immunity does not apply to the President's conduct prior to taking office.

(2)   Executive Privilege

(a)   Absolute Privilege

As a general rule, the President possesses an executive privilege of confidentiality with respect to certain activities and operations of that office. Thus, the President usually is not obligated to disclose privileged information to third parties who are outside of the President's administration. The executive privilege fully applies in terms of issues such as diplomatic, military, or certain national security interests. The President does not, however, possess an absolute and unqualified privilege of immunity from judicial process in every situation.

(i)   Civil Cases

In *Cheney v. U.S. District Court for the District of Columbia*, a civil case, the Supreme Court decided that a federal court prematurely denied then Vice-President Cheney's request to maintain confidential the details of his energy-task force meetings (e.g., the identity of non-governmental members), which he made pursuant to the *Federal Advisory Committee Act*. With respect to discovery requests to the Vice-President and others who served on this task force formed to advise President Bush, the Court noted that: "Special considerations control when the Executive's interests in maintaining its autonomy and safeguarding its communications' confidentiality are implicated." The Court also pointed out that the right to production of relevant evidence in civil cases lacks the identical "constitutional dimensions" that exist in criminal proceedings. Indeed, withholding necessary materials in ongoing criminal proceedings may impermissibly impair essential functions of another branch of government.

(b)   Qualified Privilege – Criminal

The President possesses a qualified privilege not to disclose confidential information that is otherwise subject to discovery in criminal proceedings. The valid need for protection of executive communications assists in performance of executive duties. However, the privilege is not absolute. The President must demonstrate more than a generalized need for confidentiality. A court should weigh the public interest in obtaining the truth against the need of the President to maintain confidentiality.

b)   Legislative Immunity

The Speech and Debate Clause of the *Constitution*, provides that "for any Speech or Debate in either House [all Congress members] shall not be questioned in any other Place." U.S. Const. art. I, § 6. That provision applies to the official activities of the members of Congress while they participate in the legislative function. It generally protects them by making their communications in that capacity privileged from civil or criminal suit, including grand jury proceedings. The immunity does not apply to the communication by a member:

- that occurred prior to taking office;
- that involved political functions during the member's term of office; or
- after the member leaves office.

The staff of members of Congress also may assert the privilege for their conduct that occurs in the scope of their work on behalf of their respective members of Congress.

c)   Judicial Immunity

Members of the federal judiciary, such as federal judges and the Supreme Court's justices, are protected by immunity from civil actions seeking money damages and for actions arising from statements made while acting as a member of the judiciary. The immunity does not apply to statements made, or conduct that occurred:

- before the member took office;
- in the member's term of office, but not while the member engaged in official conduct; or
- after the member leaves office.

III.   **THE RELATIONS OF NATION AND STATES IN A FEDERAL SYSTEM**

★   A.   **Intergovernmental Immunities** ⎯⎯⎤ ⎢ Question Key
                                                      7,29,36,52,126,151

★   1)   FEDERAL IMMUNITY FROM STATE LAW

a)   The Supremacy Clause

Article II contains the Supremacy Clause, which makes the *Constitution*, federal law, and treaties, the "supreme law of the land." U.S. Const. art. II, § 2. The Supremacy Clause mandates that state courts follow the *Constitution* if a state law conflicts with the *Constitution*. State governments, including state judicial branches, can neither disregard the *Constitution*, nor its interpretation by the federal judiciary. If a state officer fails to abide by a federal law, the official may be punished pursuant to federal law and the power of contempt.

(1)   Intergovernmental Immunity

The Supremacy Clause legally furthers the principle of federalism that, in certain respects, the state governments and laws are subordinate to the federal government and laws. The Supremacy Clause is the basis for the doctrine of intergovernmental immunity. Pursuant to the doctrine, states cannot enact laws that interfere with the operations and activities of the federal government. The Supremacy Clause prohibits a state from regulating in a way that affects the federal government's laws or regulations unless either:

- the state receives express consent from the federal government; or

- the state law is consistent with federal law already in effect.

(2)   Tax Immunity

The federal government is immune from direct taxation by a state. However, a state may impose an indirect and nondiscriminatory tax upon the federal government. For example, a state may impose a uniform tax upon all similarly situated taxpayers of a particular status, class, or category, that include federal government employees, but that does not treat the federal officials differently from other taxpayers.

Federal property is immune from local and state property taxes. However, the lessees of federally owned facilities are subject to non-discriminatory property-use taxes based on the value of the facility.

2)   STATE IMMUNITY FROM FEDERAL LAW

A state is immune from taxation by the federal government on property that is used in, or income that is derived from, the state's performance of basic governmental functions. For example, state park land cannot be taxed by the federal government.

	Question Key
B. The Authority Reserved to the States	5,31,32,61,74,78,79, 98,134,139,145,148

1)   NEGATIVE IMPLICATIONS OF COMMERCE CLAUSE

a)   Dormant Commerce Clause

The phrase Dormant Commerce Clause (also called Negative Commerce Clause) refers to certain negative or implicit implications of the Commerce Clause of the *Constitution*. The Commerce Clause authorizes Congress to enact laws that may affect interstate commerce. This "Commerce" power implies a negative converse — that states are restricted from legislating in a manner that improperly burdens or discriminates against interstate commerce.

b)   Types of Laws Subject to the Dormant Commerce Clause

The types of laws subject to analysis under the Dormant Commerce Clause are: 1) discriminatory laws (laws that expressly discriminate against out-of-state people or entities); and 2) laws that do not expressly discriminate, but unduly burden interstate commerce, which can be discriminatory against out-of-state people or entities. As for an expressly discriminatory law, suppose that state A enacts a statute providing that only oil from wells within its borders may be processed in refineries located in state A. This law could be challenged as expressly discriminatory by state B, which prior to the law's enactment had provided most of the oil that was refined in state A. A law that does not expressly discriminate but unduly burden interstate commerce, for example, could provide that no carbonated beverage may be sold in state A unless it was bottled within 20 miles from where it was sold in state A. The standard of review under the Dormant Commerce Clause depends upon whether it is a discriminatory law or a law that burdens interstate commerce.

(1)   Undue Burdens

A state statute may be unconstitutional if it unreasonably burdens interstate commerce. A state statute that impermissibly burdens interstate commerce treats that commerce more adversely than intrastate commerce by, for example, imposing increased regulatory obligations on out-of-state individuals or entities as compared to intrastate individuals or entities.

As a general rule, state or local laws that affect interstate commerce are unconstitutional unless the following elements are fulfilled:

- A legitimate governmental end is pursued by the law;

- A rational relation exists between the law and the end that is pursued;

- The law's benefits exceed its burden upon interstate commerce; and

- Nondiscriminatory alternatives are not available.

If compared to the following test regarding discriminatory laws, the standard for laws that unduly burden interstate commerce (but do not expressly discriminate against them) is much more relaxed. Therefore, a state law is much more likely to be upheld if it merely unduly burdens interstate commerce than if it expressly discriminates against it.

(2)   Discriminatory Favoring and Disfavoring

Generally, if a local or state law discriminates against out-of-state individuals or entities, it is unconstitutional unless it is necessary to achieve an important governmental purpose. Such a law would favor in-state and local individuals or entities and disfavor out-of-state individuals or entities. Such a law might establish different sets of laws for individuals or entities within a state or locality as compared to individuals or entities located outside that state or locality. A discriminatory law cannot be justified on the basis of economic protectionism in favor of the state or the locality.

Based on the Dormant Commerce Clause, the Supreme Court invalidated a state law that discriminated against out-of-state haulers of solid waste in favor of in-state haulers of solid waste because the law involved unconstitutional discrimination. The law was intended to preserve space in treatment facilities for in-state solid waste at the exclusion of out-of-state solid waste.

In *Granholm v. Heald*, the Supreme Court held that statutes of Michigan and New York regulating importation and sale of wine discriminated against interstate commerce contrary to the Commerce Clause. Moreover, the Court concluded that section 2 of the Twenty-first Amendment to the *U.S. Constitution* neither permitted nor authorized this discrimination by differential treatment of in-state winery interests compared to treatment of out-of-state wineries, which were burdened while in-state wineries were benefitted. The Court found that these state statutes unconstitutionally deprived citizens of their right to have access to the markets of other states on equal terms.

(a)   Government Interests/Market Participant

The following limited grounds may render constitutional a state law that otherwise discriminates against out-of-state individuals or entities in favor of in-state individuals or entities:

- The law is necessary to accomplish an important government interest; such as protecting the environment within the locality or the state; or

- A locality or a state gives preference to its citizens' receipt of government benefits, and the locality or the state is participating in a market as a business. This is known as the market participant exception.

On the exam, it is often unnecessary to determine whether a law, in practice, satisfies one of these grounds (i.e., whether it actually is necessary to accomplish an important government interest). Unless specific Supreme Court precedent has decided the specific factual scenario one way or the other, it is unlikely that you will have to make a close judgment call on the exam. Often, the exam language is termed in conditional statements referencing the appropriate legal standard. For example, an answer choice may provide that the law is valid "if the law is necessary to accomplish an important government interest." If the appropriate legal standard is used, then this answer choice must be correct. This is because the use of conditional language of the word "if," renders the answer choice correct under these circumstances.

If, on the other hand, the answer choice uses the word "because" instead of "if," then the answer requires a judgment call. For example, an answer choice may provide that the law is valid "because the law is necessary to accomplish an important government interest." By substituting the word "because" for the word "if," the answer requires an examinee to make the judgment call that the law set forth in the question actually does satisfy the required test. This is a leap of logic that requires certainty in the factual analysis regarding the required standard.

(b)   State as Market Participant

A state law that discriminates in favor of in-state entities or individuals over out-of-state entities may be constitutionally permissible under the Commerce Clause if the state has a pecuniary or proprietary interest in the financial success of an in-state business activity or industry that the state law protects. In that situation, the state is a market participant because it created, sponsored, or is in a joint venture with a particular type of business activity or industry. Consequently, the state has an economic interest in fostering the success of that business activity or industry through discriminatory regulation that favors it over out-of-state competitors.

For example, a state law may allow for a lower tuition rate at state universities for state residents as compared to non-state residents.

2)   TENTH AMENDMENT

a)   General

The Tenth Amendment to the *Constitution* ("Tenth Amendment") provides: "The powers not delegated to the United States by the *Constitution*, nor prohibited by it to the States, are reserved to the States respectively, or to the people." U.S. Const. amend. X.

b)   Limited State Sovereignty

Under the Tenth Amendment, a state possesses power to regulate the activities of its separate branches of government free from federal government interference. That power may be considered a component of state sovereignty under the Tenth Amendment. The federal government may, however, enact and enforce laws that affect a state government's activities if those laws did not contradict the state's right to regulate those activities. One example of such a law is the *Racketeer Influenced and Corrupt Organizations Act* ("RICO").

c)   States Subject to Indirect Mandates

The Tenth Amendment does not prevent Congress from indirectly obtaining a state's compliance with a valid police power objective. Thus, a federal statute may constitutionally render a state's receipt of federal highway funding contingent on the state's making of a legislative change in the legal drinking age. That condition is rationally related to a legitimate congressional interest in decreasing the amount of traffic fatalities on federal highways.

d)   No Direct Mandates

The Tenth Amendment precludes Congress from requiring states to enact laws or to administer federal law. For example, it prohibits directly mandating that a state regulatory agency take specific action. In *New York v. United States* and *Printz v. United States*, the Supreme Court ruled that federal laws may not commandeer state legislatures by obligating states to pass and execute federal legislation. Such federal laws would impermissibly deprive a state of its sovereignty under principles of federalism included in the Tenth Amendment. In *Printz v. United States*, the Supreme Court invalidated a federal statute that required state and local law enforcement officials to perform background checks on potential purchasers of handguns. Although state governments generally may not be subjected to affirmative duties by federal statutes, under *Reno v. Condon* such statutes may prohibit state governments from making unauthorized disclosure of certain personal information like the names and addresses of its licensed motor vehicle drivers.

3)   OTHER

a)   General

The powers reserved to the states under the Tenth Amendment are numerous and provide the basis for each state government's existence and activities.

b)   Police Power

One primary category of state authority under the general right of sovereign self-government is the police power. The police powers are those that a state employs to protect the public's health, safety, welfare, and morals. A state's exercise of police power generally is permissible as long as the *Constitution* is not otherwise violated. Examples of state offices that exercise police powers include law enforcement agencies, criminal justice systems, and public health and sanitation services.

c)   Non-Federal Legislation

The Tenth Amendment authorizes state and local legislatures to enact social and economic legislation, subject to two limitations:

- Federal constitutional rights may not be violated; and

- The legislation must be rationally related to achieving a legitimate governmental interest.

For example, in *Prudential Insurance Co. v. Benjamin*, the Supreme Court decided that police power authorizes states to regulate auto insurance rates.

d)   Standard of Review

A state law promulgated pursuant to the police power is valid under the following conditions:

- A conflicting federal law does not preempt the state law;

- The state law does not exceed the limits of state power with respect to interstate commerce; and

- The state law does not violate individual constitutional rights.

C.   National Power to Override or Extend State Authority

1)   PREEMPTION

a)   Constitutional Basis

| Question Key |
| 1,4,8,22,51,56, |
| 91,123,165 |

The Supremacy Clause of the *Constitution* underlies the Preemption Doctrine. The doctrine provides that federal law overrides state law if the state law conflicts with the federal law. There are two types of preemption, either express or implied.

b)   Express Preemption

Express preemption is evident when federal law explicitly states that it preempts other law. Such federal law supersedes any state law that attempts to regulate the same subject matter.

c)   Implied Preemption

Implied preemption arises when a federal law is silent about preemption and one of three circumstances is present: (1) when it is impossible to comply with both state and federal requirements; (2) when a state law impedes a specified federal objective; or (3) when federal law implicitly indicates that Congress intended to "occupy a field" of legal subject matter. To determine if a federal law impliedly preempts another law, a court will evaluate the language of the relevant statutes, as well as assess the overall statutory objectives.

2)   AUTHORIZATION OF OTHERWISE INVALID STATE ACTION

a)   Congressional Approval of Non-Federal Law

In *Gibbons v. Ogden*, the Supreme Court stated that Congress "may adopt provisions of a state [law] of any subject." For example, Congress possesses the authority to legislatively approve or adopt local or state legal provisions that affect commerce. Congress may do that even if the provisions otherwise would conflict with or violate the Dormant Commerce Clause.

b)   Federal and State Regulation

Congress may exercise its plenary power under the Commerce Clause in the following ways:

- delegate to the states certain power to regulate commerce;

- share with the states its power to regulate commerce; or

- prohibit the states from exercising the power to regulate commerce.

c)   Congressionally Authorized Laws

Congress is not required to outlaw all state laws that burden, or are discriminatory with respect to, interstate commerce. Congress may authorize a burdensome or discriminatory state law. Conversely, the following types of state laws are valid in the absence of any congressional authorization.

- a state law that does not unduly burden interstate commerce, if the local interest the law advances outweighs the burden it imposes; or

- a discriminatory state law that advances a legitimate state interest, when nondiscriminatory alternatives were unavailable.

D.   **Relations Among States**

Question Key
154

1)   INTERSTATE COMPACTS

a)   Constitutional Basis

The Compact Clause in Article I of the *Constitution* provides in part that "No State shall, without the Consent of Congress…enter into any Agreement or Compact with another State or with a Foreign Power." U.S. Const. art. I, § 10, cl. 3. The *Constitution* has been interpreted to require congressional consent for some, but not all, interstate agreements.

b)   When Consent Is Required

With respect to agreements or compacts among two or more states, congressional consent is not necessary regarding those "many matters upon which different states may agree and that can in no respect concern the United States." The consent of Congress, however, will be required if:

- an agreement tends to increase the political power;

- of those states who are parties to it;

- that might interfere with or encroach on the United States' supremacy.

For example, an agreement by adjacent states to change their common border line would need congressional consent if either state's political power consequently might be altered. Conversely, congressional consent is not required for state laws that allow for regional banking, because such laws do not increase the political power of the states in which the regional banking occurs.

c)   Means of Consent

Congress may give consent to an agreement or compact by means of legislation that approves either of them before or after their formation. When such congressional consent is obtained, the agreement or compact becomes a federal law and, by its terms, may limit the scope of judicial relief available to the parties.

d)   Limited Judicial Relief

The Supreme Court will not provide judicial relief if a properly approved agreement or compact contains terms that might seem unfair to its parties. In *Texas v. New Mexico*, the Supreme Court held that "unless the compact to which Congress has consented is somehow unconstitutional, no court may order relief inconsistent with its expressed terms."

★   2)   <u>FULL FAITH AND CREDIT</u>

a)   Constitutional Basis

Article IV of the *Constitution* includes the Full Faith and Credit Clause. The Clause states, in part, that "Full Faith and Credit shall be given in each State to the public Acts, Records, and judicial Proceedings of every other State." U.S. Const. art. IV, § 1.

b)   Legal Effect of Clause

A partial effect of the Full Faith and Credit Clause is to require that a final judgment in a legal proceeding, which was rendered by a court of one state, be recognized as valid by the courts in other states. The other states are required to deem the final judgment as *res adjudicata*. For example, the other states are obligated to allow a judgment creditor to maintain an action to enforce a valid final judgment, entered by a sister state, that is rendered for money damages. The same principal applies to judicial recognition of the official acts and records of a sister state.

IV.   INDIVIDUAL RIGHTS

★★★

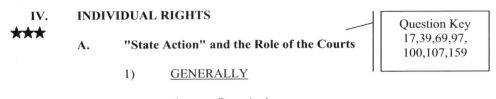

| Question Key |
| 17,39,69,97, |
| 100,107,159 |

A.   **"State Action" and the Role of the Courts**

1)   <u>GENERALLY</u>

a)   State Action

The *Constitution* places limitations on governmental conduct, not, with minor exception, on private conduct. Therefore, in order to invoke the protection of the *Constitution*, a person must demonstrate that the challenged conduct involves state action.

State action occurs when a government (federal, state, or local) engages in conduct that implicates the constitutional rights of a person. State action may or may not involve private individuals or entities. Therefore, a government may not avoid the consequences of state action by utilizing a private individual or entity to engage in unconstitutional conduct against a person. The question of when the private actions of individuals constitute state action subject to the *Constitution* is a difficult one that will be addressed in the next section on Types of State Action.

b)   Private Action

Wholly private action includes many types of conduct undertaken by individuals or entities who are not serving in any public capacity. Not all private action must comply with the *Constitution*. In fact, most do not. Only the Thirteenth Amendment expressly applies to a private action. The other provisions of the *Constitution* address limitations on state action.

2)   <u>TYPES OF STATE ACTION</u>

a)   Private Source of Information

State action may arise when a private individual or entity assists with, or engages in, conduct on behalf of a government that implicates the constitutional rights of a person. When the state action is based on private information supplied to a government by an individual or entity, the state action must comply with the same constitutional and legal requirements that would apply if the government itself had obtained that information.

b)   Entangled State and Private Activity

If an individual or entity engages in unconstitutional activity pursuant to a government's encouragement, authorization, or facilitation, then the individual or entity is subject to constitutional provisions that protect against such activity. That type of an entanglement would exist, for example, if a state police officer asks a person to obtain a box that the person's roommate keeps in his closet. More specifically, state action may exist if excessive entanglement occurs between a private individual or entity and a government.

However, state regulation or licensing of a private individual or entity, in and of itself, does not transform that private individual's or entity's conduct into state action. For example, requiring a person to obtain a fishing license does not transform that person's fishing activities into state action.

c)   Judicial Enforcement of Constitutional Rights

Courts may enforce the laws Congress enacted to protect against state action. As discussed earlier, those laws are based on certain constitutional amendments. Even if the private conduct of individuals or entities is not subject to these amendments, such private conduct may be subject to statutes enacted pursuant to these amendments. If an individual or entity uses a state's court in order to enforce a private right to discriminate, that conduct is considered tantamount to state action. Consequently, such private action will be subject to review by the federal courts under the Equal Protection Clause of the Fourteenth Amendment.

3)   <u>CIVIL LIABILITY</u>

a)   State Action

If the government acts in conformity with all relevant constitutional and legal protections, then the government will not have any civil liability to a person for its conduct. However, if state action violates a person's constitutional or legal protections, then the government may be subject to civil liability to that person.

b)   Private Activity

If a private individual or entity engages in conduct that adversely affects a person's constitutional rights without being encouraged or directed to do so by a government, then the government may avoid legal liability for state action. Similarly, a government may avoid legal liability for state action if a private individual or entity alone adversely affects a person's constitutional rights by undertaking the performance of a traditional government function. In those instances, only the private individual or entity could be civilly liable for the unconstitutional conduct.

(1)   Entangled State and Private Activity

If a government encourages or directs a private individual or entity to engage in conduct that adversely affects a person's constitutional rights, then that conduct constitutes state action for which the government will be legally accountable. In other words, the government cannot avoid legal accountability for state action that adversely affects a person's constitutional rights on the basis that an individual or entity perpetrated the state action if it occurs on the government's behalf. In that event, both the government and the private individual or entity could be civilly liable for the state action.

B.   Due Process

1)   <u>GENERAL CONSTITUTIONAL BASIS</u>

a)   Fifth and Fourteenth Amendments

(1)   Fifth Amendment (Federal)

The Due Process Clause of the Fifth Amendment to the *Constitution* ("Fifth Amendment") applies to the federal government by its terms. The Fifth Amendment provides that no person may be "deprived of life, liberty, or property, without due process of law." U.S. Const. amend. V. The Fifth Amendment applies to the conduct of the federal government.

(2)   Fourteenth Amendment (State)

The Due Process Clause of the Fourteenth Amendment applies to the states by its terms. It provides, in part, that "nor shall any State deprive any person of life, liberty, or property, without due process of law." U.S. Const. amend. XIV, § 1. The Fourteenth Amendment applies to a state government's conduct.

On the exam, an answer may hinge on whether state or federal activity is being challenged. If federal activity is being challenged, look for a reference to the Fifth Amendment. If state or local activity is being challenged, look for a reference to the Fourteenth Amendment.

b)   Selective Incorporation

The Supreme Court's case law makes many of the provisions in the Bill of Rights (the first 10 amendments to the *Constitution*) applicable to the states based on the selective incorporation doctrine, which operates through the Due Process Clause of the Fourteenth Amendment. For example, freedom of expression pursuant to the First Amendment may be selectively incorporated to apply to the states. Consequently, a state would be prohibited from violating a person's rights under the incorporated provision.

(1)   Exceptions to Selective Incorporation

The following provisions under the Bill of Rights are not extended to the states pursuant to the Due Process Clause of the Fourteenth Amendment. Therefore, a state is not required to protect individual rights under the following provisions (although states often do under their own constitutions):

- right against the quartering of soldiers in one's house. U.S. Const. amend. III.

- right in criminal cases to a grand jury indictment. U.S. Const. amend. V.

- right against excessive fines. U.S. Const. amend. VIII.

- right in civil cases to a jury trial. U.S. Const. amend. VII.

- right to bear arms. U.S. Const. amend. II.

2)   SUBSTANTIVE DUE PROCESS

| Question Key |
| 24,43,55,103,109,114, |
| 118,119,146 |

a)   Types of Due Process

State action that impairs, interferes with, denies, or deprives a person of life, liberty, or property requires substantial justification. To be constitutionally valid, that action must comply with the requirements of both substantive and procedural due process.

b)   Types of Rights

Once a court determines that a person's due process rights are being denied by a law, a court then may determine whether the government action is justified. The type of analysis a court employs to review a Due Process Clause issue will depend upon the classification of the right that is at stake or allegedly being infringed. There are two general types of rights derived from the *Constitution* – fundamental rights and other rights. The analytical standard employed by a court will depend upon whether the implicated right is a fundamental right or other right.

c)   Standards of Review

Under the doctrine of judicial review, the Supreme Court has developed different types of analysis (i.e., levels of scrutiny) for the review of laws and government conduct to determine if they satisfy the requirements of the relevant Due Process Clause. Those standards of review will be addressed in relation to the types of rights involved.

(1)   Fundamental Rights and Strict Scrutiny

A court will analyze government action that results in depriving a person of his fundamental rights with strict scrutiny. It is the most rigorous standard of judicial review. Under the strict scrutiny standard, a court will inquire:

- Is a law necessary to achieve a compelling government purpose?

- Is the least-restrictive means used?

- Does no less burdensome means exist to accomplish the purpose? and

- Is the law sufficiently narrowly tailored to accomplish the purpose?

- Burden of Proof

The government possesses the burden of proving the law's validity under the strict scrutiny test.

★★

(a) Fundamental Rights

Several rights are classified as fundamental rights which, if implicated, require analysis under the strict scrutiny standard. For exam purposes, these include: 1) the right to freedom of association; 2) the right to privacy; 3) the right to vote; and 4) the right to travel, (as well as most rights in the bill of rights). On the exam, those rights generally are analyzed under right- or fact-specific standards that are covered in other portions of this outline.

(i) Right to Privacy

For exam purposes, fundamental rights implicated in substantive due process analysis often are related to the right to privacy. Although the *Constitution* contains no express right to privacy, the Supreme Court has held that in many personal affairs, such an implied right to privacy exists. For example, in *Pierce v. Society of Sisters*, the Supreme Court provided for a parent's fundamental right to choose the manner in which the parent's child is educated (not the right to an education itself). In *Loving v. Virginia*, the Supreme Court protected the fundamental right to marry a person of one's choosing regardless of his and her respective racial background. In *Griswold v. Connecticut*, the Supreme Court recognized the right of individuals to acquire and utilize contraceptives.

(A) Sexual Conduct

In *Lawrence v. Texas*, the Supreme Court struck down a Texas law that made it a crime to engage in homosexual sodomy. The Court expressly overruled *Bowers v. Hardwick*, which had upheld a similar Georgia statute by not recognizing a constitutional protection of sexual privacy.

(B) Right to Abortion

In *Roe v. Wade*, the Supreme Court recognized a woman's right of privacy as the legal basis for limiting the regulation or banning of abortion. *Roe v. Wade* protects a woman's right to obtain an abortion on demand prior to the viability of a fetus, which occurs at the beginning of the third trimester. During the first trimester, a state cannot impose any law that limits a woman's right to an abortion. During the second trimester, a state can only impose a law that protects its interest in the mother's health. However, after the point of fetal viability (i.e., when the fetus can survive outside the womb), no fundamental right to an abortion exists. Beyond this point, states may regulate or outlaw abortion unless, in order to protect the woman's health or life, abortion is necessary.

(I) Undue Burden

Pursuant to *Roe v. Wade*, for substantive due process purposes, a woman possesses a fundamental right to an abortion before fetal viability. Accordingly, in that case, the Supreme Court applied the strict scrutiny standard of review. However, in the subsequent case of *Planned Parenthood v. Casey*, the Supreme Court did not utilize a strict scrutiny analysis of state regulations affecting abortion. Instead, the Supreme Court used the analytical test of whether the state law at issue imposes an undue burden on the woman's ability to choose to have an abortion before the fetus is viable. An undue burden exists if a state imposes legal restrictions that are substantial obstacles to obtaining an abortion before the fetus is viable. If the state law imposes such an undue burden on a woman's right to an abortion during that period, a court will invalidate it.

In *Stenberg v. Carhart*, the Supreme Court held that a Nebraska law criminalizing partial birth abortion, unless necessary to save the mother's life, violated the *Constitution*. Partial birth abortion is a surgical abortion wherein an intact fetus is removed from the uterus via the cervix. The Supreme Court's majority opinion stated and applied two rules from *Planned Parenthood v. Casey*. First, a woman possesses the right to an abortion before the fetus is viable. Second, a law that imposes an undue burden on the woman's abortion decision before the fetus is viable is unconstitutional. This opinion also stated and applied the rule from *Roe v. Wade*, that after the fetus is viable, the state can regulate or prohibit abortion unless it is necessary for the woman's health or life. The Supreme Court found the Nebraska law unconstitutional for two reasons. First, it lacked an exception for the preservation of the woman's health. Second, it caused those who performed abortions to "fear prosecution, conviction, and imprisonment," which resulted in an "undue burden upon a woman's right to make an abortion decision."

However, in *Gonzales v. Carhart*, the Supreme Court held that the federal *Partial-Birth Abortion Ban Act of 2003,* which banned partial birth abortions, was constitutional because, among other reasons, it did not impose an undue burden on a woman's right to abortion under the rules of *Planned Parenthood v. Casey*.

According to the Supreme Court's decision in *Ayotte v. Planned Parenthood of Northern New England*, "if enforcing a statute that regulates access to abortion would be unconstitutional in medical emergencies, invalidating the statute entirely is not always necessary or justified, for lower courts may be able to render narrower declaratory and injunctive relief."

(II)   Resolved
         Issues

- Waiting Period

In *Planned Parenthood v. Casey*, the Supreme Court decided that requiring a woman to wait 24 hours before obtaining an abortion is not an undue burden on the woman's right to an abortion.

- Minors and Parental Consent

A parental consent requirement is not an undue burden on a pregnant minor's (i.e., female under 18 years old) right to an abortion. If parental consent is required, there must be a satisfactory judicial bypass procedure. Such a procedure may allow a judge to approve an abortion for a minor: (1) even if the minor is not sufficiently mature and emancipated to make an independent decision to obtain an abortion, and (2) if she convinces the judge that the abortion would be in her best interest. If the judge is so convinced, he must override any parental veto.

- Spousal Consent

The Supreme Court has ruled that requiring a married female to obtain consent from her husband to obtain an abortion constitutes an undue burden.

- State Funding

A state is not obligated to provide funding so that a woman may exercise the right to an abortion.

- State Interest

The state has a legitimate interest in encouraging child birth. Therefore, a state may take action to advance this interest, provided they do not create an undue burden on a woman's right to an abortion.

(ii)   Rights to Vote and Travel

The rights to vote and to interstate travel are fundamental rights. Any law infringing upon these rights is subject to strict scrutiny. Exam issues involving these rights often are addressed in the context of equal protection, because they often involve laws classifying individuals. For a discussion regarding such laws, refer to the section of this outline addressing equal protection.

(2)   Rational Basis Review

A deprivation of rights that are not fundamental must be rationally related to a legitimate government interest. Thus, the applicable standard of judicial review is rational basis analysis. Under that standard, a court will inquire:

- if a contested law is rationally related to;

- achieving a legitimate or hypothetically conceivable government interest.

 A law subject to rational basis review rarely will be invalidated. On the other hand, a law subject to strict scrutiny rarely will be upheld.

- Burden of proof

A challenger of the law possesses the burden of proving its invalidity under rational basis review.

(a)   Other Rights

The non-fundamental rights include matters of economic regulations and entitlements to government benefits. On the exam, they often are referred to as "economic rights." These rights are not fundamental rights and, therefore, are rarely a basis for invalidating a law. Examples of those types of rights include:

- tax laws;

- welfare benefits;

- right to loiter or panhandle;

- practicing a trade or profession; and

- participating in physician-assisted suicide.

3)   <u>TAKINGS</u>

a)   Just Compensation

The Fifth Amendment provides, in its Takings Clause, that private property shall not "be taken for public use, without just compensation." U.S. Const. amend. V.

b)   Obtaining Compensation

Just compensation generally is defined as the reasonable market value of a landowner's real property. Often, the government provides just compensation to a landowner pursuant to a mutual agreement. If no such agreement is reached, and the landowner seeks to obtain just compensation through litigation with a government, a trier of fact will determine what amount of compensation is just. A landowner may bring a "reverse condemnation" action alleging that a government has effectively taken his property and, as such, the landowner is seeking compensation for it. If, on the other hand, a government initiates legal proceedings against a landowner to obtain real property, the action is considered a "condemnation" action. In that action, a government seeks to assert its power of eminent domain against the landowner. Usually, the rational basis standard of review applies to such cases.

The government also may relinquish the taken property and pay damages.

c)   Public Use Requirement

The *Constitution* provides that private property shall "not be taken for public use, without just compensation." The public use requirement is satisfied if the government's action is rationally related to a legitimate public purpose (such as providing for public safety, welfare, health, or other public reasons).

(1)   Public Purpose of Economic Development

In *Kelo v. City of New London*, the Supreme Court broadly interpreted the words "public use" in the Takings Clause as meaning a public purpose. The Court held that "[p]romoting economic development is a traditional and long accepted function of government" in terms of its public purpose. Accordingly, pursuant to a public development plan not adopted "to benefit a particular class of identifiable individuals," contrary to its owner's wishes a government may take private property for the purpose of economic development.

d)   Types of Takings

A government must pay a landowner just compensation for all real property that it takes from the landowner. There are two types of compensable takings: 1) a possessory taking; and 2) a regulatory taking.

(1)   Possessory Taking

A possessory taking involves a government's physical confiscation or occupation of real property. For example, a permanent physical occupation by the government of any private property is a possessory taking. Another example of a possessory taking is when the government takes property to expand a highway from four to six lanes.

(2)   Regulatory Taking

A regulatory taking occurs when a government's regulation eliminates the investment-backed expectation and economic value of an individual's property. Such action constitutes a taking within the meaning of the Fifth Amendment (or as applied to the state by the Fourteenth Amendment). If a regulation constitutes a regulatory taking, the government must provide just compensation.

If the investment-backed expectation and economic value is merely limited, but not eliminated, a taking will not exist (so long as some economically viable interest remains).

4)   <u>PROCEDURAL DUE PROCESS</u>

a)   Nature of Due Process

Question Key
16,25,48,71,72,
127,140,153

The goal of due process is to afford fairness, accuracy, security, and autonomy to each person. A fundamental feature of due process is the provision of notice and a hearing to a person whose legally protected interest in life, liberty, or property is subject to impairment, infringement, deprivation, or denial by a government agency. Even in the absence of a statutory provision for notice and hearing, a due process right under the *Constitution* may afford a person a right to notice and hearing from an agency. *Goldberg v. Kelly*, 397 U.S. 254 (1970) (case involving cancellation of government benefits).

b)   General Considerations

A government must utilize adequate and fair procedures when its action results in an intentional or reckless deprivation of a person's life, liberty, or property. It is important to understand how procedural due process differs from substantive due process.

Substantive due process analysis is concerned with the actual individual right that is impaired, and whether the government possesses the authority to impair that right. Procedural due process analysis, by contrast, is concerned with what procedural mechanisms of challenge the state must provide to an individual before taking a person's protected rights (life, liberty, or property).

c)   Due Process Test

The two-part test for procedural due process includes: 1) determining whether a deprivation of life, liberty, or property occurred; and 2) determining what process is due.

(1)   Did a deprivation of life, liberty, or property occur?

- Life

A deprivation of life occurs when a person dies as a result of state action.

- Liberty

A deprivation of liberty results from a person's incarceration or other denial of a person's physical freedom of mobility. Examples of such deprivation include losses of the right to:

- drive a motorized vehicle for which an operator's license is required;

- engage in a profession for the purpose of earning a living; or

- raise one's own children in a manner that one deems appropriate.

- Property

A deprivation of a personal property interest occurs when a government takes an individual's occupational license, a public employee's job, or a citizen's entitlement to a public benefit. For example, a professor at a public institution who is employed at will possesses no entitlement to continued employment. Therefore, the interest is not subject to due process protections, and the person can be terminated without due process considerations. However, if the professor has tenure, the tenure may create an entitlement to the benefit (i.e., continued employment), such that the state must provide procedural due process safeguards for any potential termination of the professor's employment.

(a)   Law Defines Property Rights

The Supreme Court has permitted a state's local government to delineate the scope and nature of the interest(s) that this government created in an ordinance regarding public employment. Accordingly, a state or local government may describe a benefit by law or contract in a manner that does not confer any property or liberty interest. When a government does this, then an individual recipient of the benefit may not be entitled to judicial relief on claims of a deprivation of an interest.

(2)   What procedures are due under the circumstances?

The Supreme Court in, *Mathews v. Eldridge*, declared that a government must utilize certain procedures of due process in order to deny a person of life, liberty, or property. Determining those procedures involves a balancing of the following considerations:

- What interest is a person seeking to protect?

- What interest is a government seeking to advance?

- What fiscal or administrative burdens would the government incur to use other procedures?

The minimum constitutionally required procedural due process requires:

- the provision of advance notice of a government's anticipated activity; and

- an opportunity for the party subject to that activity to be heard in some type of official proceeding.

d)   General Precedent Examples

(1)   General

In *Santosky v. Kramer*, the Supreme Court decided that a termination of a parent's custody of a child requires both a notice and the presentation at a hearing of clear and convincing evidence of a lack of fitness of the parent.

In re Ruffalo holds that a hearing is required before a professional license is revoked.

The Supreme Court ruled in *Goldberg v. Kelly*, that a hearing is required to end an individual's welfare benefits.

The Due Process Clause also guarantees the rights of criminal procedure. For example, a state prosecutor possesses the burden of establishing every element of a charged crime beyond a reasonable doubt.

    (2)   Public Employees

In *Cleveland Board of Ed. v. Loudermill*, the Supreme Court held that the proper termination of a tenured public employee requires that the employee first receive a notice and an opportunity to be heard before the termination occurs. Public employment constitutes a protected personal property right if an employee is subject to termination only "for cause" pursuant to a public employer's informal customs or policies, an employment manual and/or agreement, or a controlling statute.

Tenure is a protected personal property interest in public employment. A public employee who has not fulfilled an employer's criteria for obtaining tenure and who is under an "at-will" contract lacks a protected property interest in employment. Thus, such an employee is not entitled to receive notice or an opportunity to be heard when the employer terminates that employment relationship.

★★★

C.   **Equal Protection**

1)   <u>FOURTEENTH AMENDMENT</u>

The Fourteenth Amendment includes the Equal Protection Clause, which provides, in part, that: "No State shall...deny to any person within its jurisdiction the equal protection of the laws." U.S. Const. amend. XIV, § 1. Of course, this Fourteenth Amendment provision applies to the states rather than the federal government. The Supreme Court has applied the same principle of equal protection of the laws with respect to the actions and laws of the federal government by means of the Due Process Clause of the Fifth Amendment. In one case, the Court held that racial segregation in the public schools of the District of Columbia violated the Fifth Amendment's Due Process Clause. U.S. Const. amend. V and *Bolling v. Sharpe*, 347 U.S. 497 (1954).

a)   Equal Protection Principle

The Supreme Court basically construes the Fourteenth Amendment as requiring that all laws treat similarly situated people in the same manner. If such people do not receive equal treatment either under the laws or from a government, then a violation of equal protection may have occurred. In other words, a government's regulation or conduct may have interfered with or infringed upon the right to equal protection.

★★★

b)   Standards of Review

Determining whether a classification violates the Equal Protection Clause depends, in part, upon the standard of review used by the court. The type of analysis a court utilizes to review an Equal Protection Clause issue will depend upon either: 1) the classification of the right at stake or allegedly being infringed or 2) how the law classifies people. First, we will examine the nature of the protected right. There are two general types of rights derived from the *Constitution* — fundamental rights and other rights. The Supreme Court has developed three primary types of analysis, or levels of scrutiny, for the review of laws and government conduct to determine if they satisfy the requirements of the Equal Protection Clause. In the following sections, those standards of review will be addressed in relation to the types of rights at issue.

c)   Distinguished from Substantive Due Process

Although both substantive due process and equal protection concern the protection of individual liberties, they are distinguishable. Equal Protection analysis applies when a law treats one class of people different from another class of people. For exam purposes, substantive due process generally applies when a law that treats all people equally, infringes upon protected rights. That is why substantive due process is applicable to laws regulating abortion, an issue affecting women of all races, and equal protection applies to laws governing suspect classifications, such as race, that may treat all people of one race differently from all people of another race.

| 2) | FUNDAMENTAL RIGHTS |

Question Key
12,89,90,141

    a)   Types of Rights

One basis for asserting a claim under the Equal Protection Clause is a violation of a basic, or fundamental, right. Testable issues may include, for example, alleged infringement of the rights to vote, to travel interstate, or to access the courts.

    b)   Strict Scrutiny Review

A court considering cases in which parties are challenging laws infringing upon fundamental rights or laws involving a suspect classification will apply the most rigorous standard of review. It is known as strict scrutiny review. Under the strict scrutiny standard, a court must determine:

- Is a law necessary to achieve a compelling government purpose?

- Is the least-restrictive alternative means used?

- Does no less burdensome means exist to accomplish the purpose? and

- Is the law sufficiently narrowly tailored to accomplish the purpose?

Under strict scrutiny review, it is important to remember that the government possesses the burden of proving the law's validity under the above test. This test is very difficult for the government to satisfy. Thus, most laws fail under a strict scrutiny analysis.

    (1)   Right to Vote

The right to vote is a fundamental right protected under the Equal Protection Clause and the Fifteenth Amendment. A reviewing court generally will apply strict scrutiny to any challenged law that limits that right (except with regard to voter age, residency, and citizenship). In *Bush v. Gore*, the Supreme Court ruled that in a presidential election, the counting of votes without uniform standards violates the Equal Protection Clause.

    (a)   One Person, One Vote

    (i)   General

The one-person, one-vote rule is not found in the *Constitution*. Rather, this principle of equal protection stems from case law. Prior to these cases, some legislative voting districts had grossly unequal numbers of people. Consequently, in some states, a minority of the voters could elect a majority of the state legislature's members. Today, however, congressional districts must be drawn to be almost mathematically equal, and state legislative districts cannot vary more than a few percentage points.

(A)   Apportioned
Voting Districts

Geographically defined voting districts must be apportioned based on population. To provide for equality of representation, any deviation of population levels in those districts should be minor. A greater deviation may be constitutionally valid if a state proves that it is warranted by a legitimate governmental interest. One example of such an interest would be to maintain a voting district's integrity.

(I)   Racial
Considerations

Any use of racial considerations in drawing voting districts is subject to strict scrutiny.

(B)   Water   Storage
Districts

The one-person, one-vote principle may not apply in certain circumstances, such as when a state elects certain functionaries whose duties are so far removed from normal governmental activities and so disproportionately affect different groups that the principle should not apply.

The Supreme Court has specifically held that a water storage district, by reason of its special limited purpose and of the disproportionate impact of its activities on landowners as a group, is an exception to the rule.

(b)   Durational Residency Restrictions

In *Marston v. Lewis*, the Supreme Court sustained a 50-day requirement of durational residency as a prerequisite for a person to exercise the right to vote. Any durational residency period that is longer than 90 days may unconstitutionally infringe on the fundamental right to vote if no compelling government interest is furthered by that requirement.

(c)   Poll Taxes

Poll taxes, or taxes people pay to exercise their right to vote, are unconstitutional pursuant to the Twenty-Fourth Amendment.

(d)   Property Ownership Requirement

A property ownership requirement would allow a person to vote only if the person owned taxable property within a voting district. Such a law generally would be invalid unless an exception applies.

(i)   Exception

Absent a narrowly tailored and compelling government interest, a court will hold that a property requirement is an unconstitutional violation of the Equal Protection Clause. Elections for positions that are of special interest to the community may be valid exceptions to the general rule prohibiting property ownership requirements.

(2)   Right to Travel

The right to travel from state to state is protected by the Equal Protection Clause. A reviewing court will apply strict scrutiny to any challenged law that restricts people from traveling or moving between states or that imposes a durational residency prerequisite in order to qualify for government benefits.

(3)   Licenses

The right to seek work (as opposed to the right to work) is protected by the Equal Protection Clause. If a state law treats its residents differently from non-residents for the purpose of issuing an occupational license, then the state must provide a substantial reason for that different treatment for the state law to be upheld as constitutionally valid.

★★

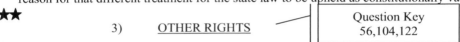

3)   <u>OTHER RIGHTS</u>

Question Key
56,104,122

If an alleged violation of the Equal Protection Clause does not involve a fundamental right, or a suspect or quasi-suspect classification, then the level of judicial review is rational basis analysis.

a)   Rational Basis Review

Under the rational basis standard of review, a court will inquire:

- if a contested law is rationally related to

- achieving a legitimate or conceivable government interest.

A person challenging the law possesses the burden of proving its invalidity under the rational basis test. This standard is very difficult for a challenger of the law to satisfy. A court would be reluctant to second-guess a legislature's means of furthering a legitimate government interest. Thus, almost any law would satisfy rational basis review.

b)   Education

The *Constitution* does not provide a fundamental right to education. Thus, laws that regulate education are subject to rational basis review. A state may limit its allocation of funding for public education to school districts on the basis of residency when:

- the allocation of educational funds is rationally related to;

- a legitimate interest in allocating funds to only genuine state residents.

★★

4)   <u>SUSPECT CLASSIFICATIONS</u>

Question Key
37

Equal protection principles are applicable not only to fundamental rights and other rights, but also to certain legal classifications. Under equal protection analysis of a contested law involving a class of people, a court would inquire into the nature of the classification. The standard of review a court could use may depend upon whether a classification is of a suspect, quasi-suspect, or non-suspect class.

a)   Suspect Classes

Race, ethnicity, and national origin are the fully suspect classifications of individuals with respect to government laws or conduct affecting individual liberties. A court ordinarily will apply strict scrutiny to test the constitutionality of a statute that includes a suspect classification.

(1)   Facially Discriminatory Laws

A legal provision such as a statute that involves a facially discriminatory classification is one that, by its terms, regulates or bans some activity in an unequal and unconstitutional manner. A relevant example is a statute prohibiting interracial marriages. A facially discriminatory gender classification would allow men to work a job that women are prohibited from working. A legal provision including a facially discriminatory classification is subject to strict scrutiny review. Because the provision is discriminatory on its face, a challenger of such a provision does not need to prove discriminatory purpose or intent.

(a)   *De Jure* Discrimination

Discrimination by, or as a matter of, law (i.e., *de jure* discrimination) occurs under circumstances involving a discriminatory purpose. Circumstances in which such intentional, or *de jure,* discrimination may occur include when a government's legal provision discriminates:

- on its face, as a matter of law; or

- as applied under the facts (e.g., in its implementation); or

- when a discriminatory purpose or intent led to its enactment, even though the law is facially neutral.

(2)   Facially Neutral Laws

A legal provision such as a statute that contains a facially neutral classification may be discriminatory due to the discriminatory purpose or intent of its enactment and because it will produce an invidious effect of a discriminatory impact upon a particular class. In this situation, a challenger of the law must produce evidence of the law's discriminatory purpose or intent.

(3)   *De Facto* Discrimination

De facto discrimination may occur when a legal provision is not based on a discriminatory purpose or intent, although discrimination results from the affect of the legal provision. For example, suppose there are eight elementary schools in one public school district. The student enrollment at six of those elementary schools is divided equally between students in the racial majority and students in the racial minority. However, in the other two elementary schools, which are in adjacent neighborhoods, the enrollment of one is almost entirely of students in the racial majority, and the enrollment of the other is almost entirely of students in the racial minority. If the difference in those two school's enrollment results from a legal provision that is not based on a discriminatory purpose or intent, the apparent discrimination in those schools would be *de facto*. Generally, *de facto* racial discrimination resulting from racial segregation in public school systems cannot be remedied by the federal courts, but *de jure* discrimination can be.

(4)   Affirmative Action

(a)   General – Strict Scrutiny Review

Affirmative action is a method of using race as a factor to remedy past discrimination. For example, an affirmative action program could apply to favor black applicants in the awarding of contracts to contractors for the provision of goods or services to the government. Affirmative action may be referred to as a type of reverse or benign discrimination.

In *Richmond v. Croson*, the Supreme Court ruled that affirmative action programs are subject to a type of strict scrutiny review. Generally, such a program will be upheld only if it fulfills the compelling governmental interest of remedying past discrimination. Note that this interest does not include governmental goals of racial diversity or a racially balanced workforce.

(b)   Quotas and Set-Asides

(i)   Generally Prohibited

The Supreme Court's decision in *California v. Bakke*, provides that quotas, or the setting aside of a specified number of positions for minorities to be admitted to a university, are usually not constitutional. In *Gratz v. Bollinger*, the Supreme Court ruled that race may be considered as a factor in terms of preferential college admissions provided that the factor's role in the formula does not operate as a virtual quota. To withstand strict scrutiny analysis, a party must prove that the use of race as a factor in making admission decisions is narrowly tailored to further the compelling governmental interest in educational diversity.

(ii)   Permissible under Limited
Circumstances

(A)   Discrimination in
Community

Under certain circumstances, a government may establish a race-conscious set-aside program to remedy documented past discrimination in a community. Such a program will, however, be unconstitutional if that same remedy may be accomplished instead by race-neutral means. To determine the program's constitutionality, consider:

- Does the evidence demonstrate a history of racial discrimination in a community?

- Is a race-based program required to remedy that past discrimination?

- Is a race-neutral means available to achieve that objective?

(B)   Discrimination by Employer

Under certain circumstances, a court may order "affirmative race-conscious relief as a remedy for past discrimination." Such circumstances might include "where an employer or labor union has engaged in persistent or egregious discrimination, or where necessary to dissipate the lingering effect of pervasive discrimination."

(C)   Evidence of Past Discrimination

In *Parents Involved in Community Schools v. Seattle School District No. 1*, the Supreme Court prohibited solely using racial classifications to assign students to public schools in order to attain racial integration when no effects of past intentional racial discrimination were being remedied.

(5)   Federal Prisoners

The Fifth Amendment's Due Process Clause prevents the federal government from depriving a federal prisoner of equal protection of the law. For example, a prison policy of dividing prisoners into cell blocks based on their race creates a suspect classification under the Fourteenth Amendment's Equal Protection Clause. The policy may unconstitutionally violate the prisoner's right to equal protection of the law if the prison's officials might have developed a less-restrictive alternative to reduce violence among the prisoners.

Thus, prisoners cannot be deprived equal protection rights. However, this does not mean any law that classifies people as prisoners is subject to strict scrutiny. Federal prisoners are not a suspect or quasi-suspect class.

5)   OTHER CLASSIFICATIONS

Question Key
20,30,54,60,62,64,112, 119,128,133,160

a)   Alienage

The Naturalization Clause of Article I provides Congress with plenary and sole power regarding aliens, naturalization, and citizenship. U.S. Const. art. I, § 8, cl. 4. Alienage is a quasi-suspect type of classification. Consequently, it may be subject to two different standards of review.

(1)   Federal Law Standard

A federal law that classifies based on alienage (alien status, naturalization, or citizenship), is subject to rational basis review on account of congressional authority over aliens. Thus, federal laws affecting aliens as a class only need to be rationally related to a legitimate government interest. Such review applies to congressional determinations and issues regarding discrimination based on alienage in the following contexts:

- government employment;

- national security;

- foreign policy;

- immigration; and

- the naturalization of citizens.

For example, an agreement by the federal government to process refugees and place them in the United States is permissible under the federal power to establish conditions for aliens to be in the country. Additionally, a classification based on alienage is permissible to render aliens ineligible for federal employment that requires a top-secret security clearance that would provide them access to information vital to national defense.

(2)   Two State Law Standards

(a)   General Rule - Strict Scrutiny

State alienage classifications generally are subject to strict scrutiny review. Thus, a state law or action classifying people by alienage violates the Equal Protection Clause of the Fourteenth Amendment if the state:

- cannot prove a compelling state interest in a state law that discriminates against aliens; and

- cannot prove that the least-restrictive means available were used to fulfill that interest.

For example, the Supreme Court invalidated a state law that prevented resident aliens from practicing law because that law did not satisfy strict scrutiny. Additionally, the Supreme Court held that a state could not deny welfare benefits to aliens because that classification did not advance a compelling government interest.

(i)   Exception - Rational Basis

Certain state alienage classifications are subject to less stringent rational basis review if they involve the state's:

- governmental functions;

- representative government;

- political processes; or

- public policy.

To that extent, both a state government and the federal government may use an alienage classification if it is rationally related to a government interest in a "policy-making position" or a "function at the heart of representative government."

For example, a government may discriminate against aliens with respect to the terms of their employment as a probation officer, teacher, police officer, as well as their serving on a jury or voting. Such discrimination may be based on the effect those positions may have on the development or implementation of state policy.

Conversely, the Supreme Court decided that the job of a notary public is not a government function because that job's duties are "essentially clerical and ministerial." Thus, strict scrutiny will be applied to local or state government regulations that limit or prevent aliens from becoming notary publics.

            b)   Gender

                             (1)   Intermediate Review

Gender is a quasi-suspect type of classification. Legal provisions, such as statutes, containing gender classifications usually are subject to a heightened or intermediate level of judicial review scrutiny. A law's disparate impact on a gender, without more, does not constitute discrimination and is insufficient to trigger heightened judicial scrutiny. A challenger of the provision must show that the provision's *intent* and *impact* are both discriminatory, or that the provision, on its face, is discriminatory.

Under the intermediate scrutiny standard, a court generally will inquire:

- if a contested law is substantially related to;

- achieving an important government interest?

The government possesses the burden of proving the provision's validity under intermediate scrutiny.

In *Craig v. Boren*, the Supreme Court struck down a law that prohibited the sale of beer to males less than 21 years of age and to females less than 18 years of age. The Supreme Court found that the law's different treatment of each gender lacked a substantial relationship to an important government interest.

(a)   Exceedingly Persuasive
Justification

In gender classification cases, the government must also satisfy another element – that an "exceedingly persuasive justification" exists for the challenged classification. An exceedingly persuasive justification for a statute with a classification resulting in reverse (i.e., benign) discrimination could be the remedial purpose of rectifying prior discrimination against women.

c)   Nonmarital Children

(1)   General

Classifications of nonmarital children are also a quasi-suspect classification. Nonmarital children are those born out of wedlock and also are referred to as "illegitimate" children.

(2)   Intermediate Review

Laws that discriminate against nonmarital children on the basis that they are illegitimate are subject to intermediate scrutiny review. This type of heightened scrutiny provides that, in order to be upheld, a legislative classification that differentiates between nonmarital children and legitimate children must be substantially related to a legitimate state interest.

(3)   Precedent

Laws that completely bar nonmarital children from receiving government benefits or damages in a wrongful death action will be invalidated under the intermediate scrutiny review.

Laws that do not completely bar nonmarital children from receiving an inheritance, government benefits, or damages in a wrongful death action, may be sustained under intermediate scrutiny review. A court, however, may hold that statutory discrimination against a nonmarital child that precludes that child's recovery of wrongful death damages, is substantially related to an important government interest of proving paternity before a parent dies.

d)   Miscellaneous Classifications

The following types of discriminatory classifications are not suspect. Thus, they are subject to rational basis judicial review:

- wealth or financial;

- age;

- disability;

- education; and

- any other classification.

For example, a mandatory retirement age law is subject to rational basis review.

(1)   Political Candidates

A court will review government action that prevents indigent people from participating in the electoral process because of a government-imposed policy. Political candidates, however, may be subject to reasonable burdens imposed by state and local governments. Such legally permissible burdens include:

- the requirement that a candidate must obtain registered voters' signatures in order for the candidate's name to be put on the voting ballot;

- paying a fee to file an application for candidacy if the candidate is not indigent; and

- releasing information about the candidate's financial connections to entities that may have interactions in the voting district the candidate may represent.

(2)   Life Partners

Laws of an economic nature that do not consider unmarried life partners as relatives or family members in the same manner as a married couple are subject to rational basis review. A state may defend such a law by contending that it possesses a legitimate interest in promoting marriage that is advanced by not including nonmarital partners in statutory provisions for survivors, heirs, or beneficiaries.

★★   **D.   Privileges and Immunities Clauses**

> | Question Key |
> | :---: |
> | 61,154,162 |

1)   ARTICLE IV PRIVILEGES AND IMMUNITIES

a)   Equal Treatment of Citizens and Non-Citizens

Article IV of the *Constitution* provides that: "The Citizens of each State shall be entitled to all Privileges and Immunities in the several States." U.S. Const. art. IV, § 2, cl. 1. According to the Privileges and Immunities Clause of Article IV, a first state may not deprive a citizen of any other state the fundamental privileges and immunities enjoyed by the citizens of the first state.

b)   Types of Privileges and Immunities

The privileges and immunities (i.e., rights) may be of an economic nature. For example, a state cannot charge a non-citizen substantially more for a commercial license than it charges a citizen. The rights may be of a constitutional nature. For example, a state's residency requirement for an abortion is unconstitutional. Fundamental rights of state citizenship may include:

- access to state courts;

- real estate ownership and sales;

- seeking employment; and

- access to certain licenses.

         c)   Licenses

In *Toomer v. Witsell*, a case involving a commercial license, the Supreme Court held that a state may discriminate against the fundamental rights of the state's non-citizen only if two elements are satisfied:

- A state proves that a non-citizen is a "peculiar source of evil" that the state enacted a regulation to remedy; and

- The regulation is substantially related to the state's objective.

In *Baldwin v. Fish & Game Com'n of Montana*, a case involving a recreational license, the Supreme Court held that a state may discriminate by charging a non-resident a higher cost for that license than a resident. The Supreme Court concluded that the Privileges and Immunities Clause of Article IV did not apply, because a non-resident did not have a right to "equality in access" for the purpose of hunting elk in the state. Rather, the Privileges and Immunities Clause of Article IV protects non-citizens of states from discrimination only with respect to essential activities and basic rights.

         d)   Employment

A state's licensing laws and local income tax laws may not invalidly restrict the fundamental right of a non-citizen to seek work. For example, if a state law treats its citizens differently than non-citizens for the purpose of issuing an occupational license, then the state must provide a substantial reason for that different treatment in order for the state law to be upheld. For example, a municipal income tax upon a city's workers who reside beyond city limits unconstitutionally discriminates based on residency, contrary to the Privileges and Immunities Clause of Article IV.

        2)   FOURTEENTH   AMENDMENT   PRIVILEGES   OR IMMUNITIES

         a)   Restriction of State Legal Authority

The Privileges or Immunities Clause of the Fourteenth Amendment provides in part that: "No State shall make or enforce any law which shall abridge the privileges or immunities of citizens of the United States." U.S. Const. amend. XIV, § 1. This provision does not incorporate any of the Bill of Rights. In comparison, the Due Process Clause of the Fourteenth Amendment does incorporate some of the Bill of Rights.

         b)   Protection of Federal Privileges or Immunities

The Privileges or Immunities Clause of the Fourteenth Amendment applies only to certain federal rights. Specifically, this provision prevents a state from depriving its citizens of the privileges or immunities of national or federal citizenship, which include:

- the right to vote in federal elections;

- the right to petition the federal government to address grievances; and

- the right to travel interstate.

        c)   Right to Travel and Take up Residency in New State

A court will apply strict scrutiny to a state law that restricts people from traveling or moving between states, because the right to interstate travel is fundamental. A state's durational residency requirement is also such a law because a state's new citizen has a right to be treated in the same way as a long-term citizen of the state.

        (1)   Duration of Residency Restrictions on Benefits

For example, the Supreme Court declared unconstitutional a state's law that restricted the state's new citizen's welfare benefits as compared to the welfare benefits available to long-term citizens of the state. In another case, the Supreme Court invalidated a state law that required a person to reside in a state for one year prior to receiving medical benefits from the state. Medical care is considered a "vital government benefit." Thus, a state may not deny it without proof that:

- the denial was required to fulfill a compelling state interest; and

- no less-restrictive means existed to accomplish that objective.

★

E.   **Obligation of Contracts, Bills of Attainder, *Ex Post Facto* & *Habeas Corpus***

Question Key
24,60,65,127

The *Constitution* prohibits the enactment of three types of retroactive legislation by Congress and state legislatures. These types of prohibited retroactive legislation either impair the Obligation of Contracts or are Bills of Attainder and *Ex post facto* laws.

        1)   CONTRACT CLAUSE

        a)   Limitation upon State and Local Laws

The Contract Clause of the *Constitution* states, in part, that: "No State shall...pass any...law impairing the Obligation of Contracts." U.S. Const. art. I, § 10, cl. 1. The Supreme Court relies on this provision to avoid state laws that retroactively impair contractual duties and rights. The Supreme Court applies the Contract Clause to generally limit the ability of local and state governments to alter or modify: (1) private contracts; (2) public charters; and (3) contracts involving private and public parties.

b)   Limitation upon Federal Laws

The Fifth Amendment states, in part, that a person shall not be "deprived of life, liberty, or property, without due process of law." U.S. Const. amend. V. This provision bars any federal law that would retroactively impair a contractual obligation.

c)   Impairment of Private Contracts

A local and state government may enact legal provisions that impair private contracts only for the police power purposes of protecting the public health, safety, welfare, and morals. A court would ask the following questions to determine if such impairments are legally permissible:

- Does the legal provision substantially impair a contractual relationship?

- Is that provision designed to promote a significant and legitimate social purpose?

- Is the provision reasonably and narrowly tailored to promote the significant and legitimate social purpose?

- Is the provision an unjustifiable attempt to alter the obligations of the parties to a private contract?

In sum, a state may justify a law that impairs an obligation of private contracts only by making a showing of necessity. To do that, the state possesses a burden of proving:

- the existence of an important state interest; and

- that the law will not substantially impair existing contract rights.

d)   Impairment of Public Contracts

The following test applies to determine if impairments of public contracts are legally permissible:

- Does the legal provision substantially impair a contractual relationship?

- Is that provision justified by a significant and legitimate social purpose?

- Does the provision use a method to promote that purpose and not an unnecessarily broad repudiation of its contract obligations to private persons?

- Is the provision narrowly tailored and reasonably necessary to promote the significant and legitimate social purpose?

Generally, a court will permit a reasonable extent of impairment of contractual obligations when a local or state law modifies a contract's terms. A state may justify a law that impairs an obligation of public contracts only by making a showing of necessity. To do that, the state possesses a burden of proving:

- the existence of an important state interest; and

- that less-restrictive means cannot serve that interest; and

- the impairment is required due to unforeseeable circumstances.

2) BILLS OF ATTAINDER

a) Definition

A Bill of Attainder is a retrospective law that imposes punishment on named individuals or a readily identifiable group of individuals. It is an impermissible legislative penalty that precludes a person from receiving a minimum degree of procedural due process, such as notice and a hearing. For example, a law that imposes a retrospective income tax on bonuses received by employees of companies that are the recipient of federal aid, such as legislation contemplated after the enactment of one of the stimulus acts of 2009, may be challenged as an unlawful bill of attainder.

b) Constitutional Prohibition

Article I of the *Constitution* states, in part, that: "No Bill of Attainder…shall be passed." U.S. Const. art. I, § 9. That provision applies to and is controlling upon Congress. Article I further provides that: "No State shall…pass any Bill of Attainder." That provision applies to and is controlling upon the states. U.S. Const. art. I, § 10, cl. 1.

3) *EX POST FACTO* LAWS

a) Definition

The Constitution's prohibition of *ex post facto* laws prevents the federal and states' governments from punishing people for conduct that was lawful when it occurred and before a federal or state law subsequently rendered that conduct unlawful. Like a bill of attainder, an *ex post facto* law is an impermissible legislative penalty that precludes a person from receiving a minimum degree of procedural due process, such as notice and a hearing.

b) Constitutional Prohibition

Article I of the *Constitution* states, in part, that: "No…*ex post facto* Law shall be passed." U.S. Const. art. I, § 9, cl. 3, 9. This provision applies to and is controlling upon Congress. Article I also provides that: "No State shall…pass any…*ex post facto* Law. U.S. Const. art. I, § 10, cl. 1. This provision applies to and is controlling upon the states.

4) *HABEAS CORPUS*

a)   Definition

The Latin term *"habeas corpus"* can be literally translated to the phrase "you shall have the body." Generally, a person may file a petition for a Writ of *Habeas Corpus* in a federal court directing the government to produce and/or release a detained individual from unlawful imprisonment. Procedural and substantive federal and state law governs the availability of *habeas corpus* relief in various circumstances.

b)   Suspension Clause

The Suspension Clause of Article I of the *Constitution* states, in part, that: "The Privilege of the Writ of Habeas Corpus shall not be suspended, unless when in Cases of Rebellion or Invasion the public Safety may require it." U.S. Const. art. I, § 9, cl. 2. Note that, in contrast to a constitutional right, *habeas corpus* relief constitutes a privilege subject to suspension. In that sense, it can be compared to a driver's license or professional license. Pursuant to the Suspension Clause, certain people were not entitled to *habeas corpus* relief during the Civil War pursuant to federal law suspending the privilege. More modernly, in the context of the War on Terror, a controversial issue has arisen as to the scope of availability of *habeas corpus* relief that illustrates the interplay between the legislative, executive, and judicial branches of the United States government.

c)   Supreme Court Decisions

Congress passed a resolution authorizing President Bush to use military force in response to the terrorist attacks of September 11, 2001. The President issued a military order asserting the authority to detain, as an enemy combatant, people suspected of being terrorists or engaging in terrorism against the United States or people who were part of, or supporting, certain terrorist groups. Pursuant to the order, such detained enemy combatants lacked traditional constitutional due process protections such as any right to legal counsel, presentment of formal charges, a hearing about their detention, and incarceration for a period of specified duration. Consequently, people designated as enemy combatants theoretically could be held indefinitely without legal recourse. As a result, several enemy combatants challenged their detentions on various grounds.

(1)   Due Process for Citizens

In 2004, in *Hamdi v. Rumsfeld*, the Supreme Court held that a citizen of the United States detained as an enemy combatant possesses due process rights to counsel and "a meaningful opportunity to contest the factual basis" for this detention before a neutral decision-maker. Moreover, the executive branch lacks authority to detain a citizen indefinitely without certain fundamental due process protections subject to judicial review.

(2)   *Habeas Corpus* for Non-Citizens

The same year, in *Rasul v. Bush*, the Supreme Court held that federal statutory *habeas corpus* jurisdiction extended to an individual who was not a citizen of the United States (i.e., a foreign national), during the individual's detention as an enemy combatant in the detention center at the United States Naval Station at Guantanamo Bay, Cuba because the United States exercises control and jurisdiction there.

(a)   Detainee Treatment Act of 2005

Congress passed the *Detainee Treatment Act of 2005*. The Act, among other things, strips federal courts of *habeas corpus* jurisdiction over enemy combatants held at Guantanamo Bay. In 2006, in *Hamdan v. Rumsfeld*, the Supreme Court held that a United States military commission lacked power to try Hamdan, who was not a citizen of the United States, because its procedures and structures violated both the *Uniform Code of Military Justice of the United States* and the *Geneva Conventions*. The Court reversed the federal court of appeal's reversal of the federal district court's decision to grant Hamdan's petition for *habeas corpus*. The Court held that the federal *Detainee Treatment Act of 2005* did not remove federal statutory *habeas corpus* jurisdiction over appeals by enemy combatants pending at the enactment of the statute.

(b)   Military Commissions Act of 2006

In response, Congress enacted the *Military Commissions Act of 2006*. That Act attempted to avoid the effect of the *Hamdan* decision by eliminating the invocation of the Geneva Convention to *habeas corpus* cases and applying the law to pre-existing cases. In the 2008 decision of *Boumediene v. Bush*, the Supreme Court held that the Act unconstitutionally suspended the Writ of *Habeas Corpus*. The Court decided that federal constitutional *habeas corpus* protections extend to individuals designated as enemy combatants and/or detained in the detention center at Guantanamo Bay, Cuba. The Court explained that Congress must comply with the requirements of the Suspension Clause in order to deny individuals the privilege of *habeas corpus* relief by providing "an adequate and effective substitute for the *habeas* writ."

★★   F.   **First Amendment Freedoms**

1)   FREEDOM OF RELIGION AND SEPARATION OF CHURCH AND STATE

The First Amendment to the *Constitution* ("First Amendment") states, in part, that: "Congress shall make no law respecting an establishment of religion, or prohibiting the free exercise thereof..." U.S. Const. amend. I. These two consecutive provisions are respectively referred to as the Establishment Clause and the Free Exercise Clause. They apply to the states under the Due Process Clause of the Fourteenth Amendment. They apply to the federal government directly and under the Due Process Clause of the Fifth Amendment.

The Supreme Court construes the First Amendment as requiring governmental neutrality with respect to religion.

Case law and scholarly writings consider the First Amendment as a primary basis for the concept and practical effect of maintaining religions and governments as distinct and unconnected entities. Despite their different purposes and meanings, the Free Exercise

Clause and the Establishment Clause of the First Amendment both mandate legal standards to preserve general church and state separation.

★

a)   Free Exercise Clause

Question Key
125,131

The Free Exercise Clause prevents a government from interfering with:

- the religious theology, doctrine, or beliefs of religious denominations, sects, or individuals;

- the religious practices, rituals, activities, and conduct of religious denominations, sects, or individuals;

- the internal disputes of an organized religion concerning its doctrines or practices; and

- a person's freedom to select any type of religion.

In essence, the Free Exercise Clause is implicated when government action or state action limits, penalizes, interferes with, or burdens the religious beliefs or practices of individuals. Thus, the Free Exercise Clause may, for example, prevent the government from legislatively outlawing a religion or all religions.

(1)   Sincerely Held Beliefs Generally Protected

A court may not consider the reasonableness or truthfulness of any religious belief because a person's freedom to select a religion is absolute. If a law infringes upon a person's right to freely exercise religious beliefs, then a court adjudicating the person's case may consider only the sincerity of the person's beliefs. If the person sincerely holds those beliefs, they may be legally protected.

(2)   Prohibited Religious Activity

The Free Exercise Clause does not completely protect all types of religious expression. A government may constitutionally regulate or outlaw some types of religious conduct, such as the use of a controlled substance in a religious ritual. In that event, the government may take into consideration health and safety concerns with respect to state action that interferes with religious conduct.

(a)   Rational Basis - Broadly
Applicable Laws

A rational basis level of scrutiny applies to determine the constitutionality of a broadly applicable law that incidentally affects religious conduct. Such a law will be valid if it applies to all persons and entities and does not target a particular religious group. A government's regulation that affects religious conduct will be constitutionally permissible if it:

- directly concerns and affects the general public;

- only indirectly impacts religious conduct, and

- advances a legitimate state interest.

       (i)   Generally Applicable Criminal Law

In *Employment Division v. Smith*, a highly controversial decision, the Supreme Court upheld a state statute that imposed criminal liability for possessing peyote, a controlled substance. The statute lacked a religious exemption for Native Americans, who use peyote in their religious activities. The Supreme Court stated that "the right of free exercise does not relieve an individual of the obligation to comply with a valid and neutral law of general applicability on the ground that the law proscribes . . . conduct that his religion prescribes . . . ." If a law falls under this generally applicable law exception to the constitutional principle of free exercise of religion, it is subject to a rational basis standard of judicial review. A law rationally related to promoting a legitimate state interest is constitutional. Given that this is a low threshold, a law to which this variation from the constitutional principle of free exercise of religion applies will likely be constitutional.

       (ii)   Unemployment Cases

The Supreme Court has held that the government cannot deny unemployment benefits to a person who has quit or lost a job as a result of a sincere religious belief. For example, suppose a person's employment is terminated after the person refuses to work on Saturdays, pursuant to the person's religious beliefs. In such a case, under *Sherbert v. Verner*, the Supreme Court employed a balancing test under which the Court balanced the government's interest in regulating religious expression with an individual's interest in religious expression. This balancing test was the widespread test used to analyze free exercise cases until it was deviated from in *Employment Division v. Smith*. However, in *Sherbert*, the Court limited the balancing test to unemployment compensation cases.

       (b)   Strict Scrutiny - Compelling Interest

          (i)   Intentional Burdens or Interference

The courts will use strict scrutiny in reviewing laws that intentionally burden or interfere with the free exercise of religion, as well as in cases involving laws that are not laws of general applicability (i.e., laws that carve out secular or religion-based exceptions). These are laws that can be said to "target" a religion or religious practice.

For example, a state would be prohibiting the free exercise of religion if it attempts to ban acts only when they are engaged in for religious reasons, or only because of the religious belief that they may display. The Supreme Court has provided that "it would be unconstitutional to ban the casting of 'statutes that are to be used for worship purposes,' or to prohibit bowing down before a golden calf." If a law intentionally burdens the free exercise of religion, then the government must demonstrate a compelling interest for it.

(ii)   Statutorily Required Strict
Scrutiny

Gonzales v. O Centro Espirita Beneficente Uniao Do Vegetal involved a challenge by a religious group to the constitutionality of a generally applicable law that incidentally burdened its religious practice. The Court sustained the challenge on the basis that the government failed to show a compelling interest for its seizure of hoasca, a sacramental tea regulated by the federal *Controlled Substances Act*, as required by the federal *Religious Freedom Restoration Act of 1993*. Also, the federal *Religious Land Use and Institutionalized Persons Act* essentially imposes the strict scrutiny standard of review to government actions that interfere with religious exercise by institutionalized individuals (e.g., inmates or prisoners).

(c)   State Constitution Prohibition

In *Locke v. Davey*, the Court held that the State of Washington's denial of funding to students seeking 'devotional' degrees, pursuant to the anti-establishment provision of the State's Constitution, did not improperly infringe upon a student's rights under the First Amendment's Free Exercise Clause. The Court explained the "State's interest in not funding the pursuit of devotional degrees is substantial and the exclusion of such funding places a relatively minor burden on" the student.

★★   b)   Establishment Clause

Question Key
23,42,70,95,96,157

The Establishment Clause of the *Constitution* prevents Congress from legislatively establishing or directly assisting a religion or religions in general. It can be viewed as the converse of the *Constitution's* provision for the free exercise of religion. Under this free exercise provision, the government may not punish or impede religious beliefs or entities. Under the Establishment Clause, the government generally may not promote or assist religion.

(1)   Sect Preference

A law's preference of one sect could indicate or be a tendency toward promoting or assisting religion. If a law possesses a sect or denominational preference, it will be subject to strict scrutiny. Thus, it will be upheld only if it is necessary to promote a compelling interest. It would be difficult, if not impossible, for a law with a sect preference to satisfy this standard.

(2)   No Sect Preference

If government takes action or passes a law that possesses no sect preference (i.e., it is neutral on its face), then, according to *Agostini v. Felton*, (a case about government aid to religious schools), a court would examine the law's purpose and effect to determine if the action violates the Establishment Clause:

- Secular Purpose

The law must have a "secular legislative purpose" or intent, not a sectarian legislative purpose or intent. If it does not have a secular legislative purpose or intent, it is unconstitutional.

- Effect

The law's primary effect must be one that neither advances nor inhibits religion. In determining whether the law satisfies this requirement, a court would examine whether the law fosters an excessive government entanglement with religion.

A government action or law is unconstitutional if it fails either prong. In other words, the law cannot have either a sectarian legislative purpose or intent, or have the primary effect of advancing or inhibiting religion.

(3)   Establishment Clause Analytical Tests

Three main types of analytical tests apply to cases based on the Establishment Clause: (A) the *Lemon* test, (B) the coercion test, and (C) the endorsement test.

First, the three-part test of *Lemon v. Kurtzman*, resembles the foregoing one in that: (1) the statute's legislative purpose must be secular; (2) its primary or principal effect must neither inhibit nor advance religion; and (3) the statute must not "foster an excessive entanglement with religion." Note that this test separates out the factor of excessive entanglement as a third element in addition to those regarding secular purpose and effect.

Second, the coercion test inquires whether an individual feels coerced to engage in religious conduct due to government action.

Third, the endorsement test assesses the effect of government action upon an individual's standing in the community. This action will not be constitutional when it suggests that insiders are believers and outsiders are non-adherents.

The Law of Church and State: U.S. Supreme Court Decisions Since 2002, Congressional Research Service, Cynthia M. Brougher, October 30, 2007, p. 4 at http://www.au.af.mil/au/awc/awcgate/crs/rl34223.pdf.

(a)   Public Displays of Symbolic Items

In *Lynch v. Donnelly*, the Supreme Court ruled that public displays involving religious themes (e.g., Christmas or Easter) were lawful provided that primarily secular symbols surrounded the other religious symbols. To analyze if a public display is constitutional, consider:

- Does the display including religious symbols depict and commemorate a religious event or season as a primarily secular holiday?

- Are many different faiths reflected by the religious symbols?

- Viewed in its entirety, does the display endorse religion(s) or represent a holiday season?

(i)   Examples

The test is one that depends upon an analysis of the totality of the circumstances, such as the context in which the display appears. For example, in *Van Orden v. Perry*, the Court upheld the legality of a display of the Ten Commandments at the Texas state capitol because of the monument's secular purpose. This display was found constitutional as one of several other types of historical monuments placed near each other for the purpose of exhibiting state identity.

On the other hand, in *McCreary County v. ACLU of Kentucky*, the Supreme Court ruled that displays of the Ten Commandments in several Kentucky courthouses were unconstitutional because they were not clearly integrated with a secular display. Thus, the Court held that they had a religious purpose. The Court stated that when "the government acts with the ostensible and predominant purpose of advancing religion," it violates the Establishment Clause if a religious purpose of the government's acts is observable from the facts.

(b)   Relationship between Religion and Schools

(i)   Religious Education

The Establishment Clause generally prohibits a government from presenting religious education in public schools. Under *Flast v. Cohen*, a federal taxpayer challenging the use of federal funds to benefit religion needs to show that a congressional appropriation promotes religion, such as a federal funding of religious schools. If this type of claim is established, the federal government then must prove that a compelling government interest exists to promote religion or to discriminate against nonbelievers (a difficult standard to satisfy).

(A)   Tuition Vouchers

In *Zelman v. Simmons-Harris*, the Supreme Court upheld the constitutionality of school tuition vouchers issued by the government for use at either public or private schools.

(ii)   Officially Sponsored Prayer

The Supreme Court has held that officially sponsored prayers at activities of public elementary and secondary schools violate the Establishment Clause of the First Amendment even if the idea for the prayer originates from the students rather than, for example, school administrators.

(iii)   Transportation Cost Reimbursement

In *Everson v. Board of Education*, the Supreme Court upheld a state law that authorized school boards to reimburse parents for the costs of their children's transportation to private schools on public buses. The boards could equally reimburse these transportation costs of parents of all school children, regardless of whether these children attended public schools or private religious schools. The Supreme Court determined that the statute that authorized the reimbursements had:

- a primarily secular objective and effect of transporting all children; and

- an incidental result of benefiting religion.

          (iv)   Educational Diagnostic Services

The federal government may furnish public funds for educational diagnostic services if those services advance a state's educational objectives, and if the federal government only incidentally furnishes assistance to a religion by providing such funding to parochial (religious) schools.

          (v)   Access to School Facilities

If a government provides non-religious groups with access to school facilities for meetings, then religious groups may be afforded the same access.

          (c)   Validity of Tax Exemptions

In *Walz v. Tax Commission*, the Supreme Court decided that:

- a tax exemption that equally applies to both nonprofit organizations and religious groups is constitutionally valid; and

- a tax exemption that only applies to a religious group but not to nonprofit organizations is constitutionally invalid.

The Supreme Court evaluates aid to religious groups in the form of tax exemptions to ascertain if the law:

- possesses a secular objective and impact; and

- avoids excessive government entanglement.

          (d)   Mandatory Business Closure

Generally, the Establishment Clause is not violated by a law requiring a merchant's business to remain closed on Sundays.

          (e)   Limited Accommodation

In *Cutter v. Wilkinson*, the Court declared that the limited governmental accommodation of religious practices does not *per se* violate the Establishment Clause. The Court upheld part of the federal *Religious Land Use and Institutionalized Persons Act*, which essentially imposed the strict scrutiny standard of review to government actions that interfere with religious exercise by institutionalized individuals. The Court found that this part of the Act did not "exceed the limits of permissible government accommodation of religious practices."

★★   2)   FREEDOM OF EXPRESSION AND ASSOCIATION

The First Amendment provides, in part, that: "Congress shall make no law...abridging the freedom of speech, or of the press, or the right of the people peaceably to assemble." U.S. Const. amend. I. The First Amendment includes the Freedom of Speech Clause and the Freedom of the Press Clause. Although the First Amendment expressly refers to "freedom of speech," the Supreme Court construes that phrase to include freedom of expression by means other than speech, such as communicative conduct and graphic presentations. Freedom of association includes the right of one or more individuals or entities to communicate, meet, have relationships, and create organizations. First Amendment case law provides legal standards for the judicial review of regulations upon the freedom of expression and association. The relevant standard that applies will depend upon where, when, and how the regulated expression and/or association occurs.

a)   General Considerations ┐┌─────────────────┐
                                     │ Question Key   │
                                     │   80,85,163   │
★★   (1)   Overbreadth └─────────────────┘

A law may be held unconstitutional if it is impermissibly overbroad. The doctrine of overbreadth is implicated when a law restricts or prohibits a wider scope of expression than is necessary to prohibit. For example, suppose a state law prohibits people from wearing "any clothing that resembles any type of government issued or required uniform." This law is overly broad in terms of its blanket prohibition on wearing any such clothing. This law also lacks sufficient specificity in terms of identifying what types of government uniforms it applies to. As a result, a security guard's uniform arguably could violate this law if that uniform resembles a law enforcement officer's uniform. If a legal provision is overbroad contrary to the First Amendment by unduly limiting a first party or a third party's freedom of expression, then the first party or third party has standing to bring a civil action for the third party's benefit.

(a)   Substantial Overbreadth

In order to invalidate a law, the law must be substantially overbroad. It is, therefore, not easy to invalidate a law on overbreadth grounds. A court would examine the totality of the facts of each case in making such a determination. Additionally, a challenge to a law regulating commercial speech almost certainly would fail.

★★
(2)   Vagueness

A law may be held unconstitutional if it is impermissibly vague. The doctrine of vagueness is implicated when a law that prohibits expression fails to clearly define conduct – so that a reasonable person could not ascertain what expression is allowed and what expression is prohibited. In other words, a reasonable person must be able to discern what is prohibited by reading the law, so the person can act properly. If the law is too vague as written, the law may be void for vagueness. For example, an ordinance prohibiting assembly on the sidewalks in a manner that is "annoying to persons passing by" is unconstitutionally vague. A reasonable person cannot be expected to know what is "annoying," and as such, this subjective standard could not be enforced because it is vague.

(3)   Symbolic Speech

Symbolic speech occurs through nonverbal activity. Symbolic speech, or even the right to not speak at all, generally is constitutionally protected under the First Amendment. A regulation of symbolic speech is unconstitutional unless the following two requirements are met:

- A government possesses an important interest not related to suppressing the symbolic speech; and

- The regulation's effect on a communication is not more than is necessary to accomplish its purpose.

For example, the federal government cannot ban burning of the United States flag in order to suppress this type of symbolic speech that protests federal government policy.

(4)   Expressive Conduct

In *United States v. O'Brien*, the Supreme Court held that an individual may constitutionally be convicted for expressive conduct constituting the offense of burning a draft card. The Court stated that if a regulation prohibits expressive conduct which involves elements of both "nonspeech" and "speech," "a sufficiently important governmental interest in regulating the nonspeech element can justify incidental limitations on First Amendment freedoms." For the regulation to be sufficiently justified so as not to be unconstitutional:

- it must be within the government's constitutional power to promulgate;

- it must further an important or substantial governmental interest;

- the governmental interest must be unrelated to the suppression of free expression; and

- the incidental restriction on alleged First Amendment freedoms must be no greater than is essential to the furtherance of that interest.

(5)   Equal Access

(a)   Military Recruiters

In *Rumsfeld v. Forum for Academic and Institutional Rights*, the Supreme Court decided that Congress could, without violating the First Amendment freedoms of speech and association, legislate that law schools receiving federal funding must allow military recruiters equal access to their institutions and students as afforded to every other type of employer. The Court concluded that the federal *Solomon Amendment*, which conditioned receipt of federal funding upon a university's allowance of equal access to military recruiters as other employers, did not violate the university's First Amendment rights to freedom of association and freedom of speech, notwithstanding the university's contention that the military's "Don't ask, don't tell" policy regarding homosexuality violated the nondiscrimination policy of the university. The Court determined that the *Solomon Amendment* did not require the university to speak or deny the university the right to speak. Moreover, in *Grove City v. Bell*, the Court held that no First Amendment violation occurred by conditioning a college's receipt of federal funding upon the college's compliance with federal law.

(6)   State's Ideological Message

The Supreme Court, in *Wooley v. Maynard*, held that a state may not constitutionally mandate that an individual participate in the dissemination of an ideological message by displaying it on the individual's private property in a way, and for the explicit purpose, that the public observe and read it. Moreover, the "First Amendment protects the right of individuals to hold a point of view different from the majority and to refuse to foster," in the manner the state requires, an idea individuals find morally objectionable such as the New Hampshire state motto of "Live Free or Die." Consequently, the state could not constitutionally enforce criminal sanctions against individuals who covered that motto on their vehicle license plates on the basis of moral or religious grounds.

★ | Question Key 15 |

      b)   Content-Specific Regulation (Strict Scrutiny)

A regulation is content-based when a government's application of a law is contingent upon the viewpoint or subject matter being expressed. For example, a law that prohibits the communication of a particular theory or viewpoint is content-based. Content-based regulation means the government is restricting some speech but not others, based on the content of the expression.

If the government attempts to impair free expression in a content-based manner, then a court will use the strict scrutiny standard to review the law. The strict scrutiny standard provides that the law will be upheld only if necessary to achieve a compelling purpose. This standard is rarely satisfied in the First Amendment context. As a result, a court almost certainly will strike down the content-based law or regulation.

(1)   Unprotected Expression

Some types of speech, including obscenity and certain words of provocation, generally are not constitutionally protected.

(a)   Unprotected Obscenity

In *Miller v. California*, the Supreme Court ruled that obscene expression, as a form of speech, usually is not protected under the First Amendment. Thus, a state may constitutionally regulate such expression included within sexually oriented materials or communications. The Supreme Court declared that such a "work" of expression is obscene if the following three factors are met:

- "an average person, applying contemporary community standards, would find the work, taken as a whole, appeals to the prurient interest" [in sex];

- "the work depicts or describes, in a patently offensive way, sexual conduct specifically defined by the applicable state law;" and

- "the work, taken as a whole, lacks serious literary, artistic, political, or scientific value" as determined by a national, rather than a local, standard.

An obscene "work," as defined by those factors, may include a variety of materials such as magazines, books, and films that fulfill the Supreme Court's following two examples that distinguish the "work" from what could be constitutionally protected pornography:

- "Patently offensive representations or descriptions of ultimate sex acts, normal or perverted, actual or simulated."

- "Patently offensive representations or descriptions of masturbation, excretory functions, and lewd exhibition of the genitals."

If those two factors are met, the obscene work can constitutionally be prohibited.

(i)   Child Pornography

Even though a legal provision cannot criminalize an adult's private possession of obscenity, it can criminalize private possession of child pornography by an adult. Although pornography that does not constitute obscenity generally cannot constitutionally be prohibited, child pornography may constitutionally be prohibited when it does not constitute obscenity.

(ii)   Internet Filtering

In *United States v. American Library Association*, the Supreme Court held that the First Amendment rights of a public library patron are not violated by a library's use of Internet filtering software in order to qualify for certain federal funding under the *Children's Internet Protection Act (Act)*. The Court did not find the Act unconstitutional because the Act allowed adults to request that librarians unblock specific websites or disable the filters, the use of which was mandated for the purpose of protecting children from exposure to obscene, pornographic, and harmful websites and webpages.

- Conditional Federal Funding

Therefore, the Court decided that the Act, which "forbids public libraries to receive federal assistance for Internet access unless they install software to block obscene or pornographic images and to prevent minors from accessing material harmful to them," does not induce libraries to violate the *U.S. Constitution*. Consequently, the Court found that Congress validly exercised its spending power by conditioning public libraries' receipt of federal funding upon compliance with the Act. Congress, of course, may not induce recipients of such funding to engage in unconstitutional conduct.

(iii)   Swear Words

Swear words, including those indecent or profane, generally do not constitute obscene speech.

(b)   Provoking   Imminent   Lawless
Conduct

In *Brandenburg v. Ohio*, the Supreme Court held that a state may not prohibit or regulate the "advocacy of the use of force or of a violation of law except when such advocacy is directed to inciting or producing imminent lawless action, and is likely to incite or produce such action." In other words, the expression of speech may be regulated if the following elements are met:

- The individual or entity engaged in the expressive conduct intends to produce imminent lawless conduct; and

- The expressive conduct will probably incite or produce the lawless conduct.

Lawless conduct that may be incited by such unprotected speech includes rioting, mayhem, insurrection, or even the clearing of a public gathering place by yelling "fire" or similar words of alarm.

(c)   Fighting Words

Government may also prohibit or regulate the use of "fighting words." Along the same lines as the rule regarding imminent lawless conduct, a court may uphold the validity of a legal provision that bans "fighting words," or statements that a speaker deliberately makes to provoke a physically violent reaction from a listener.

★★

Question Key
38,47,59,149,152

c)   Content-Neutral Regulations (Intermediate Review)

Content-neutral restrictions exist when a government's application of a general law does not hinge upon the viewpoint or type of subject matter being expressed. Content-neutral restrictions may be permissible under the First Amendment if they are reasonable in terms of regulating the time, place, and manner of expression. A court will apply the following version of the intermediate scrutiny test when reviewing such restrictions:

- Does the content-neutral restriction reasonably serve a significant governmental interest?

- Is the restriction narrowly tailored to not exclude other content?

- Does the restriction allow for alternative channels to communicate the information?

(1)   Time, Manner, and Place of Expression

A government's legal restrictions on the time, place, and manner of expression of speech in any type of public forum generally must, at a minimum, be reasonable and content-neutral. The four main types of places or forums and their relevant standards are as follows:

(a)   Private Property

An individual or entity lacks any constitutional right to enter upon the privately owned land of another to engage in expressive conduct, such as speech. A government may prohibit such an entry by an individual or entity that would occur for the purposes of directing expressive conduct at the owner. Because such an entry would violate an owner's right of privacy, it is subject to reasonable regulation in terms of time, place, or manner. An individual or entity may, however, obtain permission from an owner to use the owner's land to engage in expressive conduct, such as speech, on the land.

(b)   Non-Public Forums

A non-public forum is government property that traditionally has not been open as a place for expressive conduct such as speech. Examples of a non-public forum include, but are not limited to, prisons or military compounds. A government may regulate expressive conduct on its own property if the regulation satisfies the rational basis rule and is content-neutral.

(c)   Limited or Designated Public Forums

A limited or designated public forum is a place with a limited history of expressive activity, typically used only by certain groups or regarding certain topics. Examples of a limited public forum may include a public school auditorium or a town-owned meeting room.

Another example of a limited or designated public forum is a government-owned building or place to which a private individual or entity temporarily obtains access from a government for purposes of the expressive conduct of speech. If a government otherwise could preclude such free expression in the particular building or place, then the government may regulate the expression in that place on the following grounds:

- A government's regulation of expression is content-neutral;

- The regulation is narrowly tailored in terms of time, place, and manner to fulfill a significant government interest; and

- The regulation provides ample alternative channels for communication.

United States v. Grace. A government possesses the burden to prove a regulation furthers a substantial government interest by reasonable means. This three-part analysis also applies with respect to general public forums.

(d)   General Public Forums

A general or open public forum is a place with a long tradition of freedom of expression, such as speech. Examples of general public forums include public parks, sidewalks, and street corners. A government must make such forums available for the expression of speech if the speech satisfies the test regarding limited or designated public forums.

(i)   Content Based

A government may regulate the content of that speech in a general public form only when:

- the Supreme Court has decided that the First Amendment does not protect that type of speech; and

- a government proves that it possesses a compelling interest in suppressing the speech.

(2)   Permit or License Requirements

A permit or license requirement obligates an individual or entity to obtain governmental approval in order to engage in expressive conduct, such as speech. Also, a permit or license can be required to lawfully conduct certain public events, such as a parade or rally. The criteria for the issuance or revocation of a permit or license generally must be content-neutral in terms of regulating the viewpoints of an individual or entity that seeks its issuance. Refusal of a permit or license is generally permissible only if it will be used for expressive conduct that is not constitutionally protected. A court analyzes content-neutral permit requirements under a semi-intermediate scrutiny standard of review to determine if:

- an important reason exists to require permitting; and

- a legal provision affords no discretionary authority to a permitting authority.

(a)   Laws Requiring Permits for Public Protest

In *Schneider v. State*, the Supreme Court ruled that if a legal provision requires the issuance of a permit as a prerequisite to the occurrence of a public protest event, then that provision must satisfy the following prongs:

- unambiguous criteria exist for obtaining the permit; and

- an official or office that issues the permit lacks discretion with regard to the decision-making about permit issuance.

(b)   Challenging Permit Requirements

(i)   Facially Valid Permit

If a provision of law that requires a permit is facially valid, then an applicant for a permit must comply with the permit requirement, legally challenge it, or disobey it and be subject to prosecution for violating that law.

(ii)   Facially Invalid Permit

A law that provides an official with absolute discretion regarding issuance of a permit to engage in expressive conduct is facially invalid. Such a law is void. Consequently, a person who fails to request a permit before engaging in expressive conduct will not be convicted of violating a facially invalid law.

(3)   Compelled Speech Violations

A compelled speech violation may occur if, as a condition of permitting expression, the government requires an individual to add a non-comporting message to his expression. In *Hurley v. Irish-American Gay, Lesbian and Bisexual Group of Boston, Inc.*, the Supreme Court held that application of the Massachusetts public accommodations law by state courts to obligate "private citizens who organized a parade to include among the marchers a group imparting a message that the organizers do not wish to convey violates the First Amendment." The Court further stated that "disapproval of a private speaker's statement does not legitimize use of . . . [state] power to compel the speaker to alter the message by including one more acceptable to others."

★   d)   Commercial Speech

> Question Key
> 136

Commercial speech is speech that occurs in advertising or business transactions. It is speech that advertises a product or is made for a business purpose. The First Amendment only protects truthful commercial speech that advances a lawful activity. Of course, untruthful commercial speech and/or commercial speech that advances an unlawful activity is not protected by the First Amendment. For example, a government may outlaw commercial speech that is false, untruthful, deceptive, misleading, or that advertises illegal activity.

Generally, commercial speech is afforded less protection than non-commercial speech and, accordingly, can be subject to more regulation than non-commercial speech.

(1)   Standard of Review

A court reviews commercial speech under a type of intermediate scrutiny standard.

A law or government action regulating commercial speech will be upheld if the law is:

- *narrowly tailored*;

- to serve a *substantial government interest*.

The narrowly tailored requirement in the commercial speech context requires that there be a reasonable fit between the ends, and the means chosen to accomplish those ends. For example, a law barring the solicitation of accident victims within a limited time period following an accident is narrowly tailored to serve the state's substantial interest in protecting the privacy of the victims.

The narrowly tailored standard replaced the prior standard – that the government use the least-restrictive means available to accomplish this objective. The newer standard, therefore, is easier for the government to satisfy.

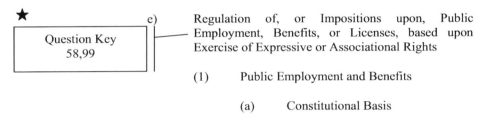

★

| Question Key |
| 58,99 |

     e)   Regulation of, or Impositions upon, Public Employment, Benefits, or Licenses, based upon Exercise of Expressive or Associational Rights

          (1)   Public Employment and Benefits

               (a)   Constitutional Basis

                     (i)   No Religious Test

Article VI of the *Constitution* ("Article VI") provides, in part, that "no religious Test shall ever be required as a Qualification to any Office or public Trust under the United States." U.S. Const. art. VI, cl. 3. Therefore, an individual's exercise of religious expressive rights or associational rights cannot impact:

- the individual's eligibility for an elected office of the federal government; or

- an employment decision concerning the individual in working for the federal government.

For example, the fact that an individual is a member of a religion who regularly attends religious events cannot impact his eligibility for federal elected office or a federal employment decision regarding the individual.

                     (ii)   First Amendment and Public Employees

                         (A)   Public Employment Decisions

The First Amendment's provisions of freedom of speech and association generally protect a public employee from a denial of a promotion or raise, or from being fired or demoted, on the basis of membership in a political party. An exception to that rule applies when that membership is a valid prerequisite for a position of employment that is at issue. Membership is a valid prerequisite only if the position of employment:

- concerns policy making at an advanced level; or

- involves closely advising an elected official.

(B)   Public Employee Speech

The First Amendment's provisions for freedom of speech for private citizens do not protect a public employee from discipline by a public employer, (e.g., denial of a promotion or raise or from being fired or demoted), imposed for speech occurring pursuant to the employee's official duties.

(b)   General Rule

As a general rule, a person's exercise of expression or association rights may not be a basis for denying the individual a job, a license (e.g., to practice law), or another public benefit, such as employment.

(i)   Exception

The exception to the general rule applies if the individual's exercise of those rights would be unlawful, such as the individual's membership in an outlawed organization. Accordingly, an employee may not be penalized in terms of employment status or in the terms and conditions of employment based on the employee's association with an organization unless:

- the employee belongs to an organization involved with unlawful activity not constitutionally protected; and

- the employee is aware of that unlawful activity and the organization's intent to achieve its unlawful objectives.

(2)   Law and other Occupational Licenses

(a)   General Rule

Generally, the fact that an applicant for an occupational license or admission to a state bar organization previously belonged to a subversive organization does not create an irrebuttable presumption of unfitness for bar membership.

(i)   Exception for Subversive Group

This general rule is subject to an exception for an applicant's membership in a subversive group. The First Amendment cannot protect the free expression right of a bar applicant who is a knowing and active member of an organization dedicated to the illegal purpose of violently overthrowing a government. Such an applicant may be disqualified from becoming an attorney on the basis of lacking loyalty to the principles of a constitutional system of government.

(ii)   Loyalty Oath Requirement

A loyalty oath may be required in some situations. A loyalty oath to uphold the federal constitutional form of government involves an affiant's affirmation of personal opposition to violently overthrowing the federal government. If it is not vague or overbroad, a constitutionally permissible loyalty oath may be required:

- as a condition of public employment or public service, or

- to acquire an occupational license or hold an elected office.

(iii)   Constitutionally Required Disclosures

Certain disclosures may constitutionally be required to obtain a law license. In *Konigsberg v. State Bar of California*, (Konigsberg II), the Supreme Court declared that "the State's interest in having lawyers who are devoted to the law . . . [is] clearly sufficient to outweigh the minimal effect upon free association" resulting from compulsory disclosure of evidence relevant to determining a bar applicant's membership in political organizations. A bar applicant who refuses to provide such disclosure is subject to a denial of bar membership.

(iv)   Revocation of License

Under some circumstances, a license can constitutionally be revoked. A state licensing board possesses the power to revoke a commercial license if its employment endangers the public. Such a license is a personal property interest that the state may not revoke without affording procedural due process to the licensee. At a minimum, the licensee is entitled to notice and an opportunity to be heard.

f)   Association Membership

Association membership may be constitutionally protected under the First Amendment's provision for freedom of association. If a government imposes restrictions upon individuals obtaining memberships in groups, a court will apply strict scrutiny in reviewing those restrictions.

(1)   Small, Exclusive Organizations

In *Rotary Club International v. Rotary Club of Duarte*, the Supreme Court held that laws (including state laws) precluding an organization from discriminating are generally valid. Such laws would outlaw discrimination based on suspect and quasi-suspect classifications, for example. There are two exceptions to this rule:

- The organization is an "intimate association," meaning small in size; or

- The discrimination is integral to the organization's purpose.

Therefore, a government cannot mandate that a private and selective organization with just a few members allow someone to be a member contrary to the organization's right to freely associate under the First Amendment. In that situation, the First Amendment essentially would trump the operation of other anti-discrimination laws. But in an opposite situation, the First Amendment may not apply to that affect.

        (2)   Large, Discriminatory Organizations

For example, *Roberts v. United States Jaycees* involved a challenge to the U.S. Jaycees' policy of not accepting women into membership. The policy was challenged as violating the *Minnesota Human Rights Act*. The Supreme Court decided that the government may intervene and require that an organization accept someone as a member if required under state law under the following circumstances:

- A big, nationwide organization discriminates against a suspect class; and

- A compelling state interest warrants judicial interference with the organization's right to freely associate.

        g)   Media Outlets

        (1)   General Right to Communicate News

A media outlet possesses a First Amendment right to disseminate an accurate representation of a newsworthy event, even if that event is depicted in a distasteful or disgusting manner. Examples of media outlets include, but are not limited to, newspapers, radio stations, and television broadcasters.

        (2)   Government Cannot Force Publication

As a general matter, the government cannot force publication by a media outlet. Under *Miami Herald Co. v. Tornillo*, the Supreme Court concluded that a state may not force a newspaper to publish certain content because compelling certain speech would violate the newspaper's right to free expression under the First Amendment.

        (3)   Prior Restraint

        (a)   General Considerations

Prior restraint exists when a law or court order prevents the communication of speech in advance of the planned speech's occurrence. It is analyzed most often in the context of freedom of the press as protected under the First Amendment. For example, a government may seek to enjoin the publication of a newspaper article on the basis that it contains confidential or classified information.

        (b)   Post Statement Remedies

The freedom of the press is a fundamental right afforded by the First Amendment. However, punishment for the abuse of the liberty accorded to the press is essential to the protection of the public. The common-law rules that subject a defaming party to responsibility for the public offense of defamation are not abolished by the protection extended in either state or federal constitutions. These limitations upon freedom of the press are post-statement limitations.

(c) Prior Restraint is Extraordinary

An instance of prior restraint would be extraordinary because it is done before the speech or expression is permitted, not after. Thus, the permissibility of prior restraint is limited.

(i) Exceptions

This does not mean, however, that an instance of prior restraint would never be upheld. Prior restraint may be permitted in exceptional cases. For example, if the nation is at war, the government could prevent, by prior restraint, the publication of the flying dates of planes or the number and location of ships. On similar grounds, the primary requirements of decency may be enforced by prior restraint against obscene publications. Likewise, the security of the community may be protected by prior restraint against incitements to acts of violence and the overthrow by force of orderly government.

(4) Generally Applicable Laws

Generally, the First Amendment will not protect the press from liability resulting from generally applicable laws not directed at suppression of free speech. For example, a reporter who commits trespass or otherwise breaks the law in the course of reporting the news cannot avoid legal liability for such misconduct only by relying upon the First Amendment.

The Supreme Court declared that "generally applicable laws do not offend the First Amendment simply because their enforcement against the press has incidental effects on its ability to gather and report the news . . . [E]nforcement of such general laws against the press is not subject to stricter scrutiny than would be applied to enforcement against other persons or organizations." *Cohen v. Cowles Media Co.,* 501 U.S. 663 (1991).

★

| Question Key | h) | Defamation and Other Privacy Matters |
| 26,137 | | |

On the MBE, a question testing defamation or other privacy torts may be classified as either a constitutional law or torts question. Expressive speech or conduct that is defamatory, or causes an invasion of privacy, is subject to some regulation under the First Amendment. The extent of First Amendment protection depends upon the content of the expression and the individual or entity engaged in the expression.

(1) Defamation

Defamation consists of either slander (by spoken words), or libel (by printed words). To be actionable, both types of defamation must be published or communicated to two or more individuals or entities by its speaker or writer. There are two main categories of defamation that differ based on what type of person is subject to defamation, and the state of mind of the person who published the communication.

(a)   Public Matter, Figure, Official

In order for a public figure or official to prevail in a defamation action, or if the matter communicated is a matter of public concern, a plaintiff must prove with clear and convincing evidence that a defendant published a defamatory communication with actual malice. Actual malice includes: 1) knowledge of the falsity of the statement; or 2) a reckless disregard as to falsity of the statement, such that the defendant doubts the truth of that statement.

(b)   Private Figure

In order for a private figure to prevail in a defamation action, the plaintiff must prove that a defendant made a false statement and that the statement was at least negligently made. If that statement's subject matter involves a public concern, then the private figure plaintiff may not recover punitive damages without proving that the statement was made with actual malice.

(2)   Privacy Protections

In *Zacchini v. Scripps-Howard Broadcasting Co.*, the Supreme Court established four types of legally protected privacy:

- false-light depiction of a person;

- appropriation of a trade name or likeness;

- publication of private facts about a non-newsworthy event or person; and

- a "right of publicity" of a performer with a commercially valuable name.

Expressive conduct that implicates any of these four types of legally protected privacy interests may constitute an invasion of privacy not protected under the First Amendment. A plaintiff who suffers from any of those types of invasions of privacy may seek to recover damages in a tort lawsuit. Two of these topics, right of publicity and publication of private facts, will be examined further.

(a)   Right of Publicity

The Supreme Court held that the plaintiff in *Zacchini* fell under the fourth category of protected privacy interest, right of publicity, in his capacity as a "human cannonball." Thus, an unauthorized television broadcast of his paid public performance, which was recorded without his consent, violated his proprietary interest despite the favorable commentary that accompanied it. That broadcast did not constitute protected speech under the First Amendment.

(b)   Publication of Private Facts

(i)   Information of Public
Record

In *Cox Broadcasting Corp. v. Cohn*, the Supreme Court determined that a person's privacy interest about information that existed in the public record did not prevail over the strong interests of:

- a free press in not having to censor itself; and

- the public's need to know about activities of a government.

In *Cox*, the Supreme Court concluded that a state could not impose liability for:

- public dissemination of true information (e.g., a crime victim's name);

- contained in and obtained from official court records;

- that were open to public inspection.

Accordingly, the First Amendment protects a defendant who lawfully obtains a private fact provided that the defendant's news story addresses a matter of public concern. Id. In certain jurisdictions, the tort rule expressly includes this type of First Amendment protection.

(ii)   Truthful Publication
Protected

In *Landmark Communications, Inc. v. Virginia*, the Supreme Court construed the First Amendment as precluding criminal punishment of anyone – who did not participate in a judicial disciplinary inquiry – for their disclosing of or publishing of truthful information concerning a judicial inquiry board's confidential proceedings.

i)   Campaign Finance

The Supreme Court held in *Randall v. Sorrell,* that *Vermont Act 64*, a campaign financing law, unconstitutionally violated the First Amendment's free speech protections under *Buckley v. Valeo*, by restricting how much money political parties and individuals could contribute to a political candidate and how much money the candidate could spend in a campaign.

(1)   Contribution Limitations & Expenditure
Limitations

Pursuant to *Buckley*, the government's interest in preventing "corruption and the appearance of corruption" may provide sufficient justification for contribution limitations imposed by the *Federal Election Campaign Act of 1971* (FECA) on campaigns for federal office, although the FECA expenditure limitations violated the First Amendment.

The difference between contribution limitations and expenditure limitations is that the latter "'impose significantly more severe restrictions on protected freedoms of political expression and association than' do contribution limits. Contribution limits, though a 'marginal restriction,' nevertheless leave the contributor 'fre[e] to discuss candidates and issues.' Expenditure limits, by contrast, impose '[a] restriction on the amount of money a person or group can spend on political communication,' and thereby necessarily 'reduc[e] the quantity of expression by restricting the number of issues discussed, the depth of their exploration, and the size of the audience reached'." *Randall v. Sorrell*, 126 S.Ct. 2479 (2006) (internal citations omitted).

(a)   Soft-Money Contributions

In *McConnell v. Federal Election Commission*, the Supreme Court upheld as constitutional much of the *Bipartisan Campaign Reform Act of 2002* (i.e., *McCain–Feingold Act*). The Court followed *Buckley's* rules that strict scrutiny applies to restrictions on campaign expenditures, while a lower level of "closely drawn" scrutiny applies to restrictions on campaign contributions. The Court stated that contribution limits are based on the "important governmental interests in preventing 'both the actual corruption threatened by large financial contributions and . . . the appearance of corruption'" that such contributions could cause. The Court upheld as constitutional "the general ban on soft-money donations directly to federal candidates and officeholders and their agents."

j)   Public Schools

(1)   Compulsory Recitation of Pledge

In *West Virginia Board of Education v. Barnette*, the Supreme Court decided that, pursuant to the Free Speech Clause of the First Amendment to the *U.S. Constitution*, public school students may not be compelled by law to recite the Pledge of Allegiance to the United States flag or salute it in public schools.

(2)   Public Display by Student

In *Morse v. Frederick*, the Supreme Court held that no First Amendment violation occurred when Alaska public school officials confiscated a pro-drug banner stating "Bong Hits 4 Jesus" and suspended the student responsible for it being displayed in public during an event supervised by the school. The Court stated that the state possesses an "important—indeed, perhaps compelling interest" in preventing illegal drug use by students. In this case, the Court stated that:

> "[S]tudents do not shed their constitutional rights to freedom of speech or expression at the schoolhouse gate. [T]he constitutional rights of students in public schools are not automatically coextensive with the rights of adults in other settings. . . [T]he rights of students must be applied in light of the special characteristics of the school environment. [S]chools may take steps to safeguard those entrusted to their care from speech that can reasonably be regarded as encouraging illegal drug use."

Morse v. Frederick, 551 U. S. 393 (2007) (internal citations omitted).

G.   Second Amendment Rights

1)   RIGHT TO BEAR ARMS

The Second Amendment to the *Constitution* ("Second Amendment") provides that: "A well regulated Militia, being necessary to the security of a free State, the right of the people to keep and bear Arms, shall not be infringed." U.S. Const. amend. II.

a)   Judicial Holding

In a landmark case involving the Second Amendment, *District of Columbia v. Heller*, the Supreme Court held that the Second Amendment protected an individual's right to bear arms. The Court's decision found a District of Columbia ban on the possession of handguns in the home to be unconstitutional. Also, the District's "prohibition against rendering any lawful firearm in the home operable for the purpose of immediate self-defense" violated the Second Amendment.

b)   Limited Right to Possess Guns

The Court, however, made clear that this case did not afford individuals an unlimited right to possess guns and stated that:

> Nothing in our opinion should be taken to cast doubt on longstanding prohibitions on the possession of firearms by felons and the mentally ill or laws forbidding the carrying of firearms in sensitive places such as schools and government buildings, or laws imposing conditions and qualifications on the commercial sale of arms.

c)   Restrictions upon Weapon Possession

Moreover, the types of weapons that individuals may possess may be subject to restrictions. Some types of weapons subject to restrictions include those:

- deemed usual and dangerous; and

- "not typically possessed by law abiding citizens for lawful purposes, such as short barreled shotguns."

d)   Standard of Review

The Court stated that it would have made its decision under any standard of scrutiny, but declined to set forth a controlling standard for reviewing legal restrictions upon the Second Amendment.

AMERIBAR BAR REVIEW

Multistate Bar Examination Preparation Course

CONTRACTS AND SALES

TABLE OF CONTENTS

INTRODUCTION

There are two main sources of contract law – common law and statute. Common law is traditional law. For exam purposes, it is law set forth by judges in case opinions (as opposed to statutory law created by the legislature). Modern common law governs most contracts unless the statutory law of the Uniform Commercial Code ("UCC") displaced it and instead applies. UCC § 1-103.

Common law governs most contracts including, but not limited to, construction, service, and employment contracts. Article 2 of the UCC governs contracts for the sale or lease of goods, even when neither of the parties to the contract is a merchant. Goods generally are most items other than real property and services. When resolving any contracts question, you first must determine whether the contract is governed by common law or by the UCC.

In this outline, provisions and governing law of the UCC are presented in shaded text boxes.

I. FORMATION OF CONTRACTS

- Definition of Contract

A contract is a legally enforceable promise. The *Restatement Second of Contracts ("Restatement")* defines a contract as "a promise or set of promises for the breach of which the law gives a remedy, or the performance of which the law in some way recognizes as a duty."

To be enforceable, a contract must be based on the parties' mutual assent that is generally manifested by an 1) offer and 2) an acceptance, as well as the existence of 3) legally sufficient consideration.

- Express, Implied, and Constructive Contracts

There are three primary contract formation methods – 1) express, 2) implied, and 3) constructive. Express formation occurs when the contract's terms are either written or spoken. Implied formation is derived from the parties' conduct. Constructive formation results when the courts find that, under the circumstances, the parties have an enforceable contract.

★★ - Bilateral Contracts

Formation of a bilateral contract occurs when two parties exchange mutual promises. Their promises may be implied from the surrounding circumstances. For example, if Bob promises to paint Barbara's house in exchange for Barbara's promise to pay Bob $1,000, then a bilateral contract exists.

A bargained for exchange of promises occurs if 1) a promisor makes a promise to convince a promisee to perform; and 2) a promisee is convinced to perform based on the promise that the promisor made.

★★   •   Unilateral Contracts

A unilateral contract is created by an exchange of one party's promise for another party's performance of certain conduct. For example, if Barbara promises to pay Bob $1,000 if Bob paints her house, then an offer for a unilateral contract has been made. What is the difference between this proposed unilateral contract and the earlier bilateral contract? In the bilateral contract, a promise is exchanged for a promise. Both parties have made promises. In a unilateral contract, a promise is exchanged for an act that may be, but need not be, undertaken. In other words, a promise is exchanged for an act (that is not promised). A unilateral contract cannot be formed when an offeree makes a promise in return for an offeror's promise. In other words, if Barbara promises to pay Bob $1,000 if he paints her house, then Bob generally cannot accept the proposed unilateral contract by saying he promises to paint the house. He can accept only by actually painting the house.

★★★   A.   **Mutual Assent**

An essential basis for forming a contract is mutual assent to identical terms and conditions by the parties involved. This assent is often described as a meeting of the minds. Mutual assent usually is achieved by an offer and acceptance. Although unusual, mutual assent may exist even when the parties have not exchanged an offer and an acceptance. For example, the parties may simultaneously agree to a proposal that a third person made, or to a written agreement that incorporates all of the terms they would like to include.

               •   Objective Assent

In adjudicating contract law issues, the courts usually evaluate objective assent by each party's words and deeds. Such conduct must be intentional. The test of a first party's intent is: what would a reasonable person in a second party's position consider the first party's actions to mean? The parties do not need to make any other manifestation of their intent to be bound if they have expressly exchanged an offer and acceptance.

The majority rule is that when two parties objectively manifest their lack of intent to be bound, the courts will find that no contract exists. Conversely, when the parties objectively manifest their intent to be bound, a contract may exist. The following factors are considered objective manifestations of intent:

- definite propositions from one party to another party;
- a direct method of communicating a proposition between the parties;
- conduct manifesting an intent to enter into an agreement;
- the parties' prior dealings; or
- the parties' custom or usage of trade.

For example, suppose Mike usually mows the lawn of his own home. Suppose also that Melinda operates a lawn care service. When Mike's lawnmower stops working, he asks Melinda to mow his lawn. Melinda promises that she will do so for the standard fee. Mike promises to pay her that fee. Melinda mows Mike's lawn, and he pays her the standard fee. Here, the parties' communications and conduct objectively manifest their assent to form a contract.

★★★★   1)   OFFER AND ACCEPTANCE

★★★★   a)   Offer

Question Key
20,21,36,62,67,102,103,121,123,124,141,142,143,144,153,157,180,199,206,207,223

(1)   Objective Approach

A valid offer to enter into a contract exists when a reasonable person would objectively believe that an offer is open for acceptance. For example, suppose Offeror says to Neighbor, "If you promise to wash my car on Saturday, I promise to pay you $30." A reasonable person in the shoes of Neighbor would believe that the offer is open for acceptance. On the other hand, suppose after ingesting several alcoholic beverages in a tavern, Offeror says to Waitress, "If you bring me another beer, I promise to give you a million dollars!" Because Offeror likely is intoxicated, a reasonable person in the position of Waitress would not believe that the offer is genuine and open for acceptance. Therefore, the statement by Offeror to Waitress is not a valid and binding offer.

An offer enables an offeror to form an agreement by inviting an acceptance of the offer. An offer is an offeror's promise to do, or to refrain from doing, something specific in the future.

★★   (2)   Definiteness of Offer

(a)   General

An offer must be a clear, unequivocal, and direct approach to another party to enter into a contract. An offer needs to be sufficiently definite that an offeree may understand it. Normally, an offer to enter into a contract needs to incorporate certain terms of identification including: the parties, the subject matter, and the price. Ordinarily, if the parties to a contract agree that its price will be subsequently ascertained using some reasonably objective basis, such as fair market value, the courts would enforce the agreement.

(b)   Public Advertisements

For this reason, advertisements, catalogs, or store flyers are not considered offers. Nor is a "For Sale" sign on a used car considered an offer. The law considers these types of materials as invitations to receive offers. There are exceptions to this general rule regarding advertisements. The status depends on the wording of the advertisement and how definite it is.

An advertisement may constitute an offer to form a unilateral contract only if:

- the offer's terms of acceptance are specific and definite; and
- the types of potential offerees are clearly indicated.

(c)   Universal Contracts

An advertised public offer may provide for the formation of a universal contract. For example, a contest open to public participation may give rise to a universal contract. If an offeree performs in response to an offer for a universal contract, the offeree's death will not extinguish that offer. Conversely, with respect to an offer for a non-universal contract, the general rule is that the death of an offeree will extinguish such an offer.

     (3)   Preliminary Negotiations

(a)   General

A common issue on the exam is whether a communication made during preliminary negotiations between prospective parties is of such a substantial nature so as to qualify as an offer. Preliminary negotiations are any communications between the parties that have occurred before a formal offer is made. The following factors will determine whether a communication qualifies as an offer:

- Is an alleged offer an initial communication or an answer to an inquiry?
- Is the verbiage (i.e., wording) of the communication associated with a promise or not?
- What type of terms does the communication include? Is it detailed in terms of quantity or quality?
- Is one of the parties dealing with another party on the same subject?
- Do the parties have a familial or a professional relationship?
- Do any circumstances have an impact upon the parties' situation?
- What is the parties' prior course of dealing or usage of trade?

(b)   Prior Dealings

Prior dealings can provide evidence regarding whether specific conduct constituted an offer. In order to ascertain if a party's acts or words were intended to constitute an offer, the parties' dealings and performance under a current or past agreement will be adequate evidence of their acts and statements. The following evidence is required to establish the parties' prior dealings and performance:

- performance of a contract to sell goods on at least one previous occasion;
- awareness by both parties of the contract's terms; and
- no objections by either party to those terms.

> Under UCC § 2-208(1), evidence of acceptance and acquiescence of a course of performance of a contract for the sale of goods without making an objection will be relevant in determining this agreement's meaning.

(4)   Intent to Be Bound

When the parties in negotiations intend to reduce their agreement to writing, a question may arise as to when a contract is formed. Does that occur when they have agreed to all of the terms and conditions, or not until after they have memorialized the terms and conditions in writing? The *Restatement* provides the following factors to analyze if a contract was created:

- the extent to which express assent has been reached on all terms;
- whether the contract is a type usually put in writing;
- whether it needs a formal writing for its full expression;
- whether it has few or many details;
- whether the quantities at issue are large or small;
- whether it is a common or unusual contract;
- whether a standard form of contract is widely used in similar transactions; and
- whether either party took any action in preparation for performance during the negotiations.

If the parties seek to reach their agreement by correspondence, it is likely that the parties intend to be bound when they reach an agreement through that correspondence.

(5)   Intent Not to Be Bound

A question may arise as to whether the parties formed a contract once they separately sign duplicate originals or only when they mutually exchange signed writings. In *Aspen Acres Association v. Seven Associates, Inc.*, 29 Utah 2d 303, 508 P.2d 1179 (1973), the court held that: "The mere affixing of signatures to a document did not conclusively prove that there was a binding contract. In addition, there must be a delivery, not in the traditional sense of a manual transfer, but in the sense that it was the intent of the parties to have the document become legally operative at some definite point in time; however such intent might be indicated."

For example, suppose Dirk is negotiating to purchase Deb's home. He signs an offer and delivers it to Deb. She is unsure of whether she will accept the offer. She signs the contract, but decides to think it over for a day, so she waits until the next day to deliver it to Dirk. Even though the contract is signed, the parties do not necessarily have a binding contract. In this example, the contract must be delivered in order for Deb's acceptance to be valid.

(6)   Auctions

An auction can form the basis of a contract. An auction is with reserve if an auctioneer can withdraw an item from bidding at any time before declaring the end of bidding. An auction is without reserve if an auctioneer cannot withdraw an item from bidding unless no bids occur within a reasonable period.

The auctioneer's announcement that he will sell to the highest bidder:

- is not an offer if the auction is with reserve. In this case, an auctioneer is an offeror who makes the ultimate decision to make an offer if an auction ends having met the reserve.
- is an offer if the auction is without reserve. In this case, a bidder is an offeree, and the auctioneer decides when the contract is complete.

UCC § 2-328(3) generally incorporates the common law rules for auctions of goods. Also, the same rules apply to invitations to bid on a construction project.

(7)   Sale of Property

When potential sellers and buyers are communicating regarding the price and quantity of personal or real property, two considerations apply:

- Do their communications indicate a commitment by either of them to a specific price and quantity?
- Are any terms of their communications sufficiently definite to indicate the formation of a contract?

     (8)   Duration of Offers

An offeror may terminate an offeree's power of acceptance of an offer in several ways.

(a)   Lapse of Time

A lapse of time may terminate an offer, regardless of whether the duration of the offer is specified. When the duration of the offer's acceptance period is not specified, it is open for a reasonable time. Whether the time is reasonable depends on the subject matter, the medium of the offer, business custom, and price fluctuation. An offeror may terminate the power of acceptance upon the occurrence of a specified event.

(b)   Late Acceptance

If an offer lapses before an acceptance occurs, an offeree's late acceptance becomes another offer that may be accepted only by an offeror's timely communicated acceptance.

(c)   Death or Incapacity

A power of acceptance terminates when an offeror dies between the making of the offer and an acceptance. That power also ends when an offeror becomes incapacitated between the making of the offer and an acceptance.

(d)   Revocation

(i)   Direct Communication

Revocation is the manifestation of intent not to enter into a proposed contract made by one party after that party has already made an offer. Generally, a revocation may occur before an offeree accepts an offer. The majority rule is that a revocation is effective when received. The minority rule is that a revocation is effective when sent.

For example, suppose Offeror wishes to revoke an offer made to purchase Offeree's vehicle for $500 upon Offeree bringing the vehicle to Offeror's residence. Suppose that Offeror dispatches a courier to deliver the written revocation to Offeree. Under the majority approach, the offer is not revoked until it is received by Offeree. Under the minority approach, the offer is revoked when given to the courier. Thus, under the majority approach, if Offeree unknowingly crosses the path of the courier, and brings the vehicle to Offeror before the delivery of the revocation, the parties will have an enforceable agreement. Under the minority approach, because the revocation is effective upon dispatch, the offer cannot be accepted after dispatch.

(ii)   Indirect Communication

(A)   Implied

An offer may be revoked by implication, or indirectly, under the following circumstances:

- an offeror takes steps inconsistent with;
- an ongoing intent to enter into a contract; and
- an offeree gains knowledge of the offeror's steps.

An offer may be indirectly revoked when an offeree receives information that would cause him to reasonably conclude that an offer is no longer open. For example, suppose Bob makes the following offer to Charles on January 1, in contemplation of Charles' cross-country road trip beginning on Valentine's Day: "I promise to sell you my car on February 1, if you promise to pay me $15,000." Charles decides to think it over for a reasonable time before accepting. On January 15, Ted, Bob's brother, tells Charles that he has just purchased Bob's car. When Charles learns of the sale from Ted, Charles has indirectly received notice that the offer has been revoked. Thus, the offer can no longer be accepted. However, suppose Charles did not hear anything about the sale from Ted or anyone else. Suppose that Charles sent a letter to Bob on January 20 stating: "I accept your offer regarding the purchase of your car." The offer, assuming 20 days is a reasonable period to accept, is still valid, and Charles has validly accepted. Therefore, Bob may be liable for breach of contract if he sold the car to Ted.

(B)   Public Offers

Another exception to the rule requiring direct communication of revocation applies to offers made to the general public. In that event, if an offer was communicated to the public, then a revocation of that announcement must be made in a similar manner to that by which it was initially communicated. Reasonable means, such as by newspaper or by broadcast media, must be used. The use of reasonable means does not require that every member of the public must, in fact, receive notice of the revocation.

(iii)   Power to Revoke

(A)   General

An offeror may revoke an offer at any time before an offeree accepts it, in the absence of:

- consideration exchanged to keep the offer open;
- detrimental reliance (reasonably suffered) by the offeree; or
- the offeror is a merchant selling goods under the UCC (firm offer rule).

Remember that generally, the revocation must be communicated to the offeree either directly or indirectly in order for it to be effective.

(B)   Unilateral Contracts

An offeror may revoke an offer for a unilateral contract at any time before an offeree begins performance. Once that occurs, then the parties' performance obligations become absolute.

For example, suppose John tells Beverly, "I promise to pay you $5,000, if you paint my house." This promise for an act is a proposed unilateral contract. The problem that arises is, until what point can John legally revoke the offer? Can he wait until Beverly has painted 90% of the house and then revoke the offer? The answer is that, because this is an offer for a unilateral contract, John can revoke until Beverly begins performance – in this case, when Beverly begins to paint the house. Once she begins to perform, however, John may no longer revoke the offer.

(C)   Power to Accept

An offeree's power to accept an offer may be terminated in the following ways:

- The offeror communicates a withdrawal or cancellation of the offer;
- The offeror takes communicated action contradictory to continuing the offer (e.g., selling a car subject to an offer);
- The conduct or statements of either the offeree or the offeror ends it;
- Conditions or terms of the offer may provide for its cancellation;
- The occurrence of certain events end it; or
- If an offer does not specify an expiration date, a proper acceptance has not occurred within a reasonable time period.

The courts will determine the length of time that is considered reasonable based on the following factors:

- Each of the parties' needs with respect to the transaction at issue; and
- The contract's subject matter.

For example, in the context of commodities trading, an offer that deals with a commodity having a volatile price may remain open for just a few minutes. This is because an offeror is concerned with variable conditions in the commodities' market. An offeree must quickly make a decision based on a product's market availability.

                        (9)   Irrevocable Offer

                                            (a)   General

An irrevocable offer arises when an offeror accepts consideration to keep an offer open for a specified duration. Thus, generally the offer cannot be revoked during that period. Unless an irrevocable offer provides otherwise, acceptance of that offer may occur when it is received by an offeror instead of when it is dispatched by an offeree.

The *Restatement* provides that termination of an irrevocable offer may occur in the following circumstances:

- lapse of time;
- death or destruction of a person or thing essential to a contract's performance; or
- subsequent legal prohibition of the contract's subject matter.

An irrevocable offer is not terminated by its rejection, revocation, or even the subsequent death or incapacity of an offeror or an offeree (if they are not essential to the performance of the contract).

Promissory estoppel may render an offer irrevocable in the absence of consideration on the basis of an offeree's foreseeable detrimental reliance on the offer.

For example, suppose Krista tells Kevin that she will pay the cost of his labor and the materials for building a shed for her. Before Kevin promises to build the shed for her, he purchases, with his own funds, the materials necessary to build it and uses them to construct its walls. When Kevin tells Krista he will build the shed and what he has done, Krista tells him she no longer wants the shed. Kevin could assert that Krista's offer was irrevocable despite the absence of consideration if he can prove that his detrimental reliance upon Krista's offer was foreseeable.

(b)   "Option" Contract

An option contract results when an offeror receives consideration from an offeree in order to keep an offer open for a certain period. An option contract is the functional equivalent of an irrevocable offer and those words generally are synonymous.

An offeree's consideration for an option contract may be minimal and/or provided in the form of services.

(i)   Acceptance

- Communication of Acceptance

The majority rule provides that the acceptance of an option contract is effective only when an offeror has received a communication of that acceptance, rather than when an offeree dispatched it.

- Acceptance by Performance

If an offer allows for acceptance by performance, commencement of performance by the offeree makes the agreement an option contract that the offeror may not subsequently revoke. Restatement (Second) of Contracts § 45.

- Contractor's Reliance upon Bid

An option contract may exist, for example, when a contractor uses a subcontractor's bid for work on a construction job to determine its own complete bid for the project. The subcontractor should reasonably anticipate that the contractor's reliance on the bid will create an option contract between the contractor and subcontractor. If the subcontractor retracts the bid, requiring the contractor to procure the work from an alternative source, the contractor may recover that loss from the subcontractor.

★★   (10)   Firm Offer Rule (UCC ARTICLE 2 ONLY)

Under UCC § 2-205, a merchant's (one who deals in such goods) offer contained in a signed writing usually is irrevocable for up to three months without consideration. Such an offer by a merchant is called a firm offer.

If a merchant provides a signed writing that offers to sell or buy goods and provides assurances that the offer must remain open for a certain period, then the offer is irrevocable for:

•   either a reasonable time not exceeding three months (if the offer states no period); or

•   for the period that is stated in the offer (but not for more than three months); and

•   no consideration is required.

                             (11)   Counter-Offer

                                         (a)   Rejection of Offer (Common Law)

An offeree may respond to an offer with a counter-offer, which, under the common law, works as a rejection of the initial offer. The counter-offer terminates the original power of acceptance, unless the offeree states that the original offer continues to be considered under advisement. The counter-offer is distinct from other responses by an offeree to an offeror, such as a counter-inquiry, a request for a modification, or a future acceptance. A reply is a counter-offer if it manifests an offeree's willingness to agree to different terms than those that the offeree proposed.

For example, suppose Bob offers to paint Carla's house for $1,000, with a completion date of March 1. Carla sends the following reply to Bob's offer: "I would like you to paint my house for $1000, but it must be completed by February 14." Carla's reply manifests a willingness to agree to different terms than Bob's offer. Therefore, it is a counter-offer and works to reject Bob's initial offer. Suppose Carla reconsiders the day after Bob receives her first letter, and she sends Bob the following reply in another letter: "I changed my mind about the completion date. March 1 is fine." This second reply is not a valid acceptance because Bob's initial offer was rejected.

                                         (b)   Timing of Counter-Offer

The counter-offer is not effective until it is received by the original offeror.

                                         (c)   Option Contract

Question Key
6,8,26,28,38,83,101,104,105,122,125,137,195,235

An offeree possesses a right to make a counter-offer during the period that an offer in the form of an option exists. When the offeree makes such a counter-offer, the rule that treats a counter-offer as an implied rejection of the offer is inapplicable. Such a counter-offer will result in a termination or a rejection of the option only if the offeror altered his position by reasonably relying upon the counter-offer as a rejection of the offer.

> (d)   Uniform Commercial Code
>
> A seller may accept an offer that seeks a prompt shipment of goods by promptly promising to ship them or promptly shipping them (non-conforming or conforming). UCC § 2-206(1)(b). A shipment of non-conforming goods is an acceptance and breach. *Id.* However, a shipment of non-conforming goods with a reasonable notice of accommodation constitutes a counter-offer, instead of an acceptance and breach. Id. The buyer may reject or accept the counter-offer. *Id.*

                    b)   Acceptance

Generally, before a person can recover on a promise, the person must exchange his performance or promise for the promise he seeks to enforce. Usually, an offeree may be bound by acceptance only when the offeree:

- is aware of an offer;
- intended to accept the offer; and
- took steps to accept the offer according to the offer's terms.

★★★   (1)   Objective Theory

Generally, the courts will rely on the objective theory in deciding contract issues.

- What is the difference between objective and subjective evidence?

Subjective evidence is evidence one cannot independently evaluate – you have to simply accept what a party believes or thinks. For example, Fred says, "I made a valid offer." Is Fred lying? What is Fred's idea of a valid offer? Harry says, "I accepted the offer!" Generally, if a person believes something to be the case, then that person has met the subjective standard. In comparison, if there was a subjective standard for contracts, then one would only need to know what the offeror and offeree believed at the time they made their communications.

In contrast to those parties' subjective beliefs, objective evidence is evidence that outsiders can examine and evaluate for themselves. If a person hears Fred say, "I offer to sell you my home for X dollars," then an outsider may objectively conclude that Fred made a valid offer. What if Fred was joking about the offer? What if he was rehearsing for his lines in a movie? That would mean he did not meet a subjective standard. However, since the court uses an objective standard, if a reasonable person in the shoes of the offeree would believe a valid offer is intended, then it is a valid offer. The same objective standard applies to contract acceptance.

Under the objective theory, the mutual intent adequate to form a contract involves:

- offer: an offeror making a valid offer (viewed objectively); and

- acceptance: the offeree's response to the offer is adequate (viewed objectively) to render the agreement effective.

An offeree accepts an offer by objectively demonstrating assent to the offer's terms and conditions in the way the offer requires.

★★★   (2)   Offeror May Dictate Method of Acceptance

An offer may specify in whom a power of acceptance exists. That power is not transferable to a third person because it is personal to an offeree. The offeror may specify the manner in which acceptance must occur. An offer may require an offeree to accept it by performing certain conduct. For example, suppose Offeror offers his neighbor, Offeree, the following: "I promise to pay you $1,000 if you destroy your hideous car." It is possible Offeree may perform the act requested – destroying the car – without Offeror being aware of it, such as if he gets it crushed in an automobile junk yard. If the offeree has reason to know that the offeror lacks a way of discovering that conduct constituting an acceptance, with reasonable promptness and certainty, the offeror's duty is discharged unless:

- the offeree exercises reasonable diligence to notify the offeror of the performance;
- the offeror otherwise learns of performance within a reasonable time; or
- the offer expressly or by implication indicates that notification is not necessary to bind the offeror.

★★★   (3)   Acceptance of Offer

Generally, an offer for a unilateral contract may be accepted by performance. To accept an offer for a bilateral contract, an offeree's promise must be communicated to an offeror or the offeror's agent. Usually, an exchange of identical cross-offers will not result in the formation of a contract between two offerors.

(a)   Acceptance by Silence

Generally, an offeree's silence does not constitute acceptance of an offer.

(i)   Course of Dealing

Silence, however, may result in acceptance when the parties' custom, course of dealing, or usage of trade renders that type of acceptance reasonable. To determine if silence constitutes an acceptance, consider:

- if an offeror's expectation of a response is warranted by the parties' relationship; and

- if that expectation is justified by a duty to respond.

        (ii)   Utilization of Services

Under the *Restatement,* if an offeror could reasonably conclude from the circumstances that an offeree's silence constitutes acceptance, then silence will be construed as an acceptance. Silence also constitutes acceptance when an offeree utilizes services:

- with a reasonable opportunity to reject them; and

- with a reasonable belief that they were offered with the expectation of compensation.

For example, when an offeror renders service to an offeree within a family relationship, the offeree usually has no basis to expect compensation. Alternatively, when an insurance agent retains an insurance policy premium and does not reject it within a reasonable time, the agent's silence will be considered an acceptance.

        (b)   Acceptance by Conduct

        (i)   Unilateral Contracts

Under the common law and the *Restatement* rules of unilateral contract, when an offeror makes a promise in exchange for an offeree's performance, then the offeree's acceptance occurs only when the offeree begins performing for the offeror.

        (ii)   UCC Article 2 Contracts

Similarly, UCC § 2-204(1) states that a "contract for the sale of goods may be made in any manner sufficient to show agreement, including conduct by both parties which recognizes the existence of such a contract." With regard to sales contracts, an act of dominion, which does not become a conversion when it is not wrongful, may constitute acceptance by conduct. The test is whether an offeree's act of dominion relates to an offeror's power of acceptance.

Likewise, UCC § 2-606(1)(c) provides that an acceptance occurs when a buyer does any act inconsistent with a seller's ownership; but if the act is wrongful as against the seller, it is an acceptance only if ratified.

        (iii)   Bilateral Contracts

Generally, if beginning performance is a reasonable mode of acceptance, then it will constitute acceptance in a bilateral contract. However, the *Restatement* provides that if the offer mandates that acceptance may occur only by a promise in a bilateral contract, beginning performance will have no effect.

(c)   Where Seller Sends Wrong Goods

Under the UCC, when a seller sends the wrong goods, its actions constitute an acceptance and a breach. The buyer may reject the goods within a reasonable time after delivery or tender, according to UCC § 2-602(1). "The buyer has no further obligation with regard to goods rightfully rejected." UCC § 2-602(2)(c).

	Question Key
2) AVOIDANCE OF CONTRACT	34,37,54,55,89,110,232

Under certain circumstances, even if parties experience a valid offer and acceptance, the contract still may be avoided. Such contracts are either void or voidable. The courts will treat a void contract as if it did not exist. On the other hand, the lawful obligations of a voidable contract may be avoided by either party who disaffirms it. However, the parties may elect not to avoid the contract, even if it is voidable.

★★★   a)   Mistake

A mistake may arise when one or more of the parties to a contract have a misunderstanding about an existing fact relative to the contract. A mistake does not include an erroneous belief of one or more of the parties regarding what might occur in the future (such as an increase in the price of raw materials).

★★★   (1)   Mutual Mistake

Under the *Restatement*, a mutual mistake occurs when two parties make an assumption about a key fact on which their contract was premised and that assumption is incorrect. In that event, the contract may be avoided if, because of the mistake, a different transaction would have occurred than the one they contemplated. The following are some types of facts about which mutual mistakes may exist:

- existence, ownership, or identity of the subject matter;
- qualities of the subject matter and conscious uncertainty;
- real estate contracts involving a mistake in the amount of acres;
- mistakes with respect to the injuries identified in releases; and
- mistaken predictions.

For example, suppose Bob agrees to purchase Evan's painting, which both parties believe is painted by an amateur local artist, for $1,000. As it turns out, the painting is a Picasso masterpiece worth $2,000,000. Since the mistake was a mutual mistake that resulted in a different transaction than would have occurred had there been no mistake, the contract may be avoided.

                              (2)   Unilateral Mistake

If a first party makes a unilateral mistake about a fact that involves a basic assumption upon which the contract was formed, the contract will be upheld unless the non-mistaken second party:

- had knowledge of the mistake,
- should have been aware of the mistake,
- caused the mistake; or
- took advantage of the mistake.

For example, suppose Bob agrees to purchase Evan's painting, which Evan wrongly believes is painted by an amateur local artist, for $1,000. Bob knows that the painting is a Picasso masterpiece worth $2,000,000 and conceals that fact from Evan, sensing a good opportunity. Evan will be able to avoid the contract because Bob had knowledge of the mistake and attempted to take advantage of it.

b) Misunderstanding

(1) General

Misunderstanding may arise when the parties to a contract possess different subjective beliefs about the terms to which they are agreeing. When that discrepancy of belief is significant enough, it may prevent the formation of a contract. The ambiguity of a term in an agreement may give rise to a misunderstanding when that term has two inconsistent meanings. A contract may not exist when its primary term is ambiguous and the parties have differing concepts of its meaning. The *Restatement* provides that no contract exists when:

- a misunderstanding involves a material term; and
- neither party knows or has reason to know about the misunderstanding.

For example, suppose Alan and Bob, old friends, see each other in a parking lot after a movie. After making small talk, Bob motions behind him and says, "I am selling my black vehicle for $5,000." Bob is pointing to his black sedan. Next to the black sedan is a black pick-up truck, which Alan believes Bob is pointing to. Alan says, "Great, I've been looking for a vehicle like that for my son." The parties draw up a contract on the hood of Alan's car, which provides that "Alan promises to buy, and Bob promises to sell, Bob's black vehicle for $5,000." The next day, when Bob shows up to deliver the vehicle, Alan is stunned to see him driving a black sedan. In this case, the parties had a misunderstanding about a material term of the contract and, under the circumstances, the contract may be avoided.

(2) Patent Ambiguity

Ambiguity in a contract may be either latent or patent. A patent ambiguity is an obvious error, or gross discrepancy, or an inadvertent, but glaring gap (e.g., the numbers and words not matching - $50 spelled out as five hundred dollars). A patent ambiguity raises a duty to inquire about the ambiguity. In the case of a patent ambiguity, a court would allow the parties to present extrinsic evidence to the fact-finder for the purpose of determining intent.

(3)   Latent Ambiguity

On the other hand, if a contract is reasonably, but not obviously, susceptible to more than one interpretation, it is latently ambiguous. In the case of latent ambiguity, extrinsic evidence must be introduced to demonstrate the ambiguity. For example, a word may have two meanings, neither of which is readily apparent from the context in the contract. Suppose Bob and Carla agree that Bob will sell Carla his black car. If it turns out that Bob has two black cars, the ambiguity is a latent ambiguity. In such a case, extrinsic evidence may be introduced to resolve the ambiguity. A latent ambiguity also is subject to a special rule. It will be construed against the drafter if the non-drafter's interpretation is reasonable.

Suppose Bob drafted the contract with Carla to sell her the black car for $10,000, and the extrinsic evidence shows that Carla reasonably interpreted the contract to mean the first black car instead of the second black car. Further suppose that the two black cars were a Ferrari and a Yugo. Carla thought the sale was for the Ferrari, because she had only seen the Ferrari, and had never seen the Yugo. Under these facts, the contract could be construed in Carla's favor to refer to the first black car.

(4)   One Party Knows of Misunderstanding

When parties attach significantly different meanings to the same material term, the meaning that controls is the one attached "by one of them if at the time the agreement was made[,] . . . that [first] party did not know of any different meaning attached by the other [party], and the other [party] knew the meaning attached by the first party." *Restatement (Second) of Contracts* § 201.

★   c)   Misrepresentation

A misrepresentation is an untrue statement one party makes to another party. A misrepresentation is established by proving these elements:

- falsity: A false statement is made; with
- scienter: knowledge that the statement was false; with
- deception: an intent to deceive and to obtain reliance on the deception; and
- injury: a harm warranting damages results from the misrepresentation.

When there is a misrepresentation, a party can assert it as a basis for rescission of a contract or to claim damages. Alternatively, a party can raise misrepresentation as a defense in response to an action seeking to enforce a contract.

d)   Nondisclosure

In bargaining to form a transaction, generally no duty exists to disclose information to another party, although that information may be valuable to its holder. For example, suppose Jennifer is negotiating to sell her used car to Christine. Jennifer possesses no affirmative duty to tell Christine that the car's battery needed to be replaced two months earlier. The following exceptions to the rule require a person to disclose valuable information:

- disclosure is required by a statute or a regulation;
- an information holder's affirmative efforts to hide the truth.

For example, during negotiations to purchase a used car, a buyer asked a dealer whether the car had ever been in an accident. The dealer replied: "It is a fine car and has been thoroughly inspected and comes with a certificate of assured quality. Feel free to have the car inspected by your own mechanic." If it later turns out that the car had been involved in an accident that the dealer was aware of, then the contract will be voidable due to the dealer's affirmative efforts to hide the truth.

Some other exceptions to the general rule – that in bargaining to form a transaction, generally no duty exists to disclose information to another party – mandate a holder to disclose valuable information:

- an absence of full disclosure may constitute misrepresentation;
- a failure to disclose information makes a statement false; and
- a failure to disclose material facts in fiduciary or confidential relationship leads one to believe that another is helping him.

e)   Undue Influence

(1)   Confidential Relationship

An undue influence defense may stem from some types of confidential relationships, such as parent and child or attorney and client, where, by virtue of the relationship, one party cannot be said to have freely assented to the contract. In this situation, the contract is voidable at the option of that party.

A court may examine several factors when determining whether undue persuasion (i.e., influence) by a person in a confidential relationship would result in a voidable contract including:

- whether the dominant party made a full disclosure of relevant known facts;
- whether the consideration was sufficient; or
- whether the dependent party received adequate and independent advice.

For example, suppose Karen, a real estate attorney, agrees to represent John, a potential seller of real property including mineral rights, with respect to the sale of this real property. She drafts a representation agreement and presents it to John, who signs it without reading it. Karen tells John that the contract includes a standard provision granting Karen all royalties from the mineral rights if John's land is sold during the course of her representation. This provision is separate from, and in addition to, the legal fees and expenses Karen will receive for her representation. Karen did not advise John to consult independent counsel about the provision, which, in fact, is not a standard provision. As Karen added this non-standard provision and did not advise him to consult counsel about it, he could assert that this contract is avoidable on the basis of her undue influence.

(2)   Psychological Persuasion

In addition to undue influence through a confidential relationship, undue influence may be exerted by one in a dominant psychological position to another. If a person in such a dominant position exercises undue persuasion over a person of weakened intellect, mental state, or physical state, the contract may be avoided by undue influence. For example, this could occur in the foregoing example if John was senile when Karen drafted the contract.

Undue influence is an equitable defense that is defined in *Smith v. Henline* as any: "urgency of persuasion, whereby the will of a person is overpowered, and he is induced to do or forebear an act which he would not do, or would do if left to act freely."

A common situation when undue influence arises is when a decedent's surviving heirs or beneficiaries seek to set aside a will.

The following types of facts may be examined to determine whether undue influence exists.

- Susceptibility

Do facts exist indicating the susceptibility of an allegedly influenced person (e.g., physical and mental weakness or psychological dependency)?

- Opportunity

Was there an opportunity for a third party to assert undue influence over the influenced person (e.g., a confidential relationship between the third party and the person)?

- Disposition

Is there proof of the third party's disposition to exercise undue influence (e.g., the third party's initiation of the contested dealings with the influenced person)?

- Unnatural Transaction

Does the transaction seem unnatural in its terms and scope (e.g., an inadequate exchange of consideration occurred or the person's natural objects of bounty were neglected)?

- Independent Advice

Did the influenced person have reasonable access to independent advice?

- Fairness

Evidence of a transaction's fairness may rebut a circumstantial case of undue influence.

      f)   Duress

         (1)   General

Duress is a threat or a wrongful act that prevails over a person's free will. The test for duress in this context is subjective. The relevant inquiry is whether the person's will has been overcome, not whether the will of a reasonable person would have been overcome.

           (a)   Economic

If the threat or act is economic in nature, the law requires an objective answer of whether a reasonable third alternative existed for a threatened person. In that case, if the person could have obtained alternative, immediate, and sufficient relief (such as in a court of law), then no case of duress could be established.

    3)   NON-CONFORMING ACCEPTANCE

      a)   Communication of Acceptance

         (1)   In-Person Acceptance

When an offeror and an offeree are in each other's presence, an acceptance is not effective unless the offeror hears it or is at fault for not being able to hear it.

         (2)   Mailbox Rule

Question Key
15

As a general rule, if an offeree separately sends both a rejection and an acceptance to an offeror, the first of those two received by the offeree will be effective. For purposes of this rule, receipt of such a communication occurs when the party to which it was addressed obtains possession of it, even if the party does not read or open it.

           (a)   Acceptance upon Dispatch

The mailbox rule provides that an offeree's written communication of an acceptance (not rejection) occurs when it is placed into the mail in an authorized manner.

(i)   Exceptions

That rule's operation is suspended when an offeree expressly includes a provision with an executed and sent contract stating that the contract will become effective only when the offeror provides written notice that he has received that letter and contract. It is also inapplicable to option contracts, for which acceptance occurs upon receipt. A rejection is effective upon receipt.

(b)   Acceptance Then Rejection

Under the *Restatement*, an acceptance also is effective when sent, provided it is seasonably dispatched and received within the time that such an item would have arrived. Therefore, once an acceptance is dispatched, an offer may not be rejected (because it has already been accepted). For example, if an offeree mails an acceptance on Monday, and calls the offeror later in the day to reject, but before the acceptance is received, the rejection is ineffective. Additionally, an offeror may avoid a contract if he detrimentally relies on a rejection received prior to receipt of a controlling acceptance. For example, suppose an offeree mails an acceptance on Monday and a rejection on Tuesday. The acceptance controls because it was dispatched first. However, suppose the post office delivers the rejection on Wednesday and the acceptance on Thursday. If the offeror relies on the rejection and contracts with a substitute party on Wednesday, the offeror may avoid the contract with the offeree.

(c)   Rejection Then Acceptance

The *Restatement* provides that an acceptance sent after a prior rejection has been sent is not effective until received, and only if received before the rejection. If the acceptance is not received before the rejection, the offer is rejected.

For example, if an offeree mails a rejection on Monday, and then hand delivers an acceptance on Tuesday before the rejection is received, the acceptance controls because it was received first. However, suppose the post office delivers the rejection on Tuesday, before the acceptance is hand-delivered. In that event, the rejection controls because it was received first.

(d)   UCC Approach

Under the UCC, if the acceptance of an offer occurs by any medium reasonable in the circumstances, the acceptance is effective when it is dispatched out of an offeree's possession. If an offeree uses an unauthorized means of acceptance, then the acceptance is effective when it is received instead of when it is sent.

★★   (3)   Mirror Image Rule

| Question Key |
| See Acceptance |

At common law, the "mirror image" rule requires an acceptance that is "positive, unconditional, unequivocal, and unambiguous, and must not change, add to, or qualify the terms" of an offer. *Gyurkey v. Babler*. An acceptance that changes the offer's terms is construed as a counter-offer. Hence, an offeree's counter-offer that does not match an offeror's terms and condition constitutes a rejection of the offer and a counter-offer.

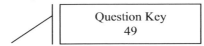

Question Key
49

b)   "Battle of the Forms" – UCC Rejects Mirror Image Rule

A "Battle of the Forms" arises under the UCC when an offeror presents an offer for the purchase or sale of goods, and an offeree responds by "accepting" the offer but providing an accepting document that contains different or additional terms. Remember, under the common law, such a response would serve as a rejection and counter-offer. In a contract subject to the UCC, however, UCC § 2-207's Battle of the Forms rule, rather than the common law's "mirror image" rule, applies to the contract's formation.

Under UCC § 2-207(1), "[a] definite and seasonable expression of acceptance or a written confirmation, which is sent within a reasonable time operates as an acceptance even though it states terms additional to or different from those offered or agreed upon, unless acceptance is expressly made conditional on assent to the additional or different terms." This rule completely alters the result of the mirror image rule, which provides that such an acceptance is a rejection and counter-offer. Remember that contracts governed by common law are subject to the mirror image rule, but contracts for the sale of goods are governed by the UCC.

(1)   Type of Acceptance Required

UCC § 2-207(1) allows any "expression of acceptance" or "written confirmation" to be an acceptance even though it states terms that are "additional to or different from" those within an offer or those agreed upon. Section 2-207(1) further provides that the "expression of acceptance" or "written confirmation" does not form a contract if it was "expressly made conditional on assent to the additional or different terms." Generally, if an offeree provides an offeror with an "expressly conditional" acceptance, and the offeror accepts those changes, then they will be added to the contract.

(2)   What Happens to New Terms

UCC § 2-207(2) states that "[t]he additional terms are to be construed as proposals for additions to the contract.

(a)   Special Rule for Merchants

Under UCC § 2-207(2), when both the offeror and the offeree are merchants, the additional terms will become part of the agreement automatically unless it is excluded by one of the three exceptions of:

(a) the offer expressly limits acceptance to the terms of the offer;

(b) they materially alter it; or

(c) notification of objection to them already has been given or is given within a reasonable time after notice of them is received.

(i)   Material Alterations

Under UCC § 2-207(2)(b), additional terms that are material alterations contained in offeree's response are excluded automatically from the agreement unless expressly agreed to by the offeror.

(A)   Examples

Examples of material alterations include, among other things: indemnification provisions; arbitration provisions; a different choice of law or venue provision; or a clause negating warranties.

(ii)   Additional Terms

Under UCC § 2-207(2)(c), additional terms contained in the offeree's response become a part of the parties' agreement unless the offeror objects to them within a reasonable time after receipt of notice of them.

Also, under UCC § 2-207(2)(a), additional terms become part of the contract unless the offer expressly limits acceptance to the offer's terms.

(b)   Non-Merchants

If either party is a non-merchant (or both are non-merchants), the contract that results from an offeree's conditional acceptance or written confirmation includes only the terms that were contained in the offer. In that event, the different or additional terms of acceptance are only considered proposals that may be individually rejected or accepted.

(c)   Terms of Documents Govern

The terms of either the offer or the corresponding conditional acceptance or written confirmation may vary the Battle of the Forms result. For example, if the offer is expressly limited to its terms, then only an unconditional acceptance or confirmation counts as an acceptance. Under the same logic, if the offeree's response by a conditional acceptance or written confirmation clearly indicates it is only effective if the alterations are accepted, then the response is not treated as an acceptance.

★   4)   <u>INDEFINITENESS</u>

Question Key 31,219

When a contract is not reasonably certain regarding its material terms, a fatal indefiniteness occurs that may void the agreement. The material and essential terms of a contract include its subject matter, price, payment terms, quantity, quality, duration, the work to be performed, and the parties' names and addresses. Indefiniteness regarding an immaterial term will not void an agreement. The question of definiteness is whether the agreement is sufficiently explicit so that the courts could ascertain the parties' respective obligations. A contract that lacks an essential term usually is unenforceable.

a)   Common Law

Incomplete contracts always have been viewed as raising a challenge for contract law. Does the incompleteness or indefiniteness rise to such a level that renders the agreement legally unenforceable? Under the common law, when the indefiniteness concerns important terms, it is presumed that the parties have not reached an agreement to which they intend to be bound. When, by contrast, the indefiniteness concerns less important terms, courts can supplement the agreement with gap fillers and enforce the supplemented contract. Moreover, if a court finds that the parties intended to be bound, the court will supply reasonable terms.

Sources the court may use to fill gaps include, but are not limited to: standard terms, usages that bind the parties, and their course of dealing or performance. For example, the terms of a contract may not specify a time for performance. In that event, the courts will apply the reasonable time standard rather than impose a condition that "time is of the essence." If, however, a contract states that a specific time is set for performance, then that time will be enforced.

b)   UCC

Under the UCC, a contract does not fail for indefiniteness if the parties intended to make a contract and there is a reasonably certain basis for giving an appropriate remedy. Certain open terms are permitted to be read into sales and lease contracts. Under the UCC, open terms can include price, payment, delivery, time, and assortment of goods. UCC § 2-204(3); UCC § 2A-204(3).

(1)   Price

UCC § 2-305(1) provides for the existence of a written agreement that lacks a price term if the parties intended to create a contract and any of these three factors exist:

- The contract lacks a price term;

- The contract provides that the parties will agree to the price and they disagree about it; or

- "The price is to be fixed in terms of some agreed market or other standard as set or recorded by a third person or agency and it is not so set or recorded." UCC § 2-305(1)(c).

(2)   Payment

In the absence of a written agreement's provision, such as that a seller extended credit to a buyer, the buyer must pay for the goods when and where the buyer will receive them, even if "the place of shipment is the place of delivery" (e.g., either party's place of business). UCC § 2-310(a).

(3)   Delivery

In the absence of a written agreement's provision regarding the location of delivery, a buyer must obtain the goods wherever they may be. The goods are usually at a seller's place of business. If the seller lacks a place of business, then the goods can be picked up at the seller's residence. UCC § 2-308(a). When, however, the parties know at the time of contracting that the goods are not at the seller's business or residence, then the goods need to be picked up wherever they are.

(4)   Time

If neither a written agreement, nor Article 2 of the UCC, indicates when a delivery or a shipment must occur, or when any other performance of the agreement is due, then any such performance must occur at a reasonable time. UCC § 2-309(1).

(5)   Assortment of the Goods

The buyer possesses the duty to cooperate by specifying the assortment of goods when the parties' agreement lacks a relevant provision. UCC § 2-311(2). If the buyer's failure to specify the assortment of goods materially affects the seller's performance of their contract, the seller can consider this failure a breach of their contract by failure to accept the agreed upon goods.

B.   Capacity to Contract

Question Key
78,179

★   1)   INFANTS

a)   Common Law

Infants, or minors, are children whose legal status and rights are defined by statutes that establish when they reach the age of majority and legally are considered adults. Generally, infants have the capacity to enter into contracts and transactions that are voidable, not void. The power of avoidance by means of disaffirmance resides in an infant until his death. At that point, it lies in the infant's heirs, administrators, or executors. When an adult is a party to a minor's transaction, the adult alone cannot avoid the contract based on infancy. Only the minor possesses that right to avoid the contract.

b)   Exceptions

Under the UCC, an infant's power of disaffirmance does not apply to a sale of goods to a subsequent *bona fide* purchaser of the goods for value. Other statutes and public policy provisions limit or eliminate an infant's power to disaffirm specified types of contracts, such as insurance contracts.

c)   Ratification

(1)   General

A proper ratification terminates an infant's power of disaffirmance. To be effective, ratification must occur after the infant has reached the age of majority. Note that a disaffirmance may be oral. It could be any other type of manifestation of unwillingness to be bound by the transaction. An infant cannot selectively ratify and disaffirm parts of a contract. No consideration is required to ratify a contract. Ratification may occur in three ways:

- failure to timely disaffirm a contract;
- express ratification; or
- acts that exhibit intent to ratify.

(2)   Extent of Ratification

If a minor expressly ratifies a contract after reaching the age of majority, the minor will be liable only to the extent acknowledged in the ratification. For example, suppose, at age 16, Kevin enters into a contract to purchase a bicycle for $500 to be paid in installments. Kevin never pays an installment for the bicycle. When Kevin turns 18 years of age, the age of majority in his jurisdiction, Kevin agrees to pay the bicycle shop $300. The bicycle is then worth $400. How much is Kevin legally obligated to pay the shop? The answer is that he must pay the amount he agreed to pay when he ratified the contract. In this case, the amount is $300.

d)   Necessaries

An infant is liable, on a quasi-contractual basis, for necessaries furnished to him. Necessaries include clothing, food, shelter, and a basic public school education.

2)   MENTALLY INFIRM PEOPLE

Generally, a contracts with a mentally infirm person is voidable. It is voidable when, before entering into the contract, the person has been judicially determined incompetent and a guardian has been appointed for the person. Mentally infirm includes a variety of conditions, such as mental retardation, insanity, senility, delirium resulting from physical injuries, the side effects of medication, and/or intoxication.

a)   Common Law

Under the common law, a person is insane when he does not understand the nature and consequences of the person's conduct when a transaction occurs. Incompetence also may be proved by a disparity of value in the consideration that is exchanged.

b)   Restatement

The *Restatement* provides that a contract is voidable if a person, due to a mental illness or defect, is unable to act in a reasonable manner in relation to the transaction, and the other party has reason to know of this condition.

c)   Ratification

An infirm person possesses the power of avoidance and ratification and this power passes on to his heirs after the infirm person's death. If the person recovers from an infirmity, he may ratify the contract entered into during the infirmity.

3)   DEALING WITH ONE'S SELF

A person cannot enter into an enforceable contract with one's self. A person must enter into a contract that includes himself or herself and other people.

C.   Improper Contracts

1)   ILLEGALITY

Generally, the courts will not enforce an illegal contract, and will consider it void. According to the *Restatement (First) of Contracts (First Restatement)*, an illegal agreement is one that is, in "either its formation or performance,…criminal, tortious, or otherwise opposed to public policy."

A supervening illegality is a change in the law that renders a party's performance of a contract unlawful under the contract's original terms. A supervening illegality is considered a type of impossibility.

2)   UNCONSCIONABILITY

Question Key
216

a)   Common Law

In equity, the doctrine of unconscionability affords relief for a palpable unilateral mistake. Parties have sought to avoid contracts as unconscionable if the pricing of the contract is so outrageous that it should not be enforced. However, courts are reluctant to disturb an agreement, even when its terms are grossly disproportionate. At law, an unconscionable agreement is defined by *Hume v. United States* as one "such as no man in his senses and not under delusion would make on the one hand, and as no honest and fair man would accept on the other." This standard is not easy to meet. As a result, it is quite rare that a contract would be deemed unconscionable at common law. The problem of unconscionability usually will be the consideration for the agreement, but it also could be the terms, interest payments, or other obligations the court determines unfair.

b)   UCC

The comment for UCC § 2-302 states that the courts may directly determine if a contract or a contract provision is unconscionable. The UCC's test is if, under the commercial background and needs of a specific case or trade, the provisions at issue are sufficiently one-sided so as to be unconscionable under the circumstances that existed when the contract was formed. The UCC generally enables courts to strike down unconscionable provisions of contracts.

c)   Types of Unconscionability

(1)   Substantive

A contract provision that is unduly one-sided in favor of one party, such that it is harsh or unfair to another party, may be considered substantively unconscionable.

(2)   Procedural

A provision of a contract into which one party was induced by another party without the one party exercising any meaningful choice may be deemed procedurally unconscionable. For example, the terms and conditions of a standard "take it or leave it" type of agreement on a pre-printed form contract may subject the one non-drafting party-- who cannot negotiate with the other drafting party about those terms and conditions--to procedural unconscionability.

3)   PUBLIC POLICY

a)   *Restatement* Approach

The *Restatement* eliminates the term "illegal" and includes any type of unenforceable bargains under the category of those prohibited by public policy. Public policy includes constitutional and statutory provisions, as well as case law. Some of the public policy grounds that may be asserted to invalidate contracts and their terms include: unconscionability, economic policy, immorality, unprofessional conduct, and paternalism.

(1)   Violation of Law

A contract that violates a law is not automatically against public policy. In determining if a specific agreement violates public policy, the courts may balance legally recognized policies against the effect on the parties and the public when declaring a particular bargain to be against public policy.

(2)   No Frustration of Policy

Enforcement of a contract that violates public policy can occur for the purpose of not frustrating the policy underlying the statute when the policy is intended to benefit the contracting party seeking relief. In other words, public policy will not prevent enforcement of a contract by parties included in the class of persons that the statute is intended to protect. Restatement (Second) of Contracts § 179 cmt. c, illus. 4; E. Allen Farnsworth, Contracts § 5.6 (4th ed. 2004).

★★   **D.   Implied-in-Fact Contracts and Quasi-Contracts**

          1)   IMPLIED-IN-FACT CONTRACT

> Question Key
> 24,70,126,211

An express contract is one for which the parties use words to form their agreement. By contrast, an implied-in-fact contract arises from an agreement manifested by the parties' conduct. A contract will be implied-in-fact when an intention is not manifested by words between the parties, but may be gathered by deduction from their conduct, language, or other circumstances.

For example, by going to Dan's dental office, Paul agrees to pay the reasonable cost of the services provided by Dan, the dentist. Paul will breach an implied-in-fact contract if he refuses to pay for the services after they are rendered.

Depending upon the circumstances, an offeree may accept an offer by means of acts or silence to form an "implied-in-fact" contract. Implied-in-fact contracts usually are treated like express contracts.

★★   2)   QUASI-CONTRACT

An implied-in-law contract or "quasi-contract" is not an express agreement, but an obligation that the law imposes to do justice even when the parties neither made nor intended any promise. It is a non-contractual obligation that is treated like a contract and serves to prevent unjust enrichment to one party from another party. In the absence of an express contract, a promisee's claim for recovery will be based on a promisor's unjust enrichment through the promisee's conduct.

For example, Al suffers injuries in a traffic accident that render him unconscious. Vicky, a medical doctor, arrives on the scene and provides emergency care. Due to her heroic efforts, Al recovers from his serious injuries. Here, Vicky can recover the reasonable value of the care she rendered for Al on a quasi-contract basis even in the absence of any actual agreement that she care for him.

The courts utilize the quasi-contract doctrine as a legal fiction to prevent a defendant's benefit to a plaintiff's detriment. Although a quasi-contract is a legal remedy, usually equitable principles govern the granting of quasi-contractual relief. The quasi-contract doctrine also applies when a contract is unenforceable because it has failed. The doctrine is directly applicable to cases regarding the provision of services.

E.   Pre-Contract Detrimental Reliance

Even before parties enter into a formal agreement, an offeree may proceed to perform in detrimental reliance upon an offer.

For example, suppose Kate tells Chris she will pay the cost of his labor and the materials for replacing her car's transmission. Before they enter into a formal agreement, he purchases a replacement transmission with his funds. When Chris tells Kate a reasonable time after Kate's offer that he will replace the transmission and what he has done, Kate tells Chris she already sold the car. Chris could assert that he detrimentally relied upon Kate's offer when he bought the transmission if his actions in doing so were reasonable.

The common law and the *Restatement* provide that an offeree who takes actions in detrimental reliance upon an offer may make the offer temporarily irrevocable in three situations:

- An offeree commences performance in response to an offer for a unilateral contract;
- An offeree starts to perform on an agreement when it is unclear if the offer is for a unilateral or a bilateral contract; or
- An offeree prepares to perform under a contract, regardless of whether the acceptance is to occur by promise or by performance.

For example, suppose Alvin promises to pay Theodore $1,000 if Theodore paints Alvin's home (a unilateral offer). Once Theodore begins to paint the home, Alvin's offer becomes temporarily irrevocable. This rule is designed to prevent Alvin from waiting until the painting is almost completed to revoke his offer, thus receiving the benefit of Theodore's work without incurring his obligation to pay.

F.   Warranties

Contracts for the sale of goods may be subject to certain warranties under the UCC. The UCC defines a warranty as a type of guarantee or promise by a seller of goods that the goods will have particular characteristics.

1)   EXPRESS

Any seller, whether or not he is a merchant, may provide express warranties under UCC § 2-313(1)(a). It provides that any affirmation of fact or promise made by a seller to the buyer that relates to the goods and becomes part of the basis of the bargain creates an express warranty that the goods must conform to the affirmation or promise.

2)   IMPLIED

a)   Implied Warranty of Merchantability

UCC § 2-314(1) provides that a merchant seller of goods provides an implied warranty of merchantability. It states that: "Unless excluded or modified, a warranty that the goods shall be merchantable is implied in a contract for their sale if the seller is a merchant with respect to goods of that kind." UCC § 2-314(2)(c) provides that merchantable goods are ones "fit for the ordinary purposes for which" such goods are used.

> b)   Warranty of Fitness for a Particular Purpose

UCC § 2-315 provides an implied warranty of fitness for a particular purpose. In order to recover for a breach of that warranty, a buyer must prove that:

- a seller had reason to know the buyer's purpose for the goods;

- the seller had reason to know that a buyer is relying on the seller's skill or judgment to select or furnish suitable goods; and

- the buyer relied on the seller's skill or judgment.

> c)   Discovery after Delivery

After accepting the goods, a buyer may find that an applicable breach of warranty has occurred. In that event, under UCC § 2-714(2), he may recover damages in the amount of the difference — at the time and place of acceptance — "between the value of the goods accepted and the value that they would have had if they had been as warranted, unless special circumstances show proximate damages of a different amount."

II.   CONSIDERATION

A contract must possess consideration. Consideration is required to enforce a promise. Generally consideration consists of a bargained for exchange of legal value in return for legal benefit(s) between two contracting parties. The following items are not valid consideration:

- past conduct;
- a promise of a future gift; or
- an illusory promise.

A.   Bargained for Exchange and Legal Detriment

1)   BARGAINED FOR EXCHANGE

A bargained for exchange exists when there is:

> Question Key
> 16,46,90,91,93,
> 150,161,208

- a promise to perform by a promisor;
- that causes a promisee to perform pursuant to that promise.

★★   2)   LEGAL DETRIMENT OR BENEFIT

a)   General

Under the majority rule, a promisee must incur a legal detriment (i.e., an obligation to do something he otherwise would not be obligated to do or refrain from an act from which he has a legal right).   Under the minority rule, even if no legal detriment exists, consideration will be found if the promisor gains a legal benefit.

For example, if Phil is allowed to park his car in a particular space every day and refrains from doing so in exchange for getting a free meal every day from Sara, who in return is the only one allowed to use that parking space, each party experiences both a legal detriment and a legal benefit.

b)   Refraining from Pursuing Legal Claim

A bargained for promise to relinquish a valid legal claim is adequate consideration to support a reciprocal promise. A bargained for promise not to assert a defense to a legal action also is adequate consideration to support a reciprocal promise.

A promise to refrain from pursuing an invalid claim generally is not adequate consideration to support a reciprocal promise. However, a promise to relinquish an invalid claim constitutes adequate consideration only when in good faith, a promisor thinks:

- the claim is valid; and
- that a legal detriment may arise only in that manner.

c)   Promise Premised Upon Future Event

A conditional promise premised on the occurrence of a future event will be enforceable if:

- adequate legal detriment is established; and
- a promisor lacks complete power to control whether or not a future event will occur.

For example, suppose Pete promises to sell his boat to Bruce for $10 if Bruce enrolls in and graduates from college. Bruce's enrollment in and graduation from college would be adequate legal detriment to provide consideration to enforce Pete's promise, and Pete lacks power over whether Bruce enrolls in and graduates from college.

★   B.   "Adequacy" of Consideration ────┐ | Question Key |
                                          | | 1,3,5,44,45,79,107, |
      1)   GENERAL   │ | 140,148 |

Generally, courts presume that any degree of detriment is adequate to sustain a promise. In other words, a court is reluctant to invalidate a contract because one person receives a seemingly beneficial bargain because he gave up too little. Such inadequacy may, however, provide circumstantial evidence of mistake, fraud, undue influence, or over-reaching. It also may serve as a basis for relief from a contract on the basis of unconscionability.

★ ### 2)   MUTUALITY OF OBLIGATION

The doctrine of mutuality of obligation provides that unless both parties to a contract are bound, neither is bound. If performance of a contractual obligation by one party, which is the consideration for the contract, is elective, rather than mandatory, and the other party is required to perform some other duty, then there is no mutuality of obligation and, therefore, no valid enforceable contract.

For example, mutuality of obligation would exist when Susan promises to buy Luanne's camping trailer for $10,000, and Luanne promises to sell the camping trailer to Susan for $10,000. Under their agreement, the promises or duties of both Susan and Luanne are mutual. If, however, Susan promises to buy Luanne's camping trailer for $10,000, and Luanne promises that she will think about selling her camping trailer to Susan for $10,000, then their agreement is not mutual because Luanne is not obligated to sell the camping trailer to Susan, and doing so would be optional for Luanne.

★★ ### 3)   IMPLIED PROMISES

a)   Common Law

Some contracts do not precisely spell out the obligations of each party. However, an examination of the facts may indicate that an obligation is presumed. For example, suppose Acme contracts to be the exclusive agent of Mega Widgets. Suppose, as provided in the contract, Mega Widgets must pay Acme a percentage of all sales of its widgets. The contract provides that Acme is the exclusive agent of Mega Widgets, but does not expressly provide that Acme must affirmatively attempt to sell the widgets. A strict reading of the contract may demonstrate that Acme possesses no legal duty to do anything. If that is the way the contract is interpreted, however, then the contract would be deemed illusory. This would be because Acme possesses no express duty to do anything, yet according to the contract, is entitled to a percentage of sales. However, under the doctrine of implied promises, it may be implied from the circumstances that ABC possesses a duty to use reasonable efforts to obtain sales for Mega Widgets. A court may find that such a contract contains a promise that may be implied from the parties' conduct.

b)   UCC

UCC § 2-306(2) states that: "A lawful agreement by either the seller or the buyer for exclusive dealing in the kind of goods concerned imposes unless otherwise agreed an obligation by the seller to use best efforts to supply the goods and by the buyer to use best efforts to promote their sale."

UCC § 2-306 concerns requirement contracts, which are supported by sufficient legal detriment to be enforceable. Under such a contract, the promisor undertakes to supply all of output that a promisee needs. Such a contract implies that both of those parties will make a good faith determination of the requisite quantities.

★

4) DISPROPORTIONATE EXCHANGES

One type of disproportionate exchange provides an exception to the rule of presumed adequacy of detriment. A court will weigh the adequacy of consideration when a promisor agrees to transfer a certain sum of funds or quantity of goods for a lesser sum or quantity at the same time and place. For example, suppose A contracts with B to provide 1,000 widgets of Grade A quality. In exchange, B agrees to provide A with 40 widgets of Grade A quality. Such a disproportionate exchange, absent other evidence justifying the discrepancy, is evidence of inadequacy of consideration. Such a contract is an exception to the general rule that courts are reluctant to inquire into the adequacy of consideration.

C. Modern Substitutes for Bargain

1) MORAL OBLIGATION

> Question Key
> 149

a) Miscellaneous Rules

The general rule is that a moral obligation constitutes insufficient consideration to render a promise enforceable. If a promisee already has received performance, a promise that a promisor made based on a moral obligation to the promisee may not be enforced. Many courts follow the *Restatement* § 86. It provides for the enforcement of promises made based on moral obligation, only to the degree that is required to prevent injustice. Moreover, no enforcement is permitted if the initial benefit was conferred as a gift.

b) Debtor and Creditor

A majority of jurisdictions rule that a debtor's promise to pay a creditor for a pre-existing debt – that otherwise a statute of limitations would preclude – may be enforced:

- although no new consideration supports it; and
- if the debtor made the new promise in a signed writing.

The creditor's claim against the debtor may rest only upon the new promise. The creditor will be restricted to recovering the amount stated in the signed writing.

> Question Key
> 35.50.51.230

2) PROMISSORY ESTOPPEL/DETRIMENTAL RELIANCE

★★

In the absence of a bargained for exchange, a promise is subject to enforcement if grounds exist for a court to find the existence of a substitute for consideration, such as promissory estoppel, resulted in the promisee's reasonable detrimental reliance. Promissory estoppel applies if:

i)   an offeror makes a promise to an offeree;

ii)   under circumstances that the offeree reasonably would anticipate the promise to be fulfilled; and

iii)   the offeror reasonably would anticipate that the offeree would alter positions based on that promise.

Promissory estoppel may apply when a party alters it position after relying on a promise. This reliance may be detrimental to the promisee. Generally, the promise relied upon will be enforced only to the extent required to avoid injustice. Therefore, the damages permitted under such an action are limited, and usually not equivalent, to the amount that may be received from a breach of a contract with consideration. Under the doctrine of detrimental reliance, the injured party may recover reliance damages as a result. In no case may an injured party receive more reliance damages than he would have been able to recover as expectation damages. For a thorough discussion of remedies, see Section VIII below herein.

3)   STATUTORY SUBSTITUTES

Certain laws render particular promises enforceable without consideration. For example, traditional statutes permit promises without consideration to be enforced if made under seal. However, most states and the UCC have rejected such statutes.

★★   **D.   Modification of Contracts**

Question Key
23,40,41,66,77,97,202,204

The parties to a contract may modify their contractual duties at any time after they have entered into the contract.

1)   COMMON LAW

For a modification to be valid, the traditional common law required that mutual assent and consideration support it. The law's modern trend allows a modification in the absence of consideration if unanticipated problems arise that could make it impractical to form a contract without altering the expected performance. The question one would ask is whether the modification is fair under the circumstances.

Under the common law, contract modification requires the following elements:

* mutual assent: This requires an agreement of both parties to the new terms; and

* consideration: Additional consideration must be provided to make the modification binding.

For example, suppose Duke and Diane entered into a valid contract for Duke to mow Diane's lawn on a regular basis. Due to significant increases in the cost of fuel after their contract's execution, Duke requests a modification of their contract's price term. Duke promises to also edge the lawn each time he mows, in return for Diane's promise to pay the increased fuel cost. They both sign a valid agreement including those terms. Here, both parties agreed to the new terms and provided additional consideration to make the modification binding.

          a)   Pre-existing Duty Rule

The pre-existing duty rule usually precludes the enforcement of a contract modification if no new consideration is provided in support of that modification. The pre-existing duty rule provides that when a party to a contract does or promises to do that which the party had a legal obligation to do, or promises not to do something or refrains from doing that which the party is not legally privileged to do, then he has not suffered detriment. The legal obligation may arise from a contract, the common law, or a statute.

A more recent rule is that modification may occur if:

- unanticipated or unforeseen problems occur that would cause an impracticable situation for one party; and
- the modification is considered to be fair.

         b)   Oral Modification

A written contract may be orally modified by the parties to it only if:

- no contractual provision prevents that type of modification; and
- the contract is not subject to the Statute of Frauds.

An oral modification that is otherwise invalid under the above test may be enforceable if one of the parties to the contract materially alters his position based on that modification. In that event, the oral modification constitutes a waiver of the contract's provision against oral modification.

      2)   <u>RESTATEMENT</u>

The *Restatement* has an exception to the pre-existing duty rule, which provides that a modification to an existing contract will be judicially sustained, despite a lack of consideration, if the modification occurred subsequent to unforeseen difficulties that arose during the original agreement's performance.

       3)   <u>UCC</u>

         a)   No Consideration

UCC § 2-209(1) provides that no consideration is necessary to modify an agreement subject to the UCC. Moreover, if the subject matter of the contract qualifies under the UCC's Statute of Frauds, for goods worth $500 or more, the modification must be in writing. UCC § 2-209(3).

b)   Modification or Rescission

UCC § 2-209(4) applies when an oral modification or rescission does not satisfy the requirements of either (A) a UCC provision regarding signed agreements that exclude oral modification or rescission or (B) the UCC's Statute of Frauds. It provides that although an attempted modification or rescission does not satisfy those requirements, it may result in a waiver.

Under UCC § 2-209(5), a party that makes a waiver affecting an executory part of the contract can retract the waiver with "reasonable notification received by the other party that strict performance will be required of any term waived, unless the retraction would be unjust in view of a material change of position in reliance on the waiver."

★   **E.   Compromise and Settlement of Claims**

Question Key
30,82,85,151,201

A promise to relinquish a valid claim is a detriment and, when bargained for, is consideration. A promise to relinquish an invalid claim is a detriment if a claimant makes it in good faith and a reasonable man could believe the claim was well founded. The *Restatement* provides that either good-faith or objective uncertainty as to a claim's validity is sufficient. A settlement agreement is enforceable if the parties to it:

- had a good-faith dispute when;
- they entered into a valid contract that resolved the dispute.

III.   THIRD-PARTY BENEFICIARY CONTRACTS

Question Key
13,14,33,39,57,88, 92,113,127,129,159, 169,175,215,217,231

Under a third-party beneficiary contract, a promisor and a promisee agree that a third party, instead of the promisee, will receive the promisor's performance. For example, suppose Bob enters into an agreement with Alan. Alan promises to provide 20 piano lessons to Edgar, Bob's cousin. In return, Bob promises to pay Alan $500.

Additionally, as a general rule, any party to a contract may transfer a right to receive performance to a third party. For example, suppose Bob enters into an agreement with Alan. Alan promises to sell Bob his car for $5,000. As a general rule, Bob can transfer his right to receive the car to a third party.

A minority of the states follow the *First Restatement's* beneficiary categories:

Incidental Beneficiary: An incidental beneficiary is a third party who receives a benefit that arises as an indirect effect of the obligations of the parties to a contract.

Donee Beneficiary: A donee beneficiary is a third party who, under a contract, is an intended recipient of a gift from a promisee and may bring an action against a promisor to recover. The *Restatement* provides that the promisee's gift to a third party renders the third party a donee beneficiary. The promisee may alter or cancel a third party's rights before they become vested.

Creditor: A third party is considered a creditor beneficiary when a promisor enters into a contract to pay a debt that a promisee owes to the third party. The creditor beneficiary receives an assignment of a promisee's right of performance from a promisor. A creditor beneficiary's rights vest as a result of altering its position by relying on the contract.

Most states have rejected the *First Restatement's* categories of beneficiaries. Instead, they follow the *Restatement's* two categories of intended beneficiaries and incidental beneficiaries.

If a contract does not name or identify a third- party beneficiary when it is signed, the third party who will benefit under the contract needs to be identified only when that party's performance is due, rather than when the contract is formed.

★★★   A.   **Intended Beneficiaries**

            1)   GENERAL

Intended beneficiaries are those third parties whom the first and the second parties to a contract designate to receive the primary benefit of the contract. A presumption applies that the first and the second parties have entered into a contract for their own benefit and not for the third party's benefit. A court, however, will enforce the parties' express contract for a third party if that contract confers actionable rights upon that individual or entity as an intended beneficiary.

            2)   DETERMINATION

When a third party asserts a right to enforce a contract as its beneficiary, the courts may consider evidence using the following factors to ascertain if a third party is an intended beneficiary:

- Does the contract expressly identify the third party?
- Does the performance run from the promisor to the third party?
- Does the contract reflect an "intent to benefit" the third party? and
- May the third party reasonably rely on the contract as conferring an intended benefit?

★   B.   **Incidental Beneficiaries**

When the performance under a contract will not run directly to the third party to the contract, that individual or entity is an incidental beneficiary. For example, suppose Bob contracts with Evergreen Landscaping to treat his land for fire ants. The treatment is aroma-based and will result in the death of fire ants within 100 yards of the land. Bob's neighbors are incidental beneficiaries of the contract. An incidental beneficiary may not sue to enforce rights under a contract, because a promisee did not intend the contract to benefit the third party, and a promisor's performance of the contract did not run to the third party.

Consider the following factors to ascertain if a third party is an incidental beneficiary:

- Does the contract show the promisee's "intent to benefit" the third party?
- Does the agreed upon performance run to the third party?
- May the third party reasonably rely on the contract as conferring an intended benefit?

★★   **C.   Impairment or Extinguishment of Third-Party Rights**

1)   CONTRACT MODIFICATION

The first and second parties to a contract may mutually alter or eliminate third-party rights under the contract before those rights vest. A majority of the states follow the *Restatement* on that issue, which provides that a third party's contractual rights vest when a third party:

- discovers a third-party contract and assents to it;
- materially alters his position based upon a promise; or
- commences a suit to enforce a promise.

Accordingly, the power of the first and second parties to modify their duties terminates when the third-party (e.g., an intended beneficiary), materially relies upon the promise.

2)   MUTUAL RESCISSION

The first and second parties to a contract may mutually agree to cancel the contract either only with respect to the third party or regarding all parties to the contract. A mutual rescission agreement may be verbal. Absent evidence to the contrary, the courts presume that neither party intended to pay for benefits that they received before the mutual rescission.

3)   ENFORCEMENT OF RIGHTS

An intended beneficiary may be entitled to enforce the contract, although he did not assent to or know about it when it was made. A first party or second party to a contract possesses the right to modify or terminate the third party's rights before those rights vest. The beneficiary's contract enforcement action may seek either damages or specific performance. A promisor may raise any affirmative defense against the beneficiary, as he could against the promisee.

D.   Enforcement by the Promisee

The promisee of a third-party beneficiary contract may bring a suit against the promisor to enforce the contract or, if applicable, for damages.

IV.   ASSIGNMENT OF RIGHTS AND DELEGATION OF DUTIES

Contract rights (or benefits) may be assigned to another person or entity under certain circumstances. Contract duties (or obligations) may be delegated under certain circumstances.   Sometimes the term "assignment" is used interchangeably with "delegation." However, each term is unique as it refers to either rights or duties. Be sure to understand the context of the question to determine whether duties have been delegated, rights have been assigned, or both.

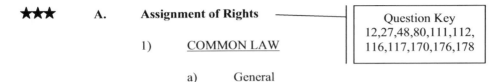

★★★   A.   **Assignment of Rights** ——— | Question Key
                                                 | 12,27,48,80,111,112,
              1)   <u>COMMON LAW</u> | 116,117,170,176,178

                    a)   General

An assignor, as a promisee in a valid contract, may transfer contractual rights to a third-party assignee. An assignment of contractual rights occurs when the assignor manifests the intent to presently transfer those rights to an assignee. However, a contract right may not be assigned if doing so would materially alter a promisor's duty.

The objective test of whether an effective assignment occurred is if both:

- the assignor intended that the assignee receive the contractual rights; and

- the assignment was immediate and complete.

                    b)   Provisions Prohibiting Assignment

Contractual provisions against assignment are usually unenforceable. Most contract rights are assignable. Even if the assignor violates a covenant with a promisor, the assignment still may be validly made, such that the promisor must continue to perform its contractual duties for the assignee. However, the promisor may bring an action against the assignor to obtain damages for violating the covenant.

                    c)   Writing Requirement

Usually, an assignment does not need to be written to be enforceable. Under certain circumstances, such as when the Statute of Frauds applies, an assignment must be in writing in order to render an assignment valid. No consideration is needed to make an assignment valid. An assignor does not ordinarily need the contract's other party, a promisor, to consent to make an assignment.

                    d)   Enforcement by Assignee

Once the assignor transfers contractual rights to an assignee, the assignee may enforce them against a promisor or others. A sub-assignee, which is a person to whom an original assignee sub-assigns the already assigned rights, lacks rights against the original assignor due to an absence of privity of contract between the sub-assignee and the assignor. Thus, while the sub-assignee cannot enforce its contractual rights against the assignor, the sub-assignee can enforce its rights against the assignee.

e)   Notice of Assignment

A promisor is required to render performance to an assignee only if the promisor possesses knowledge of the assignment. If this assignment is valid, then the assignee possesses a right to expect performance from the promisor. Conversely, the assignor loses any right to receive performance from the promisor. The promisor who receives notice of the assignment must perform a contract for an assignee. Until the promisor receives that notice, the promisor may continue to render performance to the promisee. If the promisor is aware of the assignment, then the promisor's performance of contractual duties for a promisee (or assignor) does not discharge those duties with respect to the assignee.

f)   Enforceability of Assignments

If consideration supports a purported assignment, it will be enforceable against an assignor. If a purported assignment is gratuitously made, it is not enforceable against an assignor.

g)   Termination of Gratuitous Assignments

Gratuitous assignments are terminable by a notice of termination from the assignor to the assignee, by the death of the assignor, or by a subsequent assignment of the same right. However, the assignment must be terminated before the gift is completed. A gift is completed when it is delivered to the assignee.

2)   UCC

UCC § 2-210(1) generally allows for assignment, but prohibits assignment on certain grounds such as when it "would materially change the duty of the other party." This part of the rule is, for practical purposes, basically the same as the common law limitation.

★★   **B.   Delegation of Duties**

| Question Key |
| 11,63,64,171,183,214,215 |

A "delegator" or "obligor" is one of a contract's original parties that delegates its duties under the contract to a "delegate" or "delegatee." The delegate is a third party that assumes the duties of an original party to the contract. The delegator's duty is discharged only after the delegate's performance. If the delegate fails to perform, the delegator may be held liable to the obligee. The "obligee" is the person to whom performance is owed.

1)   COMMON LAW

Contractual duties generally are delegable by a party to a contract. However, a duty is not delegable when a delegate's performance would materially vary from a promisor's performance.

a)   Delegable Duties

The following types of agreements are delegable because the parties understand that someone other than a promisor may perform the duties:

- construction contracts or subcontracts involving objectively measurable performance;
- a seller's obligation to deliver goods to a buyer or another designated recipient;
- a duty to pay money; and
- a corporation's duty.

A delegator's duty will be discharged if the delegate performs the duty. If the other party to the contract rejects the delegate's satisfactory performance of the duty (and such duty is deemed properly delegable), then the rejecting party commits a repudiation.

b)   Non-Delegable Duties

If a duty is not delegable either by the contract's terms or otherwise, then the other party may refuse to perform when a delegator attempts to have that duty performed by a delegate. That failed delegation attempt does not, however, amount to a repudiation of the duty.

The following types of contractual duties are not delegable by a party to a third party:

- those between a professional and a client that involve a personal and confidential relationship;
- those involving the exercise of special or unique talents; and
- those requiring personal skill, knowledge, or judgment.

The duties under a personal services contract ordinarily are not delegable, especially when a promisee's interest in a promisor's taste, reputation, or personality is intended to achieve a certain outcome. If a promisee is not significantly interested in a promisor's personal performance, then the obligee must accept the delegatee's performance if it is satisfactory. Conversely, if a promisee is significantly interested in a promisor's personal performance, such that the delegatee's performance could materially breach a contract, those duties may not be delegated. The fact that a contract contains a provision preventing delegation can indicate that the contract was for personal services.

V.   STATUTES OF FRAUDS

| Question Key |
| 18,73,76,86,130,160, |
| 166,196,222,234 |

★★★   **A.   Common Law**

Verbal agreements are valid and enforceable if they do not cover topics subject to the Statute of Frauds. With regard to the topics subject to the Statute of Frauds, agreements must be made in writing. The topics subject to the Statute of Frauds are as follows:

- Suretyship

An agreement to answer for another's legally enforceable debt or duty must be in writing. A surety has a collateral obligation relative to a separate arrangement between a creditor and a debtor. The Statute of Frauds requires that the collateral obligation be reflected in a written agreement to be enforceable. Contracts of suretyship also have broad disclosure requirements.

One exception, the Main Purpose Rule, provides that when a promisor's primary reason for making the suretyship promise is to further some interest of the promisor, that promise does not fall under the Statute of Frauds. The question to answer is: does the promisor's consideration directly benefit the promisor? If yes, then the promisor's verbal suretyship agreement may be enforceable without the requirement that it be in writing.

- Executor or Administrator

An agreement by either of them to answer for a duty of his decedent must be in writing. This provision applies in the same manner as that for suretyship.

- Land Contracts

An agreement for a sale of, a transfer of, or a promise to pay for, any interest in land must be in writing. Parcels, leases of one year or more, and mortgages are subject to this provision, but crops are not.

- Equal Dignities

The Equal Dignities Rule provides that in order to satisfy the Statute of Frauds, written notification of an agency contract is required. A majority of jurisdictions follow that rule, which requires proof of the following two elements: 1) a written agency contract is required for an agent to enter into an agreement to sell real estate on behalf of a principal; and 2) the principal is required to furnish a written notification that would ratify the acts of its agent.

- Marriage

An agreement made in consideration of marriage must be in writing. If two parties exchange mutual verbal promises of marriage without any related promises of property transfer, then that agreement is enforceable.

- One Year

An agreement that is not to be performed within a year of its making must be in writing. The writing requirement applies if a promise within the agreement cannot, under any circumstances, be performed within a year after the contract is made. The time period is measured from the contract's date of execution.

★★★   **B.   Writing Requirement**

When the parties have not executed a formal written agreement, a written memorandum may satisfy the Statute of Frauds if it contains the following four elements:

- identification of a contract's subject;
- indication that the parties formed a contract;
- states the contract's terms with reasonable certainty; and
- is executed by the party to be charged.

The memorandum may consist of more than one document if:

- a party to be bound executed each document; and
- the documents all relate to the same transaction.

Under those circumstances, the documents' terms may be combined to determine if, in conjunction, they contain all of the contract's essential terms.

★   **C.   UCC**

       1)   SALE OF GOODS (for $500 or more)

Under UCC § 2-201(1), a writing is required to enforce an agreement regarding the sale of goods for a sum of $500 or more. In order for a writing to satisfy the UCC's Statute of Frauds, at a minimum it must be signed by the party against whom enforcement is sought and include the essential terms of a contract for the sale of goods. In other words, the writing would be sufficient if it identifies the parties, quantity of goods, and is signed.

A court will enforce the contract only to the extent of the stated quantity amount. Conversely, the courts will not enforce the contract if the contract fails to state a quantity.

       2)   EXCEPTIONS

The UCC's Statute of Frauds is subject to three critical exceptions to its specific requirements.

a)   Merchant's Confirmatory Memo

A form of writing that will satisfy the Statute is a confirmatory memo between two merchants that the first merchant signs, and to which the second merchant makes no objection. The merchant that received the memorandum of confirmation will be bound by it if that merchant:

- had reason to know of the memorandum's contents; and

- failed to object to it in writing within 10 days after receiving it.

UCC § 2-201(2).

b)   Performance

A sale of goods exception applies to the extent of performance by payment for the goods that was made and accepted or to the degree that the goods were received and accepted.

c)   Specialty Goods

Under the UCC, a contract for specialty goods is not subject to the Statute of Frauds. Specialty goods under UCC § 2-201(3) are goods that:

- a seller specially manufactured for a buyer; and

- are not suitable for sale to others in the ordinary course of business.

VI.   PAROL EVIDENCE AND INTERPRETATION

> **Question Key**
> 9,29,43,71,87,95,158,
> 165,193,210,218,222

A court generally interprets a written contract against the party that drafted it. The Parol Evidence Rule ("Rule") is an exclusionary rule that requires the parties to incorporate into a contract all of the terms and conditions to which they have agreed. The Rule provides that if the parties intend that a writing represent their agreement's final terms and conditions, the writing cannot subsequently be contradicted with extrinsic evidence of previous or contemporaneous agreements that supplement or contradict a contract's terms.

Exceptions exist under several circumstances. For example, evidence is otherwise admissible to show:

- that the writing was not intended to be final; and

- the existence of additional consistent terms that supplement the parties' written agreement if the agreement is final but incomplete.

Additionally, the Parol Evidence Rule does not operate to exclude the following types of evidence:

- what the parties understood to be the meaning of an ambiguous contractual term;
- of inadequate consideration or a failure of consideration;
- the existence of separate agreements that were made after contract formation;
- regarding a condition precedent to the parties' integrated written contract;
- that the contract was voidable;
- that the contract was not enforceable; or
- that there was fraud, duress, or mistake.

In essence, the Rule applies if a party attempts to add new, or contradictory, substantive terms to a written contract.

A.   Four Corners Rule

This original common law rule provides that if an agreement is complete and unambiguous on its face, then the agreement is presumed to be a total integration. In that case, a court would not look beyond the four corners of the agreement. That rule gave rise to the collateral contract rule.

B.   Collateral Contract Rule

The Collateral Contract Rule provides that the existence of a total integration does not preclude the introduction into evidence of "collateral agreements" that do not contradict the main agreement. Collateral agreements are independent of the total integration.

C.   Evidence of Usage of Trade

According to the UCC, usage of trade is "any practice or method of dealing having such regularity of observance in a place, vocation or trade as to justify an expectation that it will be observed with respect to the transaction in question."

Evidence of usage of trade is admissible for the following reasons:

- to assist in construing contractual terms;
- to contradict contractual terms; or
- to supplement the contract.

This is admissible even if the contract is a complete integration.

The *Restatement* §§ 220-221 allows the introduction of evidence of a usage of trade to construe or add terms to a contract: "(i) if both parties manifest assent that the usage shall be operative, or (ii) if one of the parties intends the usage to apply and the other knows or has reason to know of this intent, or (iii) if each party knows or has reason to know that the other has an intent inconsistent with usage." Thus, a party is bound by usage of trade if the party is, or should be, aware of it.

VII.   CONDITIONS

> Question Key – Sub-Parts A-D Only
> 10,52,53,56,72,96,98,99,108,109,115,
> 138,139,145,146,189,194,209,222

A condition is an event that must occur to obligate a party to perform under a contractual term or condition. If conditions are not fulfilled by a breaching party that should have been fulfilled, then a non-breaching party may be relieved of any legal obligation under a contract.

A party to a contract is entitled to waive a condition or conditions of the contract. By waiving a condition, the party relinquishes any right to that condition being satisfied. The waiver must occur before the duty to perform that condition becomes absolute. The condition subsequently may be withdrawn by a party if that party provides proper notice to the other parties. Generally, a condition that a first party must fulfill may be excused if a second party waives the condition or breaches a contract.

★★★   **A.   Express Conditions**

1)   GENERAL

An express condition is an explicitly stated condition in a written or verbal agreement. An express condition also can be implied in fact. A promisee must strictly comply with an express condition in order for a promisor's duty of conditional performance to arise. This duty will not arise unless either the condition occurs or the non-occurrence of the condition is excused.

a)   Doctrine of Prevention

The doctrine of prevention provides a basis for excusing the non-performance of an express condition precedent. This doctrine provides that a party must abstain from activity that hinders or prevents the condition's occurrence. Restatement (Second) of Contracts §§ 225, 245 cmt. a.

b)   Communication of Express Condition

An express condition is clearly communicated, either verbally or in a written agreement, by terms, such as "on condition that" or similar language. For example, an employment agreement may stipulate that an employee must have worked for a specified duration to qualify for a benefit.

c)   Conditions Precedent and Subsequent

A condition precedent is an event that must happen before a duty to perform under a contract becomes due. A condition subsequent is an event that the parties agree will discharge a duty of performance after it has become absolute.

The courts may liberally, rather than literally, construe a contractual provision as a condition precedent or a condition subsequent in order to avoid its operation from causing forfeiture. A court may excuse a party's performance of a condition if the condition's nonperformance was due to no fault of the party.

2)   SATISFACTION

a)   Contract for Personal Services

A services contract may include a term requiring that payment to a promisee by a promisor be made subject to the paying party's satisfaction, which is a question of quality. A court will uphold and enforce such a term provided that the determination of satisfaction is made in good faith (subjective standard). Thus, the obligation to pay a promisee may not be absolute.

b)   Contracts for Mechanical Fitness or Suitability for Purpose

A contract may include a term requiring that a payment to a promisee by a promisor be made subject to that paying party's satisfaction, which is a question of mechanical fitness or suitability for a particular purpose. In these types of contracts, a court will use an objective standard to determine whether the work done would be satisfactory to a reasonable person.

★★★   B.   **Constructive Conditions**

A constructive condition is implicitly contained in a written agreement or is judicially determined (i.e., it is implied by law) from the agreement and/or the factual circumstances of a transaction. A constructive or implied condition may be included in an agreement because its nature suggests that the parties intended it to be part of the agreement. A promisee must substantially comply with an implied condition in order for a promisor's duty of conditional performance to apply.

1)   CONDITIONS OF EXCHANGE

a)   General

All contracts include a constructive condition that if a first party expects reciprocal performance from a second party, then the first party must perform its contractual duties. If the first party materially breaches the contract, then the constructive condition is not fulfilled, and the first party may not recover damages from the second party.

Once a party's absolute duty to perform exists, the party's lack of performance will constitute a breach of contract. The type of breach that has occurred will depend on the timing and nature of the breach.

> b)   Excuse or Suspension by Material Breach

The two types of breaches are material and partial breaches. The type of breach will determine the appropriate remedy for that breach. In the event of a breach of contract, a non-breaching party must prove that it was ready, willing, and able to perform its contractual duties or had performed them before filing a legal action against a breaching party. If a party commits a material breach of a contract, then the other party may be excused from performing under the contract (or suspend performance). Upon the happening of a material breach, the innocent other party may sue for breach of contract.

> 2)   IMMATERIAL BREACH

Under some circumstances, a party may commit a minor or immaterial breach if it partially performs a contract. An immaterial breach gives rise to remedies such as damages. Thus, a non-breaching party could neither suspend performance nor terminate a contract in the case of an immaterial breach by the other party. Rather, the non-breaching party must continue on with the contract and sue for damages (but it cannot suspend performance).

As a defense, a breaching party may assert good-faith conduct or that a non-breaching party did not suffer great hardship due to an alleged immaterial breach. If the breaching party establishes those defenses, then the breach would be considered minor. Remember, in the event of a minor breach, the non-breaching party is required to continue performance of the contract and may recover some damages for the breach.

> 3)   INDEPENDENT COVENANTS

Covenants in a bilateral contract may be independent of one another. In those instances, the promises made by a first party in a contract are not conditional upon any promise by a second party.

For example, suppose Bob, a landowner, entered into a contract with Manny, a builder, to have three different buildings built on separate pieces of property owned by Bob. Each structure is distinct from the other two, and the parties agree on a specific price for each. After completing the first structure in accordance with the terms of the contract, Manny demands payment of the specified price for that structure. At the same time, Manny informs Bob that he is "sick of the construction business" and will not even start building the other two buildings. Bob cannot refuse to pay anything to the builder, because the three buildings can be viewed as independent covenants.

The following four subtopics describe further examples of covenants.

> a)   Insurance Contracts

A policy of insurance provides that an insurer will pay a policy's proceeds to a beneficiary upon the occurrence of a particular event. If that policy lacks a provision that expressly conditions the insurer's obligation to pay proceeds upon an insured's full payment of every premium, a beneficiary may recover from the insurer despite the insured's failure to make some payments. Ordinarily, the courts do not consider that failure a non-occurrence of a constructive condition that would avoid the insurer's duty to pay on the policy.

b)   Real Property Lease Agreements

The courts consider the promises in an ordinary real property lease to be independent of one another. Therefore, a landlord's covenant to maintain a property in a habitable condition is not conditioned upon a tenant's payment of rent.

c)   Covenant Not to Sue

A covenant not to sue restricts a promisor or creditor from bringing an action or a claim against a promisee or debtor. If the covenant is for an unlimited duration, it operates as a discharge, like a release. If the covenant runs for a limited period, it may be raised as an affirmative defense to an action that violates the covenant.

d)   Covenant Not to Compete

A covenant not to compete obligates a promisor not to provide goods or perform services that a promisee provides or performs. It also may restrict the promisor's taking of good will or utilization of trade secrets. The *Restatement* provides that the covenant must be reasonable in duration, geographic range, and in the scope of any competing activity.

4)   <u>DUTIES REGARDING CONSTRUCTIVE CONDITIONS</u>

A first party's substantial performance of a contract is a constructive condition of a second party's performance of the contract. Thus, if the first party fails to substantially perform the contract, then the second party may consider that a failure of a constructive condition and may not be obligated to perform under the contract. When performance by the first party will take a period of time, the first party must finish its performance before the second party is obligated to perform, unless the circumstances or the contract's terms provide otherwise. Restatement (Second) of Contracts § 234.

a)   Non-Prevention

Parties to a contract have an implied duty not to wrongfully prevent the performance of a contract, nor prevent the fulfillment of a condition of each other's performance of the contract. The test is, did one party's conduct wrongfully prevent the other party's fulfillment of contractual duties?

b)   Non-Hindrance

Parties to a contract have an implied duty not to substantially hinder the performance of a contract, nor hinder the occurrence of a condition of each other's performance of the contract. The test is whether one party's conduct substantially hindered the other party's fulfillment of contractual duties.

<blockquote>c)   Cooperation</blockquote>

Parties to a contract have an implied duty of cooperation in performing a contract, as well as in the occurrence of a condition of each other's performance of the contract.

C.   Obligations of Good Faith and Fair Dealing

Kirke La Shelle Co. v. Paul Armstrong Co. provides "that in every contract, there exists an implied covenant of good faith and fair dealing." Generally, the courts consider violations of those duties to be a breach of contract. Such violations also may give rise to tort claims: for example, when an insurer violates an insurance contract or an employer abusively terminates at-will employees.

<blockquote>1)   <u>GOOD FAITH</u></blockquote>

<blockquote>a)   Common Law</blockquote>

It is presumed that all contracts contain a requirement of good-faith performance. Each party is obligated to remain faithful to a mutual purpose and to perform in accordance with their mutually warranted expectations. For example, Kim's contract to represent and sell ACME, Inc.'s products requires her to perform the contractual duties in good faith. This obligation is important with respect to exclusive agency agreements, as well as to output or requirement contracts.

<blockquote>b)   UCC</blockquote>

UCC § 1-304 states that every contract or duty under the UCC imposes "an obligation of good faith in its performance or enforcement." UCC § 1-201(20) defines good faith as "honesty in fact" in the conduct or transaction concerned. UCC § 2-306(1) provides, in part, that output and requirement contracts involve "such actual output or requirements as may occur in good faith."

<blockquote>2)   <u>FAIR DEALING</u></blockquote>

<blockquote>a)   Restatement</blockquote>

The *Restatement* provides, in part, that: "Every contract imposes upon each party a duty of fair dealing in its performance and its enforcement."

<blockquote>b)   UCC</blockquote>

UCC § 2-103(1)(b) provides that a merchant's good faith involves "honesty in fact and the observance of reasonable commercial standards of fair dealing in the trade."

★★   **D.   Suspension or Excuse of Conditions**

If a party's contractual duty is conditional, the party's performance or a condition may be suspended or even excused under certain circumstances. A suspension or excuse of conditions also may result from waiver, election, or estoppel.

1)   WAIVER

Realty Growth Investors v. Council of Unit Owners defines waiver as "a voluntary and intentional relinquishment of a known right." The *Restatement* provides that a promisor who makes a waiver must do so knowing, or with reason to know of, the right. A waiver may be implied from the factual circumstances or expressly made. In the latter situation of an express waiver, a promisor may inform a promisee that he will waive the promisee's performance of a condition.

2)   ELECTION

a)   Common Law

An election is a non-breaching party's choice to waive a condition after a breaching party's failure to fulfill the condition. Generally, a non-breaching party's election to continue performing a contract despite a material breach will:

- neither prevent that party from bringing a breach of contract action;
- nor necessarily constitute a renunciation of damages.

b)   UCC

The following UCC provision requires a buyer to provide notice to preserve remedies for a breach. UCC § 2-607(3)(a) states that: "the buyer must within a reasonable time after he discovers or should have discovered any breach notify the seller of breach or be barred from any remedy." This section pertains to accepted goods.

UCC § 1-107 provides that a claim or right arising from a breach of contract can be discharged without consideration by a written waiver or renunciation that is signed and delivered by the aggrieved (i.e., non-breaching) party.

3)   EQUITABLE ESTOPPEL

Generally, a first party who objects to, or rejects a, second party's contractual performance is not obligated to give reasons for the objection or rejection. If the first party provides more than one reason for the objection and does not provide other reasons, and the second party reasonably understands the stated reasons to be a complete listing, then the first party will be estopped from asserting the unstated reasons if the other party relied, to his injury, on the stated reasons.

★★★   E.   **Prospective Inability to Perform and Anticipatory Repudiation**

1)   COMMON LAW

★★★

a)   Anticipatory Repudiation

Question Key
74,75,131,163,
164,177,185,203
,213,225,226

When a first party communicates to a second party an unequivocal anticipated lack of ability or willingness to perform contractual obligations (e.g., "I will not perform."), it may be considered an anticipatory repudiation of the contract. In that situation, the second party is entitled to suspend its own performance of the contract. The second party also may bring an immediate breach of contract suit against the repudiator.

A first party's future inability or unwillingness to perform a contract with a second party may be demonstrated in the following ways:

- the first party's words or conduct;
- the first party's insolvency;
- the destruction of a contract's subject matter;
- preexisting or subsequent illegality of performance under the contract;
- encumbrance on a title of, or a lack of a title in, a vendor when he entered into a contract with a vendee;
- illness or death of a person whose performance is essential under a contract; and
- under the UCC, defective performance rendered under other contracts of the parties or with third parties.

(1)   Retraction of Repudiation

Under the common law of contracts, however, the repudiation can be retracted by the promising party so long as there has been no material change in the position of the other party in the interim. Such a material change in the other party's position, however, terminates the promising party's ability to retract the repudiation. Restatement (Second) of Contracts § 256. In the absence of such a termination, a retraction of the repudiation restores the other party's obligation to perform on the contract. The other party's request for a retraction of the repudiation does not operate as a waiver of the repudiation if it is not retracted.

★★   b)   Mere Expression of Doubt

A mere expression of doubt about a party's willingness or ability to perform a contract will not serve as an anticipatory breach (e.g., "I doubt I will be able to perform."). If such an expression occurs, then the first party, who anticipates a breach, may request a written assurance of performance from a second party if the first party possesses a reasonable basis to believe the second party may not perform the contract. If no written assurance is provided, then the first party can deem the contract repudiated and then file a lawsuit for breach of contract. In that event, when no written assurances are provided, the first party is not obligated to wait until the agreed-upon date of performance before he can file the lawsuit.

2)   UCC

a)   Anticipatory Repudiation

Under UCC § 2-610, when either party repudiates the contract, an aggrieved party basically may suspend its own performance and:

- await performance by the repudiating party for a reasonable time; or

- resort to any remedy for a breach.

b)   Reasonable Grounds for Insecurity

UCC § 2-609(1) provides that when reasonable grounds for insecurity arise with respect to the performance of either party to a contract, a first party may make a demand for "adequate assurances of due performance" and, if commercially reasonable, suspend performance until the assurances are received. When the second party fails to provide adequate assurances within 30 days, the first party may consider the contract repudiated. In that event, the first party could:

1)   cancel the contract,

2)   refuse to perform under the contract, or

3)   sue for breach of contract.

c)   Insolvency

UCC § 2-702(1) states that: "When the seller discovers the buyer to be insolvent, he may refuse delivery except for cash including payment for all goods theretofore delivered under the contract." UCC § 1-201(23) identifies the following three factual circumstances that indicate a party's insolvency:

1)   ceasing to pay debts in the ordinary course of business;

2)   an inability to pay debts as they mature; or

3)   insolvency as defined by the *United States Bankruptcy Code* (i.e., a party's debts exceed assets).

VIII.   REMEDIES

    A.   **Election of Substantive Rights and Remedies**

   1)   <u>COMMON LAW</u>

The common law of contracts requires a non-breaching party to elect what type of remedy he will pursue if two potential remedies are inconsistent. For example, a party could not bring an action for breach of contract on the one hand, and rescission of the contract on the other, because one action presumes a contract exists, while the other does not. The purpose of the rule is to avoid double recovery. The doctrine of election of remedies should be confined to cases where: (1) double compensation of the plaintiff is threatened, or (2) the defendant actually has been misled by the plaintiff's conduct, or (3) *res judicata* can be applied.

   a)   Options upon Breach

A non-breaching party may elect to respond to an anticipatory repudiation or breach in the following ways:

- Request Compliance

The non-breaching party may elect to provide the breaching party with an opportunity to retract the repudiation or rectify the breach. Those corrective steps may be taken by a breaching party before a non-breaching party has filed an action or changed his position based on the repudiation or the breach.

- Attempt to Cure

When a breaching party's repudiation or breach is material, the non-breaching party may obtain the requisite substitute performance of the contract if that response to the repudiation or breach is proportional.

- Sue Later

The non-breaching party may wait until the agreed-upon performance date before bringing the claim or action on the contract. A breaching party may retract the repudiation or rectify the breach of contract while that party is able to begin or resume performance, and if the non-breaching party's position did not change due to the repudiation or breach.

- Immediately Sue

The non-breaching party may bring a claim or action on the contract against a breaching party without waiting until the agreed-upon date of performance. The non-breaching party must prove that, but for the repudiation or breach, he was ready, able, and willing to perform. In order to retract a repudiation or rectify a breach, the breaching party must manifest willingness and ability to perform under the contract.

- Rescind the Contract

The non-breaching party may elect to cancel the contract by rescinding it.

2)   RESTATEMENT

Under the *Restatement*, "[i]f a party has more than one remedy under the rules . . . his manifestation of a choice of one of them by bringing suit or otherwise is not a bar to another remedy unless the remedies are inconsistent and the other party materially changes his position in reliance on the manifestation." *Restatement (Second) of Contracts* § 378 (1981).

3)   UCC

The UCC has rejected the rule of election of remedies, and provides that remedies are cumulative. Therefore, in an action for fraud, for example, the plaintiff may seek rescission of a contract, restitution of benefits, and damages due to the fraud. Nonetheless, a party still may not recover twice for the same damage.

★★★   **B.   Total and Partial Breach of Contract**

Under the common law, a breach results from a failure of a party to a contract to abide by the contract's terms or conditions.

★★★   1)   MATERIAL BREACH

> Question Key
> 42,47,81,132,233

A total, absolute, or material breach of a contract threatens its value and warrants a non-breaching party in ceasing to perform or terminating the contract. Generally, the damages available to a non-breaching party are in an amount that will place the non-breaching party in the position that he would have been in if the contract had been fully performed.

a)   Substantial Performance

A total breach of contract occurs when a breaching party fails to substantially perform the contract, and a non-breaching party has no means to cure that breach. If a breaching party performs in bad faith or willfully fails to perform contractual duties, then the non-breaching party may:

- suspend performance;
- refuse performance by the breaching party; and
- commence a lawsuit to recover damages.

A material breach usually harms or eliminates the value of a contract. A material breach gives rise to remedies including damages, as well as the suspension, discharge, or cancellation of a contract.

To analyze if a breach is material, consider:

- Did a party fail to abide by the contract's terms?
- To what degree is a non-breaching party deprived of a reasonably expected benefit? (Consider the purpose or reason of the contract.)
- To what degree will damages sufficiently compensate a non-breaching party? (Consider if any damages will adequately cover the loss)
- To what degree has a breaching party partially performed?
- How probable is it that a breaching party will cure the breach?
- How willful is the breach under the circumstances?
- To what extent is a there a delay in performance? and
- To what degree will a breaching party suffer forfeiture?

     2)   <u>PARTIAL BREACH</u>

Question Key
19,84,119

A partial or immaterial breach of a contract is one that does not fully impair its value and usually does not justify a non-breaching party in ceasing to perform under the contract. The non-breaching party may bring an action against a breaching party to recover damages that resulted from the immaterial breach. The ordinary purpose of receiving damages for a breach of contract is to place a non-breaching party in the position he would have been in had no breach occurred. For example, the typical amount of damages a non-breaching employer would receive from a breaching employee will be equal to the amount of compensation a substitute employee receives, above and beyond the amount of compensation the breaching employee would have received.

     3)   <u>UCC</u>

a)   Perfect Tender Rule – Non-Installment Contract

The Perfect Tender Rule is a stark contrast to the common law doctrine of substantial performance. Under UCC § 2-601 (the perfect tender rule for non-installment contracts): unless the parties agree otherwise, "if the goods or the tender of delivery fail in any respect to conform to the contract, the buyer may: (a) reject the whole, (b) accept the whole, or (c) accept any commercial unit or units, and reject the rest."

b)   Mitigation of Perfect Tender Rule

Some UCC rules that mitigate the UCC perfect tender rule basically provide that the:

- seller may cure if time for performance has not expired. UCC § 2-508.

- If the buyer already has accepted the goods, under certain circumstances the buyer can revoke the acceptance if the non-conformity of the goods "substantially impairs" the good's value to the buyer. UCC § 2-608. This provision mitigates the perfect tender rule by requiring that, in order for the buyer to revoke acceptance, the goods' non-conformity must substantially impair their value to the buyer. This is a different standard than providing that the buyer can revoke acceptance because the goods are not perfect.

- In an installment contract for the sale of goods, the buyer can: (1) reject an installment only if its non-conformity "substantially impairs" the value of the installment and cannot be cured, and (2) can claim a breach of the whole contract only if the non-conformity of one or more installments "substantially impairs the value of the whole contract." UCC § 2-612. This provision also mitigates the perfect tender rule on the same basis as the previous provision, but also further requires that the non-conformity as to one installment must substantially impair the whole contract's value.

c)   Conversion

A buyer of goods who rightfully rejects them but subsequently continues to exercise ownership of them, causing the seller to otherwise dispose of them before receiving them back, commits conversion by wrongfully selling the goods to a third party without returning them to the seller. The seller may recover the fair market value of the goods for the conversion. The sale price received by the buyer for the goods constitutes credible evidence of their value when the conversion occurred. UCC §§ 2-601 cmt. 2, 1-103.

★★   **C.**   **Equitable Remedies**

> Question Key
> 68,168

Although ordinarily, a non-breaching party's remedy for a breach of contract is a recovery of money damages, occasionally the non-breaching party may obtain equitable relief against a breaching party. An equitable remedy is usually available only when:

- no adequate remedy at law exists;
- the obligations and rights of parties to a contract are described with sufficient definiteness; and
- the relief requested is not too difficult to supervise or enforce.

Consider the following factors to determine if the damages are adequate to protect an injured party:

- They are too speculative in nature and difficult to calculate with sufficient certainty;
- Money damages cannot buy a substitute for the promised performance (e.g., land, a business, controlling shares of stock, intellectual property); or

●   Performance involves forbearance, as with a non-competition agreement.

★★   1)   <u>SPECIFIC PERFORMANCE</u>

                a)   Common Law

A court may order a breaching party to perform a contract if the court may enforce that type of contract and money damages would not provide an adequate remedy. The more unique an item is, the more probable it is that the court will specifically enforce a contract for that item. For example, a court may enforce an agreement for a real estate conveyance because it involves unique real property and/or a special structure on that land. Real estate conveyances often are the subject of specific performance actions on the exam.

The courts cannot properly order specific performance in the absence of adequate knowledge of what type of conduct is sought to be enforced. Thus, the terms of the parties' contract must be sufficiently definite for the courts to know how to order enforcement of contractual duties. Such an order must inform the nonperforming party of precisely what that party must accomplish to comply with the order.

The following elements are required for a court to grant specific performance of a contract:

●   the absence of a sufficient legal remedy;
●   breach of contract;
●   a mutuality of remedy;
●   a reasonable decree; and
●   the lack of another defense to enforcement.

A court usually will not enforce a personal services contract, or duties under such contracts that have been assigned or delegated to another party, for the following reasons:

●   the Thirteenth Amendment prohibits involuntary servitude;
●   the complexity of evaluating the quality of a performance by a musician, artist, or painter; and
●   the difficulty of forcing two adverse parties to collaborate on a project.

An exception to the rule against the enforcement of personal services contracts applies if an offeror promises to pay an offeree to render professional services, and the offeree renders those services. In that event, their unilateral contract is irrevocable and specifically enforceable if either party fails to perform.

                                      b)   UCC

UCC § 2-716(1) states that "Specific performance may be decreed when the goods are unique or in other proper circumstances." A buyer who cannot secure substitute goods after a reasonable time beyond a breach probably will receive specific performance, even if a seller proves that the goods were not exactly "unique."

Section 2-716, Comment 2, provides that "output and requirements contracts involving a particular or peculiarly available source or market present today the typical commercial specific performance situation, as contrasted with contracts for the sale of heirlooms or priceless works of art which were usually involved in the older cases. However, uniqueness is not the sole basis of the remedy under this section for the relief may also be granted "in other proper circumstances" and inability to cover is strong evidence of 'other proper circumstances'"

2)   INJUNCTION AGAINST BREACH

A court may order an affirmative injunction directing a breaching party not to breach a contract. A court may order a negative injunction requiring a breaching party to cease breaching a contract. For example, if a non-competition agreement is being violated, the court may grant a non-breaching party the relief of enjoining a breaching party from performing services for the non-breaching party's competitor.

3)   DECLARATORY JUDGMENT

An action seeking a declaratory judgment may be instituted to seek the court's opinion regarding the parties' rights under the law or under an instrument, such as a contract. Essentially, the parties ask the court whether a certain action is prohibited before a contract is breached or a law is violated. The declaration may be either affirmative or negative in form and effect, and such declarations must have the force and effect of a final judgment.

A declaratory judgment is an equitable judicial decree that establishes a party's rights with respect to an actual dispute. For example, if an ambiguity exists under a written contract and is disputed, a party may file an action for a declaratory judgment so that the court may resolve the ambiguity.

★ **D.   Rescission and Reformation**

| Question Key |
| 25,54,55 |

Rescission and reformation are two different ways of addressing contractual issues.

★   1)   RESCISSION

Rescission is the cancellation of a contract such that it no longer binds the parties to it. When neither party has fully performed the contract, they may mutually agree to rescind it without giving each other any other consideration. A mutual rescission may not occur after one of the parties has fully performed a contract, because of an absence of mutual consideration for that rescission. In such a case, the appropriate course is for the rescinding party to provide a release supported by new consideration. The common law requires that a rescission of a contract that is subject to the Statute of Frauds must be in writing. The *Restatement* allows for a verbal rescission. A court may grant the relief of rescission of a contract based on either a mutual mistake or a unilateral mistake.

a)   Mutual Mistake

An adversely affected party may seek judicial rescission of a contract on the basis that both of the parties to the contract were mistaken regarding a basic assumption on which the contract was formed. The result of rescission is to return each party to their respective positions that existed before the contract's execution. Consequently, a party may need either to return the benefits that were received or provide restitution to the other party.

Judicial relief from a mutual mistake may occur when a mistaken party establishes the following elements:

- a mistake in a basic assumption, upon which the contract is premised;
- the mistake materially affects or imbalances the parties' performances; and
- the plaintiff does not bear the risk of mistake.

The risk of mistake may arise when the party possessed only some knowledge of the facts about the mistake and considered that knowledge as sufficient. A court may allocate the risk of mistake to a party. Alternatively, the risk of mistake may be placed upon one of the parties by the contract.

b)   Unilateral Mistake

Judicial relief from a unilateral mistake may occur when a mistaken party establishes the following elements:

- a mistake in a basic assumption, upon which the contract is premised; and
- the mistake materially affects or imbalances the parties' performances; and
- the plaintiff does not bear the risk of mistake; and
- either the non-mistaken party knew of or had reason to know of the mistake; or
- the mistake makes enforcing the contract unconscionable.

★   2)   REFORMATION

Reformation is a judicial modification of a written contract's original provisions in order to conform it to the parties' agreement. The courts will not use reformation to alter or to avoid a bargain that allegedly was entered into due to a mistake. The courts use reformation to give a correct expression to the parties' intent. Thus, reformation is available to rectify a mistake in drafting or transcription, a misunderstanding, or duress and similar types of misconduct. A party seeking reformation of a contract for mistake must establish, with clear and convincing evidence, the following:

- the parties reached an agreement;
- they decided to reduce their agreement to writing;
- a variance exists between their agreement and the writing; and
- the variance is a mutual mistake.

One party's mistaken belief that the contract will contain a missing element is not a valid basis for reformation. Reformation is an exception to the Parol Evidence Rule.

 E.   **Measure of Damages**

Question Key
2,6,7,26,32,61,69,118,120,135,162,172, 173,184,186,195,220,224,227,228

When a party prevails in a breach of contract action seeking a recovery of damages from a breaching party, a court must determine the amount of damages to award to the non-breaching party.

          1)   <u>EXPECTATION DAMAGES</u>

a)   Common Law

          (1)   Benefit of the Bargain

When expectation damages are awarded, a court seeks to afford a non-breaching party with the benefit of the bargain from a breaching party. With that relief, the non-breaching party will be placed into the position he expected to have been in if the parties' contract had been performed. This includes any profits that would have been received.

To fulfill the non-breaching party's expectations, the amount awarded may be measured by the sum required to obtain substitute performance. Reasonable substitute performance must be provided to the extent that the circumstances warrant.

For example, suppose Jill contracts with Bob to replace the central heating and cooling unit in her house for $2,000. Bob failed to replace the unit within a reasonable time from the date scheduled in their contract. Consequently, Jill had to contract with Bill to replace the unit for $3,000. In all respects other than price, the contracts of both Bob and Bill were identical. Jill could sue Bob for breach of contract seeking to recover expectation damages in the amount of $1,000 for the additional cost of Bill's substitute performance. This amount of damage would provide Jill with the benefit of her bargain.

(2)   Construction Contracts

(a)   Breaching Property Owner

As a basic principle, the standard measure of damages for a contractor from a breaching property owner is an expected profit on the cost of building a structure for the owner, plus any costs incurred in that construction until the owner's breach occurred. The contractor must cease work upon learning of the breach in order to mitigate damages.

                                        (i)   Expectation Damages
                                                   Formula

A more detailed formula also exists for calculating expectation damages to provide the contractor the benefit of the bargain—the sum that would put the contractor in the position the contractor would have occupied but for the breach (i.e., the cost of restoration). This formula adds the amounts of loss in value and any other loss and subtracts from those losses any cost avoided and any loss avoided. Each element of this formula merits further description and explanation.

The loss in value (LIV) consists of the difference between value of the performance that in fact occurred and the performance that should have occurred. The other loss (OL) that must be added to the loss in value consists of any incidental damages plus consequential damages suffered by the non-breaching party. The cost avoided (CA), which needs to be subtracted from the sum of combining both loss in value and any other loss, consists of those costs that the non-breaching party can mitigate by properly ceasing to perform under the contract on account of the other party's breach. The loss avoided (LA), which needs to be subtracted from the cost avoided, consists of the positive impact of the breach attributable to the non-breaching party's reallocation of or ability to salvage resources that, but for the breach, would have been used to perform contractual obligations. In summary, this formula for calculating general expectation damages is LIV plus OL minus CA minus LA. Restatement (Second) of Contracts § 347; E. Allen Farnsworth, Contracts § 12.9 (4th ed. 2004).

        •   Example

Suppose, for example, that a contractor and a landowner make an agreement. The contractor promises to build a three-car garage for the landowner. The landowner agrees to pay $50,000 for this construction project. The contractor expects to receive a $5,000 profit upon completion of this project. The contractor expended $25,000 in time (i.e., labor) and materials, including $6,000 for three garage doors. Subsequently, the landowner provided proper notice that he had suffered a major, unexpected financial setback. Additionally, the landowner's notice stated that he could not pay the contractor as promised and that all work on the project must cease. By this time, the reasonable market value of time and materials furnished by the contractor for the project was $20,000. The contractor installed the three garage doors in other garages that he built. If the contractor brings an action against the landowner, the amount of damages recoverable will be calculated according to the above formula. The LIV is $50,000. The LA is 0 because the contractor suffered no consequential or incidental damages. The CA is $20,000, the sum of $45,000 minus $25,000. The LA is $6,000. Thus, $50,000+$0-$20,000-$6,000 = $24,000.

                                        (b)   Breaching Contractor

A contractor may breach a construction agreement by providing incomplete or poor performance. In that event, if the cost of finishing the building would be disproportionate to the owner's benefit from the contractor's work, then the owner may recover from the contractor only the decreased value of the completed construction. The contractor may receive a benefit for the effort made before the breach, to avoid a complete forfeiture of that effort. If the contractor's performance decreases the anticipated value of the completed construction, the owner may recover the amount of diminution or loss.

(3)   Some Measures of Expectation Damages

(a)   Difference in Value

If an award of expectation damages might be wasteful, such as when the cost to restore the party to the same position as if the contract had been performed as specified (i.e., restoration damages) would far exceed the difference in value due to performance not as specified, damages may be measured by the difference in value between both of those types of performance. *Jacob & Youngs v. Kent*, 129 N.E. 889 (N.Y. 1921) (breach of contract to install certain brand of pipe in home by installing another comparable brand of pipe in home).

(b)   Cost of Completion

Cost of completion damages are proper if a breach of contract seems to be willful and only the contract's completion as promised will allow the non-breaching party to use the land for its intended purposes. *American Standard, Inc. v. Schectman*, 439 N.Y.S.2d 529 (App. Div. 1981) (breach of contract to remove foundations and subsurface structures from land and grade land).

b)   UCC

Under the UCC, usually either a non-breaching seller or a non-breaching buyer may recover expectation damages from a breaching party in a contract action. UCC § 1-106(1) provides that the UCC's remedies "shall be liberally administered to the end that the aggrieved party may be put in as good a position as if the other party had fully performed."

★★   2)   RIGHTS OF BUYERS AND SELLERS UNDER THE UCC

★★   a)   Buyer's Preliminary Rights

(1)   Right to Inspect

UCC § 2-512(2) recognizes that a buyer may be required to pay for a seller's goods before inspecting them. Section 2-512(2) provides that such a payment before inspection of the goods does not "constitute an acceptance of goods or impair the buyer's right to inspect or any of his remedies." Thus, a buyer possesses a right to inspect the goods purchased after their delivery, notwithstanding a contractual provision that requires prepayment for the goods.

(2)   Reasonable Right to Inspect

Under UCC § 2-606(a), a buyer possesses a reasonable right to inspect goods purchased from a seller. A buyer's unreasonable exercise of that right would be inconsistent with the seller's ownership of the goods. Therefore, an unreasonable inspection will result in the buyer's acceptance of the goods. When a party's transaction involves a large quantity of goods, the number of goods inspected is a relevant factor in determining the reasonableness of the inspection.

              b)   Perfect Tender Rule - Non-Installment Contract

(1)   General

UCC § 2-601, provides, in part, that "unless otherwise agreed…, if the goods or the tender of delivery fail in any respect to conform to the contract, the buyer may: (a) reject the whole; or (b) accept the whole; or (c) accept any commercial unit or units and reject the rest." This is known as the "perfect tender rule." It is in stark contrast to the common law's substantial performance test.

(2)   Whole or Part

The UCC's perfect tender rule applies to a contract for a sale of goods that does not require multiple deliveries or installments. It permits a buyer to reject or accept a full shipment of goods. Alternatively, a buyer may reject or accept some of the commercial units that were received.

(3)   Defective Tender

Under UCC § 2-208, the courts may consider the parties' usage of trade, course of dealing, and course of performance when determining if a seller's tender to a buyer was defective.

(4)   Reasonable Time for Rejection

Under UCC § 2-602(1), "Rejection of goods must be within a reasonable time after their delivery or tender. It is ineffective unless the buyer seasonably notifies the seller." So, the rejection must occur within a reasonable time from when the goods were delivered or tendered. For the rejection to be effective, the buyer must seasonably notify the seller of the rejection.

              c)   Tender Rule - Installment Contract

(1)   General

Under UCC § 2-612(1), an installment sales contract "requires or authorizes the delivery of goods in separate lots to be separately accepted," even if the contract "contains a clause [stating that] 'each delivery is a separate contract' or its equivalent." In other words, the UCC allows for separate acceptance of each delivery of goods in separate lots, even if the parties' contract provides that each delivery is a separate contract.

(2)   Basis for Rejection of Installment

UCC § 2-612(2) provides that under an installment contract for a sale of goods, "the buyer may reject any installment which is non-conforming if the non-conformity substantially impairs the value of that installment and cannot be cured, or if the non-conformity is a defect in the required documents." In other words, any non-conforming installment can be rejected by the buyer when the non-conformity substantially impairs that installment's value and cannot be cured, or a defect in the required documents is the non-conformity.

When a seller informs a buyer that the seller will cure any non-conforming installment(s), and provides the buyer with adequate assurances about that cure, the buyer has to accept the installment unless the non-conformity or default substantially impaired the entire contract's value such that there is a breach of contract. UCC § 2-612(2)-(3). Further, when a non-conformity or default in any installment(s) substantially impairs the value of an entire contract, a breach of that contract occurs. UCC § 2-612(3). An aggrieved buyer will reinstate a contract if the buyer: (1) accepts a non-conforming installment without "seasonably" notifying the seller that the buyer is canceling the contract; or (2) brings an action against the seller regarding only past installments; or (3) demands performance of future installments.

(3)   Cancellation of Contract

Under UCC § 2-612(3), if a "non-conformity or default with respect to one or more installments substantially impairs the value of the whole contract," then a breach of the entire contract has occurred. If the buyer does not reinstate the contract in any of those ways, the buyer may reject the seller's other installments and cancel the contract.

★★   d)   Buyer's Acceptance or Rejection

If a buyer accepts a seller's goods pursuant to UCC § 2-606(1), the buyer may relinquish the right to reject them. Section 2-606(1)(a) considers an acceptance to have occurred if "after a reasonable opportunity to inspect the goods [the buyer] signifies to the seller that the goods are conforming or that he will take or retain them in spite of their non-conformity." Section 2-606(1)(b) deems it an acceptance if a buyer does not make an effective rejection, "but such acceptance does not occur until the buyer has had a reasonable opportunity to inspect" the goods. A buyer also can accept the goods by performing any act inconsistent with the seller's ownership. UCC § 2-606(1)(c). But if such an act by a buyer is wrongful as against the seller, it only is an acceptance if it is ratified by the seller.

UCC § 2-711(3) provides that a buyer who rightfully rejects a seller's goods or justifiably revokes acceptance of them may sell them at a public or private sale if the buyer already paid for the goods. The buyer only must provide the seller with notice of his intent to resell the goods in a private sale.

     e)   Buyer's Revocation of Acceptance

A buyer may revoke acceptance of goods if the buyer subsequently discovers a non-conformity in them that substantially impairs their value to the buyer, under two situations when the goods were accepted:

- "On the reasonable assumption that [their] non-conformity would be cured and it has not been seasonably cured;" or

- "Without discovering [their] non-conformity [and] if his acceptance was reasonably induced either by the difficulty of discovery before acceptance or by the seller's assurances."

UCC § 2-608(1).

In the first situation, the seller fails to seasonably cure the defect in the goods although the buyer reasonably assumed this non-conformity would be cured. In the second situation, the buyer did not discover the good's non-conformity when the goods were accepted, and either the difficulty of making that discovery before their acceptance or the seller's assurances reasonably induced the buyer's acceptance.

(1)   When to Revoke

UCC § 2-608(2) states, in part, that revocation must occur "within a reasonable time after the buyer discovers, or should have discovered the ground for it and before any substantial change in the condition of the goods which is not caused by their own defects. It is not effective until the buyer notifies the seller of it." In other words, the buyer must revoke acceptance within a reasonable time after he discovers, or should have discovered, the basis for the revocation and before any substantial change occurs in the goods' condition not caused by the goods' own defects. The buyer's revocation is not effective until the buyer notifies the seller of it.

     f)   Buyer's Remedies

The UCC provides remedies to a buyer who receives non-conforming goods from a seller and correctly either rejects them or revokes his acceptance of them. Under all circumstances, a non-breaching party must act reasonably to mitigate damages. The buyer's remedies include: cover, price difference, consequential damages, breach of warranty, and refund.

(1)   Cover

If a non-breaching buyer acts in good faith within a reasonable time period to obtain conforming goods, the buyer could cover a seller's breach of providing non-conforming goods by acquiring substitute goods at a reasonable price. UCC § 2-712(1). The buyer subsequently could recover damages from the seller in the amount of a difference between the cover price and the contract price, plus incidental or consequential damages. UCC § 2-712(2). The buyer would be able to recover those expenses when the cover price exceeded the market price.

(2)   Price Difference

If a seller fails to deliver on, or repudiates, a contract, a buyer may recover from the seller the difference between the contract price and "the market price at the time when the buyer learned of the breach." UCC § 2-713(1). The buyer is further allowed consequential and incidental damages, minus the expenses the buyer avoids. Such damages may include, for instance, the buyer's reasonable commercial costs arising from the seller's breach of contract, or the buyer's storage of, or inspecting of, the goods.

(3)   Consequential Damages

UCC § 2-715(2)(a) defines consequential damages as "any loss resulting from general or particular requirements and needs of which the seller at the time of contracting had reason to know and which could not reasonably be prevented by cover or otherwise." UCC § 2-715(2)(b) defines consequential damages as "injury to person or property proximately resulting from any breach of warranty."

(4)   Breach of Warranty

A rejecting buyer usually may not recover from a seller for a breach of warranty when no injury to a person or property results from the breach. Under UCC § 2-714, a breach of warranty recovery usually is available only when a buyer has accepted non-conforming goods. In other words, goods that were not as they were warranted to be.

(5)   Refund

A buyer who rejects non-conforming goods is entitled to recover any prepayment from the buyer to the seller of those goods. If the seller declines to issue a refund of the buyer's prepayment, then the buyer may resell the goods and credit the sale's proceeds to the balance the seller owes to the buyer.

g)   Seller's Right to Cure

(1)   Right to Cure

UCC § 2-508 generally provides for a seller's cure of improper tender or delivery. Accordingly, it limits a buyer's rights to reject a seller's non-conforming goods and to revoke an acceptance of those non-conforming goods. If the parties' contract allows the seller a certain amount of time for performance in which the seller can cure the non-conformity, then the seller may do so by shipping to the buyer conforming goods within that period. If the seller properly exercises that right, then the buyer may not reject the shipment of conforming goods made during the time for performance.

(2) Before Time for Performance

Specifically, UCC § 2-508(1) states that "when any tender or delivery by the seller is rejected because it is non-conforming and the time for performance has not yet expired, the seller may seasonably notify the buyer of his intention to cure and may then, within the contract time, make a conforming delivery." In other words, if the buyer rejects a non-conforming tender within the time for performance, the seller can seasonably provide the buyer with notice of the intention to cure and to make a conforming delivery within the contract time for performance.

(3) Notice for Extension

UCC § 2-508(2) provides, in part, that when the buyer rejects a non-conforming tender that the seller had reasonable grounds to believe would be acceptable, with or without a money allowance, the seller may – if he seasonably notifies the buyer – have a further reasonable time to substitute a conforming tender. Therefore, pursuant to seasonable notice to the buyer, and with or without a money allowance, the seller can obtain additional reasonable time to make a conforming tender that substitutes for a non-conforming tender rejected by the buyer, but only when the seller had reasonable grounds to believe the tender would be acceptable to the buyer.

 h) Seller's Remedies

(1) Standard Measure

The measure of damages for non-acceptance of goods or repudiation by the buyer is the difference between the market price at the time and place for tender and the unpaid contract price together with any incidental damages, but less expenses saved in consequence of the buyer's breach. Thus, a seller may receive any profit, including reasonable overhead the seller could have made if full performance of the contract had occurred.

(2) Lost Volume Sale

What if the seller deals in volume of one product? Suppose the seller, Circuit Country, is a retail seller of computers. If Bob agrees to purchase a computer for $1,000, and subsequently breaches this agreement, will the seller be unable to recover damages from Bob if Carla buys the same computer the next day? In the case of a lost volume sale, the standard measure of damages would not be sufficient because the seller would lose the opportunity for the potential profit from the sale once the good is resold to someone who could have purchased another equivalent good from the same seller (resulting in two sales if the original buyer did not breach).

If this standard measure of damages is inadequate to put the seller in as good a position as performance would have done, then the measure of damages is the profit (including reasonable overhead) the seller would have made from full performance by the buyer, together with any incidental damages.

Therefore, in the case of Bob and Circuit Country, Circuit Country will be entitled to recover its lost profit even if the computer is resold to someone else.

(3)   Seller's Action for the Price

A seller may bring an action on the price of goods provided under contract to a buyer:

- when, within a commercially reasonable time after transfer of risk of loss to the buyer, the goods are lost or damaged;

- after the buyer's acceptance of the goods; or

- if the seller fails to resell the goods after making reasonable efforts to do so.

UCC § 2-709.

★   **F.**   **Consequential and Other Damages**

                 1)   GENERAL

> Question Key
> 32,136,221

To calculate the non-breaching party's award of damages, a court will consider a contract's value, the actual damages sustained, subtract those costs that were avoided, and add any consequential and incidental damages.

Actual damages consist of lost profits or the cost of replacing the subject of a contract.

Avoided costs are those costs that a breaching party's conduct allowed a non-breaching party to save. As a practical matter, the avoided costs can be determined from the costs of performing under the contract if the breach had not occurred.

Incidental damages are those damages a non-breaching party sustains in attempting to mitigate damages or secure a contract's value. UCC § 2-715(1) provides that a buyer may recover incidental damages resulting from a seller's breach, and defines them as "expenses reasonably incurred in inspection, receipt, transportation and care and custody of goods rightfully rejected, any commercially reasonable charges, expenses or commissions in connection with effecting cover and any other reasonable expense incident to the delay or other breach."

Consequential damages are those damages resulting from a breach of contract, even if they are not part of the contract. Consequential damages arise in the ordinary course of events that flow from the breach of contract. A breaching party is not required to have in fact foreseen those damages. The non-breaching party possesses the right to recover consequential damages only when the breaching party could have reasonably foreseen these damages. Generally, the question is: Could a breaching party have reasonably foreseen the damages based on what they knew at the contract's formation?

For example, if an employee breaches an employment agreement that is for a specific term, an employer may obtain a substitute employee to perform the breaching employee's obligations for the remaining duration of the specific term. The usual measure of damages is any additional compensation the employer paid to the substitute employee, in excess of what compensation the breaching employee would have received. However, suppose the employee's breach resulted in the employer losing a contract with a supplier. Would the employee be liable for such consequential damages? The answer depends upon whether the employee could have reasonably foreseen the loss as a result of the breach. If so, the employer may be able to recover such damages.

2)   UCC APPROACH

Under UCC § 2-715(2), a buyer's consequential damages resulting from a seller's breach are described as "any loss resulting from general or particular requirements and needs of which the seller at the time of contracting had reason to know and which could not reasonably be prevented by cover or otherwise; and…injury to person or property proximately resulting from any breach of warranty."

3)   LIMITATIONS ON DAMAGES

Limitations on a recovery of damages may be based on the following three factors: causation, certainty, and foreseeability.

a)   Causation

A breaching party may be liable to a non-breaching party for damages when the evidence shows that the breach of the parties' contract caused the damages. Conversely, a breaching party may be able to avoid liability for damages if he can demonstrate that the damages sought did not result from such breach.

b)   Certainty

In order to be recovered in a breach of contract action, damages must be established with reasonable certainty. Damages that are speculative, remote, contingent, or just possible may not be recovered. For example, proof of damages for harm to an existing business is more certain than proof of damages for harm to a newly formed business, because the damages can be more readily verified if the business has an ongoing history.

c)   Foreseeability

A non-breaching party may recover consequential damages only to the extent that a breaching party could have reasonably foreseen that those damages probably would have resulted from the breach. This is a limitation on a recovery of consequential damages.

★   **G.   Liquidated Damages and Penalties**

Question Key
58,188

Liquidated damages are damages provided for in the contract that may be recovered if a breach of that contract occurs. For example, instead of having to prove actual damages, the parties may stipulate that a breaching party will owe the non-breaching party $10,000 in the event of a breach. Liquidated damages provisions generally are disfavored by the courts, because they are often intended to be punitive, as opposed to compensatory. A court will enforce a contract's liquidated damages provision only when actual damages are:

- difficult to ascertain or uncertain in amount; and
- reasonably estimated either at a contract's formation or when the contract was breached.

The courts will not enforce an unreasonably large liquidated damages provision, because it is void as a penalty. Penalty or punitive damages are not recoverable in an action for breach of contract.

★★   **H.   Restitution and Reliance Recoveries**

Question Key
100,190,192,205

If a contract has not been properly formed, an action for breach of contract will not be judicially sustained. A court may, however, allow a party to collect based on a reliance or restitution theory of damages. When a contract action arises from an existing and enforceable agreement, it is "on the contract." When no such agreement exists, a contract action may be filed "off the contract," on a quasi-contract basis.

The following list includes circumstances when quasi-contractual relief may be sought:

- an unenforceably vague agreement;
- an illegal agreement;
- an agreement involving impossibility and frustration of purpose; and
- a plaintiff materially breaches a contract.

        1)   RELIANCE INTEREST

                a)   Common Law

There are two main circumstances when a party may be able to recover reliance damages. The first circumstance is if the party can demonstrate detrimental reliance (i.e., promissory estoppel). The second circumstance is when, due to a lack of evidence, a court cannot determine a non-breaching party's expectation interest (e.g., speculative lost profits of a new business). When determining reliance damages, the court will seek to place the non-breaching party in a position equivalent to the position that party had before the breach occurred. Reliance damages can be distinguished from expectation damages, which are designed to place the party in the position he would have been in had the contract been performed. As for reliance damages, usually the non-breaching party will recover its out-of-pocket costs, but not his speculative lost profits. Rather, a claim for reliance damages provides for a non-breaching party's recovery of those costs incurred due to a breaching party's action or inaction.

For example, ACE Co. developed a new type of fuel cell. ACE Co. plans to demonstrate the fuel cell at a trade show in Detroit. ACE Co. intends to sell the fuel cell to vehicle manufacturers at the trade show. ACE Co. contracts with Green, a courier service, to deliver the fuel cell to the trade show. The contract is breached when the fuel cell is destroyed while in Green's possession in transit to the trade show. As a result, ACE Co. cannot demonstrate the fuel cell or sell it as planned. In ACE Co.'s breach of contract action against Green, ACE Co. probably will not be awarded any profits that it could have generated from sales of fuel cells that might have been made at the trade show if Green had delivered the fuel cell as agreed. But ACE Co. could be awarded reliance damages for all costs incurred with respect to participating in the trade show and its attempted shipping of the fuel cell.

b)   UCC

When a non-breaching party cannot prove lost profits with certainty, that party may recover those reasonable expenses the party incurred under the contract.

2)   RESTITUTION INTEREST

When a plaintiff is not entitled to recover either expectation damages or reliance damages from a defendant, the plaintiff instead may seek to recover its restitution interest. Restitution damages may be available in the following circumstances:

- No contract exists, but a plaintiff deserves a recovery;
- A contract is unenforceable;
- Plaintiff is the party that materially breached an enforceable contract and cannot recover for breach of contract; or
- Defendant breached the contract, but the plaintiff was not entitled to recover damages.

a)   Common Law

Under the quasi-contract doctrine, a plaintiff may recover for the value of his services in *quantum meruit*, which means "as much as he deserves." The usual measure of quasi-contract recovery is the reasonable value of a benefit that a plaintiff conferred on a defendant. Market value of a plaintiff's performance is the general standard to measure the amount of damages to award. If a plaintiff fully performed its duties under a contract, then the contract price is the best evidence of the contract's reasonable value. If, however, no contract exists and a plaintiff's efforts have conferred value upon a defendant, the plaintiff is entitled to recover the amount of that value from a defendant to prevent unjust enrichment.

Under a quasi-contract theory, the following elements must be satisfied for a plaintiff to receive restitution from a defendant:

1)   The plaintiff conferred a benefit on a defendant (e.g., services, items);

2)   Under a reasonable expectation of receiving compensation for it; and

3a)   The defendant expressly or implicitly requested the benefit; or

3b)   The plaintiff did not voluntarily confer the benefit;

4)   The defendant would be unjustly enriched if the defendant was not obligated to compensate the plaintiff; and

5)   It would be inequitable for the defendant not to pay for the benefit (e.g., services rendered, goods transferred, increased property value).

In several states, a party to a contract who has willfully and materially breached the contract may not recover damages on the basis of restitution.

I.   Remedial Rights of Defaulting Parties

If a party justifiably refuses to perform on the ground that his remaining duties of performance have been discharged by the other party's breach, the party in breach is entitled to restitution for any benefit he has conferred by way of part performance or reliance in excess of the loss he has caused by the breach.

For example, suppose Bob contracts with Manny. Manny agrees to paint Bob's house in exchange for $4,000. Manny paints half of the house and stops. He informs Bob that painting houses is not for him, and he will not complete the project. Manny is entitled to restitution for the benefit he has conferred by way of the partial performance. Suppose Manny's paintjob confers a $2,000 benefit to Bob, and Bob must pay Carl $2,000 to complete the job. Manny may be entitled to $2,000 (the value of the benefit conferred on Bob).

The defaulting party has the burden to prove the net benefit.

J.   Avoidable Consequences and Mitigation of Damages

1)   COMMON LAW

The doctrine of avoidable consequences requires a non-breaching party to make reasonable efforts to avoid and/or mitigate damages that stem from a breaching party's conduct. The doctrine is also sometimes referred to as the Doctrine of Mitigation of Damages. A non-breaching party has a duty to take reasonable efforts to mitigate the harm that results from a breach. Those efforts do not necessarily have to succeed. The non-breaching party may recover from a breaching party those reasonable expenses incurred in mitigating damages. The non-breaching party, however, should not take steps to mitigate damages if doing so will result in other worse types of harm.

K.   Risk of Loss

> Question Key
> 155,156

1)   UCC - SHIPMENT OF GOODS

Under the UCC, a carrier's risk of loss of goods subject to an agreement, is contingent upon whether the parties to the agreement established a "destination contract" or a "shipment contract." If the agreement mandates shipment of the goods by the carrier and lacks any other provisions, then a presumption exists that the agreement constitutes a shipment contract. UCC § 2-503, cmt. 5.

a)   Destination Contract

A destination contract exists when the parties' agreement provides that a seller must deliver the goods to a certain location. In that event, a seller bears the risk of loss until the goods are delivered free on board ("F.O.B.") to a buyer. For example, a contract may provide goods to be delivered "F.O.B. Springfield." The seller would bear the risk of loss until the goods are delivered on board the buyer's carrier in Springfield. If the agreement does not expressly state the delivery location, then it is a shipment contract.

b)   Shipment Contract

A shipment contract exists when the parties' agreement provides that a seller is to ship the goods F.O.B. by a common carrier (e.g., "F.O.B. United States Postal Service"). In that event, a seller bears the risk of loss until the goods are delivered to the carrier. Once the carrier takes possession of the goods, then the buyer is subject to the risk of loss. If the contract provides for the sale of goods "F.O.B." only, then the risk of loss passes at the seller's place of business when the goods are to be delivered.

c)   Destruction of Goods

Goods are identified at the time of a contract's formation when, for example, the parties to the contract agree to the delivery of a particular item. UCC § 2-501. If goods identified when the contract was formed are completely destroyed without the fault of either party prior to when the risk of loss of the goods has shifted to the buyer, the contract is avoided. UCC § 2-613(a). Then each party no longer must perform its respective contractual obligations. Id.

2)   PERSONAL PROPERTY

If a first party requires some specific item of personal property to perform an absolute duty under a contract, the destruction of that item due to no fault of the second party before the contract's performance date will excuse that duty. In that event, the issue arises as to who bears the risk of loss. If none of the parties to a contract are responsible for an item's destruction, then they are all free from liability for its risk of loss. An "act of God," such as a tornado, would be an instance of such a situation. Just those parties responsible for the item's destruction are liable for its risk of loss.

Usually, a contractor who enters into a contract with an owner to repair an existing structure will be discharged from performing the repairs if the building is destroyed without any fault of the contractor. The owner is liable for the risk of losing the structure in the absence of any fault attributable to a party other than the owner.

IX. IMPOSSIBILITY, IMPRACTICABILITY, AND FRUSTRATION OF PURPOSE

The doctrines of Impossibility of Performance, Impracticability, and Frustration of Purpose may apply when a contract does not expressly apportion certain risks among the parties to the contract. Generally, if a contract properly addresses those risks, its provisions will govern instead of these doctrines.

★★   **A.   Impossibility of Performance**

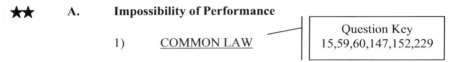

1)   <u>COMMON LAW</u>

Question Key
15,59,60,147,152,229

The common law doctrine of impossibility of performance basically pertains to situations in which a contract cannot be performed on account of certain circumstances beyond the control of the parties.

a)   Impossibility from Facts that Existed Before Formation

When impossibility arises from facts that existed before a contract's formation, but the parties did not know of them, the doctrines of mistake or fraud will apply. A mutual mistake occurs when neither party is aware of the impossibility when they enter into their contract. A fraud occurs when only one party is aware of the impossibility when both parties enter into their contract, and that party fails to disclose the impossibility to the other party.

b)   Impossibility from Facts that Arose After Formation

The Impossibility of Performance doctrine applies if the impossibility results from events or circumstances that occurred after formation of a contract.

(1)   Temporary versus Permanent Impossibility

A party's contractual duty may be discharged by impossibility when an unforeseen event occurs or unexpected circumstances arise that render the duty permanently impossible to perform. For example, suppose Alvin, a professional artist, and Carol, an heiress, enter into a valid contract for him to paint her portrait for a fair price. Before Alvin starts painting Carol's portrait, he is involved in a traffic accident and is killed. Because this agreement for personal services requires Alvin's special, non-delegable artistic ability to perform, its performance would be permanently impossible due to his death. If, however, Alvin suffered only personal injuries in that accident, from which he is expected to recover within a predictable duration, his performance of the contract would be subject only to a temporary impossibility.

The doctrine of temporary impossibility provides that if circumstances render performance impossible only for a limited duration, then an affected party's performance is not excused. That duty is instead suspended.

(2)   Non-Material Condition

If an express condition is not a material part of a contract, and its occurrence becomes impossible due to neither party's fault, then the condition is legally excused. In that event, the intended beneficiary of the condition still must otherwise perform under the contract.

(3)   Objective and Subjective Impossibility

An objective impossibility is a valid basis for nonperformance of a contractual duty, but a subjective impossibility is not. In the former instance, the contemplated performance must be something that literally "cannot be done" by anyone. Examples of objective impossibility include the situation described *supra* involving Alvin's death, as well as the unavailability or destruction of the contract's irreplaceable subject matter. When the subject matter is property, either:

- it must be expressly referenced in a contract; or
- both parties understand that that is the property being used.

Subjective impossibility exists when the performance is something one party asserts that the party cannot accomplish. Examples of subjective impossibility include insolvency and, under some circumstances, illness, and death. An instance of a subjective impossibility arises when a contractor under a construction contract becomes disabled. Although the contractor could no longer fulfill any contractual duties, those duties could be transferred to and fulfilled by a third party. The alleged impossibility was subjective because the contract could have been performed by another party. An impossibility is objective only when the contract could not be performed by anyone, as in the example *supra* of Alvin who died before he could paint Carol's portrait.

B.   Impracticability   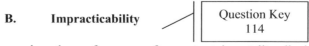 Question Key 114

Sometimes when the performance of a contract is not literally impossible, it may be sufficiently burdensome or extremely difficult in the sense of being, for example, so time-consuming or costly as to render the contract's performance impracticable.

For example, suppose Tony operates a water-well drilling and installation service. Maria purchases a new house located in an arid area. The house is not connected to any municipal water system. Maria and Tony enter into a valid contract by which he agrees to drill and install a water well on her property for a fair price. Before the date scheduled for Tony to perform the contract, it is accurately reported in a reliable government document that the water aquifer below Maria's house has run dry, but that another one over twice as deep underground has been discovered. As a result, Tony's performance of the contract probably would be excused as commercially impracticable because, in light of the newly released official data, it would cost more than twice as much as the price term in the parties' contract for him to perform. Maria and Tony, however, may be able to modify their contract to take into account the increased costs.

1)   COMMON LAW

In order for a contract to be excused under the grounds of impracticability, a party must demonstrate that: 1) an extreme burden has arisen that 2) was not foreseen. The standard is high and, under the common law, is rarely met. It arguably is met, however, in the example *supra* involving Tony and Maria.

The doctrine of temporary impracticability provides that if circumstances render performance impracticable only for a limited duration, then an affected party's performance is not excused. That duty is instead suspended.

2)   UCC

UCC § 2-615(a) provides, in part, that a seller's non-delivery, or a delay in delivery, is excused if "performance as agreed has been made impracticable by the occurrence of a contingency the non-occurrence of which was a basic assumption on which the contract was made." Thus, the UCC utilizes a type of "failure of basic assumptions" test.

UCC § 2-615 does not clearly define the term "basic assumption" for UCC purposes. A basic assumption may be an unforeseeable delay in the delivery of construction materials. A change in market conditions (e.g., mere price fluctuation) generally is not a basic assumption. For example, UCC § 2-615 and UCC § 2-616 enable a farmer to reduce any liability for breach of contract or contracts for the sale of crops by allocating the actually harvested portion of an anticipated crop among the buyers in a fair and reasonable manner after providing them with sufficient notification of the shortfall in the expected amount of the crop.

C.   Frustration of Purpose (or Commercial Frustration)

> Question Key
> 190

Frustration of Purpose occurs when events that occur before the contract's performance result in destroying a party's purpose of entering into the contract, even if performance of the contract is not rendered impossible. For example, suppose a promisee rented his apartment to a promisor for two days. The promisor's known purpose for the rental was to secure a good vantage point from which to observe a monarch's coronation. Because of the coronation's cancellation, the promisor neither occupied the apartment nor paid the promisee. The promisee may not be entitled to recover because frustration of purpose had occurred.

To succeed on a theory of frustration of purpose, a party must demonstrate:

- principal purpose of contract has been frustrated;
- frustration is total (i.e., not partial);
- non-occurrence of the frustrating event in question was a basic assumption on which the contract was entered into;
- frustrating event occurred without the fault of the party; and
- contract does not negate any defenses under the circumstances.

X.   DISCHARGE OF CONTRACTUAL DUTIES

Performance is the most common method of discharging contractual obligations. Other means of discharging contractual obligations that were described earlier include:

- the non-occurrence of a contractual condition;
- rescission of a contract;
- illegality of a contract;
- unconscionability of a contract;
- a public policy violation;
- impossibility of performance;
- impracticability of performance; and
- frustration of purpose.

Other methods of discharging contractual duties include substituted agreement, novation, account stated, accord and satisfaction, and covenant not to sue.

A.   Substituted Agreement

Question Key
200

A substituted agreement discharges a prior agreement between the parties and replaces it with a new agreement. Consequently, any subsequent claims of breach of contract must arise under the parties' new agreement, rather than under the former, replaced agreement. The parties' intent to substitute the agreement is indicated by the degree of the new agreement's formality.

When the new agreement is deemed a modification of a prior agreement, the element of consideration is required by the common law.

Under UCC § 2-209(1), however, consideration is not required to modify a contract for the sale of goods.

UCC § 2-209(1) states that: "An agreement modifying a contract within this article needs no consideration to be binding." If, however, consideration was issued with respect to the modification, it would not invalidate a modification. When the new agreement is subject to the Statute of Frauds, both the common law and UCC 2-209(3) require that the modification be in writing.

★   **B.**   **Novation**

> Question Key
> 128,187

A novation is a type of substitute agreement that replaces at least one of the parties to a prior agreement with a new party. The new party becomes a successor promisor to the original obligee under the subsequent agreement, which releases the predecessor obligor from the prior agreement. A novation may occur in the context of delegable duties when the original obligee accepts the predecessor obligor's delegate as a substitute for the purpose of performing the contract's duties. A novation discharges the original part(ies) that are not a part of the substitute agreement.

    C.   **Account Stated**

The *Restatement* provides that if a debtor receives and holds a creditor's bill for an unreasonably long time and does not contest the bill, the creditor may bring an account stated action against the debtor. The creditor carries the burden of proving that he sent the account, and the debtor did not object to it. The debtor possesses the burden of proving that the bill does not correctly express the parties' contract.

★   **D.**   **Accord and Satisfaction**

> Question Key
> 22,65,94,212

An accord is an agreement to accept substituted performance (e.g., less money). A satisfaction occurs when the substituted performance occurs. A debtor is not discharged from an existing duty until the debtor has performed pursuant to the accord's terms. If the creditor breaches an accord agreement, a debtor may bring an action either for breaching an original contract or for breaching the accord.

        1)   <u>COMMON LAW</u>

A traditional accord and satisfaction occurs when a debtor tries to obligate a creditor to take less than a debt's entire amount in full satisfaction of the debt by writing, in good faith, on a check or in an accompanying letter, "payment in full." A creditor who deposits or cashes such a check is subject to a valid accord and satisfaction if the debt:

- is subject to an honest dispute; or
- is unliquidated (i.e., not definite in amount).

Accordingly, a party cannot catch another party "by surprise" by noting a check for a random bill in full satisfaction unless the parties hold the amount due in an honest dispute (or its amount is not definite). Traditionally, a creditor could reserve its right to obtain a debt's unpaid balance from a debtor by noting on the check that it was processed "under protest." Most states no longer permit such a reservation, and the party accepting the check would be held to have acquiesced in the accord and satisfaction.

2)   UCC – ELIMINATING PROTEST RIGHTS

A majority of states have enacted laws based on UCC § 3-311. It provides that by depositing or cashing a qualifying check, even if the check was noted to be "under protest," a creditor fully discharges a debt. A creditor may, however, preserve its right to obtain a full payment of the debt by returning the debtor's payment within 90 days of receiving it.

E.   **Miscellaneous Discharges**

1)   GENERALLY

A party to most contracts may be discharged from its performance based on:

- impossibility;
- impracticability; or
- frustration of purpose.

If one of the parties to the contract rendered partial performance before such a discharge occurred, a court may allow a recovery of damages for restitution on a quasi-contract basis.

2)   PERSONAL SERVICES

A promisor may be excused from performing a contractual obligation for a promisee under a personal services contract if an absolute duty to perform exists and the following events or circumstances prevent performance:

- disability;
- death;
- illegality; or
- commercial frustration.

Thus, if a promisor becomes disabled or dies before a performance is scheduled under a personal services contract, then the obligation to perform is discharged.

A promisor in a personal services contract cannot be discharged from contractual duties on the basis of its delegation of duties to a delegate, because a promisee entered into the contract based on a significant interest in the promisor's talents and the results they would achieve.

3)   PERSONAL PROPERTY

If a first party requires some specific item of personal property to perform an absolute duty, the destruction of that item due to no fault of the second party before the performance date will discharge that duty.

AMERIBAR BAR REVIEW

Multistate Bar Examination Preparation Course

CRIMINAL LAW

TABLE OF CONTENTS

Criminal Law & Criminal Procedure are treated as one subject on the examination.

INTRODUCTION

A crime is conduct society considers to be, and legally defines as, unlawful and subject to enforcement and punishment pursuant to public law and official process and procedure.

Criminal law in the United States is derived primarily from the common law of England. Modern case law, along with state and federal statutes, build the criminal law upon this foundation. Some of those court decisions and statutory provisions were influenced by, or have followed provisions of, the Model Penal Code (the "MPC"). Approximately half of the states of the United States have adopted some component of the MPC.

I.   HOMICIDE

Homicide is defined as the unlawful killing of a living human being by another human being. Homicide does not include the legally sanctioned killing of a living human being by another human being, such as those that occur in combat during a lawful war.

A.   Intended Killings

The most severe degree of homicide is murder. A murder may result from an accused's intentional deadly conduct toward a living human being. In preparing for the MBE, you should be aware of the treatment of homicide under the common law, as well as under the modern statutory degree modification system.

1)   MURDER

Under the common law, there are three types of homicides: 1) murder; 2) voluntary manslaughter; and 3) involuntary manslaughter (involuntary manslaughter will be detailed in the section addressing unintended killings).

For an exam question testing murder, it is crucial to identify whether the jurisdiction follows the common law or statutory degree system. In many cases, the question will provide the type of jurisdiction involved, or will provide the text of a relevant statute. Be alert when reading these questions. On past questions, the examiners even have provided statutes with text that follows the common law approach instead of the degree system. Therefore, carefully read the fact patterns, as well as any relevant statute, to determine what approach governs in the jurisdiction. For questions indicating a defendant is charged with "murder," without any reference to statutes or degrees, the examiners traditionally have been testing common law murder.

★★★★   a)   Common Law Murder

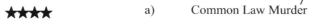

Question Key
15,16,18,19,36,37,51,57,61, 80,101,111,112,118,133, 137,148,154,161,165,169

Under the common law, a murder is defined as the unlawful killing of another human being with malice aforethought. The common law requires proof of these elements to establish that a person committed a murder:

- an act or failure to act if a duty exists;
- malice aforethought;
- causation (legal and actual cause); and
- in certain jurisdictions, the death must occur within a year and a day after the conduct of the accused caused a victim's fatal injury.

(1)   Act or Failure to Act if Duty Exists

The defendant must take some affirmative act or fail to act if a duty to act exists. For example, suppose Billy the Bystander watches Dave the Defendant brutally attack Victor the Victim. David leaves, and Billy sees Victor lying in a pool of blood in great pain. Even if Billy does nothing to help, and Victor dies as a result, Billy is not guilty of murder because he took no affirmative action resulting in Victor's death (unless a duty to act exists, such as when the person needing help is the child or spouse of the bystander). Of course, Dave may be guilty of murder, but not Billy.

★★★★   (2)   Express versus Implied Malice

A defendant is not guilty of common law murder unless he acts with malice aforethought. The malice may be either express or implied from the factual situation surrounding the offense. In most jurisdictions, the concept of malice generally requires a finding that a defendant possessed one or more of the following four of types of mental states or *mens rea*:

- Intent to kill a living human being (or knowledge that defendant's acts would kill a human being);
★★★★ • Intent to inflict serious bodily injury on a living human being (causing death);
- Depraved heart by reckless conduct (i.e., done with knowledge of substantial risk of causing death) that manifests "extreme indifference to the value of human life"; or
- Death that occurs during the commission of an inherently dangerous felony (felony-murder rule). The examiners may omit the felony-murder rule as a basis for common law murder in the text of the question

 These four malice alternatives for common law murder are tested very often. Take the time to learn and understand them. They are the four main ways in which a defendant can be found guilty of common law murder.

★★★   (a)   Depraved Heart Murder

With the exception of depraved heart murder, the intent standards are self-explanatory (e.g., intent to kill or intent to inflict serious bodily harm).

Finding a depraved heart murder requires that an accused possess a *reckless disregard* for human life.

A situation in which an accused encourages a victim to play "Russian Roulette" with a revolver illustrates a wanton and willful disregard of a risk to human life and a depraved heart. Another example would include discharging explosives in a public area without posting warnings that notify people of the danger. The death of a human that results from such conduct would constitute a depraved heart murder. Additionally, shooting a gun into a crowd of people, discharging an automatic weapon into a crowded room, or driving a car at high speeds onto a sidewalk full of people would certainly qualify. However, suppose a person standing in a deserted field shoots a gun into the sky. If the bullet falls to the ground killing a person hiding in an underground ditch, this action probably would not qualify as depraved heart murder because, although the action may be negligent, it does not exhibit a reckless disregard for human life.

The issue of whether a killing qualifies as a depraved heart murder is another commonly tested issue. Read the fact pattern carefully and try to determine whether a substantial risk to human life existed and was disregarded. If so, the defendant may be guilty of murder. If not, the defendant may be guilty of involuntary manslaughter or another crime.

★★   b)   Statutory Degrees

Question Key
9,29,64,155

Some jurisdictions follow the common law rule regarding murder. Other jurisdictions have statutorily modified the rule regarding murder, and classified murder into various degrees. Jurisdictions vary on the number of degrees, but most jurisdictions following the degree approach have two or more degrees of murder.

On the exam, it is unlikely you will have to employ the default degree rules set forth below. This is because, on many questions, the examiners provide the text of the actual rules regarding what type of murder classifies as which degree. Therefore, be sure to carefully read the text of classifications in the question. Default rules regarding the degrees of murder in jurisdictions employing the degree system are as follows:

Questions Generally Testing
Statutory Interpretation
9,10,42,62,81,82,90,155

(1)   First & Second Degree Murder

As a default, most murders will be classified as second degree murder. If, however, one of a few alternative circumstances exists, the murder will be classified as first degree murder.

(a)   Premeditation & Deliberation

If the murder is committed with *premeditation and deliberation*, it will be classified as first degree murder. Premeditation & deliberation exist when an accused takes time to reflect, to some extent, on the thought of the killing.

★★   (i)   Duration of Premeditation

The law does not require that either premeditation or deliberation must exist for a specific duration. A determination of whether an accused acted with either premeditation or deliberation will depend upon an analysis of all the factual circumstances surrounding the occurrence of a homicide. The focus of that analysis should be upon the duration between when an accused formed the intent to commit the act and when the act occurred. The greater the length of that time period, the more likely it is that the accused acted with premeditation and deliberation.

(ii)   Intoxication

If the defendant is intoxicated, the intoxication may work to negate the finding of premeditation required for first degree murder. However, intoxication generally will not reduce second degree murder to manslaughter because of the different intent required for second degree murder.

★   (b)   Felony Murder

In many jurisdictions, if the murder is committed during the perpetration of a dangerous felony, it will be classified as first degree murder. Dangerous felonies include arson, burglary, kidnapping, rape, and robbery. Be careful on the exam, however, because past questions have provided statutes under which felony murder was listed as second degree murder.

(c)   Other Statutory Circumstances

Some jurisdictions provide additional circumstances under which murder may be classified as first degree murder. For example, the murder of certain types of individuals may qualify. On any exam question, carefully read any applicable provided statute to ascertain if any other types of homicide qualify as first degree murder.

★★ | Question Key
121 (also often tested in
questions testing murder) | (2)   Voluntary Manslaughter

Voluntary manslaughter is a lesser degree of homicide that includes an element of provocation in addition to the requisite element of intent for homicide. The intent for homicide usually consists of intent to kill, or intent to do serious bodily injury, or a recklessly depraved heart. Provocation serves to mitigate the level of intent and severity of the homicide offense when the following elements are satisfied:

- A victim provoked an accused;
- The accused intentionally killed the victim;
- During the accused's heat of passion;
- The heat of passion would have overcome a reasonable person;
- No time transpired in which the accused could have reduced the passion.

(a)   Heat of Passion

"Heat of passion" is a reasonably induced emotional disturbance. The following situations may give rise to an accused's experiencing a "heat of passion" provoking a homicide: (1) assault or battery; (2) an illegal arrest; (3) adultery; (4) threats; (5) injuries to third parties; and (6) any other circumstance of a legally sufficient nature.

(b)   Cooling Off Period

Even if an accused actually experiences sufficient provocation, it must occur concurrently with the criminal act. The provocation defense will not succeed if a reasonable person would have cooled off between when he experienced the provocation and when he subsequently committed the homicide.

B.   Unintended Killings

Involuntary manslaughter is an unintended killing of a living human being. It is a lesser degree of homicide because it does not require that an accused possess a specific level of intent to kill another human being. It instead involves a reckless or careless type of criminal negligence.

★★   1)   INVOLUNTARY MANSLAUGHTER

a)   Intent to Injure

Question Key
22,63,82,95,102,143

Unlawful act manslaughter occurs when an accused kills a victim in the course of an unlawful act that does not constitute a felony. Such an unlawful act typically occurs when the accused intends only to inflict injury (but not serious bodily injury) upon a human being, but the human being dies as a consequence of the injury. For example, suppose an accused punches a human being, who dies from that injury because the punch happened to impact him in a vulnerable part of the body. The accused may be guilty of involuntary manslaughter.

b)   Reckless and Negligent Killings

(1)   Lawful Act

Criminal-negligence manslaughter occurs when an accused kills a human being in the course of a lawful act, because of the accused's failure to use due caution and circumspection.

The standard is not the same as the standard required for civil negligence. In order to be criminally liable, the accused must act with a high degree of risk of death or serious injury. Moreover, the defendant must be conscious that he has created the risk.

(2)   Omission to Act

(a)   General

An accused may be found liable for an omission only if the law imposes a duty to act upon the accused. Additionally, if the accused creates circumstances that endanger a person, the accused possesses a legal duty to help the person. Such a legal duty may arise from the following sources:

- public law, such as a statute or ordinance;
- private law, such as a contract or deed; or a
- significant relationship between a victim and an accused (e.g., parent-child, husband-wife).

(i)   Parent and Child

An omission, such as a parent's failure to furnish medical attention to an ill child, may constitute criminal negligence or recklessness based on the parent's duty of care. The test is:

- did an accused have a legal duty to act to assist an injured victim; and
- but for the accused's failure to do that, would the victim have survived?

c)   Misdemeanor-Manslaughter

(1)   Common Law Elements

An accused that causes the unintended death of a human being while attempting to commit a misdemeanor, committing a misdemeanor, or as the result of committing a misdemeanor, is criminally liable for that death:

- if the misdemeanor was inherently dangerous to life;
- if the death naturally and probably resulted from the misdemeanor; and
- if the misdemeanor was independent of the death.

(a)   *Malum in Se* versus *Malum Prohibitum*

The misdemeanor-manslaughter rule's application is limited to misdemeanors that are inherently wrong, or *malum in se* offenses. Examples of such misdemeanors are assault and battery.

The misdemeanor manslaughter rule does not apply to a *malum prohibitum* offense, which only is illegal because a legislature made it illegal. Examples of *malum prohibitum* offenses are ordinance violations and traffic offenses.

(b)   Prosecution's Burden of Proof

If the prosecution fails to establish the underlying *malum in se* manslaughter, then the accused cannot be liable for that misdemeanor or the related homicide. Even if an accused is not aware of the entire risk of his criminal conduct, the accused will be liable for the full extent of its outcome.

★★   2)   <u>FELONY-MURDER</u>

Question Key
2,32,43,49,125

a)   Common Law

The common law felony-murder doctrine renders an accused who has committed a felony criminally liable for any unintended killing of a living human being that result from the accused's dangerous and felonious misconduct. If the prosecution fails to establish the underlying inherently dangerous felony, then the accused cannot be liable for that felony or for the related murder.

(1)   Testable Elements

An accused is criminally liable for an unintended death of a living human being while attempting to commit a felony, committing a felony, or as a result of committing a felony if: 1) the felony is inherently dangerous to life; 2) the death naturally and probably results from the felony; and 3) the felony is independent of the death.

•   Inherently Dangerous Felonies

Inherently dangerous felonies include rape, robbery, arson, kidnapping, and burglary. However, many states have added additional qualifying offenses by statute. The inherently dangerous requirement is a quasi-foreseeability requirement. If a felony is inherently dangerous, then a potential death would be foreseeable.

•   Natural and Probable Result

An intervening or superseding cause would break the chain of causation and limit criminal liability for the homicide.

•   Felony Must Be Independent of Death

The felony must be independent of the death. For example, the felony of aggravated assault that results in the death of the victim is not independent of the death.

(2)   Places of Temporary Safety

If the defendant flees from the place of the felony and reaches a place of temporary safety, the felon will not be liable for subsequent deaths.

(3)   Death of Co-Felons

In most states, one felon will not be criminally liable for the death of a co-felon through the felony murder rule.

(4)   The Death Penalty and Felony Murder

There is no flat prohibition against the imposition of the death penalty for felony murder. The Supreme Court has held that the death penalty generally may not be imposed on a person who did not kill, attempt to kill, or intend that a killing take place. However, the death penalty may be imposed on someone who was a major participant in the underlying felony and acted with reckless indifference to human life.

b)   Statutory Modifications

Certain felony-murder statutes often specify and limit the types of felonies to which their provisions apply. The most commonly listed felonies are arson, rape, kidnapping, robbery, and burglary, which usually are likely to result in considerable violence. An exam question also may include a felony-murder statute with specific provisions contrary to those of a majority of jurisdictions.

II.   OTHER CRIMES

A.   Theft

1)   GENERAL

Theft is a category of common law offenses involving an accused's unlawful taking of another person's property. The Model Penal Code, and some states, combine many of the originally separate common law offenses under the one topic of theft, including the offenses of larceny, embezzlement, and false pretenses. On the MBE, however, the different classic theft crimes are often tested.

Question Key
17,45,46,58,89,97,98,103,108,
115,116,127,140,162

★★★★   2)   LARCENY

Larceny is defined as the taking and carrying away of the personal property of another with the intent to steal the property. It generally involves a trespass by an accused against personal property in the possession of a victim by intentionally physically taking the property, either directly with the accused's body, or indirectly when the accused uses an item or another person to take the property. Note that the victim does not need to own the property, just be in possession of it. Larceny is distinguished from robbery because it does not involve a use of force.

★★★   a)   Elements

Proof of the following elements, even with circumstantial evidence, is required to establish the offense of larceny:

- trespassory taking and carrying away of
- personal property of another
- with the intent to steal the property

The two most heavily tested elements of the larceny offense are the taking and intent requirements.

★★   (1)   Trespassory Taking and Carrying Away

The accused must take and carry away the property in a trespassory manner. Therefore, if the victim consents to giving the property, there is no trespass and, consequently, no larceny. The taking requirement is satisfied when the accused exercises dominion over the property, such as by taking possession of it. The carrying away requirement is satisfied by even the slightest movement of the property.

For example, if a thief picks up another person's ring off the floor, even for only a second, with the intent of stealing it, a larceny has been committed. Exam questions often test the duration or distance of the carrying away requirement. Remember, even a slight duration or distance is sufficient.

★★★   (2)   Intent to Steal

The intent to steal element requires that the accused intend to deprive the owner of the property permanently or for an unreasonable length of time. Alternatively, if the accused acts in a manner making the recovery of the property unlikely, then the intent requirement is satisfied. For example, a person may be guilty of larceny if he trespassorily takes another's car and drives it across the country (unreasonable length of time). However, the same person may not be guilty of larceny if he intends to drive it across town and back.

Defenses to the element of intent include an accused's:

- intent to return the property without creating risk of loss;
- belief of his own or another's claim of right to the property (even a belief that nobody owns the property may be sufficient);
- attempt to satisfy a claim or collect a debt.
- other defenses that negate the required intent, such as insanity, mistake of fact or law, intoxication, and others.

                                      b)   Larceny by Trick

A similar and related offense, larceny by trick, applies when an accused:

- acquires possession of a victim's property through lies;
- intends to fraudulently convert the property; and
- does fraudulently convert the property.

                                      (1)   Reliance on Falsehood

An accused must know that a victim relied on a false statement when the victim transferred the property to the accused.

(2)   Exception for Mistaken Opinion

The accused is not culpable if he made a statement of mistaken opinion to a victim, rather than a false representation.

★★   (3)   Possession not Title

For a person to be guilty of larceny by trick, the person must acquire possession, not necessarily title, to the property. If the person obtains title, he may be guilty of false pretenses.

(4)   Conversion

For a person to be guilty of larceny by trick, he must, at the time of acquiring the property, intend to convert the property. Additionally, the person must actually subsequently convert the property. Keep in mind, however, that the conversion requirement does not mean the accused actually must abide by any formalities. The accused only must seriously interfere with the owner's rights to the property in order to convert it. In one question, for example, it was sufficient that the accused drove another person's car for two days without the intent to return it. However, merely intending to drive it down the block and back would not be an act of serious interference.

3)   <u>EMBEZZLEMENT</u> ———| Question Key
                                                        5,8,103,104,108,140

a)   Common Law Elements

Proof of the following elements is required to establish an embezzlement offense:

- Intent: An accused must specifically intend to take possession;
- Lawful Possession: The accused is entrusted with an owner's property;
- Fiduciary Relationship: Exists between the accused and the owner;
- Conversion: The accused fraudulently converts the property; and
- Interference: The accused interfered with the owner's rights.

This offense may arise in a factual context involving an employer and an employee.

b)   Common Law Defenses

Defenses to the element of conversion, include an accused's intent to: return the property; provide an equivalent of the property; collect a debt; or exercise a claim of right to the property.

4)   <u>FALSE PRETENSES</u>

Question Key
30,45,103,108,122

a)   Common Law Elements

Proof of the following elements is required to establish the false pretense offense:

- Misrepresentation: An accused makes a false representation of a fact, which the victim actually believes to be true;
- Obtaining Title to Personal Property: Title to the personal property or chattel must pass to the accused;
- Scienter: The accused knew his representation was false; and
- Intent to Defraud: The accused intended to defraud the victim. An accused does not intend to defraud if he: 1) believes the property is his own; 2) intends to return the property within a reasonable time; or 3) obtains the property in satisfaction of a debt he honestly believes the victim owes him.

(1)   Invalid Defenses to False Pretenses

The following claims are not valid defenses to false pretenses:

- The victim did not sustain a monetary loss.
- The victim engaged in illegal conduct.
- The victim acted in a gullible manner.

                      (2)   Difference between Larceny and False Pretenses

A defendant commits larceny when he obtains possession of the property of another. A defendant commits false pretenses when he obtains title to the property of another. If a person steals money and intends to keep it, he is obtaining title to the money. Therefore, he is guilty of false pretenses.

5)   <u>FORGERY</u>

Question Key
151

a)   Common Law Elements

Proof of the following elements is required to establish a forgery offense:

- Intent: An accused intends to defraud a victim, even if no victim is defrauded;
- Writing: An accused creates a writing or alters (i.e., materially changes) an apparently valid writing; and

- Apparent legal significance: The writing, if authentic in whole or in part, could have legal effect by establishing a legal right, duty, or liability.

For example, suppose Erin crafts a letter on very old paper. She includes details that would lead a knowledgeable reader to believe the letter had been written by Thomas Edison to a friend. Using a sophisticated software program, Erin makes the signature and other writing on the letter almost identical to Edison's. She knew the letter would attract the attention of Edison memorabilia collectors worldwide. Almost immediately, she was contacted about selling the letter. As she had anticipated, a collector paid her $10,000 for the letter. Did Erin commit forgery?

Erin intended to, and did ultimately defraud, the collector who purchased the letter. However, even if the letter was authentic, it lacked any legal effect because it did not establish a legal right, duty, or liability. Thus, under these facts, Erin is not guilty of forgery (although she may be guilty of another crime).

B.   Receiving Stolen Goods

> Question Key
> 12

A person is guilty of receiving stolen property if he receives the personal property of another knowing it has been stolen. The elements for receiving stolen goods are:

- an accused receives personal property;
- a thief stole the property from its true owner;
- the accused knows the property was stolen; and
- the accused intends to permanently deprive the owner of the property.

The element of intent to deprive is not fulfilled if an accused acts based on a claim of right that the item belonged to him. Therefore, it is a defense that the property was received with purpose to restore it to the owner. "Receiving" means acquiring possession, control, or title to the property.

Property that was once stolen but has been restored to its true owner or to the police is no longer stolen property. Therefore, if a thief works with the police to sell once stolen property to a third party, the third party will not be guilty of receiving stolen property because the property has lost its characterization as stolen.

C.   Robbery

> Question Key
> 41,67,68,74,92,97,98,124,139

★★   1)   <u>ELEMENTS & DEFINITION</u>

Robbery is a felony under the common law and modern statutes. It consists of the elements of larceny and adds the additional requirement of a use of force. The force does not necessarily need to be employed or be truly effective to fulfill that element. For example, an accused's use of a fake weapon that resembles a real weapon may constitute a use of force if a victim reasonably believed the gun was real.

Proof of the following elements is required to establish the offense of robbery:

- Taking: The trespassory taking and carrying away;
- Personal Property: Of the personal property of another;
- Intent to Steal: With the intent to steal the property.
- Force: Without any consent and using violence, intimidation, or force. The victim must subjectively feel threatened.

2)   CLAIM OF RIGHT

The element of intent to deprive is not fulfilled if an accused acts based on a claim of right that the item belonged to him.

3)   AGGRAVATED ROBBERY

Aggravated or armed robbery is a modern statutory offense that requires an accused to have committed robbery using a dangerous weapon.

★★★ **D.   Burglary**

Question Key
17,46,90,120,127,134,163,166

1)   ELEMENTS

Common law burglary is defined as the breaking and entering of the dwelling of another at night with the intent to commit a felony inside. Thus, proof of the following elements is required to establish the offense of burglary:

- Breaking

A forceful entry is not required. However, the defendant must open a door, a window, or create some other opening. Under the common law, if the accused walks through a door left open by the occupant, a breaking does not occur.

- Entering

The defendant must physically place his body, some part of his body, or an instrument (in order to further the felonious intent) into the dwelling.

- Dwelling of Another

Only a dwelling or a building used for sleeping can be the subject to a common law burglary claim (and it must be a dwelling of another person, not the accused).

- Nighttime

At common law, a burglary could occur only at night.

- Intent to Commit Felony

The accused specifically must intend, at the time of entry, to commit a felony in the dwelling. Entering without such an intent, and later forming the intent is not sufficient. Also, not actually committing the felony is no defense. All that is required is that the person enters with the intent to commit a felony.

 Every element of the common law burglary rule is easily tested. However, many questions define burglary in the jurisdiction, and generally omit the nighttime, dwelling, or some other requirement. Read the question and any pertinent statute carefully.

2) AGGRAVATED BURGLARY

Modern statutes provide for an aggravated burglary offense that includes various degrees of the offense depending upon its seriousness, based on certain factors of culpability.

E.	**Assault and Battery**	Question Key 56

Under the common law, assault and battery are two separate crimes. However, on some exam questions, and in some jurisdictions, the phrase "assault and battery" actually may refer only to the common law crime of battery. Because assault and battery are also tested as separate offenses, it is important to distinguish between the two crimes. As a general matter, battery requires a physical contact, but assault, by definition, requires an absence of contact. Therefore, an assault may become a battery upon physical contact with the victim.

1) ASSAULT

There are two separate rules that would qualify an action as an assault.

a) Attempt to Commit Battery

First, an attempted battery qualifies as an assault. Therefore, if a person specifically attempts to cause a battery, but fails to cause contact, he may be guilty of assault.

b) Reasonable Apprehension

Second, if a first person intends to place another person in a reasonable apprehension of imminent physical harm, even if the first person does not intend to touch the other person, the first person may be guilty of an assault. Under this rule, the accused need not actually intend to commit a battery. However, an accused needs to have taken an overt act against the victim to cause a fear of injury. Words alone, such as rude or suggestive terms, are insufficient.

 On the exam, in the absence of a specific direction, either approach can be used to establish assault. However, some questions may specifically state that the jurisdiction follows one or the other approach.

c)   Conduct of Assault

The following types of conduct may constitute an assault:

- an intentional scaring of another person;
- an assault that involves a conditional threat; and
- an assault that involves intent to commit a worse offense like robbing, raping, or killing.

One example of an assault is when an accused targets a toy gun at a victim's head with the intent to make and, in fact, making the victim believe the gun is real and that a shooting may occur.

2)   BATTERY

a)   Definition & Elements

Battery involves an unlawful use of physical force upon another person resulting in a physical injury or a harmful touching. Battery is distinguished from assault by its requirement that a victim suffer an offensive physical touching or a harmful injury.

Proof of the following elements is required to prove the offense of battery:

- Conduct: An accused engaged in an intentional act or failure to act if a duty exists;
- State of Mind: The accused intends to injure a human being or engages in criminal negligence; and
- Harmful Result: A victim suffers an offensive touching or a bodily injury.

b)   Aggravated Battery

Common statutes provide for aggravated battery arising from additional factors, such as the use of weapons or the protected status of a victim, such as a law enforcement officer.

c)   Consent

A defense to the offense of battery is a victim's consent to the touching. An example of such consent is an alleged battery that occurs during a contact sport, such as ice hockey (assuming the act is normal for the sport and does not exceed the consent).

F.   **Rape - Statutory Rape** ─── Question Key 21,168

1)   RAPE

★   a)   Definition & Elements

Common law rape is established by evidence of the following:

- A male gains carnal knowledge (sexual intercourse including vaginal penetration) of a female victim;
- The accused is not married to the victim;
- The accused obtains the knowledge forcibly, by coercion, or without consent.

The common law definition of carnal knowledge is sexual intercourse between a male and a female. The common law requires that the male's sexual organ penetrate the female's sexual organ.

 The law regarding rape has changed in many jurisdictions. For example, under modern statutes, rape may be committed by both males and females, the marital exception has been eliminated, and other acts, such as oral or anal penetration, also qualify as rape. Because of the limited applicability of the common law doctrine, it is likely that a question testing rape will provide the pertinent statute in the jurisdiction.

b)   Consent Defense

Because rape is a general intent offense, an accused may be acquitted on the basis of a reasonable and genuine belief that the victim consented to the offense.

2)   STATUTORY RAPE

               a)   General

Statutory rape is a strict liability offense based on the ages of the victim.

Statutory rape laws usually, at a minimum, criminalize an adult male's conduct of engaging in sexual intercourse with a minor female. Some statutory rape laws allow either gender to be an accused or be a minor victim. Many states have criminal sexual conduct statutes that include and define all types of sexual misconduct between either or both genders, adults, and minors.

b)   Elements

The general elements of statutory rape include:

- Sexual intercourse between an adult and;
- A minor who has not reached the age of consent;
- Regardless of whether the minor participated willingly or consented to the intercourse.

As a strict liability crime, the accused need not be aware of the fact that the person is a minor. The liability is termed strict liability because defendants may be convicted even though they were genuinely unaware of one or more factors that made their acts or omissions criminal (such as the age of the sexual partner). An accused, therefore, may not be culpable in the traditional sense of possessing criminal *mens rea*.

c) Defenses

Statutory rape is a strict liability crime. Therefore, defenses to statutory rape, such as how old the victim looked or claimed to be, are unavailable to the accused. Also, the statutory rape laws do not allow a defense of whether the minor consented to the alleged offense. Moreover, the law considers the following factors irrelevant: (1) The extent of the minor's sexual experience; and (2) The minor's initiation of sexual activity.

G.   Kidnapping

Question Key
23

★   1)   ELEMENTS

Proof of seizure and transportation are required to establish a simple kidnapping:

- Seizure: An accused must confine and detain a victim for duration; and
- Transportation: The accused must transport the victim for some distance.

a) Related Offenses

Although a showing of a use of force or a ransom demand is not required to prove a kidnapping offense, it may be considered as a factor of an aggravated kidnapping.

The difference between kidnapping and false imprisonment is that kidnapping requires the movement of a victim, while false imprisonment involves the confinement of a victim.

Question Key
2,10,55,134

H.   Arson

★★   1)   ELEMENTS

The common law defines arson as the malicious burning of another's dwelling.

a) Malice

The malicious element is satisfied if an accused:

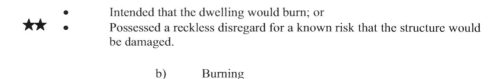

- Intended that the dwelling would burn; or
- Possessed a reckless disregard for a known risk that the structure would be damaged.

b) Burning

The burning element is not limited to setting a fire. The element is satisfied only by actual combustion or "charring" of the material that comprises the dwelling. Any amount of burning is sufficient, so no percentage of the dwelling needs to have been destroyed. The cause of the burning is irrelevant.

c)   Dwelling

Under the common law, only a dwelling may be subject to the crime of arson.

d)   Of Another

Under the common law, a person would be convicted of arson only if the dwelling belonged to somebody besides the accused. Therefore, the common law definition of arson does not include a homeowner's conduct of burning his own home to collect on a homeowner's insurance policy.

★★   e)   Modern Modifications

Modern statutes have made the crime of arson applicable to any building, not just a dwelling. Additionally, a person could be guilty of burning his own building, eliminating the requirement that the dwelling be owned by someone else. In these jurisdictions, arson is defined as maliciously burning property for an improper purpose. Some jurisdictions also have added an alternative negligence standard for arson, such as when a person discards a lit cigarette in a forest.

The modern approach is now the most commonly accepted approach to arson. Therefore, the Examiners can and do test both the common law elements and the potential modern modifications. As with most questions, watch for a statute that defines the crime.

I.   Trespass   ⟋ | Question Key
46 |

An accused commits a criminal trespass upon a victim's real property by: 1) loitering, prowling, or wandering, 2) on the property of another, and 3) without permission. Trespass may be either direct, with the accused's body, or indirect, when the accused causes an item or another person to enter upon the property. Although trespass usually is considered a tort under civil law, it may be a criminal offense under statutory law. However, it is not a crime in all jurisdictions.

J.   Bigamy

Bigamy is a strict liability crime. A person is guilty of bigamy if he marries somebody while being married to someone else.

III.   INCHOATE CRIMES AND PARTIES TO CRIMES

A.   Inchoate Crimes

Attempt, solicitation, and conspiracy are inchoate crimes.   Inchoate crimes are preparatory offenses. A charge cannot be brought for the inchoate crime alone, such as for "attempt" or "conspiracy". An inchoate crime involves another crime. For example, a person may be charged with attempted murder, or conspiracy to commit robbery.

★★   1)   <u>ATTEMPT</u>

Question Key
19,33,41,113,131,138,140,164

An accused may be guilty of attempting to commit a crime. Attempts may consist of taking preliminary steps for the commission of a crime without actually committing the crime. For example, a person may be guilty of attempting to commit burglary, robbery, larceny, as well as other statutory and common law crimes. However, no criminal liability can exist for an attempt to commit an attempt.

★★   a)   Elements

As a general rule, proof of intent and proof of an act are required to establish an attempt to commit a crime.

- Intent

A person guilty of attempt must possess the specific intent to commit a crime. Thus, the intent element generally prevents an imposition of culpability for attempt with respect to criminal offenses that arise from recklessness or negligence. Accordingly, an accused may not be criminally liable for attempting to commit a strict liability offense, because that type of offense does not require a showing of intent.

- Act

Under the common law approach, a person guilty of attempt to commit a crime must commit an act in furtherance of the crime beyond mere preparation. How far beyond mere preparation is the source of some confusion among jurisdictions and commentators. Some states provide that any act in furtherance of the commission of the crime is enough. Others require that the defendant become close to committing the crime (how close, again, differs from jurisdiction to jurisdiction). Perhaps the most commonly accepted modern approach is the test found in the Model Penal Code. Under the MPC, the defendant must take a *substantial step* toward the commission of the crime. Even though the MPC approach may be more widely accepted, the common law standard requiring "more than just mere preparation" is still tested.

★   b)   Model Penal Code's "Substantial Step" Test

The Model Penal Code altered the common law requirement that the defendant commit an act beyond mere preparation. Under the MPC, the defendant is guilty if he commits a substantial step toward the commission of the crime.

              c)   Defenses to Attempt

★★   (1)   Impossibility

Factual impossibility generally is not a valid common law defense. It exists when an accused's intentional conduct, which would otherwise constitute a crime, fails because of circumstances outside of the accused's control. Factual impossibility is not a valid defense to the offense of attempt. For example, if a person attempts to commit larceny of a watch, it is no defense that the watch was not in its usual place, thus making the larceny impossible. Also, it is no defense to the crime of attempting to purchase illegal narcotics that the substance purchased is not actually an illegal narcotic.

Legal impossibility is usually a viable defense under the common law. It occurs when an accused intentionally engages in conduct based on a mistaken belief that such conduct constitutes an offense. If the conduct is legal, then the accused cannot be criminally liable for it. For example, suppose Adam believes it is illegal to sell a prescription-strength drug in his state. He sells the drug to Arnie, a friend and acquaintance. Although Adam is not aware of it, last week, the state legislature altered the prescription requirement, making the drug available to be sold without any regulation. Due to legal impossibility, Adam would not be guilty of attempting to sell a controlled substance.

★   (2)   Abandonment

The defense of abandonment is not a valid defense under the common law of attempt (which is what applies by default on the exam). The rationale behind denying this defense is that the crime is complete upon the creation of the intent and the act and, therefore, abandonment comes too late. The modern trend in some states, and under the Model Penal Code, is that the defense of voluntary abandonment is available if an accused has voluntarily and completely renounced his purpose to commit a crime. Abandonment does not exist if it results from a third party's interference, a victim's resistance, or other circumstances that make the accused believe success is unlikely. Abandonment applies with respect to both principal and accessory liability.

★★★   2)   <u>CONSPIRACY</u>

               a)   Elements

Question Key
56,70,91,94,115,116,117,133,168

A conspiracy exists when more than one person agree to, and intend the commission of, an illegal act or a legal act by illegal means.

The elements of agreement and intent must be established to prove the existence of a conspiracy.

               (1)   Agreement

★★★   (a)   Common Law Requires Plurality

In order for a conspiracy to exist, there must be an agreement by two or more people to complete an unlawful act or lawful act by unlawful means. This is referred to as "plurality of agreement." The plurality element is heavily tested. Under the common law approach relevant on the exam, *two guilty people* must agree. Therefore, under the common law, a person will not be guilty of conspiring with an undercover police officer, who does not intend to commit the crime, or a good samaritan who intends to report the action to the police.

- Wharton's Rule

Under Wharton's Rule, an agreement by two people to commit a particular crime cannot be prosecuted as a conspiracy when the crime is of such a nature as to necessarily require the participation of two persons for its commission, such as adultery.

- Conspiracy with Protected People

A person will not be guilty of a conspiracy to commit a crime if the agreement is made only with a person who is protected by the crime. For example, a person convicted of statutory rape will not be guilty of conspiracy to commit statutory rape if the victim consented to the sexual intercourse.

★★   • Effect of Acquittal of Co-Conspirators

Under the common law approach, if all of the alleged co-conspirators have been acquitted of the conspiracy charge, a remaining lone defendant cannot be convicted of conspiracy.

★★   • Commission of Underlying Crimes

A conspirator does not need to be present at the commission of every crime that is the object of a conspiracy (such as a series of robberies).

★★   (b)   MPC

The MPC presents the "unilateral theory" of conspiracy, which requires an agreement to commit a crime between an accused and someone else in order to establish a conspiracy. Unlike the common law, the accused would be guilty of conspiracy to commit a crime even if the other person did not, in fact, agree to commit a crime (such as an undercover police officer).

(2)   Intent

A defendant must intend to complete an unlawful act or a lawful act by unlawful means.

(3)   Overt Act

Unlike the common law, some statutes require a third element to prove conspiracy. Under these statutes, the third requirement is that there must be an overt act performed in furtherance of the conspiracy. This requirement may be fulfilled by the conduct of only one of the co-conspirators. The overt act that is required is less than that required for attempt. Mere preparation will generally be sufficient.

★★★   b)   Liability for Co-Conspirator Crimes

A conspirator may be held liable for criminal offenses committed by a co-conspirator if those offenses are: 1) in furtherance of the conspiracy, and 2) reasonably foreseeable as a necessary or natural consequence of the conspiracy. The conspirator need not even be present during the commission of the crime if it satisfies this two-prong test.

★★   c)   Withdrawal

If a person withdraws from a conspiracy, he is no longer vicariously liable for the co-conspirators' subsequent criminal conduct in carrying out the conspiracy. Withdrawal will be effective only if the withdrawing person takes affirmative steps to notify the co-conspirators of the withdrawal in time for them to abandon the object of the conspiracy. Although the withdrawing party may not be liable for subsequent crimes of co-conspirators, withdrawal from the conspiracy does not eliminate the person's criminal liability for the conspiracy itself. Once the elements of conspiracy are established, the offense of conspiracy is complete, and withdrawal will have no impact.

★   3)   SOLICITATION

Question Key
3,4,147

★   a)   Elements

Solicitation is an inchoate offense. A solicitation consists of demanding, encouraging, insisting, or advising that someone else perform an illegal act on behalf of the accused. The accused must have been actively involved in facilitating the crime.

The elements of intent and the act must be established in order to prove the offense of solicitation.

• Intent: An accused possesses the intent that another person commit a crime;
• Act: The accused asks or directs the other person to commit the crime.

The accused may be found criminally liable for solicitation even if the other (solicited) person neither:

• agrees to perpetrate the crime; nor
• responds to the solicitation.

If the intent is present, the crime is complete upon the happening of the act.

★   b)   Vicarious Liability

The offense that is solicited does not need to be committed by the other person in order for the accused to be criminally liable for solicitation. If the solicited offense is committed by the other person, then the solicitor will be criminally liable for the ultimate offense.

          c)   Defenses

There is no clear common law rule on whether renunciation of the solicitation is enough to limit liability of the solicitor. By statute, however, jurisdictions have adopted varying approaches.

          d)   MPC

             (1)   Rule

Under MPC § 5.02, a solicitation occurs when an accused requests that another person commit an offense. The solicitation is punishable to the same extent as the solicited offense.

             (2)   Defense

The MPC provides that it is a defense to criminal liability for solicitation if an accused voluntarily renounces the criminal purpose that the accused asked the other person to perform.

★★★ **B.**   **Parties to Crimes**

> Question Key
> 3,4,5,40,87,99,100,107,126,132,159

        1)   <u>COMMON LAW</u>

Under the common law, parties to a crime are classified as principals and accessories.

★★   a)   Principals

A principal in the first degree is a person who engages in the act constituting the offense. Under the common law, a principal in the second degree is a person who aids a principal in the first degree during the commission of an offense, and is actually present at the scene of the crime. Under the modern approach, principals in the second degree are classified as accessories to the crime.

★★   b)   Accessories

Accessories (also called accomplices), are people who aid a principal in perpetrating an offense, by conduct such as planning, participation, or evasion of apprehension. The test of an accomplice's criminal liability is:

- Intent - Did an accessory have the intent to encourage or assist a principal in perpetrating an offense? and

- Assist - Did the accessory encourage or assist the principal in perpetrating the offense? and
- Crime - Did the principal actually perpetrate the offense charged?

If the three prongs are met, then the accessory may be criminally liable for the offense committed by the principal.

(1)   Accessories Before & After the Fact

An accessory before the fact encourages, supports, assists, abets, aids, or facilitates the commission of the offense. An accessory after the fact knowingly aids a principal who perpetrated a felony, to prevent or hinder the principal's capture, prosecution, or conviction by the lawful authorities. This distinction is critical. An accessory after the fact is not criminally liable for the actual substantive offense, but for another, less serious crime of being an accessory after the fact.

c)   Modern Developments

Under the modern approach to accomplice liability, which is most likely to be tested on the exam, the actors to a crime are classified principals and accomplices. Second degree principals under the common law are now classified as accomplices. All accomplices can be liable for the substantive offense, except that accomplices after the fact cannot be convicted of the offense committed by the principal. They can, however, be convicted of a lesser crime.

d)   Extent of Vicarious Liability

An accomplice may be held vicariously criminally liable for a principal's completed crime. Such derivative liability applies only when an accomplice could be culpable if a principal was actually convicted of an offense. Even if an accomplice is not aware of the entire risk of an accused criminal conduct, the accomplice will be liable for the full extent of its outcome.

(1)   Innocent Instrumentality

The innocent instrumentality doctrine provides a defense to criminal liability for accessories that are insane or for children and who were coerced into aiding a principal.

(2)   Natural   and   Probable   Consequences
            Doctrine

The natural and probable consequences doctrine provides that an accessory may not be prosecuted merely for the planned offense. It provides that an accessory also is liable for all offenses that were a natural and probable consequence of the planned offense for which the accessory provided aid. However, if a bystander or the police cause the death of a co-accused of an accused, the accused may not be held liable for that death under the natural and probable consequences doctrine.

IV.   GENERAL PRINCIPLES

To prove an accused's liability for a criminal offense, the common law requires the prosecution to establish, at a minimum, that the accused possessed the requisite mental state (*mens rea*) and committed a legally prohibited act (*actus rea*). Sufficient proof of those two prerequisites, as well as any other elements of an offense, may establish the accused's responsibility for the crime.

The prosecution may impose responsibility for a criminal offense only by carrying the burden of proof at trial. A trial court cannot impose a burden of proof upon an accused or shift that burden to an accused. However, the burden of proof regarding an affirmative defense, but not an element of the crime, may be shifted to the defendant.

★★   •   Reasonable Doubt Standard

The United States Supreme Court declared in *Patterson v. New York*, 432 U.S. 197 (1977), and *In re Winship*, 397 U.S. 358 (1975), that the *Constitution* obligates the prosecution to establish every element of a criminal offense beyond a reasonable doubt.

A.   Acts and Omissions

1)   COMMON LAW

a)   Acts

An *actus reus* is a prohibited criminal act. A criminal act must meet the following criteria:

- It constitutes a crime when it occurs;
- It occurs voluntarily; and
- It causes a prohibited result.

b)   Omissions

(1)   Moral Duty

An accused's failure to act when a moral duty exists does not give rise to any criminal liability. For example, suppose Fisherman is fishing on the Franklin Pier when a child, who is playing alone on the pier, stumbles and falls into the water. The child struggles and calls for help, yelling that he cannot swim. If Fisherman has never met the child, he generally possesses no legal duty to help the child, although Fisherman may have a moral duty to assist the child. If he does nothing, and the child drowns, under traditional law, Fisherman generally will not face criminal liability because a moral duty cannot give rise to criminal liability. However, some jurisdictions with "Good Samaritan" laws may impose liability under certain circumstances.

★   (2)   Legal Duty to Act

A failure to act generally does not give rise to criminal liability. However, an accused's failure to act when a legal duty to act exists, does give rise to criminal liability. A legal duty to act exists in the following circumstances:

- Contractual relationships, such as those between law enforcement officers and the public, health care providers and patients, or lifeguards and swimmers, for example, establish a legal duty and level of care.

★★   - Family relationships, such as those between parents and children, may establish a duty of care or assistance that must be provided.

- Voluntary assistance to a victim of a crime or accident from a bystander who assumes responsibility for rescuing the victim, renders the bystander criminally liable if the bystander's conduct results in increasing the extent of the victim's harm.

★   - Creation of peril creates a legal duty to assist when a first party places a second party in harm's way.

- Some jurisdictions have adopted Good Samaritan Laws that require a bystander to assist a victim of a crime or accident, provided the bystander will not be subject to a risk of harm from rendering assistance. Unless an exam question expressly provides that a Good Samaritan Law exists, you should assume it does not.

B.   State of Mind

1)   REQUIRED MENTAL STATE

a)   Common Law

An accused's bad or wicked thoughts cannot alone, without any act, constitute a crime. Conversely, some acts of an accused may, without any bad thoughts, constitute a crime.

★★★   (1)   Strict Liability Offenses  Question Key 27,119,131

A strict liability offense does not require proof of any criminal state of mind. The important consideration in determining whether a strict liability crime occurred is whether the actus reus occurred. The circumstances surrounding the act are irrelevant with regard to proving the offense. The classic tested example of a strict liability offense is statutory rape. In a jurisdiction that has adopted traditional statutory rape law, if a person over the legal age has sexual intercourse with a protected person under the age of consent, then the older person is guilty of statutory rape regardless of whether the older person was aware of the age of the younger person.

Strict liability crimes generally are limited to crimes protecting minors, such as statutory rape and selling alcohol to minors. Traffic infractions are also strict liability offenses. That is why a driver need not be aware of the fact that she is speeding in order to get a ticket. Such conduct is prohibited in order to protect or preserve the public's welfare. The following features are typical of a strict liability offense:

- It is regulatory;
- It has a minimal penalty; and
- Allocating fault might be difficult.

(2)   Negligence Offenses

A negligence offense requires proof of a failure to perform some legal duty. The important consideration is if the accused either does not know or fails to remember something he should have known or remembered. The circumstances giving rise to that failure are relevant to establishing the level of culpability for the offense. For example, suppose a person is operating an automobile unreasonably and in a manner that a reasonable person should have known was dangerous to others. If the person, as a result of the negligence, strikes and kills a pedestrian, the driver may be criminally liable for negligent homicide.

★★★   (3)   Intentional Offenses

Mens rea is the term used to describe a criminal state of mind that must coincide with a bad act in order to commit an intentional crime. There are two types, or levels, of intentional crimes – general intent crimes and specific intent crimes.

★★★   (a)   General Intent | Question Key 65 |

General intent exists when an accused intends to make the physical action that comprises the act of the crime. Unlike specific intent, it does not require the desire to achieve the consequences of that act. If the accused lacks the general intent to commit a criminal act when actually committing a criminal *actus rea* (i.e., if the accused commits an involuntary action), then the accused cannot be guilty of a general intent crime for that act.

Common general intent crimes include:

- Battery
- Kidnapping
- Rape

★★★   (b)   Specific Intent | Question Key 68,84 |

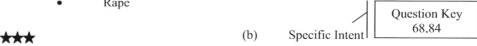

Specific intent exists when an accused both intends to commit a criminal act and does desire to achieve that act's consequences. If the accused does not possess specific intent when committing a criminal act that requires specific intent for its commission, then the accused cannot be guilty of the crime.

Common specific intent crimes include:

- M- Murder (First Degree only)
- A- Assault
- R- Robbery
- L - Larceny
- A- Attempt
- C- Conspiracy
- B- Burglary
- E- Embezzlement
- F- Forgery
- F- False Pretenses

You can try to remember the specific intent crimes by memorizing the name Marla C. Beff. Each letter in the name represents a specific intent crime.

★★   (c)   Malice   Question Key
                                                                      35

For some crimes, most notably arson, a standard slightly above general intent, but not quite specific intent, is required. This standard is called malice. Malice exists if a person knowingly disregards a substantial risk that the prohibited consequences would come about. For example, suppose a person starts a fire in the wooded backyard of another's home, and fans the flames to grow the fire, resulting in the home burning down. Even if the person can demonstrate that he did not intend to burn the home, in other words, he had no specific intent, he may nonetheless be criminally liable for the arson. The person will be criminally liable if he knew of the risk to the building and knowingly disregarded the risk (i.e., he acted with malice). Of course, proof of general intent (e.g., he intended to start the fire), would be insufficient to ground criminal liability for a malice crime.

The main malice crimes are arson and depraved-heart murder.

★   Question Key   (d)   Transferred Intent Doctrine
              18,29,61

The doctrine of transferred intent provides that an accused who possesses any criminal state of mind (*mens rea*) when he engages in illegal conduct (*actus rea*) will be liable for the results of that crime, even if it is perpetrated against someone other than the intended victim. Thus, if the accused engages in a criminal act against a first person and, instead, mistakenly perpetrates the act against a second person, that mistake will not relieve the accused of liability. This doctrine applies to most intentional offenses.

★★   b)   Model Penal Code   Question Key
                                                                    38,62,109

The MPC has done away with the common law specific and general intent standards. Instead, it sets forth the culpability level required to commit a specific offense. The four

MPC culpability levels set forth below apply to the three MPC elements for each offense. The three elements of each MPC crime are: (1) conduct; (2) circumstance; and (3) results.

 An MBE question may cite a relevant statute that defines criminal conduct. The text may contain one of the four culpability levels of the MPC. For example, a question may provide that a law in the jurisdiction makes it a crime to "knowingly sell alcohol to a minor." This type of question is usually designed to test knowledge of the MPC culpability standards. In order to resolve the question, you must apply the requirement for the culpability level to the facts in the question.

(1)   Purposely

Purposeful criminal conduct or results arise from an accused's "conscious objective to engage in conduct of that nature or to cause such as result." The accused must be "aware of the existence of such circumstances, or he believes or hopes that they exist."

(2)   Knowingly

★★
Knowing criminal conduct or circumstances exist when an accused is "aware that his conduct is of that nature or that such circumstances exist." With respect to a result element, the accused must be "aware that it is practically certain that his conduct will cause such a result." This standard may be satisfied even if the person does not act with the express purpose to bring about the prohibited results. Thus, the MPC differentiates between purpose and knowledge.

(3)   Recklessly

★
Reckless criminal conduct occurs with respect to all elements when an accused "consciously disregards a substantial and unjustifiable risk that the material element exists or will result from his conduct." The risk must involve "a gross deviation from the standard of care that a reasonable person would observe in the actor's situation."

(4)   Negligently

★
Negligent criminal conduct occurs with respect to all elements if an accused "should be aware of a substantial and unjustifiable risk that the material element exists or will result from his conduct." The risk must also involve "a gross deviation from the standard of care that a reasonable person would observe in the actor's situation."

★★   2)   <u>MISTAKE OF FACT OR LAW</u>

Question Key
14,42,69,78,149

★★   a)   Mistake of Fact

Generally, ignorance of the law and mistake of fact are not valid defenses to a crime. A mistake of fact occurs when, if the facts were as an accused considered them to be when an offense occurred, the accused could not have committed the offense. The accused may be exculpated from criminal liability based on such a mistake of fact when the mistake eliminates the required *mens rea* to commit the offense. The test depends upon the required type of *mens rea*:

★★   •   Specific Intent

Regardless of how reckless and negligent an accused's mistake of fact is, the accused will not be guilty of an offense if the mistake of fact negates an element of specific intent for the offense. For example, suppose Ted kills Barney by injecting him with poison. Ted will not be guilty of common law murder under the specific intent to kill ground if Ted honestly believes that he is administering medicine to Barney. In effect, Ted's mistake of fact negates the specific intent to kill.

★★   •   General Intent

An accused will not be guilty of a general intent offense if the defendant acts without the intent to commit the actus reus based on a reasonable mistake of fact.

★★   •   Strict Liability

★★ An accused's reasonable mistake of fact will not preclude the accused's guilt for strict liability offenses, because those offenses do not require any proof of intent.

★★   •   Negligence

An accused's reasonable mistake of fact may preclude the accused's guilt for negligence offenses, because those offenses require proof of negligence. In other words, if an accused makes a reasonable mistake, the accused has not acted negligently. This is because negligence, by definition, requires unreasonableness.

★   b)   Mistake of Law

An accused who believes that the law does not prohibit his conduct is nonetheless guilty of a committed crime, regardless of whether she possesses a mistake regarding the law (even if reasonable or based on the advice of a lawyer).

                (1)   Common Law Exceptions

Two exceptions apply to the rule that a mistake of law is not a valid defense to a crime.

                (a)   Reasonable Reliance

Reasonable reliance is a valid defense for a person who relies on an incorrect official interpretation of the law. The accused person, however, will not prevail with the defense of relying on the accused's own interpretation of the law or on that of the accused's legal counsel.

(b)   Negate Specific Intent

With respect to a specific intent offense, mistake of law is a valid defense if it negates the crime's specific intent. For example, suppose that a defendant is accused of robbery. Suppose that the defendant was actually trying to retrieve money that the victim owed him and that the defendant believed that the law permits self-help in such situations. This mistaken belief about the law may negate the specific intent required for the crime of robbery because the defendant did not possess the specific intent to gain control over another's property.

C.   **Responsibility**

1)   <u>GENERAL</u>

Under certain circumstances, an accused may not be held fully legally responsible for his criminal conduct. Usually, these circumstances pertain to the accused's mental state at the time of the offense. Two circumstances that may impact the accused's responsibility for intentional crimes are mental disorder and intoxication. These circumstances do not, however, impact an accused's responsibility for strict liability offenses.

2)   <u>MENTAL DISORDER</u>

At the time of committing an offense, an accused may suffer from a mental disorder that is less severe than insanity. The accused's insanity defense will not succeed in such a case.

a)   Alternative Doctrines

Many jurisdictions provide alternative doctrines variously described as partial insanity, diminished capacity, or partial responsibility. These doctrines permit the admission of evidence regarding the accused's state of mind relative to the intent element of any alleged criminal offense. For example, such evidence may be relevant when determining the intent possessed by the accused for a particular homicide. An individual who prevails using this defense may be found responsible for a lesser offense than that originally charged by the prosecution.

b)   Burdens of Proof

The mental disorder doctrines permit an accused to prove that an element of a crime does not exist due to the accused's mental condition at the time of the act. The prosecution must overcome the defense by proving the requisite elements beyond a reasonable doubt.

★★★   3)   <u>INTOXICATION</u>

Question Key
52,81,83,96,139,160

An accused may raise intoxication by alcohol or drugs as a defense that seeks to excuse an instance of the accused's criminal conduct. Intoxication may give rise to additional defenses, such as insanity, diminished capacity, or mistake of fact.

a)   Common Law

(1)   Voluntary Intoxication (Majority)

Voluntary Intoxication may be available as a defense, under certain circumstances, if an accused knowingly ingests a substance (i.e., alcohol or drugs) that causes the intoxication prior to the accused commission of a criminal offense.

(a)   Burden of Proof

The accused's burden of proof depends upon the type of intent the prosecution must prove in order to establish criminal liability for the alleged offense.

- Specific intent offenses: An accused has to prove an absence of specific intent that resulted from voluntary intoxication.

- General intent offenses: An accused is not required to prove an absence of general intent that resulted from voluntary intoxication. Voluntary intoxication does not negate the intent element of general intent crimes. It is not available as a defense to general intent crimes.
- Strict liability offenses: Voluntary intoxication may not be used as a defense to strict liability crimes.

(2)   Voluntary Intoxication (Minority)

In some jurisdictions, intoxication is not an excuse when it results in an accused's insanity, unconsciousness, or absence of a correct state of mind. However, if this defense is sustained in a murder case, the accused could be convicted of a lesser homicide crime.

★   (3)   Involuntary Intoxication

Involuntary intoxication exists when an accused becomes intoxicated due to trickery, coercion, or an unanticipated response to a prescription drug. In that event, the accused will not be blamed for his conduct that occurred under the influence of the intoxication.

The test of involuntary intoxication is that the accused:

- did not appreciate the quality and nature of an act; and
- did not know that the act was wrong.

      4)   INVOLUNTARY ACTIONS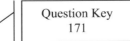

Voluntary conduct results from an accused's exercise of free will, and subjects the accused to criminal liability, if he possesses the requisite intent to perform the illegal conduct. A voluntary act is volitional and includes habitual conduct. Voluntary conduct is subject to prosecution and punishment, while involuntary conduct is not.

Involuntary conduct is not an accused's volitional act, and will not subject the accused to criminal liability even if he possesses the requisite intent to perform that illegal act. Involuntary conduct may occur during unconsciousness, while asleep, or when a first person is being moved by a second person. Involuntary conduct may also result from a seizure, reflex, convulsion, or spasm.

D.   Causation      Question Key 77

Criminal liability arises when an accused's act produces an illegal result. The act must be both the actual and proximate cause of the illegal result, and no intervening act may exist.

1)   PROXIMATE CAUSE (ALSO CALLED LEGAL CAUSE)

An act is the proximate cause of the result if the victim's harm is a natural and probable consequence of the action of the accused.

2)   ACTUAL CAUSE

An action is the actual (or factual) cause of a result if the harm would not have occurred "but for" the accused's act. Alternatively, if two independent actions contributed to the result, but each could have caused the result alone, then each will be the actual cause if it was a substantial factor in bringing about the result.

3)   INTERVENING ACTIONS

The existence of an intervening or supervening cause may relieve the accused from responsibility if the action was sufficiently outside the scope of foreseeability. As a general rule, the intervening event must be bizarre or abnormal in order to preclude a defendant's initial act from constituting the proximate cause of a victim's death.

4)   INTENDED ACTION MUST CAUSE RESULT

For criminal liability to attach, the intended action must cause the result. For example, if David shoots a bullet at Victor, intending to kill him, he may be criminally liable for murder if the bullet hits and kills Victor. However, if David, driving to Victor's house intending to shoot him inside, mistakenly drives into the structure of the house, killing Victor by mistake, David may not be criminally liable for Victor's murder. Note that David may be criminally liable for attempted murder.

E.   Doctrine of Merger   Question Key 6,114

★★

The doctrine of merger mandates that lesser included charges merge into more serious offenses. For example, a defendant may not be convicted of both assault and robbery stemming from a single event, because a robbery includes the elements of assault. The offenses merge, and the defendant may be convicted of only the robbery, or only the assault, but not both. Additionally, a defendant may not be convicted of both larceny and robbery, because robbery includes the elements of larceny.

Solicitation to commit a crime and attempt to commit a crime also merge into the completed crime.

However, a major exception to the doctrine is the crime of conspiracy. Conspiracy, unlike the other two inchoate offenses, does not merge into the completed crime. Therefore, a defendant may be convicted of both a crime and conspiracy to commit the crime.

V.   DEFENSES

The accused possesses the burden of proving the existence of an affirmative defense. This is in contrast to the rule that the prosecution must prove every element of the charged offense. This burden is not on the prosecution because the absence of an affirmative defense is not treated as an element of the crime. The accused must prove the existence of the affirmative defense by a "preponderance of the evidence."

A.   Justification and Excuse

1)   GENERAL

If an accused commits an offense with the required mental state, the accused may not be subject to criminal liability if the act is justified or the mental state is excused.

2)   JUSTIFICATION

The common law provides that justified criminal conduct is not subject to punishment. The rule of justification for criminal acts is similar to the principle of necessity. The rule arises from a case in which the crew of a capsized vessel ate their cabin boy in order to avoid starvation and survive on the high seas.

Criminal conduct that occurs due to necessity may be considered justified if an accused proves that:

- The criminal conduct served to escape unavoidable results to the accused, or others whom the accused is obligated to protect;
- Those results would have been irreparable;
- The accused did nothing beyond what was absolutely necessary; and
- The evil inflicted was not disproportionate to the threatened evil.

3)   EXCUSE

The common law provides that an accused may not be subject to punishment for crime under the doctrine of excuse. That doctrine provides that some people cannot be blamed for their conduct if the accused lacks the requisite mental state for culpability. Such a situation that will excuse culpability may flow from compulsion, such as duress.

B.   Duress

Question Key
9

1)   GENERAL

a)   Elements

An accused may attempt to avoid criminal liability by alleging that he suffered duress resulting in committing an offense because another person forced the accused to commit the offense.

To escape criminal liability, an accused must establish duress in the following manner:

- A third person presented an immediate threat to an accused causing;
- The accused to feel a well-based fear of serious bodily injury or death;
- The accused did not negligently or recklessly place herself into that situation;
- The accused lacked any reasonable legal options; and
- A direct causal connection exists between avoidance of the threatened harm and the criminal action.

                 b)   Exception for Murder

A duress defense cannot be presented in response to a charge of murder. This defense may be used in response to all other criminal charges.

C.   **Necessity**

1)   GENERAL

a)   Elements

Under a necessity defense, an accused may contend that the wrong his unlawful conduct sought to prevent constituted a greater wrong than the wrong intended to be avoided by the law the accused violated.

To escape criminal liability, an accused must establish necessity in the following manner:

- An accused faced a clear and present danger;
- The accused reasonably believed the action taken would prevent harm;
- The accused lacked a lawful means of avoiding the harm;
- The accused caused a less serious harm than that which she sought to avoid; and
- The accused did not place herself where she participated in the criminal conduct.

 D.   **Insanity**

> Question Key
> 105,136

If a defendant can demonstrate that he was insane at the time the crime was committed, the defendant may be deemed not guilty of the crime by reason of insanity.

1)   GENERAL

The law defines and determines an accused's sanity differently than the medical profession. There are several different approaches to insanity that have been adopted in various jurisdictions. For exam purposes, it is a good idea to be familiar with all of them.

The underlying considerations common to all of these approaches involve resolving whether the accused suffered from a mental defect or illness when the accused committed an offense, and whether that defect or illness altered the accused's mental condition to the extent that the accused should not be held criminally liable for the offense.

2)   IRRESISTIBLE IMPULSE

Under the irresistible impulse test, the accused will be able to successfully assert the defense if:

- the defendant had a mental disease;
- which kept him from controlling his conduct.

Under this test, a not guilty verdict may be obtained even if the accused knew what he was doing was wrong. All that is required is that the accused did not possess the capability to control his behavior.

★   3)   M'NAGHTEN

Some form of the M'Naghten rule is adopted by a plurality of jurisdictions. Under the rule, an accused will be not guilty by reason of insanity if, as a result of a mental disease or defect, either:

- The accused did not know the quality and nature of the act; or
- The accused did not know the action was wrong.

4)   NEW HAMPSHIRE TEST

Under the New Hampshire test approach, an accused must demonstrate that, but for a mental defect or disease, he would not have committed a crime.

In other words, the relevant inquiry is whether a causal link exists between the mental disease and the criminal act. This test encompasses more circumstances than the other approaches because it makes knowledge of the wrongfulness of the conduct irrelevant.

5)   MPC APPROACH

The Model Penal Code meshes the M'Naghten and Irresistible Impulse Tests.

Under the MPC approach, a person is insane if, at the time of the crime, due to a mental defect or disease, the accused lacked substantial capacity to:

- appreciate the wrongful or criminal nature of her conduct; or
- conform that conduct to the law's requirements.

 E.   Self-Defense & Defense of Others

> Question Key
> 1,34,52,66,75,85,149

       1)   <u>COMMON LAW</u>

          a)   General

Self-defense and defense of others are additional possible defenses to a criminal charge. Self-defense may apply to mitigate the severity of an accused's offense or to entirely exculpate the accused from criminal liability. An aggressor who attacks someone cannot assert self-defense if the initial victim fights back.

          b)   Elements

The elements of self-defense are:

- an aggressor presents an immediate threat to an accused;
- the accused possesses an objectively reasonable belief that the aggressor is about to use force against the accused; and
- compared to the aggressor's threatened harm, the accused cannot use excessive force.

          c)   Majority Rule

          (1)   Self-Defense

An accused may only use an extent of force reasonably necessary to prevent or stop an attack. If the accused genuinely and reasonably feels he is under attack, the accused is entitled to self-defense of non-lethal force. The accused must possess a reasonable belief that he was threatened with imminent harm. The accused's honest but unreasonable belief is not a sufficient justification for that harm.

          (2)   Defense of Others

With regard to coming to the defense of others, a person's belief that another is in danger must be reasonable under the circumstances. For example, suppose Sid is walking to work and sees Buzz attacking Woody on the sidewalk. Sid, being an honorable person, comes to Woody's aid and fends off Buzz. Although Sid does not realize it, the whole fight is being filmed for a movie. Therefore, Woody does not actually possess a right of self-defense against Buzz. If Sid's belief that Buzz is attacking Woody is reasonable, Sid would be able to assert the defense of others doctrine. If Sid's belief is not reasonable, Sid would not be able to assert the defense.

★

|d)|Minority Rule|

The minority of states follow an "alter ego" rule with respect to the rule for the defense of others from criminal charges of assault, battery, and murder. That rule provides that an accused who claims he acted to defend someone else stands in the place of someone who is being defended. Thus, the accused's right to defend someone is equivalent and dependent upon someone else's right of self-defense. The accused lacks a defense when someone whom he defends lacks a legal right to use force for self-defense.

Therefore, in the prior example, Sid would not be able to use the defense because he would stand in Woody's shoes. Woody would possess no right of self-defense. Thus, even if Sid's belief was reasonable, he would not be able to assert the defense in a minority of jurisdictions under these circumstances.

★

|e)|Imperfect Self-Defense|

An accused's unreasonable but honest belief that her life is in danger from another person would provide a basis for an imperfect self-defense to the charge of murdering that person. The defense cannot fully excuse the accused's criminal liability for the homicide, but it may be used to mitigate a murder charge to manslaughter.

★★

|f)|Deadly Force - General|

★★

|(1)|Self Defense|

A use of force that results in death, regardless of whether death is intended, is deadly force. An accused is warranted in using deadly force in self-defense only if the accused reasonably believes that deadly force is necessary to avoid the aggressor's immediate and unlawful use of deadly force.

|(2)|Defense of Others|

A person is entitled to use deadly force to defend someone else if:

- the person reasonably believes such force is essential;
- to protect someone else from the threat of immediate death or serious bodily harm; and
- the person reasonably and honestly believes someone else possesses a legal right to use deadly force to defend himself or herself.

In that event, the person may use his protection of someone else as a defense, even if that person's belief is wrong.

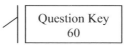

★★   (3)   Duty to Retreat

Most jurisdictions provide that a person does not possess a duty to retreat before using deadly force in self-defense. A minority of jurisdictions provide that a person possesses a duty to retreat, if a safe way exists, before resorting to the use of deadly force in self-defense. Even in this minority, however, the duty to retreat does not exist before resorting to non-deadly force.

★★   (a)   Attack in Home

Even in the jurisdictions that recognize doctrine duty to retreat, an accused has no duty to retreat if an aggressor attacks the accused in the accused's home.

                                        g)   Defense of Property

                                        (1)   General Defense

A valid defense to a charge of criminal battery is that the purported battery occurred for the purpose of defending property. Thus, an accused whose property is placed at risk by a person's illegal activity may exercise force against the person to protect the property. Even if an accused is warranted in using force to prevent interference with the lawful possession of the personal property, the accused may use only the degree of force that is reasonably necessary.

                                        (2)   Regain Possession

An owner of property may not exercise force to regain possession of any personal property that another person wrongfully took.

                           2)   <u>MPC</u>

The MPC provides that an accused may use force "upon or toward another person . . . when the actor believes that such force is immediately necessary for the purpose of protecting himself against the use of unlawful force by such other person on the present occasion." In contrast to the common law, the accused may act based on a subjective belief. The MPC permits a use of deadly force only when the accused faces "death, serious bodily harm, kidnapping, or sexual intercourse compelled by force or threat." The MPC follows the common law's retreat rule.

     F.   Entrapment | Question Key 60 |

Entrapment may be a valid defense to a crime. A valid entrapment defense possesses two elements: (1) state inducement of the crime; and (2) the defendant's lack of predisposition to engage in the criminal conduct. *Mathews v. United States*, 485 U.S. 58, 63 (1988).

                           1)   <u>INDUCEMENT</u>

Mere solicitation does not constitute inducement. Rather, inducement requires a showing of at least persuasion or mild coercion. Inducement is shown if the government's behavior was such that a law-abiding citizen's will to obey the law would have been overborne.

2)   PREDISPOSITION

Even if inducement is demonstrated, a finding of predisposition destroys an entrapment defense. The predisposition inquiry focuses upon whether the defendant was an unwary innocent or, instead, an unwary criminal who readily availed himself of the opportunity to perpetrate the crime. Predisposition should not be confused with intent or *mens rea;* a person may have the requisite intent to commit the crime, yet be entrapped.

AMERIBAR BAR REVIEW

Multistate Bar Examination Preparation Course

CRIMINAL PROCEDURE

TABLE OF CONTENTS

We have provided case names for reference purposes.
However, an examinee is not generally expected to know the names of cases.

I.   CONSTITUTIONAL PROTECTION OF ACCUSED PERSONS

★★★   A.   **Arrest, Search and Seizure**

1)   <u>GENERAL CONSIDERATIONS</u>

a)   General

The Fourth Amendment to the *U.S. Constitution* ("Fourth Amendment") provides constitutional rights that serve as bases for certain legal protections. U.S. Const. amend. IV. The Fourth Amendment states, in part, that:

> "The right of the people to be secure in their persons, houses, papers, and effects, against unreasonable searches and seizures shall not be violated, and no warrants shall issue, but upon probable cause supported by oath or affirmation, and particularly describing the place to be searched, and the person or things to be seized."

b)   Fourth and Fourteenth Amendments

By its terms, the Fourth Amendment applies to the federal government and protects a person if the federal government's conduct violates the person's rights. Under the judicial doctrine of selective incorporation, as applied by the United States Supreme Court ("the Court"), the Fourth Amendment provides fundamental rights that may be judicially protected from state action, as opposed to federal action under the Fourteenth Amendment to the *U.S. Constitution* ("Fourteenth Amendment").

★★   c)   State Action

The Fourth Amendment protects against state action, not the action of private individuals working on their own accord. State action describes at least two types of situations. The first and primary situation occurs when a public officer of a government (federal, state, or local) takes law enforcement action that affects the constitutional rights of a private person. That situation arises in a variety of factual circumstances involving various government officers and people. When the state action is based on information supplied to the officer by a private entity or individual, the state action must comply with the constitutional requirements.

The second situation arises when a private entity or individual engages in conduct on behalf of a government officer. An officer may not avoid the state action rule by utilizing a private entity or individual to conduct a search and seizure. If the probable cause used to support a warrant is obtained illegally by a private entity or individual on behalf of an officer, the warrant will be invalid. If, however, the private entity or individual conducts a search and seizure without being encouraged or directed by an officer, that search and seizure is not subject to the provisions of the Fourth Amendment.

d)   Warrant Requirement

Warrants usually are required under the Fourth Amendment to conduct legally valid arrests, searches, and seizures. The Court interprets the Fourth Amendment as mandating that all warrants be supported by the following essential elements:

- sufficient probable cause;
- an oath or affirmation by the officer requesting the warrant that the warrant's contents are accurate;
- a particular description of either the area to be searched or the items or person to be seized; and
- a statement of when, where, and how the warrant will be executed.

                        (1)   Steps to Obtain a Warrant

The following steps are necessary to obtain a valid warrant.

                        (a)   Affidavit

First, an officer prepares a written affidavit or sworn statement stating with specificity the factual basis that provides probable cause to issue the warrant. The requirement that an affidavit be written may be waived only under extraordinary circumstances, where time is of the essence. In such an instance, a verbal statement may suffice if the officer swears that the statement is true.

                        (b)   Neutral and Detached Magistrate

Second, the *Constitution* requires that a "neutral and detached" magistrate review the affidavit to determine if it fulfills the warrant requirements set forth above. In *U.S. v. Leon*, the Court stated that a magistrate who issues a warrant may not:

- be a participant in an investigation;
- serve as a "rubber stamp" of a warrant request; and
- cannot be paid for each warrant that is issued.

Although a magistrate does not need to be a bar member, the magistrate cannot be involved with an officer's execution of the warrant. The magistrate may question the officer regarding the affidavit's contents before deciding whether to sign the affidavit.

                        (c)   Execution

Third, an officer executes, or performs, an arrest, search, or seizure pursuant to the warrant's terms and subject to its scope. The warrant may grant the officer limited authority to search in terms of the particular item sought and the particular area in which the search may occur. The officer must execute a warrant properly in order for an arrest, search, or seizure that is made based on the warrant to be legally valid.

(2)   Informants and Determination of Probable Cause

General standards apply to a magistrate's determination of whether probable cause exists. The primary requirements of probable cause are that the information contained in the affidavit be of an adequate quality and quantity.

(a)   Direct Information

An officer may provide direct information based on personal knowledge or firsthand observation. Direct information is considered trustworthy unless it is "bald and unilluminating." Such untrustworthy information would involve, for example, conclusory statements not sustained by additional facts. In order to be valid, an application for a warrant must:

- state those facts necessary to allow a magistrate;
- to independently evaluate an informant's conclusions;
- about the location of evidence such as a person, place, or thing.

(b)   Informant

If an informant supplies hearsay information, then, to be considered valid, the information must satisfy the requirements of reliability under the totality of the circumstances test set forth in *Illinois v. Gates*. A magistrate must weigh the reliability of the informant's statements based on the informant's veracity and basis of knowledge. The magistrate may afford greater weight to one of those elements to compensate for the other one's weakness.

Veracity is established if the information regarding the informant convinces a magistrate that the informant is both credible and reliable. Veracity may be shown by proof of either the informant's positive prior track record or corroborating evidence that supports the informant's statements.

Basis of knowledge may be established in two manners including: 1) if an informant obtained direct information based on personal knowledge or firsthand observation; or 2) if the informant provides hearsay evidence. If the informant provides hearsay evidence, then there are two means of ensuring its accuracy. One way is self-verifying detail, such that a magistrate would be convinced of the accuracy. Another way is the existence of corroborating evidence that supports the informant's statements.

(c)   Quantity

The information's quantity will be sufficient for a magistrate to find probable cause if it would lead a person of reasonable caution to believe that:

- a person possesses, or a location contains, items subject to a search and seizure; or
- a person perpetrated a crime subject to an arrest.

            e)   Exceptions to Warrant Requirement

Despite the warrant requirement of the Fourth Amendment, many arrests, searches, and seizures occur without warrants based on exceptions to that requirement, one of which is described here. Other exceptions to the general requirement of a warrant for arrests and searches are set forth elsewhere in this outline.

(1)   Consent

Consent is a general exception to the warrant requirement. To be valid, a person's consent to an arrest, a search, or a seizure must be voluntarily given without any use of fraud, duress, or coercion by an officer. An example of coercion by an officer would be threatening a person, beating a person, or firing a gun above the head of a handcuffed accused.

(a)   Who May Consent

The determination of who has lawful authority to consent to a search initially will depend on the object of the intended search. If law enforcement officers want permission to search a person, then only the person to be searched has the authority to consent. If, on the other hand, officers desire to search premises, vehicles, or items of personal property that can be shared by two or more people, then the determination of who may consent to the search will require an analysis of who has a Fourth Amendment right of privacy in the area.

Because consent is a waiver of the Fourth Amendment right of privacy, only an individual with that right of privacy may consent to a search. The Fourth Amendment right of privacy, however, is not a function of ownership. Thus, the fact that an individual owns an apartment building does not automatically give this individual a Fourth Amendment right of privacy that he then can waive by consent regarding a rented apartment in that building.

Rather than ownership, the courts look for lawful access and control when determining authority to consent. For example, if individuals share access and control over an area, there is common authority to consent to search of that shared area.

(b)   Consent by Co-Occupant

The Supreme Court decided in *United States v. Matlock*, that one co-occupant of a premises may, in the absence of the other co-occupant, consent to the entry into the premises by an officer for a warrantless search without that entry and search violating the Fourth Amendment's prohibition against unreasonable searches and seizures.

Subsequently, in *Georgia v. Randolph*, the Court ruled that one co-occupant of a premises may not, over the objection of a present co-occupant, consent to entry into the premises by an officer for a warrantless search without that entry and search violating the Fourth Amendment's prohibition against unreasonable searches and seizures.

In *Randolph*, a husband refused to grant an officer consent to search his marital residence before his estranged wife, who was present then and there, granted consent. The Court held that the husband's refusal to allow the warrantless search made the officer's entry and search unreasonable and invalid as to the husband. The Court stated that "[a] warrantless search of a shared dwelling for evidence over the express refusal of consent by a physically present resident cannot be justified as reasonable."

(c)   Right to Refuse

A person who gives consent to an arrest, search, or seizure, is not required to know, in advance of providing consent, of the person's right to refuse to provide consent. An officer is under no obligation to inform a person of the right to refuse consent. An officer may overcome a person's refusal to provide consent by obtaining and executing a valid warrant.

f)   Administrative Searches

> Question Key
> 150

A reduced level of probable cause applies to administrative searches an officer conducts for the purpose of enforcing safety and health regulations. For example, for a code enforcement compliance search, the only required showing is that probable cause exists to believe that buildings in an area are sub-code.

★★
2)   <u>ARREST</u>

> Question Key
> 53,72,93,167

An arrest is a seizure of a person that requires probable cause and/or an arrest warrant.

★★
a)   *Terry* Stop and Situations Other Than Arrest

Many situations exist when an officer has an encounter with a person that does not constitute an arrest. For example, a mere social greeting and exchange between an officer and a person she knows obviously could not constitute an arrest.

(1)   Investigative Questioning

An officer is not entitled to stop and detain a person for any duration without possessing a reason to do so. An officer's temporary investigative stop of a person that is based on reasonable suspicion does not necessarily or automatically constitute an arrest. One factor that may distinguish an arrest from such a brief detention for questioning is an absence of restraint of a person.

(a)   Self-Identification to Officer

An officer may request that a suspect identify himself during a *Terry* stop. In *Hiibel v. The Sixth Judicial District Court,* the Supreme Court upheld a defendant's conviction for violating a Nevada statute requiring an individual to identify himself when detained by an officer in an investigative stop based on an alleged assault. The Fourth Amendment right against unreasonable searches and seizures does not permit an individual under suspicion of committing a criminal offense to refuse to identify himself to an officer, which refusal can constitute a crime.

(2)   Reasonable Suspicion Test

The Court's decision in *Terry v. Ohio* dictates that, under certain circumstances, no probable cause or warrant is required for an officer to approach a person to inquire about his identity or awareness of criminal activity. *Terry v. Ohio* gives rise to the following test of whether an officer lacking probable cause or a warrant may briefly stop a person for questioning:

- Does the officer have reasonable suspicion?
- That supports a belief that criminal activity is pending?
- That is based on specific articulable facts?

Even if the requirements are met, if there is a disproportionate use of force or the officer subjects the person to custodial detention, then an arrest has occurred.

The following facts *alone* do not give rise to reasonable suspicion: (1) a person's refusal to disclose his identity to an officer; and (2) an anonymous tip about a person's alleged illegal activity.

The following facts may give rise to reasonable suspicion justifying a brief *Terry* investigative stop: (1) evidence that corroborates an anonymous tip about a person's alleged illegal activity; or (2) a person's "unprovoked flight" from an officer within high a crime area, pursuant to *Illinois v. Wardlow.*

(3)   Extent and Duration of Seizure

The test to determine whether police conduct constitutes an arrest or seizure is would a reasonable person consider himself free to leave? If a reasonable person would not consider himself free to leave, an arrest has occurred, and the requirements for an arrest must be satisfied. If a reasonable person would consider himself free to leave, then an arrest has not occurred.

b)   Elements of an Arrest

An arrest of a person by an officer may occur properly only under specific circumstances. Those circumstances involve:

- the officer's execution of an arrest warrant identifying the person; or

- the officer's: a) probable cause to believe that the person committed a crime, and b) the officer's seizure of the person (i.e., a physical taking of his body).

★★   (1)   Probable Cause Requirement

To be constitutionally proper, an arrest generally requires that an officer possess a valid warrant or, in the absence of a warrant, probable cause to make an arrest. The test of probable cause for an arrest warrant or for a warrantless arrest is:

- Does an officer know of certain circumstances and facts about which;
- The officer possesses reasonably trustworthy information; and
- Those circumstances and facts are sufficient to permit a person of reasonable caution to believe;
- That a crime has been committed? and
- That the person committed the crime?

(a)   Pre-Textual Stops

In *Whren v. United States*, the Court concluded that even if an officer engages in a traffic stop on an improper or pre-textual basis, that stop cannot be considered unreasonable if it occurred based on another proper basis for probable cause. For example, suppose a police officer stops an automobile on the pretext that a headlight is broken, but the police officer really believes that the occupants are engaging in drug trafficking (but no probable cause for drug trafficking exists). Suppose the officer discovers cocaine on the dashboard in the vehicle. Would the stop be valid despite the pre-textual stop? The Court, in a similar case in *Whren,* considered the officer's subjective intent in making the stop to be irrelevant because the objective requirement of probable cause was fulfilled. In other words, if an officer could have stopped the vehicle on such a basis, then the stop is valid.

(2)   Seizure of the Person

Usually an officer will physically seize (i.e., restrain) a person immediately before or after making an arrest. In *California v. Hodari D.,* the Court defined such a seizure under the Fourth Amendment as "a laying on of hands or application of physical force to restrain movement, even when it is ultimately unsuccessful" or a person's "submission to the assertion of authority." The Court further stated the requirement in *United States v. Mendenhall* that "a reasonable person would have believed that he was not free to leave . . . states a necessary, but not a sufficient, condition for seizure . . . effected through a 'show of authority.'" An officer is entitled to use reasonable force to apprehend a fleeing felon.

(a)   Reasonableness of Seizure

In *United States v. Place*, the Court set forth objective reasonableness as the standard for analyzing the manner in which a seizure occurs. This standard involves balancing the "nature and quality of the intrusion on the individual's Fourth Amendment interests against the importance of the governmental interests alleged to justify the intrusion." A seizure results, for example, when a police vehicle intentionally sideswipes a fleeing vehicle causing it to crash, thereby ending its occupant's freedom of movement.

(i)   Termination of High-Speed Vehicle Chase

In *Scott v. Harris*, the Court ruled that a "police officer's attempt to terminate a dangerous high-speed car chase that threatens the lives of innocent bystanders does not violate the Fourth Amendment, even when it places the fleeing motorist at risk of serious injury or death."

c)   Arrests Requiring Warrants

(1)   Arrest Where a Person Lives

In *Payton v. New York,* the Court decided that generally, for an officer to arrest a person in the person's dwelling, the officer must both: 1) possess an arrest warrant, and 2) have "reason to believe [that] the suspect is within" the dwelling. An officer cannot forcibly enter a dwelling to make a warrantless arrest if the officer has sufficient time to obtain a warrant.

(a)   Arrest Where another Person Lives

The Court held in *Steadgold v. United States,* that usually for an officer to arrest a person in another person's dwelling, the officer must have a search warrant to search the other person's dwelling for the person who is intended to be arrested in that dwelling.

(2)   Knock and Announce Rule

In *Ker v. California,* the Court decided that an officer who seeks to serve an arrest warrant at a dwelling must notify its occupant of the officer's purpose and authority before entering the dwelling to arrest a person. In *Hudson v. Michigan*, the Court concluded that a violation of the knock and announce rule does not require, as a remedy, the application of the exclusionary rule to suppress all evidence obtained during a search conducted after the violation occurred.

(a)   Exceptions to the Rule

The Court, in *United States v. Ramirez*, provided exceptions to the above-stated requirement of notice from arresting officers when they "had a 'reasonable suspicion' that knocking and announcing their presence might be dangerous to themselves and others." The officers can avoid the notice requirement if they know that:

- the person owns or possesses a weapon; or
- the person's criminal conduct involves readily destructible evidence.

In *Wilson v. Layne,* the Court decided "that police actions in execution of a warrant [must] be related to the objectives of the authorized intrusion."

(3)   Exigent Circumstances Exception to *Payton*

(a)   Definition and Elements

Exigent circumstances may justify a warrantless arrest at someone's home. Exigent circumstances are similar to those that exist in an emergency, and include situations requiring urgent attention or warranting an immediate response. *Dorman v. United States* describes the following factors as considerations in determining if exigent circumstances exist:

- "a grave offense is involved";
- "the suspect is reasonably believed to be armed";
- "a clear showing of probable cause";
- "strong reason to believe that the suspect is in the premises";
- "likelihood that the suspect will escape if not swiftly apprehended";
- if an entry is "made peaceably"; or
- "made at night."

(b)   Arrest Where a Person Lives

A corollary of the rule in *Payton v. New York* is that an officer may arrest a person in the person's dwelling without an arrest warrant if the officer possesses consent to enter the dwelling, or if exigent circumstances support the officer's entry into the dwelling. Exigent circumstances to enter a dwelling may exist if evidence of illegal activity may be removed or destroyed before an officer arrives and/or discovers it.

(c)   Arrest Where another Person Lives

A corollary of the rule in *Steadgold v. U.S* is that an officer may arrest a person in another person's dwelling without an arrest warrant if the officer possesses consent to enter the dwelling, or if exigent circumstances support the officer's entry into the dwelling.

      d)   Warrantless Arrests

(1)   Probable Cause Required

An officer may arrest a person without a warrant, on the basis of sufficient facts to constitute probable cause that the crime was committed and that the accused committed the crime. In *United States v. Watson,* the Court ruled that no warrant is needed for an officer to arrest a person outside of a home pursuant to a statute, even if the officer possesses probable cause to make the arrest and could have obtained an arrest warrant.

(a)   Flight of Suspect

Running away from police, alone, generally is not sufficient probable cause to justify a seizure. However, the Supreme Court has held that if a person runs away from an officer, upon the approach of the officer, the flight may elevate the officer's reasonable suspicion to probable cause. In other words, by running away upon seeing an officer, a person may increase the officer's reasonable suspicion of criminal activity to the level of probable cause if the person's conduct is not otherwise ambiguous to the officer. Thus, under certain circumstances, the officer may chase and seize the person who flees from the officer.

(b)   Non-Jailable   Offenses   (Justify Lawful Seizure)

In *Atwater v. City of Lago Vista*, the Court concluded that an officer possesses discretion about whether to make an arrest for only a minor legal infraction. For example, an officer may arrest a person for violating a law, such as failing to wear a seatbelt, even if the crime is punishable only by fine. That ruling also applies to render constitutional similar arrests made for other equivalent non-jailable offenses, such as civil infractions and misdemeanors.

(c)   Arrest Prohibited by State Law

In *Virginia v. Moore*, the Court held that officers do not violate the Fourth Amendment by arresting a person based on probable cause, although state law prohibits the arrest for a minor offense, so that evidence seized as a result of the arrest does not need to be suppressed. The Court stated in part that "[t]he arrest rules that the officers violated were those of state law alone, and . . . it is not the province of the Fourth Amendment to enforce state law."

e)   Use of Force

(1)   Preventing a Person's Escape

Ordinarily, an officer is permitted to utilize only reasonable force to arrest a person.

(a)   Reasonable Force Standard

In *Graham v. Connor*, the Court analyzed the acceptable standard of reasonable force.

It "requires careful attention to the facts and circumstances of each particular case, including the severity of the crime at issue, whether the suspect poses an immediate threat to the safety of the officers or others, and whether he is actively resisting arrest or attempting to evade arrest by flight."

It also must "embody allowance for the fact that police officers are often forced to make split-second judgments—in circumstances that are tense, uncertain, and rapidly evolving—about the amount of force that is necessary in a particular situation."

(b)   Deadly Force

In *Tennessee v. Garner*, the Court discussed the use of deadly force in apprehending a fleeing felon.   It held that the use of deadly force to prevent escape generally is constitutionally unreasonable.

However, an exception exists if the officer has probable cause to believe that the suspect poses a threat of serious physical harm, either to the officer or to others. Under those circumstances, it is not constitutionally unreasonable to prevent escape by using deadly force.

Therefore, if the suspect threatens the officer with a weapon, or there is probable cause to believe he has committed a crime involving the infliction or threatened infliction of serious physical harm, deadly force may be employed, if necessary, to prevent escape, and as long as, where feasible, some warning has been given.

★★   3)   GENERAL SEARCHES

a)   Probable Cause Is Required

(1)   Legal Standard for Probable Cause

The basic test of probable cause for a search warrant or for a warrantless search is:

i)   Does an officer know of certain circumstances and facts about which;
ii)   The officer possesses reasonably trustworthy information; and
iii)   Those circumstances and facts are sufficient to permit a person of reasonable caution to believe;
iv)   That an item subject to a search will be in a particular location at a specified time and is any one of the following types of items:

- contraband;
- an instrumentality of an offense;
- a fruit of an offense; or
- evidence of an offense.

(2)   Fresh Evidence Must Show Probable Cause

Evidence used to provide probable cause, and that supports a search warrant or a warrantless search, is subject to becoming stale due to its time- and place-specific nature. Thus, the timeliness of a search with respect to obtaining of the evidence of probable cause may affect the validity of the search and the admissibility of the evidence obtained in the search. To determine the staleness of probable cause, the following considerations should be analyzed:

- What type of property will be searched or seized?

- Relative to the passage of time, what extent of opportunities exist for the disposal, removal, or destruction of seizeable property?
- What type of offense is at issue?

Generally, a search warrant must be executed during a 10-day period after its issuance in order to avoid it being considered stale.

            b)   Search Warrants

The warrant requirement of the Fourth Amendment applies to some, but not all, types of searches. If a search is conducted under a valid warrant, it usually will be considered reasonable in the absence of a contrary evidentiary showing (e.g., that the warrant was improperly executed, etc.).

            (1)   Knock and Announce Rule

As with an arrest warrant, proper execution of a search warrant at a person's dwelling usually requires an officer to knock and announce his presence before executing (i.e., conducting) a search.

            (a)   Exceptions

The officer may enter a place without knocking to conduct a search pursuant to a warrant only if the officer reasonably suspects that:

- to knock would be futile;
- to knock would endanger the officer;
- to knock would endanger someone who is inside of the dwelling;
- to knock would make the destruction of evidence highly probable.

During the execution of a search warrant, an officer is entitled to detain and/or arrest people who are in a residence that is subject to the search.

            (2)   Warrant Defines Range and Term of Search

The scope of a search is limited to the areas particularly described in a warrant, and the contents of any container located within the searched areas if the container is of the proper size to hold the specified types of items to be searched. The search must end after the property that is the object of the search has been seized.

            (3)   Exceptions to Search Warrant Requirement

A warrant is not needed under the following main exceptions: 1) consent; 2) stop and frisk; 3) search incident to lawful arrest; 4) automobile search; 5) exigent circumstances; 6) plain view; and 7) some administrative inspections.

          (a)   Lack of Consent for Warrantless Search

A hotel manager lacks authority to permit a law enforcement officer to enter the room of a hotel guest when the officer lacks a warrant to enter the room and no exceptions to the warrant requirement apply. *Stoner v. California*, 376 U.S. 483 (1964). In that situation, the officer may not reasonably rely upon the manager's unauthorized consent as lawful authority for the entry. *Illinois v. Rodriguez*, 497 U.S. 177 (1990).

★★★   4)   <u>SEARCHES OF PLACES AND THINGS</u>

> **Question Key**
> 25,44,47,76,
> 86,130,142

           a)   Dwelling Searches

The Fourth Amendment protects a person's expectation of privacy in a dwelling. Absent exigent circumstances, the Fourth Amendment would require an officer to obtain a warrant before entering and searching a dwelling. Even a temporary hotel room would qualify as a dwelling. An officer does not need a warrant to lawfully gain access to a first person's dwelling in the following five situations:

         (1)   A second person, other than a landlord, who has the right to use the first person's dwelling may provide the officer with consent to enter the dwelling;

         (2)   The officer is engaged in "hot pursuit" of a second person who is suspected of having committed a felony and who has entered into the dwelling.

         (3)   Probable cause exists to believe that:

              i)   the first person's dwelling contains contraband;
              ii)   another person in the dwelling will remove or destroy the contraband;
              iii)   before the officer could obtain a search warrant to enter the dwelling.

         (4)   An officer could prevent injury to another person who is within the dwelling.

         (5)   An officer could prevent another person from escaping the officer.

           b)   Privacy Expectations in Places and Things

★★★★   (1)   Reasonable Expectation of Privacy Standard

In *Katz v. United States*, the Court held that a person's protection from "unreasonable searches" under the Fourth Amendment applies when the person possesses a "reasonable expectation of privacy" in the area that is searched. The appropriate analysis for determining if that expectation exists is as follows:

i) Does a person display a subjective expectation that he will not be subject to government intrusions?

ii) Will society objectively accept the person's expectation of privacy as reasonable based on the following considerations:

- the type of property that is searched;
- the means the person employed to safeguard the property;
- the extent of an officer's intrusion by means of surveillance.

(2) Warrant Requirement for Electronic Surveillance

In *Katz,* the Court ruled that an officer needed a search warrant in order to lawfully use a wiretap to record conversations in a public phone booth. The Court declared that a search warrant is required to conduct electronic surveillance. The Court declared that warrantless searches by electronic means are *per se* unreasonable. Conversely, an officer's use of a pen register to record all phone numbers a person dials does not violate any expectation of privacy that the person has in those numbers.

(a) Consent is Exception to Warrant Requirement

An exception to those holdings may apply if the parties to the conversations consented to the recording of their conversations.

★   c) Privacy Expectation around Dwellings

A person's expectation of privacy with respect to a dwelling is greatest within the person's dwelling, but decreases as the distance from the dwelling increases. Thus, a lesser expectation of privacy exists in the curtilage, which is the area that directly surrounds and is closely related to a dwelling. That expectation diminishes with respect to outbuildings on the person's property around the dwelling.

★   (1) Legal Standard for Curtilage

In *U.S. v. Dunn*, the Court set forth the following factors for determining if an area constitutes curtilage:

- the area's proximity to a dwelling;
- the extent that enclosures around the dwelling encompass the area;
- the dwelling owner's use of the area; and
- the owner's efforts to maintain the area's privacy.

(2)   Aerial Surveillance of Curtilage (Usually Permissible)

The Court held in *California v. Ciraolo*, that an officer's viewing of marijuana plants within a person's fenced-in curtilage from an airplane flying at a 1,000-foot altitude did not constitute a search for three reasons. First, that over-flight "took place within public navigable airspace." Second, the officer viewed the "plants readily discernable to the naked eye as marijuana." Third, "any member of the public flying in this airspace who glanced down could have seen everything that these officers observed."

In *Florida v. Riley,* the Court decided that an officer's observation of marijuana in a greenhouse on the curtilage of a person's dwelling from a helicopter flying at a 400-foot altitude did not constitute a search. The Court ruled that an unlawful search does not occur when an officer views the curtilage:

- through aerial surveillance from navigable airspace;
- that occurs in a non-intrusive way and
- does not expose any "intimate activities" that
- typically are related to the use of a dwelling.

The Court, however, declined to rule "that an inspection of the curtilage of a house from an aircraft will always pass muster under the Fourth Amendment simply because the plane is within the navigable airspace specified by law."

                    (3)   Open   Fields   Doctrine   (No   Privacy Expectation)

In *Hester v. United States*, the Court stated that: "the special protection accorded by the Fourth Amendment…is not extended to the open fields." Thus, a person lacks a reasonable expectation of privacy in certain yard areas of the person's dwelling. The Court defined open fields in *Oliver v. U.S.*, as an undeveloped or unoccupied area located beyond the curtilage of a dwelling, regardless of whether it is a field or if it is open. In that case, the Court reasoned that "an individual may not legitimately demand privacy for activities conducted out of doors in fields, except in the area immediately surrounding the home."

              d)   Privacy Expectation in Business Property

A business owner possesses a reasonable expectation of privacy in that part of the owner's commercial business property not generally open to the public. The Court, in *Dow Chemical Co. v. United States,* stated that open areas between business buildings in a fence-enclosed industrial site "can perhaps be seen as falling somewhere between 'open fields' and curtilage, but lacking some of the critical characteristics of both."

              e)   Privacy Expectation in Public Areas

              (1)   Closed Public Areas

A search requiring probable cause occurs when a police officer surreptitiously obtains views of unlawful activity within a closed public area, such as a stall in a public rest room or a fitting room of a clothing store.

(2)   Open Public Areas

No search occurs if the officer obtains views of unlawful activity within an open public area. A prisoner lacks any reasonable expectation of privacy in the prisoner's personal property in a prison cell.

f)   Privacy Expectation in Abandoned Property

A person has an interest in property protected by the Fourth Amendment only if he possesses an expectation of privacy in the property. If no expectation of privacy exists, then any search of the property is not protected by the *Constitution*.

(1)   Household Refuse

The Court concluded in *California v. Greenwood*, that a person who places a bag of garbage out for collection lacks a reasonable expectation of privacy in the bag's contents. Thus, no search subject to constitutional protections occurs if an officer observes the contents of such a bag.

(2)   Litter

In *Hester v. United States*, the Court decided that a person who discards containers into a field abandons them, and they are subject to a search.

(3)   Trash in Lodgings

In *Abel v. United States*, the Court concluded that items placed in a hotel's waste basket before someone checked out were lawfully subject to a search.

(4)   Abandoned Vehicle

A person who abandons a vehicle loses a reasonable expectation of privacy in it. Two indications are used to determine the existence of vehicle abandonment:

- a person's conduct manifests an intent to relinquish any interest in the vehicle; and
- the person deals with the vehicle in a manner that privacy in it would not be justifiably expected.

g)   Privacy Expectation in Information

          (1)   Exposed   Information   (No   Privacy
                Expectation)

If a person or business owner voluntarily and knowingly exposes information to the public, then the privacy protection of the Fourth Amendment does not apply. That rule applies even if the exposure occurred within the person's dwelling or office. Examples of such information include papers or documents that may be readily observed within a dwelling or office through a window. Conversely, a reasonable expectation of privacy exists with respect to hidden information.

          (2)   Non-Privileged Information (No Privacy
                Expectation)

A person who voluntarily and knowingly conveys non-privileged information to another person or entity assumes the risks that:

- the other person or entity may either transmit the information (e.g., a letter or a business record) to an officer; and
- the other person is an officer.

          (3)   Federal Patriot Act

Pursuant to the *Federal Patriot Act*, generally in terrorism cases, the Federal Bureau of Investigation (FBI) may secretly issue a national security letter to obtain certain information, rather than obtaining a search warrant for this information. This information may be requested from financial institutions, credit reporting agencies, and internet service providers. Such information may include the name and address of an individual, any e-mail addresses with which the individual has corresponded, and the websites visited by the person. The *Patriot Act* includes a "gag rule" which prohibits the recipient of a national security letter from communicating with anyone about this letter, except for the recipient's lawyer. The constitutionality of the controversial national security letter provisions of the *Patriot Act* is subject to legal challenge.

★★   5)   <u>SEARCHES OF PERSONS</u> /  Question Key 156,158

Modern case law generally construes the Fourth Amendment as protecting a person's privacy interests from a search to a greater extent than its protection of places or things.

★★   a)   Reasonable Suspicion Justifies Limited Search

          (1)   Criminal Conduct or Danger

In *Terry v. Ohio*, the Court held that an officer may detain a person temporarily for questioning, and frisk or "pat down" the person's clothing for weapons on the basis of reasonable suspicion, rather than probable cause. The Court stated that reasonable suspicion exists "where a police officer observes unusual conduct which leads him to reasonably conclude, in light of his experience as a policeman, that criminal activity may be afoot and that persons with whom he is dealing may be armed and presently dangerous; and where in the course of investigating this behavior he identifies himself as a policeman and makes reasonable inquiries; and where nothing in the initial stages of the encounter serves to dispel his reasonable fear of his own or others' safety."

(2)   Legal Standard for Pat Down Search

An officer may stop a person who is behaving in a strange or hazardous manner. The officer may perform a frisk based on reasonable suspicion that the person is armed and dangerous. The *Terry* test of whether an officer may frisk or "pat down" a person for weapons is:

- Does the officer have reasonable suspicion?
- That the person stopped is armed and dangerous?
- And the reasonable suspicion is based on specific articulable facts?

(3)   Frisk for Weapons

A pat down search must be limited to the purpose of finding any concealed weapons. The search must be restricted in scope to the exterior of the person's clothing and the inside of his pockets, only if the pockets apparently contain a weapon. The purpose of such a pat down search is to protect the officer and others by discovering a weapon on the person that may be used against the officer. It may not be used as a general means to obtain evidence.

(4)   Pat Down Search Providing Probable Cause

If, however, the situation surrounding the pat down search gives rise to probable cause, such as when an officer discovers a container of contraband in a person's pocket, then the officer will not need to obtain a search warrant to seize the contraband if it is inherently destructible and, thus, could be destroyed while a search warrant was obtained.

★★   b)   Warrantless Search Incident to Lawful Arrest

Even in the absence of probable cause, a warrantless search for weapons or evidence that occurs incident to lawful arrest is constitutionally permissible. The prerequisites for this type of search are that:

- the search must occur concurrently with an arrest; and
- the arrest must be of a custodial nature.

(1)   Purpose of Search Incident to Lawful Arrest

In *Chimel v. California,* the Court stated that "it is reasonable for the arresting officer to search the person arrested in order to remove any weapons that the latter might seek to use in order to resist arrest or effect his escape." The Court further declared that the officer may "search for and seize any evidence on the arrestee's person in order to prevent its concealment or destruction."

(2)   Scope of Search Incident to Lawful Arrest

The scope of a search incident to a lawful arrest depends upon the factual context.

(a)   Search of a Person

An officer may search for weapons and contraband in the person's possession. That search may include the clothing a person is wearing when arrested, as well as inside the person's pockets or in any containers within those pockets.

(b)   Search of Surrounding Area

The search may extend into the space under a person's "immediate control," where the person could reach to grasp a weapon or evidence, to protect the officer from injury and to protect any evidence from potential destruction. If the search of the person occurs inside a building, then the scope of a search incident to that arrest is limited to the space that surrounds the place of arrest and from which another person may attack the officer. The officer may not move the person in order to expand the area of the search that is incident to the arrest. The scope of that search may not extend to looking inside closets and cabinets within the building.

(c)   Protective Sweep of a Home

In *Maryland v. Buie*, the Court concluded that a when a person is subject to a lawful arrest in a home, an officer may conduct a protective "sweep" search of the home if the officer reasonably believes it contains another person who would present a risk of danger to the officer. As with a search of person incident to a lawful arrest, the scope of the protective sweep must be reasonable in terms of what the officer is looking for and where the officer looks within a home.

(d)   Inventory Search of a Person

A search incident to a lawful arrest may occur in order to inventory the clothing and belongings of a person prior to a custodial detention of the person. Incriminating forensic evidence may be obtained from that clothing pursuant to *United States v. Edwards*.

(e)   Search for Physical Characteristics

In *United States v. Dionisio*, the Court concluded that no search results from requiring a person to give a voice sample. The Court stated that: "the physical characteristics of a person's voice, its tone and manner, as opposed to the content of a specific conversation, are constantly exposed to the public...[such that] no person can have a reasonable expectation that others will not know the sound of his voice." On similar grounds, the Court reached a similar conclusion regarding a person's handwriting.

c)   Searches for Bodily Fluids

(1)   General Circumstances

In *Skinner v. Railway Labor Executives' Ass'n,* the Court concluded that a search occurs when a person's bodily fluids are obtained by an officer and tested for the presence of contraband.

In *Cupp v. Murphy*, the Court allowed a warrantless search based on probable cause (even without an arrest) involving an officer's removal of dried blood he observed on a person's fingernails.

The Court held in *Winston v. Lee* that a surgical procedure to remove a bullet for evidence from a person under general anesthesia was unreasonable because of: 1) a considerable risk to the person's health; 2) an invasion of the person's privacy; and 3) other evidence of an offense existed.

As a general rule, the following three factors are considered in determining the reasonableness of a bodily search:

- the prosecution's need for the evidence;
- the severity of the medical invasion of the person's body; and
- the threat to the individual's health, safety, and dignity.

(2)   Emergency Circumstances

Under exigent circumstances in which lives are at risk or evidence may be destroyed, an officer who possesses probable cause is not required to obtain a warrant to search inside a person's body. Such probable cause must be based on a clear indication that evidence of criminal activity exists beneath the person's skin. The officer who acts under this rule must employ a reasonable method of search to obtain bodily fluids.

The Court decided in *Schmerber v. California* that an officer who lacked a warrant properly had a physician obtain a blood sample from an injured person who was under arrest for driving while intoxicated. The Court considered the fact that the blood-alcohol content decreases with the passage of time.

In *Rochin v. California*, however, the Court held that the method of seizure an officer used "shocked the conscience." The officer unsuccessfully attempted to forcibly remove capsules from a person's mouth. The officer had a physician administer an emetic fluid into the person's stomach to cause the person to regurgitate the capsules.

★★   6)   <u>SEARCHES OF VEHICLES</u> ─────┐ ┌─────────────┐
                                                     │ Question Key │
                                                     │   7,8,110   │
★★   a)   Warrantless Vehicle Searches ────┘ └─────────────┘

(1)   Vehicle Stop and Frisk

The Fourth Amendment does not authorize an officer to randomly stop cars just to inspect any driver's license and registration. An officer must possess a reasonable belief that an automobile's driver is, and/or its occupants are, engaged in criminal activity (e.g., a traffic law infraction), in order to justify stopping the automobile.

(a)   Reasonable Belief Standard

In *Michigan v. Long*, the Court concluded that when an officer approaches a stopped and occupied vehicle, the officer may "frisk" inside the vehicle's passenger compartment and in those areas that may contain a hidden weapon, if the officer:

- reasonably believes a person in the vehicle is dangerous; and
- reasonably believes the person may quickly obtain a weapon.

(b)   Permissible Observations (Incident to a Stop)

Pursuant to a lawful vehicle stop, an officer may observe the vehicle's exterior, take note of any peculiar odors emanating from the vehicle, and record any openly visible vehicle identification number (VIN). Under *New York v. Class,* if an officer stops a vehicle for a traffic violation, then the officer may even enter the vehicle in order to discover a VIN that is concealed within the vehicle.

(2)   Vehicle Search Allowed Incident to Lawful Arrest

In *New York v. Belton,* the Court ruled that when an officer lawfully arrests a person who occupies a vehicle, the officer may completely search the vehicle's passenger compartment, as well as any containers within it that could hold a weapon or contraband. Under *Belton*, this search is permitted even after the occupant has been removed from the automobile. The scope of the search does not include the vehicle's trunk. Keep in mind, however, that there must be an actual custodial arrest of the occupant. Providing the occupant with a citation alone, without an arrest, does not provide grounds for this search.

(3)   Vehicle Search without Arrest or Warrant

(a)   Motor Vehicle Warrant Exception

The fact that an officer makes a valid stop of a vehicle for a traffic violation does not, in itself, provide grounds to conduct any type of search of the vehicle. Of course, an officer may search a vehicle if she obtains a warrant based upon probable cause. However, a vehicle also may be lawfully searched by an officer without a warrant, and not incident to an arrest, either based on consent to search, or if probable cause exists that the vehicle contains an item subject to seizure. The exception to the warrant requirement has been justified on many grounds, including the fear of removal of the vehicle from the area, as well as the openly visible nature of the contents of an automobile.

(b)   Option to Seize Vehicle

The officer may elect to seize the vehicle and obtain a search warrant before conducting a warrantless search. If probable cause for the search exists, then a search of a vehicle could occur within a reasonable time and away from the scene after the vehicle is seized and towed to another place. Containers in the vehicle may be searched if they are of the size that could hold the contraband that is the focus of the search.

(c)   Scope of Search

If probable cause justifies the search of a vehicle, then it justifies the search of all parts of the vehicle and its contents that may conceal the object of the search. For example, if an officer has probable cause to believe that the vehicle contains a stolen computer chip, then the officer can search any container that may hold the chip. However, if the officer has probable cause to believe that the vehicle contains a stolen big-screen plasma television, the officer cannot search a container that is too small to contain the television.

In *Wyoming v. Houghton*, the Court held that the personal belongings of a passenger also can be searched, if those belongings may hold the items sought.

(d)   Applicability to Mobile Homes and
           Other Vehicles

In *California v. Carney*, the Court held the motor vehicle exception to apply to a motor home. The court, however, distinguished between mobile motor homes and parked motor homes. A court must examine several factors to determine whether the exception applies including: 1) whether the mobile home is elevated on blocks; 2) whether the mobile home is a licensed vehicle; and 3) whether the mobile home is connected to utilities. The motor vehicle exception has been applied to trucks, trailers pulled by trucks, boats, houseboats, and airplanes.

(4)   Inventory Search of Impounded Vehicles

A vehicle may be subject to lawful impounding for several reasons, including being present at the scene of a crime. In *South Dakota v. Opperman*, the Court declared that if a vehicle is lawfully impounded, then the vehicle may constitutionally be subject to an inventory search without probable cause or a warrant, provided the search is made in good faith and pursuant to standard procedures.

7)   MISCELLANEOUS CONCEPTS

a)   Border Searches (No Warrant or Suspicion Required)

The Court in, *United States v. Ramsey*, decided that even without a warrant or suspicion of wrongdoing, a person can be subject to being stopped and having his luggage searched on the United States side of an international border crossing or entry point.

b)   Non-Searches

The following types of law enforcement activities do not constitute a search:

- an officer's use of ordinary physical senses for detective work.
- an officer's use of equipment that magnifies objects to photograph.
- an officer's use of a trained sniffing dog to detect evidence.

However, note that an officer's thermal imaging scan of a dwelling constitutes a search for which a warrant is required.

8)   SEIZURE OF THINGS

a)   General Definition

A seizure is a meaningful interference with a person's possessory interest in property by someone other than the person. Such interference may occur when an officer takes control of property by removing it from the person's constructive or actual possession or by destroying it. Usually a seized item is taken into an officer's possession and may be used as potential evidence in a criminal trial. A slight movement of a person's property is not a seizure of it because no meaningful interference has occurred.

b)   Types of Seizures

(1)   Lawful Seizure

A lawful seizure of property occurs if it is based on sufficient probable cause or a valid warrant. The seized property must have been discovered either within the scope of a lawful search based on valid probable cause or described within the warrant.

(2)   Unlawful Seizure

An unlawful seizure of property occurs if it is based on insufficient probable cause or an invalid warrant. The seized property must have been discovered in an unlawful search, or beyond the scope of a lawful search, or if that property was not described within the warrant. Some of the consequences arising from an unlawful seizure of property, such as suppression of the evidence, are described under the subtopic of the exclusionary rule.

(3)   Seizure of Vehicle

A vehicle is seized if an officer renders it unavailable to its owner(s) and occupant(s), or impounds it to make it inaccessible to them.

(4)   Seizure of Dwelling

A dwelling is seized if an officer seals it off in a manner that prevents its occupants from ingress or egress to obtain their personal property.

(5)   Seizure of Item

An officer or a private actor may seize an item of property during a search of a person's place of business, vehicle, dwelling, personal effects, or the clothes he is wearing.

★   c)   Plain View Doctrine

Under the plain view doctrine, an item or contraband may be seized by an officer from a person's dwelling without a warrant or the person's consent when:

- the officer sees the item in plain view while lawfully present in the place where the item is located;
- the item is found in a searchable area that the officer may lawfully access;
- the officer believes probable cause exists to seize the item; and
- the basis for the officer's probable cause to believe the item may be seized is "immediately apparent."

In *Arizona v. Hicks*, the Court decided that an officer may not search further than observing an item in plain sight in order to determine if that item may be seized. In that case, an officer who lawfully entered a home in response to a gunshot and noticed a stereo that resembled a stolen stereo improperly looked at that stereo's serial number. The officer seized it as evidence, which was ruled inadmissible partially because the officer moved the stereo in order to get a better look at it.

★★   9)   <u>STANDING TO RAISE CONSTITUTIONAL ISSUES</u>

a)   Standing to Contest Search or Seizure

A person must have standing in order to make an in-court challenge to a violation of constitutional rights. To obtain standing, a person generally must have a reasonable expectation of privacy in an item that was seized or in a place that was searched.

(1)   Traffic Stop and Seizure of Person

Like the driver of a car, a passenger in the car subject to a traffic stop by an officer possesses standing to challenge the constitutionality of the stop because it constitutes a seizure of a car occupant's person for purposes of the Fourth Amendment because such an occupant is not free to end this encounter with the officer and leave the scene.

b)   Derivative Standing to Contest Search or Seizure

Generally, a first person lacks standing to legally contest a violation of a second person's constitutional rights. The second person cannot necessarily obtain standing on the basis that the first person possessed that reasonable expectation of privacy. Usually, only the person whose rights may have been violated by an arrest, search, or seizure may challenge that government action.

(1)   Vehicle Search and Seizure

A person lacks standing to challenge a vehicle search due to an absence of a reasonable expectation of privacy if the person:

- was not present when the search occurred; and
- lacked an ownership interest in the vehicle.

(2)   Dwelling Searches and Seizures

In *Rakas v. Illinois*, the Court concluded that a first person's standing to challenge evidence unconstitutionally obtained from a second person depends on whether the first person possessed a reasonable expectation of privacy in the second person's area that an officer searched. The fact that the first person was "legitimately on the premises" that were searched does not necessarily provide standing. Such derivative standing is not automatically available to challenge the introduction of evidence. Rather, the first person must prove that her constitutional rights were violated by the search that was directed toward the second person.

c)   Plain View from Neighbor's Property

When police see a defendant's contraband (e.g., marijuana plants) in plain view from the property of the defendant's neighbor and consequently seize the contraband, the defendant lacks standing to complain of trespass by the police on the neighbor's property. *Horton v. California*, 496 U.S. 128 (1990).

★★★   **B.**   **Confessions and the Privilege against Self-Incrimination**

★★★   1)   <u>GENERAL CONSIDERATIONS</u>

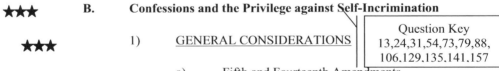

> Question Key
> 13,24,31,54,73,79,88,
> 106,129,135,141,157

a)   Fifth and Fourteenth Amendments

The Fifth Amendment to the *U.S. Constitution* ("Fifth Amendment") provides constitutional rights that serve as a basis for certain legal protections. The Fifth Amendment provides, in part, that: "No person…shall be compelled in any criminal case to be a witness against himself." Under the doctrine of selective incorporation, the Fifth Amendment's protections apply to all the states pursuant to the Due Process Clause of the Fourteenth Amendment.

(1)   Self-Identification to Officer

An officer may request that a suspect identify himself or herself during a *Terry* stop. In *Hiibel v. The Sixth Judicial District Court,* the Supreme Court upheld a defendant's conviction for violating a Nevada statute requiring an individual to identify himself or herself when detained by an officer in an investigative stop based on an alleged assault. The Fifth Amendment right against self-incrimination does not permit an individual under suspicion of committing a criminal offense to refuse to identify himself or herself to an officer, which refusal can constitute a crime. Only in unusual circumstances could an officer's request that a suspect disclose his name be significant enough to incriminate the suspect. Note that this concept is also detailed in the outline section covering the Fourth Amendment, which is equally applicable.

>   b)   Sixth and Fourteenth Amendments

The Sixth Amendment to the *U.S. Constitution* ("Sixth Amendment") provides, in part, that: "In all criminal prosecutions, the accused shall enjoy the right to…have the assistance of counsel for his defence." U.S. Const. amend. VI. The Supreme Court, in *Gideon v. Wainwright,* applied the selective incorporation doctrine to rule that the Sixth Amendment afforded rights that applied to all of the United States under the Due Process Clause of the Fourteenth Amendment. In *Rompilla v. Beard,* the Supreme Court decided that a death penalty imposed upon a defendant convicted of murder may be overturned when the defendant's counsel did not provide a defense that satisfied basic constitutional standards.

>   c)   Fifth and Sixth Amendments Apply at Different
>   Points

The Fifth Amendment right to counsel applies before formal charges are filed against a person. The Court stated in *Rothgery v. Gillespie County, Texas*, that the Sixth Amendment right to counsel "applies at the first appearance before a judicial officer at which the defendant is told of the formal accusations against him and restrictions are imposed on his liberty." Moreover, the attachment of this right to counsel does not depend upon whether the prosecution is involved in or aware of the initial proceeding. The right to counsel under either of the Amendments may be violated if an officer obtains a confession from a person without first having obtained a waiver of the right to counsel. In that event, the confession will be suppressed pursuant to the exclusionary rule.

★★★   2)   <u>CONFESSIONS</u>

A confession is a person's self-incriminating statement. It may or may not have been made while the person is in legal custody. If it is voluntarily made when the person is neither in custody nor under interrogation, then the confession will not need to be suppressed under the exclusionary rule. It will be admissible. However, if a confession is involuntarily made when the person is in custody and under interrogation, then the confession may need to be suppressed under the exclusionary rule.

>   a)   Voluntary Confession is Generally Admissible

If a confession is voluntarily made when a person is not under custodial interrogation, then the confession is admissible. For example, suppose a police officer knocks on someone's door to inform them of a neighborhood PBA event. When the occupant opens the door, he says, "I did it! I killed my friend. How did you know so quickly?" Because the occupant was not under custodial interrogation, if the confession is deemed voluntary (not coerced), it will be admissible.

To ascertain whether a person made a voluntary confession, consider the totality of the circumstances of the confession, including the person's situation and an officer's conduct.

(1)   The Person's Situation

Considerations that relate to a person include gender, education, mental state, physical state, age, and race.

(2)   The Officer's Conduct

Considerations regarding an officer's conduct may involve the type and scope of any questioning, as well as where, and for how long, it occurred. Courts will measure the voluntariness of a confession in relation to how the conditions of an officer's questioning restrict a person's liberty interests.

(3)   Deception

The fact that a person's confession resulted from an officer's scheme of deception (e.g., regarding the evidence against the person) does not automatically render the confession involuntary and invalid. Similarly, under *United States v. Kontny*, a confession will not be inadmissible simply because the officer used deceit or trickery. "Far from making the police a fiduciary of the suspect, the law permits the police to pressure and cajole, conceal material facts and actively mislead." *United States v. Rutledge*, 900 F.2d 1127 (7th Cir. 1990).

(4)   Coercion

However, in *Arizona v. Fulminante*, the Court concluded that a person's confession is coerced if it results from a threatened physical violence against the accused. Likewise, a confession that results from actual physical violence against the accused certainly would be coerced and, thus, involuntary. *Rodgers v. Richmond* provides that when an officer used coercive conduct, the issue becomes whether such conduct is sufficient to overcome the person's will. Pursuant to *Schneckloth v. Bustamonte*, this question may be answered by an analysis of the totality of the circumstances, including but not limited to, the officer's conduct and the person's familiarity with the criminal justice system, level of education, and age.

b)   Confession Made During Custodial Interrogation

Under the Court's decision in *Miranda v. Arizona*, a statement by a person during custodial interrogation will be considered to be compelled in violation of the person's

Fifth Amendment right against self-incrimination, if the police has not provided legally sufficient procedural safeguards of that right.

(1) Custodial Interrogation

(a) Custody

Custody exists when a reasonable person would believe that the person's freedom of action is restricted to the extent of an arrest. Custody may involve a period of detention or confinement, such as while a person is in shackles, in an officer's vehicle, or in some building under the officer's control.

(b) Interrogation

Interrogation occurs when an officer questions a person using words or actions that the officer reasonably would anticipate provoking an incriminating reply by the person. Interrogation does not occur when an officer presents preliminary inquiries to a person in the context of an investigatory stop or when obtaining background information such as a person's name. However, the questioning does not need to be explicit. For example, a group of officers engaging in a conversation intended to provoke the suspect into providing an incriminatory remark constitutes questioning.

(2) Procedural Safeguards

The following conditions must have existed when a person answered an officer's questions in a custodial interrogation in order for those answers to be admissible in a criminal proceeding: 1) an adequate warning occurred; and 2) a waiver occurred.

(a) Adequate Warning Obligation

Miranda v. Arizona requires that an officer make all of the following warning statements to a person: "You have the right to remain silent. Anything that you say can and will be used against you in a court of law. You have a right to consult with a lawyer and to have a lawyer present during interrogation. If you cannot afford a lawyer, one will be appointed for you." The officer lacks any obligation to give these warnings to a person only subject to a *Terry* stop.

(i) Right to Silence Applies
to Charged Offense

In *Michigan v. Mosley*, the Court decided that after a person invokes the right to silence, an officer may not question the person about the offense for which the person is in custody. The officer, however, may later question the person about a separate offense after providing another adequate warning.

(ii) Fifth Amendment Right
Must Be Asserted

In *Davis v. United States,* the Court ruled that a person must clearly and unequivocally invoke the right to counsel under the Fifth Amendment. When a person does request the assistance of counsel, an officer must carefully honor that request and cease questioning the witness.

(iii)   Delay Between Warnings and Confession

Under *Davis,* if the officer waits for a significant period before seeking to obtain the person's confession in the absence of counsel, the officer must then provide new *Miranda* warnings before engaging in a conversational interrogation. *Miranda* warnings provided after a confession is made are ineffective.

(iv)   Questioning Cannot Occur Without Counsel

After a defendant asserts his right to counsel, unless the defendant voluntarily initiates a subsequent conversation, answers to subsequent questioning will not be admissible. In *Oregon v. Bradshaw*, the Court concluded that if a person voluntarily initiates communication with an officer in the absence of legal counsel, then the officer could obtain a valid waiver of the right to counsel.

(v)   Public Safety Exception

Under the Court's decision in *New York v. Quarles*, a person is not entitled to receive an adequate warning (e.g., to enable the accused to request counsel) before an officer begins an interrogation of the accused regarding public safety concerns.

(vi)   Consecutive Questionings

In *Missouri v. Seibert*, the Supreme Court rejected the approach used by officers of initially questioning and getting an inadmissible statement from a suspect before providing *Miranda* warnings prior to subsequently questioning and getting another similar statement from the suspect after he received *Miranda* warnings. This approach to obtaining a confession impermissibly deprives a suspect of receiving *Miranda* warnings before questioning by the officer.

b)   Waiver of the Rights

If a person elects to make a statement after receiving an adequate warning, then to properly waive the right against self-incrimination, the person's waiver must be voluntary, knowing, and intelligent.

(i)   Voluntary

A person's waiver is voluntary if it did not occur as a result of coercion. To analyze if coercion existed, consider the totality of the circumstances. The types of facts subject to that analysis include an officer's conduct and a person's age, maturity, and intelligence. A person's confession that results from an officer's deliberate deception or coercive threat of serious injury or death may not be considered voluntary.

(ii)   Knowing & Intelligent

A person's waiver occurs knowingly if the person understands the nature of the person's rights and the results of relinquishing them.

★★   3)   PRIVILEGE AGAINST SELF-INCRIMINATION

a)   Scope of Right Not to Testify

Under the Fifth Amendment, an individual has the right to refuse to answer any questions or make any statements, when to do so would help establish that the person committed a crime or is connected to any criminal activity. This right applies to testimonial communications in the context of judicial, congressional, and grand jury proceedings. The person may either completely decline to testify or decide to testify subject to selectively invoking the privilege. Additionally, a person does not need to be charged with a crime in order to invoke the right.

b)   Improper Comments or Inferences about Silence

In *Griffin v. California*, the Court decided that references to a person's failure to testify in her criminal trial, both by the prosecution and in jury instructions, violated her right to Due Process under the Fourteenth Amendment. The Court considered such a comment upon the person's silence a "penalty imposed by courts for exercising a constitutional privilege." The Court, in *Mitchell v. United States*, extended the rule of *Griffin v. California* to preclude a sentencing judge from drawing a negative inference from a person's refusal to testify at her criminal trial.

c)   Jury Instructions or Inferences about Silence

The Court, in *Lakeside v. Oregon*, concluded that a trial court may instruct a jury, on that person's behalf, that a person possesses the Fifth Amendment right not to testify. The Court ruled that the jury could not draw an inference of guilt from the person's exercise of that right. The Court decided that the instruction, even if provided contrary to a person's objections, did not violate the person's privilege against self-incrimination. However, the Court acknowledged that it may be advisable for a trial judge not to give such a cautionary instruction over a defendant's objection.

d)   Accused Person's Right to Testify

A person on trial for a criminal offense possesses a constitutional right to "testify on one's own behalf at a criminal trial" under the Court's decision in *Rock v. Arkansas*. That right is derived from the following grounds:

- The Fifth Amendment's right of a person not to incriminate himself or herself includes the related right to testify in his discretion.
- The right to compulsory process under the Sixth Amendment.
- The Court stated, in *Rock v. Arkansas* that a legal basis supports a person's right to testify on his own behalf.
- The Due Process Clauses of the Fifth Amendment (federal offenses) and the Fourteenth Amendment (state offenses) protect the right to a fair trial, which includes an opportunity to be heard.

The Court stated, in *Rock v. Arkansas*, that a legal restriction upon an exercise of the right to testify "may not be arbitrary or disproportionate to the purposes that they are designed to serve."

★   **C.**   **Right to Counsel and Identifications**

> Question Key
> 59

★   1)   <u>SIXTH AMENDMENT RIGHT TO COUNSEL</u>

The Sixth Amendment provides, in part, that: "In all criminal prosecutions, the accused shall enjoy the right to…have the assistance of counsel for his defence."

         a)   Procedural Considerations

            (1)   Applies to Federal Proceedings

In *Johnson v. Zerbst*, the Court ruled that a person in a federal criminal proceeding possesses a Sixth Amendment right either to retain legal counsel or, if the person is indigent, to have a court-appointed counsel.

                 (a)   Federal Grand Jury Proceedings

A federal grand jury witness lacks a constitutional right to counsel within the grand jury room. *United States v. Mandujano*, 425 U.S. 564 (1976).

            (2)   Applies to State Proceedings

The Court, in *Gideon v. Wainwright*, applied the selective incorporation doctrine to rule that the rights under the Sixth Amendment exist in all of the states pursuant to the Due Process Clause of the Fourteenth Amendment. The Court considered those rights fundamental, and decided that these required judicial protection from state action under the Sixth Amendment. Thus, a person in a state criminal proceeding possesses a Sixth Amendment right either to retain legal counsel or, if the person is indigent, to have a court-appointed counsel.

            (3)   Applies to Critical Phases

In *Massiah v. U.S.*, the Court extended the right to counsel to all critical phases of a criminal proceeding. For example, the taking of a statement constitutes a critical phase.

Although an arrest is not such a phase, if it results in custodial interrogation, then the Sixth Amendment right to counsel may apply. The Court decided, in *Texas v. Cobb*, that under the Sixth Amendment, a person's counsel only needs to be present at an interrogation if the interrogation concerns an offense that the person retained the counsel to defend.

> (4)   Criminal Proceedings Commence Critical Phases

The critical phases of a criminal proceeding begin when adversary proceedings are formally initiated. Examples of when those phases begin are: a formal charge, an indictment, an arraignment, or a preliminary hearing.

> (5)   Right to Counsel if Misdemeanor Requires Incarceration

An accused possesses a right to counsel for all felony cases. In *Scott v. Illinois*, the Court construed the Sixth Amendment's right to counsel to provide that a person who is charged with a misdemeanor is not entitled to an attorney unless imprisonment actually is imposed. The accused, therefore, may not be incarcerated if the accused has been denied the right to counsel in the case. In addition, a court may not activate a suspended or probated sentence of a defendant who was denied the right to counsel in the underlying case.

> (6)   Representation by Counsel of Choice

Pursuant to *United States v. Gonzalez-Lopez*, a wrongful deprivation of a defendant's right to be represented by counsel of the defendant's choice under the Sixth Amendment entitles the defendant to a reversal of his conviction.

> b)   Waiver of Right to Counsel - Three Elements

To be valid, an unrepresented person's waiver of the Sixth Amendment right to counsel must be made knowingly, voluntarily, and intelligently. Such a waiver does not need to be express to be considered valid. Such an implied waiver may be valid if it may be inferred from the surrounding circumstances and a person's conduct. A represented person may only effectively waive the Sixth Amendment right to counsel in the presence of the person's counsel.

★   2)   <u>LINEUPS & SHOW-UPS</u>

> a)   No Right to Counsel before Charge

If no formal charges are brought against a person before a show up, then the person's Sixth Amendment Right to Counsel does not attach, pursuant to *Massiah v. U.S.* That right applies only after the prosecution files charges against the person. Therefore, a person can be compelled to participate in a lineup against their will. Additionally, an accused's Fifth Amendment right not to incriminate himself does not apply to lineups. That right is testimonial, and therefore, does not apply to lineups.

> b)   Sixth Amendment Right to Counsel in Pre-Trial Identifications

The Court, in *U.S. v. Wade*, concluded that a "post-indictment lineup was a critical stage of the prosecution" in which a person is entitled to the assistance of counsel. In *Moore v. Illinois*, the Court held that the rule in *U.S. v. Wade* governed an identification of a person during a pre-trial proceeding.

> c)   Right to Counsel in Criminal Proceedings

The Court, in *Kirby v. Illinois*, decided that the rule of *U.S. v. Wade* applied only to identifications occurring "at or after the initiation of adversary judicial criminal proceedings — whether by way of formal charge, preliminary hearing, indictment, information, or arraignment." Usually, the filing of a formal charge by the prosecution will be the first step of such proceedings. Thus, no Sixth Amendment right to counsel exists for a person who is placed in a line-up before adversarial judicial criminal proceedings occur. That right exists for a person who is questioned by an officer after commencement of those proceedings. The right does not exist if the person unilaterally volunteers such information in an outburst.

> d)   Right to Counsel in One-on-One Show-ups

In *Moore v. Illinois*, the Court decided that a person generally possesses a right to counsel at a one-on-one show up at the person's preliminary hearing because such an identification procedure typically is impermissibly suggestive. However, in subsequent case law, the Court has required that the accused show some police misconduct that made the show-up procedure impermissibly suggestive. A show-up procedure is not suggestive when an officer did not engage in improper conduct during the process.

> e)   Right to Counsel Violations & In-Court Identifications

When there has been a lineup or show up in which the right to counsel has been improperly denied, all testimony relating to the out-of-court identification is inadmissible. *Gilbert v. California*; *Moore v. Illinois*. A subsequent in-court identification is inadmissible unless the government can show by clear and convincing evidence that the in-court identifications were based upon observations of the suspect other than at the lineup identification. In determining whether there is an independent source for the in-court identification, the court will consider factors including the witness' opportunity to observe the criminal act, any discrepancy between a pre-lineup description and the defendant's actual appearance, any identification by picture of the defendant prior to the lineup, the failure to identify the defendant on a prior occasion, the lapse of time between the criminal act and the lineup, and the circumstances surrounding the conduct of the lineup. *United States v. Wade*.

3)   OTHER FORMS OF IDENTIFICATION

a)   Photographic Identification

In *United States v. Ash*, the Court ruled that no right to counsel exists while an officer shows pictures of a person and others to witnesses without the person being present. That rule applies even if the photographic identification occurs after the person already has been indicted. The Due Process Clause of the Fourteenth Amendment may preclude the admission into evidence of photographic identification evidence at trial if an "unduly suggestive" procedure was used to obtain that evidence.

b)   Scientific Identification

The right to counsel under *U.S. v. Wade*, does not extend to the following scientific identification procedures: fingerprints, hair, blood samples, and clothing. The key distinction between scientific identification and in-person identification is that a scientific identification does not rely on the recollections of a witness for its validity, but rather upon the accuracy of the instrumentation.

D.   Fair Trial and Guilty Pleas

1)   GENERAL CONSIDERATIONS

a)   Pleading Guilty or Going to Trial

A person who is charged with a criminal offense by the prosecution may either defend the charge at a trial or plead guilty to the offense. If the person enters a guilty plea, then the person forfeits the right to a trial for the purpose of determining his guilt or innocence. Both a guilty plea and a trial that results in finding a person guilty normally are followed by a separate sentencing proceeding that determines the type and scope of punishment that will be imposed upon the person.

★★   2)   FAIR TRIAL

Question Key
26,152

a)   General Grounds for Fair Trial Requirement

The concept of a fair trial is derived from common law principles, rules of civil procedure, rules of evidence, statutes, and constitutional rights.

b)   Constitutional Grounds for Fair Trial Requirement

In combination, the constitutional rights under the Sixth Amendment are intended to provide an impartial determination of a person's guilt or innocence in a criminal trial. The Due Process Clauses of the Fifth Amendment (federal offenses) and the Fourteenth Amendment (state offenses) also provide bases for the requirement of a fair trial.

       (1)   Sixth Amendment Grounds for Fair Trial Requirement

The Sixth Amendment provides in part that:

> "In all criminal prosecutions, the accused shall enjoy the right to a speedy and public trial, by an impartial jury of the State and district wherein the crime shall have been committed…and to be informed of the nature and cause of the accusation; to be confronted with the witnesses against him; to have compulsory process for obtaining witnesses in his favor, and to have assistance of counsel for his defense."

The several protections included in that language are addressed separately below.

       c)   Requirement of Proof beyond a Reasonable Doubt

Part of the due process right to a fair trial is the requirement that the prosecution must show that a defendant is guilty, beyond a reasonable doubt, of all elements of a charged offense. *Mullaney v. Wilbur* provides that a person cannot, without violating constitutional due process, be required to establish adequate provocation to reduce a homicide from murder to voluntary manslaughter. The reason for that decision is that adequate provocation is an element of voluntary manslaughter.

       d)   Right to Trial by Impartial Jurors

A defendant has a right to a trial by jurors who were not subject to unfair influences. For example, a juror could be unfairly biased against a person due to awareness of prejudicial media coverage regarding the accused.

       3)   <u>TRIAL BY JURY</u>

       a)   Determination of Judge or Jury

Whether a judge or a jury will decide a person's guilt or innocence in a criminal trial depends upon the nature of the person's alleged offense. Constitutional provisions and laws will determine if a particular offense includes a right to a jury trial.

       b)   Constitutional Grounds for Trial by Jury

       (1)   General Federal Constitutional Basis

Article III of the *Constitution* provides, in relevant part, that:

> "The Trial of all Crimes, except in Cases of Impeachment, shall be by Jury, and such Trial shall be held in the State where the said Crimes shall have been committed."

(2)   Sixth Amendment Basis

The Sixth Amendment provides, in part, that: "In all criminal prosecutions, the accused shall enjoy the right to a …trial, by an impartial jury…"

The "impartial jury" provision of the Sixth Amendment applies to the federal government. In *Duncan v. Louisiana*, the Court used the selective incorporation doctrine to apply the "impartial jury" provision of the Sixth Amendment to the states pursuant to the Due Process Clause of the Fourteenth Amendment. In criminal cases to which the "impartial jury" requirement applies, the jury determines a person's guilt or innocence. The requirement does not apply to "petty offenses."

c)   Jury Requirement for State Law Offenses

(1)   Serious Offenses Exceed Six Months

The Sixth Amendment provides state defendants a right to a jury trial for serious offenses. A serious offense generally is an offense that involves potential imprisonment for at least six months. In *Baldwin v. New York*, the Court provided that "no offense can be deemed 'petty' for purposes of the right to trial by jury where imprisonment for more than six months is authorized." If the punishment exceeds a minimum of six months, then an offense is considered "serious."

(2)   Petty Offenses Are Less Than Six Months

Thus, the determination of whether an offense is "petty" depends upon:

- the nature of the offense; and
- the maximum potential penalty for the offense.

In *Dyke v. Taylor Implement Manufacturing Co.,* the Court concluded that if a statute only authorizes a maximum penalty of a fine or imprisonment for less than six months, then a jury trial is not required.

(3)   Contempt Offenses as Serious or Petty

Under *Cheff v. Schnackenberg*, the Court concluded that no jury trial right exists in two situations involving cases of criminal contempt:

- the statutory penalty provides that criminal contempt is a petty offense; and
- absent a statutory penalty, the penalty imposed is less than six months.

In *Codispoti v. Pennsylvania,* the Court determined that when several acts of contempt occurred at a trial, and the combined sentences for convictions of those acts of contempt could exceed six months, then the Sixth Amendment mandated a jury trial about them.

But in *Lewis v. United States,* the Court concluded that the Sixth Amendment did not require a jury trial where Congress expressly identified the offense of obstructing the mail as a petty offense.

      d)   Jury Composition

           (1)   Number of Jurors

The constitutional number of jurors on a jury ranges from 6 to 12 persons.

           (a)   Unanimity

In *Burch v. Louisiana,* the Court held that a guilty verdict by a six-person jury must be unanimous. However, a guilty verdict by a jury composed of 10-12 jurors need not be unanimous. The line of how many jurors requires unanimity is unclear, but the requirements involving the two extremes now are established.

           (2)   Fair Cross-Section Requirement

Although the jury pool (i.e., the potential jurors) needs to represent a fair cross-section of the community, the selected jury (i.e., the actual jurors) does not need to constitute a fair cross-section of the community.

           (3)   Burden of Proof for Fair Cross-Section

The Court, in *Taylor v. Louisiana,* observed that a jury's function "to guard against the exercise of arbitrary power," will not be fulfilled "if the jury pool is made up of only segments of the populace or if large, distinctive groups are excluded from the pool." In order to show that the fair cross-section requirement is not fulfilled, a person must prove the following elements that the Court provided in *Duren v. Missouri*:

> (1) that the group alleged to be excluded is a 'distinctive' group in the community; (2) that the representation of this group in venires from which juries are selected is not fair and reasonable in relation to the number of such persons in the community; and (3) that this under-representation is due to systemic exclusion of the group in the jury-selection process.

           (4)   Challenges to Jurors

           (a)   For Cause

Jurors may be challenged and excused for general cause or bias, implied or actual. Examples of general causes to excuse jurors include felony convictions, and defects of physical senses or reason (e.g., unsound mind).

           (b)   Peremptory Grounds

Generally, jurors may be challenged and excused based on a party's discretion without the party having to articulate any reason(s) for making such peremptory challenges. The prosecution's exclusion of jurors on the basis of race, however, may violate the Equal Protection Clause of the Fourteen Amendment to the *U.S. Constitution.*

(1)   Batson Procedure

The decision in *Batson v. Kentucky*, prohibits the prosecution from using peremptory challenges to strike jurors in a racially discriminatory manner. A defendant needs to present the following evidence to make a *prima facie* case of unconstitutional racial discrimination in the exercise of peremptory challenges:

- The defendant is a member of a specific racial group;
- The prosecution has eliminated other members of that group by peremptory challenges;
- Such peremptory challenges could be for discriminatory purposes; and
- All relevant circumstances raise an inference of intentional racial discrimination by the prosecution.

After a *prima facie* case is presented, the prosecution is entitled to present a racially neutral reason for its exclusion of certain jurors. After the prosecution presents the reason, the burden shifts back to the defendant to prove that the reason is actually a pretext for discrimination. The trial court must then decide if racial discrimination has been established and, if it is, the trial court could disallow the racially discriminatory strikes. Also, if a *Batson* violation has occurred, the defendant could move for a new array of jurors. Moreover, the making of a *Batson* objection, the presentation of evidence about this issue, and the trial court's decision about it, create a record for appellate review.

e)   Waiver of Right to Jury Trial

A person may agree to waive a right to trial by jury and instead submit to a bench trial that is conducted and decided by a trial judge. A person may make a valid waiver of a jury trial if doing so is not prohibited by a constitution, statute, or court rule.

(1)   Methods of Waiving the Jury Trial Right

In *Patton v. United States*, the Court stated that a valid waiver of a jury trial requires "the express and intelligent consent of the defendant." A person's silence cannot operate as a waiver. A person's written waiver of a jury trial is required in both the federal courts and in the courts of several states. A few states provide a person an unconditional right to a trial without a jury.

(a)   Consent Requirement

Other states and the federal courts require either consent of the court or consent from both the court and the prosecution for a trial without a jury. The Court, in *Singer v.*

United States, upheld the latter type of approval requirement. A person may, however, waive the requirement of a 12-member jury for a constitutionally lesser number of jurors.

f)   Right to a Jury for Sentencing

In *Apprendi v. New Jersey,* the Supreme Court held that: "Other than the fact of a prior conviction, any fact that increases the penalty for a crime beyond the prescribed statutory maximum must be submitted to a jury, and proved beyond a reasonable doubt." Thus, the jury instead of the sentencing court must consider such facts.

(1)   Effect upon State Sentencing Guidelines

The Court later applied this rule in *Blakely v. Washington* and invalidated a sentence imposed pursuant to the sentencing guideline system of the State of Washington.

(2)   Effect upon the Federal Sentencing Guidelines

Subsequently, in *United States v. Booker,* the Court applied *Blakely* to the Federal Sentencing Guideline system and held that the mandatory application of these Guidelines violated the Sixth Amendment right to trial by jury because they permit the sentencing court to make factual findings that might enlarge the sentence over the maximum allowed by the jury. The *Booker* Court found that the federal statute that made these Guidelines mandatory was incompatible with the Court's Sixth Amendment "jury trial" holding and thus, must be removed from the *Federal Sentencing Reform Act of 1984.* According to these changes, the Guidelines effectively were rendered advisory upon a sentencing court, such that they provide the range of sentences which may be considered, but the sentence may be customized by the sentencing court in light of other statutory considerations.

4)   <u>RIGHT TO SPEEDY TRIAL</u>

a)   Constitutional Basis

The Sixth Amendment's speedy trial provisions apply to criminal prosecutions by the federal government. In *Klopfer v. North Carolina*, the Court applied the selective incorporation doctrine to rule that the speedy trial provision of the Sixth Amendment applied to the states' conduct pursuant to the Due Process Clause of the Fourteenth Amendment.

b)   Attachment / Suspension of Speedy Trial Right

The speedy-trial right attaches when the earlier of the following two events occur: 1) a person is either arrested; or 2) formally charged with a crime. The right is suspended either when a trial commences, or the prosecution's charges are dismissed and the person is discharged.

c)   Challenging Violation of Speedy Trial Right

A violation of the right to a speedy trial must be raised by a motion to dismiss the charges. If a person goes to trial or pleads guilty before filing such a motion, the person forfeits the right to raise that issue, even on appeal. In *Strunk v. United States*, the Court ruled that "the only possible remedy" for denial of the right to a speedy trial is a dismissal of the charges.

(1)   Did a Violation of the Speedy Trial Right Occur?

The Court, in *Doggett v. United States*, declared that a violation of the speedy trial right occurs when pretrial delay prejudices a person's ability to present a defense to criminal charges.

The Court, in *Barker v. Wingo*, established a balancing analysis that applies to delays that exceed one year. That test seeks to determine what constitutes a speedy trial based on a consideration of the following factors:

•   How long did the delay last?

The impact of the delay depends upon the reason for the delay.

•   Why did the delay occur?

Although a failure to assert the speedy trial right does not waive it, it is a valid consideration.

•   Did the delay occur despite good faith, and was it justifiable?

•   Did a person assert the right to a speedy trial?

A significant consideration is if the person experienced the delay while in custody.

•   Did the accused suffer any prejudice as a result of the delay?

In *Dillingham v. United States*, the Court held that a person is entitled to a speedy trial even though the person is not indicted for a lengthy time after being arrested and released. In that event, the above analytical factors will be applied to determine the reasonableness of the delay.

d)   Remedy for Violation of Speedy Trial Right

If the person experienced a deprivation of the speedy trial right, then the charges should be dropped and the person should be discharged.

5)   COMPULSORY PROCESS

        a)   Constitutional Basis for Access to Evidence

The compulsory process provision of the Sixth Amendment affords a person access to certain evidence to prepare a defense in a criminal trial. To protect that right of access and ensure fundamental fairness in criminal trials, the Court either directly uses the Due Process Clauses of the Fifth and Fourteenth Amendments or it applies the Sixth Amendment under the selective incorporation doctrine.

        b)   Required Evidentiary Disclosures

A person is entitled to the following types of protections regarding compulsory process:

- production of relevant and inculpatory or exculpatory evidence in the prosecution's possession;
- the prosecution may not, in bad faith, destroy relevant and exculpatory evidence;
- the subpoena power to require the production of witnesses and physical evidence;
- the provision of information to enable a person to fully exercise the subpoena power; and
- no prosecutorial conduct preventing a person's use of subpoenas.

In *Pennsylvania v. Richie*, the Court considered the extent of a person's right to obtain evidence from the prosecution. The Court decided that a person is not entitled to access the records of a public agency that a state statute required remain confidential, despite the person's claim that the records could be useful for the person's purpose of cross-examining the prosecution's witnesses. The Court ruled that the relevance of evidence to the person's guilt was contingent upon the following test:

- did a reasonable probability exist that;
- if the prosecution had disclosed the evidence;
- a proceeding would have had different results?

★   6)   RIGHT TO CONFRONTATION

Question Key
39

        a)   General

                (1)   Constitutional   Basis   for   Right   to
                        Confrontation

The Sixth Amendment's provision of a right of confrontation applies to criminal prosecutions by the federal government. In *Pointer v. Texas,* the Court used the selective incorporation doctrine to apply the witness confrontation provision of the Sixth Amendment to conduct by the states, pursuant to the Due Process Clause of the Fourteenth Amendment. That provision entitles a person to be present in criminal proceedings against him in order to face any accusers, including the prosecution and any witnesses against the person.

(2)   Right of Cross-Examination

The Sixth Amendment also permits a defendant to cross-examine witnesses in criminal proceedings. *Pointer v. Texas* dictates that if a person is not afforded an opportunity to cross-examine a witness at a pretrial hearing, then the prosecution may not introduce such pretrial testimony at trial.

(3)   Confrontation Right in all Trial Proceedings

The Court's decision in *United States v. Gagnon*, stands for the proposition that the due process aspect of the Sixth Amendment extends its protections beyond instances in which a person is "actually confronting witnesses against him." This provision applies to any trial-type proceeding in which the person's presence "has a relation, reasonably sustainable, to the fullness of his opportunity to defend against the charge."

(4)   Out-of-Court Testimony/Hearsay

Any out-of-court statement that is "testimonial" in nature is not admissible, unless: 1) the declarant is unavailable to testify in court; and 2) the defendant has had a prior opportunity to cross-examine him. If a statement is "non-testimonial," then a court may use its discretion to determine the reliability of a statement and whether it should be admitted. An out of court statement is "testimonial" in nature if it is the result of police interrogation, or given under circumstances in which the intended use for the statement is criminal prosecution.

b)   Exceptions or Limitations on Right to Confrontation

(1)   Disorderly Conduct

The Court, in *Illinois v. Allen*, concluded that a person's Sixth Amendment right to be present at a trial of the person for a felony offense may be forfeited if:

- the person engages in such disorderly conduct that
- a trial could not proceed with that person remaining in the courtroom.

A judge possesses discretionary authority to employ other lesser means than removal to control a person's disruptive conduct, such as physically restraining a person, gagging the person, or citing the person for contempt.

(2)   Waiver of Right to Confrontation

In *Taylor v. United States*, the Court concluded that if a person voluntarily removes himself or herself from the courtroom, a judge may consider that removal a waiver of the right to confrontation without the judge providing any other notice to the person.

(3)   Co-Defendant's Confession

If two accused are tried together and only the first accused testifies at trial, the second accused's confession may not be admitted at trial if it implicates the first accused. The reason for excluding the confession is that the first accused would be denied an opportunity to cross-examine the second accused concerning his statements' truth or falsity.

(4)   Witness Competency Hearing

A person lacks any right to attend a witness competency hearing that occurs out-of-court if the person's attorney represented the person in that hearing and provided effective cross-examination of the witness.

(5)   Child Witness

Some state laws allow a trial court to permit a child to testify against a defendant outside of the defendant's presence. A trial court may determine that a one-way closed circuit television procedure is necessary to protect the welfare of a particular child witness who seeks to testify in an action. The trial court must find that the child witness would be traumatized, not by the courtroom generally, but by the presence of the defendant.

7)   PUBLIC TRIAL

a)   Sixth Amendment Constitutional Basis

The Sixth Amendment's provision of a right to a public trial applies to criminal prosecutions by the federal government. The Court's decision, in *In re Oliver*, invoked the selective incorporation doctrine and ruled that the public trial provision of the Sixth Amendment applied to the states' conduct pursuant to the Due Process Clause of the Fourteenth Amendment.

b)   Purpose of Public Trial Right

The public trial requirement is intended to provide a fair trial. Secret trials are prohibited to prevent the possibility that the prosecution and/or judge could engage in improper conduct or fail to follow proper procedures, which would violate a person's rights.

8)   PRETRIAL PUBLICITY

A person's general right to a fair trial – in federal courts under the Due Process Clause of the Fifth Amendment, and in state courts under the Due Process Clause of the Fourteenth Amendment – may be affected by issues arising from two other related rights. Those are: a person's right to a public trial under the Sixth Amendment, and the freedom of the press under the First Amendment to the *U.S. Constitution* ("First Amendment"). U.S. Const. amend. I. Both of those provisions apply directly to the federal government. They also apply to the states through the incorporation doctrine under the Due Process Clause of the Fourteenth Amendment.

> a)   Restraints on Free Speech (Provide a Fair Trial)

A gag order is a judicial means of preventing a person from making any statements about ongoing judicial proceedings to the public or the press. The following two decisions of the Court, *Gentile v. State Bar of Nebraska* and *Nebraska Press Association v. Stuart*, supply the following elements that warrant imposing a gag order against a criminal defense attorney who represents a person:

- Possible statements of the attorney to the press having a reasonable or "substantial likelihood" of causing prejudice in a criminal trial;
- The order must be "narrowly tailored" to limit only the statements that present that potential for prejudice; and
- Alternatives that involve lesser restrictions are inadequate to prevent the threatened harm.

In *United States v. Ford*, the Sixth Circuit Court of Appeals concluded that imposing a gag order on a person in a criminal proceeding required a finding of a "clear and present danger" of prejudice that may result from the person's statements.

Nebraska Press Association v. Stuart stands for the proposition that only rare circumstances may justify a prior restraint against the press' publication of information that may be prejudicial to a person who is subject to a hearing.

> b)   Limitations on Press Access (Provide a Fair Trial)

In both *Richmond Newspapers v. Virginia* and *Globe Newspapers v. Superior Court for Norfolk County*, the Court determined that the First Amendment right of the press to access a criminal trial was "qualified" or "presumptive," and not absolute. The proceedings could be closed based on a proper showing of a compelling need, such as a person's need for a fair trial.

In *Press-Enterprise Co. v. Superior Court*, the Court established the following test to ascertain if the First Amendment right of the press to access a proceeding applied:

- experience: "Whether the place and process have historically been open to the press and the general public?"
- logic: "Whether public access plays a significant positive role in the functioning of the particular process in question?"

> c)   Transfer of Venue

> > (1)   Actual Prejudice

In *Irvin v. Dowd*, the Court held that if prejudicial pretrial publicity jeopardizes a defendant's right to a fair trial by an impartial jury, the trial judge should grant a change of venue. According to the Court's decision in *Murphy v. Florida*, a defendant may challenge a trial court's denial of a change of venue by showing that pretrial publicity created either "actual prejudice" or "inherent prejudice" among the jurors. A showing of actual prejudice focuses on the voir dire responses of the jurors, as in *Irvin*, and establishes actual prejudice if the responses demonstrate actual juror partiality or hostility that cannot be laid aside. For example, in *Irvin*, eight of the 12 jurors in the case indicated during voir dire that they thought the defendant was guilty of the murder for which he was being tried.

> (2)   Inherent Prejudice

To establish inherent or presumed prejudice, on the other hand, the focus is on the content, volume, and distribution of the publicity regardless of voir dire responses. In *Rideau v. Louisiana*, the Court concluded that where highly prejudicial publicity may deprive the defendant of a fair trial, the Court will apply the inherent prejudice test. In *Rideau*, the Court decided "that it was a denial of due process of law to refuse the request for a change of venue, after the people of Calcasieu Parish had been exposed repeatedly and in depth to the spectacle of Rideau personally confessing in detail to the crimes with which he was later to be charged. For anyone who has ever watched television the conclusion cannot be avoided that this spectacle, to the tens of thousands of people who saw and heard it, in a very real sense was Rideau's trial - at which he pleaded guilty to murder. Any subsequent court proceedings in a community so pervasively exposed to such a spectacle could be but a hollow formality."

In *Patton v. Yount*, the Court indicated that the inherent prejudice test is applied only in cases where extreme and inflammatory publicity is distributed immediately prior to trial, creating a "huge . . . wave of public passion." Otherwise, the inquiry is limited to the actual prejudice standard.

> (3)   Attempts   to   Limit   Venue   Transfer
>   Disfavored

In *Groppi v. Wisconsin*, the Court invalidated a state law that prohibited venue changes in misdemeanor cases because no other available remedies were sufficient to protect a person's right to a fair trial.

> d)   Television Access to Trials

Any criminal case that generates a great deal of publicity presents some risks that the publicity may compromise the right of the defendant to a fair trial by improperly influencing a jury member.

> (1)   Limited Televised Proceedings

In *Chandler v. Florida*, the Court decided a person's challenge to the televising of some phases of a criminal proceeding against him. The Court concluded that no violation of the person's right to a fair trial under the Due Process Clause of the Fourteenth Amendment had occurred. The Court did not strike down an experimental televised proceeding program that the Florida Supreme Court had authorized. The program survived judicial scrutiny because the "guidelines placed on trial judges positive obligations to be on guard to protect the fundamental right of the accused to a fair trial." In order to prevent such a broadcast, a defendant must demonstrate that "the media's coverage of his case – be it printed or broadcast – compromised the ability of the particular jury that heard the case to adjudicate fairly."

9)   SEQUESTRATION OF JURORS AND WITNESSES

a)   Jurors

(1)   General Policy Considerations

A person may request a trial judge to sequester the jurors during a criminal proceeding to avoid any influences upon them by publicity about a case on which they are sitting. Sequestration imposes costs upon the government that is providing the trial, as well as on the jurors, who are isolated from their personal lives. Sequestration may adversely affect a person's rights due to the potential for jurors to resent the person or to feel pressured to reach a decision.

(2)   Motion to Sequester the Jury

The denial of a motion to sequester a jury does not present a due process issue unless:

- a movant establishes proof of having suffered actual prejudice; and
- the movant proves that adverse publicity actually tainted a juror.

b)   Witnesses

(1)   General Considerations for Sequestration

At a minimum, the sequestration of witnesses involves preventing a witness from hearing the testimony of another witness who also is testifying in the same proceeding. The type and extent of sequestration limitations depends upon the controlling statutes, court rules, case law, trial judges, and the parties in a trial.

(2)   Sequestration to Provide Fair Trial

In *Perry v. Leeke*, the Court described the following reasons to justify the sequestration of witnesses: "to lessen the danger that their testimony will be influenced by hearing what other witnesses have to say, and to increase the likelihood that they will confine themselves to truthful statements based on their own recollections."

(3)   Sequestration per Federal Rules of Evidence

Federal Rule of Evidence 615 allows either party to request and obtain the mandatory sequestration of witnesses. There are at least four types of witnesses who may be exempted from sequestration: (1) victims; (2) any witness who is essential to proving the prosecution's case; (3) the parties to a trial; and (4) the parties' representatives.

★   10)   <u>GUILTY PLEAS</u>

> | Question Key |
> | :---: |
> | 20 |

  a)   Definition and Legal Consequences

A guilty plea is a person's admission of culpability for an offense, and acceptance of responsibility for criminal conduct. The result of a guilty plea is to avoid any trial and proceed directly to the sentencing stage of a proceeding. Sometimes, a guilty plea may result from a negotiated plea agreement or bargain with the prosecution.

  b)   Result of Waiving Several Rights

In *Boykin v. Alabama*, the Court held that a guilty plea results in a person's waiver of the following federal rights that are incorporated to the states under the Due Process Clause of the Fourteenth Amendment:

- the Fifth Amendment right against self-incrimination;
- the Sixth Amendment rights of a jury trial and the confrontation of witnesses.

  c)   Intelligent and Voluntary

The *Boykin* Court ruled that for a plea to satisfy the requirements of due process, "the face of the record" of the plea must contain "an affirmative showing that it was intelligent and voluntary." Further, in order for a guilty plea to be valid, a person must comprehend both the potential maximum and minimum periods of incarceration that might be required for a charged offense.

  d)   Voluntariness Depends on Promises

In *United States ex rel. Thurmond v. Mancusi*, the Court decided that a person who entered into a plea agreement based on his counsel's assurance that the prosecutor would recommend a suspended sentence could introduce subjective evidence that his plea was not voluntary. A judicial inquiry into the voluntariness of a person's plea may include consideration of the circumstances of the plea.

  e)   Counsel Must be Present at Plea

The Sixth Amendment right to counsel applies to: 1) the plea negotiation process, 2) a person's decision to waive certain rights, and 3) the process of entering a guilty plea. Thus, the person should be represented by counsel during the plea negotiation process, as well as during entry of the plea that must occur on the record in open court.

  f)   Avoiding Plea after Its Entry

In *McMann v. Richardson*, the Court stated that "a deal is a deal." Thus, a person generally is bound by a plea agreement even if the person subsequently considers it to be disadvantageous. To avoid a plea agreement, the Court requires a person to prove a "serious dereliction on the part of counsel sufficient to show that his plea was not…a knowing and intelligent act." The following considerations will not warrant the avoidance of a plea agreement:

- the fact that a different counsel might have utilized a different strategy; and
- the fact that the statutory or case law changed after entry of the plea.

(1)   Validity of Plea to Death Penalty Offense

In *Brady v. United States*, the Court decided that a person's agreement to enter a plea due to the person's fear of receiving a death sentence, and based on another person's testimony, does not invalidate the guilty plea. The Court declined to hold that the person's fear rendered the plea involuntary when the person received the assistance of counsel during the plea negotiations and the entry of the plea. Thus, the person could fully consider the advantages and disadvantages of the plea. Subsequent legal developments did not warrant a reversal of the conviction.

(2)   Prosecutorial Vindictiveness (Will Not Invalidate Plea)

In *Bordenkircher v. Hayes*, the Court concluded that the prosecution does not violate the Due Process Clause of the Fourteenth Amendment by increasing the number and severity of criminal charges against a person in response to the person's refusal to accept a plea bargain involving fewer or less severe charges.

(3)   Violation of Judge's Promise (May Invalidate Plea)

In *United States ex rel. Elkins v. Gilligan*, the Court decided that a person suffered a due process deprivation when the person entered into a plea agreement based in part on a judge's promise of a specific sentence term of incarceration. The judge stated on the record that he imposed a different sentence based on facts about the person's criminal history that surfaced after the plea's entry. The Court decided that the judge's failure to fulfill the promise could have been remedied only if the judge had, on his own motion, reinstated the person's plea of not guilty.

(4)   Promises Made by Prosecution

Under *Santobello v. New York,* the Court provided that if a promise by, or inducement from, the prosecution is consideration for a guilty plea, then the plea will not be voluntary unless the prosecution's promise is fulfilled. If a person's plea relies on the prosecution's promise to a substantial extent, even if the promise is implied, then the promise must be fulfilled or the person should be permitted to withdraw the guilty plea.

(5)   Penalty Increase Permitted (after Violation of Plea)

In *Ricketts v. Adamson*, the Court ruled that when a person who has pled guilty and started a sentence violates a plea agreement, the person may be prosecuted again for the original charge and a greater charge.

★   **E.   Double Jeopardy**

| Question Key |
| 114, 145 |

1)   <u>GENERAL</u>

a)   The Double Jeopardy Clause

"[T]he Double Jeopardy Clause protects against three distinct abuses: [1] a second prosecution for the same offense after acquittal; [2] a second prosecution for the same offense after conviction; and [3] multiple punishments for the same offense." *U.S. v. Halper*, 490 U.S. 435, 440 (1989).

b)   Fifth and Fourteenth Amendments

The Double Jeopardy Clause ("Clause") applies to criminal prosecutions by the federal government. Under the selective incorporation doctrine, the Double Jeopardy Clause applies to the state's conduct through the Due Process Clause of the Fourteenth Amendment.

c)   Application of Double Jeopardy

The protection of the Double Jeopardy Clause is usually limited to when:

- the same "sovereign" government seeks to prosecute;
- the same person more than once for;
- the same offenses arising from a person's unlawful conduct.

d)   General Rule of Double Jeopardy

The Double Jeopardy Clause prohibits a second trial after a valid trial results in a conviction, an acquittal, or a pardon. The Clause prohibits the same government from twice and consecutively prosecuting a person for one and the same instance of an offense. The Clause prohibits the same government from imposing multiple punishments for the same offense.

e)   Dual Sovereign Doctrine

Under the dual sovereign doctrine, however, a person may be consecutively prosecuted in a state court and in a federal court for one and the same offense. Similarly, the person may be consecutively prosecuted in the courts of two different states for one and the same offense.

f)   Attachment of Double Jeopardy

A person is usually entitled to Double Jeopardy protections once jeopardy "attaches." Attachment of the Double Jeopardy protections occurs:

- In a criminal trial by a judge, either at the beginning of the introduction of evidence or when a witness is sworn.
- In a criminal trial by a jury, the protection attaches when the jury swears its oath.
- When a person pleads guilty to an offense, the protection attaches when a trial judge unconditionally accepts the person's plea and renders a judgment of conviction.

Jeopardy does not attach when a person appears at an initial preliminary hearing. Jeopardy does not attach to grand jury proceedings.

g)   Exclusions from Double Jeopardy

The Double Jeopardy Clause does not apply to prohibit a second trial in the following instances:

- hung jury: The results of a trial are that a jury cannot agree on a verdict.
- mistrial: A mistrial results due to the misconduct of one or both of the parties or a trial judge of a case.
- plea agreement: If a person's conduct breaches a plea agreement, the other potential criminal charges that the prosecution reduced or dropped in the agreement could be reinstated. The person would again be subject to prosecution for those other charges.
- successful appeal: An appellate court decides that a person is entitled to a new trial.

2)   DOUBLE JEOPARDY ISSUES

a)   Different Offenses Require Proof (of Additional Element)

To fall under the protection of the Due Process Clause, a person's conduct subject to subsequent prosecutions must consist of a single act, occurrence, or transaction. In *Blockburger v. U.S.,* a sentencing case, the Court stated that: "where the same act or transaction constitutes a violation of two distinct statutory provisions, the test to be applied to determine whether there are two offenses or only one, is whether each provision requires proof of an additional fact that the other does not." The point of that rule is that two offenses will not comprise the same offense if each offense mandates proof of an element that the other offense does not mandate. That point applies if some of the identical facts are needed to establish the elements of both offenses.

b)   Motion for Mistrial (Generally Waives Double Jeopardy)

A mistrial results when circumstances render it impracticable or not possible to complete a trial. In *United States v. Dintz*, the Court stated that "a motion by the defendant for mistrial is ordinarily assumed to remove any barrier to re-prosecution, even if the defendant's motion is necessitated by prosecutorial or judicial error. When a person moves for a mistrial, the person generally waives the protection of the Double Jeopardy Clause. If, however, the person makes that motion due to the bad-faith conduct of the prosecution or the trial judge, then the Clause will protect the person from a retrial." Such conduct may include overreaching or harassment by the prosecution.

c)   Defective Indictment (Double Jeopardy Does Not Apply)

In *Illinois v. Somerville*, the Court concluded that a second trial would not result in double jeopardy when a defective indictment required a mistrial. The Court stated that: "A trial judge properly exercises his discretion to declare a mistrial if an impartial verdict cannot be reached, or if a verdict of conviction could be reached but would have to be reversed on appeal due to an obvious procedural error in the trial. If an error would make reversal on appeal a certainty, it would not serve the "ends of public justice" to require that the Government proceed with its proof, when, if it succeeded before the jury, it would automatically be stripped of that success by an appellate court."

d)   Manifest Necessity (Double Jeopardy Does Not Apply)

In *United States v. Perez*, the Court decided that retrial of a person is not precluded by Double Jeopardy when a jury cannot render a verdict of either acquittal or conviction. The test is, does a "manifest necessity" require a retrial? In applying that test, the courts weigh:

- a person's interest in not being subjected to a successive proceeding;
- the prosecution's interest in having an adequate opportunity to prove its case; and
- the validity of the reasons for not completing the adjudication of a case.

In *Arizona v. Washington*, the Court stated that "manifest necessity" is the prosecution's burden of proof to show that a retrial is necessary. The Court, however, decided that the absence of the trial court's finding of "manifest necessity" did not invalidate its granting of the prosecution's motion for a new trial. The Court stated that the: "strictest scrutiny is appropriate when the basis for the mistrial is the unavailability of critical prosecution evidence."

e)   Dismissal of Charges (Not Necessarily Double Jeopardy)

The prosecution's dismissal of charges against a person may be of two types: A dismissal with prejudice prevents the prosecution from bringing those charges again. That type of dismissal bars a retrial and may be appealed because it constitutes an acquittal. A dismissal without prejudice allows the prosecution to re-file those charges.

★★   F.   **Exclusionary Rule**   Question Key
                                                                 11,25,48, 146
            1)   GENERAL

                        a)   Constitutional Basis to Exclude Evidence

The exclusionary rule affords a person with a remedy that prevents the prosecution's admission at trial of evidence gathered in violation of the person's rights under the Fourth Amendment, Fifth Amendment, and Sixth Amendment.

                        b)   Fifth and Fourteenth Amendments

The Exclusionary Rule applies to criminal prosecutions by the federal government pursuant to the Due Process Clause of the Fifth Amendment. In *Mapp v. Ohio*, the Court declared "that all evidence obtained by searches and seizures in violation of the [U.S.] *Constitution* is, by that same authority, inadmissible in a state court. . . . Since the Fourth Amendment's right of privacy has been declared enforceable against the States through the Due Process Clause of the Fourteenth [Amendment], it is enforceable against them by the same sanction of exclusion as is used against the Federal Government."

                        c)   Motion to Suppress Evidence (with Constitutional
                                    Basis)

The Court stated in *Rakas v. Illinois* that "one whose Fourth Amendment rights are violated may successfully suppress evidence obtained in the course of an illegal search and seizure."

                        d)   Fruit of the Poisonous Tree Doctrine

In *Nardone v. United States*, the Court decided that evidence gathered by an officer in violation of a person's federal constitutional rights, or obtained by means of utilizing unconstitutionally gathered evidence, is referred to as "fruit of the poisonous tree." Consequently, the exclusionary rule prohibits the admission of such evidence at trial. Such inadmissible evidence may be derived from an unlawful arrest, search, identification, or interrogation.

                        (1)   Identifications of a Person

The fruit of the poisonous tree doctrine also applies to identifications of a person. The results of an out-of-court identification may not be introduced at a trial if such a line-up occurred in the absence of a person's counsel, contrary to the Sixth Amendment. In the event of such an improper out-of-court identification, the prosecution may not obtain subsequent in-court identification by the same witness until the prosecution proves with clear and convincing evidence that the in-court identification is not a fruit of the tainted out-of-court identification.

(2)   Confessions   Obtained   in   Custodial Interrogations

A confession that is made in compliance with *Miranda v. Arizona* is admissible as substantive evidence against a person. A confession that is obtained in violation of *Miranda* may be used to only impeach the accused if, before making that statement, the accused made a voluntary, knowing, and intelligent waiver of his right to remain silent.

(3)   Warrant   Obtained   Based   on   Illegally Obtained Information

When information discovered by means of an illegal search is used to obtain a search warrant based on this information, evidence seized pursuant to the search warrant must be suppressed. *Murray v. United States*, 487 U.S. 533 (1988).

2)   <u>EXCEPTIONS</u>

a)   Federal Grand Jury Proceeding

In *United State v. Calandra*, the Court concluded that the exclusionary rule is inapplicable to federal grand jury proceedings and does not provide a basis for dismissal of a federal indictment. Thus, a witness in a grand jury hearing must answer questions that arise from unlawfully obtained evidence. Furthermore, the witness will not prevail on a motion to suppress illegally obtained evidence.

b)   Fruit of the Poisonous Tree Doctrine Exceptions

The Court, in *Wong Sun v. U.S.* and in other cases, set forth three exceptions to the doctrine.

(1)   Inevitable Discovery

To avoid the operation of the doctrine, the prosecution must establish that an officer would have inevitably discovered the proffered evidence regardless of having initially obtained it by unconstitutional means. For example, suppose an officer conducts an illegal search of a person's apartment and makes a copy of a confession note that is in plain sight. The next day, the landlord makes a routine inspection of the apartment before the person returns from a week-long trip, and also finds the note. As a result, he provides the police with the note. The note may be admissible evidence because the landlord would have lawfully found it even if the officer had not engaged in an unlawful search.

In other words, if evidence is unlawfully obtained through an unconstitutional seizure, that flaw may be immaterial if that evidence ultimately would have been discovered by legal means.

(2)   Independent Source

Evidence obtained by an independent source is an exception to the doctrine. The prosecution must establish that it obtained the evidence through a lawful independent source of the evidence other than the one that is subject to the exclusionary rule.

(3)   Attenuated Taint

The prosecution must prove that any taint of illegality that affects the evidence, which resulted from its being improperly obtained, must have been attenuated or dissipated. Examples of factual considerations that would result in lessening a taint to the evidence include:

- a person's act of free will.
- a lengthy chain of causation occurred between the alleged offense and when a seizure of the evidence happened.
- a long passage of time transpired between a person's unlawful act and a seizure of the evidence.

3)   RESTRICTIONS

The exclusionary rule does not fully apply in the following circumstances.

a)   Impeachment

If a person elects to testify, then counsel may use evidence that was unconstitutionally obtained to impeach the person. This restriction applies when the defense "opens the door" to such evidence.

b)   Other Proceedings

Unconstitutionally obtained evidence may be used in the following types of non-criminal proceedings: civil, parole, and grand jury. The prosecution also may use unconstitutionally obtained evidence against a person in a criminal proceeding alleging perjury.

c)   Reliance in Good Faith

Unconstitutionally obtained evidence is admissible if an officer gathered it based on good faith reliance upon, among other things, the following types of legal authority:

- legal enactments: An officer depended upon an ordinance or statute that was valid when the officer gathered the evidence, but a court decision or legislative act subsequently invalidates that ordinance or statute.
- court opinions: An officer followed the requirements of controlling court opinions when the officer gathered the evidence but subsequent court decisions overruled those opinions.
- search and arrest warrants: In *U.S. v. Leon*, an officer executed a properly issued warrant that a court subsequently determined was defective due to no fault of the officer or the issuing magistrate. The Court held that "the Fourth Amendment exclusionary rule should be modified so as not to bar the use in the prosecution's case-in-chief of evidence obtained by officers acting in reasonable reliance on a search warrant issued by a detached and neutral magistrate but ultimately found to be unsupported by probable cause."

In *U.S. v. Leon*, the Court established a "good faith" exception to the exclusionary rule. That exception applies when a defective search warrant is not premised upon probable cause. Any evidence that is seized pursuant to that warrant will not be automatically excluded if two conditions are fulfilled:

- An officer who obtained the warrant did not lie to a magistrate; and
- The officers who executed the warrant acted in good faith.

Remember, evidence generally will not be suppressed if an officer reasonably held a good faith belief that his actions leading to its discovery were authorized by a valid search or arrest warrant, even if the warrant later turns out to be invalid. For example, in *Arizona v. Evans*, 514 U.S. 1 (1995), the good faith exception to the exclusionary rule applied where the arrest and resulting search incident to that arrest were based on a warrant that was quashed almost three weeks earlier. In that case, due to a court employees' clerical error, the warrant still showed up in the computer database and was relied upon by the officer.

(1)   Exceptions

The good faith exception does not apply in the following situations:

- dishonesty: The magistrate relied upon an officer's affidavits of information that included misrepresentations or indicated a reckless disregard for the truth.
- non-judiciousness: The magistrate entirely abandoned her judicial duty in issuing the warrant by serving as a "rubber stamp" for an officer.
- insufficient affidavit: The magistrate issued a warrant pursuant to a "bare-bones" affidavit lacking in probable cause, which made an officer's reliance on the warrant unreasonable.
- deficient warrant: The magistrate issued a "facially deficient" warrant lacking in particularity regarding either a location to be searched or a person or an item to be seized. In that event, an officer could not reasonably presume that the warrant is valid.

- state rights broader than federal rights: Under *Michigan v. Long,* where the state has granted broader rights under its own constitution than under the federal constitution, it is irrelevant that the police thought their actions were permitted under the federal constitution.

G.   Bail

1)   EIGHTH AMENDMENT

The Eighth Amendment to the *U.S. Constitution* ("Eighth Amendment") provides constitutional rights that serve as bases for certain legal protections. The Eighth Amendment states in part that: "Excessive bail shall not be required." U.S. Const. amend. VIII. The Eighth Amendment applies to the states based on the selective incorporation doctrine, which operates through the Due Process Clause of the Fourteenth Amendment.

2)   EXCESSIVE BAIL STANDARD

According to the Court, in *U.S. v. Salerno*, bail is excessive when the conditions of release for an accused exceed those that are reasonably calculated to fulfill a "compelling interest." The Eighth Amendment provides for an accused person to receive an individualized assessment of the facts in order to ascertain the conditions of bail.

Other than in cases involving capital offenses, a person has a right to a bail that is not excessive. The amount of bail cannot exceed what is rationally calculated to assure a defendant's presence at subsequent court proceedings.

H.   Eighth Amendment

The Eighth Amendment provides in part that neither excessive fines may be imposed nor may "cruel and unusual punishment" be inflicted. U.S. Const. amend. VIII. The Eighth Amendment applies to the states based on the selective incorporation doctrine, which operates through the Due Process Clause of the Fourteenth Amendment.

1)   DEATH PENALTY

Although the death penalty does not itself violate the prohibition of "cruel and unusual punishment," this prohibition affects procedural matters about when a jury can impose this type of penalty and how it may be implemented. Cornell University Law School, Legal Information Institute, Cornell Law School Death Penalty Project, *Death Penalty*, at http://topics.law.cornell.edu/wex/Death_penalty.

a)   Requirement of Proportionality

A violation of the Eighth Amendment occurs when a penalty imposed for a crime contradicts the requirement of proportionality. The following factors must be considered when determining proportionality of a penalty to a crime:

- gravity of the crime and stringency of its penalty;

- how other criminals are punished in the jurisdiction; and

- how other jurisdictions penalize the same offense.

(1) Certain Rape Offenses

Based on the requirement of proportionality, the Supreme Court decided in *Coker v. Georgia* that the death penalty cannot be imposed for the offense of raping an adult woman. The death penalty also may not be imposed for the offense of raping a child when the child survives the rape, pursuant to *Kennedy v. Louisiana.*

b) Individualized Sentencing

An individualized sentencing procedure must be conducted by the trial court, and specific circumstances concerning the criminal must guide the jury, before imposition of the death sentence can occur.

(1) Aggravating Factors

A circumstance or fact that increases the culpability of a defendant for an offense constitutes an aggravating factor. When aggravating factors support a trial court's decision to sentence the defendant to death, instead of any other penalty, the jury rather than the trial court must determine the existence of an aggravating factor pursuant to *Ring v. Arizona.* With regard to aggravating factors, in *Brown v. Sanders*, the Supreme Court additionally ruled that when an appellate court finds a factor of sentencing invalid, the sentence imposed will not be constitutional without a jury finding of another aggravating factor that includes the same circumstances and facts as the invalid factor. According to the Court in *Kansas v. Marsh*, the individualized sentencing principle will not be violated when the death penalty applies to an equal balance of mitigating and aggravating factors.

c) Means of Execution

Although the method of execution may be legislatively established, this method must not cause a defendant wanton or unnecessary pain. To ascertain whether the means of execution employed constitute cruel and unusual punishment contrary to the Eighth Amendment, the analytical standard is whether these means are objectively intolerable. A modern case decided by the Court, *Baze v. Rees*, decided that cruel and unusual punishment does not include a death penalty inflicted by means of lethal injection. Other means of the death penalty, such as electrocution and hanging, have withstood legal challenges in lower federal courts and state courts.

d) Categories of People Ineligible for the Death Penalty

Unconstitutional cruel and usual punishment results from imposing the death penalty upon mentally retarded defendants, pursuant to *Atkins v. Virginia.* The Court reached this decision based upon the requirement of proportionality because such defendants' disability reduces the seriousness of their crime, making the death penalty too severe relative to it. The Court outlawed the death penalty against juvenile defendants in *Roper v. Simmons* based on their reduced culpability for offenses in light of their lesser responsibility and maturity, partial development of character, and increased susceptibility to harmful influences.

I.   Appeal

1)   SCOPE OF APPELLATE REVIEW

Normally, the scope of appellate review is restricted to those legal issues that were raised in a trial court. Similarly, usually only those issues properly preserved for appellate review will be considered on appeal. For example, if a person wishes to challenge the prosecution's introduction of a statement into evidence, the accused's counsel must correctly make a timely and specific objection in response to the attempted entry of the evidence.

2)   PLAIN ERROR DOCTRINE

One exception to the rule requiring preservation of error is the "plain error" doctrine that exists in both state and federal appellate courts. That doctrine allows a party to raise an issue for the first time on appeal if the issue is characterized as a plain error. A plain error is an error that impacts a party's substantial rights.

In *United States v. Atkinson,* the Supreme Court held that the plain error doctrine enables a court, "[i]n exceptional circumstances,...in the public interest" to "notice error to which no exception has been taken, if the errors are obvious, or if they otherwise seriously affect the fairness, integrity or public reputation of judicial proceedings." In *United States v. Frady*, the Court limited the plain error doctrine to "those circumstances in which a miscarriage of justice would otherwise result."

The doctrine may apply, for example, if the prosecution improperly comments upon a person's failure to testify in a criminal trial. Those comments would violate the accused's privilege against self-incrimination, which would affect the accused's substantial rights.

AMERIBAR BAR REVIEW

Multistate Bar Examination Preparation Course

TABLE OF CONTENTS

INTRODUCTION

There are two main bodies of evidence law you should generally be familiar with – the common law and the *Federal Rules of Evidence*. The common law applied in most jurisdictions before evidentiary rules and statutes were adopted. The common law was very rigid in its requirements. In other words, the rules were strict and did not provide much leeway for liberal interpretation by judges. They also generally were more restrictive in what type of evidence may be admitted. The *Federal Rules of Evidence*, which will be referred to in this outline as the "*Federal Rules*" (not to be confused with the *Federal Rules of Civil Procedure*), are applied by the federal courts. The *Federal Rules* generally are more liberal in terms of their requirements. Compared to the common law, generally more types of evidence will be admitted, and it will be up to the jury to weigh the credibility of that evidence. Many states have adopted statutes or rules of evidence that are based on the *Federal Rules.*

For the Multistate Bar Exam or MBE, unless otherwise noted, the *Federal Rules of Evidence* govern. This outline, therefore, focuses on the *Federal Rules of Evidence*. However, some common law concepts are also included if necessary to provide context. You may find it easier to remember the federal rule on point if you can contrast it with the generally more rigid common law rule. That is why we will, on occasion, cover both the common law and the Federal Rules. Additionally, answers containing the common law rule on point are often used as distractor answers on the MBE. Remember, however, by default, on the MBE, the *Federal Rules* govern unless otherwise noted.

Evidence law applies to the admissibility of evidence in both civil and criminal actions. Evidence law does not apply to the discoverability of evidence in these actions. Remember, discovery, which is broader in scope than admissibility, is governed by the applicable rule of civil or criminal procedure. In other words, there are items or testimony that may be the subject of discovery in an action, which, nonetheless, may not be admitted into evidence in a case.

In this outline, selected provisions of the *Federal Rules of Evidence* are presented in shaded text boxes. On the MBE, you generally do not need to know rule numbers, but we have provided selected rules for reference purposes.

I.   PRESENTATION OF EVIDENCE

A.   Introduction of Evidence

> Question Key
> 46,121,164,166

1)   REQUIREMENT OF PERSONAL KNOWLEDGE

★

A proponent of evidence (someone seeking to introduce the evidence) is required to establish a proper foundation in order to introduce evidence at a trial in a civil or criminal proceeding. To introduce testimonial evidence from a witness, a proponent must be able to demonstrate that the testimony will be supported by the personal knowledge of the witness.

Under both the common law and *Federal Rule of Evidence* ("FRE") 602, a witness must have personal knowledge regarding the subject matter of his testimony. For example, if the witness testifies about observing a thing or event, the witness must have firsthand knowledge about it as a result of seeing or experiencing the thing or event. In other words, the testimony should regard matters he has perceived or about which he personally knows.

Personal knowledge includes any knowledge witnesses have gained though personal observations they are recounting when they provide testimony. FRE 602 states that:

> A witness may not testify to a matter unless evidence is introduced sufficient to support a finding that the witness has personal knowledge of the matter. Evidence to prove personal knowledge may, but need not, consist of the witness' own testimony.

For example, suppose John sees that Sally's car is red. John would have personal knowledge that the car is red. However, suppose John never sees the red car, but is told that the car is red by Sally. In that case, John lacks personal knowledge that the car is red.

	2)	REFRESHING RECOLLECTION	Question Key 115,137

        a)   FRE 612

If a testifying witness cannot clearly remember something, or recall an event about which the witness is questioned, then an examining attorney may present an item to the witness for review. Items that may be used for that purpose and examined by a witness include documents, tangible objects, sounds, and smells. The attorney must provide the item with intent to cause the witness to recollect the subject about which the witness is needed to testify. The purpose for the rule is that, upon being provided with the item, the witness may recall the subject and testify about it.

For example, suppose a prosecutor calls Danny to the stand to testify about a crime he witnessed at Coney Island one summer afternoon. Danny witnessed the crime 18 months ago, so his memory of the event is not perfect. Under the rule permitting refreshing recollection, the prosecutor may provide Danny with items in order to refresh his mind. For example, the prosecutor can provide him with a newspaper article about the crime or a map of the area. The prosecutor can use almost anything to refresh Danny's recollection, so long as it is intended to actually refresh his recollection. For example, although extreme, the prosecutor even can provide Danny with an authentic Coney Island hot dog if he thinks it will jog his memory from that day.

                    (1)   Admission as Evidence

The item may be presented to the witness. Only the party-opponent's attorney who did not use the item to refresh the recollection of the witness may have the item that the witness uses to refresh recollection admitted as evidence (e.g., an exhibit) in the case. Generally, if the item is a document, the party-opponent's attorney is permitted:

- to inspect the document; and

- to have any unrelated information excised from the document before it is admitted.

(2)   Prohibition on Reading

If an examining attorney presents a document to a testifying witness to refresh the witness' recollection, the witness may not read from it while testifying. In particular, the document may not be read aloud to the jury when it is otherwise inadmissible. FRE 612(2) provides two means to prevent the witness from providing testimony that merely repeats the contents of a document shown to the witness to refresh his recollection:

- A trial judge possesses discretion to ascertain if a witness' testimony is simply restating the document's contents; and
- A party opponent is entitled to examine the document to determine if the witness, in fact, possesses, and is testifying based upon, his independent memories regarding the document's contents.

(3)   Pretrial Review

An examining attorney may present documents to a testifying witness for review before a trial. Such pretrial refreshing of recollection may be disclosed upon cross-examination of the witness at trial. A cross-examining attorney generally is not entitled to production of any documents the witness reviewed before the trial.

(a)   Mandatory Production Exception

FRE 612 affords a trial judge the discretion to order the production of any document a witness reviews prior to a trial.

(4)   Hearsay Evidence Reviewable

A document used to refresh recollection may otherwise constitute hearsay evidence, but its permitted use under FRE 612 is not for asserting the truth of a matter.

(5)   Best Evidence Rule Inapplicable

An item used to refresh recollection does not need to be an original in order to satisfy the Best Evidence Rule if it will not be used as evidence.

(6)   Text of FRE 612

Except as otherwise provided in criminal proceedings by section 3500 of title 18, *United States Code*, if a witness uses a writing to refresh memory for the purpose of testifying, either —

(1) while testifying, or

(2) before testifying, if the court in its discretion determines it is necessary in the interests of justice, an adverse party is entitled to have the writing produced at the hearing, to inspect it, to cross-examine the witness thereon, and to introduce in evidence those portions which relate to the testimony of the witness. If it is claimed that the writing contains matters not related to the subject matter of the testimony the court shall examine the writing in camera, excise any portions not so related, and order delivery of the remainder to the party entitled thereto. Any portion withheld over objections shall be preserved and made available to the appellate court in the event of an appeal. If a writing is not produced or delivered pursuant to order under this rule, the court shall make any order justice requires, except that in criminal cases when the prosecution elects not to comply, the order shall be one striking the testimony or, if the court in its discretion determines that the interests of justice so require, declaring a mistrial.

3) OBJECTIONS AND OFFERS OF PROOF

a) Objections

(1) Definition

An objection is a declaration by a party in a judicial proceeding in opposition to an act or statement of a party opponent in the proceeding. Usually, objections are made on the record at a trial in response to a party's proffered evidence.

(a) Objectionable Questions

An attorney should not ask a witness objectionable questions at a trial. Those types of questions include ones that are argumentative, compound, misleading, or conclusory.

(2) Timely & Specific

The two main requirements for making an objection are that the objection must be timely and specific.

(3) Rulings on an Objection

If a judge sustains an objection, the proffered evidence will not be admitted into evidence. If the judge overrules the objection, the evidence will be admitted. A trial judge has discretion to decide whether to admit evidence.

(4)   Absence of, or Incorrect, Rulings

Otherwise inadmissible evidence may, nonetheless, be admitted as evidence in three different situations:

- No opportunity exists for a party opponent to object to the proffered evidence;
- A party opponent fails to object when a party proffers the evidence; or
- A trial judge incorrectly admits the evidence over an objection.

b)   Objection not Automatic

FRE 103(a)(1) requires the making of an objection by a party because no objections will occur automatically.

c)   Offers of Proof

(1)   Definition

An offer of proof is a presentation made on the record for the purpose of preserving a contested issue of certain evidence's admissibility for appellate review. An offer of proof is made by a proponent of evidence (i.e., a proffering party) after a trial judge has excluded (i.e., ruled as inadmissible) evidence in a legal proceeding. In an offer of proof, the proponent seeks to demonstrate on the record, and outside of a jury's presence, the type and nature of the evidence that would have been presented in the proceeding and why it is admissible. Again, this must be done to preserve the issue for appeal.

(2)   Elements

Two steps are required for a proponent to make an offer of proof regarding the excluded evidence.

- The proponent must describe the proposed evidence.
- The proponent should explain the evidence's relevance to a disputed issue when its materiality is not apparent on its face.

(3)   FRE 103(a)(2)

FRE 103(a)(2) provides for the making of an offer of proof by a party to create a record for an appellate court to consider a trial judge's ruling on the admissibility of evidence.

d)   Standard of Review

Generally, federal courts of appeal apply an abuse of discretion standard of review to an alleged error in an evidentiary ruling by a federal district court. *United States v. Alexander*, 849 F.2d 1293 (10th Cir. 1988). Although the federal court of appeal would make a different ruling, if the challenged ruling falls within the realm of reasonable disagreement, the federal court of appeal should affirm the ruling.

e)   Text of FRE 103(a)

(a) Effect of erroneous ruling.

Error may not be predicated upon a ruling which admits or excludes evidence unless a substantial right of the party is affected, and

(1) objection - In case the ruling is one admitting evidence, a timely objection or motion to strike appears of record, stating the specific ground of objection, if the specific ground was not apparent from the context; or

(2) offer of proof - In case the ruling is one excluding evidence, the substance of the evidence was made known to the court by offer or was apparent from the context within which questions were asked.

Once the court makes a definitive ruling on the record admitting or excluding evidence, either at or before trial, a party need not renew an objection or offer of proof to preserve a claim of error for appeal.

---

4)   <u>LAY OPINIONS</u>

Question Key
65

a)   Common Law

(1)   General Rule

The original and strict common law rule provides that a lay witness may testify only to facts and not relate any opinions or conclusions. The reason for this rule is that only a trier of fact, and not a witness, may form opinions, inferences, or conclusions based on the facts of the case.

(2)   Exception

An exception to the general common law rule applies when a witness provides a "shorthand rendition" of the facts.

b)   Federal Rule is Less Restrictive

(1)   Distinguished from Common Law

FRE 701 is less strict than the common law because it does not preclude a lay witness from testifying regarding a limited scope of opinions or conclusions. On the MBE, remember that the FRE, not the common law rule, governs, unless otherwise noted.

(2)   Opinion Testimony Rule

Under the *Federal Rules*, a lay witness may present opinion testimony that will:

- assist in obtaining a clear understanding of the witness' testimony; and
- be rationally based on the witness' perception.

Accordingly, a lay witness generally may testify regarding her opinion about intoxication, sanity, weight, speed, and height. The lay witness generally can provide opinion testimony that does not require an expert. A fact-finder, either a trial judge or jury, must analyze and evaluate the lay witness opinion testimony.

(3)   Shorthand Rendition Rule

A liberal construction of FRE 701 allows for the admissibility of lay opinion that is presented in a "shorthand rendition." In that event, lay opinions may be admitted on the basis of convenience or expediency instead of as a matter of necessity.

(4)   Text of FRE 701

> If the witness is not testifying as an expert, the witness' testimony in the form of opinions or inferences is limited to those opinions or inferences which are (a) rationally based on the perception of the witness, and (b) helpful to a clear understanding of the witness' testimony or the determination of a fact in issue, and (c) not based on scientific, technical, or other specialized knowledge within the scope of Rule 702.

5)   <u>COMPETENCY OF WITNESSES</u>

| Question Key |
| 51 |

A witness is considered competent if the witness possesses the requisite legal qualifications to provide testimony. A considerable difference exists between the common law rules of competency and those under the FRE.

a)   Common Law

The common law provides that a witness will necessarily be found incompetent if the witness fits into any of the following categories:

- minors or infants;
- insane persons;
- convicted felons;
- non-believers in a supreme being;
- parties to, or persons interested in, litigation; or
- persons presenting the statements of a decedent in a lawsuit regarding the decedent's estate.

b)   Federal Rule is Less Restrictive

(1)   No Automatic Incompetency

Unlike the common law, FRE 601 does not provide that any status of a witness will automatically result in disqualification of the witness. The FRE effectively eliminates the common law categories of incompetency.

(2)   Grounds for Impeachment

The common law grounds for the disqualification of a witness as incompetent may be used only to impeach the credibility of the witness at trial. The jury will factor the existence of the ground when determining the weight of the evidence. In other words, the strict common law rule resulted in a prohibition against the admission of the testimony. Under the FRE, the testimony is more likely to be admitted into evidence. However, the fact-finder determines whether the evidence is trustworthy.

(3)   State Law Applies in Diversity Actions

FRE 601 provides that, for civil litigation in federal courts that are exercising diversity jurisdiction and applying state law to claims and defenses, state law on the subject of the competency of witnesses is controlling.

(4)   Presumption of Competency

FRE 601 deems all witnesses competent unless another provision of the FRE states otherwise. In effect, under the *Federal Rules of Evidence*, a witness is presumed competent.

(a)   Ability to Understand and Convey

Under FRE 601, the question of a person's competency will depend upon the person's capacity to understand the facts and the person's capability to convey them. For example, a trial judge must determine the competency of a mentally impaired person to be a witness based on the evidence of record in a hearing on that issue. In that hearing, the trial judge will examine that person's capacity to comprehend information and ability to communicate it.

(b)   Automatic   Grounds   of
                Incompetency

The *Federal Rules* also provide that witnesses, excluding a trial judge and jurors who may be called as witnesses, are automatically incompetent to testify on only two grounds:

*   lack of personal knowledge of a matter about which the witness may testify as required by FRE 602; and

- inability or refusal to solemnly swear (by affirmation or oath) to tell the truth under FRE 603. Inability may result from a lack of understanding. A person need not swear to a supreme being, but the oath or affirmation must demonstrate an appreciation for the obligation to tell the truth.

        (c)   Challenging Competency

A witness' competency may be attacked by another person who also heard or observed what the witness heard or observed, and then states in court something different from what the witness heard or observed.

        (5)   Text of FRE 601

> Every person is competent to be a witness except as otherwise provided in these rules. However, in civil actions and proceedings, with respect to an element of a claim or defense as to which State law supplies the rule of decision, the competency of a witness shall be determined in accordance with State law.

        (6)   Text of FRE 603

> Before testifying, every witness shall be required to declare that the witness will testify truthfully, by oath or affirmation administered in a form calculated to awaken the witness' conscience and impress the witness' mind with the duty to do so.

        c)   Interpreters

The *Federal Rules of Evidence* permit a witness to testify using the assistance of an interpreter for the purpose of communicating with a jury. Rule 604 states that: "An interpreter is subject to the provisions of these rules relating to qualification as an expert and the administration of an oath or affirmation to make a true translation."

        d)   Judge as Witness

The *Federal Rules of Evidence* prohibit a judge from testifying as a witness in a case over which the judge is presiding. FRE 605 states that: "The judge presiding at the trial may not testify in that trial as a witness. No objection need be made in order to preserve the point."

        e)   Juror as Witness

        (1)   Trial Testimony Prohibited

Under the *Federal Rules of Evidence*, jurors may not be witnesses in a case that they will be deciding.

(2) Confidential Deliberations

Jurors generally cannot, either in an affidavit or by direct testimony, testify in an inquiry into the validity of an indictment or a verdict about statements or matters that they considered in their deliberations that produced the indictment or the verdict.

(a) Exceptions

The exceptions to the prohibition against jurors giving testimony apply:

- when a juror was subjected to an improper outside influence (e.g., an effort to tamper with the jury is discovered.); or
- when a juror was exposed to extraneous prejudicial information (e.g., a juror in sequestration reads a newspaper editorial asserting that a criminal defendant is not guilty.); or
- whether a mistake occurred when entering the verdict onto the verdict form.

(3) Contesting Jury Conduct

A party may challenge alleged jury errors or a verdict attributed to those errors by either moving for a new trial or appealing from that verdict.

(4) Appellate Review of Jury Conduct

A trial or appellate court will analyze the following issues when disposing of a party's challenge to the conduct of a juror or a jury:

- What evidence demonstrates the alleged juror's or jury misconduct?
- Does a juror's misconduct justify a new trial or the relief that is requested on appeal?

(5) Text of FRE 606

(a) At the trial.

A member of the jury may not testify as a witness before that jury in the trial of the case in which the juror is sitting. If the juror is called so to testify, the opposing party shall be afforded an opportunity to object out of the presence of the jury.

(b) Inquiry into validity of verdict or indictment.

> Upon an inquiry into the validity of a verdict or indictment, a juror may not testify as to any matter or statement occurring during the course of the jury's deliberations or to the effect of anything upon that or any other juror's mind or emotions as influencing the juror to assent to or dissent from the verdict or indictment or concerning the juror's mental processes in connection therewith. But a juror may testify about (1) whether extraneous prejudicial information was improperly brought to the jury's attention, (2) whether any outside influence was improperly brought to bear upon any juror, or (3).whether there was a mistake in entering the verdict into the jury form. A juror's affidavit or evidence of any statement by the juror may not be received on a matter about which the juror would be precluded from testifying.

      f)   Dead Man's Statutes

Some exam questions indicate that a Dead Man's Statute does, or does not, apply to the fact pattern. If it does apply, the question may provide the text of the statute. Read it carefully to understand exactly what type of testimony is, or is not, prohibited.

        (1)   Strict Statutes

Strict Dead Man's Statutes preclude a survivor from testifying about a transaction involving her and a decedent when the survivor is a plaintiff and the decedent is a defendant in the same litigation.

        (2)   Moderate Statutes

Moderate Dead Man's Statutes allow a survivor to testify about a transaction involving her and a decedent when the survivor is a plaintiff and the decedent is a defendant in the same litigation. Moderate Dead Man's Statutes permit the decedent's estate to present hearsay statements that the decedent made regarding the transaction.

          (a)   Applicable State Statute

In federal cases when diversity jurisdiction exists, federal courts will apply the relevant state's Dead Man's statute.

     6)   <u>JUDICIAL NOTICE</u>

Question Key
31,177

Generally, not all facts need to be established in a trial through the introduction of evidence by the parties seeking to prove those facts. Judicial notice is the recognition by the court of a fact that is of common knowledge from sources that guarantee accuracy or are a matter of official record, without the need for the introduction of evidence establishing the fact. Thus, the principle of judicial notice enables a trial judge to accept as true a generally known fact, although neither party has offered evidence to prove that alleged fact. Examples of matters given judicial notice are public and court records, times of sunset and sunrise ascertainable in an almanac, government rainfall and temperature records, and a known historic event, such as 9-11.

a)   Judicial Notice of Facts

(1)   General

FRE 201 provides that the parties in a trial need not produce evidence to establish particular types of facts because a trial judge is entitled to take "judicial notice" of those facts.

(a)   Without Request

In the absence of a party's request for a trial judge to exercise judicial notice, the judge may do so on a discretionary basis.

(b)   Upon Request

When a party requests that a trial judge take judicial notice, the judge is required to do so when the party provides sufficient information for the judge to take that notice.

(2)   Conclusivity of Established Fact

(a)   Criminal Jury Instructions

In a criminal case, a trial judge should instruct a jury that it may, but is not required to, consider the fact of the judicial notice to be conclusive. In a criminal case, due to the defendant's constitutional right to a trial by jury, the fact subject to judicial notice may be brought to the attention of the jury. However, the jury must be free to reject it. Any instruction using the term "presumption" may be inappropriate under these circumstances. The judge may instruct that the fact creates a permissible inference, but no more.

(b)   Civil Jury Instructions

In a civil action, FRE 201(g) requires a trial judge to instruct the jury to accept any judicially noticed fact as conclusive.

(3)   Adjudicative Facts Subject to Judicial Notice

Judicial notice under the *Federal Rules of Evidence* concerns adjudicative facts. Facts subject to judicial notice must be beyond "reasonable dispute" such that a status of certitude may be attained because the fact is not reasonably disputable. The fact must be generally known within the trial judge's jurisdiction or be capable of accurate and ready determination through sources whose accuracy cannot reasonably be questioned.

- "Generally Known" Within a Trial Judge's Jurisdiction

If the action is in New York City, for example, the fact that the Hudson River runs along the west side of Manhattan is generally known in the jurisdiction. Such a fact would not be generally known, for example, in Nebraska.

- "Capable of Accurate and Ready Determination" Through "Sources Whose Accuracy Cannot Reasonably be Questioned." FRE 201

Tidal times that are easily ascertainable in an almanac are capable of accurate and ready determination through a source whose accuracy cannot reasonably be questioned (the almanac).

(4)   Timing of Judicial Notice

Judicial notice may be taken at any stage of a proceeding, even on appeal.

b)   Judicial Notice of Law

Judicial notice of law is treated differently from judicial notice of fact. The rules of evidence governing admissibility and proof of documents generally do not make sense to apply to statutes or judicial opinions – which are technically documents. This is because, unlike documents intended to prove facts, documents intended to prove law are presented to the court as such, not to the jury as evidence. However, judicial notice of law may still be taken through common law rules, even though it is not addressed in the *Federal Rules*. In the federal system, "[t]he law of any state of the Union, whether depending upon statutes or upon judicial opinions, is a matter of which the courts of the United States are bound to take judicial notice, without plea or proof." *White v. Gittens*, 121 F.3d 803, 805 n.1 (1st Cir. 1997).

In addition to state or federal law, for which courts *must* take judicial notice, federal courts may take judicial notice of local laws, such as municipal or county ordinances, and foreign laws.

Although judicial notice of fact and judicial notice of law share the phrase "judicial notice," they draw on different rules of practice. Rule 201 "governs only judicial notice of adjudicative facts." Fed. R. Evid. 201(a). Judicial notice of law is outside the scope of Rule 201, and derives from practical considerations and case law that do not rely on Rule 201.

★★   7)   ROLES OF JUDGE AND JURY

| Question Key |
| 1,34,39,47,64,168,172 |

a)   Role of Trial Judge

FRE 104(a) provides that a trial judge may determine preliminary questions of fact that bear on witness competency, testimonial privilege, and the admissibility of evidence. In deciding admissibility issues, a trial judge is limited only by the FRE with respect to determining testimonial privileges. Accordingly, a trial judge could consider hearsay evidence when deciding on the admissibility of other types of evidence. In addition, any hearing on a preliminary question of fact that involves the admissibility of a confession should be conducted outside the presence of the jury. In addition, the jury should not be present in any such hearing when justice requires the jury's absence.

(1) Hearsay Evidence

According to FRE 104 and FRE 103, the issue of admissibility of hearsay evidence is a question for a trial judge, not a jury, to decide. Such a determination should occur in the jury's absence.

b) Role of Jury

Generally, a jury determines issues of fact. The jury determines the credibility and weight of admissible evidence. The jury may make inferences from the evidence and draw conclusions about it. When the admission of evidence is contingent on an issue of fact, the common law and FRE 104(a) provide different tests for allocating the responsibility to determine the evidence's admissibility. In a bench trial, the judge also acts as the fact-finder, taking the place of the jury.

8) LIMITED ADMISSIBILITY

Limited admissibility means that while specific evidence may be admissible by a party for one purpose, it must be excluded from admission by a party opponent for any other purpose.

a) Text of FRE 105

> When evidence which is admissible as to one party or for one purpose but not admissible as to another party or for another purpose is admitted, the court, upon request, shall restrict the evidence to its proper scope and instruct the jury accordingly.

B. Presumptions

Question Key
11, 35

1) GENERAL CONSIDERATIONS

a) Definition

A presumption arises when a basic fact may be established by a party and from that fact another presumed fact may be inferred. A presumption is a definite proposition that a fact-finder must accept, or an inference that a jury must make, unless contrary evidence is produced that rebuts the presumption.

(1) Permissive Inference

A permissible inference may arise when a basic fact is established and a finder of fact may or may not decide that a presumed fact exists. In other words, the finder of fact may reject the presumption.

(2) Conclusive Presumption

A conclusive presumption results when, after a foundation is laid to establish a basic fact, a finder of fact must decide that a presumed fact exists. A jury must accept the facts that are provided under that presumption. A conclusive presumption may exist, for example, with respect to matters of public policy.

(a) Jury Instruction on Presumption

A trial judge will instruct a jury regarding a presumption if a party provides the proper foundation to support the presumption and no contrary evidence is introduced.

2) CIVIL PROCEEDINGS

a) Common Law

(1) Establishing a Presumption

In order for a connection between a basic and a presumed fact to give rise to a presumption in a civil case:

- The burden of production must be shifted to a party that opposes the presumption; and
- The presumption must be rebuttable.

(2) Conclusive Presumptions

Generally, few presumptions are strong enough to be conclusive, such that a fact-finder has to accept them if the laying of a solid foundation establishes those facts.

(a) Public Policy Exception

Established foundational facts will have a conclusive effect when matters of public policy are under consideration.

b) Rebuttable Presumptions and the Bursting Bubble

(1) Rebuttable Presumptions

Generally, a presumption shifts the burden of production and is rebuttable. Many presumptions may be rebutted by using evidence that contradicts the presumed proposition.

(2)   Bursting Bubble Approach

The *Federal Rules of Evidence* use a "bursting bubble" approach to presumptions. Under that method, if a party establishes a foundation for a presumption and no contrary evidence is introduced, a trial judge will instruct a jury on the presumption. If, however, a party-opponent produces sufficient credible evidence in opposition to the presumption, the "bubble bursts," then the judge will not instruct the jury about the presumption. The jury may determine a contested proposition based on the jury's evaluation of both parties' evidence.

3)   CRIMINAL PROCEEDINGS

Federal case law governs the use of presumptions in federal criminal cases because the Federal Rules do not address their use in criminal trials. An example of a conclusive presumption in criminal law is one providing that a certain blood content level constitutes being "under the influence" of an intoxicating controlled substance. Even when a prosecutor establishes such a conclusive presumption against a criminal defendant, a fact-finder is not obligated to find the defendant guilty despite the lack of any rebuttal evidence on the issue of whether the defendant was "under the influence."

4)   GOVERNING LAW

Generally, federal courts applying the doctrine of *Erie Railroad Co. v. Tomkins* follow the common law regarding presumptions in federal actions. That is, when an issue is to be decided under state law, the law of that state should be applied to both burdens and presumptions. However, in civil actions grounded in diversity jurisdiction, the federal court should apply the presumption law of the state whose substantive law is applied.

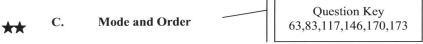

★★   **C.   Mode and Order**

| Question Key |
| 63,83,117,146,170,173 |

1)   CONTROL BY COURT

Pursuant to relevant legal authority, such as statutes, court rules, common law, and rules of evidence, a trial judge controls the sequence and scope of trial proceedings. In particular, the trial judge rules on evidentiary questions, such as admissibility and objections.

2)   PHASES OF EXAMINATION

All parties have an opportunity to call, examine, and cross-examine witnesses. There are four main phases of witness examination in a trial. Each phase involves a different scope of permissible questioning.

Direct Examination is conducted by a party who has called a witness to testify.

Cross-Examination occurs after direct examination. It is conducted by a party who did not call a witness to testify. Cross-examination is an absolute right. The cross-examining party need not accept the first answer that the witness provides. A defendant possesses a right to confront any witness that testifies against the defendant in criminal proceedings. That right to cross-examine a witness is derived from the Sixth Amendment to the *U.S. Constitution*.

Redirect examination occurs after cross-examination. It is conducted by the party who called the witness to testify.

Re-Cross examination occurs after re-cross examination. It is conducted by the party who did not call the witness to testify.

a)   Questioning by a Trial Judge

FRE 614(a)-(b) authorizes a trial judge to call and question witnesses. This is called judicial examination. The rule in most states is that the trial judge may not comment on the weight of the evidence.

(1)   Text of FRE 614

(a) Calling by court.

The court may, on its own motion or at the suggestion of a party, call witnesses, and all parties are entitled to cross-examine witnesses thus called.

(b) Interrogation by court.

The court may interrogate witnesses, whether called by itself or by a party.

---

3)   <u>SCOPE AND FORM OF QUESTIONS</u>

a)   Direct Examination

The permissible types of questions on direct examination include specific inquires about the facts or general queries to obtain a narrative answer from a witness.

(1)   Leading Questions Exceptions

Under FRE 611(c), leading questions usually are not permitted in a direct examination unless they are necessary to obtain testimony. That exception to the general rule applies when a witness is experiencing difficulty in answering a question due to a personal situation. Examples of those types of witnesses include: children, individuals with a severe speech impediment, mentally disabled individuals, or hostile witnesses. Courts also may permit leading questions for the purpose of obtaining preliminary information, such as the person's name and address.

An often tested point is that leading questions may be permitted when the witness is being examined by the attorney who called the witness if that witness is a "hostile" witness.

b)   Cross-Examination

Leading questions are a generally permitted type of inquiry on cross-examination. A leading question suggests to a witness the answer that is sought. Such questions attempt to limit the scope of answer to a "yes" or a "no." For example, "was the color of the vehicle red?", is a leading question. On the other hand, "what color was the vehicle?", is not a leading question.

(1)   Scope of Questioning

FRE 611(b) generally restricts the scope of cross-examination to those issues that were testified to on direct examination, subject to a trial judge's discretion. However, the subject matter of the direct examination is often read broadly to include the essential elements of the cause of action, crime, or defense mentioned on direct. The credibility of a witness, however, is subject to attack on cross-examination. As a result, it can be said that there are three purposes for cross-examination: (1) eliciting testimony that will shed additional light to facts raised in direct examination; (2) in states applying the "wide-open" rule, to elicit testimony on any additional facts that are relevant to an issue in the case; and (3) to impeach the credibility of the witness' direct testimony.

c)   Redirect-Examination

The scope of questioning on redirect examination is limited to questions regarding a witness' testimony on cross-examination that raised significant new issues, such as by impeachment evidence.

d)   Re-Cross-Examination

The scope of questioning on re-cross examination is limited to questions regarding a witness' testimony on redirect-examination that raised significant new issues, such as by rebutting impeachment evidence.

e)   Improper Questions

In addition to questions seeking to introduce otherwise inadmissible evidence, the following types of questions should not be used in any examination of witnesses, and are subject to sustainable objections:

- conclusory, argumentative, harassing, misleading, or compound questions; and
- questions that assume facts not in evidence.

4)   EXCLUSION OF WITNESSES

a)   General Considerations

A party may request that a witness be excluded from the courtroom while other witnesses are testifying. The purpose of permitting the exclusion is to prevent the testimony of another witness from influencing or affecting the subsequent testimony of the witness sought to be excluded. Witnesses may be excluded from the courtroom during part or all of a judicial proceeding. Under the FRE, unless an exclusion applies, the trial judge must exclude a witness at the request of a party.

b)   Inclusion of Witnesses

A trial judge may not exclude the following types of witnesses:

- a party who is a natural person; or

- an officer or employee of a party who is not a natural person designated as its representative by its attorney; or

- a person whose presence is shown by a party to be essential to the presentation of the party's cause; or

- a person authorized by statute to be present.

(1)   Text of FRE 615

> At the request of a party, the court shall order witnesses excluded so that they cannot hear the testimony of other witnesses, and it may make the order of its own motion. This rule does not authorize exclusion of (1) a party who is a natural person, or (2) an officer or employee of a party which is not a natural person designated as its representative by its attorney, or (3) a person whose presence is shown by a party to be essential to the presentation of the party's cause, or (4) a person authorized by statute to be present.

★★★★   **D.   Impeachment, Contradiction, and Rehabilitation**

★   1)   IMPEACHMENT   Question Key
                                                                   144,152

a)   Common Law

The common law prohibits a party from impeaching its own witness on direct examination.

b)   FRE 607

The *Federal Rules* and most states now reject the common law rule prohibiting a party from impeaching its own witness. This is a commonly tested rule. Under the FRE, as a ★★general rule, any witness may be impeached by either party.

(1)   Impeachment with Hearsay Evidence

Hearsay evidence offered to impeach a witness is being used to show discord between the witness' original testimony and the hearsay evidence. Accordingly, such evidence is not being offered to prove the truth of the underlying hearsay statement. Thus, it is not being used for a purpose that falls within the hearsay definition. Therefore, the hearsay evidence may be admissible to the extent that it is being used to impeach a witness, rather than as substantive evidence.

★★   (2)   Impeachment of Hearsay Declarants

If a trial judge admits an out-of-court statement into evidence for the purpose of proving the truth of that statement, which is hearsay, the declarant of that hearsay is subject to impeachment in the same manner as if the declarant were a witness testifying at that trial. Thus, the declarant may be impeached, for example, with inconsistent statements -- even though the statements otherwise would be hearsay -- for the purpose of attacking the declarant's credibility.

(a)   Text of FRE 806

> When a hearsay statement, or a statement defined in Rule 801(d)(2)(C), (D), or (E), has been admitted in evidence, the credibility of the declarant may be attacked, and if attacked may be supported, by any evidence which would be admissible for those purposes if declarant had testified as a witness. Evidence of a statement or conduct by the declarant at any time, inconsistent with the declarant's hearsay statement, is not subject to any requirement that the declarant may have been afforded an opportunity to deny or explain. If the party against whom a hearsay statement has been admitted calls the declarant as a witness, the party is entitled to examine the declarant on the statement as if under cross-examination.

 ★   2)   <u>IMPEACHMENT BY CONTRADICTION</u>

Question Key
95

Although no federal rule directly addresses impeachment by contradiction, under the common law, a party may not impeach a witness by contradiction on a collateral matter with extrinsic evidence.

a)   Contradiction

Contradiction evidence is that which goes against the testimony of a prior witness, and it may be used to show that the testimony of a prior witness lacks credibility, and to establish the facts to which the subsequent witness is testifying.

b)   Collateral Matters

Collateral matters are factual issues that have no bearing on the case but for the purpose of undercutting the credibility of a prior witness by contradiction, rather than one of the other means of impeachment discussed below.

        c)   Extrinsic Evidence

In this context, extrinsic evidence means any evidence that does not come from the witness who is being impeached.

     3)   <u>INCONSISTENT STATEMENTS AND CONDUCT</u>

        a)   Establishing a Foundation

Question Key 6,23,66

In order to impeach the credibility of a witness with a prior inconsistent statement of the witness, a foundation must be established using verbal or written statements.

        b)   Verbal Statements

Testimony of a second witness may be used to establish that a first witness made statements prior to testifying that were inconsistent with the first witness' trial testimony.

        (1)   Common Law

The common law provides that a prior inconsistent statement may not be admitted into evidence until after:

- A witness is informed of the statement, and the place, time, and person to whom it was made; and
- The witness receives an opportunity to either explain away the statement or deny making it.

         (2)   Federal Rules

Under the *Federal Rules*, a witness is not required to possess the opportunity to explain or deny a statement before it is introduced. The witness, however, must have the opportunity to explain or deny the statement at some point, even after the statement has been established.

The testimony about the prior inconsistent verbal statement may be used to impeach the first witness, but may not be used as substantive evidence in the case. In other words, the prior inconsistent statement, which may consist of an out-of-court statement, is probative to reflect on the truthfulness of the witness. Additionally, if the first witness made the prior inconsistent statement under oath, then it could be admitted as substantive evidence under FRE 613.

The credibility of a first witness may be questioned when the testimony of a second witness contradicts the first witness' testimony. Generally, the testimony of a second witness will be admissible if it is relevant to contradict the first witness' testimony.

c)   Written Statements

(1)   Common Law

Under the common law, a witness must be shown an inconsistent written statement and be provided with an opportunity to explain or deny it before it is admitted into evidence. A witness who is subject to impeachment by a prior inconsistent statement is entitled to an opportunity to explain or deny it.

(2)   Federal Rules

Rule 613 allows for the laying of a foundation for the admission of a witness' prior consistent or inconsistent statement, either before or after a witness is impeached. Under the *Federal Rules*, a witness need not have the opportunity to explain or deny a written statement before it is introduced.

★★

(a)   No Requirement to Show Statement First

Unlike the common law, FRE 613(a) allows for the admission of a prior statement into evidence without a requirement that the witness has already seen it and received an opportunity to explain or deny it. However, FRE 613(a) affords an opposing counsel a right to request and review a prior statement.

(b)   Opportunity to Explain Still Exists

Extrinsic evidence of a prior inconsistent statement by a witness will not be admissible unless the witness is afforded an opportunity to explain or deny it, and the opposite party is afforded an opportunity to interrogate the other witness, if any. Although the Federal Rule eliminates the requirement that the witness be able to explain the statement before it is introduced by an opposing party, the witness still must possess such opportunity at some time.

★★★   4)   <u>BIAS AND INTEREST</u>

| Question Key |
| 18,50,54,70,81,139,174 |

      a)   Impeachment for Bias and Interest Generally

The *Federal Rules of Evidence* lack an express provision that addresses bias and interest as grounds for impeachment of a witness. Nonetheless, in civil or criminal proceedings subject to either the common law or the *Federal Rules of Evidence*, a witness always may be asked questions that would reveal a bias or an interest of the witness. Specifically, a party-opponent may try to impeach the credibility of a witness on cross-examination by inquiring about partiality, bias, interest, or motivation.

Generally, a witness' testimony may be influenced by an improper motive that results from:

- a relationship between the witness and another party, or
- the witness' interest in the results of a trial; or
- feelings or emotions regarding parties or issues in a case;

which cause the witness to desire a specific outcome of the case. In addition, in a criminal trial, an indictment, or a promise of leniency or immunity for a witness charged with a crime, is evidence of bias or interest and, therefore, admissible as impeachment evidence.

b)   Evidence of Bias and Interest

Evidence of an impeaching nature may be used to show the bias of a witness either for or against a party, as well as the interest of the witness in the litigation's outcome. For example, evidence that an expert witness is receiving a fee may show the expert's interest in a case's outcome.

(1)   Permissible Types of Evidence

Extrinsic and direct evidence of bias and interest may be produced if a proper evidentiary foundation is laid. Such a foundation may be provided by questioning a witness regarding the facts that indicate bias or interest. If that witness denies being biased or interested, a cross-examining attorney may call other witnesses to prove bias or interest. A party-opponent also may introduce evidence of any relationships or conduct that may provoke a witness' emotions of bias or interest.

c)   Scope of Impeachment

Under FRE 403 and FRE 611, a trial judge may exercise discretion in controlling cross-examination regarding bias or the use of evidence to establish bias. Re-direct examination may be used to rebut any inference of bias that is raised during a cross-examination.

★★   5)   <u>CONVICTION OF CRIME</u>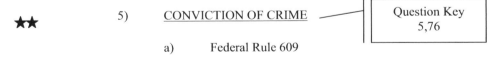

Question Key
5,76

a)   Federal Rule 609

The character for truthfulness of a witness may be attacked with evidence of conviction of the witness for either offenses for which a false statement or act of dishonesty is a required element, or other offenses under certain circumstances.

(1)   Offenses not Requiring Evidence of Dishonesty or False Statement

Under FRE 609(a)(1), under certain circumstances, a witness is subject to impeachment by evidence of a prior conviction for an offense that did not require evidence of dishonesty or false statement to establish the offense's elements--under certain circumstances. Specifically, such evidence may be used for impeachment purposes if these two factors are fulfilled:

- The law that a witness violated provides as potential penalties either a death sentence or imprisonment for more than one year; and
- The court determines that the probative value of admitting this evidence outweighs its prejudicial effect to the accused

The second prong of the test is important and has been tested often on the exam. Once the offense is established, the evidence of the conviction is not admitted automatically. The court must determine that the probative value of admitting the evidence outweighs its prejudicial effect to the accused.

(2)   Offenses Requiring Evidence of Dishonesty or False Statement

Under FRE 609(a)(2), any witness is subject to impeachment by evidence that the witness was convicted of a misdemeanor or felony offense if it readily can be ascertained that proving the elements of the offense required admission or proof of an act of "dishonesty or false statement." Such offenses show that the witness' conduct involved a lack of veracity or truth. Examples of such offenses include, but are not limited to, perjury, embezzlement, and fraud. A prior conviction that falls under FRE 609(a)(2) is available for impeachment purposes regardless of the duration of imprisonment involved. Also, admission of evidence of this type of offense does not require a FRE 403 probative value analysis.

(3)   Methods of Impeachment

A party seeking to impeach a witness may introduce a prior conviction of the witness by asking the witness about it on cross-examination. Extrinsic evidence of a prior conviction may be established by the testimony of someone who observed the conviction. A certified copy of a judgment of conviction may establish that occurrence. FRE 902 renders such a judgment self-authenticating.

(4)   10 Year Limitation

The *Federal Rules of Evidence* provide that if a person who was convicted of a felony or a misdemeanor, or released from incarceration, over 10 years prior to a proceeding in which that person was called as a witness, that duration of time may preclude the admission of a prior conviction of the witness. Such a prior conviction, however, may be admitted if its probative value outweighs that evidence's prejudicial effect under FRE 403.

(a)   Notice Requirement

Prior to presenting such evidence, a prosecutor is required to notify the defense of that intent in order to allow the defense time to contest the use of that evidence.

(5)   Text of FRE 609(a)-(b)

(a) General rule.

For the purpose of attacking the character for truthfulness of a witness,

(1) evidence that a witness other than an accused has been convicted of a crime shall be admitted, subject to Rule 403, if the crime was punishable by death or imprisonment in excess of one year under the law under which the witness was convicted, and evidence that an accused has been convicted of such a crime shall be admitted if the court determines that the probative value of admitting this evidence outweighs its prejudicial effect to the accused; and

(2) evidence that any witness has been convicted of a crime shall be admitted regardless of the punishment, if it readily can be determined that establishing the elements of the crime required proof or admission of an act of dishonesty or false statement by the witness.

(b) time limit.

Evidence of a conviction under this rule is not admissible if a period of more than ten years has elapsed since the date of the conviction or of the release of the witness from the confinement imposed for that conviction, whichever is the later date, unless the court determines, in the interests of justice, that the probative value of the conviction supported by specific facts and circumstances substantially outweighs its prejudicial effect. However, evidence of a conviction more than 10 years old as calculated herein, is not admissible unless the proponent gives to the adverse party sufficient advance written notice of intent to use such evidence to provide the adverse party with a fair opportunity to contest the use of such evidence.

 ★★★   6)   SPECIFIC INSTANCES OF CONDUCT

> Question Key
> 2,32,129,170,
> 175,176

Evidence of specific instances of conduct, such as prior bad acts not resulting in conviction, may be admitted to impeach a witness under certain circumstances.

a)   Common Law

The common law provides that, on cross-examination, an attorney may question a witness about prior bad acts that did not result in a criminal conviction. However, the attorney may not use extrinsic evidence for this purpose. A party must have a good-faith basis to believe a witness committed the prior bad act.

b)   Federal Rules

FRE 608(b) generally follows the common law, but limits an attorney's questions on cross-examination to only the prior bad acts of a witness that are probative of truthfulness (e.g., lying on a job application). The allowance of such questions is in a trial judge's discretion.

(1)   Prior Bad Acts

Prior bad acts are specific instances of misconduct by a witness that do not result in a criminal conviction. For example, a party may seek to introduce evidence that the witness lied on a state permit application, to reflect negatively on the witness' truthfulness. FRE 608(b) provides that these acts may be the subject of questioning only during the cross-examination.

(a)   Extrinsic Evidence

Extrinsic evidence in the form of witness testimony is not permitted. For example, a party may ask an initial witness about the prior bad act on cross-examination if the party has a good-faith basis that the prior bad act occurred. However, a party cannot call a second witness after the initial witness testifies that she did not commit the prior bad act. ★★In effect, the questioning party is "stuck" with the witness' answer. Certain federal courts consider any document as extrinsic evidence. Other federal courts do not consider a document as extrinsic evidence if the initial witness can authenticate the document.

(2)   Text of FRE 608(b)

> Specific instances of the conduct of a witness, for the purpose of attacking or supporting the witness' character for truthfulness, other than the conviction of a crime as provided in rule 609, may not be proved by extrinsic evidence. They may, however, in the discretion of the court, if probative of truthfulness or untruthfulness, be inquired into on cross-examination of the witness (1) concerning the witness' character for truthfulness or untruthfulness, or (2) concerning the character for truthfulness or untruthfulness of another witness as to which character the witness being cross-examined has testified.

★★   7)   CHARACTER FOR TRUTHFULNESS

a)   Common Law

The common law permits the credibility of a first witness to be impeached by testimony of a second witness indicating a bad reputation for truthfulness of the first witness. Such impeaching testimony may neither relate specific examples of an alleged lack of truthfulness nor be a statement of opinion.

b)   Federal Rules Permit Opinion and Reputation

FRE 608(a) allows the credibility of a witness to be attacked by evidence in the form of both opinion and reputation that refers to that witness' character for truthfulness or untruthfulness.

        c)   Impeachment

A testable impeachment issue involves the use of evidence to prove that a witness does not have a good character regarding truth and veracity. Taking all of the provisions discussed above together, evidence may be proffered for the purpose of impeaching a witness in the following ways:

- Evidence of a witness' reputation for truthfulness (FRE 608(a));
- Opinion evidence to establish that a witness lacks a good character for truth and veracity (FRE 608(a));
- Evidence of particular acts to prove a witness' bad character for truth and veracity. Such evidence may include prior inconsistent statements, previous conduct (FRE 404), or prior criminal convictions (FRE 609). That evidence cannot just be used to show that the witness generally has a bad character; and
- Specific instances of prior bad acts that did not result in criminal conviction, as long as those instances of misconduct are probative on the issue of truthfulness (untruthful conduct per FRE 608(b)). A cross-examining attorney, however, cannot introduce extrinsic evidence of a witness' misconduct. The cross-examiner must accept a witness' answer to a question if the witness admits or denies the act.

        d)   Bolstering Credibility

           (1)   Generally Permissible

A party whose witness' character for truthfulness has been specifically impeached on cross-examination may call a witness to either bolster or rehabilitate the credibility of that witness. However, a party opponent's presentation of other witnesses or evidence that generally contradicts the testimony of a witness does not warrant rehabilitating the witness' credibility.

           (2)   Types of Permissible Evidence

The type of attack on an impeached witness' character will dictate the type of evidence that is available to support the rehabilitation. Character evidence used for the purpose of bolstering needs to be logically connected to the evidence that was used to impeach a witness. Evidence presented to bolster the credibility of a witness is inadmissible if credibility of that witness was not previously challenged at trial.

           (3)   Text of FRE 608(a)

> The credibility of a witness may be attacked or supported by evidence in the form of opinion or reputation, but subject to these limitations: (1) the evidence may refer only to character for truthfulness or untruthfulness, and (2) evidence of truthful character is admissible only after the character of the witness for truthfulness has been attacked by opinion or reputation evidence or otherwise.

8)   IMPAIRMENT OF SENSORY CAPACITY OF WITNESS

A witness may suffer from an impairment of a sensory capacity that affects the ability to accurately observe, remember, or relate events. Evidence of that impairment may be used to attack the credibility of the witness during cross-examination.

9)   REHABILITATION OF IMPEACHED WITNESSES

a)   Bolstering not Permitted until Attack

Under FRE 608(a)(2), a witness' credibility cannot be bolstered by one party's attorney until after it has been attacked by another party's attorney on cross-examination. The evidence to use for rehabilitation must "meet the attack." For example, evidence of the untruthfulness of a witness may be met with evidence of truthfulness of the witness (not evidence of peacefulness or good general moral character of the witness).

b)   Exceptions

Two exceptions to the rule exist. First, an out-of-court identification of someone by a witness may be presented in a direct examination of the witness. Second, a rape victim may bolster her testimony in a direct examination by stating that she immediately filed a police report after the incident.

E.   Proceedings to Which Evidence Rules Apply

1)   STATE EVIDENCE LAW

When so provided by state law, common law evidence rules apply to civil and criminal proceedings in state court before either a trial judge or a jury. Most states have, however, adopted rules or statutory evidentiary compilations. The state law rules apply in both state trial actions and, to a limited extent (e.g., privilege and other "substantive" evidence rules), in federal actions grounded in diversity jurisdiction. Those rules also may apply in appellate proceedings that are subject to a *de novo* standard of review.

2)   FEDERAL RULES

FRE 101 provides that the FRE apply to any trials in federal courts. The federal courts apply the FRE when they are exercising federal question jurisdiction. A federal court exercising diversity jurisdiction must determine which laws apply to the merits of a case. In such a case, the federal court applies the law of the state where that court sits to substantive issues in the case. The federal court will apply federal law to procedural issues, which generally results in the application of the FRE.

3)   CONSTITUTIONAL BASIS

In criminal proceedings, evidentiary rules may not contradict either the Compulsory Process Clause or the Confrontation Clause of the Sixth Amendment to the *U.S. Constitution.* In civil proceedings, evidentiary rules cannot infringe upon a litigant's fair trial right under the Due Process Clause of the Fourteenth Amendment.

II.   RELEVANCY AND REASONS FOR EXCLUDING RELEVANT EVIDENCE

★★★★

A.   Probative Value

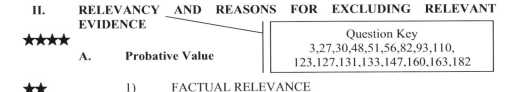

Question Key
3,27,30,48,51,56,82,93,110,
123,127,131,133,147,160,163,182

★★   1)   FACTUAL RELEVANCE

Relevance is the threshold inquiry in any evidence analysis. In order for evidence to be admissible, it must be factually relevant. If evidence is not factually relevant, it will not be admitted.

a)   Definition

Evidence is factually relevant if it relates to, and possesses probative value regarding an event, people, or time, at issue in litigation. Evidence is factually relevant if it possesses any tendency to make the existence of any fact that is of consequence to the determination of the action more probable or less probable than it would be without the evidence. Only relevant evidence is admissible in legal proceedings.

(1)   Text of FRE 401

> "Relevant evidence" means evidence having any tendency to make the existence of any fact that is of consequence to the determination of the action more probable or less probable than it would be without the evidence.

b)   Types of Relevant Evidence

(1)   Direct Evidence

Direct evidence will resolve an issue if it is believed. Direct evidence is relevant if it directly relates to a material fact. Direct evidence may be provided by witnesses who possess knowledge of a fact in dispute and whose testimony, when believed, will settle an issue. Direct evidence is admissible even if it negatively reflects on a party's character.

For example, if a witness testifies that she saw the defendant stab the victim, that evidence is direct evidence. In other words, if it is believed, the testimony settles the issue.

★★   (2)   Circumstantial Evidence

Circumstantial evidence is evidence of a collateral fact based on which a fact-finder could infer the existence of a relevant fact. That inference may be drawn only from the collateral fact or that fact when viewed in combination with other evidence.

Circumstantial evidence, although it is believed, will not resolve an issue without the use of additional reasoning or evidence.

For example, if a witness testifies that she saw the defendant's car speeding from the scene of a murder at around the time of death of the victim, the testimony is considered circumstantial evidence. It is circumstantial evidence because it requires additional reasoning or evidence to conclude that the defendant was the one who killed the victim.

Evidence may not be excluded simply on the basis that is it circumstantial. Circumstantial evidence is admissible if it is relevant, has probative value, and is not subject to exclusion on any other basis.

                    c)   Failure to Object on Relevance Grounds

If evidence is even loosely related to the controversy, but not covered by the pleadings, a party's failure to object to the admission of such evidence on relevance grounds can have the effect of adding the issue to the case. As a result, once the evidence is entered, the party who failed to object may present evidence to rebut the information without violating the relevance requirement.

★★★★   2)   LEGAL RELEVANCE

Once evidence is deemed factually relevant, the court also must consider whether it is legally relevant under FRE 403.

                    a)   FRE 403

Under FRE 403, factually relevant evidence may be excluded when its probative value is "substantially outweighed by the dangers of": (a) unfair prejudice; (b) confusion of the issues; (c) misleading the jury; (d) undue delay; or (e) cumulative evidence.

        •   Weighing Relevancy

The courts apply FRE 403 as a balancing test of proffered evidence using a reasonableness approach. The courts possess extensive discretion in applying the standard.

•   Text of FRE 403

> Although relevant, evidence may be excluded if its probative value is substantially outweighed by the danger of unfair prejudice, confusion of the issues, or misleading the jury, or by considerations of undue delay, waste of time, or needless presentation of cumulative evidence.

(1)   Unfair Prejudice

An Advisory Committee Note to FRE 403 defines "unfair prejudice" as "an undue tendency to suggest decision on an improper basis, commonly, though not necessarily, an emotional one."

Evidence meeting this test may be inadmissible because its prejudicial effect outweighs its probative value. For example, the results of a lie detector test may be inadmissible evidence because its prejudicial effect would outweigh its probative value. That effect arises from the fact that the test results may be deemed unreliable.

The risk of unfair prejudice is often cited also when excluding evidence of a prior civil judgment as proof in a subsequent civil proceeding.

(2)   Confusion

Confusion may result from the introduction of evidence similar to, but different from and not directly related to, the evidence that is at issue. Evidence that causes confusion may be inadmissible under FRE 403.

(3)   Waste of Time

The introduction of redundant or cumulative evidence results in wasting the time of a trial judge, jurors, and other parties to a case. For example, the use of more than one witness or document to establish the same facts would result in a waste of time, and may be inadmissible evidence under FRE 403.

★★★   **B.   Authentication and Identification**

> Question Key
> 24,29,38,69,77,78,84,92,107,
> 108,118,132,142

1)   GENERAL CONSIDERATIONS

a)   Definitions

Authentication is the legal requirement of establishing a foundation that evidence is genuinely what it purports to be. Identification is a prerequisite to admissibility that informs a party opponent and a fact-finder of the nature and essence of each item of proffered evidence. Under the common law and FRE 901, most real and demonstrative evidence is not assumed to be authentic or self-identifying. Indeed, all evidence needs to be identified when laying a foundation for its admission. Identification is a prerequisite for authentication because the parties and the trier of fact must be appraised of what evidence is sought to be admitted, and thus needs be authenticated. Accordingly, for the purposes of this topic and its subtopics, as under the FRE, authentication and identification will be considered related terms because of their similar requirements and purposes.

b)   Exceptions

Exceptions to the requirements of authentication and identification include the parties' stipulations to the evidence's genuine nature, admissions of the evidence's authenticity, and self-authenticating evidence.

2)   FRE 901

a)   General Rule

FRE 901 applies to all types of evidence and sets the standard of proof for its proponent to authenticate and identify evidence. Thus, evidence is inadmissible unless it has been authenticated and identified. The requirement of authentication or identification as a condition precedent to admissibility is satisfied by evidence sufficient to support a finding that the matter in question is what the proponent claims.

(1)   Example

A proponent may seek to introduce a photograph of an accident scene into evidence. FRE 901 allows for the admission of testimony from a witness who has knowledge of the accident scene for the purpose of authenticating and identifying the photograph of the scene. In order for the photograph to be admitted, a witness with knowledge must testify that the photograph correctly describes what it is purported to illustrate. If the evidence is used to show what a scene is like, then the evidence should accurately reflect the scene as it appeared at or near the time of the incident. In other words, the item cannot represent the scene in an altered form.

(2)   Text of FRE 901(a)

> The requirement of authentication or identification as a condition precedent to admissibility is satisfied by evidence sufficient to support a finding that the matter in question is what its proponent claims.

b)   Examples of Methods of Authentication of Items

FRE 901 lists several methods of authenticating physical evidence. However, the list is non-exhaustive and is not meant in any way to limit the proper methods for authenticating evidence. The examples of proper methods of authentication that apply to all forms of evidence (those that apply to documents, recordings, and pictorial evidence are addressed below) are:

- testimony by a witness that the evidence is authentic;
- distinctive characteristics in the evidence such as "[a]ppearance, contents, substance, [or] internal patterns";
- evidence of a system or process used to ensure accurate results;
- any other method provided by statute or rule.

c)   Documents

The authenticity of a document under FRE 901 may be shown in the following ways:

- A party-opponent admits or stipulates that it is genuine;
- A jury makes a comparison between two pieces of evidence;
- Circumstantial evidence indicates that the document is genuine, such as by
  o   the contents of a disputed document that disclose information that only the purported signer would know, making him the probable author; or
  o   when a letter offered into evidence appears to be a reply letter coming from the addressee of the first letter; or
- A witness testifies that the document is genuine.

The following types of witnesses may provide the testimony:

- a person who executed a document;
- a witness who saw the person execute the document;
- an expert witness who compared samples of the person's handwriting and signature with the handwriting and signature on the documents; or
- lay witnesses who are familiar with the person's handwriting; however, under FRE 901(b)(2), that familiarity may not have been acquired for the purposes of litigation.

d)   Authenticating Recordings

A witness who is familiar with the voice of a person whose voice is purportedly recorded may testify that the person's voice is on the recording. For example, testimony of a witness who recognizes the voice of someone on a recorded phone call may authenticate and identify the contents of that phone conversation. In the absence of such testimony, surrounding circumstances may provide sufficient circumstantial evidence of authentication and identification. For example, a telephone conversation may be admissible evidence if a person called identifies herself on a phone and her telephone number (the number called) is listed in a telephone directory.

(1)   Text of FRE 901(b)(5)-(6)

(5) Voice identification. Identification of a voice, whether heard firsthand or through mechanical or electronic transmission or recording, by opinion based

upon hearing the voice at any time under circumstances connecting it with the alleged speaker.

(6) Telephone conversations. Telephone conversations, by evidence that a call was made to the number assigned at the time by the telephone company to a particular person or business, if (A) in the case of a person, circumstances, including self-identification, show the person answering to be the one called, or (B) in the case of a business, the call was made to a place of business and the conversation related to business reasonably transacted over the telephone.

e)   Authenticating Pictorial Evidence

The modern majority rule provides that pictorial evidence is admissible without any supporting testimony from a witness who observed the person or event that was photographed. This "silent witness" approach allows for the pictorial evidence to "speak for itself." To authenticate pictorial evidence, however, foundational testimony is required from a witness that the technological process used to obtain it is reliable. The types of pictorial evidence that may be authenticated in this manner include films, x-rays, and images captured by automated devices (e.g., surveillance camera videos or pictures).

3)   SELF-AUTHENTICATED EVIDENCE

Certain types of evidence are self-authenticating. Therefore, the proponent is not required to authenticate the evidence.

a)   Ancient Documents

FRE 901(b)(8) makes ancient documents self-authenticating evidence if:

- the document is at least 20 years old;
- the document is not suspicious in appearance; and
- the document occupied a natural custodial location.

(1)   Text of FRE 901(b)(8)

(8) Ancient documents or data compilation. Evidence that a document or data compilation, in any form, (A) is in such condition as to create no suspicion concerning its authenticity, (B) was in a place where it, if authentic, would likely be, and (C) has been in existence 20 years or more at the time it is offered.

b)   Other Self-Authenticating Evidence

FRE 902 provides that extrinsic proof of the genuineness of certain evidence is not required to establish the admissibility of such evidence including:

- acknowledged or notarized instruments, such as deeds;

- certified copies of public records;
- statute books that appear to be from another state or nation;
- any official publication;
- newspapers or periodicals;
- labels, signs, or inscriptions of "control, or ownership"; and
- commercial paper and similar documents, such as labels that indicate the source of a product.

Question Key
9,15,22,52,57,79,88,106,110, 111,112,135,143,146,158

 C.   Character and Related Concepts

1)   ADMISSIBILITY OF CHARACTER

a)   General Rule

Evidence of a person's character or character trait usually is inadmissible to show that the person "acted in conformity therewith on a particular occasion." FRE 404(a)(1)-(3) provide exceptions to that rule. The exceptions in FRE 404(a)(1)-(2) apply to criminal proceedings.

(1)   Exceptions

Evidence of a "pertinent trait of character" is admissible in a criminal case if:

- a defendant uses it to prove his good character and innocence; or
- a prosecutor uses it to rebut the defendant's evidence of good character and innocence; or
- the prosecutor uses it to rebut the defendant's evidence of a victim's bad character.

FRE 404(a)(1).

(a)   Defendant Introduces Character Evidence

A defendant in a criminal action has the right to introduce evidence of good character. For example, if a defendant is charged with battery, he may introduce evidence that he is a peaceful person (i.e., character for peacefulness). If a defendant produces evidence of a pertinent trait of the defendant's character that is inconsistent with a charged offense, or to prove his innocence, then a prosecutor may rebut that evidence by:

- cross-examining a defendant's character witness as to the witness' knowledge of certain instances of the defendant's prior conduct;
- calling a prosecution witness to testify about his opinion of a defendant's character or about the witness' knowledge of the defendant's reputation in the community. A prosecutor may offer this extrinsic rebuttal evidence.

(2)   Character of Victim

A criminal defendant may present opinion or reputation evidence regarding an alleged victim's "pertinent trait of character" if that evidence is relevant to a defense that the defendant raised to a prosecutor's charge. FRE 404(a)(2). For example, a victim's reputation for violence is admissible to prove that a defendant acted reasonably to protect himself from harm. This rule relates to the issue of self-defense.

(3)   Character of Witness

The credibility of a witness may be attacked with evidence of the witness's untruthful character by means of questioning the witness about an alleged false statement by the witness. FRE 404(a)(3). Therefore, a court may admit non-extrinsic evidence about a prior bad act (e.g., lying), if the non-extrinsic evidence is proffered in cross-examination of the witness and is probative of the witness's untruthfulness. Conduct by the witness that involves deception or falsehood usually is probative of untruthfulness.

(4)   Text of FRE 404(a)

> Evidence of a person's character or a trait of character is not admissible for the purpose of proving action in conformity therewith on a particular occasion, except:
>
> (1) character of accused – In a criminal case, evidence of a pertinent trait of character offered by an accused, or by the prosecution to rebut the same, or if evidence of a trait of character of the alleged victim of the crime is offered by an accused and admitted under Rule 404 (a)(2), evidence of the same trait of character of the accused offered by the prosecution;
>
> (2) character of alleged victim - In a criminal case, and subject to the limitations imposed by Rule 412, evidence of a pertinent trait of character of the alleged victim of the crime offered by an accused, or by the prosecution to rebut the same, or evidence of a character trait of peacefulness of the alleged victim offered by the prosecution in a homicide case to rebut evidence that the alleged victim was the first aggressor;
>
> (3) character of witness - Evidence of the character of a witness, as provided in Rules 607, 608, and 609.

        2)   <u>METHODS OF PROVING CHARACTER</u>

a)   Reputation or Evidence is Most Common Method

Both reputation evidence and opinion evidence are admissible in any case "in which evidence of character or a trait of character of a person is admissible." FRE 405(a). In other words, under certain circumstances when character evidence is admissible, it may be demonstrated by the use of reputation or opinion evidence of the character of the person.

b)   Specific Instances of Conduct

(1)   Ultimate Issue

Evidence of specific instances of a person's conduct is admissible when character is an ultimate issue in either civil or criminal proceedings. FRE 405(b). An ultimate issue exists if a "trait of character of a person is an essential element of a charge, claim, or defense." FRE 405(b).

Evidence of specific instances of that person's conduct is also admissible. FRE 405(b). In other words, the Federal Rules increase the scope of admissible character evidence to include certain prior acts of a person that are proffered to prove the person's character with respect to an "essential element of a charge, claim, or defense" that is being adjudicated.

(a)   Criminal Proceedings

FRE 405(b) applies when a defendant's character is an "essential element" of a prosecutor's charge, or a defense to that charge, in a criminal proceeding. In that instance, FRE 405 provides for admission of all three types of character evidence:

- specific instances of the defendant's conduct (FRE 405(b);
- opinion evidence about the defendant's character (FRE 405(a)); and
- reputation evidence regarding defendant's character (FRE 405(a)).

(b)   Civil Proceedings

Character is an "essential element" of a civil claim or defense under FRE 405(b) in the following (and other similar) types of civil actions or causes of action:

- negligent entrustment: A plaintiff asserts that a defendant entrusted something or some responsibility to a third party whose character is at issue.
- child custody: The character of a parent or guardian may determine custodial rights.
- defamation: A plaintiff alleges that a communication defamed his character.
- fraud or misrepresentation. A plaintiff alleges that a false representation defrauded him.

In those four instances, FRE 405 provides for admission of all three types of character evidence:

- opinion evidence; and
- reputation evidence; and
- specific instances of conduct.

(c)   Text of FRE 405

(a) reputation or opinion.

In all cases in which evidence of character or a trait of character of a person is admissible, proof may be made by testimony as to reputation or by testimony in the form of an opinion. On cross-examination, inquiry is allowable into relevant specific instances of conduct.

(b) specific instances of conduct.

In cases in which character or a trait of character of a person is an essential element of a charge, claim, or defense, proof may also be made of specific instances of that person's conduct.

★   3)   HABIT AND ROUTINE PRACTICE

a)   General Rule

Evidence that a person consistently and predictably acts in a certain way is admissible to prove the person's act on a specific occasion conformed to any previous acts. Similarly, an entity's routine practice is admissible to prove the occurrence of a particular event that resulted from that practice. It is not necessary for a party that seeks to prove the existence of a habit to present eyewitnesses to corroborate the occurrence of particular acts or practices.

b)   Difference between Habit and Character Evidence

The main practical difference between habit and character evidence is that either party in both civil and criminal cases may introduce habit evidence, but character evidence usually is admissible only after a defendant opens the issue. Habit evidence requires proof of a very specific, frequently repeated behavioral pattern, whereas character evidence deals with either general moral character or a relevant character trait. For example, in a negligent vehicular homicide case, the defendant may present evidence about his law-abiding character trait for being a good and careful driver. Detailed testimony about the routine manner in which he executes right-hand turns would be habit evidence. Habit has a narrow focus. Habit deals with a person's response to a particular type of situation, while character evidence would allow a proponent to prove specific relevant character traits, such as honesty or peacefulness. The same type of behavior on the part of an organization is called a custom or routine practice.

(1)   Text of FRE 406

> Evidence of the habit of a person or of the routine practice of an organization, whether corroborated or not and regardless of the presence of eyewitnesses, is relevant to prove that the conduct of the person or organization on a particular occasion was in conformity with the habit or routine practice.

4)   OTHER CRIMES, ACTS, TRANSACTIONS, AND EVENTS

a)   Criminal Proceedings

In a criminal case under FRE 404(b), a prosecutor cannot use evidence of specific instances of a criminal defendant's prior wrongful conduct to prove the defendant's bad character. Evidence of prior bad acts is not admissible for a prosecutor to assert that a defendant had a propensity or predisposition to commit a charged offense similar to the defendant's prior offenses.

(1)   MIMIC KOP Evidence

Evidence of the prior wrongful acts and past crimes is admissible if the evidence possesses independent relevance and is not being used to prove character. This evidence may be used to prove one of eight things, including: 1) motive, 2) intent, 3) absence of mistake, 4) identity, 5) common plan or scheme, 6) knowledge, 7) opportunity, and 8) preparation. When the first letters of those words are combined they spell out MIMIC KOP.

MIMIC KOP evidence may be used to establish the elements of a crime. It must be presented in the form of specific acts, rather than as reputation or opinion evidence. A trial judge must determine if the risk of undue prejudice from the evidence of the prior wrongful acts and past crimes substantially outweighs its probative value so as to warrant its exclusion at trial.

Pursuant to the rule, if requested by an accused, the prosecutor in a criminal case "must provide reasonable notice in advance of trial, or during trial if the court excuses pretrial notice on good cause shown, of the general nature of any such evidence it intends to introduce at trial."

(2)   Text of FRE 404(b)

> Evidence of other crimes, wrongs, or acts is not admissible to prove the character of a person in order to show action in conformity therewith. It may, however, be admissible for other purposes, such as proof of motive, opportunity, intent, preparation, plan, knowledge, identity, or absence of mistake or accident, provided that upon request by the accused, the prosecution in a criminal case shall provide reasonable notice in advance of trial, or during trial if the court excuses pretrial notice on good cause shown, of the general nature of any such evidence it intends to introduce at trial.

b) Civil Proceedings

(1) Prior Accidents

The majority of courts exclude evidence of prior accidents proffered to establish that a defendant was negligent in a specific situation at issue in the litigation. Those courts also exclude evidence showing an absence of prior accidents to prove a defendant exercised due care in a particular instance. The rationale for such exclusionary rules is that the probative value of such evidence does not outweigh the risk of unfair prejudice and waste of court time.

(a) Exception

The evidence of prior accidents is, however, admissible when it is offered to prove either:

- the existence of a dangerous condition; or
- that a defendant was aware of a dangerous condition.

5) PRIOR SEXUAL MISCONDUCT OF A DEFENDANT

a) Sexual Assault and Child Molestation

(1) Criminal Cases

In a criminal case in which the defendant is accused of sexual assault or child molestation, evidence of the defendant's commission of another offense of sexual assault or child molestation is admissible.

(a) Notice Requirement

In a case in which a prosecutor intends to offer evidence of a prior sexual assault or child molestation, the prosecutor must disclose the evidence to the defendant, including statements of witnesses or a summary of the substance of any testimony that is expected to be offered, at least fifteen days before the scheduled date of trial or at a later time, if the court permits, for good cause.

(2) Civil Cases

In a civil case in which a claim is predicated on a party's alleged commission of an offense of sexual assault or child molestation, evidence of that party's commission of another offense of sexual assault or child molestation is admissible.

(a) Notice Requirement

A party who intends to offer evidence of a prior sexual assault or child molestation must disclose the evidence to the party against whom it will be offered, including statements of witnesses or a summary of the substance of any testimony that is expected to be offered, at least fifteen days before the scheduled date of trial, or at a later time, if the court permits, for good cause.

D.   Expert Testimony and Scientific Evidence

| Question Key |
| 16,116,128,165,169 |

1)   QUALIFICATIONS OF WITNESSES

A party may seek to introduce evidence that requires specialized knowledge. If scientific, technical, or other specialized knowledge will assist the trier of fact to understand the evidence in a case, or to determine a fact in issue, then a witness qualified as an expert may testify in the form of an opinion.

A potential expert witness must be qualified as an expert by knowledge, skill, experience, training, or education. An expert witness may testify in the form of an opinion.

There are three requirements for expert testimony: (1) the testimony must be based upon sufficient facts or data; (2) the testimony must be the product of reliable principles and methods; and (3) the witness must apply the principles and methods reliably to the facts of the case.

2)   BASIS FOR EXPERT TESTIMONY

a)   Perceived Facts

An expert witness who testifies at trial may base her opinion testimony on the facts perceived by, or made known to the expert, at or before the hearing.

★★

b)   Hypothetical Information

Alternatively, an expert witness who testifies at trial may base her opinion testimony on data or facts about which the expert learns at a trial, possibly through a hypothetical question, and data or facts made known to the expert prior to a trial. In addition, many jurisdictions require that hypothetical questions must contain all material facts in evidence that are essential to creating a rational expert opinion.

c)   Hearsay Evidence

If the facts are facts reasonably relied upon by experts in the particular field in forming opinions upon the subject, then the facts and data are not required to be admissible in evidence in order for the opinion to be admitted into evidence. However, any facts or data that are otherwise inadmissible cannot be disclosed to the jury unless the court determines that their probative value in assisting the jury to evaluate the expert's opinion substantially outweighs their prejudicial effect.

d)   Disclosure of Factual Basis

The expert may provide an expert opinion without first testifying to the underlying facts or data that the expert has relied upon, unless the court requires otherwise. However, the expert may, in any event, be required to disclose the underlying facts or data on cross-examination.

3)   <u>ULTIMATE ISSUE RULE</u>

a)   Ultimate Issue of Fact

An ultimate issue is one upon which a decision by a trier of fact will be outcome determinative in a civil or criminal proceeding. For example, in a prosecution for driving a vehicle in excess of the speed limit, the vehicle's speed is the ultimate issue. Under the common law approach, an expert witness could not testify regarding an ultimate issue of fact, because such testimony would usurp the function of the trier of fact. Modern rules, including *Federal Rule* 704, depart from the common law and generally permit an expert witness to testify about an ultimate issue of fact, unless it concerns a criminal defendant's mental state while committing an alleged offense. Therefore, because the *Federal Rules* generally apply on the MBE, ultimate issues of fact may be the subject of expert testimony.

b)   Ultimate Issue of Law

Neither a lay witness nor an expert witness may testify about an ultimate issue of law or assert what the outcome of any proceeding should be.

c)   Text of FRE 704

(a) Except as provided in subdivision (b), testimony in the form of an opinion or inference otherwise admissible is not objectionable because it embraces an ultimate issue to be decided by the trier of fact.

(b) No expert witness testifying with respect to the mental state or condition of a defendant in a criminal case may state an opinion or inference as to whether the defendant did or did not have the mental state or condition constituting an element of the crime charged or of a defense thereto. Such ultimate issues are matters for the trier of fact alone.

4)   <u>RELIABILITY, RELEVANCE, AND SUBJECT MATTER</u>

a)   Common Law *Frye* Standard for Admissibility

An issue regarding expert testimony that may arise on the exam is the standard for determining admissibility of scientific evidence. The common law *Frye* case provides the following standard to determine the admissibility of scientific evidence:

Is the principle or test being used to obtain the evidence at issue *generally accepted* in the scientific community?

The Frye standard limits the use of expert evidence based on novel scientific theories. Under the *Frye* test, most courts exclude evidence such as the results of voice prints, truth serum, lie detector tests, hypnosis, and psychological stress evaluators, because these types of tests are not generally accepted in the scientific community.

Other reliable scientific evidence, such as: speed detection equipment results, statistical probabilities, neutron activation analysis, and information based on psychiatry and psychology, are admitted because they generally are accepted in the scientific community.

        b)   Competing *Daubert* Standard for Admissibility

The common law's *Frye* standard is quite rigid and flatly works to reject novel scientific theories that have not gained general acceptance. The Supreme Court, and some state courts, have rejected or modified the *Frye* standard to permit the application and admission of expert evidence based on novel scientific theories. In the *Daubert* case, the Supreme Court rejected *Frye* and adopted a two-prong test. In order to be admitted, scientific evidence must be 1) relevant and 2) reliable.

The Supreme Court held that in order for expert testimony to be considered reliable, the expert must have derived her conclusions from the scientific method. The general observations of whether evidence is based on the scientific method include, but are not limited to, the following:

- The theory or technique must be subject to empirical testing.
- It must be subjected to peer review and publication.
- There must be a known or potential error rate and the existence and maintenance of standards concerning its operation.
- Whether the theory and technique generally is accepted by a relevant scientific community is still a factor, but not determinative.

E.   **Real, Demonstrative, and Experimental Evidence**

      1)   GENERAL CONSIDERATIONS

Question Key
167

        a)   Real and Demonstrative Evidence

Real and demonstrative evidence are two types of tangible physical evidence. They are both types of direct, as compared to circumstantial, evidence. They may consist of documents but cannot be composed of testimony. Their primary difference arises in terms of the proper means of authenticating them.

        b)   Requirement for Admissibility

To be admissible, real, demonstrative, and experimental evidence need to fulfill the general requirements of relevance: (1) factual relevance; and (2) legal relevance.

      2)   REAL EVIDENCE

Real evidence is physical evidence that was involved in, or was a part of, an incident or situation that gave rise to civil or criminal legal proceedings. Examples of real evidence include weapons that allegedly were used in committing crimes and pictorial evidence. A prerequisite to the admission of real evidence is authentication and identification.

3)   DEMONSTRATIVE EVIDENCE

Demonstrative evidence illustrates or describes an issue of significance in civil or criminal legal proceedings. Examples of such evidence include maps, diagrams, and models that serve to explain a fact or some other item of evidence that may pertain to a witness' testimony. A proponent of demonstrative evidence needs to show that the evidence truly is that which it purports to represent.

4)   EXPERIMENTAL EVIDENCE

a)   General Considerations

Experiments or demonstrations are admissible if they will provide relevant evidence that is more probative than prejudicial, wasteful, confusing, or cumulative. For example, an in-court display of an injury is considered relevant. For a demonstration to be relevant, it must prove that what is demonstrated must be similar to the matter in issue.

(1)   Out-of-Court Experiment

If an out-of-court experiment occurs before a trial, a test of its relevance is whether a sufficient similarity of circumstances exists between the test and the actual event. The experiment's results may be conveyed to a jury during the trial if they are relevant and more probative than prejudicial under FRE 403.

(2)   In-Court Experiment

A trial judge may allow an in-court experiment if a sufficient similarity of circumstances exist between the test and the actual event.

III.   PRIVILEGES AND OTHER POLICY EXCLUSIONS

> Question Key
> 13

A testimonial privilege authorizes a first party, to refuse to disclose to a third party, the contents of communications with a second party. The first party also may prevent the second party from disclosing those communications to the third party. Several privileges exist under the common law.

- Federal Question

In a case grounded in federal question jurisdiction, the federal common law of privilege applies.

- State Privilege Law

While the Federal Rules of Evidence do not specifically provide for certain types of testimonial privileges, FRE 501 provides that when an element of a claim or defense is not based on a federal question, state law determines testimonial privileges. Thus, in a federal action grounded in diversity jurisdiction, the privilege law of the state in which the federal court sits will apply.

- Traditional and Modern Privileges

FRE 501 permits federal courts to recognize and apply traditional common law privileges, as well as the following modern privileges, which exist between: attorney-client, physician/psychotherapist-patient, and spouse-spouse. The privilege against self-incrimination under the Fifth Amendment to the *U.S. Constitution* also is available to a potential witness.

- Waiver of Privilege

Generally, the holder of a privilege may waive it in any of the following ways:

- by failing to claim the privilege;
- by disclosing the privileged information to a third party; or
- by signing a written waiver of the privilege.

> Text of FRE 501
>
> Except as otherwise required by the Constitution of the United States or provided by act of Congress or in rules prescribed by the Supreme Court pursuant to statutory authority, the privilege of a witness, person, government, State, or political subdivision thereof shall be governed by the principles of the common law as they may be interpreted by the courts of the United States in the light of reason and experience. However, in civil actions and proceedings, with respect to an element of a claim or defense as to which State law supplies the rule of decision, the privilege of a witness, person, government, State, or political subdivision thereof shall be determined in accordance with State law.

A.   Spousal Incompetency and Marital Communications

1)   SPOUSAL IMMUNITY

Question Key
44,55,130

a)   General Principles

Under the doctrine of spousal immunity or incompetency, a person may not be called to testify against a spouse in any criminal prosecution. The privilege covers testimony regarding events occurring at any time, even before the marriage. The focus of the privilege is not on the content of the testimony, but rather on prohibiting testimony against a spouse. Spousal immunity is also referred to as spousal incompetency because a witness spouse cannot testify at all (as if the spouse is incompetent to be a witness).

(1)   Who Holds the Privilege?

Under federal law, the witness, not the party spouse, holds the privilege. Therefore, under federal law, the witness may waive the privilege and testify. However, in most states, the spouse who is a party in the case, not the testifying witness, holds the privilege. Therefore, in a majority of states, even if the witness wishes to testify, she cannot unless the party spouse waives the privilege.

(a)   Criminal Proceedings

A prosecutor cannot compel a witness spouse to testify against a criminal-defendant spouse during any criminal or grand jury proceeding. In a federal criminal proceeding, only the witness spouse, not the accused spouse, may assert the right not to testify. Therefore, the witness spouse may testify against the accused over the objection of the accused.

(2)   Terminates upon Divorce

A valid marriage must exist when the witness is called to testify for spousal immunity to apply. Spousal immunity ends when a marriage ends.

(3)   Family Disputes Exempt

Spousal immunity does not apply in cases involving litigation between the spouses.

b)   Applicability of the Principles

Spousal immunity does not apply when spouses are involved in litigation regarding domestic violence against, or incest with, family members. The majority of states limit the application of spousal immunity to only the context of other types of criminal proceedings, but not to civil proceedings. A minority of states apply spousal immunity to both criminal and civil proceedings.

2)   MARITAL COMMUNICATIONS PRIVILEGE

a)   General Principle

A spouse cannot be required, and neither may be allowed without the other's consent, to divulge the confidential communications between them that occurred during their marriage. The privilege protects those communications made in reliance on the intimacy of marriage. Unlike spousal incompetency, the Marital Communications Privilege concerns itself with the *content* of the testimony.

Both of the spouses hold the privilege, which applies in both criminal and civil proceedings. Either spouse may invoke the privilege not to testify regarding confidential communications, made while married, between the spouses. Each spouse may prevent the other from testifying regarding confidential communications. Additionally, unlike spousal incompetency, this privilege can be asserted even if the parties get divorced.

b)   Minority Rule

In a minority of jurisdictions, the Marital Communications Privilege may only be invoked by the "communicating spouse." In those jurisdictions, the spouse who did not make the communication cannot invoke the privilege and could be required to disclose what the "communicating spouse" said.

c)   Exceptions

The privilege does not apply to communications that occurred before the marriage or in the presence of third parties during the marriage. The rules of the Marital Communications Privilege do not apply when the spouses are involved in litigation regarding domestic violence against, or incest with, family members.

★★   **B.   Attorney-Client Privilege and Work Product**

> Question Key
> 26,42,87,99,100,
> 140,150,183

Certain *communications* made between an attorney and a client may be privileged and not subject to discovery or admissibility.

1)   ATTORNEY-CLIENT PRIVILEGE

a)   Application of the Privilege

(1)   Unprivileged Communications

A person or an entity may communicate with an attorney as a potential or existing client of the attorney. A casual communication, not conducted for the purpose of obtaining legal advice or representation, is not privileged.

(a)   Example

A routine report that a company's non-legal employee prepared for a company executive, or according to company policy, does not become privileged merely because the company provided the report to its attorney for the purpose of litigation.

(2)   Privileged Communications

The general rule is that if a communication is made between a person or an entity and an attorney, for the purpose of obtaining or providing legal representation or advice, the communication is confidential, and therefore, legally privileged from disclosure. The privilege exists even if the potential or existing client communicated with someone that he reasonably believed to be, but who, in fact, was not an attorney. The privilege applies regardless of whether the attorney ultimately provided any advice or representation to the person.

(a)   Agency Rule

An attorney may include third-party agents in confidential communications with clients without waiving the attorney-client privilege. The content of the communications between the consultant and the client, and between the consultant and the attorney, about those communications are subject to the attorney-client privilege, so long as the consultant acted as the attorney's agent. This rule applies to other relationships between a client and a third party that may or may not otherwise be privileged, such as communications between a physician and the client as a patient.

(b)   Common Interest Privilege

Parties with a common interest may hold joint discussions with all their respective lawyers present, without waiving their privilege. In addition, if there is a falling out between the parties, each individual party still holds the privilege with respect to the privileged information. Therefore, if a party holding the privilege objects to disclosure of privileged information, another party may not disclose the privileged information. This common interest privilege, however, has limitations. It is enforceable only in cases involving the parties and a third-party. It is not applicable in cases *between* the parties with a common interest.

(c)   Asserting the Privilege

(i)   General   Rule   (Client Asserts Privilege)

A client holds the privilege of confidential communications with the client's attorney. The client may exercise that privilege by preventing anyone from disclosing to any third party, or testifying about, the confidential communication. The privilege continues even after the death of either the client or the attorney.

An attorney is obligated to assert the privilege to protect a client who cannot assert it for a valid reason such as incapacity or death.

(d)   Privilege Unavailable

The privilege does not apply to:

- physical evidence that the client provides to the attorney;
- documents preexisting the attorney-client relationship;
- attorney fee arrangements, agreements, and payments; or
- the attorney's services that are requested to assist in planning or committing a crime or a fraud.

The privilege may be lost when:

- the client waives confidentiality as to one or more issues, such as by disclosing privileged communications to a third party; or
- the client or the attorney breaches a duty that is owed to each other.

2)   WORK PRODUCT

a)   Qualified Immunity

Work product immunity may protect an attorney from disclosing to a third party some of the information the attorney creates or acquires while preparing for litigation. Fed. R. Civ. P. 26(b)(3). The *Federal Rules* provide qualified immunity, which means that work product materials may be subject to discovery if the party requesting them proves:

- a substantial need for the materials; and
- an inability to obtain a substantial equivalent of those materials by another method.

b)   Absolute Immunity

Even if a party can demonstrate the need for the materials and an inability to obtain a substantial equivalent of those materials by another method, an attorney possesses absolute immunity from disclosing work product documents when they divulge the attorney's "mental impressions, conclusions, opinions, or legal theories" regarding litigation. Fed. R. Civ. P. 26(b)(3).

For example, suppose a first attorney conducts an interview with a potential witness in an action. Two weeks after the interview, the potential witness dies. If the opposing attorney can demonstrate a need for obtaining a copy of the transcript of the interview, as well as an inability to obtain a substantial equivalent (because the witness is deceased), then the court may order the first attorney to disclose a copy of the transcript of the interview. However, the first attorney may "redact" or remove anything on the document (such as the attorney's notes) that may divulge the attorney's mental impressions, conclusion, opinions, or legal theories.

3)   DISCLOSURE OF PRIVILEGED MATERIAL

A party is generally protected against inadvertent waiver of the attorney-client privilege or the work product protection resulting from disclosure of information or a communication subject to such privilege or protection under certain circumstances. A privileged document may be inadvertently disclosed, for example, in response to a document request in a civil action.

a)   Waiver

Under FRE 502(a), if a disclosure occurs during a federal proceeding or to a federal agency or office or agency, which waives the privilege or protection, the waiver applies to an undisclosed communication or information in a state or federal proceeding only when:

- "the waiver is intentional;

- the disclosed and undisclosed communications or information concern the same subject matter; and

- they ought in fairness to be considered together."

b) Inadvertent Disclosure

Pursuant to FRE 502(b), if a disclosure occurs in a federal proceeding or to a federal agency or office, the disclosure does not operate as a waiver in a state or federal proceeding if:

- "the disclosure is inadvertent;

- the holder of the privilege or protection took reasonable steps to prevent disclosure; and

- the holder promptly took reasonable steps to rectify the error, including (if applicable) following *Federal Rule of Civil Procedure* 26(b)(5)(B), which allows a party making a claim that information produced during discovery in civil litigation is subject to a claim of privilege or protection to notify the party receiving the material of the claim and the basis for this claim. Moreover, after receiving such notice, the receiving party "must promptly return, sequester, or destroy the specified information and" any copies of it in this party's possession. Also, this information may neither be used nor disclosed until resolution of this claim occurs.

c) Disclosure in State Proceeding

According to FRE 502(c), if a disclosure occurs during a state proceeding and is not the subject of an order by a state court regarding waiver, the disclosure will not constitute a waiver in a federal proceeding when the disclosure:

- "would not be a waiver under this rule [502] if it had been made in a federal proceeding; or

- is not a waiver under the law of the state where the disclosure occurred."

d) Court Orders' Controlling Effect

FRE 502(d) provides that a federal court may issue an order providing that the privilege or protection will not be waived by any "disclosure connected with the litigation pending before the court." In this event, the disclosure will not constitute a waiver in any other state or federal proceeding.

e)   Party Agreement's Controlling Effect

Under FRE 502(e), unless an agreement among parties about the effect of disclosure during a federal proceeding is incorporated into a court order, only the parties to the agreement will be bound by it.

f)   FRE 502's Controlling Effect

Pursuant to FRE 502(f), notwithstanding certain other FRE, FRE 502 generally applies to both federal and state proceedings, even when state law provides the rule of decision.

C.   **Physician/Psychotherapist-Patient**

1)   ORIGIN AND SCOPE

| Question Key |
| 49,62 |

The common law did not provide for a privilege between a patient and a physician or a psychotherapist. However, many modern state statutes now provide for the privilege. It protects, from disclosure to third parties, all confidential communications regarding medical treatment that occur between a patient and a physician or psychotherapist. The privilege commences when a patient begins a relationship with a physician or psychotherapist in order to obtain medical treatment.

2)   ASSERTING THE PRIVILEGE

A patient holds the privilege and may assert it to prevent a physician or psychotherapist from divulging confidential information obtained in the course of providing medical treatment to the patient. The physician or psychotherapist also may assert the privilege on behalf of the patient.

3)   AVAILABILITY OF THE PRIVILEGE

a)   Waiver

The patient may waive the privilege in the following ways:

- by intentionally or unintentionally disclosing the privileged information to a third party; or
- by signing a written waiver of the privilege.

b)   Discretionary Enforcement

A trial judge possesses discretion in deciding whether to enforce a privilege if a patient is either out-of-court or not aware of a disclosure of a confidential communication with a physician or psychotherapist.

        c)   Limitations

Several states do not extend the privilege of a patient and a physician or psychotherapist to the following situations:

- criminal trials;
- malpractice actions involving the patient and a physician/psychotherapist;
- proceedings in which a patient's mental competency or physical condition is at issue; and
- when an allegedly privileged communication was made to aid the future commission of a criminal offense or civil fraud.

D.   Self-Incrimination

| Question Key |
| 7,71,89,91,122,150 |

    1)   FIFTH AMENDMENT

        a)   Testimonial Privilege

The Fifth Amendment to the *U.S. Constitution* provides that no witness may be compelled to testify in criminal proceedings when doing so would incriminate the witness. The privilege extends only to compelled "testimonial" communications. Therefore, even though an act may provide incriminating evidence, a criminal suspect may be compelled, among other things: 1) to submit to fingerprinting; 2) to submit to a DNA or blood test; or 3) to make a recording of his voice.

        b)   Application of the Privilege

Despite the express text of the Fifth Amendment applying to "criminal proceedings," the privilege against self-incrimination under the Fifth Amendment "applies alike to civil and criminal proceedings, wherever the answer might tend to subject to criminal responsibility him who gives it." *Butterfield v. State*, 992 S.W.2d 448 (Tex. Crim. App. 1999).

        (1)   Proceedings

The protection may be asserted in any proceeding, whether it is civil, criminal, administrative, judicial, or investigatory. The protection applies to civil proceedings because the nature of the protection goes to the questions asked, not the nature of the proceeding itself. For example, this provision applies to the states and:

- to criminal defendants on trial;
- to witnesses in criminal trials;

- in congressional investigations; and
- in grand jury proceedings.

(a)   Adverse Inferences

In a *civil case*, but not a criminal case, the jury may draw an adverse inference from a party's invocation of the Fifth Amendment privilege against self-incrimination. Also, the jury may draw an inference that evidence destroyed by a party was adverse to the party.

c)   Required Judicial Finding

A trial judge should allow a witness to exercise her Fifth Amendment privilege to remain silent on the stand if there is a reasonable possibility that the risk of self-incrimination exists. There is not a requirement of a showing that the witness' testimony will incriminate himself or herself.

d)   Protection Must be Asserted to Each Inquiry

The Fifth Amendment protection must be asserted in response to each specific inquiry or it may be waived. Each assertion of the privilege rests on its own circumstances. General or blanket assertions of the protection are impermissible.

e)   Assertion of Innocence does not Waive Protection

The Supreme Court has held that even if a person professes innocence, he still may assert the protection of the Fifth Amendment.

f)   The Fifth Amendment and Impeachment on Cross-Examination

The Supreme Court has held that once a criminal defendant decides to take the stand in his own defense, his ability to assert the privilege may be diminished. FRE 608(b) takes the position that a criminal defendant, like other witnesses, does not lose the protection of the privilege by testifying when examined on matters related only to character for truthfulness. However, the Supreme Court generally has held that a defendant's choice to testify acts as a waiver of the privilege with regards to questions on cross-examination that concern matters touched upon in direct examination.

2)   IMMUNITY

a)   Transactional Immunity

Transactional immunity protects a witness against any prosecution for the transactions about which he has testified. For example, if a witness testifies under a grant of transactional immunity, to having robbed a bank, he cannot be prosecuted for that robbery, even if the prosecution does not directly or indirectly make use of his testimony in the prosecution.

b)   Use and Derivative Use Immunity

Use and derivative use immunity, by contrast, is much narrower. It merely protects against the direct or indirect use of the testimony in a subsequent prosecution. Thus, if the witness testifies under a grant of use and derivative use immunity that he robbed a bank, the prosecution may not use that testimony as part of the prosecution, but it may, nonetheless, prosecute him for the robbery if it can prove its case without making any use of his testimony.

(1)   Compelled Document Production

In criminal proceedings, for example, a subpoena duces tecum may require that a witness produce documents, although they may include incriminating information, because the creation of those documents was not compelled. However, the Fifth Amendment's protections extend to the witness' production of documents that would possess testimonial significance because of the compelled testimony aspect of the witness' production and authentication of those documents. *United States v. Hubbell*, 530 U.S. 27 (2000); *Fisher v. United States*, 425 U.S. 391 (1976). In the event of such compelled document production, use and derivative use immunity may adequately protect the witness' privilege against self-incrimination. If the witness is granted use and derivative use immunity in such circumstances, the witness' privilege against self-incrimination may be overcome. *Kastigar v. United States*, 406 U.S. 441 (1972).

E.   **Other Privileges**

1)   <u>PRIVATE AND PUBLIC PRIVILEGES</u>

a)   Miscellaneous Private Privileges

The general rules of testimonial privilege apply to the relationships that exist between clergy-layperson, accountant-client, and journalist-source.

b)   Federal Governmental Privileges

The federal government possesses a privilege against the disclosure of diplomatic or military secrets. The federal executive branch possesses some absolute and qualified privileges not to disclose certain information.

c)   Law Enforcement Privilege

All government law enforcement officers have a qualified privilege not to disclose the identity of confidential informants.

F.   **Insurance Coverage**

Question Key
171

1)   <u>GENERAL RULE</u>

FRE 411 provides that evidence about whether a person carried liability insurance is inadmissible regarding whether the person engaged in negligent or wrongful conduct.

a)   Exception

Evidence regarding whether a person possesses liability insurance may be admitted for the following reasons other than establishing negligence:

- to show that a witness is biased or prejudiced; or
- to show control, agency, or ownership.

(1)   Text of FRE 411

> Evidence that a person was or was not insured against liability is not admissible upon the issue whether the person acted negligently or otherwise wrongfully. This rule does not require the exclusion of evidence of insurance against liability when offered for another purpose, such as proof of agency, ownership, or control, or bias or prejudice of a witness.

★ **G. Remedial Measures**

Question Key
67,94,101,119

    1)   <u>COMMON LAW</u>

        a)   General Rule

Under the common law, certain evidence is not admissible to establish awareness of fault or liability for negligence. One type of such evidence would indicate that a defendant took measures to remedy an allegedly harmful condition after a plaintiff suffered damages resulting from that condition. For example, evidence that a defendant installed slip-resistant flooring after a slip-and-fall accident subject to litigation is evidence of a subsequent remedial measure. The problem with such evidence is that it may lead a fact-finder to believe that a defendant acknowledged fault and, thus, should be liable to a plaintiff for the earlier damages. Courts, however, prefer that a defendant take subsequent remedial measures to minimize the prospects of harm to others.

    2)   <u>FRE 407</u>

        a)   General Rule

FRE 407 provides that evidence of subsequent remedial measures is inadmissible to prove the fault or negligence of a defendant. However, the uniform application of FRE 407 allows the admission of relevant evidence of subsequent remedial measures to:

- prove a defendant owned or controlled something that harmed a plaintiff;

- prove the feasibility of precautionary measures if a defendant controverts them; or
- to impeach the defendant.

            b)   Strict Liability Rule

Both state and federal court precedent include a split of authority regarding the admissibility of subsequent remedial measures evidence in trials of strict liability claims. In jurisdictions where such evidence is inadmissible in strict liability actions, that exclusionary rule extends to preclude any showing of a design defect, a product defect, or the absence of a warning label.

            (1)   Text of FRE 407

> When, after an injury or harm allegedly caused by an event, measures are taken that, if taken previously, would have made the injury or harm less likely to occur, evidence of the subsequent measures is not admissible to prove negligence, culpable conduct, a defect in a product, a defect in a product's design, or a need for a warning or instruction. This rule does not require the exclusion of evidence of subsequent measures when offered for another purpose, such as proving ownership, control, or feasibility of precautionary measures, if controverted, or impeachment.

★

H.   **Compromise, Payment of Medical Expenses, and Plea Negotiations**

      1)   <u>COMPROMISE</u>

Question Key
19,56,68,113,126,148,159

         a)   Compromise of Civil Matters

FRE 408 prohibits the use of evidence (1) of compromising a claim in exchange for consideration or (2) of statements or conduct occurring in compromise negotiations about certain claims, subject to exceptions. These two types of evidence may not be used when "offered to prove liability for, invalidity of, or amount of a claim that was disputed as to validity or amount, or to impeach through a prior inconsistent statement or contradiction." The rationale is to allow the parties and counsel to speak freely during settlement negotiations, without having to worry that their statements will be used against them at trial.

            (1)   Admissions of Fact Excluded

Admissions of fact made by a first party to a second party during settlement negotiations of a civil case are inadmissible.

            (2)   Offers to Compromise Excluded

Evidence of a first party's offer to compromise or settle a second party's civil claim is inadmissible with respect to the validity of that claim.

(3)   What Communications FRE 408 Applies To

FRE 408 applies only to offers made as *part of a settlement negotiation*. Settlement negotiations can only take place if there is a *claim in dispute*. While these negotiations need not be conducted in a formal setting with attorneys present, they are required to be for the purpose of reaching a compromise before litigation ensues.

(4)   Text of FRE 408

> (a) Prohibited uses. Evidence of the following is not admissible on behalf of any party, when offered to prove liability for, invalidity of, or amount of a claim that was disputed as to validity or amount, or to impeach through a prior inconsistent statement or contradiction:
>
> (1) furnishing or offering or promising to furnish or accepting or offering or promising to accept a valuable consideration in compromising or attempting to compromise the claim; and
>
> (2) conduct or statements made in compromise negotiations regarding the claim, except when offered in a criminal case and the negotiations related to a claim by a public office or agency in the exercise of regulatory, investigative, or enforcement authority.
>
> Permitted uses. This rule does not require exclusion if the evidence is offered for purposes not prohibited by subdivision (a). Examples of permissible purposes include proving a witness's bias or prejudice; negating a contention of undue delay; and proving an effort to obstruct a criminal investigation or prosecution.

2)   <u>PAYMENT OF MEDICAL EXPENSES</u>

a)   Offers to Pay Medical Expenses are Inadmissible

If a first party pays for, or offers or promises to pay for, an injured second party's medical expenses, such an offer is not admissible under FRE 409 to prove the first party's responsibility for an incident that resulted in the second party's injury.

(1)   Important Public Policy

This material evidence (the offer), having probative value, may be excluded pursuant to FRE 409 on the basis of important social policies, such as encouraging the prompt payment of medical expenses.

b)   Other Statements are Admissible

Other statements that the first party made in connection with an offer or promise to pay, or a payment for, the second party's medical expenses, may be admissible. Such statements may include, for example, the first party's admission of fault or responsibility for the second party's injury.

(1)   Text of FRE 409

> Evidence of furnishing or offering or promising to pay medical, hospital, or similar expenses occasioned by an injury is not admissible to prove liability for the injury.

3)   <u>PLEA NEGOTIATIONS</u>

a)   Evidence of Plea Negotiations is Inadmissible

Neither pleas nor any other statements a criminal defendant made during plea negotiations are admissible as evidence against the defendant at a criminal or civil proceeding. Thus, if a prosecutor rejects the defendant's offer to make a plea to a criminal offense, that offer cannot be used in the same or another proceeding as evidence of the defendant's guilt.

b)   Four Types of Evidence are Implicated

FRE 410 applies to the following four types of evidence arising from, or related to, plea negotiations between a prosecutor and a criminal defendant:

- a guilty plea that is subsequently withdrawn after a trial judge has accepted it;
- a plea of *nolo contendre*;
- a statement made about a guilty plea or a plea of *nolo contendre* during proceedings under *Fed. R. Civ. P.* 11 or similar state rules; and
- the contents of discussions between the prosecutor and the criminal defendant concerning the entry or withdrawal of a guilty plea.

c)   Text of FRE 410

> Except as otherwise provided in this rule, evidence of the following is not, in any civil or criminal proceeding, admissible against the defendant who made the plea or was a participant in the plea discussions:
>
> (1) a plea of guilty which was later withdrawn;
>
> (2) a plea of *nolo contendere*;
>
> (3) any statement made in the course of any proceedings under Rule 11 of the *Federal Rules of Criminal Procedure* or comparable state procedure regarding either of the foregoing pleas; or

> (4) any statement made in the course of plea discussions with an attorney for the prosecuting authority which do not result in a plea of guilty or which result in a plea of guilty later withdrawn. . . .

I.   Past Sexual Conduct

1)   COMMON LAW PERMITTED EVIDENCE

Under the common law, a criminal defendant could introduce evidence of an alleged rape victim's "character for chastity" to establish a consent defense. Consequently, the criminal defendant could introduce evidence of the victim's prior sexual activity in order to prove consent as a defense to an alleged rape.

2)   FRE 412 AND RAPE SHIELD LAWS

"Rape shield" statutes or cases have replaced the common law in most jurisdictions. Such provisions restrict the scope of evidence of an alleged victim's past sexual conduct.

a)   Victim's Past Sexual Conduct

Under FRE 412, a defendant may introduce evidence of an alleged victim's "pertinent trait of character." However, FRE 412 restricts the admissibility of evidence of the victim's previous sexual conduct. FRE 412(a) excludes all reputation and opinion evidence regarding a victim's past sexual conduct, as well as all testimonial evidence about that conduct.

b)   Circumstances of Admissibility

Evidence of a victim's specific acts is admissible in rape trials only to show prior sexual conduct in three situations:

- when the victim's past sexual behavior with the defendant is presented to show consent;
- when the victim's past sexual behavior with persons other than the defendant is presented to show that the defendant was not "the source of semen or injury;" or
- constitutional grounds exist that warrant its admission.

(1)   Text of FRE 412

> (a) Evidence generally inadmissible.
>
> The following evidence is not admissible in any civil or criminal proceeding involving alleged sexual misconduct except as provided in subdivisions (b) and (c):

(1) Evidence offered to prove that any alleged victim engaged in other sexual behavior.

(2) Evidence offered to prove any alleged victim's sexual predisposition.

(b) Exceptions.

(1) In a criminal case, the following evidence is admissible, if otherwise admissible under these rules:

(A) evidence of specific instances of sexual behavior by the alleged victim offered to prove that a person other than the accused was the source of semen, injury, or other physical evidence;

(B) evidence of specific instances of sexual behavior by the alleged victim with respect to the person accused of the sexual misconduct offered by the accused to prove consent or by the prosecution; and

(C) evidence the exclusion of which would violate the constitutional rights of the defendant.

3)   FREs 413-415

a)   General Description

FREs 413-415 are additional provisions that apply not only to criminal rape trials, but also to other types of civil trials and criminal proceedings regarding child molestation and other types of sexual misconduct. FREs 413-415 include the elements of 412(b)(1)(A)-(B), and additionally provide that for any reason, the prosecutor may introduce evidence of sexual behavior between a defendant and a victim.

b)   Prior Acts Evidence

FREs 413-415 allow the admission of evidence of a defendant's prior acts of child molestation or sexual misconduct for the purpose of showing the defendant's disposition to commit a charged act of sexual misconduct.

★ IV.   WRITINGS, RECORDINGS, AND PHOTOGRAPHS

★   A.   **Requirement of Original**

Question Key
10,33,104,166,168

1)   COMMON LAW

a)   Common Law Best Evidence Rule

The common law Best Evidence Rule ("Common Law Best Evidence Rule") provides that no evidence is admissible unless it is the best that the nature of the case will allow. The Common Law Best Evidence Rule requires that if a party seeks to prove the actual terms of a writing, the original writing must be produced unless the original is unavailable (due to no fault of the party seeking to introduce the evidence).

b)   Collateral Writing Rule

The collateral writing rule applies when a witness' testimony describes writings that have only a peripheral relationship to any disputed issues of a trial. In that event, the original writing does not need to be produced because it lacks direct significance.

2)   <u>FEDERAL RULES</u>

a)   Federal Best Evidence Rule

In order to prove the content of a writing, recording, or photograph, the original writing, recording, or photograph is generally required.

The *Federal Rules of Evidence* have altered the Common Law Best Evidence Rule. *Federal Rule* 1002, the federal Best Evidence Rule ("Federal Best Evidence Rule"), applies if the evidence at issue is a writing, recording, or photograph. This has been expanded from the common law rule. Moreover, the Federal Best Evidence Rule applies only if a party is seeking to prove the contents of the writing, recording, or photograph.

(1)   Legally Controlling Evidence

The Federal Best Evidence Rule applies when a writing, recording, or photo is evidence of a legally controlling nature. In other words, that evidence:

- must be essential to the disposition of legal issues in controversy; and
- its proponent must seek to establish the contents of an item being presented.

Examples of such writings include a contract deed, or a will that is subject to interpretation because its contents, effect, or applicability are at issue. The evidence also may be a subject of the testimony of a witness regarding an item that she observed (a photograph), or heard (a recording).

(2)   Text of FRE 1002

> To prove the content of a writing, recording, or photograph, the original writing, recording, or photograph is required, except as otherwise provided in these rules or by act of Congress.

b)   Admissibility of Duplicates

(1)   General Rule

Under FRE 1003, a duplicate is allowed as evidence, instead of an original, unless a party-opponent presents a genuine issue regarding authenticity or in a specific situation it would not be fair to admit the duplicate. In that event, an admissible document may be any duplicate of an original document that correctly reproduces the document.

(2)   Text of FRE 1003

> A duplicate is admissible to the same extent as an original unless (1) a genuine question is raised as to the authenticity of the original or (2) in the circumstances it would be unfair to admit the duplicate in lieu of the original.

c)   Admissibility of Other Evidence of Contents

(1)   Exceptions to FRE 1002

FRE 1004 provides four exceptions to the Federal Best Evidence Rule. The exceptions apply when a plausible reason exists for a party's failure to produce an original item of evidence. Other evidence is admissible to establish the existence and/or contents of a missing or unavailable original item under the following circumstances:

- It is either destroyed or lost and its proponent did not lose or destroy the item due to bad faith misconduct (FRE 1004(1));
- It cannot be secured through normal judicial channels of procedure or process (FRE 1004(2));
- The party against whom it would have been proffered has possession of the item and failed to produce it despite receiving adequate notice that it was needed at the hearing. Such notice may be properly given by means of correspondence, pleadings, subpoena, or otherwise (FRE 1004(3)); and
- An original item of evidence does not need to be produced in order to establish a collateral matter. In that event, a writing, recording, or photograph is not closely related to a controlling issue. (FRE 1004(4)).

(a)   Collateral Matter

The Federal Best Evidence Rule does not apply with respect to proving collateral matters. Evidence is collateral to an ultimate issue when it is of minor importance. Thus, if the writing, recording, or photo would not be presented with respect to a controlling issue, the original version of that item does not need to be presented as evidence. That item may be established by means other than producing an original document.

(b)   Independent Evidence

The Federal Best Evidence Rule does not apply, and a copy of a document may be used as evidence, if events or facts exist independently of a writing (e.g., certificates of death or birth).

(2)   Text of FRE 1004

The original is not required, and other evidence of the contents of a writing, recording, or photograph is admissible if--

(1) Originals lost or destroyed. All originals are lost or have been destroyed, unless the proponent lost or destroyed them in bad faith; or

(2) Original not obtainable. No original can be obtained by any available judicial process or procedure; or

(3) Original in possession of opponent. At a time when an original was under the control of the party against whom offered, that party was put on notice, by the pleadings or otherwise, that the contents would be a subject of proof at the hearing, and that party does not produce the original at the hearing; or

(4) Collateral matters. The writing, recording, or photograph is not closely related to a controlling issue.

d)   Admissibility of Secretly Obtained Recordings

No rule automatically prohibits the introduction of evidence obtained through deception. Certain federal and state statutes govern clandestine recordings of conversations. These statutes may require the exclusion from introduction into evidence of such recordings obtained in violation of the applicable statute.

B.   Summaries

1)   GENERAL CONSIDERATIONS

a)   Definition

A summary is a compilation or other form of summarized writings, recordings, or photographs, that purports to accurately represent, and/or compile into a manageable and reduced format, all of the source material from which it was derived. A party may seek to introduce a summary into evidence instead of all the source material from which it was generated. The party's reason for proffering a summary instead of all of the originals that it consolidates, may be the considerable volume of material that the summary represents.

b)   Analysis of Admissibility

The following factors may be used to analyze the use of a summary as evidence:

- Is the evidence too voluminous to be presented into evidence?
- Is the evidence too voluminous to be examined in court?
- Has a competent witness gained familiarity with the evidence and the summary?
- Has the witness testified that the summary accurately reflects the evidence?

(1)   Text of FRE 1006

> The contents of voluminous writings, recordings, or photographs which cannot conveniently be examined in court may be presented in the form of a chart, summary, or calculation. The originals, or duplicates, shall be made available for examination or copying, or both, by other parties at reasonable time and place. The court may order that they be produced in court.

C.   Completeness Rule

1)   FRE 106

a)   General Rule

If a proponent proffers an incomplete writing or recorded statement as evidence, then a party-opponent is entitled to have the remainder of the writing or statement contemporaneously entered into evidence if fairness warrants the simultaneous consideration of that remainder by a trier of fact.

b)   Application of the Rule

In applying the rule of completeness, FRE 106, a trial judge may exercise discretion in deciding to introduce a part or all of a recorded statement or document into evidence with respect to two considerations.

- Would a misleading impression result from the taking of part of a document out of context (i.e., without the remainder of that document being introduced into evidence)?
- Would delaying until later in a trial impact a party-opponent's right to introduce any other part of a document or reduce the adequacy of the party-opponent's response?

(1)   Text of FRE 106

> When a writing or recorded statement or part thereof is introduced by a party, an adverse party may require the introduction at that time of any other part or any other writing or recorded statement which ought in fairness to be considered contemporaneously with it.

V.   HEARSAY AND CIRCUMSTANCES OF ITS ADMISSIBILITY

★★★★

A.   Definition of Hearsay

Question Key
4,28,36,43,75,104,105,
125,144,149,154,155,
157,161,162,163,180

★★★★   1)   WHAT IS HEARSAY

The basic hearsay rule does not allow the introduction into evidence of:

- an out-of-court statement (i.e., assertive act) that is;
- offered to prove the truth of a matter asserted in the statement.

FRE 802 states in part that: "Hearsay is not admissible except as provided by these rules or by other rules…"

The objective of the hearsay rule excluding such testimony is to preclude testimony from being presented without a party-opponent having an opportunity to cross-examine the witness.

a)   Definitions

★★★★

(1)   Hearsay

"Hearsay is a statement, other than one made by the declarant while testifying at the trial or hearing, offered in evidence to prove the truth of the matter asserted." FRE 801.

(2)   Witness

A witness is a person testifying in a proceeding whose testimony is subject to objection based on the hearsay rule. The hearsay rule may apply and require the exclusion of testimony by a witness about an out-of-court statement.

(3)   Declarant

A declarant is a person who makes an out-of-court statement. The declarant may either be a testifying witness or a third party who made the statement.

b)   What is Not Hearsay

The hearsay rule does not preclude the admission of evidence in four situations.

- when a statement does not assert a fact;
- when a statement is of a type that FRE 801(d) defines as not hearsay (discussed in this section).
- when a statement qualifies as an exception to the hearsay rule under FRE 803-804 (discussed later); or
- when a statement is not being offered to prove its truth under (a)-(b).

★★   (1)   Statement not Offered to Prove its Truth

A statement is hearsay only if it is offered to prove the truth of the matter asserted in the statement. For example, suppose that Al and Barb are married. They argue often. One day, their friend Carla hears Barb say, "Al, you are the scum of the earth." A few months later, at Al and Barb's divorce trial, Al seeks to have Carla testify as to the statement. Can she do so or is evidence of the statement hearsay? In this case, Carla can testify because the statement is probably being introduced to demonstrate that Barb was mean and cruel to Al, not that Al actually is the scum of the earth. This is a tough line to draw in some examples, but it is important to isolate the statement that was made out-of-court. Is the statement being proffered to prove its truth or for some other reason? If it is not being offered for its truth, it is not hearsay. If it is being offered for its truth, determine whether a hearsay exception applies.

                    (2)   "Verbal Acts"

"Verbal acts," as opposed to general verbal statements, are not hearsay because they state operable facts and are not offered to prove the truth of an asserted matter. These facts possess independent legal significance and are not inadmissible under the hearsay rule. These facts are of legal consequence.

                    (a)   Defamation

Examples of verbal acts include defamatory words in a libel or slander lawsuit. They are admissible evidence to prove that a defamatory statement (i.e., verbal act) was made because of the statement's independent legal significance and because its truthfulness is not at issue.

                    (b)   Contract Formation

Words of offer or acceptance in oral contract litigation are verbal acts because they are explanatory words that relate to and give character to a transaction. As such, they may operate with "independent legal effect" upon another person and should be admitted as not hearsay. They are admissible evidence to prove that the statement was made because its significance and its truthfulness are not at issue.

★★   (3)   Effect on Reader or Hearer

A declarant's out-of-court statement is admissible to prove its effect upon a reader or hearer instead of the statement's truth or falsity.

                    (a)   Emotion

A declarant's out-of-court statement is admissible to prove that it caused an emotional response in a reader or a hearer, rather than to prove the statement's truth or falsity. For example, suppose David is on trial for assaulting his neighbor Tim. The defense alleges that David acted emotionally. Tim picked on David for several years until one day, David snapped. David put on a disguise and attacked Tim. Among other evidence, the defense may introduce testimony by another neighbor, Mark, that he heard Tim say to

David, "David, you are a puny weakling with no spine. You don't have the guts to stand up to me." The statement may be introduced to prove that David had endured emotional trauma caused by Tim. The statement is not hearsay because it is not being offered to prove its truth – that David is a puny weakling with no spine. It is being offered to show the statement may have had an effect on David's emotions.

(b)   Notice

A declarant's out-of-court statement is admissible to prove that it provided notice of some information (e.g., fact or event) to a reader or a hearer. In that event, the statement is not being presented to establish the statement's truth or falsity. For example, suppose Javier is at a nightclub with some friends. John, Javier's brother, tells Javier, "Samuel has a gun and said he would use it before the night is over." The conversation was overheard by Michael. Later that night, Javier and Samuel argue over a law school exam fact pattern. Things get heated between the two. When Javier sees Samuel reach into his pocket, he believes Samuel is reaching for the gun. In response, Javier, a quick draw champion, draws his own gun and shoots Samuel first. In Javier's trial for murder, Javier wishes to call Michael to testify as to the statement made by John, who has fled the country on an unrelated matter. Michael's testimony about the statement made by John is not hearsay. The statement is not being offered to prove that Samuel actually had a gun and intended to use it. Instead, it is being introduced to demonstrate that Javier had notice that Samuel had a gun and intended to use it.

(4)   Action by Non-Human

The action of an animal is not hearsay. For example, the response of a drug dog to a suitcase is not hearsay.

★★★   2)   PRIOR STATEMENTS BY WITNESS

Question Key
23,66,75,96,
134,153,180

FRE 801(d)(1) allows the admission of three types of prior statements by a witness.

★★   a)   Prior Inconsistent Statements

FRE 801(d)(1)(A) permits the cross-examination of a witness as to a prior inconsistent statement. Although the witness may be questioned, an important distinction to understand, that has been tested on the exam, is whether the prior inconsistent statement can be used as substantive evidence or only for impeachment purposes.

If the previous statement is inconsistent with the present testimony, and was not made under oath subject to the penalty of perjury, it may be used in the subsequent trial only to impeach the witness or attack the credibility of the witness (not as substantive evidence in the case).

If the previous statement was made under oath in a hearing, trial, or deposition and the witness was subject to cross-examination, the statement is admissible as substantive evidence of the truth of the matter that it asserted.

b)   Prior Consistent Statements

FRE 801(d)(1)(B) applies to a witness' prior consistent statement offered to rebut an allegation of "recent fabrication or improper influence or motive" if that statement was made before the motive to fabricate existed.

FRE 801(d)(1)(B) provides that if a witness' previous statement is consistent with testimony at a trial, it is not hearsay if it is proffered to rebut a party-opponent's allegations that the witness' trial testimony constituted a recent fabrication or demonstrated an improper influence or motive.

FRE 801(d)(1)(B) requires that the witness must testify at trial subject to cross-examination regarding the statement. If that requirement is fulfilled, then the statement may be used as substantive evidence. The previous consistent statement is not required to have been made when the witness was under oath.

★   c)   Prior Identification of a Witness

FRE 801(d)(1)(C) provides that a witness' prior identification of a person that occurred out-of-court is admissible to prove its truth when the witness is presently testifying. It is not hearsay evidence. It constitutes substantive evidence. However, a witness who made a declaration of identification must personally testify in court.

FRE 801(d)(1)(C) provides that if a witness made an earlier out-of-court identification of an individual after seeing that person, the statement about the earlier identification is not hearsay. That is true even if the statement is offered to prove the truth of a matter asserted – an identification. That earlier identification statement is admissible as substantive evidence. The witness has to testify at a trial and be cross-examined.

                          d)   Non-hearsay Evidence

A prior statement by a witness that is admitted as evidence is admissible as non-hearsay evidence. In other words, it does not qualify as hearsay at all. As non-hearsay, prior witness statements are not considered an exception to the hearsay rule. This is important to note because the answer choices of MBE questions may focus on the distinction between non-hearsay and a hearsay exception.

                          e)   Text of FRE 801

The following definitions apply under this article:

(d) Statements which are not hearsay.

A statement is not hearsay if—

(1) *Prior statement by witness*. The declarant testifies at the trial or hearing and is subject to cross-examination concerning the statement,

> and the statement is (A) inconsistent with the declarant's testimony, and was given under oath subject to the penalty of perjury at a trial, hearing, or other proceeding, or in a deposition, or (B) consistent with the declarant's testimony and is offered to rebut an express or implied charge against the declarant of recent fabrication or improper influence or motive, or (C) one of identification of a person made after perceiving the person.

 3) STATEMENTS ATTRIBUTABLE TO A PARTY OPPONENT

Question Key
8,56,68,73,86,89,96,97,102,103,107,113,138,179

a) Admission of a Party Opponent

A party-opponent is an adverse party in a lawsuit. The *Federal Rules of Evidence* provide that a party-opponent's out-of-court statement may be admitted in the lawsuit if the statement is offered by another party against the party-opponent; and the party-opponent's position is inconsistent with the out-of-court statement. For example, suppose Michael sues Dwight over a car accident alleging that Dwight was negligent. A police officer on the scene asked Dwight how fast he was going and Dwight responded, "55 miles per hour," which is 10 miles per hour over the speed limit. At trial, Dwight alleges that he was going 45 miles per hour. Michael may introduce testimony by the officer as an admission of a party opponent because the two requirements are met: 1) the evidence is offered against a party opponent (Dwight); and 2) the party opponent's position is now inconsistent with the prior statement (Dwight now alleges he was going 45 instead of 55).

 b) Who Made the Statement

The party opponent himself need not be the one to make the statement. It will additionally be attributed to the party opponent in several different circumstances including:

- the party opponent has expressed an adoption or belief in the statement's truth; or
- the party-opponent authorized a person who made the statement; or
- the out-of-court statement was made by the party-opponent's co-conspirator (in a crime). If a statement was made in the course of, and in furtherance of, a conspiracy, then it is admissible as if the party-opponent had made that statement; or
- the out-of-court statement was made by the party-opponent's agent.

If an employee of a party opponent made the statement within the existence and scope of an employment relationship, then the statement is admissible as if the party-opponent had made that statement.

★★   c)   Adoptive Admission (Silent Admission)

A party's failure to respond to a statement or an act (in the nature of a provocative accusation or event) may constitute an admission if:

- the party-opponent, against whom such evidence is proffered, heard, comprehended, and had the ability to respond to the statement; and
- a reasonable person in a party-opponent's position would have responded by refuting that statement or act.

However, an adoptive admission will not result if the party possesses a constitutional right to remain silent. For example, suppose David is arrested for a crime and is read his *Miranda* warnings. One of these warnings provides that David has the right to remain silent. Can David's subsequent silence be seen as an adoptive admission, even if a reasonable person would have responded by refuting a harmful statement? The answer is no, because David possessed a right to remain silent under the circumstances, and his silence cannot be used against him as an adoptive admission.

              d)   Text of FRE 801

The following definitions apply under this article:

(d) Statements which are not hearsay.

A statement is not hearsay if . . .

(2) Admission by party-opponent. The statement is offered against a party and is

(A) the party's own statement, in either an individual or a representative capacity or

(B) a statement of which the party has manifested an adoption or belief in its truth, or

(C) a statement by a person authorized by the party to make a statement concerning the subject, or

(D) a statement by the party's agent or servant concerning a matter within the scope of the agency or employment, made during the existence of the relationship, or

(E) a statement by a coconspirator of a party during the course and in furtherance of the conspiracy.

> The contents of the statement shall be considered but are not alone sufficient to establish the declarant's authority under subdivision (C), the agency or employment relationship and scope thereof under subdivision (D), or the existence of the conspiracy and the participation therein of the declarant and the party against whom the statement is offered under subdivision (E).

★★★   4)   <u>MULTIPLE HEARSAY</u>

Question Key
20,43,60,155

a)   Definition

If an out-of-court statement that a party proffers as evidence includes an additional out-of-court statement, and both of the statements are admitted to prove their truth, a trial judge must separately analyze both levels of potential hearsay to determine their admissibility under the hearsay rule.

For example, suppose David seeks to proffer as evidence, a transcript of an interview with Wanda, in which Wanda recounts hearing Paul say that he arrived at the house at 8:30 pm (a material issue). The introduction of this transcript presents a multiple hearsay problem. The transcript is hearsay, as is Wanda's recounting of Paul's conversation. Therefore, David must overcome hearsay objections as to each level of the hearsay.

b)   Application

If either of the statements constitutes hearsay and does not qualify under a hearsay rule exception, that combination of statements is inadmissible. A double hearsay situation also arises if one party offers into evidence a written report or record of another party's oral out-of-court declaration.

(1)   Text of FRE 805

> Hearsay included within hearsay is not excluded under the hearsay rule if each part of the combined statements conforms with an exception to the hearsay rule provided in these rules.

5)   <u>GENERAL   EXCEPTIONS   (AVAILABILITY IMMATERIAL)</u>

FRE 803 describes those exceptions to the hearsay rule that apply when the availability of a declarant is immaterial at a criminal or civil proceeding. One of the main purposes of preventing the admission of hearsay is to avoid the situation when a declarant fabricates testimony, and cannot be cross examined by the party against whom the evidence is proffered. In the following cases, some factor reduces the risk of fabrication and therefore, makes the declarant's testimony more reliable under the eyes of the law. Out-of-court statements that qualify as hearsay exceptions are admissible to prove the truth of the matter asserted in the statement.

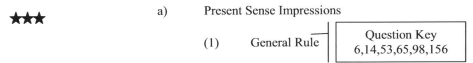

★★★

a)   Present Sense Impressions

(1)   General Rule

Question Key
6,14,53,65,98,156

FRE 803(1) provides that a declarant's sudden and extemporaneous statement that describes an event and is made when the event occurs, or soon afterward, is admissible. The applicability of this exception decreases in proportion to the length of the time lapse between the event and the statement. If the statement is sudden and contemporaneous, the likelihood of fabrication is diminished and, therefore, public policy permits the admission of the evidence.

For example, suppose Wendy, the passenger on a bus, hears the bus driver say, "We are going really fast!" Moments later, the bus collides with a truck. In the ensuing litigation, Wendy may testify regarding the bus driver's statement because it was an extemporaneous statement describing an event when it occurred.

(2)   Text of FRE 803(1)

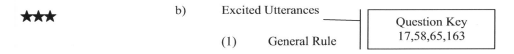

Present sense impression. A statement describing or explaining an event or condition made while the declarant was perceiving the event or condition, or immediately thereafter.

★★★

b)   Excited Utterances

(1)   General Rule

Question Key
17,58,65,163

A declarant's spontaneous and unprompted statement, which is made under the stress of an exciting or startling event and relates to that event, is admissible. Usually on the MBE, excited utterances are followed by exclamation points. One example may include the statement "Look out, that car blew the red light!"

(2)   Application of Rule

The rule applies to a declarant's statement that is made:

- in reaction to an unexpected event or condition; and
- relates to the unexpected event or condition; and
- when the declarant experienced stress that the event or condition caused.

The statement need not explain, describe, or be limited to the witness' observations of that event. The witness' excitement is a sufficient assurance of reliability.

(3)   Text of FRE 803(2)

> Excited utterance. A statement relating to a startling event or condition made while the declarant was under the stress of excitement caused by the event or condition.

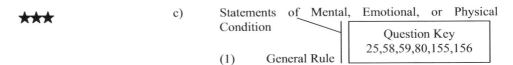

c)   Statements of Mental, Emotional, or Physical Condition

| Question Key |
| 25,58,59,80,155,156 |

(1)   General Rule

A declarant's spontaneous and impromptu statement regarding a then existing (present but not past) mental, emotional, or physical condition is admissible. That statement may be made to anyone or to a provider of health care. Under the *Hillmon* doctrine, a fact-finder, either the trial judge or the jury, may consider the statement to determine a declarant's or other person's state of mind in either civil or criminal cases. If this determination depends upon circumstantial evidence, statements regarding state of mind that were heard or otherwise understood are relevant.

(a)   Mental State at Issue in Case

A declarant's words that express the declarant's state of mind are admissible. A declarant's statement of a current state of mind or intent to do something in the near future is admissible. An example of such words is a declarant's announcement of feeling fearful when it is presented in support of the affirmative defense of self-defense.

(b)   Mental State as Proof of Subsequent Act

A declarant's statement about his state of mind is admissible to prove the declarant's conduct subsequently complied with the preexisting state of mind.

(c)   State of Mind as Non-hearsay

If a question exists as to whether a witness actually heard a declarant's statement regarding state of mind, the statement will be admissible as circumstantial evidence that is not hearsay because that out-of-court statement's truth or falsity is immaterial. In other words, an out-of-court statement regarding a declarant's state of mind that is not being offered to prove the declarant's state of mind, is not hearsay, but is circumstantial evidence.

(2)   Text of FRE 803(3)

> Then existing mental, emotional, or physical condition. A statement of the declarant's then existing state of mind, emotion, sensation, or physical condition (such as intent, plan, motive, design, mental feeling, pain, and bodily health), but not including a statement of memory or belief to prove the fact remembered or believed unless it relates to the execution, revocation, identification, or terms of declarant's will.

d)   Statements for Medical Diagnosis and Treatment

(1)   General Rule   Question Key
                             21,85,136,149

A declarant's statement of a past or present mental, emotional, or physical condition (e.g.. medical history) is admissible only if it was made for the purpose of treatment or diagnosis by a physician. The statement can concern medical symptoms "or the inception or general character of the cause" of them.

To fall under this rule, statements must be "reasonably pertinent to diagnosis or treatment", such as those regarding the medical condition subject to diagnosis or treatment. Usually, a patient's statement that identifies someone as being at fault for the patient's medical condition will be inadmissible under this rule because that other person's identity will not be relevant to treatment of the patient.

Under this rule, the declarant is usually a patient, and the person who heard the statement and testified about it would be the witness. That witness normally is a physician or another person involved with diagnosing or treating the patient. Such witnesses include, but are not limited to, nurses, paramedics, and other health care workers.

(a)   Statements to Expert Witnesses

Statements made to any physician in order to facilitate his expert testimony fall under the hearsay exception because the expert testimony will concern a diagnosis or treatment.

(b)   Statements Regarding Fault

Statements made regarding the cause of, or who is at fault for, an injury may be admitted only "insofar as reasonably pertinent to diagnosis or treatment." Such statements are also inadmissible under the business record exception of FRE 803(6) for two reasons. First, despite a physician's administrative duty to record the cause of an injury, a physician normally obtains that information from a patient, who lacks that duty. Further, a patient's statements regarding fault for an injury usually are considered to be beyond a reporter's duty to record. Therefore, a witness health care provider's notes indicating that "patient indicates that back hurts because a speeding vehicle driven by Dan hit him after running a red light," would not be completely admitted. However, the notes may be admitted partially to include "patient indicates that back hurts," while the remainder would be redacted.

(2)   Text of FRE 803(4)

Statements for purposes of medical diagnosis or treatment. Statements made for purposes of medical diagnosis or treatment and describing medical history, or past or present symptoms, pain, or sensations, or the inception or general character of the cause or external source thereof insofar as reasonably pertinent to diagnosis or treatment.

e)   Past Recollection Recorded

(1)   General Rule

A recorded past recollection (such as a written statement made by the witness several years earlier) may be admitted into evidence as an exception to the hearsay rule when the following two requirements are satisfied:

- the witness states that the witness does not recollect the recorded information (i.e., a document or an audio and/or video recording); and
- presentation of the document does not refresh the witness' recollection.

In that event, the document may be read into evidence when these four conditions exist:

- a witness possessed personal, firsthand knowledge at the time of the document's creation before the witness testifies;
- the document records the witness' knowledge at that time;
- the witness made a timely statement when the writing was created; and
- the witness testifies to the writing's reliability.

For example, suppose a case goes to trial two years after it is filed. In the intervening time, the memories of witnesses fade. Wally, a key witness for the prosecution, submits a signed affidavit in which he describes the perpetrator of a crime (e.g., hair color, height, weight, etc). When called to testify at trial, Wally has forgotten the specifics. Even when he is given a copy of his affidavit, Wally still does not remember the specifics. The prosecutor may, under these circumstances, attempt to introduce the affidavit as a past recollection recorded that Wally can read into evidence. The affidavit cannot be received as an exhibit, however, unless the defense counsel offers it as an exhibit.

(2)   Text of FRE 803(5)

> Recorded recollection. A memorandum or record concerning a matter about which a witness once had knowledge but now has insufficient recollection to enable the witness to testify fully and accurately, shown to have been made or adopted by the witness when the matter was fresh in the witness' memory and to reflect that knowledge correctly. If admitted, the memorandum or record may be read into evidence but may not itself be received as an exhibit unless offered by an adverse party.

f)   Records of Regularly Conducted Activity

(1)   General Rule

| Question Key |
| 12,60,87,109,149,178,181 |

Certain records of regularly conducted business activities are admissible as an exception to the hearsay rule when the business records were

- made contemporaneously or around the time when;
- an act, condition, or event that the records concern occurred;
- made by a person possessing personal knowledge of that occurrence;
- made in the normal course of regularly conducted business activity; and
- maintained in the normal course of regularly conducted business activity.

(a)   Supporting Testimony

The above factors must be established by testimony of a witness who either:

- was the person who possesses personal knowledge of the occurrence; or
- is the custodian of the business's records; or
- someone else possessing knowledge of the business record keeping method.

The person with personal knowledge about an occurrence and who records it does not have to be the one who enters it into the business record. That person and others who create the record proffered as evidence must be acting under a business duty. The person with personal knowledge about the occurrence does not need to testify at trial.

(b)   Definition of Business

For the purposes of the rule, a business means all commercial professions, associations, businesses, and callings of any type. The status of such entities, whether for profit or not, is irrelevant. This record can be of and concerning any events, acts, conditions, or diagnoses.

(2)   Lack of Trustworthiness

The business record will not be admitted as an exception to the hearsay rule if the source of information or the method or circumstances of preparation indicate lack of trustworthiness. For example, suppose Amy slips and falls on a water puddle at the local MegaMart. Tony, who works at MegaMart, and who had left the puddle while mopping it to take a phone call, files an accident report immediately after the incident. In the report, Tony asserts that Amy was negligent and caused the accident by not carefully watching where she was walking. Such a report suggests a lack of trustworthiness and likely will not be admitted as a business record.

(3)   Accident Reports-Records Made in Preparation of Litigation

Accident reports and records made in preparation of litigation often fall outside the scope of this hearsay exception. The Supreme Court stated, in *Palmer v. Hoffman*, 318 U.S. 109 (1943), that accident reports, though made in order to collect information on which management may act, do not constitute a regularly kept business record because they are not made systematically or as a routine business matter, such as payroll or accounts receivable. Other courts have read this holding not as creating a blanket rule, but as giving discretionary power to trial courts to decide whether such records are admissible. This decision is based on a determination of whether the record possesses the requisite trustworthiness needed to fit with this hearsay exception. Similarly, most courts have reached the conclusion that records made in preparation of litigation are not admissible under this exception because they too often lack trustworthiness.

(4)   Text of FRE 803(6)

> Records of regularly conducted activity. A memorandum, report, record, or data compilation, in any form, of acts, events, conditions, opinions, or diagnoses, made at or near the time by, or from information transmitted by, a person with knowledge, if kept in the course of a regularly conducted business activity, and if it was the regular practice of that business activity to make the memorandum, report, record or data compilation, all as shown by the testimony of the custodian or other qualified witness, or by certification that complies with Rule 902(11), Rule 902(12), or a statute permitting certification, unless the source of information or the method or circumstances of preparation indicate lack of trustworthiness. The term "business" as used in this paragraph includes business, institution, association, profession, occupation, and calling of every kind, whether or not conducted for profit.

g)   Absence of Business Records

(1)   General Rule

The lack of a business record when it would regularly be kept is admissible to prove the non-occurrence of an event or the non-existence of a fact if that event was of a type that the record usually would have been made due to its existence or occurrence. For example, in response to a loitering problem, suppose that the standard procedure at MegaMart is for an employee to file a Bathroom Inspection Report each evening, detailing that the bathroom was checked for loiterers. A Bathroom Inspection Report exists for every day of the year except the day at issue in litigation, when Mary was assaulted by someone in the bathroom. The absence of the report may be admitted to prove that the inspection did not occur on that day.

(2)   Text of FRE 803(7)

> Absence of entry in records kept in accordance with the provisions of paragraph (6). Evidence that a matter is not included in the memoranda reports, records, or data compilations, in any form, kept in accordance with the provisions of paragraph (6), to prove the nonoccurrence or nonexistence of the matter, if the matter was of a kind of which a memorandum, report, record, or data compilation was regularly made and preserved, unless the sources of information or other circumstances indicate lack of trustworthiness.

h)   Public Records and Reports

(1)   General Rule ┐ ┌─────────────┐
                         │ Question Key │
                         │   90   │
                         └─────────────┘

If public records, reports, statements, or data compilations in any form are created by public agencies and officials within the scope of their duties, then they are admissible as exceptions to the hearsay rule. Police reports, however, are inadmissible hearsay evidence against a criminal defendant. In addition, the great majority of courts exclude evidence of a prior civil judgment against a party in subsequent civil litigation. However, this rule stems not from the admissibility of the evidence under the public records and reports hearsay exception, but because the danger of undue prejudice substantially outweighs the probative value of the evidence.

(2)   Text of FRE 803(8)

> Public records and reports. Records, reports, statements, or data compilations, in any form, of public offices or agencies, setting forth (A) the activities of the office or agency, or (B) matters observed pursuant to duty imposed by law as to which matters there was a duty to report, excluding, however, in criminal cases matters observed by police officers and other law enforcement personnel, or (C) in civil actions and proceedings and against the Government in criminal cases, factual findings resulting from an investigation made pursuant to authority granted by law, unless the sources of information or other circumstances indicate lack of trustworthiness.

i)   Vital Statistics Records

FRE 803(9) makes admissible: "Records or data compilations, in any form, of births, deaths, fetal deaths, or marriages, if the report was made to a public office pursuant to requirements of law."

j)   Religious Organization Records

FRE 803(11) provides for the admissibility of: "Statements of births, marriages, divorces, deaths, legitimacy, ancestry, relationship by blood or marriage, or other similar facts of personal or family history, contained in a regularly kept record of a religious organization."

k)   Marriage, Baptism, and Similar Certificates

FRE 803(12) allows the admission into evidence of: "Marriage, baptismal, and similar certificates. Statements of fact contained in a certificate that the maker performed a marriage or other ceremony or administered a sacrament, made by a clergyman, public official, or other person authorized by the rules or practices of a religious organization or by law to perform the act certified, and purporting to have been issued at the time of the act or within a reasonable time thereafter."

★   l)   Family Records

FRE 803(13) provides for the admissibility of: "Statements of fact concerning personal or family history contained in family Bibles, genealogies, charts, engravings on rings, inscriptions on family portraits, engravings on urns, crypts, or tombstones, or the like."

m)   Records of Property Documents

FRE 803(14) allows the admission into evidence of: "Records of documents affecting an interest in property. The record of a document purporting to establish or affect an interest in property, as proof of the content of the original recorded document and its execution and delivery by each person by whom it purports to have been executed, if the record is a record of a public office and an applicable statute authorizes the recording of documents of that kind in that office."

n)   Statements in Property Documents

Question Key
45

FRE 803(15) provides for the admissibility of: "Statements in documents affecting an interest in property. A statement contained in a document purporting to establish or affect an interest in property if the matter stated was relevant to the purpose of the document, unless dealings with the property since the document was made have been inconsistent with the truth of the statement or the purport of the document."

★   o)   Ancient Documents

Question Key
90

FRE 803(16) allows the admission into evidence of: "Statements in a document in existence twenty years or more the authenticity of which is established."

p)   Market Reports and Commercial Publications

FRE 803(17) provides for the admissibility of: "Market reports, commercial publications. Market quotations, tabulations, lists, directories, or other published compilations, generally used and relied upon by the public or by persons in particular occupations."

★   q)   Learned Treatises

Question Key
41

The *Federal Rules* allow the admission into evidence of scholarly or learned materials to the extent called to the attention of an expert witness upon cross-examination, or relied upon by the expert witness in direct examination. Qualifying statements include statements contained in published treatises, periodicals, or pamphlets on a subject of history, medicine, or other science or art, established as a reliable authority by the testimony or admission of the witness or by other expert testimony or by judicial notice. If deemed reliable, the statements may be read into evidence but may not be received as exhibits. The evidence will be considered as both substantive evidence (i.e., for proof of its content in the action) and for impeachment purposes.

r)   Reputation Concerning Personal or Family History

"Reputation among members of a person's family by blood, adoption, or marriage, or among a person's associates, or in the community, concerning a person's birth, adoption, marriage, divorce, death, legitimacy, relationship by blood, adoption, or marriage, ancestry, or other similar fact of personal or family history," qualifies as exceptions to the hearsay rule. FRE 803(19).

        s)   Reputation Concerning Boundaries or General History

FRE 803(20) allows the admission into evidence of: "Reputation in a community, arising before the controversy, as to boundaries of or customs affecting lands in the community, and reputation as to events of general history important to the community or State or nation in which located."

        t)   Judgment of Prior Conviction

        (1)   General Rule

FRE 803(22) provides that a criminal defendant's prior felony conviction is admissible as substantive evidence of the facts that were necessary to support that conviction if that conviction resulted from a trial or a guilty plea, rather than a plea of *nolo contendere*. The judgment of prior conviction may be admitted into the record in a civil or criminal proceeding.

A prior felony conviction of anyone other than the criminal defendant may be used for impeachment purposes or to show the effect of collateral estoppel or *res judicata*. Unless used for those purposes, such a prior felony conviction is hearsay that is not subject to any exception. Unlike a felony conviction, a misdemeanor conviction is inadmissible hearsay.

        (2)   Text of FRE 803(22)

> Judgment of previous conviction. Evidence of a final judgment, entered after a trial or upon a plea of guilty (but not upon a plea of *nolo contendere*), adjudging a person guilty of a crime punishable by death or imprisonment in excess of one year, to prove any fact essential to sustain the judgment, but not including, when offered by the Government in a criminal prosecution for purposes other than impeachment, judgments against persons other than the accused. The pendency of an appeal may be shown but does not affect admissibility.

        6)   <u>EXCEPTIONS REQUIRING UNAVAILABILITY OF DECLARANT</u>

        a)   General Rule

FRE 804 describes those exceptions to the hearsay rule that do not apply unless a declarant is unavailable as a witness at a criminal or civil proceeding.

(1)   Unavailability

Unavailability occurs when a declarant who, through no malfeasance of the evidence's proponent, cannot testify due to privilege, a refusal to testify, a loss of memory, death or illness, or a reasonable absence.

★★   (a)   Former Testimony

| Question Key |
| 44,85,120,154 |

If a presently unavailable declarant testified under oath in a former trial, hearing, proceeding, or deposition, that testimony is admissible in a subsequent proceeding when:

- the prior testimony was given under oath;
- it concerns the same topic as does the present trial, hearing, proceeding, or deposition; and
- one of the following two parties had an opportunity and similar motive to develop the former testimony by direct, redirect, or cross-examination:

    ○ the party-opponent against whom the evidence is presented or,
    ○ in a civil action, the party-opponent's predecessor in interest.

Note that in the past, the examiners have inquired into whether a statement made in an affidavit can qualify as former testimony. It cannot because, although it may have been made under oath, the opponent could not have had an opportunity to develop the testimony.

★

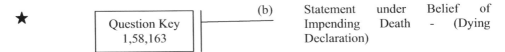

| Question Key |
| 1,58,163 |

(b)   Statement under Belief of Impending Death - (Dying Declaration)

A presently unavailable declarant's statement is admissible if it was made:

- under a certain expectation of impending death (regardless of whether death resulted); and
- regarding the circumstances or cause of that expectation.

Dying declarations are admissible in all civil proceedings, but are admissible only in criminal prosecutions for homicide. In other words, FRE 804(b)(2) applies to civil and criminal homicide proceedings at which a declarant is unavailable, and in which evidence is introduced of a declarant's statement about the cause or circumstances of what the declarant expects to be an imminent death.

The dying declaration must concern the circumstances or cause of the death. For example, suppose Gary is shot. Believing he is about to die, he tells Isabel, the paramedic on the scene, "Billy shot me." Gary's statement would be admissible as a dying declaration. On the other hand, if Gary said, "I give my house to my friend Bob," the statement would not be admissible because it does not concern the circumstances of the potential death. Additionally, remember that the person must actually believe he is going to die.

> Question Key
> 23,45,58,97,114

(c)   Statements against Interest

A presently unavailable declarant's statement is admissible if it was:

- made contrary to a declarant's pecuniary, penal, or proprietary interests;
- at the time when made by the declarant.

Unlike for admissions of a party opponent, the declarant does not have to be a party in the case.

Additionally, if a criminal defendant proffers a declarant's statement against interest, such as a third person's confession of a crime, as an exculpatory defense, then corroborating evidence is required for it to be admissible.

(2)   Text of FRE 804

(a) Definition of unavailability.

"Unavailability as a witness" includes situations in which the declarant--

(1) is exempted by ruling of the court on the ground of privilege from testifying concerning the subject matter of the declarant's statement; or

(2) persists in refusing to testify concerning the subject matter of the declarant's statement despite an order of the court to do so; or

(3) testifies to a lack of memory of the subject matter of the declarant's statement; or

(4) is unable to be present or to testify at the hearing because of death or then existing physical or mental illness or infirmity; or

(5) is absent from the hearing and the proponent of a statement has been unable to procure the declarant's attendance (or in the case of a hearsay exception under subdivision (b)(2), (3), or (4), the declarant's attendance or testimony) by process or other reasonable means.

A declarant is not unavailable as a witness if exemption, refusal, claim of lack of memory, inability, or absence is due to the procurement or wrongdoing of the proponent of a statement for the purpose of preventing the witness from attending or testifying.

(b) Hearsay exceptions.

The following are not excluded by the hearsay rule if the declarant is unavailable as a witness:

(1) former testimony. Testimony given as a witness at another hearing of the same or a different proceeding, or in a deposition taken in compliance with law in the course of the same or another proceeding, if the party against whom the testimony is now offered, or, in a civil action or proceeding, a predecessor in interest, had an opportunity and similar motive to develop the testimony by direct, cross, or redirect examination.

(2) statement under belief of impending death. In a prosecution for homicide or in a civil action or proceeding, a statement made by a declarant while believing that the declarant's death was imminent, concerning the cause or circumstances of what the declarant believed to be impending death.

(3) statement against interest. A statement which was at the time of its making so far contrary to the declarant's pecuniary or proprietary interest, or so far tended to subject the declarant to civil or criminal liability, or to render invalid a claim by the declarant against another, that a reasonable person in the declarant's position would not have made the statement unless believing it to be true. A statement tending to expose the declarant to criminal liability and offered to exculpate the accused is not admissible unless corroborating circumstances clearly indicate the trustworthiness of the statement.

(4) statement of personal or family history. (A) A statement concerning the declarant's own birth, adoption, marriage, divorce, legitimacy, relationship by blood, adoption, or marriage, ancestry, or other similar fact of personal or family history, even though declarant had no means of acquiring personal knowledge of the matter stated; or (B) A statement concerning the foregoing matters, and death also, of another person, if the declarant was related to the other by blood, adoption, or marriage or was so intimately associated with the other's family as to be likely to have accurate information concerning the matter declared.

(5) [other exceptions.][Transferred to Rule 807]

(6) forfeiture by wrongdoing. A statement offered against a party that has engaged or acquiesced in wrongdoing that was intended to, and did, procure the unavailability of the declarant as a witness.

7)   **OTHER EXCEPTIONS**

a)   General Rule

A hearsay statement that does not fall under any of the enumerated exceptions will not necessarily be excluded from evidence. It may be admitted under a "catch-all" or "residual" exception if a judge determines that, based on circumstantial evidence, the statement is:

- proffered as evidence of a material fact; and
- trustworthy evidence about that fact; and
- more probative about an issue than other evidence about the fact; and
- the purpose of the *Federal Rules of Evidence* would be served by presenting the evidence; and
- the interests of justice would be served by presenting that evidence.

A party who wishes to admit evidence pursuant to this exception must provide a party-opponent with adequate advance notice of that intent to proffer evidence.

b)   Text of FRE 807

Rule 807. Residual Exception

A statement not specifically covered by Rule 803 or 804 but having equivalent circumstantial guarantees of trustworthiness, is not excluded by the hearsay rule, if the court determines that (A) the statement is offered as evidence of a material fact; (B) the statement is more probative on the point for which it is offered than any other evidence which the proponent can procure through reasonable efforts; and (C) the general purposes of these rules and the interests of justice will best be served by admission of the statement into evidence. However, a statement may not be admitted under this exception unless the proponent of it makes known to the adverse party sufficiently in advance of the trial or hearing to provide the adverse party with a fair opportunity to prepare to meet it, the proponent's intention to offer the statement and the particulars of it, including the name and address of the declarant.

AMERIBAR BAR REVIEW

Multistate Bar Examination Preparation Course

REAL PROPERTY

TABLE OF CONTENTS

INTRODUCTION

Unless otherwise indicated, this outline covers majority legal principles. The MBE generally tests majority rules unless a question expressly provides that the minority rule applies or the question otherwise would not make sense.

I. OWNERSHIP

A primary purpose of property law is defining and establishing the nature and extent of property ownership. A useful means of understanding the concepts of ownership is looking at a parcel of real property as a bundle of sticks that represent interests, rights, or estates in the property. An individual or entity that has complete ownership, possession, and use of the parcel holds the entire bundle. But if that ownership is incomplete in some respect, then the individual or owner will not hold all of the sticks, or interests, rights, or estates in the property.

The right of ownership is the greatest interest of all. Other lesser interests include the right to possession and use, the right of transfer, and the right to exclude others from a parcel of real property.

A. Present Estates

1) GENERAL CONSIDERATIONS

a) Definitions

Present estates concern the types of rights and interests in real property that are held by individuals or entities. Present estates may either be possessory or non-possessory because an ownership interest does not necessarily require or involve possession and use of the property.

b) Types of Interests

A first party may hold title to a parcel of real property, which constitutes an ownership interest. A second party may simultaneously have a right to occupy that parcel, which is a possessory interest. If the second party seeks to transfer that interest to a third party, the second party is limited to transferring a possessory interest and cannot transfer an ownership interest. A party may only transfer the rights it possesses in property.

c) Determining Interest Type

One should consider the following factors when determining the nature and extent of an interest in property:

- the language used to establish an estate;

- the nature and type of rights the grantor conveys;
- the duration of the estate; and
- the involvement of any future interest.

(1)   Present Estates

Present estates include freehold estates and qualified estates. A fee simple estate is a freehold estate. Qualified estates, on the other hand, include defeasible fees simple, life estates, estates for a period of years, and fees tail.

 Many exam questions provide the language of a conveyance and require the examinee to identify what type of interest was created. Therefore, it is important for you to understand the different types of interests and how they are created.

★★   2)   <u>FEE SIMPLE</u>

| Question Key |
| 7,57,169 |

a)   Fee Simple Absolute

(1)   Nature and Characteristics

Most real property owners hold their property in fee simple absolute (also referred to as fee simple). A fee simple absolute is the most substantial type of property interest for three reasons. First, it neither involves, nor is subject to, a future interest. Second, its duration is for a potentially infinite period. Third, its holder may exclusively occupy and enjoy the parcel of real property.

(2)   Creation

Grantors typically transfer property by a conveyance in a written instrument. The usual language in a conveyance that creates a fee simple absolute is either "from a grantor to a grantee," or "from a grantor to a grantee and his heirs." It may also state "from Grantor to Grantee in fee simple absolute" or other similar language. A conveyance of a fee simple interest is neither qualified in any way nor limited by any other interest.

(3)   Rights of Possession and Use

The grantee of a fee simple absolute has the exclusive rights of possession and use. The grantee may share these rights with others, including invitees and licensees, or may transfer the rights to third parties.

★★   3)   <u>DEFEASIBLE FEE SIMPLE</u>

| Question Key |
| 27,30,57,114 |

a)   Nature and Characteristics

A defeasible fee simple is an estate in land in which the holder possesses fee simple title, but the title is subject to being divested upon the occurrence of a certain condition. This type of interest is also called a defeasible fee or a qualified fee. Thus, a conveyance of a defeasible fee simple includes language that may limit its duration. For example, a grantor may convey this type of estate for charitable purposes or to ensure that a parcel of real property will be used pursuant to the grantor's wishes for some duration.

A defeasible fee simple creates an accompanying future interest.

b) Creation

There are three main types of defeasible fee simple estates. The three types of defeasible fees include: 1) a fee simple determinable, 2) a fee simple subject to a condition subsequent, and 3) a fee simple subject to an executory interest. On the MBE, you must be able to identify each of them.

(1) Fee Simple Determinable

A fee simple determinable is an estate that ends *automatically* if the condition specified in the conveyance occurs. Upon the happening of the event, the interest will automatically revert back to the grantor or the heirs of the grantor. A possibility of reverter is the accompanying future interest created with a fee simple determinable and held by the grantor.

The grantor must use durational language to create this estate. The usual language that creates a fee simple determinable may include: "to Grantee and her heirs for as long as [or, alternatively, so long as, until, or while] a conveyed parcel of real property is used for a public park [or alternatively some other purpose]."

Unlike in a fee simple subject to a condition subsequent, set forth below, in a fee simple determinable the possibility of reverter automatically vests legal possession of the parcel in the grantor when the condition that limits the conveyance is no longer satisfied.

The durational language must be clear and unequivocal. Compare the following example:

QUESTION

Anders conveyed her only parcel of land to Burton by a duly executed and delivered warranty deed, which provided:

"To have and to hold the described tract of land in fee simple, subject to the understanding that within one year from the date of the instrument said grantee shall construct and thereafter maintain and operate on said premises a public health center."

The grantee, Burton, constructed a public health center on the tract within the time specified and operated it for five years. At the end of this period, Burton converted the structure into a senior citizens' recreational facility. It is conceded by all parties in interest that a senior citizens' recreational facility is not a public health center.

In an appropriate action, Anders seeks a declaration that the change in the use of the facility has caused the land and structure to revert to her. In this action, Anders should

(A)   win, because the language of the deed created a determinable fee, which leaves a possibility of reverter in the grantor.

(B)   win, because the language of the deed created a fee subject to condition subsequent, which leaves a right of entry or power of termination in the grantor.

(C)   lose, because the language of the deed created only a contractual obligation and did not provide for retention of property interest by the grantor.

(D)   lose, because an equitable charge is enforceable only in equity.

The correct answer is choice (c). This question tests the requirements for a defeasible fee simple. A defeasible fee simple is an estate in land in which the holder possesses a fee simple title, but the title is subject to being divested upon the occurrence of a certain condition. Thus, a conveyance of a defeasible fee simple includes language that may limit its duration. This durational language must be clear and unequivocal. When conveyances include language explaining the purpose of the transfer, the vast majority of courts will hold the language as precatory – not intended to have any legal significance- and will interpret the conveyance to have transferred all the interests the grantor owned, If the grantors owned a fee simple, the courts presume that is what they intended to convey. This result follows from the presumption against forfeitures and protects the interests of the grantee, placing the burden on the grantors to be clear if they intend to retain a future interest in the property. Here, the conveyance lacks any durational language. Although it may, at first glance, appear to be a defeasible estate, the language in the deed created only a contractual obligation and did not provide for retention of a property interest by Anders.

(2)   Fee Simple Subject to Condition Subsequent

A fee simple subject to a condition subsequent is a defeasible fee estate that does not end automatically upon the happening of the condition specified in the conveyance. The holder of the interest must claim the future interest in the estate. The grantor holds the accompanying future interest, which is called a "right of reentry" or "right of entry."

The language used to create this interest would include: "to Grantee, but if Grantee sells alcohol on the property, then Grantor has the right of reentry."

Remember, in order to create a fee simple subject to a condition subsequent, the grantor must provide language containing a right to reentry upon the happening of a specified event. The language must expressly state that if the grantee does not use the parcel as designated, then the grantor may reenter and occupy the parcel.

The occurrence of the condition authorizes the grantor to reenter the parcel. The grantor may or may not ultimately decide to do so. To exercise the right, the grantor must take affirmative steps in order to regain possession and use of the parcel.

(3)   Fee Simple Subject to an Executory Interest

A fee simple subject to an executory interest is a fee simple estate that is subject to divestment in favor of someone other than the grantor if a specified event happens. For example, Grantor may deed his property to Grantee providing, "To Grantee and his heirs, but if the property is ever used as a liquor store, then to Edward." If Grantee violates the terms of the deed, the property would then go to a third party.

An executory interest, which is further explained below, is an interest that automatically transfers to another grantee upon the occurrence of a certain enumerated change in the use of the specified property.

The first grantee's interest in the estate automatically terminates if the grantee does not fulfill the condition of the grant. The second grantee then obtains use and possession of that interest.

c)   Rights of Possession and Use

Under all three types of defeasible fees, the original grantee retains the right of possession and use, if it is not legally transferred, for as long as the terms of the language of conveyance are satisfied. If the grantee does not fulfill the terms of the conveyance, then the grantor may regain possession and use of the parcel under either a fee simple determinable with a possibility of reverter or a fee simple subject to a condition subsequent. If the grantee does not satisfy the terms of a grant with respect to a fee simple subject to an executory interest or limitation, the law automatically terminates the grantor's and the first grantee's interests in the parcel and transfers the interests to a second grantee who obtains the rights of possession and use.

★★★   4)   <u>LIFE ESTATE & TERM OF YEARS</u>

a)   Nature and Characteristics

> Question Key
> 7,22,45,52,58,59,
> 92,140,168

A life estate is a possessory interest in a parcel of real property that lasts for the life of some person. A conveyance of a life estate provides the grantee a right to occupy the parcel for a lifetime. The measuring lifetime may either be that of the grantee or that of a third person. Such a grantee is considered a life tenant.

b)   Creation

The usual language that creates a fee simple may include: "to a grantee for the grantee's life," or "to a grantee for the life of [another person]," or "to a first grantee for life, but [if something specific occurs], then to a second grantee."

c)   Classification of Interests

A life estate creates a corresponding future interest that may become possessory upon the end of a measuring lifetime. That future interest may either be a reversion or a remainder (reversions and remainders will be covered in another section of the outline).

(1)   *Pur Autre Vie*

A life estate *pur autre vie* is a life estate that results from the granting of a life estate where the measuring lifetime is that of someone other than the life tenant. For example, suppose that a grantor conveys a life estate to a first grantee for that grantee's life. Ten years later, the first grantee conveys her interest to a second grantee. The second grantee possesses a life estate *pur autre vie* for the life of the first grantee.

(2)   Term of Years

An estate for a term of years is another similar type of possessory estate that a grantee holds for the duration that a conveyance sets forth. For example, suppose that a grantor conveys a possessory interest to a grantee for five years. The grantee possesses an estate for that term of years.

(3)   Determinable Life Estate

An instrument that also contains a limitation creates a determinable life estate. The limitation might, for example, automatically terminate the life estate owner's interest in the property prior to the death of the measuring life. For example, suppose Harold conveys Blackacre "to Wanda for life or until she remarries." The limitation is valid, and Wanda possesses a determinable life estate.

d)   Rights of Possession and Use

A grantee of a life estate, a life tenant, retains the rights of possession, use, and profits from the parcel for the duration of the measuring life. A grantee of an estate for a term of years retains the rights of possession, use, and profits from the parcel for that number of years.

(1)   Encumbrances

A life tenant may only encumber a parcel of real property by a mortgage, lease, or other creditors' interests to the degree of the tenant's interest in that parcel.

★★ A life tenant who takes possession of real property that is encumbered by a mortgage, unless otherwise provided in the conveyance, will be responsible for paying the interest on that mortgage. The remainderman has the duty to pay the principal.

(2)   Waste

A reversionary interest holder, or remainderman, has the right to receive a parcel in essentially the same condition that a life tenant found it upon taking possession of it. Accordingly, a life tenant possesses a duty not to commit waste that would unreasonably impair the value of the parcel when a reversionary interest holder takes possession of it. An example of waste would be destruction of the parcel or any structures upon it. The law prohibits the life tenant from committing several types of waste.

(a)   Ameliorative Waste

Ameliorative waste occurs when a life tenant improves the parcel's value in a manner that violates the intent of its grantor. In order to take any lawful action to improve the parcel that is subject to a life estate, a life tenant needs to obtain the consent of all reversionary interest holders.

(b)   Permissive Waste

Permissive waste results from a life tenant's failure to fulfill legal duties. Those duties include maintaining the parcel with its structures and making property tax and mortgage payments. Those payments are limited to the degree of profits or income from the parcel, or if none, then in the amount of the parcel's reasonable rental value. The life tenant may insure the parcel, but the common law does not impose a duty to insure.

(c)   Affirmative Waste

Voluntary or affirmative waste consists of a life tenant's activity that diminishes the parcel's value. One type of such conduct would be demolishing an existing structure on the parcel that is not in a condemned condition. Another type of such activity would be an unauthorized taking of natural resources from the parcel.

(i)   Exceptions

(A)   Open   Mine
Doctrine

The open mine doctrine allows a life tenant to continue operating a previously functioning mine on the parcel of real property to extract natural resources.

(B)   Owners   in
Possession

Owners of a fee simple interest who are in possession of it are not subject to the law of waste.

e)   Legal and Equitable Remedies

If the life estate tenant, a tenant for a term of years, or someone in legal privity with such a tenant commits waste, then the grantor or the holder of the reversionary interest may, according to the common law or state statutes, seek the following remedies:

- forfeiture of possession;
- legal damages based on the parcel's diminished value or the cost of restoring the parcel's original condition; or
- equitable remedies of injunctions or accountings.

5)   FEE TAIL   ⌐ | Question Key |
                         | 45 |

        a)   Nature and Characteristics

A fee tail is an estate in land that is limited in inheritance to a particular class of heirs of the grantee. Generally this type of estate no longer exists because most jurisdictions have abolished it by law. A fee tail is similar to, or in the nature of, a fee simple absolute. The goal in creating a fee tail is to ensure that an estate remains within a family's ownership.

        b)   Creation

The following types of language of conveyance may effectively establish a fee tail: "to a grantee and the heirs of her body." Thus, a fee tail will endure as long as the grantee continues to have a bloodline.

        c)   Classification of Interests

A fee tail establishes a future interest of a reversion in a grantor that becomes effective when and if all of the grantee's heirs are deceased.

        d)   Rights of Possession and Use

A grantee of a fee tail and the grantee's heirs obtain the rights of possession, use, and profits from a parcel during the successive lifetimes of the grantee and each of the heirs.

B.   Co-tenancy | Question Key |
                  | 6,11,15,31,39,48,53,62,74,77,88,104,113,120,121,1 |
★★★★ | 33,135,145,153,160 |

The term co-tenancy refers to concurrent ownership of an estate. There are three main concurrent estates in property: 1) tenancy in common; 2) joint tenancy; and 3) tenancy by the entirety.

★★   1)   OBLIGATIONS AND ENTITLEMENTS

Regardless of the type of estate, co-tenants possess certain rights regarding the property, which they are free to modify through an agreement among themselves.

        a)   Rights of Possession and Use

A tenant possesses an unrestricted right of access to the real property. If a co-tenant wrongfully excludes another from using the property, the excluded co-tenant may bring forth a cause of action for ouster. The ousted tenant may receive fair rental value of the property for the time of dispossession.

Co-tenants may exercise these rights either concurrently or separately. Their separate and disproportionate exercise of those rights usually does not affect the validity or availability of their respective rights. For example, although co-tenant 1 owns 30 percent of a parcel with co-tenant 2 who owns 70 percent of the parcel, both co-tenants equally share the right of possession and enjoyment of the estate.

(1)   Boundary Disputes

A co-tenant in possession may, without any input from an out-of-possession co-tenant, handle situations such as boundary disputes.

b)   Costs

Each of the co-tenants may be separately assessed his ownership interest in the property maintenance expenses, insurance, and taxes. A co-tenant possesses a right of contribution from the other co-tenants for the costs of owning the property. Co-tenants may be required to contribute to the payment of expenses, such as property taxes and mortgages, on the entire property.

(1)   Right of Reimbursement for Expenses

A co-tenant in possession of a parcel possesses the right to reimbursement from a co-tenant who was out of possession of the parcel for a *pro rata* amount of the payments that were made for property maintenance, insurance, and taxes. In a partition sale, that amount may be credited towards and added to the paying of the co-tenant's share of the proceeds. That amount is subject to an offset based on the value of the paying co-tenant's use and enjoyment of the property.

(2)   No Reimbursement for Improvements

Co-tenants are not responsible for reimbursing a co-tenant for the costs of improvements to the parcel. A first co-tenant lacks a right to reimbursement from any other co-tenants who decline to help pay for the cost of improvements to part of their parcel of real property.

(a)   Enhancements and Devaluations

If a co-tenant adds something that enhances the value of the property, the co-tenant generally possesses no right to demand that the other co-tenants share in the cost of this enhancement. This is the rule even if the enhancement results in greater profits for the property. Nonetheless, if the property is partitioned, the co-tenant possesses the right to recover the value added by the improvement to the property. If, however, the co-tenant's enhancements decrease the value of the property, then the co-tenant will be responsible for the decrease in value.

c)   Income

A co-tenant possesses the right to an accounting of all profits derived from the property. If the property generates rent, for example, each co-tenant has the right to a proportion of the income.

(1)   Profits

When profits are derived from a parcel, all of the co-tenants possess a right to receive a percentage of the profits according to their ownership interest in the common estate.

(2)   Rent

If one of the co-tenants is in exclusive possession of the parcel, then the other co-tenants possess no right to receive rent from the one co-tenant. Also, a co-tenant in possession has no obligation to share any profits that result from that co-tenant's efforts with another co-tenant who did not exercise possession of the estate.

(a)   Exception for Ouster

A co-tenant possesses a right to recover rent, however, if the co-tenant is subject to an ouster from the parcel due to a wrongful exclusion. Ouster results when a first co-tenant makes a claim of ownership against a second co-tenant. Making a claim of adverse possession during an existing partition action between them will not constitute an ouster.

d)   Outstanding Title

Title to a parcel of real property that is subject to a co-tenancy may become outstanding as a result of either a foreclosure proceeding or tax sale. One co-tenant may acquire title to the parcel, and other co-tenants may assert and regain their interest in the parcel.

(1)   Mortgage Foreclosure

A co-tenant who acquires title to the parcel in a mortgage foreclosure sale may recover from each co-tenant who is obligated on the mortgage their ownership interest in its debt. Likewise, the co-tenants may recover their ownership interest by reimbursing the purchasing co-tenant.

(2)   Tax Sale

A co-tenant who acquires title to the parcel in a tax sale may recover from each co-tenant his ownership interest in the tax debt. Likewise, the co-tenants may recover their ownership interests by reimbursing the purchasing co-tenant.

★★★   2)   <u>TENANCY IN COMMON</u>

                a)   Nature and Characteristics

A tenancy in common is a form of concurrent estate in which each owner, referred to as a tenant in common, owns separate and distinct shares that may differ in proportion. The tenancy in common is the default form of concurrent estate. A tenancy in common exists when at least two co-tenants possess an ownership interest in the same parcel(s) of real property. The following factors exemplify this estate:

- each co-tenant's interest may, but is not required to be, equal in extent;
- each co-tenant's right to use and enjoy the property is equal; and
- none of the co-tenants possess a right of survivorship.

For example, suppose Bob and Carl own Blackacre as tenants in common. Bob may own a 60% interest, and Carl may own a 40% interest. Bob and Carl, however, possess the equal right to use and enjoy Blackacre.

In a tenancy in common, none of the co-tenants possess a right of survivorship. Therefore, a co-tenant's ownership interest may pass by intestacy or bequest.

                b)   Creation

                (1)   Unity of Possession

In order to create a tenancy in common, there must be unity of possession. Unity of possession means that both co-tenants must have an equal right to enjoy and possess the entire parcel when the tenancy in common is created.

                (2)   Other Means of Creation

                (a)   Presumption of Creation

Generally, a presumption exists that a conveyance to at least two unmarried individuals establishes a tenancy in common. For example, suppose O conveys "Blackacre to Edward and Josephine." Pursuant to the presumption, the conveyance establishes a tenancy in common.

                (i)   Overcoming Presumption

The typical manner of overcoming this presumption is by including in the deed's words of conveyance the phrase "joint tenants" or "joint tenancy" and the word "survivor" or survivorship." Sheldon F. Kurtz, *Moynihan's Introduction to the Law of Real Property* 282 (4th ed. 2005). Some case law finds that the word "jointly" in a deed of itself overcomes the presumption of a tenancy in common. William B, Stoebuck & Dale A. Whitman, *The Law of Property* 185–86 (3d ed. 2000). Other case law provides that the use of the word "jointly" in the deed shows intent that the grantees "own together" instead of them owning as joint tenants with the right of survivorship. Id. Use of the phrase "equally, to share and share alike" in conjunction with the word "jointly" may indicate a joint tenancy if it evidences the grantor's intent to grant each grantee an equal interest in the real property. This constitutes another key indicator of a joint tenancy that is not essential for a tenancy in common. Suppose, for example, that a grantor duly executes a deed "jointly in fee to my sons, Bob and Tom, equally, to share and share alike." In this example, the language of grant needs analysis in light of other relevant facts and the foregoing rules in order to determine whether the grantor intended to create a tenancy in common or a joint tenancy.

(b)   Creation by Succession

A transfer resulting from intestate succession may create a tenancy in common.

(c)   Automatic Creation

A tenancy in common may arise by default when a divorce of married individuals terminates a tenancy by the entirety. That subtopic is discussed below.

c)   Classification of Interests

(1)   Distinguishing Tenants from Co-tenants

The term "tenant" as used in the concurrent estate context does not have the same meaning as that of a tenant who rents or leases premises from a landlord. The term "co-tenant" means an owner of premises in common with co-tenants.

d)   Interest is Transferable or Descendible

If a tenancy in common only consists of two co-tenants, the death of one of them does not terminate their tenancy. Consequently, a deceased co-tenant's ownership interest is descendible to his heirs. The heir becomes a co-tenant in common.

e)   Legal and Equitable Remedies

(1)   Partition

A co-tenant (tenants in common or joint tenants) may bring an action for partition to divide property and obtain a final accounting of respective interests in the property. A co-tenant may seek and obtain a partition in two ways: 1) by voluntary written agreement; or 2) through a partition action by a tenant in common seeking judicial proceedings to obtain an involuntary partition. In such an action, the tenants may also seek the equitable remedy of an accounting to determine their respective financial interests relative to the estate.

(a)   Types of Partition

There are two types of partition: 1) partition in kind by means of actually dividing the parcel; or 2) partition by sale by selling the parcel and dividing the profits from that sale. Although partition in kind generally is preferred over partition by sale, a partition by sale may occur when it is not possible to physically divide the parcel equitably and fairly.

(b)   Partition Sale

In a partition sale, a co-tenant whose efforts and funds resulted in improvements to a parcel possesses the right to recover the parcel's increase in value that resulted from the improvements. That tenant has no right to recover those improvement's actual costs out of the sale proceeds. If other co-tenants contributed efforts and funds towards making the improvements, then they possess the right to a *pro rata* recovery of the parcel's consequent increased value.

★★★   3)   <u>JOINT TENANCY</u>

a)   Nature and Characteristics

A joint tenancy exists when at least two co-tenants own a parcel subject to a right of survivorship. The right of survivorship possessed with a joint tenancy is the critical distinction of the joint tenancy from other concurrent estates. As with a tenancy in common, joint tenants possess the right to concurrently enjoy and possess the parcel.

b)   Creation

(1)   Four Unities

The common law requires the existence of four unities to create a joint tenancy. These unities are: (1) unity of interest, (2) unity of title, (3) unity of time, and (4) unity of possession. All joint tenants must acquire an interest or estate by the same conveyance, commencing at the same time, and hold it for the same term of undivided possession.

(a)   Unity of Title

The joint tenants must receive their interest in land under the same document or conveyance.

(b)   Unity of Time

Each of the joint tenants' titles must vest at the same time. Suppose, for example, Blackacre was left to three brothers "upon attaining the age of 30." If they are of different ages, and therefore will attain the age of 30 at different times, then no unity of time would exist.

(c)   Unity of Possession

As with tenancy in common, the joint tenants have a right to possess the entire parcel and may not exclude each other.

(d)   Unity of Interest

The term "unity of interest" refers to the necessity that all joint tenants have interests of the same duration, and accordingly one cannot be a joint tenant for life and another joint tenant for years." 2 *Tiffany Real Prop.* § 418 (3d ed. 2001). There is no requirement of unity of equality of interest (i.e., the same proportion).

c)   Rights of Possession and Use

(1)   *Inter Vivos* Transfer

A joint tenant's attempt to make an *inter vivos* transfer of an interest in a joint tenancy cannot be valid because it would violate the four unities.

(2)   Right of Survivorship

When one of the joint tenants dies, that tenant's ownership interest automatically passes to a single surviving joint tenant or pro rata among all surviving joint tenants. This right of survivorship is the primary distinguishing feature of a joint tenancy that is lacking in a tenancy in common. If a single joint tenant survives, then the "joint" tenancy is ended.

d)   Legal and Equitable Remedies

(1)   Partition

This remedy is discussed under co-tenants in common, although it also applies to, and is available to, joint tenants.

(2)   Severance

(a)   Severance by Mortgage

A severance may occur by the taking of a mortgage on a parcel of real property that is subject to a joint tenancy. Whether the mortgage results in a severance depends upon whether the state is a title theory or lien theory state.

In a lien theory state, the taking of a mortgage merely places a lien on the property, leaving the joint tenancy undisturbed. In a title theory state, though, the mortgage actually conveys title to the mortgagor until the mortgagee pays the mortgage. In such states, the taking of a mortgage by one owner breaks the joint tenancy as to that owner.

(b)   Severance by Conveyance

A severance may occur as the result of a joint tenant making a conveyance. For example, suppose one of the joint tenants conveys his interest in the parcel to a third party. In that event, the joint tenancy transforms into a tenancy in common.

4)   TENANCY BY THE ENTIRETY

a)   Nature and Characteristics

The traditional common law approach treats husband and wife as a single legal entity. A minority of the states recognize a tenancy by the entirety between those spouses as a legal entity.

b)   Creation

In some states, a conveyance of a parcel to a married couple automatically operates to create a tenancy by the entirety. Other states require that a conveyance must clearly express an intention to create a tenancy by the entirety.

c)   Classification of Interests

Tenancy by the entirety is a type of co-tenancy because more than one person has an ownership interest in a concurrent estate. A tenancy by the entirety is only available for and applicable to a married couple.

d)   Rights of Possession and Use

(1)   Right to Transfer

The present rule that either spouse may exercise the ability to transfer rights of possession and survivorship supersedes the former rule that only a husband possessed those rights. Neither of them, however, may defeat the other's right of survivorship by making a conveyance to a grantee.

(2)   Right of Survivorship

A tenancy by the entirety provides a right of survivorship so that the entire estate transfers to the surviving spouse upon the other spouse's death.

(3)   Termination

The following events terminate a tenancy by the entirety: death of either spouse, annulment or dissolution of a marriage, divorce, or mutual agreement.

e)   Legal and Equitable Remedies

(1)   Majority Rule

In a majority of states that recognize tenancies by the entirety, one spouse's creditor may not acquire an interest in the estate of a tenancy by the entirety.

(2)   Minority Rule

In a minority of states that recognize tenancies by the entirety, a creditor may acquire an interest in one spouse's ownership interest but may not encumber the other spouse's ownership interest. In those states the creditor may not interfere with the right of survivorship.

★   **C.   Future Interests**

Question Key
See questions keyed for
present estates

1)   <u>DEFINITION</u>

A future interest is a present non-possessory estate or interest in a parcel of real property that may become a possessory interest in the parcel at some time in the future. A future interest is a right to receive possession of the parcel at a future time. A future interest follows a qualified estate and may be created in a grantee or in a grantor. There are several different types of future interests. An exam question may require an examinee to determine what type of interest has been created by a specific conveyance.

★   2)   <u>REVERSIONS</u>

a)   General

A grantor's conveyance of something less than a fee simple interest to a grantee creates a reversion interest. For example, if a grantor conveys a life estate or an estate for a term for years, the grantor reserves a reversion interest in the estate.

b)   Nature and Characteristics

A reversion is a grantor's future interest that is derived from a conveyance of an interest in real property that is of a lesser quantity than the interest that the grantor owns.

c)   Creation

A grantor may create a reversion by conveying to a grantee an interest in real property that is of a lesser quantity that the one that the grantor retains. For example, the grantor might convey a life estate or a fee tail to a grantee and retain a reversionary interest in fee simple absolute. The grantor need not explicitly reserve a future interest in a conveyance for it to exist. Operation of law, rather than the express terms of the deed, creates a reversion.

d)   Rights of Possession and Use

A grantor relinquishes a present right to possess and use a parcel of real estate but reserves that right for the future. A grantee exercises a present right of possession and use of the parcel until it reverts to the grantor pursuant to the conveyance's terms.

★★   3)   <u>REMAINDERS, VESTED AND CONTINGENT</u>

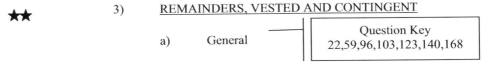

     a)   General

| Question Key |
| 22,59,96,103,123,140,168 |

A remainder interest generally follows a life estate or an estate for a term of years. A remainder will never follow a fee interest. It only comes into existence at the natural expiration of the prior estate. For example, a second grantee possesses a remainder interest in the property when a grantor makes a conveyance to a first grantee for life, then to the second grantee.

     b)   Nature and Characteristics

A remainder is a future interest that may be established in a grantee as a result of a prior estate's termination.

     c)   Creation

A single instrument, such as a deed, must establish both a future interest and a present interest in order to establish a remainder. A remainder may not prematurely end a proceeding estate. In other words, a remainder becomes a present possessory interest at the natural expiration of the prior possessory interest. Thus, the estates that a remainder may follow are life estates, estates for a term of years, or fee tails (estates that end naturally or at a pre-determined definite time).

     d)   Classification of Interests

If a remainder is not vested, then it is contingent. The distinction between vested and contingent remainders is important for several purposes, including the application of the Rule Against Perpetuities.

     (1)   Vested Remainders

     (a)   General

A remainder is a vested remainder if: 1) it exists in an ascertainable person or persons (i.e., specific and identifiable); and 2) it is not subject to an express condition precedent. For example, a grantor conveys an interest "to a first grantee for life, then to a second grantee." The second grantee possesses a vested remainder because she is ascertainable, and no specific contingency qualifies the second grantee's interest. The first grantee's death is not a contingency but rather the natural expiration of the first grantee's estate.

     (b)   Condition Subsequent

A vested remainder cannot be created as a result of the occurrence of a condition precedent. The occurrence of a condition subsequent to the creation of a vested remainder, however, will cause the vested remainder to take effect and operate to become a present possessory interest (as opposed to a future interest). For example, a grantor conveys an interest to a first grantee for ten years, then to a second grantee. The second grantee's interest is vested when the original conveyance creates the remainder, and the remainder takes effect as a present possessory interest when the ten year period ends.

(c)   Defeasance or Divestment

Vested remainders may be subject to defeasance or divestment upon the happening of a particular condition. For example, a grantor conveys an interest "to a first grantee for life, then to the second grantee and his heirs; if the second grantee dies before the first grantee, then to a third grantee and her heirs." Through this written conveyance, the first grantee obtains a life estate. Under that conveyance, the second grantee receives a vested remainder subject to divestment because the second grantee's death before the end of the first grantee's life estate will eliminate the second grantee's remainder. A vested remainder subject to defeasance or divestment is subject to the Rule Against Perpetuities.

(i)   Indefeasibly Vested

A vested remainder may be indefeasibly vested. A vested remainder that is indefeasibly vested is a remainder that is not dependent upon any condition precedent or any condition subsequent that may completely or partially defeat the remainder. If it cannot be defeated, then it is said to be indefeasibly vested.

(ii)   Vested   Subject   to
Complete Defeasance

A vested remainder subject to complete defeasance is a remainder that can be completely defeated by the occurrence of a condition subsequent or other limitation.

(d)   Subject to Open

Vested remainders may be subject to open when a specified class of persons, such as children or grandchildren, holds a remainder, and at least one member of the class is ascertainable. In that event, the number of members of the class may increase or decrease until all of its members have been ascertained. That may happen when the parents of the class members are unable to have children or have died. An open vested remainder is subject to the limitations of the Rule Against Perpetuities. A vested remainder subject to open is also called a vested remainder subject to partial defeasance.

(i)   Ascertainable Persons

Generally, if a person is named and alive, the person is ascertainable (i.e., identifiable). A person's heirs are not identifiable as such until the person's death. Thus, if a person is not identifiable or not yet born, the person is not ascertainable as heir. For example, assume that a grantor conveys an interest to a first grantee for that grantee's life, then to a second grantee's children. If the second grantee has one child who is living at the time of conveyance, then that child is ascertainable and possesses a vested remainder subject to open. If the second grantee is alive, then the second grantee's unborn children possess remainders that are contingent upon them being born.

(2)   Contingent Remainders

(a)   General

A written conveyance establishes a contingent remainder when it contains either or both of the following conditions: 1) no grantee is specified or identifiable; or 2) the grantee's receipt of the remainder interest is conditional.   For the interest to be a contingent remainder, it must potentially become possessory at the natural expiration of the prior estate. For example, suppose Otis convey Blackacre to "Bob for his life, then to Carl's heirs." If Carl is alive, his heirs cannot be specified or identified. Therefore, Carl's heirs possess a contingent remainder.

(b)   Conditional Element

If a condition in a written conveyance must be fulfilled to establish a remainder interest, then the remainder may be contingent. In other words, if a remainder interest is subject to an express condition that must be met before the interest becomes possessory in a grantee, then it is contingent. For example, "to a first grantee for the first grantee's life, then if a second grantee is alive and has two children at the time of her death, to the second grantee and her heirs." The second grantee possesses a contingent remainder because she must fulfill a condition before she may take possession.

(i)   Contingent versus Vested

If one clause in a written conveyance creates a remainder interest, and a separate and subsequent clause provides a condition that may eliminate the interest, the remainder is a vested remainder subject to divestment by a condition subsequent. For example, a grantor conveys an interest "to a first grantee for the first grantee's life, then to a second grantee and her heirs, but if the second grantee is not employed as an attorney when the first grantee dies, then to a third grantee and her heirs." The first grantee possesses a life estate.   The second grantee possesses a vested remainder subject to divestment by a condition subsequent because the provision creating the property interest comes before a separate and subsequent clause that provides for the potential elimination of the interest. The third grantee possesses a remainder that is contingent upon the second grantee's failure to satisfy the condition.

The way that a conveyance is written dictates the type of remainder the conveyance creates. For example, suppose the above conveyance was written as follows: "To a first grantee for the first grantee's life, then if the second grantee is not employed as an attorney when the first grantee dies, to the second grantee and her heirs." In this example, the second grantee possesses a contingent remainder because the clause creating the condition appears before the clause granting the interest to the second grantee. The placement of commas or clauses can make all the difference.

(c) Destructibility of Contingent Remainders

(i) Common Law (Minority)

At common law, destruction of a contingent remainder occurs unless it vests at or before the expiration of a prior life estate. Assume that a grantor conveys an interest "To a grantee for life, then to the grantee's children who reach the age of 30." If, at the grantor's death, the grantee's only child is 29, then that child's remainder is destroyed, and the property reverts to the grantor.

(ii) Modern Law (Majority Rule)

Statute or case law has abolished the harsh common law rule in a majority of jurisdictions. Today, a remainderman who fulfills a condition of a contingent remainder will generally be entitled to receive a remainder interest. For example, a grantor conveys an interest "to a grantee for life, then to the grantee's children who reach the age of 30." If the grantee's only child is 29 at the grantee's death, the child will be entitled to the property when and if she turns 30. In the interim, the grantor would be entitled to possession of the property.

e) Rights of Possession and Use

A holder of a remainder interest lacks any present rights of possession and use of the parcel. The holder's right of use only exists when the parcel becomes possessory.

f) Legal and Equitable Remedies

(1) Vested Remainders (Damages Allowed)

A vested remainder holder may file a lawsuit to enforce its property interests and seek a recovery of damages or injunctive relief.

(2) Contingent Remainders (Damages Prohibited)

A contingent remainder holder may file a lawsuit to enforce its property interest and seek a recovery of injunctive relief. That holder may not recover damages. The holder may also file a lawsuit seeking an injunction to stop waste but not a lawsuit to recover damages for the waste.

★ 4) <u>EXECUTORY INTERESTS</u>

Question Key
76,91

a) Nature and Characteristics

An executory interest cuts short the natural termination of a preceding estate. The two types of executory interests are shifting or springing.

(1)   Shifting Executory Interest

A second grantee's shifting executory interest may cut off a first grantee's interest. The interest shifts or transfers from the first grantee to the second grantee pursuant to some condition. For example, suppose Opel conveys Blackacre "to Arnold for so long as the premises are not used as a brothel, then to Charles." Charles possesses a shifting executory interest.

(2)   Springing Executory Interest

A grantee's springing executory interest may cut off a grantor's interest. A springing executory interest is an interest that "springs" from the grantor to the grantee pursuant to a condition. For example, suppose Opel, owner of Blackacre in fee simple, conveys Blackacre "to Gertrude in five years," or "to Gary two years after my death." In these examples, the grantees' executory interests cut short Opel's fee simple interest. When the interests become possessory, they "spring" directly from the grantor to the grantee.

b)   Creation

(1)   General

A conveyance may create a springing or a shifting executory interest, which follows a fee interest, in a grantee.

(2)   Shifting Executory Interest

A shifting executory interest is an interest that shifts by becoming possessory directly from one grantee to another. For example, a grantor conveys an interest to a first grantee for so long as the premises are not used as a brothel, then to a second grantee. The second grantee possesses a shifting executory interest because title passes from the first grantee to the second grantee upon fulfillment of the requisite condition.

A shifting executory interest includes language similar to the following example: "To a first grantee and her heirs, but if a second grantee gets married, to the second grantee and her heirs."

(3)   Springing Executory Interest

A springing executory interest is an interest that becomes possessory directly from the grantor to an interest holder grantee. For example, a grantor conveys an interest "to a grantee when and if the grantee reaches the age of 30." The grantee possesses a springing executory interest because title passes from the grantor to the grantee.

In another example, a grantor conveys an interest "to a first grantee for that grantee's life, then 10 years after the first grantee's death, to a second grantee." Title will pass from the grantor to the first grantee as a life estate holder, then back to the grantor for 10 years, and then finally to the second grantee. The second grantee possesses a springing executory interest because she obtains title from the grantor.

            c)   Classification of Interests

An executory interest is an interest in a third party that always follows a fee interest. For example, a grantor conveys an interest to a first grantee for so long as the premises are not used as a brothel, then to a second grantee. The first grantee possesses a fee simple determinable because the happening of the event eliminates the grantee's estate. The second grantee possesses an executory interest because, if it comes into existence, it cuts off a fee simple determinable interest.

            d)   Rule Against Perpetuities

Executory interests are subject to the limitation of the Rule Against Perpetuities.

        5)   <u>POSSIBILITY OF REVERTER, POWER OF TERMINATION</u>

            a)   Nature and Characteristics

A fee simple determinable is an interest that is subject to potential reversion to the grantor if a certain event occurs. The two types of future interests that accompany a fee simple determinable are the possibility of reverter and the power of termination.

              (1)   Possibility of Reverter

A possibility of reverter is a future interest that a grantor retains when the grantor conveys a fee simple determinable. For example, a grantor conveys an interest "to a grantee for so long as the premises are not used as a brothel." The grantee's interest is conditioned upon the premises not being used in a certain way. No additional event needs to occur before the grantor automatically regains possession of the premises other than a failure of the stated condition. Thus, the grantor retains a possibility of reverter.

The Rule Against Perpetuities is not applicable to a possibility of reverter.

              (2)   Powers of Termination

A power of termination (i.e., a right of re-entry) is similar to a possibility of reverter. For example, the grantor conveys an interest "to a grantee, but if the premises are used as a brothel, the grantor reserves the right to re-enter and terminate the grantee's interest." The additional event of the grantor's re-entry must occur for the grantor to retake the estate. In other words, with a power of termination, a grantor must take affirmative action in order for the estate to revert back to the grantor. Contrast this situation to an automatic transfer that would occur upon the happening of a condition with a possibility of reverter.

The Rule Against Perpetuities is not applicable to a right of re-entry.

b)   Creation

(1)   Possibilities of Reverter

A conveyance may create a possibility of reverter in a grantor. It may only follow a fee simple determinable. For example, a grantee conveys an interest "to a grantor subject to a provision that if the parcel ceases to be used as a park, it will revert to the grantor." If the grantee stops using the land as a park, then the interest automatically goes to the grantor, and the grantee's interest ends. Sometimes, the operation of law, instead of the express terms of a deed, may create a possibility of reverter.

(2)   Powers of Termination

A conveyance may create a power of termination or right of entry in a grantor. It may only follow a fee simple subject to a condition precedent. For example, a grantee conveys an interest "to a grantor subject to a provision that if the parcel ceases to be used as a park it will revert to the grantor." If the grantee begins to build a house on the parcel, then the grantor may re-enter the premises and terminate the grantee's estate.

c)   Rights of Possession and Use

(1)   Possibilities of Reverter

A grantor does not need to expressly communicate to a grantee that the grantor possesses a possibility of reverter in order to exercise it because of the possibility's automatic nature.

(2)   Powers of Termination

A grantor needs to expressly communicate to a grantee that the grantor possesses a power of termination or right of entry in order to exercise it.

6)   <u>POWERS OF APPOINTMENT</u>

Question Key
149

a)   Nature and Characteristics

The *Restatement (Third) of Property* states that a power of appointment is "a power created or reserved by a person (the donor) having property subject to his disposition, enabling the donee of the power to designate, within such limits as the donor may prescribe, the transferees of the property or the shares in which it shall be received."

b)   Creation

Using the appropriate language in an instrument of conveyance including, but not limited to, a will may create a power of appointment.

c)   Rights of Possession and Use

The holder of a power of appointment may or may not have a right of possession and use in the property that is subject to transfer pursuant to the power. That right of possession and use will depend upon the extent of the holder's interest in the parcel that is subject to the power of appointment. The holder possesses the right to appoint the recipients of property, or to select who will receive property. The donor usually conveys the power by will or trust to a donee as the holder. A trustee of a trust may possess a power of appointment for the purpose of disposing of the property that is held in a trust.

(1)   General Power of Appointment

The donee of a general power of appointment receives all rights to appoint the property to herself, her creditors, or any others. Therefore, if a power is exercisable in favor of the holder, it is a general power of appointment. A power of appointment is general unless the terms of its creation limit it.

(2)   Special Power of Appointment

A special power of appointment is a power that is not exercisable in favor of a donee of this power, her estate, her creditors, or the creditors of her estate. With a special power of appointment, a holder of that power cannot appropriate the property into the holder's own hands. The terms of creation of the holder's exercise of that power must limit it in order for it to be a special power of appointment.

(3)   Exercise of Power of Appointment

A power of appointment will be properly exercised if the holder intends to exercise the power. A common question is whether a power of appointment can be exercised in a general residuary clause of a will. In that event, a testatrix's will bequeaths "the rest of the property in my estate or over which I possess a power of appointment to a holder of the power of appointment and his heirs." In the absence of a requirement in that grant of the power that specific reference to the power is necessary to exercise the power of appointment, a general residuary clause may provide a basis for an effective exercise of the power only if 1) the power is a general power or 2) the testatrix's will manifests an intention to include the property subject to the power.

(4)   Subject to the Rule Against Perpetuities

A power of appointment is subject to the Rule Against Perpetuities. It must become exercisable within the perpetuities period. Any interest that is created by the exercise of a special power of appointment is valid only if the interest will in all events vest, or fail to vest, no later than 21 years after the death of a life in being at the time the power was executed.

7)   ACCELERATION OF FUTURE INTERESTS

If a party disclaims a life estate or other future interest, the issue may arise of whether succeeding interests or estates accelerate in possession or enjoyment or whether the disclaimed interest must be marshaled to await the actual happening of a contingency. For example, assume that a grantor conveys an interest "to a first grantee for that grantee's life, then to a second grantee." If the first grantee disclaims the interest, must the second grantee await the first grantee's death to take possession? Generally, under those circumstances, remainder interests accelerate, and the "future interest" takes effect as if the disclaiming grantee had predeceased the grantor, and the contingent event was satisfied. A grantor may draft a written conveyance to avoid such an acceleration of future interests.

★★   **D.   The Law of Landlord and Tenant**

Question Key
32,78,82,87,115, 164,171

1)   <u>GENERAL</u>

Landlord and tenant law concerns leasehold estates when a landlord owns real property and a structure on that property while a tenant makes a payment in return for use and possession of the property and the structure that is upon it (i.e., a premises).

★   2)   <u>FITNESS AND SUITABILITY OF PREMISES</u>

a)   Implied Warranties

(1)   Common Law

The common law provides that residential leases include an implied warranty of habitability requiring that the premises be fit and suitable for basic human habitation. A few types of failures to maintain those standards include a lack of working plumbing, running water, or heat during the winter.

(2)   Codified Provisions

State statutes or regulations may provide express warranties regarding habitability, additional rights to report a violation of proper housing standards, and procedures to address such violations. These types of codified provisions may also protect a tenant who reports a landlord's failure to comply with the legal standards for housing.

(a)   Retaliation Prohibited

The codified provisions may preclude a landlord from responding to the reporting in any of the following ways: harassing a tenant, raising the rental cost, terminating the tenant's lease, or engaging in a retaliatory eviction.

3)   <u>TYPES OF HOLDINGS: CREATION AND TERMINATION</u>

a)   General

A tenant is entitled to possession of a landlord's rented premises for a period that is agreed upon under a lease agreement ("lease"). Such a rental contract provides a tenant with a leasehold estate or interest in the premises. There are four primary types of leasehold estates. The most common types tend to be either periodic tenancies or terms of years.

b)　　　Terms for Years

A term for years may be referred to as an estate for years or a tenancy for years because its duration is fixed and established. Notice of termination by either party to each other is not required for this type of lease because each party knows the termination date. For example, the lease might provide for a term of two years, at which time the lease would expire. The parties may add a notice requirement to the lease or provide an advance notice as a matter of courtesy.

c)　　　Tenancies at Will

A tenancy at will does not provide either party with any certainty of a fixed duration of a leasehold estate. Each of the parties may elect to terminate the estate at any time. A court will conclude that a tenancy at will exists if the parties neither have a lease nor a series of rental payments from which to imply that the leasehold existed for any term.

d)　　　Holdovers and Tenancies at Sufferance

A tenant who continues to occupy a landlord's premises beyond the expiration of a leasehold interest has holdover possession as a tenant at sufferance. A tenancy at sufferance only continues until either the landlord or tenant agrees to a new term, or the landlord evicts the tenant. The landlord is entitled to recover rent from a tenant at sufferance for the period between the end of the existing tenancy and the eviction date.

e)　　　Periodic Tenancies

A periodic tenancy runs for specified duration and may continue after that period for successive intervals until either party provides a notice of termination to the other party.

(1)　　　Notice of Termination Requirement

For example, the lease might run from month to month and only require a notice of termination one month in advance of that period's end date. If the lease runs from year to year, the common law requires that a party provide a notice of termination at least six months before the current year's end. Although the common law allowed oral notice, some statutes require written notice.

(2)　　　Creation

An agreement's express terms may create a periodic tenancy, or a court may imply and enforce a periodic tenancy from the parties' conduct with respect to the assessment and payment of rent.

f)   Incapacity or Death

In the majority of states, the incapacity or death of either party to a lease does not result in an automatic termination of the lease. Instead, the party's rights, interests, and obligations in the lease pass to his estate.

(1)   Enforceability of Lease

If a lease was valid, it is enforceable by or against the administrator of a deceased party's estate, such as a personal representative. For example, an estate may enforce a valid purchase option in a lease. The majority rule provides that the option is not subject to the Rule Against Perpetuities.

★★   4)   <u>ASSIGNMENT AND SUBLETTING</u>

a)   Nature and Characteristics

(1)   Assignment

An assignment arises when a tenant transfers all or some of the leased premises to another for the remainder of the lease term, retaining no interest in the assigned premises. Thus, when a third party receives a tenant's complete interest in a lease, including its remaining duration, the third party becomes an assignee. Absent an explicit provision that prohibits assignment, the parties to a lease may assign it by means of a writing that satisfies the Statute of Frauds. Without a written prohibition otherwise, a tenant may assign his interest without the consent of his landlord.

(a)   Enforceability of Prohibition

The courts will not enforce a lease's covenant against assignment when:

- an initial landlord provides consent to an assignment, which serves as consent to subsequent assignments; or
- an initial landlord waives the covenant by allowing an assignee to pay rent.

(b)   Purchase Option

A split of authority exists on the issue of whether a party may assign a purchase option in a lease independently from the lease.

(2)   Sublease

A sublease occurs when a third party and a tenant enter into their own agreement that does not include all of the interests reflected in the lease. The third party becomes a sub-lessee for a duration that generally is less than the full term of the tenancy. Absent an explicit provision in a lease that prohibits subleasing, the parties to the lease may sublet a premises by means of a writing that satisfies the Statute of Frauds. A sublease is less than a complete assignment of rights. For example, a sub-lessor may retain possession for the last day prior to the expiration of the main lease.

b)   Privity of Contract

Parties are each bound by a contract's terms when they are in privity. Thus, a party may sue another party for breach of contract if the parties possess privity of contract.

(1)   Assignment

Privity of a landlord and a tenant continues if either the landlord or the tenant assigns the lease to an assignee. As such, the tenant remains contractually obligated to pay the rent to the landlord.

(a)   Assignment by Landlord

A landlord may assign his interest as lessor to an assignee. Although an assignee and a landlord will be in privity of contract, a tenant will not be in privity with the assignee.

(b)   Assignment by Tenant

A tenant may assign his interest as lessee to an assignee. The assignee and the tenant will be in privity of contract. Also, the landlord will be in privity with the assignee.

(2)   Sublease

With respect to a sublease, a tenant and a landlord stay in privity of contract, and a tenant and a sub-lessee continue in privity of contract.

c)   Privity of Estate

A lease contains covenants that run with the land and to which a landlord and a tenant are bound. A tenant's covenant is to pay rent. A landlord's covenant is to maintain habitability. Thus, a party may sue another party for rent due or to maintain the premises as habitable if the parties possess privity of estate.

(1)   Assignment

An assignee and a tenant are in privity of estate if a landlord assigns the lease to the assignee. An assignee and a landlord are in privity of estate if a tenant assigns the lease to the assignee. In that event, the privity of estate between the original tenant and the landlord ends. An assignee and a landlord are in privity of estate as long as the assignee stays in possession of the property. Thus, an assignee is liable for any covenants that run with the lease such as the duty to pay rent, taxes, or insurance, etc.

(2)   Sublease

Privity of estate exists between a landlord and a tenant if the tenant subleases the premises to a sub-lessee.

d)   Consent

(1)   Assignment

By agreement, a tenant may need a landlord's consent to assign a lease to an assignee. A landlord does not generally need a tenant's consent to assign a lease to an assignee.

(2)   Sublease

A lease may provide that a landlord's consent is required for a tenant to sublease the premises.

(3)   Restraints on Alienation Disfavored

The law disfavors restraints on alienation. Thus, if a lease expressly required consent for assignment of the tenant's interest, without expressly addressing subletting, a court may conclude that subletting is permissible and vice-versa.

e)   Liability

A party who possesses privity of contract with another may seek to enforce the contractual provisions. If no privity of contract exists, a party may seek to enforce covenants that run with the land.

(1)   Assignment by Tenant

When a tenant assigns a lease, an assignee becomes liable to a landlord on all covenants that run with the land. The tenant continues to be liable on the lease's other covenants.

(2)   Assignment by Landlord

When a landlord assigns a lease, an assignee becomes liable to a tenant on all covenants that run with the land. The landlord continues to be liable on all covenants in the lease.

(3)   Sublease

A tenant is liable for all covenants in a lease and may enforce them. A sub-lessee is not liable for the covenants in a lease and cannot enforce them.

5)   RENT

    a)   General Considerations

A lease includes a tenant's obligation to pay rent to a landlord in order to possess an exclusive right to occupy the premises. The tenant neither obtains nor acquires an ownership interest in the premises as a result of paying rent.

    b)   Landlord's Remedies

        (1)   Tenant Out of Possession

When a tenant fails to pay rent during the term of a lease and while not in possession of the premises, then a landlord may respond in one of three ways.

- rent the premises as soon as possible while holding the tenant liable for any deficiency during the lease term;
- disregard the abandonment and hold the tenant liable for unpaid rent; or
- acknowledge the abandonment that the tenant had communicated.

        (2)   Tenant in Possession

When a tenant fails to pay rent while in possession of the premises, then a landlord may either sue to recover the unpaid rent or seek to evict the tenant.

            (a)   Self-Help Prohibited

When a tenant fails to pay rent while in possession of the premises, a landlord may not exercise self-help remedies against the tenant, such as changing the locks or forcibly removing the tenant's clothing or possessions from the premises.

    c)   Destruction of Premises

        (1)   Partial Occupancy

If a tenant only occupied part of a premises that was entirely destroyed, then the tenant's lease duty to pay rent ended when the destruction occurred.

        (2)   Total Occupancy

If the tenant occupied the entire premises that was completely destroyed, then the tenant's lease duty to pay rent will continue if the leased premises was comprised of both land and a building.

6)   SURRENDER,   MITIGATION   OF   DAMAGES,   & ANTICIPATORY BREACH

a)   Surrender

Surrender constitutes a premature ending of a leasehold interest in either of two ways:

- the parties mutually agree to terminate the leasehold; or
- the leasehold terminates due to the operation of law.

(1)   Agreement to Terminate

Under the Statute of Frauds, unilateral notice of surrender and a mutual surrender agreement must be in writing. Some courts interpret the Statute of Frauds as allowing for a verbal surrender if the remaining duration of a lease agreement is short enough to allow for the creation of a parol agreement. Certain statutes generally require a written surrender for most leaseholds except for those of a short duration.

(2)   Operation of Law

A termination of a lease by operation of law results when two conditions are fulfilled:

- a tenant engages in a non-verbal act of abandoning a premises; and
- a landlord accepts the premises back for his own account.

Abandonment of a premises does not, of itself, result in a surrender by operation of law. The landlord must also act. A landlord has several options in responding to a tenant's abandonment. The landlord may enter the premises and rent them for the tenant's account. By taking this action, the landlord may charge the tenant with the deficit between the lease's rent and the new rent received from another party. Alternatively, the landlord may accept the abandonment as a surrender of the leased property and enter the premises for his own account. Finally, the landlord may do nothing. As a result of doing nothing, the leasehold will remain, as will the duty of the tenant to pay rent.

b)   Mitigation of Damages

A landlord may incur a financial loss when a tenant abandons a leasehold without having fully paid for the remainder of its term.

(1)   No Duty to Mitigate is Majority Rule

The majority of case law does not apply the contract law doctrine of mitigation of damages when a landlord takes no action to find a new tenant after a former tenant abandons a leasehold. The *Restatement (Second) of Property* agrees with those cases, under which a landlord will not incur any legal detriment from doing nothing. Thus, a landlord lacks an affirmative legal duty to mitigate damages by means of seeking new tenants for abandoned premises.

(2)   Modern Trend Imposes Duty to Mitigate

The minority rule, and modern trend, applies the contract law doctrine to require a landlord to mitigate damages by again seeking to lease a premises for a tenant's account. The *Model Residential Landlord-Tenant Code* and the *Uniform Residential Landlord and Tenant Act* also require some mitigation of damages by a landlord.

          (3)   Impact of Attempt to Mitigate Damage

                (a)   For Landlord's Account

If a landlord attempts to mitigate damages by re-entering the premises for his own account, then a tenant's legal liability for unpaid rent ceases because operation of law ends the leasehold.

                (b)   For Tenant's Account

If a landlord attempts to mitigate damages to re-enter and re-let "for the tenant's account," then a tenant's legal liability for unpaid rent is reduced without ending the leasehold by operation of law.

        c)   Anticipatory Breach

          (1)   Definition

Anticipatory breach occurs when either party to a lease repudiates the lease or any of its promises, terms, or covenants before their scheduled performance. Examples of covenants that are subject to repudiation include those of quiet enjoyment and habitability.

          (2)   Remedies to Breach

A promisee may consider a promisor's repudiation as a breach and exercise any available remedies such as an action for damages or specific performance, as well as termination of the leasehold. The promisee's only requirement is to respond to the repudiation before the statute of limitations' expiration. The promisee may, however, ignore the repudiation unless doing so would increase the extent of the repudiating promisor's damages.

          (3)   Non-Breaching Party's Obligation

A promisee must prove that he was ready, willing, and able to perform in the absence of a promisor's repudiation. A repudiation relieves the promisee of any obligations under the lease. To be effective, words or conduct of repudiation must be definite and unequivocal.

          (4)   Retraction of Repudiation

The promisor may retract a repudiation before the promisee:

- acts in reliance on the repudiation;
- communicates an affirmative acceptance of the repudiation; or
- files a civil lawsuit.

★   7)   DUTIES

          a)   Landlord's Duties

              (1)   Covenant of Quiet Enjoyment

An implied covenant obligates a landlord to provide a tenant with quiet enjoyment of the premises that the tenant uses, whether the premises are residential or commercial. That duty of the landlord includes:

- exercising control of any common areas;
- not evicting the tenant either actually or constructively; and
- protecting against any superior claim of possession.

              (a)   Actual Eviction

A landlord is not permitted to wrongfully evict a tenant. If a landlord wrongfully evicts a tenant, the tenant may sue for trespass, ejectment, or may even treat the lease as terminated. The tenant's obligation to pay further rent terminates. Additionally, even if the landlord's eviction of the tenant is only partial, the tenant's obligation to pay rent ends.

              (b)   Constructive Eviction

                (i)   Untenantable Condition

Just as the landlord cannot wrongfully actually evict a tenant, a landlord cannot be responsible for actions that constructively evict the tenant. "[A] constructive eviction arises where a landlord, while not actually depriving the tenant of possession of any part of the premises leased, has done or suffered some act that renders the premises untenantable and has thereby caused a failure of consideration for the tenant's promise to pay rent. In addition to proving that the premises are untenantable, a party pleading constructive eviction must prove that (1) the landlord caused the problem, (2) the tenant vacated the premises because of the problem, and (3) the tenant did not vacate until after giving the landlord reasonable time to correct the problem." *Welsch v. Groat*, 897 A.2d 710 (Conn. Ct. App 2006).

For example, a landlord who refuses to provide heat in the winter or water to an apartment may be responsible for a constructive eviction of the tenant. The landlord's action, or failure to take action, must render the property untenantable (violating the covenant of quiet enjoyment).

                (ii)   Traceability to Landlord

In order to maintain an action for damages, the tenant must demonstrate that the uninhabitability resulted from the landlord's actions, not the actions of a third party, and that the tenant vacated the premises in a reasonable time.

(2)   Covenant of Possession

A landlord has a duty to provide a tenant with physical possession of a leased premises pursuant to a lease. If the landlord fails to timely deliver possession of the premises due to a holdover tenant or fails to adequately prepare the premises for occupancy, then the tenant is entitled to recover damages for that breach of the lease.

b)   Tenant's Duties

(1)   General Obligations

A tenant possesses the primary duty to pay rent in order to be entitled to occupy a premises. A constructive eviction caused by the landlord excuses that duty. A tenant has a duty not to use the premises for illegal purposes.

(2)   Maintenance Obligations

If a lease includes an explicit covenant that a tenant must maintain the premises in good condition, then the tenant is liable for any destruction or harm to the premises that occur while the tenant occupies the premises. If a lease lacks any terms or conditions with respect to the responsibility to repair the premises, then the tenant possesses an obligation not to commit waste and to keep the premises in reasonably good condition.

(3)   Repair Obligations

The common law provides that when a lease does not address repairs, a landlord, rather than a tenant, possesses the duty to repair the premises. If, however, a tenant's negligent harm to a premises leads to extensively damaging the premises, then the courts will consider it waste. In that event, the tenant would possess the duty to repair and not be excused from the duty to pay rent.

(a)   Premises Liability Issue

In certain states, a tenant may be liable for an invitee's injuries on the leased premises despite a landlord's promise to repair the premises. Other states permit an invitee to bring a lawsuit against a landlord if the landlord received written notice of the problem.

E.	**Special Problems**		Question Key 4,72,76,91,96,97,103, 118,123,126,127
★★★	1)	<u>RULE AGAINST PERPETUITIES</u>	
	a)	General Considerations	

The Rule Against Perpetuities (Rule) is partially based on the concept that living people, and not deceased people, should control the disposition of property interests. The Rule is a clear expression of the common law's abhorrence of things uncertain. The Rule derives its name from the fact that it limits the duration of legal interests that suspend property rights in perpetuity. The common law prefers certainty in property rights and that property be fully owned by just one person at a time.

(1)   21-Year Standard

The common law will tolerate temporary contingent interests for a certain time only. Under the common law rule against perpetuities, that limitation on the duration of temporary contingent interests is no longer than 21 years after the death of a life in being at the time of the initial conveyance. If an interest in property continues to be contingent after that period, it is considered void under the Rule.

(a)   Applicable to Executory Interests

If the Rule renders an executory interest like a fee simple determinable with a vested remainder void, then courts will consider that estate a fee simple determinable with an implied possibility of reverter back to a grantor or the grantor's successors. In other words, the prohibited executory interest will fail.

b)   Common Law Rule

The Rule states that an interest must vest, if at all, within 21 years of the death of a life in being at the time of the interest's creation. If there is any possibility, no matter how remote, that the interest will not vest, or will fail to vest, within the time period, then the conveyance will be void as violating the Rule Against Perpetuities.

An interesting and educational way of looking at the Rule is to put it in modern terms. If you are going "to delay some gift, either by will or while you're still alive, full title has to land fair and square within 21 years after the death of a person alive at the time of the gift.'" *Duhaime Law*, at http://www.duhaime.org.

(1)   Scope of Application

The Rule is applicable to contingent remainders (not vested remainders as they are already vested), executory interests, powers of appointment, and options to purchase land. The Rule does not apply to interests that the grantor retains, such as a reversion or the possibility of reverter.

(a)   Charitable Conveyances Exception

The charity-to-charity exception to the Rule applies if a second charitable organization will receive a contingent future interest from a first charitable organization. Such a conveyance will not be subject to the Rule.

c)   Rule Analysis Example

Let us examine how the rule may arise in practice. Suppose a grantor conveys an estate "to a grantee for life, then to the grantee's first child who marries and the heirs of that child." The grantee is alive when the devise is made, but the grantee does not have any children. One should consider the following factors when analyzing this example under the Rule:

(1)   Is the property interest at issue subject to the Rule?

In the above situation, the grantee received a life estate, and any unborn children may receive a contingent remainder because no children are ascertainable, and a condition precedent must be satisfied.

(2)   On what date does the perpetuities period commence?

The effective date of an instrument that creates an interest in property is the starting date of the perpetuities period. In the above situation, a "devise" by the grantor indicates that the instrument that created the property interest is a will. The will's effective date is the day of the grantor's death.

(3)   Must a condition precedent occur before a future interest vests?

The important inquiry is if any event must occur before an interest will vest in a grantee. It does not matter if any event must occur before the grantee obtains possession. With respect to a class gift, all of the class members' interests must be valid before that gift will take effect. Because the condition precedent requires that a child of the grantee get married, the interest may fail if the grantee does not have children or such children do not marry.

(4)   Determine whose lives were in being on the instrument's effective date.

In other words, which of the potential devisees were alive on that date? Such devisees, if any, were either born before that date or in gestation on that date and will affect the vesting of the interest. In the above situation, only the grantor and the grantee were alive when the will became effective. Thus, either may be a life in being when applying the test.

(5)   Will validation of the interest timely occur?

The critical question is if the interest would vest or fail with respect to the lives in being during their lifetimes plus 21 years. If the interest could, under any possible scenario, vest or fail to vest outside of this period (21 years after the death of a life in being), the interest will be invalid under the Rule.

Therefore, for the interest to be valid under the Rule, there must be no possible scenario under which the contingent remainder vests, or fails to vest, more than 21 years after the death of a life in being (in this case either the grantor or grantee).

In order to reach the appropriate conclusion, one must experiment with the lives in being and determine whether there is a chance that the interest could vest, or fail to, more than 21 years after the death of a life in being. Let us return to our example. Remember, the grantor conveys the estate "to a grantee for life, then to the grantee's first child who marries and the heirs of that child." In the example, the grantee is alive with no children at the time of the conveyance. Of course, the grantee can have a child (or children) after the conveyance. Is it possible for the grantee to have a child marry more than 21 years after the grantee's death? Of course it is. For example, the grantee can have a child two years after the conveyance. The grantee can then die. Thirty years later (more than 21 years after his death), that child may marry. Thus, the interest may vest more than 21 years after the death of a life in being (the grantee). Therefore, the interest violates the Rule Against Perpetuities.

Remember, the rule does not provide that an interest is valid if it can somehow vest within 21 years of the death of a life in being. On the contrary, the interest will fail if the interest can somehow vest (or fail to) more than 21 years from the death of a life in being.

d) Wait and See Rule

Many states have reformed the harsh common law Rule and have taken a "wait and see" approach. Under those state statutes, a court will wait out the perpetuities period to determine if an interest at issue actually vests or fails within the period. In contrast, the harsh common law Rule would invalidate an interest if it is merely possible that the interest may vest or fail after the period.

e) *Cy Pres* Doctrine

In some jurisdictions by statute, under the *Cy Pres* doctrine, a court may reform a non-vested interest to assure that it will vest within the permissible period. In exercising this reformation power, the statutes direct the courts to reform the non-vested interest to most closely approximate the intention of the grantor of an interest in order that the non-vested interest will vest during the perpetuities period.

f) Other Reforms

A modern trend exists to reform the rigid common law Rule Against Perpetuities.

Some states have implemented a statute that repeals the Rule. These statutes may be based on the *Uniform Statutory Rule Against Perpetuities* (USRAP). The USRAP will validate interests that: 1) would satisfy the common law rule; or 2) would vest or fail within 90 years after the creation of an interest.

g) Shelley's Case

Most jurisdictions have abolished the Rule in Shelley's Case. It concerned conveyances which provided: "to Gertrude for life, then to Gertrude's heirs." The rule operated to merge the life estate in a person and a remainder interest in the person's heirs. As a result of the merger, for example, Gertrude would obtain both the life estate and the remainder. By operation of law, the Rule in Shelley's Case resulted in Gertrude possessing a fee simple absolute.

★   2)   ALIENABILITY,   DESCENDABILITY,   AND
                   DEVISEABILITY

Both absolute estates, such as fee simple estates, and qualified estates, such as future interests, are generally transferable (i.e., alienable, descendible, and devisable).

                   a)   Restraints on Alienation —

| Question Key |
| 72 |

The law disfavors restraints on alienation. A restraint on alienation is a restriction on a grantee's right to sell or transfer real property. Courts will only permit a restraint on alienation if it is reasonable and for a legitimate purpose and will strike down any unreasonable or undue restraint. Courts have considered keeping land ownership within a family to be a reasonable purpose.

                           (1)   Invalid Restraints on Alienation

                                    (a)   Indefinite Restraints

The common law generally prohibits restraints on alienation of fee simple estates unless reasonable and for a legitimate purpose. For example, a restraint that violates public policy will not be enforceable. Additionally, the common law usually does not countenance a forfeiture restraint that lacks any limitations upon its scope and duration. For example, suppose O conveys Blackacre "to Gary, provided that Blackacre is never sold to a person who owns a red car." The restriction, which lacks any limitation upon its scope and duration, is invalid. As a consequence, Gary possesses a fee simple absolute.

                                    (b)   Unconstitutional Restraints on
                                             Alienability

Even if a restraint on alienability is only applicable for a reasonable duration, courts will generally not enforce a restraint that discriminates against an individual or entity based on a constitutionally protected classification, such as race or religion.

II.   RIGHTS IN LAND

| Question Key |
| 13,21,25,47,65,66,81,89,90, |
| 100,101,109,110,128,150,166 |

★★★★   **A.   Covenants at Law and In Equity**

        1)   DEFINITION

A restrictive covenant is a legal obligation imposed in a deed by the grantor upon the grantee of real estate to do or not to do something. These restrictions may "run with the land" and, as such, are enforceable on subsequent buyers of the property. Examples of restrictive covenants include a duty to maintain a property in a reasonable state of repair, to preserve a sight-line for a neighboring property, not to run a business from a residence, or not to build on certain parts of the property. A covenant restricts the manner in which a parcel of land may be used.

To be binding, the grantor must place a restrictive covenant on property at the time it is conveyed. Someone who has no interest in the property cannot attach the burden to the property after the conveyance.

2)   COVENANTS AT LAW

A covenant "at law" is a covenant that can only be enforced for damages, not in equity. If a party seeks to enforce the provisions of a covenant, they may only enforce them through a covenant "at equity," called an equitable servitude. Equitable servitudes are discussed below.

a)   Nature and Characteristics

(1)   General

A covenant is a promise regarding a promisee's conduct with respect to real property. An affirmative covenant is the promise to do some act. A negative covenant is the promise to refrain from doing some act. For example, a covenant may prohibit the use of a parcel for a specific purpose, such as for a brothel.

(2)   Compared to Easements

Covenants are sometimes referred to as "negative easements" because they are comparable to easements. For example, a beneficiary of a covenant may not enter upon the burdened property, but may require the servient property's owner to do or not do something on that property.

(3)   Applicability of Zoning Ordinances

Zoning ordinances do not override a private restrictive covenant. The stricter of either the zoning ordinance or the covenant will prevail.

b)   Creation

A covenant often both provides a benefit to a promisee and imposes a burden on a promisor. The benefit is the promisee's receipt of a promised performance. The burden is the promisor's obligation to fulfill the promise.

c)   Classification of Interests

(1)   Covenants Running with Land

An initial promisee and promisor may enforce a restrictive covenant. The issue of whether the successors in interest ("successors") of an initial promisor and promisee may enforce the covenant depends on whether the covenant runs with any estates in land that the initial promisee and promisor convey to their successors. The lands at issue are either burdened or benefited, and they may either exist within the same or different estates.

(2)   Burdens Running with Land

The following elements are necessary for a burden to run with the land:

- A covenant is in writing;
- The intent of the initial promisee and promisor is for the covenant to run with the estates in land;
- The covenant relates to, or touches and concerns, the estates in land;
- The initial promisee and promisor are in horizontal privity; and
- The successors of the promisee and the promisor are in vertical privity.

The first two elements are straightforward and thus require no elaboration.

(a)   Touch and Concern

The "touch and concern" element applies if:

- the burden diminishes the use and enjoyment of the servient estate; or
- the burden increases the use and enjoyment of the benefited estate.

C. Clark, *Real Covenants and Other Interests Which "Run With Land* 97 (2d ed. 1947), states that: "If the promisor's legal relations in respect to the land in question are lessened—his legal interest as owner rendered less valuable by the promise—the burden of the covenant touches or concerns that land; if the promisee's legal relations in respect to that land are increased—his legal interest as owner rendered more valuable by the promise—the benefit of the covenant touches or concerns that land."

(b)   Horizontal Privity

The element of horizontal privity means that the initial promisor and promisee were connected in terms of their relationship, such as mortgagor and mortgagee, grantor and grantee, or landlord and tenant.

(c)   Vertical Privity

The element of vertical privity means that a connection exists between the initial promisor and promisee and their successors. For vertical privity to exist, an original promisor and each subsequent grantor must have conveyed an entire estate to each successor.

(3)   Benefits Running with Land

The following elements are necessary for a benefit to run with an estate in land ("estate") and benefit the successors:

- A covenant is in writing;
- The intent of the initial promisee and promisor is for the covenant to run with the estate;
- The covenant relates to, or touches and concerns, the estate; and
- The successors of the promisee and the promisor are in vertical privity.

TEST TIP The required elements for a benefit to run with the land in a covenant at law do not include the element of horizontal privity, which is required for a burden to run with the land in a covenant at law.

d)   Rights of Possession and Use

(1)   Covenants Running with Land

A conveyance from an initial promisee and promisor to their successors will be effective and provide for an enforceable covenant when the covenant runs with an estate.

(a)   Duration

A covenant may specify when it will end or provide a method of determining when it will end.

(2)   Rights of Successor in Interest

A successor in interest to a parcel of land may invoke rights under a covenant if:

- the successor of the burdened land received constructive, inquiry, or actual notice of the covenant;
- the covenant touches and concerns the land at issue; and
- sufficient evidence indicates that the necessary intent existed to bind successors and assigns.

(a)   Sufficient Evidence Requirement

If a covenant expressly states that the parties to it intended the covenant to run to successors and assigns, it satisfies the element of sufficient evidence. For example, a covenant might provide that every buyer of a lot in a subdivision must pay an annual fee to maintain its recreation area. Such a provision is a way to minimize potential litigation.

e)   Legal Remedies

(1)   Covenant Enforcement

The only means of enforcing rights under a covenant at law is to file a lawsuit seeking damages. No equitable remedies are available.

(2)   Covenant Avoidance

The change of neighborhood doctrine provides for judicial relief from a covenant if the neighborhood has sufficiently changed so that a court should either not enforce the covenant or consider it terminated. A test that courts use to apply the doctrine provides that:

- a change in a neighborhood has rendered;
- a covenant outmoded;
- its usefulness lost;
- its benefits substantially lost; and
- judicial enforcement of the covenant would be inequitable.

Some courts hold that changes in zoning and decreased value in benefited land are only evidence that indicates a change of neighborhood but do not serve to conclusively establish that the change occurred.

(3)   Deed as Basis of Enforcement

A deed may provide an owner of a parcel in a subdivision an independent right to enforce the restrictive covenants with respect to all other deeds in the subdivision.

(4)   Third Party Enforcement

An unintended and incidental third-party beneficiary lacks any basis to legally enforce at law a covenant running with the land. Similarly, a covenant running with the land is not enforceable at law against remote grantees. The parties must be in privity to enforce at law a covenant running with the land.

(5)   Unconstitutional Restrictions

Courts may determine that a restrictive covenant violates the equal protection clause of the Fourteenth Amendment to the *U.S. Constitution* unless "it can be shown that the particular classification involved in the unequal treatment of individuals bears some rational relationship to a permissible state objective." Allan E. Korpela, LL.B., Annotation, *Validity and Construction of Covenant Restricting Occupancy of Premises to Person Over or Under Specified Age*, 68 A.L.R.3d 1239 at 1241 (1976). Courts generally will not enforce restrictions based on protected classes because to do so would constitute state action in violation of the Fourteenth Amendment.

3)   COVENANTS IN EQUITY (EQUITABLE SERVITUDES)

a)   Nature and Characteristics

Covenants that run in equity are also known as equitable servitudes. They are promises and/or agreements regarding the use of real property that bind an initial promisor and promisee and their successors. Whether these successors may enforce the servitude depends on whether its covenant(s) run with the land that the initial promisee and promisor convey to their successors. If the covenant runs with the land, courts may consider it a cloud or "burden" on the title to the land. In that event, the covenant is not personally limited in its application to the initial promisor and promisee. When an equitable restriction runs with the burdened property, one can describe it as being rooted in that land.

b)   Creation

The Statute of Frauds applies to equitable servitudes because they affect interests in land and consequently must be in writing to be enforceable.

(1)   Burden Running with Land

The following elements are necessary for a burden to run with the land:

- A promise that is in writing;
- The initial promisee and promisor intended for the promise to be enforceable;
- The promise relates to, or touches and concerns, the land; and
- The successors of the promisee and the promisor have notice of the promise.

Unlike restrictive covenants, equitable servitudes that burden the land do not include the element of horizontal privity.

(2)   Benefit Running with Land

The following elements are necessary for a benefit to run with the land and bind the successors:

- A covenant that is in writing;
- The initial promisee and promisor intended that the promise be enforceable; and
- The promise relates to, or touches and concerns, the land.

c)   Classification of Interests

(1)   Distinguishing an Equitable Servitude

The remedy for a breach that a dominant estate owner possesses distinguishes an equitable servitude from a covenant running with the land. If the owner seeks damages, the owner must demonstrate the requirements for a covenant running with the land. If the owner requests equitable relief such as an injunction, the owner must establish the elements of an equitable servitude.

(2)   Types of Equitable Servitudes

(a)   Affirmative

A covenant to perform an affirmative act is a type of equitable servitude that may not necessarily touch and concern the land. Whether such a covenant touches and concerns the land may depend on if, or to what extent, the act affects the land.

(b)   Negative

Negative equitable servitudes impose prohibitions that will touch and concern the land.

(c)   In Gross

If an equitable servitude involves a benefit in gross to an estate, the benefit cannot run with the land. The term "in gross" means that a party that does not own adjacent land and may not even own any land receives the benefit of the servitude.

(3)   Implied Reciprocal Servitudes

An implied reciprocal servitude exists under the general or common scheme doctrine. It exists when a builder of property or real estate developer subdivides a large parcel of land into equally-sized lots. Grantors initially sell and convey those lots using a deed containing a restrictive covenant limiting use of the lots, generally for single-family dwellings. If a subsequent buyer receives such a deed for such a lot that lacks the restrictive covenant language, then the other owners may seek and obtain injunctive relief against the building of anything other than a single-family dwelling on the lot.

The parties for whom the benefit of the restrictive covenant are intended (typically other lot owners) may enforce the restrictive covenants on others similarly bound. Enforcement of such covenants, however, rests upon the existence of a common plan.

(a)   Analysis of Enforceability

The test to determine if an implied reciprocal servitude is generally enforceable is if:

- A lot was originally part of a parcel held in common ownership;
- The lot was subject to a common building plan or scheme involving a use restriction; and
- A buyer of a deed to the lot possessed inquiry notice of the use restriction.

(i)   Bases of Inquiry Notice

The following factors may provide inquiry notice:

- physical evidence that a subdivision only includes single-family homes; and
- the restriction's existence in recorded deeds,

even if a developer failed to record a map, plan or plat of the subdivision.

d)   Equitable Remedies

(1)   General

Most modern litigation involving covenants running with the land is based upon equitable servitudes and seeks an equitable remedy, rather than seeking to obtain enforcement of restrictive covenants to recover a legal (money) remedy.

(2)   Equitable Servitude Enforcement

The means of enforcing an equitable servitude is to file an action in equity seeking injunctive relief for the following reasons:

- legal remedies are inadequate;
- to halt a current breach of an equitable servitude; and
- to prevent any future breach of the equitable servitude.

(3)   Implied Reciprocal Servitudes Exception

The courts may grant injunctive relief on the basis that an implied reciprocal servitude exists. This exception is to the general rule that equitable servitudes, like restrictive covenants, must satisfy the Statute of Frauds to be enforceable. Otherwise, usually if no restriction on land use is written in a recorded deed, the courts cannot enforce that restriction at law or in equity.

(4)   Third Party Enforcement

An unintended and incidental third-party beneficiary lacks any basis to legally enforce an equitable servitude. The parties need not have privity to enforce an equitable servitude.

B.   **Easements, Profits, and Licenses**

1)   <u>GENERAL</u>

The law originally referred to easements and profits as "incorporeal hereditaments," which meant a "non-possessory" and "inheritable" estate. Easements, profits, and licenses are considered non-physical interests in land.

a)   Reduced Right of Possession

Easements, profits, and licenses are considered servitudes on the possessory interests in land. Thus, an owner of land that is subject to a servitude relinquishes the right of exclusive possession in favor of the holder of a servitude. Easements, profits, and licenses exist separately from, and are created in addition to, the "natural rights" that arise from land ownership.

★★★★   2)   EASEMENTS

Question Key
3,5,9,33,38,60,61,68,69,79,80,
83,111,136,137,142,164

a)   Nature and Characteristics

An easement is a limited right to access the real property of another.

(1)   Limited Right

An easement ordinarily exists when an owner of property grants to a non-owner of property (an easement holder) a restricted right to use or access that property. Examples of easements include driveways, walkways, and utility routes. Certain criteria, such as duration or particular purpose, may restrict the scope of use or access of an easement.

(a)   Duration

An easement may exist perpetually, for a specified duration, or for as long as it is required to continue based on the nature of the easement.

(2)   Types of Estates

The property that the easement benefits is the dominant estate. The property that is burdened by an easement is the servient estate.

(3)   Statute of Frauds

A written easement's creation generally is subject to the Statute of Frauds. The Statute, however, does not prevent the creation of an oral easement by means of a verbal conveyance or oral agreement to convey property interests.

b)   Creation

Grantors may use several different methods to create easements. For example, a reservation in a deed that conveys an interest of property from a grantor to a grantee may create an easement. The method of creation depends upon the type of easement.

(1)   Easement by Grant

A conveyance of a deed from a grantor to a grantee that allows a grantee to use the property may establish an easement by grant. To be valid, an easement by grant must:

- be written;
- be executed by a grantor;
- express the grantor's intent to provide an easement to a grantee;
- adequately describe the land that is subject to the easement; and
- identify the grantor and the grantee.

(2)   Easement by Necessity

Judicial proceedings may create a strict necessity easement. A party must make a strong showing of strict necessity for such an easement when the use and enjoyment of land in a dominant estate, which is adjacent to a servient estate, would be unavailable without that easement upon the servient estate. In other words, there is no other means of ingress or egress to the dominant estate's land. In that event, a party need not show proof of pre-existing use.

When such an easement by "way of necessity" is warranted, a court will require a servient estate's owner to make a conveyance of an easement to the party. Such an easement arises when:

- A conveyance by a grantor;
- severs part of the grantor's land into two or more parcels; and
- one of those parcels lacks access to a public road.

A strict necessity easement does not need to be in writing to be enforceable. The grant or conveyance implies this type of easement. In other words, it is implied that the grantor would have provided the grantee of a land-locked parcel with access to a public road.

(3)   Easement by Implication

An implied easement results from a non-owner's ongoing, permitted, and lawful use of an owner's estate. Although no express agreement creates such easements, they may be reduced to writing and/or judicially inferred from prior use if all essential facts exist. For example, a property development plat may provide a buyer of a parcel in that property development an implied private easement. Such an easement may allow for the use of common areas and ways of access that exist in that property development.

(a)   Subdivision Example

When lots are sold in a subdivision containing streets that access the lots, those lots include implied, appurtenant easements to use the streets for ingress and egress to their lots. This rule is an exception to the general rule that an existing use must result in an implied easement. The law usually does not permit the holder of an implied easement to improve or upgrade it further than the parties who established the easement reasonably contemplated at the time of its creation.

(4)   Easement by Prescription

Prescriptive easements allow a non-owner of an estate who is using an owner's estate to obtain a legal right to use the estate if the non-owner fulfills these conditions:

- The non-owner engages in open and notorious use of the estate;
- The non-owner's use of the estate is hostile (no permission);
- The non-owner's use of the estate is continuous; and
- The non-owner's use is uninterrupted for a legally-required period (depends upon the jurisdiction).

(a)   Requirement of Use

Some states may require that the non-owner engage in actual use of the property to obtain a prescriptive easement upon it. The doctrine of prescriptive easement focuses on the element of use, as compared with the adverse possession doctrine's focus upon the element of possession. Both doctrines may, for example, apply to an access driveway. In that case, the factual situation will determine if an adverse claimant is entitled to just use of, or full possession of, the driveway.

c)   Classification of Interests

(1)   Appurtenant Compared to In Gross

(a)   Appurtenant Easement

An appurtenant easement is an easement that is attached to a dominant estate. An owner of dominant property and an owner of servient property may create an appurtenant easement by an express written or verbal agreement. The owner of the dominant property may reasonably exercise rights that are created by and arise from the easement after it is created. This owner, as the easement holder, receives the benefit of physical use of a servient estate. The fact that those estates are adjacent does not, of itself, establish that the dominant estate owner is the holder of an appurtenant easement.

(b)   Easements in Gross

Easements in gross belong to and are attached to an easement holder. An easement in gross is not attached to its holder's real property; it only burdens a servient estate. An easement in gross benefits no dominant estate. Easements in gross, for example, authorize utility companies to place their conduits on or in an owner's property.

(i)   Creation

Operation of law or an express written or verbal agreement by an owner of servient property and either a non-owner of property or an owner of non-adjacent property may create an easement in gross. The non-owner of property or owner of non-adjacent property may reasonably exercise rights that are created by and arise from the easement after it is created.

(2)   Affirmative and Negative Easements

(a)   Affirmative Easements

Affirmative easements empower a dominant estate owner to engage in permissible conduct on the servient estate. For example, affirmative easements may enable a dominant estate owner to cross the servient estate for the purposes of ingress and egress. Generally, a written easement needs specific language to that effect to establish the appurtenant nature of those crossings. An example of an appurtenant easement is an access road that allows ingress and egress to its holder's estate by the holder, invitees, and licensees.

(b)   Negative Easements

Negative easements authorize a dominant estate's owner to prevent a servient estate's owner from engaging in some otherwise permissible conduct on the servient estate. Negative easements, for example, preclude a servient estate owner from erecting a barrier that prevents a dominant estate owner from crossing the servient estate for ingress and egress.

d)   Rights of Possession and Use

(1)   General Considerations

An easement is a right of use of land without a right of possession. For example, an affirmative easement would be a property owner's grant of permission to a holder to freely roam the property for recreational purposes. An example of a permissible negative easement is one that provides a dominant estate's owner with a right against interference with "light, air, and view."

(2)   Duration of Easements

The language that is used to establish an easement may determine the easement's duration. If the easement is created in a manner other than in writing, then its duration will depend upon the circumstances that surround its creation. For example, if a structure on a servient estate is essential to an easement, then the structure's destruction will end the easement. An easement is extinguished when the same party owns both of its estates.

(3)   Maintaining Easements

The holder of an express easement possesses a duty to maintain the easement. That holder also possesses a right to enter upon the servient estate's land to make reasonable repairs of an easement. The servient estate owner may not prohibit such repairs.

(4)   Alienability of Easements

The transferability of easements depends on the type of easement involved.

(a)   Easements in Gross

Easements in gross are alienable and may only be transferred if they are for a commercial purpose.

(b)   Appurtenant Easements

Appurtenant easements are subject to, and included with, a conveyance of a dominant estate. They also are usually conveyed with a servient estate unless the buyer lacks notice of the easement and buys the premises in good faith.

(i)   Dominant Estate

An appurtenant easement may only benefit the dominant estate to which it is appurtenant. If the easement holder uses the easement to benefit any other property, directly or indirectly, the courts may extinguish the easement.

(ii)   Servient Estate

A property owner of a servient estate is entitled to use the land in a manner that does not unreasonably or unduly interfere with an easement. The holder of an easement is not necessarily entitled to an exclusive right to use the area that is subject to the easement. That area may be subject to concurrent use.

(5)   Modification of Easements

In order to accommodate change, parties may make reasonable modifications to express rights of easement that are generally described. An easement may also, however, prohibit modifications.

(6)   Termination of Easements

(a)   Abandonment

Abandonment of an easement may result from non-use by its holder and the holder's demonstrated intention not to use the servient estate again. Note that non-use is not enough. The party must also demonstrate an intention not to use the servient estate again. For example, a railroad company might not have used its easement for many years and could remove the train tracks that are upon it. The removal of the tracks would demonstrate the intent not to use the servient estate again.

(b)   Release

A written release of an easement by its holder to the servient estate's owner will end the easement.

(c)   Adverse Possession

Adverse possession of an easement by the servient estate owner will terminate the easement if he fulfills the following elements: adverse interests, actual use, open use, notorious use, hostile use, non-permissive use, and continuous use, for the statutory period.

(d)   Destruction

Destruction of a servient estate will end an easement.

(e)   Condemnation

Condemnation of a servient estate by a government will end an easement.

(f)   Necessity

Necessity for an easement may end, and consequently the easement will expire.

(g)   Estoppel

Estoppel will end an easement when an easement holder communicates to the easement owner that the easement will not be enforced, and the estate owner acts in reasonable reliance upon that assurance.

(h)   Merger

Merger of both the dominant and the servient estates will end an easement. A merger results when the owner of the dominant estate obtains title to the servient estate. As a general rule, an owner of an estate cannot own an easement on the estate.

(i)   Misuse

Misuse of an easement does not usually terminate the easement but may give rise to claims for legal or equitable remedies.

e)   Legal and Equitable Remedies

(1)   Legal Remedies

(a)   Actions to Construe Easements

Legal proceedings may be necessary to interpret and determine the scope of easements.

(b)   Actions for Damages

(i)   Injury to Land

(A)   Unavoidable
Harm

If a dominant estate owner reasonably exercises a right to repair an easement, which results in unavoidable or necessary harm to a servient estate, the servient estate's owner cannot complain about the harm in order to recover damages.

(B)   Unreasonable
Harm

The servient estate owner may, however, recover damages from a dominant estate owner for injury to its land due to unreasonable harm that resulted from repairs of an easement that the dominant estate holder made. The damages are usually limited to the amount that is required to restore the land to its pre-existing condition.

(ii)   Tort Liability

If a holder of an express easement negligently breaches the holder's duty to maintain the easement, the holder may have tort liability for any consequent injury to property, persons, or deaths.

(2)   Equitable Remedies

(a)   Actions for Injunctive Relief

Proceedings in equity may be necessary to obtain injunctive relief regarding an easement.

With respect to prescriptive and implied easements, the majority rule is that the use of an easement that was intended for accessing a first parcel of land, but the grantee instead used to access a second parcel of land, automatically constitutes an "overburdening" of the easement, and the owner of the servient estate may enjoin its use.

(b)   Actions to Enforce Oral Easements

Courts may enforce an easement arising from a verbal conveyance or oral agreement to convey property interests on two equitable grounds. The equitable doctrines of part performance and estoppel allow for such enforcement of this exception to the Statute of Frauds. Those doctrines apply under these circumstances:

- an oral grantor informs an oral grantee that;
- the grantee possessed an easement or profit on certain land;
- the grantee relied on the grantor's representation; and
- the grantee acted in detrimental reliance upon the representation by;
- spending funds, engaging in labor, or improving the easement or profit.

3)   <u>PROFITS</u>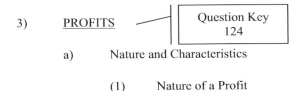

Question Key
124

   a)   Nature and Characteristics

        (1)   Nature of a Profit

A profit (i.e., a *profit à prendre*) is a legal right to enter onto certain real property ("property"), that is a servient estate, and to remove natural resources from this property such as minerals, timber, or wildlife.

        (2)   Characteristics of a Profit

A valid profit usually includes these features:

- a written instrument;
- a certain duration;
- a particular area;
- a payment of significant consideration;
- the ability to exert control over the interest by improvements; and
- not being terminable at will by an owner.

                (a)   Duration

A profit exists either perpetually or for a duration that the language used to establish it specifies.

                (b)   Statute of Frauds

The Statute of Frauds requires a legally sufficient written document to establish and enforce a profit.

   b)   Creation

A reservation in a deed that conveys some interest in property from a grantor to a grantee may create a profit.

   c)   Classification of Interests

There are two main types of profits.

        (1)   Profit Appurtenant

A profit appurtenant provides benefits to an owner of a dominant estate that arise from, and are inseparable from, a parcel of land that belongs to an owner of a servient estate. The fact that those estates are adjacent does not, of itself, establish that the dominant estate owner is the holder of a profit appurtenant. An instrument of conveyance must contain specific language to that effect to establish the appurtenant nature of the profit.

(2)   Profit in Gross

A profit in gross provides benefits that only personally serve its holder and are separate from the profit holder's use or ownership of any property. A profit in gross usually involves the removal of a natural resource from property. It does not include a dominant estate in addition to a servient estate. Sometimes the holder of a profit in gross may not own property that the servient estate benefits.

d)   Rights of Possession and Use

(1)   Rights of a Profit Holder

(a)   Possession and Use

A profit is a right of use of land without a right of possession. Thus, a profit holder lacks a right to possess the property that is subject to the profit. Instead, the profit holder has only the right to take certain resources from the property.

(b)   Alienability

A profit in gross is transferable. The intent of a grantor of a profit in gross is determinative of whether a non-exclusive profit is divisible. A transfer of a profit to two or more persons who will use a profit "as one stock" for business purposes is not a prohibited division of the profit.

(c)   Termination

A written release of a profit by its holder to the servient estate owner will end the profit.

(2)   Rights of a Property Owner

(a)   Use

The owner of a servient estate has the right to use the land in a manner that does not unreasonably or unduly interfere with a profit.

(b)   Possession

Like easements, a profit imposes a burden on a servient estate owner's right of possession. In that respect, profits are generally subject to the rules governing easements.

e)   Legal and Equitable Remedies

The courts generally seek to allow a proper use of a profit by its holder while disallowing or sanctioning its improper use.

    (1)   Legal Remedies

        (a)   Property Owner's Remedies

The legal remedies that are available to a property owner for an improper use of a profit by a profit holder may include a recovery of damages or a termination of the profit.

        (b)   Profit Holder's Remedies

A profit holder may bring an action to receive compensation from a government that takes that property interest by condemnation using the power of eminent domain.

    (2)   Equitable Remedies

The equitable remedies that a property owner may seek for an improper use of a profit may include injunctive relief from a profit holder's use of the profit.

★   4)   <u>LICENSES</u>

Question Key
64,146

    a)   Nature and Characteristics

    (1)   Nature of a License

A property owner or possessor may grant a license that enables a non-owner of a property, as a license holder, to access the property for a particular reason and duration. A license is "[a]n authority to do a particular act or series of acts upon the land of another without possessing any estate or interest therein." *Black's Law Dictionary* (3rd Ed.) A license protects a non-owner from being considered a trespasser while on the owner's property. Some examples of a license would be a temporary parking permit or a ticket for admission to an entertainment event.

    (2)   Characteristics

        (a)   General Elements

The following features identify a license:

- a specified or uncertain duration;
- a particular or general area;
- a payment of minimal consideration to obtain access;
- the inability to control a property interest by improvements or repairs; and
- terminable at will by an owner, unless it is irrevocable.

(b)   Additional Terms

A license may provide that it exists for, and ends at, the expiration of a limited duration. A license may include disclaimers of warranty regarding premises liability or responsibility for personal injury or death on the premises.

b)   Creation

(1)   Verbal or Written Licenses

The Statute of Frauds does not apply to a license because a license is not considered an interest in land. A license may be verbally granted or be reflected in a formal writing or by a ticket of admission into, or onto, a premises.

c)   Classification of Interests

(1)   Revocable License

A mere license is revocable earlier than anticipated at the will of a property owner, either by verbal or written means.

(2)   Irrevocable License

A license coupled with an interest is irrevocable for a reasonable duration.

(a)   License Coupled with an Interest

A license coupled with an interest is a privilege incidental to the ownership of an interest in a personal property located on the land with respect to which the license exists. For example, suppose Bill lets Ted borrow his snow blower. Ted tells Bill, "Feel free to take it from my garage." As a result, Bill possesses a license coupled with an interest.

(b)   Executed License

An executed license, which is a license pursuant to which some action has been taken, such as the expending of money or labor, is irrevocable.

d)   Rights of Possession and Use

(1)   Non-Owner's Rights

A license is a non-owner's limited privilege of access upon, and right' to use and occupy, a property owner's land or premises. A license does not convey any right to possess the land.

(2)   Owner's Rights

A property owner possesses the right not to issue a license. A property owner may only revoke a license under certain circumstances. The doctrine of estoppel prevents a property owner from revoking a license if a non-owner makes an expenditure in reliance on the license. Similarly, a license that a non-owner executes provides an easement by estoppel that the property owner cannot revoke if the non-owner reasonably relies on the license to its detriment.

        e)   Legal and Equitable Remedies

           (1)   Legal Remedy

A recovery of damages is a property owner's legal remedy for a non-owner's improper use of a license.

           (2)   Equitable Remedy

Injunctive relief is an equitable remedy for an improper use of a license.

    C.   **Other Interests in Land**

★   1)   <u>FIXTURES</u>

> Question Key
> 41,131,143

It is important to be able to determine if a piece of personal property becomes a fixture of the land. If it becomes a fixture, then generally, it passes with the land and cannot be removed (absent agreement).

        a)   Common Law

           (1)   Elements of a Fixture

An item is a fixture if it satisfies the following three elements:

- Chattel

It is chattel, an item originally of tangible personal property;

- Attached

It is attached to real property or a structure that is located on real property;

- Injury

It cannot be removed without injury to the freehold, such as real property or a structure to which it is attached.

Severance of a fixture from the real property does not alter its classification as a fixture.

(2)   Fixtures in Leasehold Tenancies

When a leasehold estate holder attaches a chattel to the estate property for any purpose, the courts usually do not consider this attachment permanent. The courts often allow the holder to remove such a "fixture" during the tenancy. Alternatively, the holder's representative may remove it within a reasonable period from the holder's death. Generally, the removal may not occur if it would result in:

- substantial injury to property to which it is attached; or
- substantial destruction of the attached chattel.

(3)   Trade Fixtures Doctrine

(a)   Definitions

Trade fixtures are personal property attached to the property as an essential element of conducting a tenant's business. Usually such fixtures are not especially adapted or fitted to the leased premises and may be used in other premises for business purposes.

(b)   General Rules

The trade fixtures doctrine generally allows a tenant to remove fixtures from leased premises unless that removal would cause serious harm to the premises. The tenant must remove the fixtures during the term of a lease of a specified duration or within a reasonable period after a lease ends. The tenant is liable to the landlord for the cost of repairing any damage that results from the removal of the fixtures.

(4)   Accessions Doctrine

The accessions doctrine generally provides that if a tenant expends labor and cost to attach a chattel to a landlord's property in a situation that does not allow the chattel's removal, then the landlord is entitled to ownership of the chattel.

(5)   Fee or Freehold Estates

A question may arise as to whether certain originally personal property will be transferred with an estate as a result of a sale or conveyance of the estate.

(a)   General Rule

Usually, if personal property is attached to real property, it will be considered an integral part of the real property under two conditions:

- removal of the personal property would substantially damage the real property; and
- the attaching party intended that the personal property would become a part of the real property.

(b)   Transferability

When the personal property becomes an integral part of the real property, it is subsequently owned with, and will be transferred with, the real property.

(c)   Priority of Claims

When an owner of personal property perfects a lien in that property before affixing it to real property, the owner may obtain priority over other creditors' claims against the real property, such as those of a subsequent mortgagee of the real property.

b)   Uniform Commercial Code ("UCC") Article 9

Beyond those common law rules and doctrines regarding fixtures, UCC provisions apply to fixtures and security interests in them. Generally, the UCC's provisions enable a fixture's owner or a holder of a security interest in the fixture to perfect its security interest in the fixture. Also, some provisions serve to determine the respective priority interests in the fixture.

(1)   Goods versus Fixtures

As a general rule, a secured party ordinarily has the right to repossess collateral that secures an obligation when the debtor is in default on the obligation. The presence of collateral located on real property, though, adds a wrinkle to the general rule. If goods are not classified as fixtures, then Article 9 provisions will apply. Any real property encumbrances will be irrelevant, and the priority rules of Article 9 will govern. If, however, the goods are classified as "fixtures," then the UCC requires consideration of any real property encumbrances in determining priority and rights upon default.

(a)   Classification as Fixtures

The Code provides that "goods are 'fixtures' when they become so related to particular real estate that an interest in them arises under real estate law." UCC § 9-313. In other words, fixtures are so intertwined with the real property that they become part of the real property. Article 9 generally leaves the determination of the status of goods as fixtures to the local real property law of the jurisdiction concerned.

(b)   Perfection of Security Interests in Fixtures

A party may perfect a security interest in fixtures by a regular Article 9 filing as to the goods or by a fixture filing filed at the office in the jurisdiction where real estate mortgages are recorded and that provides that it is being filed in the real estate records. In other words, a party may file a security interest in a fixture either under Article 9 or local real estate law.

        (c)   Priority of Fixtures Against Real Estate Interests

             (i)   Prior Perfected Interests Prevail

A fixture filing made before an interest of a competing real estate claimant is recorded will generally enable the secured party claiming a security interest in the fixtures to prevail over the real estate claimant if the secured party would have prevailed over the real estate claimant's predecessor in interest.

             (ii)   PMSI in Fixtures

A purchase-money security interest in goods that become fixtures will generally prevail over an existing interest of record of a competing real estate claimant if a fixture filing is made as to the goods within 20 days after the goods become fixtures.

             (iii)   Construction Mortgages

A fixture security interest will generally be subordinate to the construction mortgage of a construction mortgagee where the goods become fixtures before completion of construction. Nonetheless, a security interest perfected before the goods become fixtures has priority over a competing real estate claimant in the goods, including a construction mortgagee.

        (d)   Remedies

In some ways, the protection Article 9 provides to encumbrancers of real estate over holders of security interests in fixtures operates to limit the secured party's repossession rights. First, the secured party must have priority over all real property encumbrancers. A secured party who has priority over all owners and encumbrancers of the real estate is entitled, upon default, to remove the collateral from the real estate. Moreover, even if the secured party has priority over all real estate interests, the secured party must reimburse the real estate interests for any physical injury caused by the removal of fixtures.

★   2)   SCOPE AND EXTENT OF REAL PROPERTY

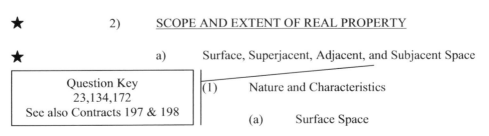

★   a)   Surface, Superjacent, Adjacent, and Subjacent Space

Question Key
23,134,172
See also Contracts 197 & 198

      (1)   Nature and Characteristics

        (a)   Surface Space

Surface space is the ground level of the land that comprises an owner's real property and surrounds the structures that are located on that property. Surface interests extend to the top and a minimal depth of the owner's real property.

(b)   Superjacent Space

Superjacent space is above the surface of an owner's real property and/or structures that are located on that land. Superjacent interests extend into the airspace that is above an owner's real property and the structures that are on that land.

(c)   Adjacent Space

Adjacent interests extend along the edge of the ground that surrounds, or borders upon, an owner's real property and the structures that are on that land.

(d)   Subjacent Space

Subjacent space is below an owner's real property and/or structures on that land.

(2)   Rights of Possession and Use

(a)   Surface Space

A surface property owner may exercise the rights of possession and use upon and within that real property and any structures on the land.

(b)   Superjacent Space

A superjacent property owner may exercise its rights of possession and use above that real property and any structures upon the land. Under the common law, those rights extended "to the heavens," although the modern trend is to limit those rights to the height that a property owner could make use of them.

(c)   Adjacent Space

An adjacent property owner's rights of possession and use extend along the edge or border of that real property and any structures upon the land.

(i)   Lateral Support

The corollary right of lateral support from adjacent land and under the ground's vertical surface is absolute. Absolute liability arises from a violation of this right. Lateral support protects real property and/or structures on the property from excavation, erosion, or other harms that are caused by acts or omissions of an owner of adjacent real property.

(A)   Exceptions

Structures: Lateral support is not an absolute right if a structure that is built upon the land artificially places weight upon the natural forces that hold the ground intact.

Act of God: Neither a landowner nor an adjacent landowner is liable if a lateral support is withdrawn as a result of some event of nature or weather such as erosion or a flood.

(d)   Subjacent Space

A subjacent property owner's rights of possession and use extend indefinitely downwards below that real property and any structures upon the land. Those are subterranean, or below surface, rights to recover natural resources like precious stones, minerals, oil, and gas.

(i)   Subjacent Support

The right of subjacent support arises from land below the ground's horizontal surface. For example, a surface owner may possess a right to subjacent support of real property and/or structures on that property from certain types of harm arising from an underlying mineral rights owner's below-ground activities, such as tunneling.

(3)   Legal and Equitable Remedies

The general interests of surface, superjacent, adjacent, and subjacent space include a right to exclusive possession and use that is free from unlawful invasions or interferences. Violation of those rights to possession gives rise to causes of action arising from trespasses upon, or nuisances that harm, those rights. A negligence or strict liability action for damage to personal property can also provide a remedy for a property owner.

(a)   Trespass

Trespass mainly involves an actual physical invasion of the property owner's possessory interest by a person or a thing. A legal privilege to enter upon land renders a trespass lawful. If a person with legal privilege takes actions beyond the permitted activities, though, such a person may become a trespasser *ab initio*.

Examples of trespass include all of the following, if done without right:

- the construction of a well or pipeline under real property;
- a tree that intrudes a possessory interest in the airspace of property;
- aircraft flights over property that cause actual damage to property; and
- physical entry upon real property.

(b)   Nuisance

Nuisance usually involves a "nonphysical" invasion of the property owner's possessory interest by vibration, noise, or odors. Liability for nuisance might result from aircraft flights over property. Depending on their frequency and the severity of those over flights, a property owner may recover damages, and/or an inverse condemnation might occur. The defense of "coming to the nuisance" is not absolute. Under this defense, a plaintiff is not entitled to recover for a nuisance if the plaintiff moved near that pre-existing nuisance.

(i)   Private Nuisance

(A)   Intentional

An intentional private nuisance is:

- an unreasonable activity or condition;
- on a neighboring owner's real property that;
- unreasonably or substantially interferes with a property owner's use and enjoyment of the land. This interference is measured by the "reasonable person" test.

(B)   Unintentional

Under the *Restatements of Torts* an unintentional nuisance is conduct that could be actionable as either negligent or ultra hazardous.

(ii)   Public Nuisance

A public nuisance is similar to a private nuisance, except it affects more than just a few property owners. It extends to the general public or a much larger number of people. Usually a property owner may bring a private nuisance action, and a prosecutor may bring a public nuisance action. A public nuisance may also arise from illegal activities in violation of an ordinance. An example of such an activity is operating a brothel.

(iii)   Remedies

(A)   Legal Remedies

A prevailing party in a nuisance action may recover damages as follows: a permanent nuisance gives rise to reduced rental value; and a temporary nuisance entitles a party to receive lost rental value.

(B)   Equitable
Remedies

Injunctive relief from a nuisance may be available within a trial court's discretion. An equitable defense to such relief is balancing the hardships or the equities. An injunction may completely prohibit the nuisance or be narrowly tailored to minimize the extent of the nuisance. The person seeking injunctive relief must assert some substantial injury to himself or herself.

(c)   Removal of Support

(i)   Strict Liability

Strict liability exists if:

- a neighboring property owner removes lateral support from another property owner's adjacent property in its natural state; and
- the other owner's property would have been adequately supported in its natural condition.

A neighboring property owner has a burden of proving that the other property owner's adjacent land would not have subsided in its natural condition. The neighboring property owner may be liable for damages to the other property owner's improvements and harms to the land.

(ii)   Negligence Liability

Negligence liability exists when a neighboring property owner engages in activities that could cause subsidence of another property owner's adjacent land. The neighboring owner has a duty to provide notice of such activities to all other property owners. The neighboring owner must conduct those activities with the exercise of reasonable care to maintain lateral support of the adjacent land. The neighboring property owner is liable for a breach of those duties if it results from the foreseeable harm that is caused by unreasonable conduct.

(iii)   Vicarious Liability

An employer of an independent contractor is not exempt from tort liability when the contractor's excavation activities were inherently dangerous, despite the employer's lack of control of those activities.

★   b)   Rights in Common Resources

| Question Key |
| 24,50,112 |

(1)   General Considerations

Generally, it is difficult for an owner of real property to obtain an exclusive right to the light and air that surrounds that real property. Usually, an owner must receive an express grant to create an easement for light and air. Property owners cannot imply such easements, despite the existence of other elements for implying a quasi-easement, because such an easement would not be evident to a buyer of the servient estate. The courts generally will enforce express negative appurtenant easements for light and air. The courts, however, usually decline to enforce a prescriptive easement for light and air.

(2)   Light

Case law provides that a property owner may erect a structure in the airspace above the property that blocks the sunlight or views of the neighboring property owners.

(3)   Air

A property owner may erect a structure in the airspace above the property that interferes with the neighboring property owners' reception of television or radio signals.

(a)   Weather Modification

Southwest Weather Research, Inc. v. Rounsaville, 320 S.W. 2d 211 (Tex. 1959), is a decision in a property owner's action seeking to prevent a neighboring property owner from modifying the weather over that land. The court concluded that a property owner has a right to all naturally existing clouds and any rainfall that those clouds produce above that owner's land. Consequently, the court held that one property owner may enjoin a neighboring property owner from engaging in weather modification in airspace above the property owner's land.

(4)   Riparian Rights

(a)   Moving Water

Moving water is water contained in rivers, streams, and creeks. Owners of property along those channels of water possess certain riparian rights to use those watercourses.

(b)   Stationary Water

Stationary water is water contained in reservoirs, lakes, and ponds. Owners of property along stationary water possess riparian rights to access those bodies of water.

(c)   Reasonable Use Doctrine (Majority Rule)

The modern reasonable use doctrine applies in a majority of the states. It provides that a riparian property owner may reasonably use the water and cannot unreasonably interfere with the other riparian owners' ability to reasonably use the water.

(i)   Balancing Test

A judicial determination on whether a particular use of the water is permissible will depend upon a balancing of the following factors:

- the purpose and importance of a use;
- the social and economic value of a use;
- the impact of a use on other riparian owners;
- the appropriateness of the use to a specific watercourse; and

● the feasibility and expense of adjusting a use or of other uses.

A domestic use usually prevails over other uses. Water use for irrigation may be of secondary importance.

(d) Colorado Doctrine (Minority Rule)

The Colorado Doctrine of prior appropriation applies in many of the western states. The doctrine provides that an initial user of water for a "beneficial purpose" acquires the right to continue that use. This right of the initial user, who need not be a riparian property owner, is subject to using a decreased amount of water if a subsequent user can show that water is needed for a preferred beneficial purpose.

(5) Underground Water

Underground water in percolating aquifers and subterranean streams may form or be a part of the water table that could extend under the surface land of several property owners.

(a) Underground Streams & Aquifers

If the water flows in a stream or aquifer, then the same riparian rules that are described *supra* will apply. The majority rule of reasonable use applies to limit any taking of underground water that harms other surface property owners.

(6) Surface Water

Diffuse surface water is water that results from the melting of snow, rainfall, overflowing springs, or a diversion of those types of water by one neighbor upon another neighbor's property.

(a) Impounding Surface Water

An owner may impound diffuse surface water, especially when this is done in the absence of any malice towards others.

(b) Expelling Surface Water

(i) Reasonable Use (Majority Rule)

There are different views regarding the way an owner may expel surface water. A property owner such as a farmer may impound surface water, especially in the absence of any malice towards others.

First, the reasonable use doctrine applies in several states. It provides that a property owner is privileged to reasonably use his land and to only modify its surface water drainage so that it would not unreasonably interfere with a neighboring property owner's use of the land.

(A)   Balancing Test

A court may determine a reasonable use issue by considering the following factors:

- the degree of necessity for a property owner to modify the drainage onto another's land;
- if the property owner made the modification with reasonable care;
- if other more beneficial modifications were possible; and
- the extent of damages that the neighboring property owner incurred.

(ii)   Common Enemy Doctrine
(Minority Rule)

A minority of states follows the common enemy doctrine. It allows a property owner to utilize any means to remove surface water without becoming liable to neighboring property owners for any resulting flood upon their land. This rule is subject to several qualifications. One imposes liability for the collection of and expulsion of surface water in greater quantities than those naturally present. Another imposes liability for a property improvement that results in greater water runoff. Lastly, an unreasonable alternative means of drainage may result in greater liability.

(7)   Navigable Water

Navigable water is subject to the federal and state governments' "navigation servitudes." They limit a riparian property owner's rights under the federal navigation power arising from the Commerce Clause of the *U.S. Constitution*.

(8)   Vegetation

(a)   Definition

Natural vegetation, or *fructus naturales*, belongs to a surface property owner. It includes perennial shrubs, grasses, and trees that grow on the ground. Adjacent property owners own trees growing along a border of real property as tenants in common.

(b)   Status and Rules

Fructus naturales is real property until it is severed from the ground. It passes with a transfer of the land and is subject to a mortgage unless otherwise agreed. In the absence of immediate severance of such natural vegetation from real property by a vendor for a vendee, the sale of that vegetation is a sale of an interest in land. Thus, the Statute of Frauds requires that a sale without a severance be reflected in writing.

(9)   Crops

(a)   Definition

Crops, or *fructus industriales*, belong to a surface property owner. They are annual plants that are cultivated through human effort and intended for human or animal consumption.

(b)   Status and Rules

Growing crops constitute personal property that is subject to the laws of wills, trusts, and intestacy. They pass with a transfer of the land and are subject to a mortgage unless otherwise agreed. They may be subject to an agreement of sale before the time of harvest.

(10)   Emblements

Qualified estates and leasehold estates of an uncertain duration include a license or right of emblements. The right applies in the following circumstances:

- A qualified estate holder or a tenant for an uncertain period (e.g., a life estate or a tenancy for an uncertain period that was not terminated for a tenant's misconduct) plants crops;
- The crops exist in one growing season when the estate ends (but not thereafter);
- The crops need to be harvested and removed from the land; and
- An instrument of conveyance, or lease, or will prohibits emblements.

The doctrine of emblements entitles a tenant or the representatives of a deceased life estate holder to harvest the crops. The doctrine applies to estates of uncertain duration but does not apply to leasehold estates of certain duration.

★   **D.**   **Taking and Aspects of Zoning**

> Question Key
> 95

1)   TAKING

a)   General Considerations

A taking occurs when a government appropriates a private owner's real property for public use. Under the Takings Clause of the *U.S. Constitution*, the owner of property that is taken for public use is entitled to just compensation. A less traditional type of taking occurs when the government appropriates private property for a specified type of public purpose, such as an economic development plan under certain limited circumstances.

b)   Application

If a property owner declines to sell or dedicate real property to a government for public use, then the government may exercise its legal power to acquire that property.

(1)   Eminent Domain

Eminent domain is one type of power that the government may assert to acquire land that is needed for the purpose of public transportation or government buildings.

(2)   Regulation

Regulation is another type of less extreme power that the government may impose to apply certain restrictions on, or zoning provisions about, land use. A regulatory taking may occur when a state enabling act and/or a local zoning provision:

- deprives a property owner of reasonable use of its parcel;
- without providing the constitutionally required just compensation.

c)   Interests Subject to Takings

A government may appropriate all types of private property interests by condemnation.

(1)   Freehold Estates

If the interest taken is a freehold estate, the taking terminates an owner's interest, and the owner is entitled to compensation.

(2)   Leasehold Estates

If the interest taken is a qualified estate, then two situations may arise.

(a)   Entire Leasehold Premises

If the government condemns the entire leased premises, the action will cancel the lease. Accordingly, if the interest taken is an entire leasehold estate, then the leasehold and all duties under the lease end. Thus, the tenant would no longer be obligated to pay rent for any remaining duration of the lease. The owner of the property would be entitled to just compensation.

In the absence of a controlling provision in the lease agreement, a tenant may be able to recover part of the compensation that a landlord receives. The part the tenant is entitled to is the amount of the leasehold's fair market value for its remaining duration that exceeds the tenant's lease obligations. Consequently, to ascertain if the tenant can recover any compensation from the landlord, one must determine if the fair market value of the lease exceeds the cost of the tenant's remaining lease obligations.

(b)   Partial Leasehold Premises

If a government condemns only part of the leased premises, the action will cancel the lease. If the interest taken is only part of a leasehold estate, then a tenant remains obligated to pay the entire rent. A landlord has no duty to abate the rent obligation as a result of the government's taking.

In the absence of a controlling provision in the lease agreement, a tenant may be entitled to recover part of a landlord's award of just compensation. The first type of recoverable compensation is the portion of the rent attributable to the taken part of the leasehold estate. The second type of recoverable compensation is the amount of the leasehold's fair market value for its remaining duration in excess of the tenant's lease obligations.

In other words, the portion the tenant can recover will be equal to the capitalized cost of remaining rent on the condemned portion and any surplus value consisting of the excess of fair market value of the condemned portion of the lease compared to the costs of the remaining lease obligations. Accordingly, if the tenant had a good bargain on the lease, he will be entitled to the fair value of the good bargain.

For example, suppose Tenant rents a warehouse for $10,000 per year. With one year remaining, before the final payment, the government exercises its power of eminent domain and takes one-quarter of the warehouse. The lease will not be cancelled. Tenant will still be required to pay $10,000 under the lease. However, he will be entitled to $2,500 from the condemnation award. This amount is the pro-rata amount of remaining rent under the lease for the condemned property. Additionally, if he had a good bargain, for example if the market value of the rental was $20,000, instead of $10,000, but Tenant negotiated a great deal, then Tenant will be entitled to the surplus value of the condemned portion of the lease. In this case, that amount would be an additional $2,500.

<blockquote>d)   Legal and Equitable Remedies</blockquote>

A property owner whose land is taken by the government without any condemnation proceedings may bring a civil action to recover damages in a reverse condemnation action or seek the equitable relief of an injunction against the taking.

<blockquote>2)   ASPECTS OF ZONING</blockquote>

<blockquote>a)   Nature and Characteristics</blockquote>

"The essence of zoning is territorial division in keeping with the character of the lands and structures and their peculiar suitability for particular uses, and uniformity of use within the division." *Katobimar Realty Co. v. Webster*, 20 N.J. 114, 118 A. 2d 824 (1955).

<blockquote>b)   Bases for Creation</blockquote>

<blockquote>(1)   Enabling Acts</blockquote>

The legal basis for local zoning provisions in the form of regulations, ordinances, or codes is usually a state's enabling act or statute. The zoning power is not generally premised upon a government's police power obligation to provide for the public's health, safety, morals, and welfare under the Tenth Amendment to the *U.S. Constitution.*

(2)   Home Rule

Sometimes, local governments, such as counties or municipalities, impose zoning provisions pursuant to home-rule powers that a state provides. Those provisions may pre-exist or follow the creation of a master plan that establishes the vicinities of, and defines the various types of, zones of use.

c)   Rights of Possession and Use

The zoning category that applies to the owner's property will determine a property owner's rights of possession and use.

(1)   Nonconforming Uses

Under some circumstances, a grandfather provision will allow the pre-existing and nonconforming use of the property that occurred before the government imposed zoning restrictions to continue.

(a)   Just Compensation

Other enabling statutes provide that zoning provisions cannot mandate the elimination of nonconforming uses without providing just compensation. Zoning statutes that eliminate nonconforming uses without providing just compensation are subject to invalidation as unconstitutional on the grounds of a denial of due process or operating as a regulatory taking.

d)   Legal and Equitable Remedies

A property owner who opposes or contests the imposition of, or restrictions upon land use that result from, a zoning category may seek a variety of legal and equitable remedies for relief from the effects of that category. Common law or statute may provide those remedies. Statutes may proscribe remedies to the use of administrative-law type procedures and processes. Three common forms of request for relief from zoning provisions are variances, special permits, and rezoning.

(1)   Variances

A variance occurs when the government office or agency that administers zoning provisions grants a property owner an exception from the zoning laws. The two types of variances include a use variance that applies to a particular parcel of real property and a bulk variance that applies to any parcels of real property that the zoning ordinance affects.

(a)   Variance Standard

A common legal standard for obtaining a variance is that the enforcement of zoning provision would result in an unnecessary hardship to a property owner. Hardship usually exists when, absent the variance, a landowner cannot make reasonable use of the land.

(2)   Special Use Permit

A special use permit is a right to conduct certain activities, termed conditional uses, within a zoning district. A property owner must obtain special approval of the zoning authority for these permits. Some jurisdictions call this type of permit a conditional use permit.

For example, suppose a local government allows, as a special use, the operation of a recreational facility within its residential zoning districts. A landowner wishing to operate a recreational facility must apply for and obtain a special use permit from the local governing authority.

(3)   Rezoning

A rezoning may occur when the government office or agency that administers zoning provisions decides to revise and modify them. Some jurisdictions refer to rezoning as amending a zoning ordinance. A property owner may challenge a rezoning that adversely affects his interest in or use of the affected land.

e)   Appellate Procedure

A property owner whose request for a variance or rezoning is denied at an initial administrative level, such as a local zoning commission, may seek agency review by a local zoning board of appeal. If no other level of agency review is available, the owner who seeks to contest the board of appeal's decision may obtain judicial review of it.

(1)   Due Process

In addition to raising substantive issues on appeal, a property owner may assert a violation of procedural or constitutional due process if the contested agency action or decision does not comply with the procedures that either the state enabling act or the local zoning provision established. At a minimum, such procedures should afford a property owner with notice and hearing in actions for rezoning or variances. Other issues include violations of constitutional equal protection or regulatory taking.

III.   REAL PROPERTY CONTRACT

★★   **A.   Types of Contracts**

| Question Key |
| 86,125,163,167 |

1)   CONTRACTS TO BUY & SELL

A buyer and a seller of interests in real property usually enter into a marketing contract reflecting the terms and conditions of their agreement. The contract may exist separately and distinct from any document regarding either: 1) the financing of the purchase of the real property interest, such as a mortgage; or 2) a conveyance thereof, such as a deed to a parcel of land. The parties may also refer to a marketing contract as a sell and buy contract.

2)   INSTALLMENT CONTRACTS

An installment contract, otherwise known as a contract of deed or a land contract, is an agreement pertaining to a purchase of real property and the financing of that purchase. Often, an installment contract requires that a buyer provide a specified down payment and make periodic payments for a particular duration. After the buyer fulfills those payment obligations, then the buyer will receive a deed for that interest in real property.

3)   OPTION CONTRACTS

a)   Right to Purchase

An option contract must be in writing to be enforceable under the Statute of Frauds. A seller (i.e., optioner) provides a buyer (i.e., optionee) with a right to purchase an interest in real property at a future time under certain conditions. An optionee may seek specific enforcement of the option contract as an equitable interest in the real property. An option is subject to the Rule Against Perpetuities.

b)   Preemptive Option

A potential seller (i.e., optioner) may provide a prospective buyer (i.e., optionee) a preemptive option (i.e., a conditional option) that constitutes a right of first refusal to purchase the seller's interest in real property if and when the seller decides to sell this interest. A preemptive option is subject to the Rule Against Perpetuities. A court may strike down as void ab initio a preemptive option that violates the Rule Against Perpetuities.

B.   Creation and Construction

| Question Key |
| 2,29,35,40,63,73,75,93, |
| 135,151 |
| See also Contracts 31 |

1)   STATUTE OF FRAUDS

a)   General Rule

A Statute of Frauds exists in all of the United States. The Statute of Frauds generally requires that, in order to be enforceable, an agreement conveying an interest in land must be in writing, signed by the party to be charged, and contain all essential terms of the parties' agreement. The Statute of Frauds also applies to an option to purchase real property and a promise to provide a right of first refusal. Courts will generally not enforce oral modifications of written agreements unless they constitute a waiver, as in terms of the time specified for performance, estoppel, or part performance.

(1)   Part Performance Exception

Part performance of a contract is an exception to the Statute's requirement of a writing. This exception applies when the parties only have a verbal agreement, and the buyer has fulfilled at least two or more of the following conditions:

- A buyer makes substantial improvements to the property;
- A buyer is in open and notorious possession of a seller's property; and
- A buyer pays the purchase price in part or in full.

In other words, many courts may grant specific performance of a verbal contract to sell land if a buyer's conduct was sufficient to constitute part performance. This exception is based on the theory that a person who has relied reasonably to his detriment on the assurances of the land owner should not suffer because the agreement was not recorded in writing.

    2)   ESSENTIAL TERMS

a)   Required Information

(1)   Sell and Buy Contract

To be enforceable, a written sell and buy contract must also be sufficiently definite by containing, at a minimum, the first four items of the following information:

- the parties' names and addresses;
- an accurate legal description of the land;
- a signature by the party to be bound;
- language indicating an intention to buy and to sell the land;
- statement of the land's selling price;
- a recital of earnest money and consideration for the purchase; and
- a covenant of marketable title.

(a)   Description of Land

The land's description must be adequate. It does not need to be as precise as the description that is contained in a deed. For example, a proper address for the property being bought and sold would generally suffice. The description must be sufficient to facilitate specific performance.

(2)   Deed of Conveyance

A deed is an instrument that represents the title to real property. The Statute of Frauds requires that, other than for short-term leases, a conveyance of a real property interest must be in writing. Thus, a grantor must transfer a valid instrument of conveyance, or deed, to a grantee to make an effective sale of real property. To be valid and enforceable, a deed must include the following information:

- the parties' names and addresses;
- an accurate legal description of the land;
- language indicating an intention to transfer possession of the land; and
- a signature by a grantor.

If a deed does not satisfy the Statute of Frauds, then recording it will not render it a sufficient writing for purposes of complying with the Statute of Frauds.

Destruction of a written deed does not affect the grantee's title, except if the law requires recording of the deed to transfer title.

A person may appoint an agent to sell his real estate. That agent, however, only possesses the authority to do acts specifically set forth in the authorization. Additionally, courts may not construe the authority to sell or to convey real estate as the authorization to execute a deed. Courts are divided as to whether agents who are authorized to sell or to sell and convey have the power to include covenants in the conveyance.

(a)   Attestation of Deed

Attestation occurs when a lay witness to a grantor's signing of a deed informally executes the deed to verify that the deed is authentic. Although attestation is not a common law requirement, some state statutes mandate it.

(b)   Acknowledgement of Deed

Acknowledgement occurs when a public witness to a grantor's signing of a deed formally executes the deed to verify that the deed is authentic. The witness may be a notary public or a judicial official. Some state statutes require acknowledgement in order for a deed to be self-authenticating as evidence or to be recorded.

★★   3)   <u>IMPLIED CONDITIONS OF TERMS</u>

a)   Time for Performance

The date and time for the parties to complete a real estate transaction is important for reasons of cost and convenience. The parties may stipulate certain dates and times for performance of certain steps that their contract requires, such as a final closing meeting. Failure to perform as stipulated may give rise to litigation.

(1)   Legal Standard

The law generally provides that, unless the parties make a contrary agreement, time is of the essence. The law may require a person who breaches a contract's requirement of time for performance to pay damages.

(2)   Equity Standard

At equity, time is not of the essence unless the contract or surrounding circumstances make it so. When time is not of the essence, a first person's tardy performance does not excuse a second person's performance that occurs within a reasonable time. In that event, the first person may obtain specific performance of the contract. A party may not rescind or abandon the contract for such a nonmaterial breach.

b)   Determining if Time is of Essence

The fact that a sell and buy contract includes a closing date does not prove that the parties considered time to be of the essence. The following may establish the existence of that term:

- a clause in the contract stating that time was of the essence; or
- the parties' conduct that indicated an implicit agreement that time was of the essence.

c)   Curing a Breach

If time is not of the essence, a party who has failed to perform contractual duties may cure that breach by substantially performing those duties within a reasonable time. Conversely, a party who breaches a time is of the essence clause will not be entitled to specific performance.

C.   Performance

1)   FITNESS AND SUITABILITY OF PREMISES

a)   Disclosure of Defects

Usually a deed does not include a covenant that warrants the fitness and suitability of a premises that is subject to a conveyance of an interest in real property. The common law doctrine of *caveat emptor* does not require a seller of such an interest to disclose any defects of the interest to a buyer. Modern case law may invoke, but does not necessarily follow, this doctrine in instances when premises contain defects. Additionally, some state statutes require disclosures of certain defects of a premises.

(1)   Seller's Disclosure Obligations

The following rules apply to a seller's nondisclosure of defects of a premises:

- A seller will be liable for fraud for making affirmative misrepresentations about a property that are relied upon by a buyer.
- A seller who has special relationship of trust with a buyer, such as a fiduciary, will be subject to a duty of full disclosure and candor about any defects on the premises.

- A seller will be civilly liable for failing to disclose material defects that cannot be easily discovered by an inspection of the property.

★★

2)   MARKETABLE TITLE

Question Key
26,28,42,117,122,127
See also Contracts 174

   a)   General Rules

Marketable title means that the title is free from reasonable doubt about its validity, any threats of litigation regarding the title's validity, or actual lawsuits relating to the title. A sell and buy contract usually includes an implied or express warranty of marketable title. If the contract does not address the issue of quality of the title, a court will imply the requirement of marketable title. Unless the sell and buy contract allows for anything other than marketable title, a seller cannot require a buyer to accept less than marketable title. The buyer may waive the requirement that the seller provide marketable title because the right to marketable title benefits the buyer. Title does not need to be marketable until when the seller must deliver it to the buyer. This point in time could be, for example, the date set for closing their real estate transaction. As a practical matter, the parties' sell and buy agreement may provide that certain circumstances may render title to the real property unmarketable.

   b)   Marketability of Title

A title is unmarketable when a reasonable person would not purchase it. Title is not marketable if, among other things, any of the following conditions exist:

- The real property violates a zoning statute, ordinance, or regulation;
- The real property is subject to an adverse possession claim;
- An encumbrance exists on the real property, such as a servitude or mortgage; or
- The real property is subject to, or at issue in, ongoing litigation.

Conversely, unpaid liens or mortgages on the real property do not render title unmarketable if:

- A seller gives a buyer reasonable assurances that any encumbrances on the title will be discharged when the seller tenders the title; and
- The proceeds of a sale under a sell and buy contract are adequate to, and actually applied to, extinguish all encumbrances.

Generally, easements do not render title unmarketable.

   (1)   Failure to Deliver Marketable Title

A seller who does not deliver marketable title at the mutually agreed upon time and/or place breaches a covenant in the sell and buy contract that marketable title will be tendered. This breach involves the failure of a constructive condition, which discharges a buyer from performing further and provides the following remedies: potential loss-of-bargain damages, rescission and restitution, specific performance and abatement, and reimbursement for out-of-pocket expenses. A maxim provides that equity will not compel a buyer to purchase a lawsuit.

(a)   Zoning and Marketable Title

If a seller's property is in violation of zoning regulations when the seller enters into a sell and buy contract with a buyer, then the title is unmarketable and the buyer may decline to perform the contract. Marketable title is not lost if the buyer plans to use the property in a manner that will violate existing zoning regulations.

(2)   Breach of Contract

Although a seller may lack marketable title at the execution of a sell and buy contract, the seller will only breach the contract by failing to provide marketable title at the closing. When the seller fails to provide marketable title on the closing date, a buyer may:

- elect to not perform under a sell and buy contract;
- rescind the contract and recover its down payment;
- commence a breach of contract action for damages; or
- file an action seeking specific performance of the contract and request a purchase price abatement as relief for the title's defect.

(a)   Curing Title Defects

Examples of title defects and their cures include:

- Applying the sale proceeds towards satisfaction of the mortgage debt may cure an outstanding mortgage.

- Obtaining a judgment that quiets title in the adverse possessor may cure a claim to title by adverse possession.

- Obtaining a termination of the easement may cure an easement that burdens the land.

c)   Insurable Title

The parties' contract to sell and buy real property may include a clause requiring insurable title, which involves a different standard than the marketable title requirement. To be enforceable, the clause language must be clear and unambiguous. The parties may also stipulate to their awareness of and acceptance of any encumbrances and other interests to which the real estate to be conveyed is subject.

★   3)   RISK OF LOSS

a)   Intervening Events

Events may occur between the formation and performance of a sell and buy contract that affect one party or reduces the real property's value. The following events may cause a loss to the property:

- natural conditions that may cause physical damage to the property (e.g., weather-related damage to structures or crops, fires, floods, and storms);
- changes in the land's legal status (e.g., a taking through eminent domain and modified zoning provisions or housing codes);
- an adverse judgment that involves judgment liens upon the land.

b)   Doctrine of Equitable Conversion

Jurisdictions are split regarding risk of loss rules. Many jurisdictions follow the doctrine of equitable conversion. Under the doctrine of equitable conversion, discussed in depth below, a purchaser of real property becomes the equitable owner of title to real property at the time he enters into a contract to purchase the property. The seller retains legal title of the property prior to the date of conveyance. Therefore, the risk of loss transfers to the buyer at the time the parties enter into the contract. Thus, if a house on the property burns down after the parties sign the contract, but before the grantor conveys the deed, the buyer will still have to pay the contract price for the land.

c)   The Uniform Vendor and Purchaser Risk of Loss Act

The *Uniform Vendor and Purchaser Risk of Loss Act* ("Act") allocates the risk of loss to a seller until the earlier of a transfer of title to the real estate to the buyer or when the buyer takes possession of the real estate. For example, if a fire damaged a seller's house before the buyer received title or possession of it, the buyer may obtain a reduction in the purchase price if the sell and buy contract is not avoidable. The Act is the minority rule and only applies in those states that have adopted it to some extent.

D.   Interests Before Conveyance

★

1)   EQUITABLE CONVERSION

| Question Key |
| 42,98,99 |
| See also Contracts 133 |

a)   Equitable Conversion Doctrine (Majority Rule)

Equitable conversion applies when parties have entered into a specifically enforceable sell and buy contract. The equitable conversion doctrine considers a buyer as the owner of real property during a contract's executory period. Thus, the risk of loss falls upon a buyer. This doctrine requires the buyer to fulfill a contract and pay the purchase price despite a major loss in the property's value due to an unanticipated event that the buyer did not cause. A minority of jurisdictions rejects the doctrine and place the risk of loss upon a seller.

b)   Effect of the Equitable Conversion Doctrine

Under the doctrine, a sell and buy contract with a seller is specifically enforceable in equity. The doctrine furthers the maxim that equity considers that as having been done that which should have been done. The doctrine provides that the execution of the contract yields the following results:

- The seller retains a legal interest in the real property.
- The seller receives a right in personal property to obtain the purchase price.
- The buyer obtains an equitable interest in the real property.
- The buyer receives a right in realty to a conveyance of that property.

(1)   Death of a Party

Equitable conversion applies to the distribution of property under both testate and intestate succession. Courts consider a seller's interest personal property secured by a lien. Courts consider a buyer's interest real property.

(a)   Exception - Option to Buy

Equitable conversion does not apply to an option that a buyer fails to exercise before a seller's death. Only an optionee (i.e., buyer) may specifically enforce an option.

(2)   Right of Possession

A buyer who obtains equitable title does not gain the right of possession that is derived from legal title. If, however, the buyer is purchasing real property under a land contract (i.e., installment contract), the buyer may occupy the property. In that event, the buyer may not cause waste harming the seller's security interest.

★   2)   <u>EARNEST MONEY DEPOSIT</u>

Question Key
34,35,158

a)   Definition

The parties' sell and buy contract may require a buyer to pay funds as a deposit to a seller or a third party who normally will apply them towards the purchase price of the interest in real property. The parties may refer to these funds as earnest money because they indicate the buyer's serious interest in completing the parties' proposed transaction.

b)   Payment

Earnest money is similar to, and may be part of, a buyer's down payment of the total purchase price. But the buyer generally pays, and the seller receives, the earnest money well in advance of closing on a real estate transaction because it serves to secure the buyer's right of priority to the property over other potential buyers.

c)   Liquidated Damages

A sell and buy contract may allow a seller to retain a down payment of earnest money if a buyer fails to complete performance of the contract. Such a provision is unenforceable if the amount retained is large enough to constitute a penalty. Such a provision is enforceable if the amount of down payment is reasonably related to the seller's actual damages.

★   3)   BREACH OF CONTRACT REMEDIES

          a)   Seller's Remedies

               (1)   Damages

A seller may seek the difference between the contract price and the market price at the time of closing while retaining the real property that is subject to the parties' sell and buy contract.

               (2)   Specific Performance

A seller may obtain specific performance of a buy and sell contract that a buyer breaches because money damages are inadequate. Specific performance is available even if the seller's title includes an immaterial defect. In that event, the buyer is entitled to an abatement in price for the value of any defect.

          b)   Buyer's Remedies

               (1)   Damages

Nearly half of the jurisdictions follow the American rule that is also used for personal property sales. If a seller intentionally breaches a sell and buy contract, a buyer may recover the difference between the real property's market value and the contract price on the date that the closing is to occur.

The other half of jurisdictions follow the English Rule, which applies when a seller does not intentionally breach a contract. In that event, a buyer can only recover damages that will restore the buyer to its original position.

               (2)   Specific Performance

A buyer may obtain specific performance of a buy and sell contract that a seller breaches if money damages are inadequate. Specific performance is not available when a buyer seeks to have a seller cure a defect. In that event, the buyer may only obtain an abatement of price in the amount of the defect.

               (3)   Rescission

If a buyer elects not to seek either damages or specific performance, the buyer may request rescission of a sell and buy contract and recover any down payment.

E.   **Relationships After Conveyance**

1)   CONDITION OF PREMISES

| Question Key |
| 14,49,51 |
| See also Contracts 191 |

a)   Seller's Failure to Disclose Defects

(1)   Seller's Decreased Liability

The following circumstances may decrease the prospects that courts will impose liability for a seller's nondisclosure of a premise's defects:

• A buyer learned of defects of premises before the purchase from an inspection or other sources; or
• Information about the defects of premises was available to a buyer.

(2)   Seller's Increased Liability

The following considerations may increase the likelihood of imposing liability for a seller's nondisclosure of a premises' defects:

• A novice buyer is acquiring a residential property;
• A property defect presents a safety or health risk;
• A seller reassured a buyer about the property's quality;
• A buyer neither received nor depended upon a professional inspection of the property; or
• A seller possesses reason to expect that the seller's nondisclosure will impact subsequent buyers despite a lack of privity between them and the seller.

b)   State Disclosure Statutes

Several state statutes deny a remedy to a buyer of a house in which an AIDS patient died or a crime occurred. Many state statutes require a house seller to make a written disclosure of the seller's knowledge of whether the items are defective or not.

c)   Contract Disclaimers

Although a seller could contractually disclaim a duty to disclose defects, courts do not usually completely enforce general disclaimers or "as is" clauses. Such a clause will prevent a lawsuit for passive nondisclosure of defects but will not prevent one for concealment of, or misrepresentations about, defects.

d)   Contractor Liability

The common law doctrine of *caveat emptor* usually does not protect contractors who build new housing in their sales of the housing. Most courts consider the contractor legally responsible for the property's quality on three theories that are similar to the bases of manufacturer's tort liability: negligence, implied warranty, and strict liability.

IV.   REAL PROPERTY MORTGAGES

A.   Types of Security Devices

1)   MORTGAGES

a)   Definition

A mortgage is an interest in land created by a written instrument providing security for the performance of a duty or the payment of a debt. *Black's Law Dictionary* 1009 (6th ed. 1990). A mortgage provides security for payment of a financial obligation or for performance of a duty. A mortgage typically is an agreement between a mortgagor and a mortgagee.

(1)   Parties' Roles and Obligations

A mortgagor requests a mortgage, borrows funds from a mortgagee, and obtains an ownership interest in real property. The mortgagee is a lender of the funds, issues the mortgage, and holds a security interest in the real property for payment of the funds. A promissory note usually reflects the mortgagor's financial obligation of payment.

b)   Statute of Frauds

In order to satisfy the Statute of Frauds, a mortgage must be in writing. At a minimum, a written mortgage instrument needs to contain certain essential information including:

- the parties' names and addresses;
- an accurate legal description of the land;
- the amount of funds that are borrowed; and
- a mortgagor's promise to pay.

2)   LAND CONTRACTS AS SECURITY DEVICES

a)   Definition

A land contract provides for a future purchase of real property through the financing of that purchase. A land contract allows a buyer to take possession of the property while making regular payments towards the property's purchase price. The seller retains a deed to the property that she neither conveys nor delivers until after the buyer completely satisfies the payment obligation.

b)   Seller's Rights

Under a land contract, a seller possesses two rights of enforcement in the event of nonpayment: 1) to recover the unpaid balance; and 2) oust the buyer from possession of the land. In either event, the seller neither loses possession of the deed that serves as the seller's security device nor is obligated to refund any of the buyer's installment payments.

c)   Default Procedures

The common law and most states require a seller to provide a buyer with fair notice of a default on a land contract prior to bringing a forfeiture action. That notice should describe the default, what steps would cure it, and how much time is allowed for the cure. The notice needs to declare that a forfeiture will occur if the default is not cured. State law determines whether a buyer possesses a right to redeem the property or to reinstate the land contract.

d)   Statute of Frauds

A land contract is subject to the Statute of Frauds. Thus, to be enforceable it must, at a minimum, be in writing, be signed by the party to be charged, and contain all of the contract's essential terms.

3)   ABSOLUTE DEEDS AS SECURITY

> Question Key
> 55

a)   Definition

Two primary transactions for the conveyance of an interest in real property are land contracts or sell and buy contracts that involve a mortgage agreement. The sell and buy contract may, instead of including a mortgage agreement, provide an absolute deed as security. The parties may even possess just an oral understanding that once the debt is paid, the creditor will convey the deed to the debtor. In other words, the creditor holds the deed in absolute form.

b)   Admissible Evidence

Neither the parol evidence rule nor the Statute of Frauds precludes the presentation of evidence that parties intended such an absolute deed to be a mortgage. In that event, the court may consider the deed as their mortgage if the evidence indicates that the deed was intended as security for the debt.

4)   DEEDS OF TRUST

A deed of trust requires three parties. The parties include the trustor (e.g., borrower), the lender, and a neutral third party. The third party is the trustee, who essentially holds temporary title until the lien is paid. Payment in full of the debt cancels the deed of trust. Until then, the trustee has the power to foreclose if the debt is not paid without having to resort to the court system. This power makes it easier and quicker than foreclosing on a mortgage.

5) EQUITABLE MORTGAGE

An equitable mortgage is a "mortgage" that lacks one or more required formalities. Under the equitable mortgage doctrine, courts may enforce such a defective mortgage as an equitable mortgage.

B.   Some Security Relationships

1) NECESSITY AND NATURE OF OBLIGATION

a)   General Considerations

A mortgage represents the security interest, and a promissory note represents the debt that the interest secures. A mortgage does not need to be recorded to create a binding legal agreement between the parties.

(1)   Recorded Mortgages

Recording acts usually classify a mortgage as an encumbrance on the title to the real property, which creates a security interest that a creditor may enforce by selling that property to recover any unpaid balance under the secured promissory note.

(2)   Unrecorded Mortgages

If a mortgagee has not recorded a mortgage, a mortgagor could convey the secured real property to a *bona fide* (good-faith) purchaser who would not be subject to the mortgage.

★   2) THEORIES: TITLE, LIEN, AND INTERMEDIATE

a)   Title Theory (Minority Rule)

> Question Key
> 161

The minority of the states follow the common law title theory. Under that theory, a mortgagor (i.e., borrower) owns the real property, although the mortgagee (i.e., lender) possesses the legal title to this property. The mortgage serves as a conveyance of legal title to the property to a mortgagee. Upon payment of the mortgage debt, that type of title is subject to defeasance. The title provides a mortgagee with a security interest until payment in full of the mortgage debt entitles the mortgagor to a return of the legal title.

(1)   Severance of Joint Tenancy

A mortgaging of a joint tenancy interest in real property will automatically sever the title of a joint tenancy in a title theory jurisdiction. For example, an equity loan creates a type of mortgage lien that will result in severance of a joint tenancy before a loan default and a foreclosure sale occurs.

b)   Lien Theory (Majority Rule)

The majority of the states follow a lien theory, which provides that a mortgagor owns the real property. This property is subject to a lien that a mortgage imposes, irrespective of a mortgage's operative language. The mortgagor retains the legal title until a foreclosure occurs.

(1)   Joint Tenancy Not Severed

A mortgaging of a joint tenancy interest in real property does not automatically sever the title of a joint tenancy in a lien theory jurisdiction. For example, an equity loan creates a type a mortgage lien that will not result in a severance of a joint tenancy unless a loan default and foreclosure sale occurs.

c)   Intermediate Theory

Under the intermediate theory, the lien theory applies prior to a default on a mortgage. The title theory applies after a default on the mortgage.

3)   RIGHTS AND DUTIES PRIOR TO FORECLOSURE

a)   Rights Prior to Foreclosure

After a mortgagor's default and prior to the foreclosure of a mortgage by a mortgagee, a mortgagor possesses a right to pay the outstanding deficiency balance and get current on the mortgage obligation. If the mortgagor does that within a notice period or prior to a deadline, then the mortgagee would not need to foreclose on the mortgage.

b)   Duties Prior to Foreclosure

Before a mortgagee commences foreclosure of a mortgage, the mortgagee must provide the mortgagor with adequate written notice of the deficiency balance that is due upon default and a reasonable amount of time to pay that amount.

c)   Mortgagee in Possession

A mortgagee may obtain possession of a parcel of real estate that secures the mortgage during its existence. The mortgagee may do so if a mortgagor is in default of a mortgage or abandons the mortgaged parcel. The mortgagee need not occupy a parcel in order to be in possession of it. The mortgagee needs to exercise some "dominion and control" of the parcel to be in possession of it.

(1)   Title Theory (Minority Rule)

A mortgagee has a right to possession of the mortgaged parcel prior to or following a mortgagor's default unless a statute or their agreement provides otherwise.

(2)   Lien Theory (Majority Rule)

A mortgagee does not have a right to possession of the mortgaged parcel prior to or following a mortgagor's default until after either a foreclosure has occurred or the duration for statutory redemption has expired, unless a statute or their agreement provides otherwise.

(3)   Intermediate Theory

A mortgagee is entitled to possession of the mortgaged parcel prior to or following a mortgagor's default unless a statute or their agreement provides otherwise.

(4)   Mortgagee in Possession's Liability

A mortgagee in possession is personally liable in tort for injuries attributable to its use of the property or lack of performing legally required duties as a landowner.

★

★   4)   REDEMPTION & CLOGGING EQUITY OF REDEMPTION

a)   Right to Redeem

> Question Key
> 152

Redemption is the right of a mortgagor to purchase the real property by fully paying the mortgage debt (and any applicable late fees or collection costs) within a certain time before the date of foreclosure. The purpose of foreclosure is to prevent a mortgagor from redeeming the default and recovering the real property.

(1)   Common Law

The common law generally provides an equitable right of redemption within a reasonable time before a foreclosure occurs.

(2)   Statutes

States may provide a statutory right of redemption within a specified interval after a foreclosure occurs. A mortgagee cannot include language in the mortgage that waives a mortgagor's right of redemption.

(3)   Title Theory States

In a title theory jurisdiction, a mortgagor possesses an equity of redemption (after defaulting on an obligation) in order to make mortgage payments to a mortgagee. Equitable principles will provide the mortgagor relief from a conveyance of the mortgaged real property that the law renders absolute in the mortgagee. The mortgagor may possess an equity interest in that property in the amount that the mortgagor has paid to the mortgagee in excess of the original mortgage debt.

(4)   Junior Creditors' Interests

A mortgagor's (borrower's) exercise of the right to redeem a default will not affect the mortgagor's obligation to junior interests. However, all junior creditors' interests will be extinguished at a foreclosure sale. Before a foreclosure sale, a redeeming party may pay off the mortgage that is being foreclosed. An exercise of the right to redeem a default will not affect the junior creditor's interests.

b)   Clogging Equity of Redemption

(1)   Definition

A clog is any impediment a mortgagee imposes upon a mortgagor's ability to redeem a mortgage. A doctrine that prevents a mortgagee from making a mortgage irredeemable prohibits clogging the equity of redemption. It is the opposite of the equity of redemption doctrine, which provides for the redemption of a mortgage.

Clogging the equity of redemption refers to a method that a mortgagee would employ to obtain fee simple title to a mortgaged interest in real estate upon a mortgagor's default. Mortgagees may, however, use the following permissible means to limit a mortgagor's late exercise of a power of redemption: 1) a deed absolute; or 2) a land contract.

(2)   Prohibited Provisions

(a)   General

Equity prohibits the following types of provisions that would "clog" the equity of redemption:

- a provision that restricts redemption to a certain time period;
- a provision restricting the power of redemption to only a mortgagor and/or the mortgagor's male heirs; and
- a provision obligating a mortgagor to provide a mortgagee with a quit claim deed upon foreclosure.

(b)   Specific Performance of Mortgagee Option

A mortgagee is not necessarily entitled to specific performance of the mortgagee's option to purchase the mortgaged real property that is contained in an agreement with a mortgagor. Courts may not enforce this option because it allows a mortgagee to obtain the real property without following the foreclosure procedures.

(3)   Permitted Provisions

(a)   Increased Interest

A stipulated provision for an increased interest amount following a default would not be an impermissible clog but may be invalid if it provides for a usurious interest rate.

(b)   Due on Sale Clause

A due on sale clause is not a clog, even if it is contained in a purchase money mortgage. A due on sale clause is a provision in a mortgage or deed of trust that permits the lender to demand immediate payment of the full balance of the mortgage if the mortgagor (i.e., borrower) sells the home.

(c)   Deed in Lieu of Foreclosure

A deed in lieu of foreclosure is an instrument in which a mortgagor (i.e., borrower) conveys all interest in real property to the mortgagee (i.e., lender) to satisfy a loan that is in default and avoid foreclosure proceedings.

A deed in lieu of foreclosure allows a mortgagor to sell the equity of redemption to a mortgagee. This type of deed refers to the use of a written agreement created subsequent to the parties' original transaction. The deed must be based on new consideration. The deed may not be based on any oppression or fraud by a mortgagee.

c)   Deeds of Trust

The deed of trust provides a trustor with an equal equity of redemption as a mortgagor possesses under a mortgage. It enables a lender to both exercise the power of sale to foreclose and to bid at sales that the lender initiates.

★★   **C.   Transfers by Mortgagor**

> Question Key
> 16,54,138,147

1)   GENERAL CONSIDERATIONS

a)   Personal Liability

The personal liability of a mortgagor (i.e., borrower) to a mortgagee (i.e., lender) continues after a transfer of the mortgage to a third party unless:

- Those parties enter into a legally sufficient agreement to the contrary;
- The mortgagor fully pays off the mortgage balance; or
- Certain other principles of suretyship or contract apply. Such principles are further discussed *infra*.

b)   Methods of Transfer

"Voluntary *inter vivos* transfer of the mortgagor's interest is ordinarily effected by a deed of conveyance in the usual form. At the mortgagor's death, transfer of his interest may be effected either by a duly executed will or by the statute of descent if [the mortgagor] dies intestate. Successive transfers of the mortgaged land may take place in any of these ways or by various modes of involuntary transfer, such as foreclosure, execution, or bankruptcy sale." Cunningham and Tischler, *Transfer of the Real Estate Mortgagor's Interest*, 27 Rutgers L.Rev. 24, 25 (1973).

c)   Types of Transfer

Three types of transfers are:

- a transfer "subject to" a mortgage;
- a transfer "assuming" a mortgage; and
- a transfer in exchange for the land's full value.

d)   Due-on Sale Clause

A due-on-sale clause in a mortgage may provide that upon the happening of certain events, the mortgagee may accelerate the mortgage debt so that it must be paid earlier than otherwise provided by the mortgage. For example, the clause can state that the mortgagee may accelerate the debt and foreclose on the mortgage in the event of a transfer of the real property subject to the mortgage by the mortgagor to a third party without the mortgagee's prior consent. In that example, the mortgagor's sale of the real property to a third party by means of an installment land contract before discharge of the mortgage could constitute a transfer that may trigger the clause and consequent foreclosure.

(1)   Legal Restraint on Alienation

If a mortgagor grants a mortgage to nationally chartered bank (i.e., a mortgagee), a due-on-sale clause contained in the mortgage is valid and a legal restraint on alienation. The *Garn-St. Germain Depository Institutions Act* preempts any state law that provides otherwise.

 2)   DISTINGUISHING "SUBJECT TO" AND "ASSUMING"

a)   Transfers "Subject to" a Mortgage

(1)   Majority Rule

If a transferor conveys real property to a transferee that is "subject to" a mortgage, the transferee does not become personally liable for the mortgage debt. The transferee may, however, lose its right to that property by failing to pay the debt when the mortgage is foreclosed.

(2)   Minority Rule

A few states, by statute or in case law, provide that a conveyance that is subject to a mortgage imposes a direct obligation upon a transferee.

b)   Transfers "Assuming" a Mortgage

(1)   General Rule

If a buyer "assumes" a mortgage when purchasing real property from a seller, the buyer becomes personally liable for a mortgage debt. Consequently, the buyer becomes primarily liable for a deficiency judgment if a foreclosure sale does not result in fully repaying the debt. In that event, the seller becomes secondarily liable unless the seller has obtained a release from the mortgagee.

(2)   Statute of Frauds

The predominant common law rule is that the Statute of Frauds does not preclude the creation of an oral assumption of mortgage agreement. Statutes in a minority of states, however, require that such an agreement be in writing in order for it to be enforced.

(3)   Novation

When a promisor agrees to assume a mortgage, a mortgagor will still be liable for its mortgage obligations to a mortgagee unless a novation expressly substitutes the promisor for the mortgagor and releases the mortgagor from any further liability. The mortgagee may recover on the mortgage from the promisor as a third-party beneficiary of the assumption. The promisor and the mortgagor will be jointly and severally liable to the mortgagee, although they will not be equally subject to the mortgage obligation among each other. Their contractual relationship will determine their respective liability.

c)   Assignment of a Mortgage

An assignor may transfer a mortgage or a promissory note to an assignee. If the assignor transfers the mortgage or the note to different assignees, then the mortgage follows the note. The note for the debt is the primary obligation, and the mortgage is a secondary provision of security for the debt.

3)   RIGHTS AND OBLIGATIONS OF TRANSFEROR

a)   Transferor's (Borrower) Rights

A transferor (i.e., mortgagor or initial borrower) may usually transfer a mortgage interest to a transferee without a mortgagee's consent, unless the mortgage document requires consent. The mortgagor's right to transfer is derived from its ownership interest in the real property.

b)   Transferor's Obligations

(1)   Non-assuming Transferee

If a transferee does not assume a transferred mortgage, then a transferor cannot make a personal claim to recover the mortgage debt from the transferee. Thus, the transferor remains entirely liable (without recourse to the transferee) to the mortgagee for the mortgage debt.

(2)   Assuming Transferee

If a transferee assumes a transferred mortgage, then a transferor can make a personal claim to recover the mortgage debt from the transferee. Therefore, although the transferor remains liable to the mortgagee for the mortgage debt, the transferor may seek a recovery for that debt from the transferee.

4)   APPLICATION OF SUBROGATION & SURETYSHIP

a)   Subrogation Principles

(1)   General Considerations

Subrogation refers to the substitution of one person in the place of another person with reference to a specific claim, demand, or right. The substituting party generally pays the debt or claim of another and, as a result, succeeds to the rights of the other in relation to the debt or claim and its rights, remedies, or securities.

Generally, three types of circumstances give rise to subrogation issues in the mortgage context:

- A subrogee voluntarily extinguishes the mortgage of another;
- A subrogee pays a debt for which the subrogee is not responsible in order to preserve some interest in the property; and
- A surety on a mortgage debt pays this debt.

(2)   Subrogation Rights

A party's payment of the obligation that a mortgage secures will result in subrogation of that party to the mortgagee's rights in the mortgage. For example, suppose Sal, a surety (guarantor) of Mac's mortgage, pays Mac's liability upon Mac's default of the mortgage. Sal would step into the shoes of the mortgagee (i.e., lender) and could exercise the right of foreclosure against Mac. The subrogee must completely pay the debt to obtain the right of subrogation.

b)   Suretyship Principles

(1)   Transfers "Subject to" a Mortgage

A transferor remains liable on the mortgage when a grantee (i.e., transferee) takes property "subject" to a mortgage. The grantee is not liable on the mortgage, but the mortgagee can still foreclose on the land to secure payment of the debt. The transferor has no recourse against the grantee if the mortgage is foreclosed.

(2)   Transfers "Assuming" a Mortgage

A transferor becomes a surety (i.e., guarantor) to a mortgagee when a transferee "assumes" a mortgage. A transferee and the land are the primary obligors on the mortgage. Additionally, the transferee may indemnify the transferor if the transferor is required to satisfy the mortgage.

c)   Subordination

(1)   Definition

A subordination agreement modifies the respective priorities of mortgage interests that the law and those documents provide. Such an agreement is subject to the recording statutes, which are discussed *infra*.

(2)   General Considerations

A subordination may be effective for any time duration. It may reverse the normal order of priority for liens. A subordination agreement may become effective upon the future execution of a mortgage that is adequately described.

5)   DUE ON SALE CLAUSES

Some mortgages include clauses providing that a mortgage is "due on sale" and "due on encumbrance" for the purpose of preventing a transfer of mortgages. Those clauses provide for acceleration of the mortgage by making the principal and interest immediately due and payable. Accordingly, a mortgage may include a clause requiring that, upon a sale of the mortgaged real estate, a mortgagor must fully pay the amount that remains due on the mortgage.

D.   **Transfers by Mortgagee**

1)   COMMON LAW

a)   Mortgagee

A mortgagee (i.e., lender) may transfer its mortgage interest to a third party.

b)   Means of Transfer

The type of mortgage and obligation involved will determine the ways in which the mortgagee may transfer an obligation. The UCC describes the means of transfer of an obligation to pay funds.

2)   UCC ARTICLE 3

a)   Negotiable Instruments

Subject to certain changes, most states have enacted statutes based on Article 3 of the UCC as the law governing negotiable instruments. The UCC defines a negotiable instrument as a writing that promises or mandates the payment of a specified sum of money. As its title indicates, parties may transfer such a writing between themselves by means of negotiation.

(1)   Promissory Notes

A promissory note is a negotiable instrument that a party may use to obtain payment in property law transactions. That type of note secures mortgages and similar loans. A note must satisfy the requirements of Article 3 to be considered negotiable.

(2)   Transfer by Negotiation

A transfer may be accomplished by negotiation if the payee-mortgagee endorses a negotiable promissory note and the payee-mortgagee physically transfers the note into the new holder's possession.

When a transferee is either ineligible for holder in due course status or would forego that status, then the parties may use methods to assign a non-negotiable instrument instead.

(3)   Holder in Due Course

A holder in due course takes possession of a negotiable instrument free from certain defenses such as payment, failure of consideration, and fraud. A holder in due course receives a note:

- in good faith;
- for value; and
- without notice that it has been dishonored, is overdue, or is subject to any claim or defense.

(a)   Defenses

A holder in due course possesses a note free from many of the defenses that a note's maker might raise against foreclosure or collection. The following "real" defenses are valid even against a holder in due course:

- misrepresentation that induces a party to execute an agreement;
- duress regarding, or the illegality of, a transaction;
- the infancy of a party to an agreement; or

- discharge in an insolvency proceeding.

b)   Derivative Title Rule

The derivative title rule prevents a property owner from transferring rights in a piece of property that exceed the owner's rights.

(1)   Exception for Negotiable Instruments

The derivative title rule does not apply to negotiable instruments. A *bona fide* purchaser who lacks awareness of a defect in title to an instrument, or any claims against it, takes that title free of any defects or claims. With respect to the inapplicability of the derivative title rule, Article 3 furnishes warranties for transactions that involve negotiable instruments.

c)   Non-negotiable Instruments

A party may only transfer a non-negotiable instrument by assignment, not by negotiation. The ways to assign a non-negotiable instrument are:

- An assignor's verbal communication that an assignment is being made;
- A written instrument of assignment that a mortgagee-payee executes to an assignee; or
- The mortgagee-payee indorses an original note; or
- A transfer of possession of a note, which is not a necessary part of the above methods.

E.   Discharge and Defenses

1)   DISCHARGE

a)   Definition

In both title theory and lien theory states, a discharge occurs when the entire mortgage debt is paid in full, such that a mortgagor and his transferee have no further payment obligation to a mortgagee.

b)   Prepayment

The majority rule provides that a mortgagor may not prepay a mortgage debt prior to its due date unless the parties have expressly stipulated to the contrary. A provision allowing prepayment may be enforceable if the parties were knowledgeable and entered into their agreement after dealing at arm's length.

c)   Late Payment

(1)   Title Theory States

A mortgagor's late payment does not discharge a mortgage lien if a mortgagee rejected it.

(2)   Lien Theory States

The majority rule is that a mortgagor's late payment discharges a mortgage lien if a mortgagee rejected it.

d)   Merger

If a fee title and a mortgagee's interest both coexist with respect to the same individual or entity, a lesser estate (i.e., a mortgage), merges into a greater estate (i.e., a fee interest). Consequently, the merger extinguishes the mortgage. This doctrine allows a mortgagor to argue that a mortgage does not exist and provides a defense in a foreclosure action.

2)   DEFENSES

a)   Payment to Assignor

A mortgagee (i.e., lender) may assign an interest in a mortgage to an assignee. The mortgage will then be payable to the assignee. A question that may arise is what happens if the mortgagor pays the mortgagee as assignor instead of the assignee.

An assignee of a mortgage may seek to recover payment of the mortgage from a mortgagor who previously paid for the balance due on the mortgage to a mortgagee. The mortgagor may potentially raise the defense of prior payment.

(1)   Notice Received

If a mortgagor receives notice of the assignment, then any subsequent payment that the mortgagor makes to the mortgagee as assignor will not serve as a defense to the assignee's action on the obligation or for a foreclosure.

(2)   No Notice

If a mortgagor (i.e., borrower) does not receive notice of the assignment, then any subsequent payment that the mortgagor makes to the original mortgagee as assignor will serve as a defense to the assignee's action on the obligation or for a foreclosure.

★   F.   **Foreclosure**

1)   GENERAL CONSIDERATIONS

| Question Key |
| 162,170 |

A mortgagor's failure to make payments will result in a default of the mortgagor's obligations to a mortgagee. A mortgagor's failure to cure a default may cause a mortgagee to seek foreclosure of the mortgage. Foreclosure is a way for a mortgagee to legally enforce a mortgage by applying the proceeds from a sale of the security, the mortgaged premises, towards satisfying the mortgagor's debt obligation.

a)   Mortgagor's Responses

A mortgagor may respond to a foreclosure either by voluntarily redeeming (i.e., paying-off) the mortgage obligation or by disputing the foreclosure.

2)   TYPES

a)   Judicial Foreclosure

A judicial foreclosure is a judgment rendered by a court in favor of foreclosure of a mortgage or deed of trust. The judicial foreclosure judgment will order that the real property that secured the debt be sold under foreclosure proceedings to pay the debt. Thus, if a mortgagee prevails in a foreclosure action to recover the balance due on a mortgage, then a trial court will direct a sale of the mortgaged interest in real property to satisfy the amount of a judgment of foreclosure.

(1)   Liability for Deficiency

If the sale proceeds are insufficient to satisfy the judgment, then the court will calculate the amount of deficiency for which it may award a decree. A mortgagor may be personally liable for the amount of that deficiency.

b)   Power of Sale

(1)   Definition

A foreclosure under power of sale only occurs if the mortgage's terms provide for this private remedy that does not involve the courts.

(2)   Statutory Protections

State statutes may provide certain procedural safeguards for a mortgagor that is subject to a power of sale. Those legal provisions apply in addition to any process or procedure that the parties stipulated in the mortgage. State statutes may also allow a mortgagor to bring a legal challenge to the results of a sale under a power of sale if:

- the sale price "shocks the conscience" because of gross inadequacy; or
- the sale involves unconscionable or fraudulent conduct.

(a)   Trust Deed Foreclosure

Some states allow a trustee to foreclose on a trust deed without judicial proceedings if the trust deed contains a power of sale clause.

c)   Strict Foreclosure

The most commonly used types of foreclosures are the judicial foreclosure and the power of sale. Another less prevalent type of foreclosure, though, is the strict foreclosure.

Under a strict foreclosure, the mortgagor is given a certain amount of time to pay the debt. If he fails to do so, under a strict foreclosure, the mortgagee (i.e., lender), takes title to the property directly instead of forcing a sale of the property.

Most states do not permit strict foreclosures.

3)   PRIORITY AMONG MORTGAGEES

Typically, the type of recording statute used in the jurisdiction will determine priority. Usually, a prior properly recorded interest is senior to a subsequent properly recorded interest.

a)   Destruction of Junior Interests

A foreclosure will destroy any interest junior to the interest being foreclosed upon if that junior interest was made a party to the foreclosure action (e.g., duly received notice of the action) and did not participate in it or take any other action. A senior interest to the one foreclosed upon, however, will remain intact. Therefore, any person who purchases property upon the foreclosure of a junior mortgagee will take the property subject to the interests of any and all senior mortgagees.

As a practical matter, if the title to a mortgaged property purchased at foreclosure sale by a buyer other than the former mortgagor is free from any mortgage liens, the buyer could subsequently sell the property to the former mortgagor. If, for example, the buyer and the former mortgagor did not act in collusion with respect to this transaction, a former mortgagee of the property with a junior interest in the property--who duly received notice of the foreclosure and did not participate in it or take any other action--cannot successfully challenge this transaction on the basis of fraud.

4)   RIGHTS OF OMITTED PARTIES

a)   Parties Possessing Right of Redemption

If a foreclosure action does not include a party possessing a right to redeem a mortgage, that action does not eliminate the party's interest. Rather, the foreclosure is void with respect to the party's right. The omission of the party from a foreclosure does not prevent a purchaser at the foreclosure sale from succeeding to all of the real property owner's rights. The omitted party may redeem the real property and title to it by paying the purchaser the amount of the mortgage debt. This rule also applies to junior lienholders who may exercise a right of foreclosure, redemption, or to recover on a surplus.

b)   Junior Lienholders

If a foreclosure action resulting in a sale does not include a junior lienholder, then the action does not automatically destroy the interest of the junior lienholder. This rule applies because the junior lienholder did not have the opportunity to be present at the foreclosure sale in order to maximize the price obtained in order to preserve his interest. Courts have primarily afforded such an omitted junior lienholder with two remedies under these circumstances. First, the junior lienholder could foreclose on the property again. The junior lienholder would be entitled to any funds in excess of funds originally owed to the senior lienholders. In that case, the original buyer would stand in the shoes of the senior lienholder. Second, the junior lienholder could pay the full amount due under the original senior lien on the property. As a result, the junior lienholder would be assigned the senior lienholder's interest. Consequently, the junior lienholder would possess rights under both the senior and junior liens.

5)   DEFICIENCY AND SURPLUS

a)   Results of a Foreclosure Sale

If a lawful forfeiture results in a sale of a mortgaged interest in real property, then at least three results could occur. First, if the amount that a buyer paid is equal to the balance that is due on the mortgage, then the mortgagee receives a full recovery. Second, if the amount that the buyer paid is less than the mortgage balance that is due, then a deficiency remains due to the mortgagee (i.e., lender). In that event, the mortgagor (i.e., borrower) remains liable to pay that balance due. Third, if the buyer pays an amount that is greater than the remaining mortgage balance, then a surplus exists.

b)   Allocation of Surplus

The junior lienholders receive first payment of the surplus, and the mortgagor receives any residue.

c)   Priority among Multiple Mortgages

Two or more simultaneously executed mortgages have equal priority to the surplus unless either a collateral agreement provides otherwise, or a recording act affects their priority. Two or more consecutively executed mortgages have priority in order of their sequence unless either a collateral agreement provides otherwise, or a recording act affects their priority.

6)   REDEMPTION AFTER FORECLOSURE

a)   Statutory Right

Some states provide a statutory right of redemption to a mortgagor whose mortgage went through foreclosure. Thus, the statute affords the mortgagor a specified time period in which to pay the mortgagee, at a minimum, the amount of the deficiency on the mortgage. A statute might also require the mortgagor to pay the costs and fees of the foreclosure. Fulfillment of the statutory requirements entitles the mortgagor to the real property.

7) DEED IN LIEU OF FORECLOSURE

Certain jurisdictions allow a mortgagor who otherwise would be subject to foreclosure to provide a mortgagee (i.e., lender), with the deed as additional security for the unpaid mortgage debt. Further, a mortgagee may purchase a mortgagor's equity of redemption (the right to redeem the property) under the following circumstances:

- The purchase occurs after the mortgage exists, not before or when it is created;
- The transaction involved no fraud;
- Sufficient consideration supports the transaction; and
- The mortgagee carries the burden of proving the transaction's fairness.

V.   TITLE

Unlike a certificate of title for a vehicle, one official paper does not necessarily represent title to real property. An owner of an interest in real property will ordinarily possess a deed reflecting that interest. This deed is a documented form of title. Despite the Statute of Frauds, adverse possession is one situation when a person may obtain a claim of title to real property in the absence of a written instrument like a deed.

★★   **A.   Adverse Possession**

Question Key
10,44,130,155

1)   DEFINITION

Adverse possession is a doctrine that allows a non-owner of a real property estate who is in possession of that estate to obtain a legal right of title to own and use the estate under certain conditions.

★★   a)   Elements

For purposes of the Multistate Bar Examination, the essential elements of adverse possession include a person's entry upon and remaining in actual possession of real property in an open, continuous, and exclusive manner under a claim of right for the legally required period during which the actual owner may assert a legal claim for possession of the real property. More specifics about these elements, as well as other general common law elements that could apply in particular jurisdictions, are set forth *infra*. Accordingly, as a general rule, adverse possession requires fulfillment of the following physical, mental, and time conditions:

(1)   Open & Notorious

The person claiming adverse possession must have engaged in open use of the estate that is visible in an inspection of the estate. This non-owner's use of the estate must also be notorious or obviously evident. In other words, the claimant must engage in acts of possession consistent with ownership of the property at issue in a manner which is capable of being seen.

(2)   Actual

The claimant's use of the estate is actual use or in the manner that an owner would use the estate. This use, however, generally does not need to be the estate's best and highest use.

(3)   Hostile

The claimant's use of the estate must be hostile. Courts determine hostile or adverse use by one of the following three types of tests:

(a)   Trespass

Did a non-owner act with a deliberate intention of obtaining title to real property while aware that the property belonged to another?

(b)   Objective

Did a non-owner use the property without permission as the owner would? (This analysis disregards the non-owner's subjective belief.)

(c)   Good Faith

Did a non-owner use the property based on a good faith belief that the non-owner held title to the property?

•   Permission Exception

Generally, an owner's permission will negate the element of hostile or adverse use unless the non-owner's occupancy exceeded the duration of the owner's permission. For example, if the owner's agents inspect the property and ignore the non-owner's presence, the owner is bound by that fact which supports the non-owner's claim of open and hostile possession.

(4)   Continuous

The claimant's use of the estate must be continuous and uninterrupted.

(5)   Exclusive

The claimant's use of the estate must be "exclusive" without sharing it with another.

(6)   Period

The possession must be for a legally-required period.

(a)   Adverse Possession Period

State statute usually dictates the period that is required for adverse possession to occur. The most common statutory periods are 10, 15, or 20 years in length. The statutory period for adverse possession commences when a non-owner makes a hostile entry onto the premises.

(i)   Tolling

(A)   Disabilities

Tolling of the statutory period may occur for the duration of an estate owner's suffering from any of the following disabilities: imprisonment, infancy (i.e., age of minority), or legal incapacity.

(B)   Statutes

State statutes may provide for a specific amount of time in which an estate owner may bring an action to challenge a claim of adverse possession after the disability ends. Certain states may require that the disability must have existed when the adverse possession began. For example, a statute may provide that the tolling period is 20 years or until the owner reaches the age of majority, whichever occurs first.

(b)   Tacking of Statutory Period

The principle of tacking combines a claimant's period of possession with a prior possessor's period of "continuous" use. In order to tack possession periods, all of the possessing parties must be in privity.

(i)   Bases of Privity

A successor will be in privity with a prior possessor, or predecessor, if, as the subsequent possessor, the successor obtains the real property by deed, devise, or descent. A successor who takes possession through a voluntary transfer from a predecessor may tack its period of possession from when the predecessor commenced possession.

(c)   Interruption of Statutory Period

Interruption of adverse possession occurs when an estate owner retakes possession before the legally-required period of adverse possession expires.

b)   Constructive Adverse Possession (Color of Title)

Constructive adverse possession applies when a non-owner takes possession of part of an owner's tract of real property under color of title. The term color of title refers to a claim based on a written instrument such as a deed, a will, or a judgment that may have been defective and invalid. The non-owner must reasonably believe that its deed was valid.

(1)   Reasonable Connection Rule

The adverse possession of part of an owner's tract will be adequate to provide the non-owner title to the whole parcel of land, provided that a reasonable connection exists between that part of the parcel that is actually possessed and the entire tract.

★★   c)   Marketability of Title

As a general matter, adverse possession secures equitable title. Equitable title to property obtained by adverse possession generally is not marketable. Title that is obtained through adverse possession is usually deemed marketable only if an adverse possessor received a judgment quieting title. Such a judgment will make the adverse possessor the owner of record, which can be the basis for issuing a deed that provides marketable legal title. Legal title to property obtained as a result of adverse possession generally is equally valid as legal title obtained otherwise.

d)   Payment of Property Taxes

The rule in a majority of states is that an owner's property taxes payment will not negate a non-owner's claim of adverse possession. Another majority rule provides that the non-owner does not need to pay property taxes to establish adverse possession. Stoebuck and Whitman, *The Law of Property* 854 (3d ed. 2000). However, in a minority of states, the non-owner cannot establish adverse possession unless he pays property taxes. *Id.* at n.7.

e)   Government Land

Government-owned land is generally exempt from adverse possession.

★★★★   **B.   Conveyancing by Deed**

★★★★   1)   DEED TYPES

Question Key
1,20,46,63,67,70,80,84,86,102, 107,108,129,132,144,157

A deed is a document that facilitates a conveyance of a property interest between a grantor and a grantee. The Statute of Frauds requires that the deed instrument be in writing, be signed by the transferor, and contain the essential terms. Those terms include the grantee's name and a sufficient description of the land to be enforceable. The main types of deeds include Quitclaim Deed, Special Warranty Deed, and General Warranty Deed.

a)   Quitclaim Deed

A quitclaim deed includes no promises or covenants from a grantor to a grantee. Consequently, a grantee takes title "as is" under a quitclaim deed.

b)   Special Warranty Deed

A special warranty deed includes six essential covenants (discussed below) for a grantee that are limited to remedying defects of title that are attributable to a transferor. It is a deed in which the grantor warrants, or guarantees, the title only against defects arising during the period of his tenure and ownership of the property. It does not warrant against defects existing before that time.

c)   General Warranty Deed

A general warranty deed provides six primary covenants to a grantee that warrant against all defects of title. A grantor is liable for a breach of any covenant. The six primary covenants include three present covenants and three future covenants. Those covenants are further discussed *infra* under the subtopic of "Covenants For Title."

2)   NECESSITY FOR A GRANTEE

In order for a deed to be valid, a grantor must specifically identify a grantee in the deed. Although use of the grantee's name may be sufficient, the grantor may also include, or be required to include, grantee's address for identification purposes. The law does not require the grantee's signature to make a deed valid.

3)   DELIVERY AND ESCROWS

Generally, to be effective, a deed must be executed, delivered, and accepted. It should also be recorded.

a)   Execution

For a deed to be a valid instrument, it must at a minimum set forth in writing:

- the parties' names;
- an accurate legal description of the land;
- language indicating an intention to convey the land; and
- a signature by a grantor.

A grantor's signature on a deed fulfills the execution requirement of item 'iv'. A deed is void if it lacks one of the essential items 'i-iv' *supra*. A deed to a grantee who does not exist is void. When the grantee's name does not appear in a deed, a court may find the deed valid if it includes language that enables the court to determine the grantee's identity, such as "to the grantor's sister."

b)   Delivery

For a deed to operate as a valid conveyance, a grantor needs to:

- show intent to immediately transfer an interest in real property; and
- engage in conduct or cause one to engage in conduct conveying a deed.

(1)   Intent Requirement

Evidence of intent may include words or conduct showing an interest in making a transfer. Physical transfer of a deed from a grantor to a grantee demonstrates intent, although it is not a necessary step in making a delivery. A grantor's agent may deliver the deed to a grantee or the grantee's agent.

(2)   Delivery Requirement

The grantor must deliver the title unconditionally. Therefore, a grantor cannot condition its delivery of title to a grantee upon the occurrence of a future event. For example, if such a condition of delivery is the grantor's decease, courts will not enforce the transfer because the grantor lacked an effective present intent to deliver title.

(a)   Presumption against Delivery

A presumption exists that there was no valid delivery of a deed if a grantor fails to transfer the deed to a grantee. The parties may introduce evidence to overcome this presumption.

(i)   Parol Evidence
        Admissible

Parol evidence is admissible to prove whether a grantor intended to make a present transfer of a deed. For example, testimony is admissible to show that a grantor instructed its agent that the grantor possessed a right to retrieve a deed before the agent delivered it to a grantee.

(A)   Detrimental
        Reliance

In the absence of a written deed, a purported grantee must establish that the grantee acted in detrimental reliance upon an alleged grantor's asserted promise to transfer the deed.

★★★

c)   Acceptance

A grantee has no obligation to accept a deed. The grantee's acceptance of the deed is a prerequisite to the completion of a grantor's delivery of the deed.

(1)   Presumption of Acceptance

A majority of states presume acceptance by a grantee if the deed would be beneficial to a grantee. A grantee must accept or reject a deed within a reasonable period from the time of delivery.

(a)   Recordation not Required

The fact that a grantee neither acknowledges a deed's delivery and acceptance nor records it will not affect the deed's validity.

(2)   Rebutting Presumption of Acceptance

The courts may consider a grantee's conduct and statements to ascertain whether the grantee accepted or rejected the delivery of a deed. Evidence of the grantee's contrary conduct may rebut the presumption of acceptance.

d)   Escrow

Escrow is a means by which a grantor may transfer a deed to a grantee. The grantor places an executed deed in the possession of a third party that lacks any conflict of interest with either the grantor or the grantee. The third party holds the deed pursuant to instructions on the conditions for release of the deed. When a grantee fulfills those conditions, such as making a payment to the grantor, then the third party will deliver the deed to the grantee.

(1)   Delivery to Agent Insufficient

The majority of courts hold that a grantor lacks a present intent to transfer title if, in an escrow situation, the grantor only provides a deed to the grantor's agent. In that event, the grantor fails to make a delivery because the grantor could require the agent to return the deed instead of providing it to a grantee.

(2)   Types of Escrow

(a)   Sales Escrow

A custodian that is a professional individual or a commercial entity processes a sales escrow. For certain purposes, and if specified conditions are fulfilled, a delivery of the deed by the custodian to a grantee will relate back to the date that the grantor put the deed in escrow.

(i)   Relation-Back Doctrine

This relation-back capability allows for a closing to occur even if the grantor dies or becomes incapacitated prior to the closing date. The relation-back feature applies if a true escrow occurred under these two conditions:

- A grantee and a grantor entered into an enforceable sale agreement; and
- The grantor failed to reserve a right to recall the deed from its custodian.

(b)   Death Escrow

A death escrow is an arrangement between a grantor and a layman custodian. A death escrow exists when a deed is put in escrow until the grantor dies and then the custodian provides it to the grantee upon the grantor's death. The requirement for a death escrow to be valid is that the grantor not be able to control the deed. Thus, a death escrow would not be valid if the grantor possessed an express right to recall the deed.

(i)   Relation-Back Doctrine

Generally, in a death escrow situation, the courts consider the grantor's delivery of the deed to the custodian as immediately conveying title to the grantee, so the relation-back doctrine does not apply.

★★   e)   Reconveyance

The courts in most jurisdictions will presume that a grantee accepted a grantor's conveyance if it was legally sufficient in terms of execution, delivery, and acceptance. Thus, in order to reconvey title to the grantor, the grantee must use a new deed that includes all of the necessary formalities. In other words, the grantee cannot effectively reconvey title simply by returning the delivered deed to the grantor.

★★   f)   Conveyance by Gift

A party may make a gift of real property. In order for the gift to succeed, the law requires a deed as well as the elements for a gift. The elements of a gift are 1) intent; 2) delivery; and 3) acceptance. The donor must possess a donative intent. Delivery (actual or constructive) must occur. Courts presume acceptance if the gift is beneficial, but the parties can rebut the presumption. Once complete, the donor or donee cannot revoke the gift. Thus, as with a conveyance for consideration, if the elements of a gift are satisfied, in order to reconvey title to the donor, the donee must use a new deed that includes all of the necessary formalities.

★   g)   Conveyance by Dedication

A landowner may choose to transfer an interest in real property to the public in the form of a dedication. Landowners may make dedications for public use for several different purposes including property dedicated for use as public schools, museums, streets, and parks. A dedication requires both an offer and acceptance to be valid. An oral offer of dedication does not fall under the Statute of Frauds. Therefore, such a dedication does not have to be in writing to be valid. The public entity must take affirmative action to accept. In other words, courts do not presume acceptance because public entities may want to avoid assuming the burdens, such as maintenance, that come with the property.

4)   LAND DESCRIPTION AND BOUNDARIES

As with sell and buy contracts, the Statute of Frauds requires that a deed contain a written identification and description of the land that a deed conveys. A more precise and accurate land description decreases likelihood of dispute over what land is conveyed and increases the likelihood of enforceability. For example, a statement that a grantor is conveying half of the land is an insufficient description of the land to allow for specific performance of a conveyance pursuant to a deed.

a)   Official Descriptions

The federal Government Survey System and the local subdivision plat are two types of official land descriptions. Official maps from local governments or boundaries described by metes and bounds are also valid types of descriptions.

(1)   Monuments and Watercourses

The use of monuments or streams and rivers as boundaries may present difficulties with land descriptions because the monuments may be removed, and the streams and rivers may change course. If the shift in a watercourse boundary is gradual, whether caused by artificial or natural processes, the boundary will likely still follow the course of the water, so long as the benefiting owner did not act to deprive the other owner.

b)   Correcting Descriptions

If a description is ambiguous, courts will allow the introduction of extrinsic evidence to aid in identifying the land; however, if there is no ambiguity, the grantor cannot introduce such evidence to show that he did not intend to convey the land described.

c)   Reformation Doctrine

(1)   Majority Approach

The majority of states recognize the doctrine of reformation, which allows for the modification of a written description that does not satisfy the parties' intentions. The modification's purpose is to fulfill the parties' intentions regarding the boundaries of the conveyed premises.

(2)   Minority Approach

The minority of states only permit reformation to limit or decrease the size of a parcel of land. In that event, a reformed deed may not convey more or different property.

5)   COVENANT OF TITLE

Covenants are promises that relate to the real property. As indicated *supra*, a warranty deed usually includes six covenants unless the terms of that deed explicitly exclude them. These covenants fall into the two categories of present covenants and future covenants.

a)   Present Covenants

The present covenants of title are 1) of seisin, 2) right to convey, and 3) against encumbrances. A breach of the present covenants may only occur at the time when the conveyance occurs. The statute of limitations for lawsuits seeking to enforce present covenants starts to run when title to real property passes in a conveyance by deed.

(1)   Covenant of Seisin

The majority of states consider a covenant of seisin as a promise that a grantor owns the estate that a deed purports to convey. The minority of states consider a covenant of seisin as a promise that a grantor has possession of land, whether or not that possession is wrongful.

(2)   Covenant of the Right to Convey

The covenant of the right to convey provides that the seller warrants that he possesses the right to convey the property. Some minor differences exist between the covenants of seisin and of the right to convey. The right to convey is a promise that no valid restraint on alienation that applies to a real property interest prevents a grantor from making a conveyance (even assuming that he is the owner of the property).

(3)   Covenant against Encumbrances

Encumbrances are the rights or interests of third parties to which a deed is subject. Examples of encumbrances are restrictive covenants, leases, easements, mortgages, and liens. The covenant against encumbrances is a promise that the deed is free from such third party interests.

b)   Future Covenants

In a future covenant, the buyer can sue a prior grantor. In other words, the buyer can sue someone who is further up the chain of title if the prior grantor deeded the property with a future covenant.

(1)   Types of Future Covenants

The three future covenants of title are of warranty, quiet enjoyment, and further assurances. They are promises that nothing will disturb a grantee's possession.

(a)   Covenant of Warranty

The covenant of warranty is that the grantor will warrant and defend the title of the grantee against rightful claims regarding the title conveyed. *See e.g.,* Utah Code Ann. § 57-1-12.

(b)   Covenant of Quiet Enjoyment

According to the covenant of quiet enjoyment, a grantor warrants that the grantee may possess and quietly enjoy the land. *See e.g.,* Utah Code Ann. § 57-1-12 (2000) (providing that grantor "guarantees the grantee, his heirs, and assigns . . . the quiet possession" of premises conveyed).

(c)   Covenant of Further Assurances

Under the covenant of further assurances, the grantor represents that he will do whatever is necessary in the future to establish title in the grantee.

(2)   Eviction

There is no breach of future covenants until a grantee is disturbed in possession, which constitutes an eviction. In the context of future covenants, eviction possesses a different meaning than this word does in the context of landlord and tenant relations. Accordingly, the consequence of an eviction is not an actual loss of possession of the premises.

(3)   Enforcing Future Covenants

No cause of action accrues until one in possession of a title superior to that of the grantee causes a grantee's eviction. An "eviction" sufficient to trigger the protection may result from several occurrences including, for example: a judicial decree that the original grantee lacks title or must leave the property; another party's interference with the original grantee's possession; or the grantee's relinquishment of possession of the real property to the third party.

(a)   Damages

Generally, the grantor cannot be liable for damages amounting to more than the grantee paid for the property. When the breach is for encumbrances, the grantee may be able to receive damages in the amount of the diminution of value.

(b)   Statute of Limitations

The statute of limitations runs from the eviction date. The covenant of quiet enjoyment, however, runs with the land. Thus, the statute of limitations does not apply to actions contesting an eviction based on a breach of the covenant of quiet enjoyment. Therefore, a remote grantee may bring a lawsuit against an initial grantor seeking damages if a third party claimant interferes with the grantee's possession and enjoyment.

(i)   Liquidated Damages

A party may enforce a deed's liquidated damages clause if it is reasonably related to the amount of damages that were foreseeable when the parties entered into the contract.

c)   Merger Doctrine

★★★   (1)   Common Law

The doctrine of merger provides that if a buyer accepts a deed from a seller, the buyer may only bring claims that arise from title defect issues that may be asserted pursuant to the deed's title covenants. The merger results in the deed's covenants of title subsuming any covenants of title in the sell and buy contract.

(2)   Modern Law

The modern application of that rule is to only merge those covenants of title in a sell and buy contract that are the same as the covenants in a deed of conveyance. Thus, any covenants in the contract that are different from those in the deed will not be merged. Although this trend is the modern trend, the common law approach is the majority approach.

6)   <u>TITLE PROBLEMS</u>

a)   Title Defects

Some title defects occur at the time of the conveyance; however, parties may discover other title defects only after a conveyance occurs. In that event, a buyer may seek a remedy against a seller. The following types of defects may render a title defective include: 1) complete claims to the land made by a third party that deprive the grantee of title, such as through adverse possession or a defect in the chain of title; and 2) undisclosed partial claims to the land, such as those of encumbrancers (easements, covenants, etc).

b)   Defective Deed Issues

(1)   Deed Construction Rule

In dealing with disputes concerning ambiguous provisions in a deed, many courts admit testimony in order to clarify those provisions. The courts generally resolve such ambiguities against a deed's drafter.

(2)   Deed Reformation

If a formally correct deed contains inadvertent errors, a court will reform the deed in equity based on "clear and convincing" evidence.

(a)   Good Faith Purchaser Exception

A court will not reform an erroneous deed in favor of a third party if a *bona fide* purchaser has relied upon that deed's provisions.

c)   Void and Voidable Deeds

If a deed involves defects regarding its execution, delivery, or that raise a question of a grantor's capacity, then the grantor and his successors might seek a declaration that the deed is void or voidable.

(1)   Voidable Deeds

A *bona fide* purchaser usually acquires valid title if a deed is voidable unless a minor executed the deed and disaffirms it in a reasonable time after attaining the age of majority.

(a)   Fraudulent Inducement

A deed is voidable due to a grantee's fraudulent inducement by means of:

- misrepresentation;
- false financial statement; or
- bad check.

(b)   Other Grounds for Deed Voidable

Specific bases upon which a deed becomes voidable are:

- execution by a minor;
- lack of capacity;
- breach of fiduciary duty;
- insanity;
- duress;
- mistake; and
- undue influence.

(2)   Void Deeds

A *bona fide* purchaser will not obtain title to a deed that includes a defect that renders it void. A deed is void under these circumstances:

- lack of delivery;
- forgery;
- fraudulent execution;
- fraudulent inducement; and
- grantor's illiteracy, senility, illness, and confusion.

C.   **Conveyancing by Will**

> Question Key
> 45

1)   <u>GENERAL CONSIDERATIONS</u>

Unlike a will, a deed cannot provide that it must take effect upon a grantor's decease. A deed and a will lack the same operative effect because they involve very different formalities. A grantor who wishes to make a conveyance effective upon his death must use a testamentary instrument, rather than a deed, to fulfill that purpose. Such an instrument may not be recorded or appear in a chain of title, which may create issues of conflicting claims of ownership under a recording act.

2)   <u>ADEMPTION</u>

a)   Doctrine of Ademption by Extinction

Under the doctrine of ademption, if the subject matter of a specific devise is not in the probate estate at the time of the testator's death, the bequest to the devisee adeems (i.e., fails). *See generally* William H. McGovern, Jr. and Sheldon F. Kurtz, *Wills, Trusts, and Estates*, p. 295, (2d ed. 2001). The doctrine of ademption by extinction applies only to specific devises. It does not apply to general or demonstrative devises. For example, suppose a testator's will leaves a fee simple estate to a beneficiary. Before the testator's death, the testator sells that estate to a third party. Under the general rule, the devisee receives nothing because the gift adeems by extinction.

(1)   Modification by Intent Theory

Some courts will temper this result and implement an intent theory to determine if the testator intended for the gift to adeem. If a beneficiary can prove that the testator did not intend for the gift to adeem, then the beneficiary will be entitled to a gift of equal value to the one that adeemed.

3)   <u>EXONERATION</u>

a)   Common Law

Under the common-law doctrine of exoneration, a specific beneficiary of encumbered real property is entitled to have a mortgage on the property paid from the estate as a debt of the decedent unless the evidence indicates that the testator had a contrary intent. *Martin v. Johnson*, 512 A.2d 1017 (D.C. 1986).

b)   Statutory Law

Today, many states have adopted statutes contrary to this common-law rule of exoneration. For example, the *Uniform Probate Code* provides that "a specific devise passes subject to any mortgage interest existing at the date of death, without right of exoneration, regardless of a general directive in the will to pay debts." Unif. Probate Code § 2-607. In states with statutes of this type, the specific devisee of encumbered real property takes it subject to a mortgage notwithstanding the fact that a will contained a clause directing an executor to pay the decedent's debts.

4)   LAPSE

If a devisee named in a testator's will predeceases the testator, the devise lapses into the residuary estate unless the jurisdiction's anti-lapse statute preserves the devise for the devisee's descendants. In many jurisdictions, a devise to a person who is a descendant of the testator's grandparents does not lapse if the deceased person's descendants survive the testator. Rather, a substituted gift is created in the deceased person's descendants.

For example, suppose Terrence passes away, leaving a will. The will provides that his stock in IBM is to be left to his cousin Sally. Unfortunately, Sally died just a few months before Terrence, and Terrence had not changed his will. Normally, the IBM stock would adeem to the estate and pass by intestacy. Many jurisdictions, though, have anti-lapse statutes that save a gift made to a descendant of a grandparent (some statutes deviate from this rule and will save gifts made to a descendant of parents or even descendants of the grandparents of a testator's spouse). If the jurisdiction possesses such a statute, then the gift of the IBM stock would be made to Sally's descendant(s). Therefore, absent a contrary intent in the will, Melanie, Sally's only daughter, would receive the stock.

★★★★ **D.**   **Priorities and Recording**

Question Key
8,18,19,37,43,46,56,71,94, 105,119,139,141,142,148, 156.159.165

1)   RECORDING SYSTEMS

        a)   General Considerations

The existence of and access to a public recording system does not usually provide a title researcher with a definitive summary statement as to all interests that exist in certain real property. Rather, those systems provide a repository for all documents that reflect ownership interests in and encumbrances upon the real property.

        b)   Types of Recording Systems

Individuals may record deeds of conveyance in either of two types of systems:

- indexes of grantor-grantee and grantee-grantor; or
- a tract index that lists properties by geographic location.

                (1)   Grantor-Grantee System

Most states possess an index of grantors and an index of grantees. In theory, one would perform a title search by beginning with the grantor index. One would look up the name of the first recorded owner of title to property. This owner is usually the government. The search would attempt to locate the first grant from the government to the first grantee. The next step is to look up the grantee's name in the grantor index to locate the deed by which it subsequently conveyed the title to the property. The search is continued with each subsequent grantor until the searcher finds no more grants. An alternative method is to reverse the process. Thus, one may search backward in the grantee index. An individual would conduct this search by beginning with the name of the person or entity who is thought to own the land to find the grantor to it. Then the individual would search the grantee index again to find the source of that grantor's title, and so on until reaching the grant from the government. These links from grantor to grantee are called the "chain of title." The last grantee found is the "record title holder."

A prospective purchaser must research the chain of title.

The holder of record-title is not automatically the owner of the land. For example, if a person conveys title to property to someone else, even though it is not recorded, he may have nothing left to transfer to any subsequent person. As a result of the various state recording laws, though, the courts will protect a purchaser who pays valuable consideration and does not have knowledge of the prior unrecorded deed from the claims of a prior grantee under that deed.

2)   <u>TYPES OF PRIORITY</u>

In the absence of a state recording act that establishes the priority of conveyances of the same interest in real property from a common grantor to different grantees, the actual sequence of the delivery of each deed may establish that priority. The recording acts may operate to alter that common law approach of "first in time, first in right" and its results. The three primary types of acts are race, notice, or race-notice.

a)   Recording Acts

(1)   Pure Race Recording Act

Some states have a pure race recording act ("act"). A pure race recording act provides that a buyer for value who is first in time to record an acquired interest in real property possesses a priority interest over any other buyers. The act is a derivative of the first-in-time rule. The act applies to situations when a grantor of a real property interest conveys a deed to a first buyer and then subsequently conveys another deed for the same interest to a second buyer. Of those two buyers, the one who records first will prevail.

(2)   Notice Recording Act

Some states have a notice recording act. A notice recording act provides that regardless of which of multiple buyers for value first records, a subsequent *bona fide* purchaser for value of an interest in real property will prevail if that purchaser lacked notice of the other buyers' prior interests. That purchaser will also prevail over a grantee or devisee who fails to record his interest.

(3)   Race-Notice Recording Act

Some states have a race-notice recording act ("act"). This type of act allows a subsequent buyer for value without notice of a prior interest in the same real property to prevail over other prior buyers for value. Under a race-notice act, a subsequent buyer of a real property interest generally will only prevail if he is a *bona fide* (i.e., good faith) purchaser, for value, who also records before the initial buyer. Typically, in a race-notice jurisdiction, a new buyer has a grace period after the sale in which to record. A grace period would prevent the prior buyer who failed to record from recording immediately upon finding out about the sale to the new owner but before the new owner has the time to record the conveyance.

Under this type of act, usually in a dispute between a subsequent good faith buyer relying upon the record title and a prior grantee (e.g., a purchaser or donee) of a previously unrecorded conveyance of the same real property, the subsequent good faith buyer prevails if he acquired the property without knowledge or notice (i.e., actual, constructive, or record) of the prior grantee's interest. However, when a party has obtained equitable title to the real property by means of adverse possession before the good faith buyer obtained legal title from the record title owner, this equitable title cannot be defeated by the later conveyance from the record title owner to the good faith buyer, even though the real property is vacant when the buyer acquires it.

QUESTION

A creditor received a valid judgment against a debtor and promptly and properly filed the judgment in the county. Two years later, the debtor purchased land in the county and promptly and properly recorded the warranty deed to it. Subsequently, the debtor borrowed $30,000 from his aunt, signing a promissory note for that amount, which note was secured by a mortgage on the land. The mortgage was promptly and properly recorded. The aunt failed to make a title search before making the loan. The debtor made no payment to the creditor and defaulted on the mortgage loan from his aunt. A valid judicial foreclosure proceeding was held, in which the creditor, the aunt, and the debtor were named parties. A dispute arose as to which lien has priority. A statute of the jurisdiction provides: "Any judgment properly filed shall, for 10 years from filing, be a lien on the real property then owned or subsequently acquired by any person against whom the judgment is rendered." A second statute of the jurisdiction provides: "No unrecorded conveyance or mortgage of real property shall be good against subsequent purchasers for value without notice, who shall first record."

Who has the prior lien?

A) The aunt, because a judgment lien is subordinate to a mortgage lien.
B) The aunt, because she is a mortgagee under a purchase money mortgage.
C) The creditor, because its judgment was filed first.
D) The creditor, because the aunt had a duty to make a title search of the property.

The correct answer is choice (c). This is a race notice jurisdiction which protects a bona fide purchaser for value without notice who records first. The creditor filed first, giving the aunt constructive notice of the judgment lien. Accordingly, the judgment lien has priority.

---

          b)   Mortgagees

Courts consider mortgagees to be buyers under the recording acts because, like ordinary buyers of real property, they provided value for their interest in real property.

★★★   c)   Types of Notice

Notice is an essential element in determining rights of priority that arise from a conveyance of an instrument that reflects an interest in real property, such as a deed. The types of notice are as follows.

          (1)   Constructive Notice

Recording acts charge grantees with constructive notice of all correctly recorded prior conveyances of interest in real property that affect the same real property. In other words, a buyer is considered to possess constructive notice of recorded prior conveyances that appear in the chain of title. A person does not have constructive notice of a conveyance that is outside the chain of title.

          (a)   Collateral Documents Rule

The collateral documents rule provides that a grantee of real property possesses constructive notice of the contents of instruments regarding adjacent parcels of land if those parcels were conveyed by a common owner.

          (2)   Record Notice

Record notice exists if a reasonable review of public records would reveal a previously recorded instrument.

          (3)   Inquiry Notice

Inquiry notice occurs when a reasonable investigation would reveal facts about claims regarding real property if a buyer is aware of circumstances or facts that would lead a reasonable person to inquire further. For example, a potential buyer could visit the real property before making a purchase to determine who is in possession of it, if it contains defects, and if it matches the description of the land and any structures that are on the land. Thus, recording acts charge a buyer with actual knowledge of those facts that would have been discovered through a reasonable investigation.

          (4)   Actual Notice

Actual notice arises from knowledge that one literally obtains from another person. For example, a seller communicates to a buyer that, before a closing occurs on their contract to buy and sell real property, the seller will remove an encumbrance from title to that property.

(5)   Imputed Notice

Imputed notice applies only to certain relationships and means that if one person in that relationship possesses certain knowledge, then another person in that relationship is imputed to possess the same knowledge. Imputed notice may run from agent to principal, employee to employer, or spouse to spouse.

★   d)   Judgment Liens

(1)   Definitions

A judgment creditor is a party who prevails in a civil action seeking damages from a judgment debtor. For example, suppose Carl sues Daryl. Before the court enters any judgment, Daryl conveys his real property interest to Tom. Tom does not record the conveyance. Carl then obtains a judgment against Daryl. What would happen to the interest in the real property?

(a)   Minority Rule

Under the above example, a minority of the recording acts would not protect a third party's interest (Tom's) over that of a creditor.

(b)   Majority Rule

Under the above example, the majority of recording acts would not protect a creditor's lien interest (Carl's) over that of the third party (Tom's). In the majority of states, a judgment creditor lacks priority as compared to a grantee of real property before the court enters judgment.

(i)   Judgment Liens

Most recording acts do not consider a judgment creditor a *bona fide* purchaser for value. Thus, a judgment creditor may only apply a judgment lien against property that a debtor owned when the court entered judgment, excluding any recorded or unrecorded conveyances unless a recording act affords special protection to judgment liens.

e)   Fraudulent Conveyances and Bona Fide Purchasers

If a grantee obtains an interest in real property from a grantor by fraudulently inducing that conveyance, then the actual owner of a real property interest may void the conveyance in a civil action against the grantee. The actual owner, though, will not prevail in such an action against a *bona fide* purchaser from the grantee.

3)   SCOPE OF COVERAGE

★★★   a)   *Bona Fide* Purchasers

| Question Key |
| 8,43,71,141,142 |

(1)   Statutory Coverage

The recording acts will only protect *bona fide* purchasers who:

- have obtained an instrument of conveyance by giving valuable consideration;
- without notice of another party's prior deed that affects title to the same real estate.

In addition to specific state statutory protections of *bona fide* purchasers, such as under recording acts and the *Uniform Commercial Code*, the common law provides certain protection to such a purchaser.

Each jurisdiction provides different rules regarding the rights of a *bona fide* purchaser relative to previous buyers of the same interest.

b)   Recorded Instruments

(1)   No Automatic *Bona Fide* Purchaser Status

Most recording acts charge a subsequent buyer of a real property interest with constructive notice that another buyer previously recorded an instrument of conveyance for the same interest, despite the subsequent buyer's failure to search the records. Thus, the subsequent buyer is ineligible for *bona fide* status and protection if the previous grantee properly registered the previously recorded instrument and entered it in the appropriate governmental office.

(2)   *Bona Fide* Purchaser Status

Conversely, the subsequent buyer may be eligible for *bona fide* status if the previous grantee did not record the undiscovered instrument or properly register or enter it in the appropriate governmental office.

(3)   Instruments Outside the Chain of Title

A previously recorded instrument must exist and appear within the chain of title. If a reasonable person is unable to locate the instrument after a standard title search, then that instrument does not afford constructive notice because it does not exist within the chain of title.

(a)   Wild Deed

In an ordinary wild deed situation, someone other than the buyer's grantor creates a prior interest in the same real property outside of the chain of title. A wild deed is a deed that is either not recorded within the buyer's chain of title or recorded out of sequence (e.g., too late or too early). Thus, recording acts do not charge a buyer with notice of the wild deed because the wild deed is deemed unrecorded.

(b)   Improperly Indexed Deed

The instrument must be correctly indexed. If a public servant improperly filed the instrument that exists outside of the proper chain of title, then it does not exist for the purpose of affording constructive notice to a subsequent buyer. Not every properly recorded instrument necessarily affords constructive notice to the world. In other words, the instrument may be ineffective to provide notice.

c)   Effective Documents

An instrument reflecting an interest in real property must be effective in order to provide notice. A deed, for example, will not be effective if it lacks any of the minimum necessary elements such as the parties' identities, a statement of a grantor's intent to convey, a sufficient property description, and the grantor's signature. For example, if the grantor executes a deed that does not identify the grantee or describe the land, the deed will only become effective to convey title if the grantee's name and a land description is added. Until then, the deed is ineffective.

d)   Parties Protected

Obtaining *bona fide* purchaser status will protect new buyers (those who pay value) of interests in real property if a diligent title search fails to disclose a prior recorded interest in real property. Recording such an interest to give constructive notice to the world protects the present owners of those interests from losing them to subsequent buyers.

4)   <u>SPECIAL PROBLEMS</u>

a)   After-Acquired Title

| Question Key 12 |

(1)   Doctrine of Estoppel by Deed

The doctrine of estoppel by deed creates an implied covenant by the grantor to convey title to the grantee when the grantor receives interest in purportedly conveyed property after he delivers the deed. The doctrine applies under two conditions:

- A grantor conveys to a grantee a greater interest in real property than that which the grantor owns at the time of the transfer; and
- The grantor subsequently acquires the interest in real property that the grantor purported to own and previously convey to the grantee.

When those conditions are fulfilled, the doctrine of estoppel by deed prevents the grantor from asserting ownership of title to that interest as against the grantee. The doctrine also prevents the grantor from denying that he conveyed the title at issue to the grantee.

(2)   Legal Remedies

The grantee may bring an action against the grantor to obtain title to the real property. The courts may conclude that the grantor's acquisition of the title to the real property automatically transfers the title to the grantee. The grantee may choose to either pursue the action for damages or accept an automatic transfer of the title.

The law is unsettled as to whether the doctrine applies to an unwilling grantee.

b)   Forged Instruments

The courts consider forged instruments to be completely void. Thus, such instruments have no legal effect and cannot convey any interest in real property to a grantee or a *bona fide* purchaser in the chain of title.

c)   Transfers by Corporations and by Agents

Corporations, like individuals, generally may acquire and dispose of interests in real property. Unless statutory law provides otherwise, corporations may authorize agents to acquire, dispose of, and manage these property interests. The agents may be disclosed or undisclosed. The agents may possess actual or apparent authority. The scope of corporate authority and the nature of the authority of corporate agents are more fully described in other outlines that cover those legal subjects.

d)   Purchase Money Mortgages

(1)   General Considerations

A purchase money mortgage is a mortgage under which the seller of the real property loans money directly to a buyer of real property. Typically, the seller conveys title to the real property in exchange for a down payment, a mortgage on the property, and a promissory note or loan for paying the remaining balance due on the purchase price. Generally, purchase-money mortgages receive priority over every other type of interest attached to the property that is subject to the mortgage.

(2)   Right of Priority

(a)   General Rule

A purchase money mortgage receives priority over any other competing claims against the real property that secures it even if the competing claims were asserted contemporaneously with, or preexisted, the competing claims. This right of precedence in the purchase money mortgage exists even if a third party, such as a lender, funded the purchase. Thus, a purchase money mortgage receives precedence over the following types of competing claims:

- homestead;
- community property;
- dower;
- judgments granted, entered or recorded prior to execution of the

purchase money mortgage;

- a vendor's lien if the vendor failed to obtain a purchase money mortgage; and
- other mortgages that were created prior to or concurrently with the purchase money mortgage, even if such mortgages include after acquired property clauses. Such clauses only establish equitable mortgages.

(i)   Exceptions

The recording acts may provide exceptions to the rule of purchase money mortgage priority. A majority of the recording acts protect a mortgagee from an earlier purchase money mortgage that was not recorded if:

- The mortgagee took the mortgage without notice of an earlier unrecorded purchase money mortgage; and/or
- The mortgagee recorded its subsequent mortgage before the other mortgagee recorded the earlier purchase money mortgage.

The fact that the earlier mortgage secured some of the purchase cost is not relevant.

AMERIBAR BAR REVIEW

Multistate Bar Examination Preparation Course

TABLE OF CONTENTS

INTRODUCTION

A tort is a wrongful act not involving a breach of contract, which may justify a civil lawsuit. The examiners classify torts into five different categories: 1) intentional torts; 2) negligence; 3) strict liability; 4) products liability; and 5) other miscellaneous torts.

I.   INTENTIONAL TORTS

A.   General Requirements

Liability for any intentional tort exists if three general elements are proven: 1) intent; 2) a volitional act; and 3) causation.

Question Key
14,37,174

1)   INTENT

Intentional tort liability arises when one person intends to bring about some mental or physical result to another person. However, intent does not require a finding of intent to harm or injure. For example, suppose Daryl points a toy gun at Paul, making Paul think that Daryl is conducting a robbery. However, Daryl is playing a practical joke. Even if Daryl intends no harm, if he intends to put Paul in fear of an imminent harmful bodily contact, the intent required for assault is satisfied. The defendant need only intend to bring about the tortious result. The intent element does not require that the tortfeasor possess a wrongful motive or the intent to harm.

★   a)   Substantial Certainty

In addition to possessing the express intent to bring about the prohibited result, sufficient intent to ground an action in intentional tort includes when a defendant knows that the consequences are substantially certain to result from his actions.

For example, suppose Doris is standing on the platform waiting for the subway. She has an old sack of garbage she wants to discard. She looks for the garbage can, but sees that Danny is blocking it. She sees a small opening, slightly larger than the bag, between Danny's arm, his torso, and his briefcase. She decides to try to throw the bag in the hole between Danny's arm, the briefcase, and Danny's torso. She does not intend to hit Danny, but she has never had great aim, and knows her chances of getting the bag through the hole are small. She throws the bag and, sure enough, it hits Danny's torso, splattering ketchup from the bag onto his brand new designer suit. Although Doris did not intend to hit Danny, in fact, she wanted to miss him completely, she nonetheless was substantially certain she would hit him. Therefore, because she was substantially certain the contact would occur, she is deemed to possess the required intent for battery.

★   b)   Transferred Intent Doctrine

The Transferred Intent Doctrine may apply to an intentional tort when the plaintiff is not the defendant's intended victim. The Doctrine provides that when the defendant acts with intent to harm a first party but instead injures a second party, the defendant becomes liable to the second party.

For example, suppose Daniel intends to punch Edward. Just before Daniel winds up, Patrick walks in front of Edward. Daniel does not see him in time and ends up striking Patrick. Under the Transferred Intent Doctrine, even though Daniel did not possess the intent to strike Patrick, his intent to strike Edward will be transferred to Patrick, and Patrick may possess a cause of action against Daniel.

           c)   Capacity to Commit an Intentional Tort

All people have the capacity to commit an intentional tort, even young children.

        2)   <u>VOLITIONAL ACT</u>

A defendant must voluntarily move his body. Seizures, reflex action, or other non-controlled action are not volitional.

        3)   <u>CAUSATION</u>

A defendant's conduct, or some chain of events the defendant initiates, must have subjected a plaintiff to fear or harm defined as a tort.

        4)   <u>DAMAGES</u>

           a)   General

Except as noted, proof of actual damage is not required to prevail in an action for most intentional torts. A plaintiff may recover at least nominal damages from a defendant.

           b)   Punitive Damages

If a plaintiff can demonstrate that a defendant acted maliciously, the plaintiff may seek punitive damages. The plaintiff may not seek punitive damages in a simple negligence case.

           c)   Injunctive Relief

A plaintiff may seek injunctive relief, such as seeking an injunction to prevent a repetitive trespass.

B.   **Harms to the Person**

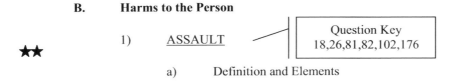

        1)   <u>ASSAULT</u>

Question Key
18,26,81,82,102,176

           a)   Definition and Elements

A person is liable for assault if he 1) acts, 2) intending to cause (a) a harmful or offensive contact with the other person, without making such contact, or (b) an imminent apprehension of a harmful or offensive contact, and 3) causes apprehension of an immediate harmful or offensive contact.

(1)   Volitional Act

A defendant must voluntarily move his body. Seizures, reflex action, or other non-controlled action are not volitional.

(2)   Intentional

A defendant must possess the intent to inflict upon a plaintiff a harmful or offensive touching or to cause apprehension of such an uninvited contact. The Transferred Intent Doctrine applies when the plaintiff was not the defendant's intended victim.

(3)   Apprehension

A defendant must have (1) placed a plaintiff in reasonable apprehension of an imminent harmful or offensive contact, and (2) the plaintiff must have subjective awareness of that harm when the defendant acted. In other words, the plaintiff must have apprehension about the contact, and that apprehension must be reasonable, meaning a person in a similar situation would have suffered the same apprehension.

The apprehension must be of imminent contact. Therefore, a person may escape liability for assault if he threatens harmful or offensive contact at some future time.

(4)   Causation

A defendant's conduct, or some chain of events the defendant initiates, must place a plaintiff in apprehension of, or subject to, an improper contact.

(5)   Damages

Proof of actual damage is not required to recover for assault. A plaintiff may recover at least nominal damages from a defendant.

b)   Words or Gestures

A defendant's menacing words alone do not constitute an assault unless, in their factual context, they give rise to a plaintiff's reasonable apprehension. A menacing gesture may not give rise to an assault when a defendant uses words to explain to a plaintiff that such conduct was harmless. For example, a person may escape liability for assault if he couples a threatening gesture with the phrase, "If I were not so nice, I would hit you."

c)   Defenses

Self-defense, defense of others, defense of property, and consent, are available defenses to an assault action. It is not a valid defense to assert that a defendant who has invaded a plaintiff's peace of mind did not actually make any harmful contact with the plaintiff, since contact is not required for assault.

★★★   2)   BATTERY

Question Key
18,27,37,41,54,101,135,136, 174,188,189,217,219

         a)   Definition and Elements

Battery is defined as 1) an act; 2) intending to cause either a) harmful or offensive contact or b) immediate apprehension of harmful or offensive contact; 3) with the person of another; and 4) actually causing such contact.

                    (1)   Intentional

A defendant must act with the intent to cause the contact or apprehension of such contact. A person is liable for battery if the person intends to cause a harmful or offensive contact with a plaintiff which results in harmful or offensive contact with the plaintiff. A person is liable for battery if the person does not intend to cause a harmful or offensive contact with the plaintiff, but intends to cause apprehension of harmful or offensive contact which results in harmful or offensive contact with the plaintiff.

Intent requires a showing that either 1) the person acted with a desire to cause a harmful or offensive touching or 2) a belief that it was substantially certain to occur. A defendant must act assertively rather than passively. Motive is irrelevant. The element of intent for battery is the same as that for assault. The Transferred Intent Doctrine also applies to battery.

                         (a)   Volitional

A defendant's unconscious act is not actionable. The defendant's reflex activity is not actionable. A legally incompetent person may have the capacity to perform a volitional act.

                    (2)   Harmful or Offensive

A determination of whether contact is harmful or offensive is based on the viewpoint of a reasonable person with ordinary sensibilities.

                         (a)   Harmful

For the contact to be harmful, it must result in an injury, but not necessarily have caused physical harm such as pain or a bodily impairment. The act may constitute battery even when it causes only indignity.

                         (b)   Offensive

A defendant's contact with a plaintiff is offensive if it would offend a reasonable person's sense of dignity. Accidental contacts, or those that are usual in human interaction, are not actionable. The question is what would an ordinary person, who is not unduly sensitive about personal dignity, consider offensive?

A contact may be offensive if a plaintiff does not permit it. A contact is not permitted if the plaintiff does not consent to it. A determination of whether a contact is unpermitted should include a consideration of the contact's factual context, such as its time and place.

(3)   Person of Another

A plaintiff's person is protected from a defendant's intentional and impermissible contact upon any part of the body, anything attached to the body, and anything reasonably connected to the body. For example, a person commits a battery if the person slaps a lunch tray out of another person's grasp, even though the tortfeasor does not touch the body of the other person.

(4)   Causation

A defendant's conduct must either indirectly or directly cause the offensive contact with a plaintiff.

(5)   Damages

Proof of physical harm is not required to recover for battery. A plaintiff may recover at least nominal damages from a defendant.

(6)   Defenses

Self-defense, defense of others, defense of property, and consent are available defenses.

★   3)   **FALSE IMPRISONMENT**

| Question Key |
| 60,112,190 |

a)   Definition and Elements

False imprisonment is defined as the intentional confinement or restraint of a person to a contained space without justification. The prohibition on false imprisonment protects a plaintiff from an unlawful restraint of freedom of movement in any direction. A storekeeper has the privilege to detain a shoplifting suspect who the storekeeper reasonably believes may have shoplifted, but may confine her only for a reasonable amount of time and in a reasonable manner to investigate such suspicions.

(1)   Intentional Confinement

A person is confined if he is in any physical location or situation in which, for a given duration, a defendant, directly or indirectly, intentionally prevents the person from going somewhere else. Confinement does not exist if the person has, and is aware of, a reasonable means of escape. False imprisonment may result from imposition of physical barriers, or the creation of a bounded area, to obstruct a person's freedom of movement. False imprisonment may result from serious threats of force against a person that are intended to prevent the person from leaving the location of confinement. The Transferred Intent Doctrine applies to false imprisonment.

(2)   Awareness

A person must be aware of the confinement. Consequently, a defendant is not liable to a plaintiff who was unconscious or asleep during the entire confinement. However, a plaintiff who is unaware of the confinement still may recover if the confinement results in harm to him (e.g. pecuniary interests).

(3)   Duration

Even a brief period of restraint is actionable because the harm to a plaintiff is the confinement itself. A plaintiff need not suffer any harm other than the confinement to bring a false imprisonment action.

(4)   Damages

Proof of actual damage is not required to recover for false imprisonment. A plaintiff may recover at least nominal damages from a defendant for false imprisonment.

4)   FALSE ARREST

False arrest occurs when a plaintiff is (1) maliciously taken into custody (2) by a person who lacks legal probable cause to detain the plaintiff. A false arrest may become a false imprisonment based on its circumstances and duration.

5)   MALICIOUS PROSECUTION

The essential elements of malicious prosecution include:

- intentionally and maliciously instituting a legal action;
- against a plaintiff without probable cause;
- for a defendant's improper purpose;
- which is terminated on the merits for plaintiff; and
- causes the plaintiff to incur monetary damages.

For example, suppose that Alan knows that his ex-wife, Judith, is considering bankruptcy. Still scorned from the divorce settlement, Alan brings a civil action against her alleging that she mentally abused him. Although he knows his allegations are false, he believes that forcing Judith to retain legal counsel will bankrupt her. Judith obtains a short-term loan and engages legal counsel. She succeeds in having the case dismissed. Judith has a case against Alan for malicious prosecution.

Terminations on the merits include dismissal by a court due to insufficient evidence or an acquittal by a fact-finder. A termination due to prosecutorial discretion, procedural defects, or technical defects will not support a malicious prosecution action.

6) ABUSE OF PROCESS

Abuse of process is the (1) malicious and deliberate misuse of (2) regularly issued judicial process that (3) is not justified by an underlying legal action. Abuse of process involves both an ulterior purpose and a willful act applying the process improperly in the proceeding's regular conduct.

For example, suppose Bob owes Beverly money but refuses to pay her despite frequent requests for payment. Beverly devises a plan under which she falsely accuses Bob of sexual assault and, as a result, Bob is arrested. Bob is charged with sexual assault and pleads not guilty. Beverly tells Bob that she will, upon his payment of the debt, drop the charges. Bob makes the payment, and Beverly admits she falsely accused Bob to get him to pay his debt to her. Consequently, the case against Bob is dismissed. Bob could prove abuse of process by showing Beverly's ulterior motive for invoking the criminal justice process in an improper manner in order to extort his debt payment. Moreover, Beverly maliciously and deliberately misused the criminal judicial process, which was not justified by her underlying claim for the unpaid debt.

The word "process" is used in the same sense as "service of process." The process can pertain to criminal or civil proceedings. It refers to an official summons or some other court-issued notice. Several types of process can be abused for an improper purpose. These include executions upon property, issuance of subpoenas, attachments of property, and garnishments of funds.

The tort is applicable if the person who abuses the process is interested only in accomplishing an improper purpose that offends justice, such as extortion, and that is collateral to the proper object of the process.

★★   7)   <u>INTENTIONAL INFLICTION OF EMOTIONAL DISTRESS</u>

a)   Definition and Elements | Key: 5,15,64,133,154, 173,175,177,203 |

Intentional infliction of emotional distress is defined as 1) extreme and outrageous conduct, 2) made intentionally or recklessly, 3) that causes 4) severe emotional distress to another.

(1)   Extreme and Outrageous

A defendant's act or words are extreme and outrageous if they exceed the ordinary bounds of behavior permitted in a decent society. Outrageous acts or words may arise from a defendant's abuse of a relation with a plaintiff, which affords the defendant power to damage the plaintiff's interests. One example is when a collection agency directs abusive language toward a plaintiff in its phone calls and letters demanding payment. Another example is when a defendant mishandles the dead body of a plaintiff's family or friend. Additionally, a court is more likely to find conduct as outrageous if it occurs in public or is persistent in nature.

(a)   Mere Insults Are Not Enough

Generally, a defendant will not liable for a mere insult, indignity, or a threat to a plaintiff. A plaintiff cannot recover for such words if they merely constituted an annoyance that arose in everyday life. A plaintiff may recover only for a defendant's profanity if such language was used in conjunction with other aggravating circumstances.

i)   Knowledge of
Susceptibility

Liability could attach if a defendant knows that the plaintiff is particularly susceptible to emotional distress.

(b)   Common Carriers

A higher standard may apply to common carriers. A passenger could hold a common carrier liable for its agent's use of profanity that an ordinary person would find insulting. In similar instances, liability may attach to innkeepers and public utilities for their agent's gross insults towards their guests or customers.

(2)   Intentional

A defendant must act either with the intent to inflict emotional distress upon a plaintiff or must act with recklessness. A person acts recklessly when he knows, or should know, that such conduct would result in severe emotional distress. This is a unique intentional tort because the "intent" requirement is satisfied by mere recklessness.

For example, suppose Paul and Pam are romantically involved with each other and live together. One day, Pam kicks Paul out of her house because he physically abuses her. Pam refuses to allow Paul back inside the house to retrieve his belongings. Afterward, Paul goes to Pam's house and, through her open windows, loudly yells, "Pam is a no good thief." Paul also threatens more violence if Pam continues to refuse him access to his belongings. During Pam's hospitalization for unrelated surgery, Paul visits her room and verbally harangues her to the extent that security guards must remove him from the hospital. Paul also tell Pam's 8-year-old daughter that Pam will go to jail for 10 years for failing to allow Paul to retrieve the belongings. From this conduct, it could be inferred that Paul either intends to cause Pam severe emotional distress or, even if his only intent was to retrieve his belongings, he knew that emotional distress would result and he acted recklessly.

A defendant's tortious intent is inferred from his reckless acts or words. Intent is inferred when the defendant knows of the plaintiff's particular sensitivity.

(3)   Causation

A plaintiff must prove that a defendant's acts or words resulted in the plaintiff's suffering from severe emotional distress.

(4)   Damages – Severe Emotional Distress

Unlike other intentional torts, intentional infliction of emotional distress requires proof of actual damages. The plaintiff must demonstrate that he suffered severe emotional distress. Severe emotional distress is emotional distress of such substantial quantity or intensity that no reasonable person in a civilized society should be expected to endure it. In determining the severity of emotional distress, consideration is given to its intensity and duration. The plaintiff need not prove that any physical suffering resulted from the emotional distress.

b)   Third-Party Claims

★★

The Transferred Intent Doctrine does not apply to this tort. However, a third party may be able to recover for the wrongful acts of the tortfeasor directed toward another person. For example, if a third party witnesses a defendant's extreme and outrageous conduct toward another person, and that conduct results in severe emotional distress to the third party, the third party may bring an action for intentional infliction of emotional distress under limited circumstances. The third party must demonstrate that he 1) was present and witnessed the act of the defendant; 2) that the defendant was aware of the third party's presence; and 3) that the third party had a close relationship to the other person.

c)   Public Figure – Actual Malice

If the plaintiff is a public figure, he must prove that the defendant acted with actual malice. For example, suppose the governor of a state signs a death warrant. An active opponent of the death penalty protests the execution by carrying a sign that states, "Governor = Murderer." A television station broadcasts coverage of the protest, including pictures of the sign. The station is not liable to the governor for intentional infliction of emotional distress absent a finding that the station acted with actual malice.

C.   **Harms to Property Interests**

    1)   <u>TRESPASS TO LAND</u>

Question Key
16,42,43,53,63,103,122

a)   Definition and Elements

A trespass to land is an act of physical invasion of the land of another with intent and causation. There are four elements:

- Physical Invasion
- Intent
- Causation
- Lack of Permission

(1)   Physical Invasion

A defendant is liable for a physical invasion of a land possessor's real property, even though the defendant has not actually entered upon the property. An invasion of the property may occur in three ways. First, the defendant may directly enter onto it. Second, she may indirectly cause a third party's entry onto the property. Third, the defendant may place an object upon the property.

(a)   Exceeding Duration of Occupancy

Trespass may occur in two ways when a defendant exceeds the duration of occupancy by intentionally remaining on land longer than permitted by the land possessor. The first way occurs if the wrongdoer's license to remain on that property has expired. For example, a licensee for a specific entertainment event is liable for trespass if the person remains on the real property longer than a reasonable duration after the event ends. The second way occurs if the defendant fails to remove his personal property from the land possessor's real property after the agreed-upon period of occupancy ends. For example, if a landowner allows a person to park a trailer on the landowner's real property for a year, the person would be liable for trespass by failing to remove the trailer upon the expiration of the year or within a reasonable time thereafter.

(2)   Intent

A land possessor must prove that entry onto the land was intentional. A land possessor does not need to prove that the trespasser knew that the land belonged to another. The Transferred Intent Doctrine applies to the tort of Trespass to Land.

(3)   Causation

A physical invasion of real property must have resulted from a trespasser's conduct or a series of events that his conduct set into motion.

(4)   Damages

Nominal damages are available for trespass to land actions. A trespasser is liable for all apparent and evident damage to a land possessor's real property that results from a trespass. The trespasser also is liable to a land possessor for any bodily harm that the land possessor or members of his household suffer as a result of the trespass.

b)   Defenses

Regardless of the extent of harm to a land possessor's real property, a trespasser's invasion of that property is actionable if it occurs without permission or legal privilege. Unless the trespasser has authorization to enter upon the property, the purpose and reasonableness of his conduct is irrelevant. The trespasser does not need to know the location of the property's boundary line. Valid defenses for a trespasser include accident, consent, necessity, and public policy. Even though necessity is a valid defense to trespass, if the trespass serves to benefit an individual or his property (private necessity), then the trespasser will be held liable for the damages caused by such trespass.

(1)   Mistake is Invalid Defense

Mistake is not a viable defense to a trespass claim. Liability for trespass is not eliminated by the fact that a trespasser acted under a reasonable and mistaken belief that he had committed no wrong. Therefore, a trespasser is liable for making a good-faith but mistaken entry onto the land possessor's real property.

c)   Land Possessor

Any person in actual and exclusive possession of land that is invaded by a trespasser is entitled to bring a trespass action against that trespasser. A landowner, lessee, tenant or even an adverse possessor may bring a trespass action. The person in possession has a right to proceed even if he is in an improper occupation situation involving adverse possession or an invalid lease. A land possessor cannot maintain a trespass action against a tenant who is in lawful possession of the premises.

d)   Directional Possession

A land possessor's interest in exclusive use and possession of land extends both vertically and horizontally from the land. No majority rule exists on the issue of the extent that such ownership extends in either direction.

(1)   Airspace Invasions

A land possessor has a legally protected interest in the airspace above the property. The protection of that interest extends for a "reasonable" distance.

(2)   Subterranean Invasions

A land possessor has a legally protected interest in the ground below the property. The protection of that interest extends for a "reasonable" distance.

(3)   Continuing Trespass

An ordinary trespass is complete when it is committed. A continuing trespass occurs when an object or items such as chattel or structures are placed onto a land possessor's real property and remain on the land for an extended period. The land possessor or a purchaser of the property may bring an action against the trespasser. The law is unsettled as to whether a land possessor may bring a single action or successive actions seeking a recovery for a continuing trespass.

        e)   Trespass Distinguished from Nuisance

Trespass is only actionable if a wrongdoer's conduct causes tangible matter to invade or enter a land possessor's real property. A trespasser's projection of light, noise, odor, or vibration over or upon a land possessor's property does not constitute a trespass. *This is heavily tested on the examination.* Such activity can give rise only to a nuisance claim.

However, a land possessor has an actionable trespass claim if a trespasser has caused harmful liquids to enter upon the land possessor's property.

2) TRESPASS TO CHATTELS

a) Definition and Elements

A trespass to chattels occurs when a trespasser intentionally interferes with an owner's chattel. Chattel is an article of movable personal property. The trespasser might damage an owner's chattel, make unauthorized use of it, or impermissibly move it between different locations.

(1) Standing

Anyone in present possession of a chattel has a valid claim to it when a trespasser interferes with that possession. Such a possessor is entitled to bring a trespass to chattels action. A person who is not in present possession of a chattel may bring such an action if he has a right to possession, either immediately or upon demand. A person who has a right to future possession of a chattel will recover only to the extent of damage to his interests.

(2) Act

A trespasser's act must result in an interference with an owner's right of possession. The act may constitute an intermeddling with the chattel that causes damage to it. The act may result in dispossession of the chattel that deprives the owner of it.

(3) Intent

An owner must prove that a trespasser intended to intrude upon or intermeddle with the chattel. The intent element does not require that the wrongdoer have a wrongful motive. The Transferred Intent Doctrine applies with respect to trespass to chattels.

(4) Causation

A trespasser's act, or some series of events that his act sets in motion, must cause the interference with the owner's right of possession of the chattel.

(5) Damages

An owner's trespass to chattels action will not succeed without proof of actual damages which is satisfied when the owner suffers a dispossession of the property.

b) Defenses

Mistake is not a defense to a trespass to chattels action. A trespasser cannot defend his misconduct based on a good-faith or innocent, mistaken belief that the chattels belonged to the trespasser when he interfered with them. Accident and consent are valid defenses because they serve to contradict the element of intent. Under certain circumstances, necessity may be raised as a defense to a trespass to chattels action.

★   3)   <u>CONVERSION</u>

> | Question Key |
> | 31,186 |

          a)   Conversion Distinguished from Trespass to Chattels

Trespass to chattels and conversion are two distinct causes of action. In contrast to trespass to chattels, a conversion action is the appropriate means of relief when a chattel owner's damages are sufficient to require a wrongdoer to pay for the chattel's full value. To some extent, it is a matter of degree. Conversion addresses a wrongdoer's interference with an owner's chattels that is significant enough to justify a forced judicial sale of them to the wrongdoer. The relevant issue in distinguishing trespass to chattels from conversion is the type and extent of the interference with the owner's chattels. Examples of interference include alteration, use, or destruction of the chattels. An analysis of the facts regarding the type and extent of the alteration, use, or destruction of the chattels will determine the significance of interference with the goods.

For example, suppose Rita sees a "For Sale" sign on Ralph's boat. Ralph lets her test drive the boat alone. Being devious by nature, Rita plans to drive it to Rico's dock and sell it to him. On the way to Rico's dock, Rita crashes the boat into a coral reef. She takes the dinghy off the boat and uses it to travel to Rico. Rico buys the dinghy but not the boat because it's damaged and she failed to deliver it. When Ralph locates his boat, it is nearly sunk and not salvageable. Rita is liable for conversion because of the destruction of Ralph's boat, which she intended to steal, and the sale of his dinghy to Rico. Rita's interference with Ralph's boat and dinghy are significant enough to justify a forced judicial sale to her. If, however, Rita did not intend to sell Ralph's boat when she test drove it, and it only became stuck upon a shoal without sustaining any damage, Rita may avoid liability by driving the dinghy back to Ralph and informing him of her mishap.

Another example may help illustrate the difference. Suppose Mario wants to play with Sonic's portable gaming system. He sees Sonic put it down on a desk in the library and walk to the restroom. Mario plays with the system and, right before Sonic returns, he removes the batteries to use in his own portable music system. At that point, Sonic may possess an action for trespass to chattels as to the gaming system, but not conversion. If, on the other hand, Mario dropped the system causing its permanent malfunction, Sonic would have an action for conversion.

★   (1)   Extent of Interference

Consider all relevant factors to determine the extent of the interference, such as:

> • the degree and length of a wrongdoer's exercise of control over the chattel;

- the wrongdoer's intent to claim a right that was contrary to the owner's right of control;
- the wrongdoer's bad intentions or good faith;
- the degree and period of the interference with the owner's control;
- the extent of injury or damage to the chattel; and
- the expense and inconvenience that the owner suffers.

        b)   Definition

Conversion is a wrongdoer's intentional exercise of dominion or control over the goods of a possessor that so seriously interfere with the possessor's right to control them that the wrongdoer is justly required to pay for the goods' full value.

        c)   Elements of Conversion

The elements of conversion are:

- a defendant's conduct interferes with a plaintiff's right of ownership;
- the interference is sufficient to constitute an assertion of dominion and control over the goods;
- the interference is inconsistent with the owner's right of possession; and
- the interference must warrant a forced judicial sale of the goods.

        (1)   Intentional Act Required

The requisite intent of a wrongdoer is to assert dominion or control over the goods in a manner that is inconsistent with the owner's rights. Conversion may result from the wrongdoer's unauthorized taking of or destruction of, the goods. A wrongdoer's intentional omission that deprives an owner of the goods affords a basis to establish conversion. The wrongdoer's negligence or nonfeasance, however, does not constitute conversion because it is not intentional.

        d)   Parties Liable

Persons who improperly exercise ownership over an owner's goods accept the risk that their conduct may lack a legal justification and, therefore, amount to conversion.

        (1)   *Bona Fide* Purchaser

Conversion occurs when a wrongdoer obtains possession and title to the goods through fraud or theft. A *bona fide*, or good faith, purchaser of such goods who obtains possession of them from such a wrongdoer is liable for conversion only when the purchaser acquires the goods in a manner that reveals the existence of an adverse claim to the goods.

        e)   Alteration of Goods

A possessor's destruction of an owner's goods constitutes a conversion. A possessor's significant modification of the goods that changes their substance or structure is also a conversion. Minor damage to an owner's goods that is attributable to a possessor may obligate the possessor to compensate the owner rather than replace the goods.

f)   Use of Goods

The greater the extent of a possessor's unauthorized use of an owner's goods, the stronger the likelihood that a conversion has occurred. Conversion occurs if a possessor's conduct substantially goes beyond the scope of possession and use that an owner has authorized.

g)   Defenses

A wrongdoer's good faith and mistake of law or fact are not valid defenses to a conversion action. A wrongdoer's return of goods to their owner with the owner's consent (or as judicially required), which occurs after the wrongdoer committed conversion against the owner, will not preclude the owner from bringing a conversion action. Courts may, however, consider a return of the goods as a factor for a reduction of the damages assessed against the wrongdoer.

D.   Defenses to Claims for Physical Harms to Persons or Property

A potential tortfeasor may have several defenses to an intentional tort claim.

★   1)   <u>CONSENT</u>

| Question Key |
| 189,217 |

Consent usually precludes a plaintiff from obtaining a recovery from a defendant in an intentional tort action. Consent may negate the existence of an intentional tort because no harm can occur to one who consciously permits the intentional tort to occur. This concept relates to the phrase *volenti non fit injuria*, which means that no wrong is done to an individual who is willing.

a)   Actual or Express Consent

Actual or express consent is consent clearly communicated to a defendant that his otherwise wrongful conduct is permissible under the circumstances.

For example, suppose a patient's actual or express consent is usually a prerequisite to authorize a physician or surgeon to perform a medical procedure upon the patient, such as surgery. The patient's actual or express consent permits the physician or surgeon to engage in conduct, such as surgery, that otherwise could constitute battery.

b)   Apparent or Implied Consent

Apparent or implied consent is consent that a reasonable person would infer from custom or from a plaintiff's activity.

For example, a participant in sports involving physical contact, such as football, boxing, wrestling, or martial arts, ordinarily will consent, apparently or implicitly, to the normally permissible types of physical contact with other participants in the same sport.

c)   Implied License

Implied license exists when, in a particular situation, a plaintiff implicitly permits a defendant to engage in the allegedly wrongful conduct in relation to the plaintiff.

d)   Consent Implied by Law

Consent may be implied by law under the following circumstances:

- a plaintiff is absent or unable to consider the matter in question;
- it is necessary that an immediate decision be made;
- no reason exists to believe that a plaintiff would withhold consent if able;
- a reasonable person in the plaintiff's position would consent to a; defendant's conduct that is at issue.

Consent may exist when a person is unable to expressly provide consent and emergency action is necessary to avoid the person's serious injury or death.

(1)   Emergency Situations

In emergency situations, a physician or surgeon's conduct that otherwise could constitute battery is justified even without the actual or express consent of the patient or the patient's agent. The patient's actual or express consent is not required to authorize the performance of certain medical procedures such as, for example, those considered necessary to save the patient's life in an emergency situation. In order to bypass the consent in an emergency situation, it must be impossible to obtain the patient's consent due to the patient's physical or mental state (unconsciousness or incapacity). A court would analyze if a reasonable person would have provided consent under the circumstances.

e)   Invalid Consent

Consent is not a defense if:

- a defendant has exceeded the consent that a plaintiff has given;
- the consent was procured by fraud;
- the consent was given under duress;
- a plaintiff lacked the capacity to consent;
- the act consented to is illegal; or

•   the consent was given as a result of a mistake of law that a defendant caused, or of a mistake that the defendant knew, such as a mistake of fact that a plaintiff caused.

A person may fail to comprehend the nature or consequences of the invasion of her person or property. For example, when a plaintiff has not consented to medical treatment, a defendant may be liable for battery. However, when the plaintiff was not fully informed of the risks and benefits of a surgical procedure before consenting to it and before it was performed, her claim arising from the surgical procedure is considered as one for negligence rather than the intentional tort of battery on account of the plaintiff's consent. Even when consent is obtained, its validity partially depends upon the extent to which the patient was informed of the risks and benefits of the procedure to which she consented.

★★   2)   PRIVILEGE

Question Key
37,41,81,122,123,188,190,219

a)   General Considerations

Privilege is a defense to an action alleging an intentional tort. A privilege exists when certain factors justify or excuse a tort. A privilege generally allows a defendant to avoid tort liability. The law provides a limited privilege of protecting one's self and others, as well as property, under certain circumstances.

★★   (1)   Protection of Self and Others

Generally, a person who acts in self-defense may employ only the force that is reasonably necessary to avoid the harm that is threatened by another person. A person is entitled to employ proportionate force against the person or the person's property to avoid an intentional tort. A person may defend a third party from an attack to the same degree the law would allow the third party to defend himself.

                       (a)   Deadly Force

Deadly force involves the use of physical means, directly or indirectly, that are likely to result in a person's death or serious bodily injury. For example, the use of a loaded gun, which could be used to kill or wound a person, is considered the use of deadly force.

                       (i)   Self-Defense

The use of deadly force is justified only when a person reasonably believes that he would suffer serious bodily injury or death from an attack of another person.

                       (A)   Duty to Retreat

The *Second Restatement of Torts* (and a minority of jurisdictions), requires a person to retreat before using deadly force in self defense, if it is safe for the person to do so. This rule of retreat is inapplicable to non-deadly force. However, even in the minority of jurisdictions that possess a duty to retreat with respect to deadly force, a person is not required to retreat if attacked in his own dwelling.

> (b)   Non-Deadly Force

>> (i)   Subjective/Objective Test

The use of non-deadly force for self-defense is permissible if:

- a defendant subjectively believes (i.e., in good faith and honestly) that;
- the plaintiff's threat warrants the use of defensive force; and
- objective grounds support that belief, such that a reasonable person would believe so under the circumstances.

>> (ii)   Reasonable Response Test

A person exercising the right of self defense or defense of others may use only the amount of force that is reasonably necessary to prevent the harm. The person's response must be reasonable and not excessive.

>> (iii)   No Duty to Retreat

A person has no obligation to retreat before using non-deadly force in self-defense.

> (c)   Defense of Others

A first person may use reasonable force to defend a second person from an attack. As with self defense, the first person can use only reasonable responsive force.

>> (i)   Effect of Mistake

There is a split among jurisdictions with regard to the effect of mistake on a person's right to defend others. For example, suppose Alan sees Bob beating up Carl. Alan attacks Bob with reasonable force. As it turns out, Bob and Carl were actors in a movie shooting a fighting scene. Is Alan liable for battery or is he excused by the doctrine of defense of others? In some states, the defender steps into the shoes of the person he is protecting. If no right to defend one's self exists, then the defender will not have the defense either. Therefore, Alan could not assert the defense because Carl could not exercise self defense under the circumstances.

Under the modern approach, a defender will possess the defense if a reasonable person would have believed the person he is protecting is entitled to defend himself. Therefore, pursuant to the modern approach, Alan could assert the defense if a reasonable person would have believed that Carl was entitled to defend himself from Bob. Jurisdictions are fairly evenly split between these two alternative approaches.

★

(2)   Protection of Property Interests

(a)   Deadly Force Prohibited

A person may not employ deadly force against another person for the purpose of protecting his property. No privilege exists to utilize force that would likely cause death or serious bodily injury in order to preserve land or chattels. The defender cannot use indirect deadly force such as a trap or spring gun to protect his property.

(b)   Non-deadly Force Permitted

A person must advise another person to leave his premises before the person may use non-deadly force to defend a property interest. If the other person fails to leave in response to that warning, then the person can use only reasonable means of defense, but never deadly force.

(i)   Mistaken Use of Force

A person may make a reasonable mistake in using force with respect to whether (1) another person entered onto the land, or (2) a request to desist was required under the circumstances.

(3)   Parental Discipline

The modern rule in certain jurisdictions allows a child to bring an action against, and recover from, a parent for a personal tort. In most jurisdictions, a parent or guardian may raise the defense of discipline in such a tort action. The parent or guardian will escape liability if the discipline imposed was reasonable under the circumstances.

(a)   Generally Permitted

A parent has the legal authority to discipline her child. However, the punishment must stay within the bounds of moderation. If the parent exceeds the bounds of moderation, she may incur criminal or civil liability.

(b)   Moderation is Question of Fact

Whether the punishment exceeds the bounds of moderation is a question for a trier of the facts who may take several factors into account including, but not limited to, the age of the child, the injuries inflicted, and conduct of the child.

(4)   Official Privilege

An officer of the law must act reasonably in carrying out the duties of protecting the public interest. A suspect cannot hold an officer liable in tort for properly performing an act (e.g., an arrest) that was directed by an enforceable law. The officer possesses immunity in such a situation.

(a)   Deadly Force

An officer of the law may not use deadly force unless: (1) it is necessary to prevent a suspect's escape, and (2) the officer has probable cause to believe that the suspect presents a significant threat of death or serious physical injury to the officer or others.

(b)   Physical Force

An arrest using physical force is permissible when it is based on a reasonably mistaken belief that a felony was about to be committed, or was being committed, by a suspect in the officer's presence.

★   (5)   Necessity

Necessity exists when a defendant acts to avoid an impending harm from some force of nature, or another independent cause that is not connected with a plaintiff. A land possessor may not resist a person's entry onto real property on the basis that it is a trespass when that entry occurred as a result of necessity. The two types of necessity are private and public necessity.

(a)   Private Necessity

Private necessity provides a person with a privilege to interfere with the property rights of another to avoid greater harm to his person. For example, a pedestrian may raise the defense of private necessity in a land possessor's trespass action when the pedestrian entered upon the land possessor's real property to avoid being struck by an out-of-control automobile.

(i)   Incomplete Defense

Private necessity is an incomplete defense. Consequently, a defendant must compensate a plaintiff for any actual damage that results from the interference with the plaintiff's property rights.

(b)   Public Necessity

Public necessity is a defense that exists when a person interferes with the property interests of another to avoid an impending harm to the community at large. For example, a municipality may raise the defense of public necessity to a trespass action when its fire-fighters need to enter upon a land possessor's real property in order to fight a fire that exists at an adjacent land possessor's premises.

(i)   Complete Defense

Public necessity is a complete defense. Consequently, a defendant is not obligated to compensate a plaintiff for any actual damage that results from the interference with the plaintiff's property rights.

3)   <u>IMMUNITY</u>

a)   General Considerations

Immunity is a defense to a lawsuit or liability for an adverse legal claim. It is generally, but not necessarily, available in tort actions for defendants such as governments and their agents. Immunity also may be asserted as a basis to avoid communicating (i.e., testifying) about confidential information that is subject to a legal privilege from compulsory disclosure. Immunity is also a defense in certain defamation actions.

b)   Intra-Family Immunities

(1)   Inter-Spousal Immunity

For many years, husbands and wives could not sue each other in tort. In the vast majority of jurisdictions, however, inter-spousal immunity has been abolished. The usual reasons for such immunity were that such suits were destructive to marital harmony and would encourage fraud and collusion against insurance companies. Homer Harrison Clark, The Law of Domestic Relations In the United States § 11.1 (2d ed. 1987). In the vast majority of jurisdictions, however, inter-spousal immunity has been abolished as courts have dismissed fears of disrupting familial harmony and of collusion. John DeWitt Gregory et al., Understanding Family Law § 6.02 (2d ed. 1993).

(2)   Parent-Child Immunity

Historically, just as husbands and wives could not sue each other, for comparable concerns about family harmony, minor children could not sue their parents for personal injury torts. Many jurisdictions have abolished this absolute immunity. Even where it does still exist, there are exceptions for willful and wanton action as opposed to mere negligence.

★   (3)   Child Immunity

(a)   General Rule

Generally, a child's status as an infant does not provide the child with immunity from tort liability. A child is ordinarily liable for intentional and negligent torts that the child commits. For an intentional tort, the relevant inquiry is whether the child possessed the required intent for the tort. If the child did possess the required intent, then the child will be liable regardless of age.

Some test questions provide answers that contain age restrictions for torts (e.g., "a child under 7 years of age is incapable of committing a tort"). These are often red herrings, as a child of any age will be liable for a tort, if he possesses the requisite intent.

Despite the general rule permitting tort liability, this liability is subject to some limitation.

(i)   Intentional Tort Limitation

The primary limitation applies to intentional torts for which the child lacks intent to commit the tort due to the child's absence of mental capacity. Absence of mental capacity could result from inexperience and/or ignorance. If the child did not possess the required mental capacity, then the child may have immunity from tort liability.

c)   Charitable Immunity

Originally, the common law applied charitable immunity to protect charitable organizations from tort liability. However, the modern majority rule is that charitable organizations are subject to tort liability. One reason for the evolution of the rule is that the common law rule shielded charitable organizations when they caused harm through negligent rendition of services, such as health care. A few jurisdictions, however, follow a minority rule either recognizing general charitable immunity from tort liability or limiting charitable immunity to specific types of cases under certain circumstances.

II.   NEGLIGENCE

★★★★   A.   General Considerations

Question Key
75,80,85,86,92,95,98,117,153,157, 161,162,171,199,202,208

In contrast to an intentional tort, the tort of negligence applies when a person, though not intending to cause a harmful result: 1) *acts unreasonably*, which causes a harmful result; or 2) unreasonably *fails to act*, and the failure to act causes a harmful result.

1)   ELEMENTS

In order to prevail on a negligence claim, a plaintiff must prove the following four elements:

- Duty - A defendant owed the plaintiff a legal duty of care;
- Breach - The defendant's conduct breached that duty;
- Causation - The defendant's conduct caused (actual and proximate) the plaintiff's injury; and
- Damages - The plaintiff suffered harm from the defendant's conduct. Damages cannot be presumed.

a)   Avoiding Directed Verdict

If the plaintiff fails to produce sufficient evidence in support of a *prima facie* (i.e., at first glance) case, the defendant may move for a directed verdict. A court will grant a directed verdict for a defendant if the evidence, when considered in the light most favorable to the plaintiff, is insufficient for submission to the jury. In other words, in order to avoid a directed verdict dismissing the claim, the plaintiff must show that a reasonable fact-finder could decide the issues of fact for the plaintiff. A court will rarely grant a directed verdict in a negligence case because it is the duty of the jury to apply the test of a person using ordinary care.

b)   Damages

Damages must be proven as an element of a claim for negligence.

(1)   Physical Injury

A plaintiff who suffers a physical injury or incapacity resulting from a defendant's negligence can recover compensatory damages for pain and suffering, medical expenses, and other adverse pecuniary consequences resulting from the injury or incapacity. The available damages for a plaintiff also include recovery for the aggravation of pre-existing conditions or disabilities. The type of damage sustained by a plaintiff does not have to be foreseeable by the defendant, as defendants must take plaintiffs as they find them, with all of their physical qualities, susceptibilities, and disabilities.

(2)   Property Damage

A plaintiff who experiences property loss or damage resulting from a defendant's negligence can recover damages in the amount of the property loss. The plaintiff may not, however, recover damages for the emotional distress that arises from the property loss.

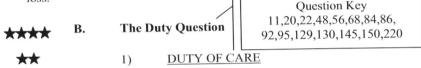

★★★★   B.   The Duty Question

| Question Key |
| 11,20,22,48,56,68,84,86, |
| 92,95,129,130,145,150,220 |

★★   1)   DUTION OF CARE

a)   Foreseeable Plaintiffs

A person who engages in an activity has a legal duty to act in accordance with the legal standard of care that applies to that activity. The majority of states follow Justice Cardozo's rule in *Palsgraf v. Long Island Railroad Company*, that a defendant only owes a duty to "foreseeable" plaintiffs. Foreseeable plaintiffs are those individuals or entities to whom a defendant could have reasonably expected to be harmed as a result of the defendant's act or omission. A defendant has a duty to avoid reasonable risks of harm created by his own negligent behavior.

b)   Unforeseeable Plaintiffs

Under the majority rule, a person does not owe a duty of care to unforeseeable plaintiffs. Unforeseeable plaintiffs are those individuals or entities whom a defendant reasonably could not have expected to be harmed as a result of the defendant's act or omission. The minority of states follow the proposed rule of Justice Andrews' dissent in *Palsgraf*, which asserted that "[e]veryone owes to the world at large the duty of refraining from those acts which unreasonably threaten the safety of others." This minority rule extends the duty of care to unforeseeable plaintiffs.

★★   2)   FAILURE TO ACT / IMPROPER ACT

A claim for negligence may arise from either an act or an omission (failure to act). A passive failure to act when a duty to act exists is classified as *nonfeasance*. An improper performance of a proper or lawful act is deemed a *misfeasance*. For example, if a person possesses a duty to assist and does nothing, this inaction is deemed nonfeasance. However, if a person undertakes to assist another, and acts unreasonably in providing that assistance, the action may be deemed misfeasance.

The issues of a failure to act or an improper act often arise in the context of a rescue.

★★   a)   Defendant Did Not Endanger Plaintiff

A first person or defendant lacks a general duty to make affirmative efforts to assist a second person or plaintiff that the first person knows is in a situation of danger that the first person did not create. In that event, the defendant who *gratuitously promises* to assist such a plaintiff lacks a legal duty to render that promised aid. However, the defendant who *undertakes* to provide such assistance possesses a duty to exercise the necessary level of due care in rendering such aid to the plaintiff.

★★   b)   Defendant Endangered Plaintiff

If a defendant's conduct placed a plaintiff in a situation of danger, then the defendant possesses a duty to assist the plaintiff to either avoid the danger or to be delivered from that dangerous situation. The defendant possesses a duty to exercise due care in rendering such assistance.

★★   c)   Self-Endangered Defendant

A defendant who has jeopardized his own safety has an obligation of due care to a plaintiff who seeks to rescue the defendant. The defendant is not liable, however, for the plaintiff's injuries that result from the rescue if the plaintiff engaged in "wanton" behavior in assisting the defendant.

                            d)   Good Samaritan Laws

Some states have enacted "Good Samaritan" statutes that shield a defendant from liability for voluntary efforts to rescue a plaintiff that are made with due care under certain circumstances.

★★   e)   The Rescue Doctrine

The circumstances surrounding a rescue attempt of a party who has been injured by a wrongdoer do not supersede the liability of the original wrongdoer who caused the original injury. An original wrongdoer will be held liable for the reasonably foreseeable events that occur in connection with the immediate consequences of the wrongdoer's actions. An attempt to aid a person injured by the wrongdoer is considered to be a foreseeable course of events. Further, an independent duty of care is owed to the rescuer by a wrongdoer and the wrongdoer will be held liable to any subsequent parties who are injured in the course of a rescue attempt that occurs in connection with the wrongdoer's actions.

★★   3)   PRE-NATAL DUTIES

a)   Wrongful Conception

A plaintiff can prevail on a claim for wrongful conception (also known as wrongful pregnancy) from the improper performance of a contraceptive procedure. A plaintiff may recover damages for the labor and delivery of the child, as well as compensation for the botched procedure. The availability for recovery of damages in connection with rearing of the child is an issue that has not been determined uniformly by the courts.

b)   Wrongful Birth

A claim for wrongful birth arises in a situation where a child is born with serious birth defects. It is a claim against the doctor for failure to diagnose, properly treat, or inform the parents of medical issue that culminated in the birth defect and prevented the parents from being able to avoid conception or terminate the pregnancy. This claim seeks damages for the cost of raising a child with birth defects. Most courts recognize this cause of action.

c)   Wrongful Life

A claim for wrongful life arises in a situation where a child is born with serious birth defects. It is a claim against the doctor for failure to diagnose, properly treat, or inform the parents of medical issue that culminated in the birth defect and prevented the parents from being able to avoid conception or terminate the pregnancy. This claim seeks damages for the child being born at all. Most courts have completely rejected this cause of action as repugnant to public policy.

C.   **Standard of Care**

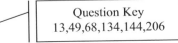

Question Key
13,49,68,134,144,206

1)   REASONABLY PRUDENT PERSON

Once a court determines that a person owed a duty to another person, the next questions that arise are what is the required standard of care and was it satisfied?

a)   Legal Standard

A person possesses a general legal duty to act reasonably and with prudence in every situation in order to avoid causing an unreasonable risk of injury to other people. The usual standard of care for a negligence case is that of a *"reasonably prudent person"* under the same or similar circumstances.

(1)   Determining Reasonableness

In order to determine reasonableness, a court would determine the standard of care that would be exercised by a person who possesses the average cognitive skills of, and an equal level of knowledge with, a typical community member. Physical limitations, such as blindness, are taken into account when determining reasonableness. A reasonable person understands his physical capabilities and mental ability and exercises them within their normal range in the context of any activity.

★★   b)   Children

If a child is a defendant in a negligence action, the standard of care is that of an ordinary child of similar age, education, intelligence, and experience. If, however, the child is involved in what is usually an adult activity, such as operating a motor vehicle, then the adult standard of care for that activity applies.

                            c)   Impaired Individuals

                                (1)   Physically Impaired

The standard of care for physically impaired individuals is that of a reasonable person who has knowledge of the particular infirmity and its effect upon his activities.

                                (2)   Mentally Impaired

The standard of care for mentally impaired individuals usually is that of a reasonable person. The law considers a mentally impaired person like a child with respect to the standard of care.

                            d)   Professional People

★★

                                (1)   Heightened Standard

The standard of care for a professional defendant is greater than that of the standard of care for a reasonable person because professionals are considered to possess superior intelligence, knowledge, and skill.

                                (2)   Legal Standard

The standard of care for professionals is that they must employ reasonable care and exercise a certain level of special knowledge and ability. Professionals must utilize the knowledge, skill, and care that are ordinarily possessed by others in good standing in the same profession.

                                (3)   Application of Standard

If a defendant has greater knowledge or expertise than an average person, it must be determined if the defendant acted as a reasonable person by exercising the standard level of knowledge and expertise of someone in good standing of the same or an identical trade or profession as the defendant.

(4)   Professions Covered

Many types of professionals are subject to this standard, including skilled tradespersons, lawyers, accountants, engineers, architects, veterinarians, dentists, psychiatrists, and pharmacists.

(5)   Medical Doctor Rules

An additional requirement applies to medical doctors (e.g., physicians, surgeons), who must perform good medical practice as measured by what is standard and usual in that profession.

(a)   Majority Rule

A majority of jurisdictions now measure the conduct against that of a reasonable doctor on a nationwide basis.

(b)   Minority Rule

The traditional rule in the minority of states measures a doctor's conduct against that of a reasonable professional in the local community.

(c)   Disclosure Rule

A medical doctor is obligated to disclose material risks to a patient with respect to potential medical treatment or surgery. The patient is entitled to sufficient information in order to give informed consent. The doctor breaches that duty of disclosure when she fails to provide the patient with the required information.

(i)   Patient's Burden of Proof

In order for a patient to prove that the doctor breached her duty of disclosure, the patient must establish proximate cause that he would have rejected treatment if the doctor had sufficiently informed the patient of the risk that the treatment presented.

(6)   Legal Profession

In order to prevail in a claim for legal malpractice, a plaintiff must show that the defendant lawyer was negligent and but for his negligence, the plaintiff would have prevailed and recovered from the original wrongdoer.

e)   Common Carriers

Common carriers provide transportation services to passengers by the operation of vehicles such as planes, trains, and buses. The common law imposes a higher standard of care upon them and their vehicle operators than that of a reasonably prudent person. That heightened obligation is to avoid harm to the passengers by exercising the greatest degree of "vigilance, care and precaution," or "the utmost caution characteristic of very careful prudent persons."

f)   Innkeepers

An innkeeper provides public accommodations to customers. An innkeeper possesses a duty of special care to a customer to provide safe lodging. An innkeeper may have a duty to reasonably assist a customer who is in peril.

g)   Tavern-Keepers

A tavern-keeper possesses a duty of reasonable care to provide a safe environment to a patron. A tavern-keeper may have a duty to reasonably assist a patron who is in peril.

h)   Shopkeepers

A shopkeeper possesses a duty of reasonable care to provide a safe shopping environment to a customer. A shopkeeper may have a duty to reasonably assist a customer who is in peril. However, this duty is not absolute.

For example, suppose a customer fell and injured himself when he slipped on a banana peel while shopping at a grocer's store. The parties agree that the banana peel was fresh and clean except for a mark made by the heel of the customer's shoe. In a negligence action brought by the customer against the grocer, if these are the only facts in evidence, there is insufficient evidence to ground liability against the grocer. Evidence that the banana peel was fresh and clean indicates that it was not on the floor for a significant time, which would result in a directed verdict for the grocer, absent additional evidence of negligence.

i)   Employers

An employer possesses a duty of reasonable care to provide a safe workplace to an employee. An employer may have a duty to reasonably assist an employee who is in peril.

j)   Educators

An educator possesses a duty of reasonable care to provide a safe educational environment to a student. An educator may have a duty to reasonably assist a student who is in peril.

k)   Jailers

A jailer possesses a legal duty to protect a prisoner from injury that may occur while the prisoner is in custody.

2)   RULES OF CONDUCT DERIVE FROM CUSTOM AND
        STATUTES

a)   Custom

Evidence of custom or usage may be introduced in a negligence action to prove the standard by which to measure a defendant's conduct. Such evidence may support a defense but that evidence is not conclusive. The reasonableness of a custom or usage may be analyzed on the basis of whether a reasonable person would have engaged in it.

b)   Statutes

Statutes may impose a standard of care upon a special class of individuals. Proof that a defendant violated a statute may be used to show that the defendant breached a duty that he owed to a plaintiff. That type of evidence is used to establish negligence *per se*.

★★★   (1)   Negligence *Per Se*

Question Key
29,32,100,126,146, 149,185,197,209

Negligence *per se* is a method of establishing negligence (e.g., that a defendant breached a duty of care because he violated the law in some manner). Negligence *per se* may be established in a civil action by invoking a criminal or civil statute that describes a special standard of care for the specified conduct that is at issue.

(a)   Elements

In the majority of states, in order to subject a defendant to tort liability based on negligence *per se*, a plaintiff must prove that:

- the plaintiff is within the class of individuals that a statute is designed to protect;
- the defendant's conduct violated the statute;
- the defendant's conduct violated the reason for the statute;
- that conduct constitutes the type of risk that the statute covers; and
- the conduct is not excused.

For example, suppose Danny is driving his car down the road when he swerves across the median and collides with Peter's car. A statute in the jurisdiction makes it unlawful to drive a car across a median. A reasonable analysis of the elements would conclude that: 1) Peter is in the class of individuals designed to be protected as he is a driver of a car; 2) Danny violated the statute by swerving across the median; 3) Danny's violation of the statute presumably violated the purpose of the statute – to prevent accidents; 4) Danny's violation is the type of risk covered by the statute; and 5) No excuse is apparent from the facts. Therefore, Peter could prevail in a negligence *per se* action.

(b)   Rebuttable Evidence

Evidence of negligence *per se* raises a prima facie case of negligence. However, the opponent may successfully rebut the negligence *per se* evidence by providing an explanation of how the accident happened that is inconsistent with a finding of negligence.

D.   Problems Relating to Proof of Fault

1)   ROLES OF JUDGE AND JURY

a)   Questions of Fact and Law

In a jury trial, the jury determines questions of fact. In a bench trial, the judge decides questions of fact. In jury and bench trials, the judge determines questions of law.

b)   Burden of Proof

A plaintiff in a civil proceeding possesses the burden of proof. The cause of action or claim at issue will determine the nature of the burden of proof. A common burden of proof in civil claims is a preponderance of the evidence.

★★   2)   *RES IPSA LOQUITUR*

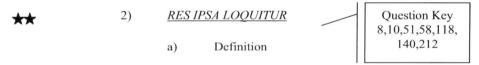

Question Key
8,10,51,58,118,
140,212

a)   Definition

Res Ipsa Loquitur is a Latin phrase that literally translates into "the thing speaks for itself." *Res Ipsa Loquitur* refers to an event that otherwise would not have occurred without someone's negligence, fault, or culpability. By invoking the doctrine, a plaintiff asserts that an act occurred, the act does not occur without negligence, and the defendant is responsible for the act.

b)   Elements

Res Ipsa Loquitur applies under the following circumstances:

- it is highly likely that a plaintiff's injury could not have occurred absent a negligent act;
- the instrumentality of harm was within the defendant's exclusive control; and
- neither the plaintiff nor a third party's conduct contributed to the plaintiff's injury.

For example, suppose Tom was standing on the sidewalk in front of a skyscraper. Tom was struck and injured by a pane of glass that fell on him from above. Above where Tom was standing when the pane of glass hit him, there was a hole in the skyscraper's exterior where a window should have been. The window fell while Tina was attempting to install it. *Res Ipsa Loquitur* would apply here for three reasons. First, it is highly likely Tom's injury could not have occurred without Tina's negligent act of dropping the window.

Second, the window was within Tina's exclusive control before it hit Tom. Third, neither Tom nor anyone else contributed to his injury.

The rule provides that adequate evidence of *res ipsa loquitur* raises a prima facie case of negligence. However, the opponent may successfully rebut the evidence by providing an explanation of how the accident happened that is inconsistent with a finding of negligence.

★★★★   **E.   Problems Relating to Causation**

In order to prevail on a negligence claim, the plaintiff must prove that the defendant's conduct caused the plaintiff's injury. There are two types of causation, *both of which must be established.* First, the defendant's conduct must be the cause in fact or "actual" cause (also called factual cause). Second, the conduct must be the legal or "proximate" cause of harm to the plaintiff. There can be more than one actual and proximate cause of a plaintiff's injury.

> Question Key
> 25,34,59,89,115,125,126,127,131,
> 132,138,139,147,201,206,216
> Includes Proximate Cause

1)   ACTUAL CAUSE

Several different approaches are used to determine whether a defendant's conduct is the actual cause of a plaintiff's injury. A common mistake many examinees make is thinking that the plaintiff's harm has only one actual cause. On the contrary, that harm can have many actual causes.

a)   "But for" Causation

"But for" causation is the most commonly used test for actual cause. That test inquires if a plaintiff would not have been injured "but for" a defendant's conduct.

For example, suppose Tim's bike is properly parked in front of a multiple-level hotel. Tara's hotel room has a balcony with a view of the city skyline. Tara accidentally loses her grip on her binoculars while observing the skyline. Tim's bike is struck and damaged by Tara's dropped pair of binoculars. Here, Tim's bike would not have been injured "but for" Tara's failure to hold onto the binoculars. Thus, Tara's failure to hold onto the binoculars is an actual cause of the damage to Tim's bike.

b)   Substantial Factor Test

The substantial factor test applies if a plaintiff's injury has several causes that contributed to that harm. For example, if two independent fires converged to create one larger fire that burned down a home, neither fire would be the "but for" cause of the larger fire if either small fire would eventually have burned down the house. The substantial factor test provides that if two or more acts combine to cause one result, a defendant will be deemed the actual cause of that result if his acts were a substantial factor in causing the injury.

c)   Harms Traceable to Multiple Potential Causes

Under *Summers v. Tice*, when it is not clear which one of multiple negligent defendants caused a plaintiff's injury (e.g., two people shoot a gun at a victim but only one unidentifiable bullet hits the victim), a trial court will shift the burden to each defendant to prove that he did not cause the injury. Then each defendant must show that his negligence did not cause the injury.

d) Harms Traceable to Multiple Defendants

Pursuant to the "joint enterprise" or "joint venture" doctrine, one defendant's negligence may be imputed to other defendants who also are involved in a common enterprise or project and who possess an implied or explicit understanding about how the project will be conducted. Dan Dobbs, *The Law of Torts* § 340 (2001).

2) LEGAL CAUSE

In order to demonstrate causation, a plaintiff must show that the defendant's act was both the actual and legal cause of the plaintiff's harm. In the prior section, we covered actual (or factual) causation. In this section, we will cover legal (or proximate) causation.

a) Remote or Unforeseeable Causes

Generally, no tort liability arises for negligence if a defendant could not have reasonably foreseen that an injury would have resulted from his conduct. Also, there may be no tort liability for negligence if the defendant's conduct was reasonable in terms of what injury from it was foreseeable. The issue of the defendant's liability may depend on whether the ultimate harm that a plaintiff suffered was reasonably foreseeable from the allegedly negligent conduct. As a practical matter, the more remote or unforeseeable the cause of the plaintiff's injury is, the less likely it is that the defendant will be liable for negligence.

★★★ ### b) Legal or Proximate Causes

Sometimes, several levels of analysis must be conducted to determine if a defendant's conduct proximately caused an injury to a plaintiff.

(1) Reasonable Foreseeability

Foreseeability is the threshold test of legal or proximate causation and should be analyzed on every exam question that presents the issue of legal or proximate causation. If a plaintiff's injury is a reasonably foreseeable consequence of the defendant's action, then the defendant's action is a proximate cause of the injury. If a plaintiff's injury is too unforeseeable or remote under the circumstances, then the defendant is not liable.

For example, suppose Kevin, seeking to impress Kelly, offers her a ride on his motorcycle. He tells her that it should be safe on a warm and sunny summer day, and that they will stay on side streets. Kelly accepts his offer and Kevin reasonably drives the motorcycle in compliance with the law. During this ride, Kelly receives a gunshot wound from a random shooter in a passing car. Kelly survives and files a tort action for negligence against Kevin, seeking damages for her injury.

There is no doubt that two of the four elements of negligence are satisfied because: 1) Kevin owed Kelly a duty of care; and 2) Kelly was injured. The ride was also an actual cause of the injury, as the injury would not have resulted if Kelly did not go on the ride. Legal causation is one of two remaining issues (breach is the other). Specifically, the issue is whether Kelly's injury was a reasonably foreseeable result of Kevin taking her on the ride. Arguably, it is not reasonably foreseeable that Kelly would be injured by a gunshot wound while riding a motorcycle. Her injury may be too unforeseeable or remote under the circumstances to make Kevin liable for it on the basis of negligence. This analysis of that issue could be affected, however, by other factual considerations, such as whether other similar incidents have recently occurred, where they were riding, and if Kevin was driving through an ordinarily safe neighborhood when the shooting occurred.

(a)   Jury Issue

The issue of foreseeability is an issue for the jury in a jury trial.

★★   (2)   Intervening Causes

An intervening cause is an act that occurs after a defendant's negligent conduct and increases a plaintiff's injury. A defendant will not be held liable when he could not have reasonably foreseen a risk of harm that arose from an intervening cause. However, a negligent defendant will be held liable for a foreseeable intervening cause.

(a)   Superseding Cause

An intervening cause becomes a superseding cause if it breaks the causal connection between a defendant's negligence and a plaintiff's final status. An intervening cause may directly precipitate a final result which will relieve the defendant of tort liability to a plaintiff. For example, if a third party commits an unforeseeable criminal act that increases a plaintiff's injury that resulted from a defendant's negligence, that act is considered an intervening and superseding cause. In that event, the defendant may not be held liable for the plaintiff's injury (unless the third-party criminal conduct was foreseeable).

(i)   Criminal Acts of Third Parties

A negligent tortfeasor generally is not liable for the criminal acts of other people made possible by the tortfeasor's negligence. However, there is an exception to this rule if the tortfeasor should have realized the likelihood of the crime.

For example, suppose a construction company was digging a trench for a new sewer line on a street in a high-crime neighborhood. During the course of the construction, there had been many thefts of tools and equipment from the construction area. One night, the construction company's employees neglected to place warning lights around the trench. A delivery truck drove into the trench and broke an axle. While the delivery driver was looking for a telephone to summon a tow truck, thieves broke into the delivery truck and stole $35,000 worth of goods. In this case, the construction company's negligent failure to place warning lights around the trench may be deemed a proximate cause of the theft. Although the general rule breaks the chain of causation for crimes of third parties made possible by the negligence, the exception that exists if the tortfeasor should have realized the likelihood of the crime may apply. A jury could find that the construction company should have realized the likelihood of the crime because "there had been many thefts of tools and equipment from the construction area."

(b)   Independent Intervening Cause

An independent intervening cause is an act that does not result from a defendant's breach of duty. An independent intervening cause that is reasonably foreseeable would not supersede the defendant's responsibility for a negligent act. For example, after a defendant starts a campfire, unpredicted heavy winds arise causing a forest fire. The defendant may be held liable for a plaintiff's harm from the forest fire that resulted from a foreseeable independent intervening cause - the heavy winds.

(c)   Dependent Intervening Cause

A dependent intervening cause occurs as a result of a defendant's conduct. The defendant will be found responsible for causing a normal or foreseeable intervening force. A negligently executed rescue is considered a foreseeable or normal dependent intervening force, as is negligence on the part of a medical professional rendering assistance

★★★   3)   <u>RESPONSIBILITY AMONG MULTIPLE TORTFEASORS</u>

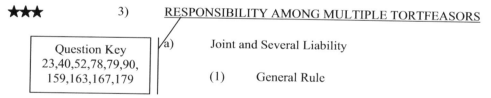

a)   Joint and Several Liability

Question Key
23,40,52,78,79,90,
159,163,167,179

(1)   General Rule

The doctrine of joint and several liability provides that when there is more than one defendant whose concurrent negligence results in harm to a plaintiff, they each may be found liable for the *entire* amount of damages caused by their indivisible wrongful conduct. The doctrine was created because the law prefers to hold a wrongdoer responsible for harm, rather than an innocent plaintiff.

For example, suppose Abbie is hit and injured by a truck driven by Bill, who was served alcohol in Charlie's bar in a jurisdiction with a dramshop law. Suppose that Bill and Charlie are found jointly liable for Abbie's injuries from the accident. It is determined at trial that Abbie should receive $10 million in damages and that Bill was 90 percent at fault and Charlie was 10 percent at fault.

In this situation, under the traditional law of joint and several liability, Abbie can recover the entire amount of damages from either Bill or Charlie. For example, if Abbie only sued and prevailed against Charlie, he would have to pay her the entire $10 million, although he was only 10 percent at fault, which actually would equate to a $1 million share of the liability. But, in the majority of jurisdictions, to protect his interests, Charlie could join Bill as a co-defendant in Abbie's suit against him. Also, if Abbie only sued and prevailed against Charlie, who did not join Bill as a co-defendant, Charlie could bring a separate action against Bill seeking to recover $9 million. In that event, Charlie would remain liable to Abbie for the entire $10 million pursuant to her separate action.

(a)   Joint Liability

Joint liability, rather than joint and several liability, exists when each joint party is liable up to the entire amount of an obligation such as a debt. A wife and husband that receive a loan from a credit union, for example, may have to sign a loan agreement making them "jointly liable" for the loan's entire balance.

The chief distinction between the two kinds of shared liability – "joint" liability and "joint and several" liability - is procedural. If liability is joint, then the plaintiff usually must proceed against all who share liability in the same proceeding. If liability is joint and several, then the plaintiff may elect to proceed against defendants separately.

(b)   Several Liability

In contrast to joint liability, under "several" liability, a defendant is liable only for her own apportioned share of the injury. When liability is "joint and several," an injured party can recover an entire judgment or just the several amount from one tortfeasor.

(2)   Application of Rule

The doctrine of joint and several liability applies in two factual situations: (1) when at least two defendants harm a plaintiff while acting separately; or (2) when at least two defendants engage in conduct together that injures a plaintiff. If the plaintiff's damages cannot be allocated to specified defendants, then all of them are liable for the plaintiff's injury.

(3)   Statutory Modification

A growing number of jurisdictions have rejected joint and several liability, and instead make a strict apportionment of fault and liability. In those jurisdictions, each defendant would be liable for his apportioned amount of responsibility. Other jurisdictions have limited the availability of joint and several liability. For example, joint and several liability may apply for damages resulting from physical injury, but not mental anguish.

b)   Contribution

If the plaintiff recovers the entire award of damages from one of the defendants, and other defendants also are found liable to the plaintiff for damages, then that defendant from whom the plaintiff recovered the damages can seek to recover from the other defendants their respective share of the damages by means of contribution.

Thus, the doctrine of contribution may require one of several defendants to pay his respective share to another defendant who paid more than his share of joint and several liability. For example, suppose that an automatic security gate, made by Ace Co., located at the end of Jill's driveway, severely injures Jack's hand. Jack could bring a tort action against Jill, and ACE Co., for the damage to his hand caused by the gate. Suppose that ACE Co. is found 90 percent at fault and Jill is found 10 percent at fault. Jack is awarded $100,000 that he recovers in full from ACE Co. ACE Co. could then bring an action for contribution against Jill to recover $10,000 - her amount of apportioned fault.

c)   Indemnification

A right of indemnification exists when a defendant pays to discharge the liability of another person when the defendant is held liable through a form of derivative liability. For example, if a principal is held liable for the tort of an agent, the principal will be entitled to indemnification from the agent. An action for indemnification differs from an action for contribution. Contribution applies when the doctrine of joint and several liability results in one defendant paying the damages attributable to another defendant. Indemnification applies when the paying defendant is held *directly liable* for the tort of another party through a form of *derivative liability*, such as vicarious liability. The person whose liability is discharged must fully reimburse the defendant who paid to discharge the liability.

★★★★   **F.   Special Liability Rules**

       1)   <u>CLAIMS AGAINST LAND OWNERS AND OCCUPIERS</u>

> Question Key
> 12,36,45,70,96,128,155,178,193,204,207 See also Property 36,85

In this section, we will generally describe rules regarding claims against owners and occupiers of land by referring to them both together as landowners. Note that such tort claims can be made based on harms that a person suffers near, and/or on, the land.

As for harm suffered near the land, an owner or occupier of land has a duty not to cause any unreasonable risks of harm to others near the land. A defendant's liability for a breach of that duty may arise from a plaintiff's claims of intentional wrongful conduct, negligence in creating a condition of risk, or activities that are subject to the rules of strict liability.

The other more typical type of premises liability involves harms that occur on the land. Under the common law rule, the duty owed to a person entering upon land of another is dependent upon the legal status of the person as a trespasser, invitee, or licensee. Additionally, the legal status of a person who enters upon a landowner's real property may change if the nature of the person's visit changes.

a)   People Not on Property

(1)   Natural Conditions

Generally, landowners have no duty to protect someone not on their property from any natural conditions that exist upon the property.

(2)   Artificial Conditions

Ordinarily, landowners have no duty to protect someone who is not on their property from any artificial conditions that exist upon it. Examples of artificial conditions include excavations, buildings, and cultivation. However, landowners are liable for harm that someone suffers as a result of *unreasonably dangerous* conditions on, or structures upon, their real property or adjoining it. Thus, a landowner is obligated to use reasonable care to prevent an injury to a person not on the landowner's property, and injuries due to an unreasonably dangerous artificial condition that protrudes upon, or abuts, adjacent property.

(a)   Pedestrian as Example

A landowner must exercise reasonable care to protect pedestrians and others on a public street from injuries that arise from dangerous artificial conditions that are located on the landowner's real property that is, for example, adjacent to the street.

b)   Trespassers

(1)   Undiscovered Trespassers

A landowner generally owes no duty of care to an undiscovered trespasser. A landowner is not obligated to inspect his real property to discover a trespasser. However, a landowner may never willfully or wantonly injure a person on her land. An exam issue may involve determining if an undiscovered trespasser's injury resulted from a landowner's activity on, or the condition of, the property. If such an activity caused an injury, then the trespasser's undiscovered status will be relevant to determining the landowner's liability.

(2)   Discovered Trespassers

A landowner has a duty to warn known trespassers, or anticipated trespassers, of dangerous artificial conditions on her real property. A trespasser is an "anticipated" trespasser if a landowner knows, or has reason to know, that the trespasser regularly enters upon the property.

(a)   Means of Discovery

The landowner has reason to know of a discovered trespasser by either observing the trespass or obtaining information that would lead a reasonable person to believe that a trespasser is on the property.

(b) Artificial Condition Rule

A landowner possesses a duty to warn of, and to make safe, an artificial condition on the real property if the landowner knows, or has reason to know, that a trespasser is regularly entering upon that property.

(3) Adult and Children Trespassers

(a) Natural Conditions

Landowners owe the same duty of care to adult or children trespassers with respect to activities and natural conditions on real property.

(b) Artificial Conditions

An increased standard of care applies with respect to children and artificial conditions that are on the property. In that case, a landowner must exercise reasonable care to prevent injury to the children. The utility of a landowner's dangerous artificial condition (also known as an attractive nuisance) must be slight in comparison with the risk that it presents to trespassing children.

(i) Attractive Nuisance Rule

The attractive nuisance doctrine is an exception to the general rule that a landowner has no duty to trespassers. A landowner may be held liable for a trespassing child's injuries caused by an attractive nuisance on the property. An attractive nuisance is any inherently dangerous object or condition of property that can be reasonably expected to attract children. In order to ground liability, the following five factors must be present:

- the place where the condition exists is one upon which the possessor knows or has reason to know that children are likely to trespass; and
- the condition is one of which the possessor knows or has reason to know and which he realizes or should realize will involve an unreasonable risk of death or serious bodily harm to such children; and
- the children because of their youth do not discover the condition or realize the risk involved in intermeddling with it or in coming within the area made dangerous by it; and
- the utility to the possessor of maintaining the condition and the burden of eliminating the danger are slight as compared with the risk to children involved; and
- the possessor fails to exercise reasonable care to eliminate the danger or otherwise to protect the children (such as putting up a prominent sign, unless the injured child could not read).

(A)   Awareness
Exception

A landowner possesses a duty to take reasonable precautions based upon the normal behavior of children. A landowner must exercise reasonable care to ensure the safety of trespassing children. The relevant issue is whether a child trespasser recognized the danger that the risk represented. If the child trespasser was aware of the condition, understood its risk of danger, and could have avoided it, then the landowner lacks a heightened duty to prevent injury to such a child.

c)   Licensees

A person is a licensee if he is on a landowner's real property: (1) with express or implied permission of the landowner; (2) but not for the benefit of the landowner. For example, a social guest is a licensee.

(1)   Duty of Care

Landowners possess a duty of reasonable care to a licensee to warn of any known, non-obvious, natural or artificial harmful conditions on the real property. The landowner, however, possesses no duty to a licensee to inspect for unknown dangers on, or to repair, the real property. The landowner also must exercise reasonable care in any ongoing active operations on the property.

d)   Invitees

A person is an invitee if he is on a landowner's real property: (1) by invitation of the landowner; and (2) for a purpose connected with the landowner's use of the property or for the landowner's benefit. The invitee may receive an express or implied invitation to enter onto the land. For example, an employee or business customer is an invitee.

(1)   Duty of Care

Landowners possess a duty of reasonable care to an invitee to warn of a known dangerous condition on the real property if that condition presents an unreasonable risk of harm to the invitee. Landowners also possess a duty of making reasonable inspections to identify and repair any dangerous condition that exists on the property.

e)   Landlord and Tenant

(1)   Patent Defects

A patent defect is a defect that is reasonably apparent from an inspection of the premises. A landlord is not obligated to warn a tenant about, or repair, patent defects.

(2)   Latent Defects

A latent defect is a defect that would not be discovered by a reasonable inspection of the premises. A landlord possesses a duty to inspect the property for latent defects. If the landlord knows of the defect, the landlord is obligated to warn the tenant about it, or to repair it. If the landlord conducts a reasonable inspection of the premises and does not discover the latent defect, the landlord will not be liable to the tenant for injury caused by the latent defect.

2)   <u>CLAIMS FOR MENTAL DISTRESS NOT ARISING FROM PHYSICAL HARMS AND OTHER INTANGIBLE INJURIES</u>

★   a)   Negligent Infliction of Emotional Distress

(1)   General Rule

Question Key
35,50,61,196,211

A person who suffers *severe emotional distress* as a result of a person's conduct may be able to recover under a theory of negligent infliction of emotional distress ("NIED"). This claim differs from intentional infliction of emotional distress ("IIED") because, in IIED cases, the plaintiff must demonstrate that the defendant acted with the intent to cause the distress or in a reckless manner. In NIED cases, the plaintiff only needs to demonstrate negligence on the part of the defendant. The substantive elements of negligent infliction of emotional distress are: "(1) the defendant negligently engaged in conduct, (2) it was reasonably foreseeable that such conduct would cause the plaintiff severe emotional distress . . . , and (3) the conduct did in fact cause the plaintiff severe emotional distress." *Johnson v. Ruark Obstetrics*, 327 N.C. 283, 304, 395 S.E.2d 85, 97 (1990).

(a)   Duty and Foreseeability

A plaintiff must prove that the surrounding circumstances and a defendant's negligent conduct both resulted in a particular probability of causing the plaintiff real and significant emotional distress. The plaintiff also must demonstrate that the defendant owed the plaintiff a duty of care under the circumstances.

(b)   No Physical Impact Required

The examiners have indicated that a majority of states have rejected the physical impact rule, which requires the plaintiff to have some physical harm or impact resulting from the distress. Thus, pursuant to that majority rule, a plaintiff may recover from a defendant for a negligent infliction of emotional distress in the absence of physical harm or impact to the plaintiff.

(i)   Minority

In a minority of jurisdictions, the plaintiff may recover for emotional distress only when it results in a physical harm or impact that could support a separate tort action.

(2)   Witnessing Injury

A relative of a physically injured person may recover if the relative suffered emotional distress as a result of seeing the injury occur.

(a)   Majority Rule

The majority rule provides that a person may recover for emotional distress from observing his close family member being injured by a negligent defendant only if the person was in the zone of danger of that incident. The zone of danger rule permits recovery for emotional distress if a plaintiff can show that he was threatened with bodily harm by a defendant's negligence and emotional distress resulted from reasonable fear of personal physical injury.

(b)   Minority Rule

The minority rule provides that a person who observed a relative being injured may recover for that distress even when he observed the incident from a position of safety.

3)   CLAIMS FOR PURE ECONOMIC LOSS

The economic loss rule provides that a cause of action for negligence does not lie when the only damage resulting from the alleged negligence is to the subject matter of a contract. In that event, the plaintiff's action generally is limited to claiming a breach of contract. *Southwestern Bell Telephone Co. v Delanney*, 809 S.W.2d 493 (Tex 1991); *Hininger v Case Corp.*, 23 F.3d 124 (5th Cir 1994).

In determining whether to apply the rule regarding pure economic loss due to negligence, a court assesses whether the cause of action is for contract or tort. If a plaintiff suffers only an economic loss to the subject matter of the contract, the action must stand in contract alone.

4)   FIREFIGHTER'S RULE

> Question Key
> 44

Public servants, including firefighters and police officers, who are injured in the line of duty may be limited in recovery by the common law firefighter's rule. This rule provides that public servants at risk of injury by the perils that they have been employed to confront assume all ordinary and inherent risks of their highly dangerous employment. As a result, they may not sue in common law when those dangers result in injury. On the exam, it is important to determine whether the injury is a result of the special risk associated with the employment. If not, then the firefighter's rule is no bar to recovery.

★★   **G.**   **Liability for the Acts of Others**

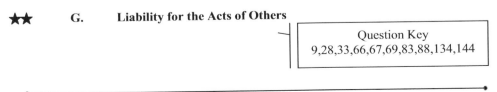

> Question Key
> 9,28,33,66,67,69,83,88,134,144

The law provides many circumstances under which one party may be liable for the acts of another party. For example, a person may be liable for failing to control third persons over whom she possesses the power of control and an obligation to control.

★★   1)   <u>EMPLOYEES AND OTHER AGENTS</u>

         a)   Employees

The doctrine of *respondeat superior* imposes vicarious liability on a master (e.g., employer) for certain tortious acts of a servant (e.g., employee) that occur during the course of, and in the scope of, the employment.

         (1)   Scope of Employment

The scope of employment includes an employee's acts that are:

- closely related to the purpose of the employee's work;
- reasonably incidental to the employee's work; and
- are means of fulfilling the employer's goals or purposes.

         (a)   Detour (Vicarious Liability)

Generally, a master (e.g., employer) will be liable for certain tortious acts that the servant (e.g., employee) commits during a "detour." The word detour refers to situations in which a servant departs from performing a master's itinerary in order to do the servant's personal chore and then the servant resumes performance of the master's itinerary. For example, suppose that an employee makes a delivery as required by an employer using the employer's vehicle. Without the employer's permission, the employee drives the employer's vehicle to a shop to buy a gift for her friend, who has no connection to the employer. In the shop's parking lot, the employee hits a pedestrian with the employer's vehicle before returning to make other deliveries for the employer. The issue is whether the employer could avoid liability for the injury to the pedestrian caused by the employee because the injury occurred during an apparent detour by the employee from her delivery work.

Jurisdictions employ different approaches to determine whether the employee's conduct is within the employer's scope of employment. The traditional rule is that an employee goes beyond the scope of employment when departing from the scope by engaging in the employee's personal chores. However, the employee remains within the scope when partially intending to serve her employer during or through the departure or when she begins to resume her work itinerary. Under a modern rule, one considers the foreseeability of the employee's departure from her itinerary. The employer is liable for tortious conduct when this conduct happens within a risk zone in which the employee is reasonably expected to depart from the itinerary, even for completely personal purposes.

         (b)   Frolic (No Vicarious Liability)

Generally, a master will not be liable for the tortious conduct of a servant, if the conduct occurs on the servant's personal "frolic" to engage in some conduct unrelated to business activity for the master. This could happen, for example, when an employee uses her employer's vehicle with her employer's permission to run a personal errand *after* business hours.

The decisive issue in determining whether conduct occurs on a detour or a frolic is whether the employee has any intention to serve the employer when engaged in such conduct. If the employee completely lacks such intent at that time, but rather only intends to achieve some personal purpose, then this conduct is outside of the scope of the employment relationship. In that event, the employer lacks liability for this conduct. Instead, only the employee has liability for this conduct because it is not within the scope of the employment relationship. However, if to some extent the employee intends to serve the employer's purpose when engaged in such conduct, then the employer may be liability for this conduct.

(2) Intentional Torts

An employee's intentional torts generally are considered to have occurred outside of the scope of employment, unless the employee committed them in furtherance of the employer's business activities.

(a) Use of Force

In other words, if an employee commits an intentional tort within the scope of employment, it usually will not be given *respondeat superior* effect. If, however, the employee entirely or partially uses force to advance the employer's goals, even inadvertently, that use of force will fall under the scope of employment. It will result in the employer being vicariously liable to a plaintiff who is harmed as a result of the employee's conduct.

(3) Scope of Liability

A vicariously liable defendant (e.g., an employer) who pays the entire amount of a plaintiff's judgment may recover that amount of damages from a defendant who is directly liable to the plaintiff (e.g., an employee).

(4) Direct Liability

An employer also may be directly liable to the plaintiff for negligently hiring or managing an employee.

b) Other Agents

A principal may be liable to a plaintiff for the conduct of its agents who are not employees to the extent that the principal has the power to control their work. Such liability is imputed or vicarious. The *respondeat superior* doctrine imposes liability on a principal for certain tortious acts of an agent that occur within the scope of the agent's work for the principal. Conversely, the agent's intentional torts generally are considered to have occurred outside of employment, unless the servant committed them in furtherance of the principal's business activities.

★★   2)   INDEPENDENT CONTRACTORS

                   a)   General Rule

Usually, a person will not be held liable for a tort that his independent contractor commits. The rationale is that the defendant lacks a right to control an independent contractor's activity.

                        (1)   Contractors and Employees

It is important to be able to distinguish between independent contractors and employees or agents of a party. An independent contractor, as distinguished from an employee, is responsible only for delivering a finished product to an employer. Generally, independent contractors are not directly supervised by the employer. They normally provide their own place of work, tools, supplies, and pay their own expenses. The business of an independent contractor usually requires specialized or professional skills.

                   b)   Exceptions

An employer of an independent contractor generally is not vicariously liable for the acts of its independent contractor. However, the employer may be liable to a plaintiff for the tortious acts of its independent contractor under certain circumstances.

                        (1)   Non-delegable Duties

In certain instances, an employer's business activities and his relationship to a plaintiff impose a duty upon the employer that cannot be delegated to an independent contractor. In such a case, the employer cannot be relieved of liability by hiring the independent contractor to perform the non-delegable duty. Consequently, an employer will be liable for the torts that an independent contractor commits while performing a non-delegable duty for the employer. Non-delegable duties may arise from public law (e.g., regulations) and private law (e.g., contracts).

                             (a)   Inherently Dangerous Activities

Inherently dangerous activities, such as blasting or fumigating, involve a significant amount of risk relative to the circumstances. That risk is ascertainable in advance. An employer cannot escape liability for an independent contractor's negligence in conducting an inherently dangerous activity.

                             (2)   Apparent Authority

A plaintiff may bring a tort action against an employer to recover damages for an independent contractor's tort when: (1) the employer presented the appearance of having authority over that contractor without informing the plaintiff that the contractor was not an employee; and (2) the plaintiff justifiably relied on the employer's representation regarding the working relationship between the employer and the contractor.

(3) Implied Authority

Implied authority exists when an employer states that a worker is an independent contractor, but the employer controls the worker's conduct. One test of the extent of that relationship is that the greater the degree of the employer's supervision of the worker, the greater the likelihood that the worker is not an independent contractor.

3) PARTNERS AND JOINT VENTURES

a) Partners

Partners in a partnership have a mutual right of control and share a common proprietary, financial, or economic purpose. Each partner in a partnership is vicariously liable to outsiders for the conduct of any other partner within the scope and course of the partnership. To be subject to that liability, each member of the partnership must: (1) have, with all of the other members, a mutual right to control its operations; and (2) share a common business purpose with all the other members.

b) Joint Ventures

A joint venture involves an undertaking of at least two people jointly to carry out one business enterprise for profit. Generally, the rules of tort liability for partnerships also apply to joint ventures.

★ 4) PARENTS

a) Common Law

Under the common law, a parent is not vicariously liable for a child's negligent torts.

(1) Exceptions

(a) Child Serving as Agent for Parent

An exception to the common law rule applies when a child's tortious conduct occurred while serving as an agent of his parent. For example, such conduct may occur while the child carries out a task pursuant to the parent's assignment.

(b) Negligent Supervision

A parent may be liable directly to an injured party for negligently supervising a child. Parents have a general duty to control the behavior of their children. The scope of the duty may depend upon the circumstances. For example, a higher standard may be required when a parent has reason to know or does know of dangerous propensities of the child and fails to exercise reasonable care to warn others or alleviate the situation.

b)   Statutes

Some state's parental liability statutes impose imputed liability on parents for their child's willful or wanton tort that causes malicious damage. These statutes usually contain specific dollar limitations, such as $2,000 or $10,000.

5)   TAVERN-KEEPERS

a)   Tavern-Keepers

(1)   Common Law

A tavern-keeper possesses a degree of control over a patron who becomes sufficiently intoxicated that the patron cannot control himself and safely get from the tavern to a place of shelter or dwelling. Under the common law rule, however, a tavern-keeper was not liable for an off premises injury caused by an intoxicated patron (even if the tavern-keeper was negligent).

(2)   Statutes

Today, many states have enacted statutes to modify the common law regarding tavern-keepers. Some state statutes require a tavern-keeper to stop serving drinks to an obviously intoxicated person. Under these statutes, a tavern-keeper may be held liable when he sells alcohol to an intoxicated person under circumstances where the tavern-keeper knows, or should know, that such conduct creates an unreasonable risk of harm to others who may be injured either on or off premises.

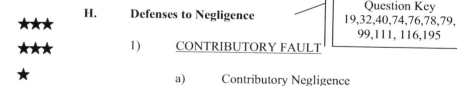

H.   Defenses to Negligence

Question Key
19,32,40,74,76,78,79,
99,111, 116,195

1)   CONTRIBUTORY FAULT

a)   Contributory Negligence

Contributory negligence is defined as a plaintiff's conduct that contributed as a legal cause to her injury and which fell below the standard to which she should have complied to avoid that harm. In a traditional contributory negligence jurisdiction, the plaintiff is barred from recovering from a defendant when the plaintiff's negligence caused the injury, *regardless of how minimal that contributory negligence might have been.* Only a very small minority of states still follow this pure form of contributory negligence based upon the common law.

For example, suppose Dave, a van driver, and Deb, a cyclist, were traveling forward in the same direction along a street. Dave drove the van in the vehicle lane, and Deb rode her bike alongside the van in the bicycle lane. When they reached a traffic light that was green for both of them, Deb attempted to continue riding straight, but after braking and using his turn signal Dave made a right turn directly across the cyclist lane. Deb tried to avoid colliding into the side of the van but could not stop quickly enough. This resulted in her hitting the van and falling off her bicycle. Deb filed a tort action against Dave seeking to recover damages for her personal injuries from this collision. In a pure contributory negligence jurisdiction, Deb would be barred from a recovery of damages if she was even only one percent negligent, such as by failing to slow down enough to a timely stop in order to allow the van to turn in front of her bicycle and across the cyclist's lane.

        (1)   Exceptions to Contributory Negligence

        (a)   Last Clear Chance Doctrine

A plaintiff's contributory negligence will not bar recovery against a defendant if the defendant possessed the *last clear chance* to avoid an accident involving those parties. Let's further consider the last example involving Dan's van and Deb's bicycle. In that situation, Deb could assert that her tort action is not barred by contributory negligence because Dan had the last clear chance of avoiding the accident by simply being observant enough to see her riding next to the van and waiting to turn right until after Deb had passed the van.

The focus of inquiry should be if the duration between a plaintiff's act of contributory negligence and the plaintiff's injury was sufficient for the defendant to exercise due care to prevent the injury. If the answer is yes, then the defendant possessed the last clear chance to avoid the injury and the plaintiff's contributory negligence will not preclude a recovery of damages. So, in the example of Dan and Deb, one analytical question could be if the period between Deb's application of the bicycle brakes and her colliding into the van was long enough for Dan to exercise due care to stop the van and allow Deb to continue riding the bike and pass in front of and beyond the van.

        (b)   Imminent Peril

A plaintiff's contributory negligence will not bar recovery if it occurred in a stressful context that a defendant produced. A plaintiff can recover damages from a defendant if the defendant knew that the plaintiff was helpless and the defendant realized or had reason to realize that peril, or the defendant should have realized that peril if the defendant had used reasonable care. In other words, a plaintiff can recover damages despite being negligently inattentive when a defendant:

- knows of the plaintiff's situation of peril;
- realizes or has reason to realize that the plaintiff is unlikely to avoid the harm; and
- negligently fails to use reasonable care to avoid the harm.

(c)   Willful and Wanton Conduct

A plaintiff's contributory negligence will be ignored if a defendant's conduct was willful and wanton.

★★★   b)   Comparative Negligence

The common law rule of contributory negligence proved to be unfairly harsh to plaintiffs and was rejected in most jurisdictions. The doctrine of comparative negligence, an alternative approach to allocating fault, has been adopted in some form in most jurisdictions.

In comparison to pure contributory negligence, the comparative negligence approach provides that when a plaintiff and a defendant, or multiple defendants, are each partially negligent, the amount of damages that are awarded to the plaintiff is subject to a reduction in the amount of the plaintiff's apportioned liability. Also, when the defendant, or multiple defendants, are seeking a recovery by means of a counterclaim and/or cross-claim, the amount of damages that are awarded to the defendant or multiple defendants is subject to a reduction in the amount of their respective liability. Under the comparative negligence approach, each party is attributed a percentage of fault.

(1)   Pure Comparative Negligence or Fault

Comparative negligence approaches are either pure or modified. The allocation of liability for damages in a pure comparative negligence jurisdiction is assessed in proportion to each party's fault, despite the fact that a plaintiff's degree of fault may exceed that of a defendant. Under this approach a percentage of negligence (i.e., fault) is allocated to any party responsible for damages and then the award of damages is accordingly apportioned among the parties. Consequently, an injured or damaged party can recover although this party was even 99 percent negligent. This party's recovery of damages is, however, reduced by the amount of the party's extent of fault.

For example, suppose there was a collision between Kevin's boat and Katrina's boat. Kevin filed a tort action against Katrina. At trial, Kevin was determined to be 99 percent at fault and Katrina was determined to be only 1 percent at fault. The judge held that Kevin sustained $100,000 in damages. This award of damages would be decreased by Kevin's 99 percent fault in causing the collision. Consequently, in a pure comparative negligence jurisdiction, Katrina would be obligated to pay one percent of Kevin's damages, or $1,000.

Another example may help illustrate the rule. Suppose that Dorothy walked across the street while the pedestrian crosswalk's flashing light was red for her. Nick drove his motorcycle under the speed limit along the street through a green light. Nick's motorcycle hit Dorothy before she finished crossing the street, knocking him off of the motorcycle onto the street. Both Nick and Dorothy sustained personal injuries, although hers were about 10 times worse than his. Dorothy filed a tort action against Nick worth a potential of $1,000,000 in damages. Nick filed a counterclaim worth a potential of $100,000 in damages. Dorothy prevailed in her action for $1,000,000 but she was found

70 percent negligent for unlawfully crossing the street. Consequently, Dorothy's award of potential damages could be reduced to $300,000 based on her percentage of negligence. Nick prevailed in his counterclaim for $100,000 but was found 30 percent negligent for failing to see Dorothy and avoid hitting her. Therefore, Nick's award of damages could be reduced to $70,000 by his negligence. Accordingly, when Nick's damages are subtracted from Dorothy's damages, Dorothy's net recovery from him would be $230,000.

(2)   Modified Comparative Negligence or Fault

In a modified comparative negligence jurisdiction, the plaintiff's comparative negligence or fault will not preclude the plaintiff's recovery of damages if the plaintiff's negligence or fault is lower than a specific percentage of the total fault.

Modified comparative negligence generally is divided into two types - either the "greater fault bar" or the "equal fault bar." Pursuant to the "greater fault bar," a plaintiff cannot recover if the plaintiff's fault is greater than the defendant's fault. Pursuant to the "equal fault bar," a plaintiff cannot recover if the plaintiff's fault is the same as or greater than the defendant's fault.

(a)   51 Percent or Greater Approach

In a majority of states that utilize a modified comparative negligence approach, a plaintiff is barred from a recovery from a defendant if the plaintiff is 51 percent or more negligent. This is the "greater fault bar" approach, under which the plaintiff cannot recover if the plaintiff's fault exceeds the defendant's fault. In other words, a plaintiff only can recover if the plaintiff's fault is less than 51 percent. Accordingly, if a plaintiff was 50 percent or less at fault, then the plaintiff can recover. The party's recovery would be decreased by the plaintiff's degree of fault. This rule does not apply only to plaintiffs, but to any injured or damaged party seeking to recover an award of damages.

If the situation described in the last example took place in one of the majority of states, Dorothy would be barred from recovering an award of damages from Nick based on the fact that she was 70 percent negligent. Nick would be entitled to $70,000 – a drastic change from the result in pure comparative negligence jurisdiction under which Nick would have owed Dorothy $230,000.

(b)   50 Percent or Greater Approach

In a minority of states, a plaintiff is barred from a recovery from a defendant if the plaintiff is more than or equal to 50 percent negligent. This is the "equal fault bar" approach, in which the plaintiff cannot recover if the fault is equal to or greater than the defendant's fault. In other words, in this type of jurisdiction, a plaintiff can recover only if the plaintiff's fault is not 50 percent or more. Accordingly, if a plaintiff was 49 percent or less at fault, then the plaintiff can recover. The plaintiff's recovery would be decreased by the plaintiff's degree of fault. This rule does not apply only to plaintiffs, but to any injured or damaged party seeking to recover an award of damages.

2)   ASSUMPTION OF RISK

A plaintiff's recovery can be denied on the basis that the plaintiff voluntarily assumed a risk of harm by: 1) knowing the risk existed; and 2) voluntarily proceeding with the activity anyway. However, a plaintiff does not assume the risk if there is no other reasonable alternative than to proceed with the activity, such as in the case of an emergency.

a)   Express Assumption of Risk

An express assumption of risk is a complete defense to the specific risks that a plaintiff agrees to assume. A court may uphold an express assumption of risk when the plaintiff's participation in an activity is voluntary or when the plaintiff expressly agrees to assume the risk.

(1)   Exception

An exception to this rule applies when such a gross disparity exists between the parties' bargaining power that the plaintiff did not really choose to assume the risk.

(2)   Limitations on Express Assumption of Risk

A plaintiff must be aware of a written provision for an assumption of risk. Thus, its placement in fine print will not suffice to bind her. The plaintiff must freely consent to the provision. The provision is not enforceable when it is contained in a contract of adhesion between the plaintiff and a defendant.

(a)   Invalidation

The provision for an assumption of risk may be judicially invalidated if it contravenes public policy. The courts will invalidate the provision if the plaintiff assumes the risk of very reckless conduct.

b)   Implied Assumption of Risk

An assumption of risk may be implied from the circumstances surrounding an incident that gives rise to a tort action. Specifically, an implied acceptance of risk can occur when a plaintiff voluntarily and freely enters into a situation in which a defendant's negligence is obvious, so that the plaintiff can be held to have consented to and accepted that negligence, such that the plaintiff has undertaken to beware of risks so that the defendant is relieved from that duty. For example, a spectator in the front row of a basketball game has implicitly assumed the apparent risk of being hit by the basketball.

3)   INTOXICATION

A plaintiff's voluntary intoxication may constitute a type of contributory fault.   A defendant's voluntary intoxication does not affect the application of the reasonable person standard.

III.   STRICT LIABILITY

A.   Common Issues Regarding Strict Liability

1)   GENERAL

a)   Definition

Under the principle of strict liability, under limited circumstances, a defendant may be liable for a plaintiff's injury without having done anything morally wrong or without failing to follow a reasonable standard of care.   Under the doctrine, a plaintiff is not required to establish intent or all of the elements of negligence.   At a minimum, a plaintiff must show some harm and seek a remedy for it.

b)   Types of Strict Liability Cases

Strict liability actions are mainly actions for damages resulting from harm caused by:

- ultra-hazardous or abnormally dangerous activities;
- animals; or
- products.

c)   Elements of Strict Liability

The elements of strict liability are:

- a defendant's absolute duty to make a something safe;
- the defendant's breach of that duty (which in most states is owed only to a foreseeable plaintiff); and
- the defendant proximately causes injury to a plaintiff's person or property.

2)   ABNORMALLY DANGEROUS ACTIVITIES

| Question Key |
| 21,87,160, |
| 183,184 |

A person involved in an abnormally dangerous activity may be held to a strict liability standard for any injuries resulting from the activity.   An abnormally dangerous activity is ultra-hazardous because it presents a substantial risk of serious harm to persons or property regardless of the degree of care that is exercised in carrying out that activity. Whoever engages in an abnormally dangerous activity has an absolute duty to safely perform the activity.

a)   *Rylands v. Fletcher*

Rylands v. Fletcher, sets forth the test for determining what qualifies as an abnormally dangerous activity. (*Rylands* is the only case name that the examiners specifically cite in the MBE's scope of testing). The test requires a case-by-case examination of several questions.

- Does the activity involve a risk of serious harm to persons or property?
- Can one perform the activity without risk of serious harm regardless of the degree of care?
- Do persons in the community not commonly engage in the activity?
- How appropriate is the activity with respect to the location?
- How does the activity's risk compare to its benefit for the community?

b)   Defenses

A defendant may assert assumption of the risk as a defense to an action alleging an abnormally dangerous activity. A defendant cannot assert contributory negligence as a defense through an allegation that a plaintiff failed to realize a hazard or guard against its existence.

        3)   <u>LIABILITY FOR ANIMALS</u>   Question Key 30.205

Under certain circumstances, a person may be held strictly liable for injuries caused by an animal.

a)   Trespassing Animals

(1)   Strict Liability

(a)   Majority Rule

The majority rule is that a defendant who owns or keeps animals that may escape, trespass, and cause harm to a plaintiff, is strictly liable for their harm. Such animals include both wild animals in captivity and livestock. Strict liability does not, however, apply to domestic animals.

(b)   Fencing In Statutes

Some jurisdictions have adopted "fencing in" statutes. A "fencing in" statute imposes strict liability if a defendant who owns or keeps specified types of animals fails to keep them within a fenced area.

(c)   Minority Rule

The minority rule is that an animal's owner is strictly liable for the damage resulting from the animal's trespass if the trespass was reasonably foreseeable.

(2)   Negligence

In addition to potential liability under a strict liability theory, a defendant who owns or keeps animals that may escape, trespass, and cause harm to a plaintiff, may be liable for the harm the animals cause based on a claim for negligence.

b)   Wild Animals

A wild animal's owner is strictly liable for injuries to a plaintiff if:

- the injury is attributable to a dangerous propensity of that type of animal; and
- the plaintiff did nothing voluntarily or consciously to bring about the injury.

An owner of a wild animal is liable even for an injury caused to a person attempting to escape from a wild animal, if the injury was foreseeable.

c)   Domestic Animals

An owner of a domestic or inherently non-dangerous animal generally is not strictly liable for the injuries that it causes. However, the owner's liability attaches if the owner knows of, or has reason to know about, a domestic animal's particularly dangerous propensities.

d)   Defenses

A plaintiff is precluded from recovering if a defendant proves the plaintiff assumed a risk of injury from a defendant's animal and the plaintiff:

- knew about and recognized the danger that justified strict liability; and
- voluntarily subjected himself to that danger.

4)   OTHER COMMON LAW STRICT LIABILITY CLAIMS

a)   Fire

American courts generally reject the common law rule that a possessor of land is strictly liable for damages that result from a fire that escapes from the land. Some states, however, have enacted statutes that impose strict liability for starting a fire under certain circumstances, such as during dry conditions. For example, some statutes provide that a railroad company is strictly liable when a train's engine starts a fire.

IV.   PRODUCTS LIABILITY CLAIMS

An overview of the history of products liability is helpful in understanding current law.

A.   Warranty Claims

Under the common law, a user of a product could only recover from an injury the product caused under a breach of warranty claim based in contract law. This type of claim remains available today. However, because of its privity requirement, it is very limited.

1)   TYPES OF WARRANTY CLAIMS

a)   Express Warranties

An express warranty arises from a manufacturer's express representation about the product's nature or quality. The express warranty may exist on a package or in product advertising. For example, a car manufacturer may provide a purchaser with a written warranty that the manufacturer will replace defective brakes for free until the car reaches 40,000 miles. If a product fails to fulfill the standards that a warranty establishes, the warranty is breached and a defendant is liable. A plaintiff does not need to prove the defendant's fault with respect to the breach.

b)   Implied Warranties

Products are sold with an implied warranty that the goods are "merchantable." Merchantable goods are goods fit for the ordinary purposes for which such goods are used. For example, if a consumer purchases a beer mug, there is an implied warranty that the mug will hold liquid. If the mug has a hole which causes the liquid to leak out, the consumer could allege a violation of the implied warranty of merchantability.

2)   PRIVITY REQUIRED

A manufacturer of goods is not liable to a third party under a breach of warranty claim if the third party has no contractual relationship with the manufacturer. For example, suppose Barney purchases cologne from ABC Co. He gives it to Ted who uses it before his big date with Robin. If the cologne is defective and causes Ted to suffer an allergic reaction, Ted is not able to recover on a warranty theory because he has no contractual relationship with ABC Co. He may, however, attempt to recover on negligence or strict liability grounds. Remember, a contractual relationship is not a requirement for liability based on negligence or strict liability in which any foreseeable user is protected.

3)   AVOIDING LIABILITY

a)   Disclaiming Warranty

A seller, by disclaiming all warranties, may not avoid liability for a purchaser's personal injuries that are attributable to a product. For example, a seller cannot avoid product liability by marking and selling a product "as is."

b) Limiting Responsibility

It is unconscionable for a defendant to attempt to restrict a plaintiff's remedies for a breach of warranty in a manner that precludes a recovery for personal injuries. The defendant cannot limit responsibility for a breach regarding the repair or replacement of consumer goods.

B. Second Restatement of Torts - Unreasonably Dangerous Standard

The common law requirement of a contractual relationship proved to be too limiting. An innocent user of a product who suffered injury as a result of a product defect was left without any remedy. This proved unacceptable for the policy reason that a person profiting from a defective commercial product, not an innocent consumer, should bear the loss of injury caused by a product defect.

The *Second Restatement of Torts* (the "*Second Restatement*") provides that a manufacturer of a product will be liable for the harm it causes if the product is "*unreasonably dangerous*." In determining whether a product is unreasonably dangerous, a court would consider the expectations of a reasonable consumer.

Under the *Second Restatement*, a plaintiff could bring a products liability claim under three theories: 1) warranty; 2) negligence; and 3) strict liability.

1) WARRANTY CLAIMS

Common law breach of implied warranty and breach of express warranty claims are still available under the *Second Restatement*.

2) NEGLIGENCE

a) Elements

In the context of a product's liability action, a plaintiff asserting a negligence claim must show:

- the existence of a legal duty owed to a plaintiff;
- a breach of the duty;
- that the defendant proximately caused the breach; and
- damages resulted to the plaintiff from the breach.

b) Duty of Care

If a reasonable person would foresee a risk of harm if the product is not carefully made or supplied, then the product's manufacturer or supplier owes a duty of due care to all foreseeable users of the product.

c)   Duty to Inspect

A product dealer, middleman, supplier, wholesaler, or retailer has no duty to inspect or test the products of a manufacturer or assembler unless there is a reason to know of a defect in the products. Therefore, in order to prevail in a manufacturing defect case grounded in negligence against a retailer, wholesaler, or another party in the chain of supply, except the manufacturer, a plaintiff must demonstrate that the party had a reason to know of a defect in the product that created a legal duty to inspect it. Otherwise, it is difficult to prevail in a manufacturing defect case grounded in negligence against such a non-manufacturer party.

(1)   Rebuilt or Reconditioned Goods

An individual or entity that reconditions or rebuilds used goods is considered the legal equivalent of a manufacturer and is held strictly liable for injuries that result from defectively rebuilt or reconditioned goods.

(2)   Leased Goods

Commercial lessors are subject to strict liability for defects in new and used leased goods.

(3)   Used Goods

Under the *Second Restatement*, courts are divided on the issue of whether a retailer of used goods is strictly liable for the defects in those goods.

        3)   <u>STRICT LIABILITY</u>

| Question Key |
| 7,22,24,73,104,105,106,107,108,120,141, 142.143.152.156.168.170.181.187.213 |

In most cases, a plaintiff brings an action for a product defect on a strict liability theory.

a)   General Rule

Under a strict liability theory, the manufacturer and any commercial supplier (e.g., middleman, supplier, dealer, or retailer) is held strictly liable for a plaintiff's injuries from a commercial product if the product is dangerously defective.

(1)   Commercial Product Seller

A commercial product seller is a "person engaged in the business of selling products for use or consumption." *Second Restatement* § 402A comment f (1966); *Restatement (Third) of the Law of Products Liability* § 1 (1998).

A commercial product seller who sells a defective product is strictly liable for injuries caused to the "ultimate user or consumer" even though the seller did not make the product and the injured person did not buy it from the seller.

(2)   Noncommercial Product Seller

A noncommercial product seller is not strictly liable for injuries caused by products it sells. A noncommercial product seller is, for example, a charitable organization that holds a bake sale of donated baked goods.

b)   Scope of Liability

A manufacturing defect exists if a product is not produced in its intended form. A plaintiff who suffers personal injury or property damage due to a manufacturing defect may seek to impose strict liability on a manufacturer and everyone else in the chain of distribution.

Today, products liability law applies to purchasers, as well as to bystanders, because all jurisdictions have abandoned the former "privity of contract" approach. *Second Restatement* § 402A; 2 Dan Dobbs, The Law of Torts § 353 (2001).

c)   Dangerously   Defective   and   the   Consumer
        Expectation Rule

A manufacturer that assembles parts into a completed product is strictly liable for defects in those parts. Under the Consumer Expectation Rule, a product is defective if it is more dangerous than an ordinary consumer would have anticipated. A product is dangerously defective if a reasonable person would not have expected it to present the danger that resulted in his injury.

(1)   Elements

To prove a defendant's strict liability for a defectively manufactured product, a plaintiff must demonstrate that:

- injury in fact resulted from a condition of the product;
- the condition existed when the product left the defendant's hands;
- the product was not materially altered before the injury occurred;
- the condition rendered the product unreasonably dangerous for its use; and
- the defendant could foresee its use, or its misuse was reasonably foreseeable.

A plaintiff who makes a *prima facie* case of strict liability does not need to show that a defendant could have manufactured a better a product.

(2)   Product Misuse

A defendant is liable for a plaintiff's reasonably foreseeable misuse of a product.

(3)   Economic Losses

The majority of courts decline to entertain strict product liability claims alleging economic losses.

(4)   Chain of Supply

If a manufacturer is held liable, then any commercial seller in the chain of supply, such as a retailer, distributor, or wholesaler, is liable. The defendant must sell the product in the course of doing business. The purpose behind this rule is that the law prefers a party who profits from the product, rather than an innocent plaintiff, to suffer a loss. For example, suppose Carl brings an action against Mega-Mart and Shanghai Toy Co. for strict liability after a basketball manufactured by Shanghai Toy Co. and purchased at Mega-Mart injures Carl because of a manufacturing defect. Carl obtains a judgment for one million dollars. Due to Shanghai Toy Co.'s lack of assets in the country, Carl cannot recover from them. He can, however, recover the full judgment from Mega-Mart. Mega-Mart, in turn, may seek indemnification from Shanghai Toy Co.

A plaintiff does not have to be in privity with the supplier in order to able to recover from the supplier for damages. For example, suppose a person buys a defective product and lends the product to another person; the other person uses the product and is injured by it. The injured person can recover directly from any supplier for damages.

C.   Third Restatement of Torts Approach to Products Liability

The *Third Restatement of Torts: Products Liability* (the "*Third Restatement*"), expands on the *Second Restatement* by incorporating case law principles since the establishment of the *Second Restatement*. Generally, the legal rules established by the *Second Restatement* still apply under the *Third Restatement*. The *Third Restatement* holds a seller or distributor of a defective product liable for harm the defect causes to persons or property. The *Third Restatement* does not classify products liability claims by fault grounds (e.g., negligence and strict liability).

Many of the rules regarding strict products liability, such as the chain of supply, and the rule regarding economic losses, generally also apply to products liability claims under the *Third Restatement*. Additionally, as with those cases, the plaintiff also must demonstrate:

- the injury in fact resulted from a condition of the product;
- the condition existed when the product left the defendant's hands; and
- the product was not materially altered before the injury occurred.

Although not yet adopted in all U.S. jurisdictions, the *Third Restatement* approach to products liability is relevant for MBE purposes. The scope of testing addresses the three types of products liability claims set forth in the *Third Restatement*. Additionally, the most recent released MBE questions directly test *Third Restatement* concepts.

The *Third Restatement* specifically identifies three types of product defects: manufacturing defects, design defects, and failure to warn defects.

★   1)   <u>MANUFACTURING DEFECTS</u>

Question Key
119.151.169

A product contains a manufacturing defect if the product departs from its intended design even though all possible care was exercised in the preparation and marketing of the product. *Third Restatement*, § 2. For example, a properly designed car brake that fails to brake when installed on a car because of a defect in the manufacturing process, may qualify as a manufacturing defect.

★   2)   <u>DESIGN DEFECTS</u>

Question Key
1,192,210

Even if a product is properly manufactured, its defective design may make it dangerous. A product possesses a design defect when the foreseeable risks of harm it poses could be reduced or avoided with the adoption of a reasonable alternative design and the omission of the alternative design renders the product not reasonably safe. A product is defective in its design if, as designed, it poses a danger to people or property.

       a)   Risks-Benefits Test

In order to prove a design defect exists, a plaintiff must satisfy the risk-benefits test. Under the risk-benefits test, a plaintiff must establish that the design caused the injury. The defendant could rebut this showing by demonstrating that the benefits of the design outweighed the risks of the design and the feasibility of a safer design. In other words, a court would determine whether the benefits of a design outweigh the risk of danger inherent in the design. Was there a feasible alternative that would have reduced the risk?

★   3)   <u>FAILURE TO WARN</u>

Question Key
2,46,71,72

A product is defective because of a failure to warn if the foreseeable risk of harm the product poses could have been reduced or avoided by the provision of reasonable instructions or warnings and as a result, the omission of the instructions or warnings renders the product not reasonably safe.

A supplier of a product is liable to foreseeable users for harm that results from foreseeable uses of the product if the product is not reasonably safe, the danger is not obvious, and the supplier fails to inform the user of the danger. For example, a knife possesses an obvious danger, and thus requires no warning.

       a)   Inadequate Warning

A product is dangerously defective if its warning is inadequate in the following respects:

- the warning is inconsistent with the product's usage instructions;

- the warning does not convey its message to a user (e.g., a person unable to read); and
- the warning neither sufficiently defines nor fails to note all dangers.

★   4)   ADDITIONAL CONCEPTS

The *Third Restatement* specifically addresses a few additional products liability concepts.

a)   Claims Supported with Circumstantial Evidence

The *Third Restatement* introduces a concept similar to the negligence topic of *res ipsa loquitur* to products liability claims. Specifically, it can be inferred that the harm a plaintiff sustains was caused by a product defect existing at the time of sale or distribution, without proof of a specific defect, when the incident that harmed the plaintiff:

- was of a kind that ordinarily occurs as a result of product defect; and
- was not, in the particular case, solely the result of causes other than a product defect existing at the time of sale or distribution.

Third Restatement, § 3.

b)   Compliance with Product Safety Laws

The *Third Restatement* also introduces a concept similar to negligence per se. For design defect and failure to warn cases, a product's noncompliance with an applicable product safety law renders the product defective. On the other hand, a product's compliance with an applicable product safety law can be considered in determining whether the product is defective. However, by itself, compliance does not preclude a finding of a product defect. *Third Restatement*, § 4.

c)   Liability of Manufacturer of Product Components

A seller or distributor of a product component is subject to liability for harm caused by a product into which the component is integrated if the component is defective and the defect causes the harm. Additionally, the seller of the component is liable for harm caused by the product if the seller substantially participates in the integration of the component into the design of the product, the integration causes the product to be defective, and the defect causes the harm.

d)   Seller of Used Products

Unlike the *Second Restatement*, the *Third Restatement* specifically addresses the sellers of used products. Under the *Third Restatement*, a seller of a used product may be held liable for damage caused by the used product under certain circumstances including:

- the seller fails to exercise reasonable care (negligence); or
- the product contains a manufacturing defect; or

- the product is remanufactured by the seller or a party in the chain of supply of the seller and the product contains a manufacturing, design, or inadequate warning defect; or
- the seller fails to comply with product safety laws.

★ **D.   Defenses**

Question Key
46,73,106,108,187

There are defenses to a strict products liability action.

1)   MISUSE

A plaintiff cannot recover on the basis of strict products liability if she misuses the product and the misuse is not reasonably foreseeable.

2)   ASSUMPTION OF RISK

A plaintiff's voluntary and unreasonable assumption of a known risk precludes the plaintiff from recovering on a strict products liability basis. Such an assumption of risk will occur if: (1) a plaintiff is warned about or discovers a product's dangerous defect; and (2) the plaintiff unreasonably and voluntarily proceeds to use the product.

3)   CONTRIBUTORY NEGLIGENCE

Contributory negligence is not a defense to strict liability when a plaintiff fails to:

- discover the defect;
- guard against its existence; or
- properly use the product and the misuse is reasonably foreseeable.

★ ### 4)   COMPARATIVE NEGLIGENCE

Most states that use a comparative negligence approach apply it to products liability cases. In those states, assumption of the risk does not bar recovery of damages. A court will examine all factors, including assumption of the risk, in determining a proper allocation of fault.

V.   OTHER TORTS

Question Key
17,39,47,94,113,114,
121,180,194,214,215
See also Property 106

★★★ **A.   Claims Based on Nuisance and Defenses**

1)   GENERAL

A nuisance is a wrongdoer's interference with the real property rights of another person, absent a physical invasion of the other person's real property. Nuisance actions are classified as public or private.

2)   PRIVATE NUISANCE

a)   Definition

A person commits a private nuisance when he *substantially* and *unreasonably* disturbs the right of another to use and enjoy land. A plaintiff may seek a civil remedy from a defendant for that disturbance. The various types of actionable disturbances may include disruptive noises and vibrations, as well as physical harms to a landowner's real property and the structures and chattel on that property. Other forms of disturbance may include the uninvited presence of odors, particulates, and gases, as well as liquids, lights, and fluids. So long as the interference is substantial and unreasonable, and such as would be offensive or inconvenient to the normal person, virtually any disturbance of the enjoyment of the property may amount to a nuisance. One basis for bringing a private nuisance action is the decrease in the use and value of the plaintiff's property due to a defendant's adverse conditions or activities.

b)   Elements

The elements of private nuisance action are:

- the defendant intentionally interfered with a plaintiff's use and enjoyment of the land;
- the defendant's conduct resulted in the type of interference with the plaintiff's land that the defendant intended;
- the plaintiff suffered a substantial interference due to the defendant's conduct;
- the interference would be offensive to a community member of normal sensitivity, rather than only to a person of abnormal sensitivity;
- the extent of the defendant's interference constitutes an unreasonable interference with the plaintiff's use and enjoyment of the land.

(1)   Scope of Interference

Two questions are used to determine the impact of a defendant's "interference" with a plaintiff's physical or mental comfort:

- would a reasonable person residing where a plaintiff lives consider the interference offensive, seriously bothersome, or unbearable?
- would the significance of the interference outweigh the usefulness of the defendant's conduct?

c)   Nuisance Distinguished from Trespass

Unlike trespass, liability for nuisance does not require proof of damage to the plaintiff's property; proof of interference with the plaintiff's use and enjoyment of that property is sufficient. Liability for private nuisance requires proof of two additional elements. First, the plaintiff must prove that the invasion in use and enjoyment of the land was substantial in that it caused plaintiff to suffer substantial actual damage. Second, the plaintiff must prove that the interference with the protected interest is unreasonable.

d)   Coming to the Nuisance

The "coming to the nuisance" defense may protect a defendant under certain circumstances when a plaintiff comes to where the defendant has been using his property in a manner that the plaintiff alleges constitutes a nuisance. In most jurisdictions, the general rule is that coming to the nuisance will not bar a nuisance action. However, it is a defense if the plaintiff came to the nuisance *for the purpose* of litigating about the defendant's pre-existing use.

e)   Contributory Negligence

If a defendant deliberately causes a nuisance to interfere with a plaintiff's interest, the defendant is not allowed to invoke contributory negligence as a defense. If the defendant negligently causes a nuisance, then the defendant may raise a contributory negligence defense.

f)   Legislative Authority

Legislative authority, such as a zoning provision regarding the land use alleged as a nuisance, may be a defense to a nuisance action. However, the defense is not automatic. The court will examine the totality of the circumstances to determine whether the action was unreasonable in light of the zoning provision and the land use.

g)   Remedies

When a plaintiff succeeds in establishing that a defendant is liable for a private nuisance, the plaintiff may seek and recover damages, injunctive relief, or abatement by self-help.

3)   PUBLIC NUISANCE

a)   Definition

A public nuisance arises from a defendant's interference with the rights and interests *of the community*. The various types of interferences may include activities that would adversely affect the public's health, safety, morals, peace, comfort, or convenience. Many of those activities also could qualify as a private nuisance and are analyzed under the elements of the private nuisance test. Other additional and different activities, such as certain criminal offenses (e.g., operating an illegal brothel), are public nuisances. The interference resulting from those activities must affect the public's common interest.

b)   Proper Plaintiff

(1)   Government

The right to relief from a public nuisance usually lies with a government entity because it is a type of offense, and often a criminal act, from which some or all of the community needs protection.

(2)   Individual

A private individual cannot bring an action for a public nuisance unless the individual shows that he either: (1) suffered a different harm that is distinct from the harm that the public sustained; or (2) suffered a far greater degree of *special damages*.

c)   Compliance with a Statute or Regulation

Under certain circumstances a defendant may raise compliance with a statute or regulation that the defendant allegedly violated as a defense in a public nuisance action.

d)   Remedies

A plaintiff in a public nuisance action may seek either an abatement of the offending activity or condition through injunctive relief or by means of a criminal prosecution when the conduct at issue constitutes a criminal offense.

★★★   **B.   Claims Based on Defamation**

1)   <u>DEFINITION</u>

Question Key
3,4,38,55,57,77,93,109,
137,158,165,172,182

Defamation includes the torts of slander and libel. Defamation is generally a communication that is likely to subject a person to public hatred, shame, disgrace, and obloquy. The *Second Restatement of Torts* defines defamation as a communication tending to injure a person's reputation by diminishing his standing in a community.

a)   Publication

The communication must involve publication (oral or written) to a least one third party other than the communication's source and its recipient. An actionable communication cannot have occurred only between one plaintiff and one defendant. Otherwise, the plaintiff's recourse is limited to a tort action alleging emotional distress that resulted from the defendant's insulting communication.

(1)   Communication to Third Party

A statement is published if a defendant, either intentionally or inadvertently, allows its communication to a third party other than the plaintiff. If the third party repeats the defamatory statement, then he may be liable for defamation based on that subsequent publication. The third party's liability exists despite his subsequent qualification of that statement indicating that it was "alleged" or just constituted his opinion.

(2)   Living Person Rule

Only a living person may be defamed. A deceased person's estate may not bring a defamation action for a statement about the deceased person that was made after he died.

(3)   Group or Class of People

Generally, no defamation action is available in response to a published communication that refers to a large group or class of people when no specific individual member of that group or class was mentioned in that communication. If, however, a defendant makes a defamatory statement regarding a very small group of people, every member of the group may be deemed adequately identifiable to allow any one or more of them to file a defamation action against the defendant.

(4)   Entities or Organizations

Business entities and other organizations may bring defamation actions under certain circumstances. A statement defames such an entity if it causes customers to stop doing business with the entity. The statement also may defame an organization when it results in people ceasing to make charitable donations to, or dissuades them from joining, the organization.

b)   Requirements of Proof

(1)   Defamatory on its Face

When a published communication is defamatory on its face, a plaintiff need not prove either inducement or innuendo.

(2)   Inducement and Innuendo

If a communication is only defamatory in light of outside facts or circumstances, then a plaintiff has the burden of establishing that the communication is defamatory by means known as either inducement or innuendo. "Inducement" is a negative implication given to a published communication when outside facts are brought to light. The plaintiff is obligated to plead the extra facts needed to make the statement defamatory.

2)   ELEMENTS OF DEFAMATION

The elements of defamation are:

- a publication to a person or people other than to a defamed plaintiff;
- of a defamatory statement of fact that is understood by people as;
- being of and concerning the plaintiff;
- tending to harm the reputation of the plaintiff; and/or
- tending to dissuade others from associating with the plaintiff.

a)   General Considerations

A third party who receives a defamatory publication must understand it. This does not, however, require that a defamatory message be believed. Recipients do not need to have a rational response to the statement.

b)   Public Figures

If the plaintiff is a public figure, the plaintiff must also must prove that the defendant acted with actual malice and that the statement is false.

3)   FAULT STANDARDS

a)   Common Law

Pursuant to the common law, if a published statement concerns private, instead of public, facts, a plaintiff is not required to prove either negligence or malice. The common law required a defendant to prove the truth of a defamatory statement as a defense.

Modern constitutional principles have modified the common law to require that in all cases, a plaintiff must prove the falsity of a defamatory statement. A defamation action is treated differently if it involves a defamatory statement about (1) a public person (i.e., public official or public figure) or (2) a public event concerning a private person (i.e., newsworthy event).

b)   Negligence Standard

In the absence of a constitutionally required standard of proving fault, most states require a showing of negligence. Mere negligence on account of the defendant with regard to the truth is sufficient to ground liability. This standard generally applies when a plaintiff is a private individual, rather than a public figure or official, and the statement concerns public facts. Note that a private individual involved in a public event need not prove malice, but must still demonstrate falsity.

c)   Malice Standards

(1)   Public Officials and Figures

New York Times v. Sullivan provides that, in order for a public official to prevail in a defamation action, the official must prove with clear and convincing evidence that a defendant published a defamatory communication with *actual malice*. Actual malice includes: 1) knowledge of the falsity of the statement; or 2) a reckless disregard as to the truth or falsity of the statement.

4)   SLANDER

Slander requires a verbal, rather than a written, communication that adversely affects a plaintiff's good name and reputation among persons having an interest in the plaintiff. Defamation law principles generally apply to both slander and libel.

5)   LIBEL

a)   Definition

Libel involves a written, rather than an oral, communication. The *Second Restatement of Torts* describes libel as: "a publication of defamatory statements in a written, printed, or other physical format having the same harmful qualities of the written or printed word, based on the area of dissemination, the deliberate character of its publication, and persistence of the defamatory conduct. Libel includes the broadcasting of defamatory matter by means of radio or television."

b)   Minority Approach

In a minority of jurisdictions, courts differentiate between libel *per se* and libel *per quod*.

(1)   Libel *Per Se*

Libel *per se* occurs when the defamatory meaning of a communication is evident on its face.

(2)   Libel *Per Quod*

Libel *per quod* exists when a publication is innocent on its face and becomes defamatory only to those individuals with knowledge of facts that were extrinsic to a published matter.

6)   DAMAGES

a)   Libel

(1)   Majority Approach

Generally, in a majority of jurisdictions, a libel action does not require the proof of special damages. Damages are presumed in those jurisdictions.

(2)   Minority Approach

Usually, a plaintiff must produce evidence from which harm to reputation can be inferred or provide direct proof of injury to the plaintiff's reputation. When a libel *per se* occurs, a plaintiff need not establish that the plaintiff suffered any harm to his reputation. The existence of such harm is presumed from the publication of the libel without any evidence of actual harm.

b)   Slander

(1)   General Rule of Proving Damages

Most types of slander require proof of special damages (i.e., those that flow from the natural and proximate consequence of the harm).

(2)   Four Exceptions

Proof of special damages is not required in four exceptions that are classified as slander *per se*. Those exceptions are verbal communications that impute:

- a crime or criminal conduct to any plaintiff;
- a loathsome disease to any plaintiff;
- something negative about any plaintiff's business, trade, profession, office, or calling;
- serious sexual misconduct including the unchastity of a woman.

Once special damages are established, a plaintiff may recover actual or compensatory damages.

c)   Generally

When a private person demonstrates that a defendant acted with negligence, that private person may generally recover only actual damages. Pecuniary damages are the monetary losses that a plaintiff sustains due to an injury to reputation like humiliation and loss of friends. General damages are presumed if the injury does not involve any pecuniary interests. Punitive damages are imposed to punish and to prevent prospective misconduct. Generally, they are not imposed in a simple negligence case.

7)   DEFENSES

a)   Absolute Privilege

An absolute privilege may shield certain individuals from liability for defamation.

Judicial proceedings provide absolute immunity to judges, jurors, witnesses, and attorneys who are involved with, and while they are working on, a case.

Legislative proceedings provide absolute immunity to legislators and witnesses in committee hearings and on the floor of the legislature. The immunity applies regardless of the communication's subject matter.

Communications within the political executive branch of government generally are absolutely privileged, subject to certain limited exceptions.

Husbands and wives have absolute immunity with respect to their private communications, even if they are defamatory in nature.

b)   Qualified Privilege

A qualified or limited privilege may shield an individual from liability for defamation under limited circumstances. In those circumstances, if a defendant acts on a good-faith belief that the information is true, and the communication possesses a socially useful purpose, it will be privileged.

(1)   Speaker's Interest

A speaker's interest may justify a defamatory communication that defends the speaker's reputation.

(2)   Third Party's Interest

Protecting another party's interest may justify a speaker in making a defamatory communication (e.g., a negative letter of recommendation).

(3)   Common Interest

Furthering a common interest of a speaker and another party, especially when a legal and moral obligation to communicate exists (e.g., a fiduciary relationship), may warrant a defamatory statement.

(4)   Public Interest

The public interest privilege also protects public officials who make defamatory publications in the course of conducting their official duties. A defamatory publication is allowed if it is a fair comment in a public discussion regarding matters of public concern.

c)   Truth

A defamatory statement is considered false unless a defendant proves its truth.

(1)   Majority Rule

In most jurisdictions, truth is a complete affirmative defense to a defamation action, even if the defendant published the statement with ill will.

(2)   Minority Rule

A few jurisdictions impose liability on a defendant who publishes a true defamatory statement if the defendant acts out of improper motives, ill will, or spite.

d)   Privity

A defamatory statement that a defendant publishes regarding a third person is actionable only to the degree that it also defames a plaintiff. If the defendant's defamatory statement just concerns the third person, even if it is someone who is related to the plaintiff, it will not defame the plaintiff.

e)   Consent

Consent (i.e., waiver) of a plaintiff to defamation exists when he caused, invited, or allowed publication of the defamatory material. If the defamation involves an invasion of privacy, then a plaintiff's consent to it, or authorization of it, is irrevocable if based on a valid contract and revocable if gratuitously given.

For example, suppose a general manager of a franchise restaurant is denied a promotion to regional manager. He asks a law firm to represent him in efforts to have the promotion decision reversed. In response to a letter from the firm on the general manager's behalf, the CEO of the company writes to the firm explaining truthfully that the general manager had been denied the promotion because of reports that he had verbally abused two former customers. Several weeks later, after an investigation, the allegations are proven untrue, and the general manager receives the promotion. The general manager had remained working at the restaurant at full pay during the review process and, thus, suffered no pecuniary harm. Would he be successful in a claim for libel? Under these facts, the answer is no because his letter "invited" the defamatory statement. He is deemed to have consented to limited publication by the CEO.

★   **C.**   **Claims Based on Invasion of Privacy and Defenses**

Question Key
110,124, 200,218

The following four tort claims may be actionable if a defendant invades a plaintiff's reasonable expectation of privacy: 1) commercial appropriation; 2) intrusion upon seclusion; 3) false light publication; and 4) private facts disclosure.

1)   COMMERCIAL APPROPRIATION

a)   Definition

An appropriation by a defendant of a plaintiff's likeness (picture or image), or identity (name) for the defendant's commercial advantage is an invasion of privacy and actionable in tort. The scope of liability usually is restricted to the use of that picture or name for the promotion of an advertisement of a product or a service. For example, this tort could arise if a famous actor's name and photograph were used to advertise a product or service without the actor's permission.

b)   Elements

The plaintiff may establish a *prima facie* case of commercial appropriation with evidence of the following elements:

- a defendant makes unauthorized use of a plaintiff's likeness (picture or name) or identity (name);
- for the defendant's commercial advantage;
- the defendant's conduct proximately causes an invasion of the plaintiff's interest in privacy.

(1)   Likeness Element

An appropriation does not require that a defendant use a plaintiff's true likeness. The likeness element is fulfilled if a defendant appropriates any characteristic or object that would identify the plaintiff. The likeness or identifier used must enable a third party to recognize the plaintiff. A drawing resembling a photograph of an actor could satisfy the likeness requirement.

(2)   Promotion Requirement

The unauthorized use of the plaintiff's likeness or identity must relate to the defendant's promotion of a product or service. The fact that the defendant received economic benefit by using plaintiff's identity is not actionable if it is not related to the defendant's promotion of a product or service.

c)   Defense

The defense of consent to, or authorization of, a commercial appropriation is irrevocable if based on a valid contract and revocable if gratuitously given. Statutes generally require written consent to a commercial appropriation.

2)   INTRUSION UPON SECLUSION

a)   Definition

The second type of privacy invasion involves a defendant's intrusion upon a plaintiff's personal affairs or activities.

b)   Elements

The plaintiff may establish a *prima facie* case with evidence of the following elements:

- intentional intrusion, physical or otherwise;
- upon the plaintiff's solitude or seclusion or private affairs or concerns;
- that would be highly offensive to a reasonable person.

c)   Defense

The defense of consent to, or authorization of, an intrusion on seclusion is irrevocable if based on a valid contract and revocable if gratuitously given. Statutes generally require written consent.

3)   <u>FALSE LIGHT PUBLICATION</u>

a)   Definition

The third type of privacy invasion occurs when a defendant publishes facts regarding a plaintiff that portray the plaintiff in a false light in the public eye.

b)   Elements

The plaintiff may make a *prima facie* case by presenting evidence of these elements:

- a publication by the defendant about the plaintiff;
- made with actual malice;
- that places the plaintiff in a false light;
- that would be highly offensive to a reasonable person.

c)   Defenses

Truth is a complete defense in a false light publication action. Privilege is also a defense to making a false or defamatory publication. The defense of consent to, or authorization of, a false light publication is irrevocable if based on a valid contract and revocable if gratuitously given. Statutes require written consent.

4)   <u>PRIVATE FACTS DISCLOSURE</u>

a)   Definition

The fourth type of privacy invasion occurs when a defendant publicly discloses private facts about a plaintiff.

b)   Elements

The plaintiff may make a *prima facie* case by presenting evidence of these elements:

- the facts disclosed are private facts;
- the defendant disclosed them to the public generally or to a large number of persons;
- the disclosure was in a form of publicity of a highly objectionable kind.

c)   Defenses

The fairness and accuracy of the disclosure is a defense in an action alleging public disclosure of private facts. The defense of consent to, or authorization of, a public disclosure of private facts is irrevocable if based on a valid contract, and revocable if gratuitously given. Statutes generally require written consent.

★   **D.   Claims Based on Fraudulent Misrepresentation and Defenses**

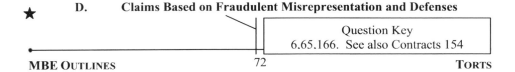

Question Key
6.65.166. See also Contracts 154

1)   <u>GENERAL</u>

Under certain circumstances, a plaintiff may bring a tort action for a fraudulent misrepresentation of fact.

2)   <u>INTENTIONAL MISREPRESENTATION</u>

a)   Definition

Fraudulent misrepresentation is a defendant's false statement of fact with the intent to mislead or deceive another person. A statement of fact does not include opinions, judgments, or puffery.

(1)   Exception

In most jurisdictions, a defendant is not liable for active concealment if a transaction with a plaintiff is indicated to be "as is."

b)   Elements

A plaintiff must prove the following elements to succeed on an action for intentional misrepresentation.

- Material Misrepresentation

A material misrepresentation is a defendant's false statement that a reasonable person (e.g., the plaintiff) would find of significant import under the circumstances.

- Scienter

The defendant knows, or should know, that the statement is false and that the plaintiff would consider it true. Alternatively, the defendant is liable if he makes the statement with reckless disregard for its truth or falsity.

- Intent

The defendant intends to induce the plaintiff's reliance on the statement.

- Reliance

The misrepresentation causes the plaintiff's actual and justifiable reliance.

- Damage

The plaintiff suffers pecuniary damages as a result of the statement.

c)   Defenses

Three defenses are available including:

- a defendant made a truthful or innocent representation;
- the defendant made the representation to protect a person's welfare; and
- the defendant made the representation to avoid a public policy violation.

Contributory negligence is not a defense to the intentional tort of fraudulent misrepresentation.

3)   NEGLIGENT MISREPRESENTATION

Under certain circumstances, a person may be liable for a negligent misrepresentation.

a)   General

If a business relationship exists between two parties, one of the parties could assert liability for negligent misrepresentation.

b)   Elements

The elements of negligent misrepresentation are: 1) business capacity; 2) breach of duty; and 3) causing damages.

(1)   Business Capacity

The business capacity element requires that the defendant have made a representation in the course of his business or in a transaction in which the defendant possesses a pecuniary interest.

(2)   Breach of Duty

The plaintiff must prove that the defendant owed a duty to a foreseeable plaintiff and the defendant did not exercise reasonable care or competence in obtaining or communicating information.

(3)   Causing Damages

The plaintiff must suffer a financial, physical, or other loss by justifiably and actually relying on the representation.

c)   Real Property Disclosure Rule

No general duty exists to disclose certain material facts to a buyer of real property except when its seller knows that:

- the real property contains a material defect;
- a buyer lacks knowledge of the defect;
- the buyer could not reasonably discover the defect; and
- the seller possesses a duty to disclose the defect to a buyer.

d)   Defenses

The following defenses also are applicable to the tort of negligent misrepresentation:

- a defendant made a truthful or innocent representation;
- the defendant made the representation to protect a person's welfare; and
- the defendant made the representation to avoid a public policy violation.

Contributory negligence is not a defense to the tort of negligent misrepresentation.

4)   NEGLIGENT NONDISCLOSURE

If a relationship exists between two parties, a person is liable for negligent nondisclosure if:

- a defendant fails to reveal a known risk of danger to a plaintiff;
- the plaintiff suffers harm as a result of the undisclosed and known risk;
- the defendant should have anticipated that;
- the plaintiff would rely on an appearance of safety.

E.   Claims Based on Interference with Business Relations

1)   INTERFERENCE WITH CONTRACTUAL RELATIONS

a)   General

A plaintiff has a right to redress when a defendant impermissibly interferes with the plaintiff's rights under a business contract with a third party. Such interference may include the loss of a right, or making the plaintiff's exercise of those rights more expensive or less beneficial.

b)   Elements

The elements of an interference with contractual relations are:

- Contract: a valid contract exists between a plaintiff and a third party;
- Knowledge: a defendant has knowledge of the contract;
- Intent: the defendant intends to interfere with the contract;
- Interference: the defendant causes interference with the contract;
- Damages: the plaintiff consequently suffers damage.

    c)   Defenses

    (1)   Privilege to Induce Breach

The defense of a privilege to induce a breach applies when a defendant's interference is justified under certain circumstances including:

- giving truthful information within the scope of a request;
- interfering with a contract that violates public policy;
- if it arises from a disinterested desire to protect an obligor; or
- when a fiduciary encourages a party to breach (because a fiduciary is considered independent and not acting for personal economic advantage).

    (2)   Privilege to Improve Financial Interest

A defendant is privileged to act to further his own financial interest. However, the defendant's breach-inducing conduct must occur for a justifiable purpose, and the defendant must use warranted means to accomplish the purpose.

    2)   <u>INTERFERENCE WITH PROSPECTIVE CONTRACTUAL RELATIONS</u>

    a)   General

A plaintiff has a right to redress when, before a business contract is actually formed, a defendant impermissibly interferes with the plaintiff's rights to form the contract with a third party. Such interference may include the loss of that economic opportunity or the making of the entering into that contract more expensive or less beneficial.

    b)   Elements

The elements of the tort of interference with prospective contractual relations are:

- Expectancy: an economic expectancy exists between a plaintiff and a third party;
- Knowledge: a defendant possesses knowledge of the economic expectancy;
- Intent: the defendant intends to interfere with the contract;

- Interference: the defendant causes interference with the contract; and
- Damages: the plaintiff suffers damage from the defendant's conduct.

      c)   Defenses

Interference with a prospective contract is justified under the following circumstances:

- a defendant provides truthful information about a contract within the scope of a request;
- the defendant acts to protect a person's welfare; or
- the defendant interferes with a contract that violates public policy.

6775733R0

Made in the USA
Charleston, SC
06 December 2010